More Praise for *The Second Emancipation*

"It would be as impossible to overstate the importance of Nkrumah as it would be to overstate the brilliance of this study. For too many, Africa as a whole remains an enigma. Howard W. French's masterwork clarifies the continent, both its history and the backstory to its current conflicts, with remarkable precision. French's book is particularly good at illuminating the ways in which the civil rights movement in the United States and the African freedom movements influenced and inspired each other. An indispensable work."
— **Greg Grandin**, winner of the Pulitzer Prize for *The End of the Myth*

"A brilliant examination. . . . Howard W. French illuminates a period of time when people believed that standards of justice and equality could prevail for African people on the continent and in the diaspora, especially in the United States during the civil rights movement, despite the centuries-old ascendance of the ideology of global white supremacy. It is a timely story for our own currently difficult racial moment."
— **Annette Gordon-Reed**, winner of the Pulitzer Prize for *The Hemingses of Monticello*

"An original, provocative, and important work of history. . . . With meticulous research and crisp writing, Howard W. French helps us see and understand the modern world anew. An extraordinary achievement."
— **Jonathan Eig**, winner of the Pulitzer Prize for *King: A Life*

"Kwame Nkrumah founded a country and became the leading African statesman of the twentieth century. French tells Nkrumah's story wonderfully well, in all its greatness and complexity." — **Odd Arne Westad**, Yale University, and author of *The Cold War: A World History*

"An epic history of the struggle to free Africa from the grip of colonial rule and Black America from the grip of Jim Crow, deftly told through the life and times of Kwame Nkrumah. In prose both lyrical and personal, Howard W. French reveals how civil rights and decolonization were bound together by Garvey's ghost, Du Boisian internationalism, a long dream of Black power, and a vision of pan-Africanism based less on returning home than on rejecting the world order and the color line that belts it. A tour de force."
— **Robin D. G. Kelley**, author of *Freedom Dreams: The Black Radical Imagination*

THE SECOND EMANCIPATION

ALSO BY HOWARD W. FRENCH

Born in Blackness
Africa, Africans, and the Making of the Modern World,
1471 to the Second World War

Everything Under the Heavens
How the Past Helps Shape China's Push for Global Power

China's Second Continent
How a Million Migrants Are Building a New Empire in Africa

Disappearing Shanghai
Photographs and Poems of an Intimate Way of Life
(with Qiu Xiaolong)

A Continent for the Taking
The Tragedy and Hope of Africa

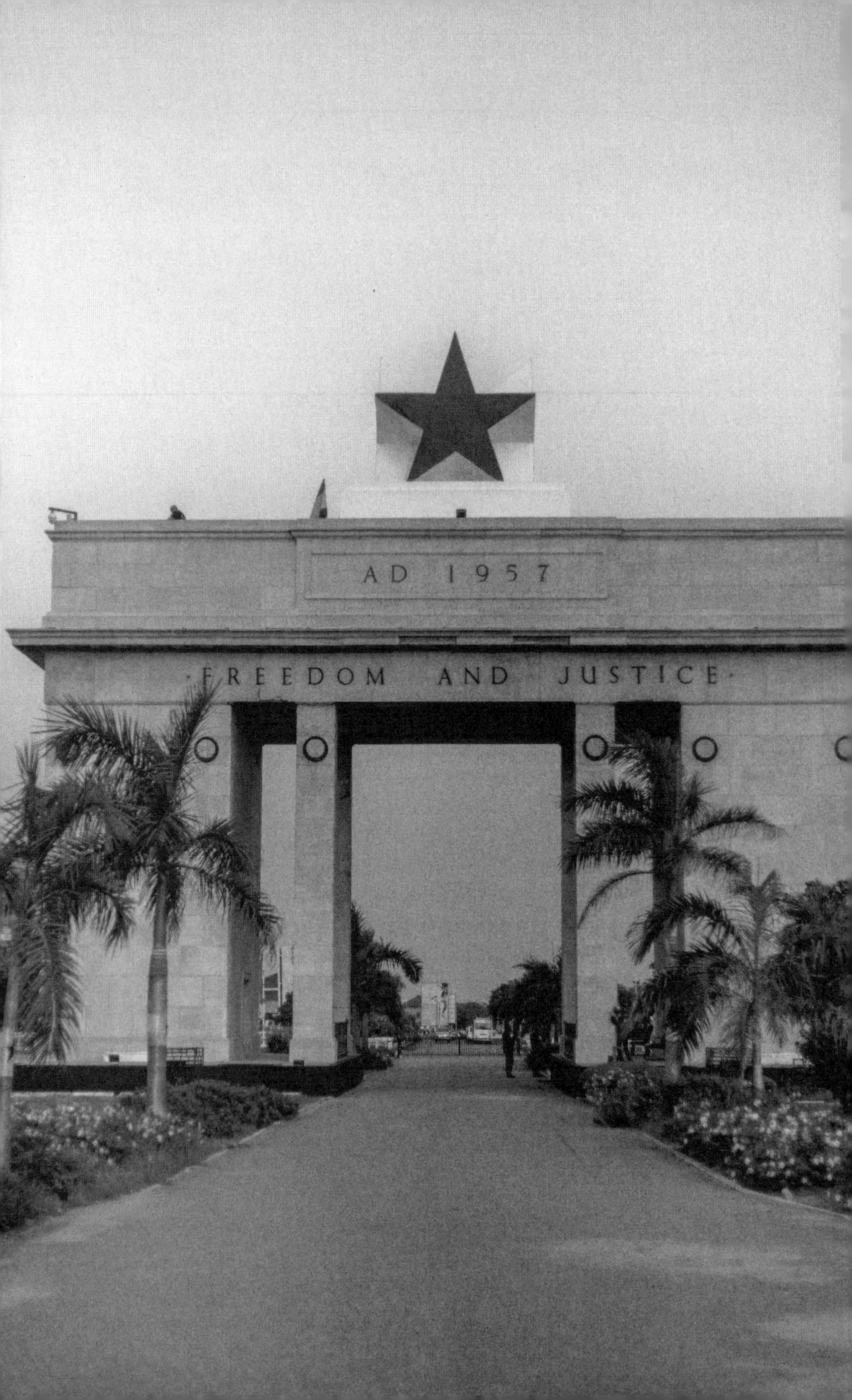
AD 1957
FREEDOM AND JUSTICE

THE SECOND EMANCIPATION

Nkrumah, Pan-Africanism,
and Global Blackness at High Tide

HOWARD W. FRENCH

Liveright Publishing Corporation

A Division of W. W. Norton & Company
Independent Publishers Since 1923

Frontispiece: Black Star Square, Accra, Ghana.
Maps created by Sebastian Ballard

Copyright © 2025 by Howard W. French

All rights reserved
Printed in the United States of America
First Edition

For information about permission to reproduce selections from this book, write to
Permissions, Liveright Publishing Corporation, a division of W. W. Norton & Company, Inc.,
500 Fifth Avenue, New York, NY 10110

For information about special discounts for bulk purchases, please contact
W. W. Norton Special Sales at specialsales@wwnorton.com or 800-233-4830

Manufacturing by Lakeside Book Manufacturing
Book design by Daniel Lagin
Production manager: Anna Oler

ISBN 978-1-324-09245-2

Liveright Publishing Corporation, 500 Fifth Avenue, New York, NY 10110
www.wwnorton.com

W. W. Norton & Company Ltd., 15 Carlisle Street, London W1D 3BS

10 9 8 7 6 5 4 3 2 1

For my sons,
Will, who was born in the West Africa of this book,
and Henry, who has been such steady company
exploring it together with me

The Negro is drawn to Africa by the necessities of his nature . . . [They] have a restless sense of homelessness which will never be appeased until they stand in the great land where their forefathers lived; until they catch glimpses of the old sun, and moon and stars, which still shine in their pristine brilliancy upon that vast domain.
—Edward Wilmot Blyden, 1832–1912

The first thing the American power structure doesn't want any Negroes to start is thinking internationally.
—Malcolm X, *Autobiography*

It has often been said that Africa is poor. What nonsense! It is not Africa that is poor. It is the Africans.
—Kwame Nkrumah in a speech at the National Assembly, Accra, August 8, 1960

One man, one vote is the African cry. It is ours too. It must be ours!
—John Lewis, speech at the March on Washington for Jobs and Freedom, August 28, 1963

CONTENTS

Preface   xiii

Author's Note   xv

Introduction   1

PART ONE
BRAIDED ROOTS

1. Saturday's Child   21
2. Black Is a Country   37
3. So Much to Do, So Little Done   57
4. Ace Boy   71
5. Yours Africanly   85
6. Euston Station   91
7. The Dawn of Action   100
8. The Darker Nations   112

PART TWO
WADING IN THE WATER

9. Land and Freedom   125
10. Nothing to Lose but Chains   129
11. Saltpond   136
12. The Mongoose   143
13. Positive Action   155
14. Seek the Political Kingdom   168
15. After the Ball (The Drums Are Heavy)   182
16. The Race Men   188

17. The Rape of Decency … 202
18. The Negro Circuit … 209
19. Land of My Fathers … 221
20. The Motion of Destiny … 228
21. Imagined Communities … 238
22. Birthday Party … 246

PART THREE
ELBOWS AT THE HIGH TABLE

23. New Africans … 253
24. Keep On Keeping On … 262
25. Frenemies … 267
26. *Quand On Refuse On Dit Non* … 273
27. Keep Your Juice … 280
28. High Water … 286
29. The Bureau of African Affairs … 293
30. Slogans and Manifestos … 299
31. Imitation Is the Sincerest Form … 310
32. Forward to Independence … 323
33. Nei Luan Wai Huan … 340
34. Dam(n) Volta … 352
35. Hard Places … 361
36. A Way in the World … 371
37. Southern Strategies … 381
38. Twenty-One Guns … 393
39. Hail Mary … 404
40. The Way Home … 417

CODA Strange Fruit … 432

Acknowledgments … 443
Notes … 447
Credits … 471
Index … 473

PREFACE

FROM THE BACK CORNER OF A MODEST-SIZED BRITISH COLONY, BORN POOR and without pedigree, Kwame Nkrumah gained access to educational opportunities that were exceptionally rare for West Africa at the time. Then, riding a voracious thirst for learning, uncanny luck with mentors, and firmness of will, he entered the slipstream of history in the middle decades of the twentieth century.

It was there that he channeled and then redefined what had been an inchoate movement of global Blackness with venerable roots in the previous century, galvanizing both his teachers and his millions of followers alike—not just in Ghana or in Africa, but throughout the Atlantic world.

In the process, Nkrumah dramatically, but peacefully, led his country to independence, prying it from the lion's grip of the world's greatest empire and making his land the first Black African nation to free itself from colonial rule.

Nkrumah's life is an epic twentieth-century story, but one that remains virtually unknown in the West save for scholars and the scattered communities of Black intellectuals and activists who still identify as pan-Africanists. This is a glaring historical omission, typical of our deliberate neglect of Africa's enormous role in the birth of the modern world, because this charismatic leader, comparable in his impact on the world of his era to Mandela and even Gandhi, has much to teach us about the Africa of the twenty-first century.

Any understanding of Nkrumah must begin with this knowledge. His untold success as a Black statesman required of him not only a vision of nation-building, but also the audacity to speak as an equal with leaders of the world's established powers: Britain, the United States, the Soviet Union, and France. He had to know when to be malleable and accommodating, and when and how to remain steadfast.

For a shining moment mid-century, Nkrumah turned Ghana into a fountainhead of emancipation from European domination, which was followed by a wave of pan-Africanism that seized the continent. Rediscovering him and his journey allow us to see how Nkrumah, like no one before him, made Africa also matter to African Americans: social leaders and intellectuals as well as ordinary people. He made them see his continent's struggle as a vital and even inseparable part of their own fight to become full citizens in the land of their enslaved forebears. Reawakened to the world of their ancestors, African Americans of that time period zealously followed Ghana's emergence into independence practically by the minute, and taking inspiration from Nkrumah, they demanded that their government fully engage with Africa for the first time. This connection, which was abundantly evident in the era of my own parents, needs to be made patently clear for a younger generation, which has grown up with a very different, not always roseate, image of Africa, or scarcely any idea of the continent at all.

The story that awaits readers in *The Second Emancipation* is quite deliberately not a comprehensive biography of Kwame Nkrumah; rather, it is an exploration of the momentous politics of his age, as well as the intellectual history of the pan-Africanist ideal, which flickers wanly in the consciousness of the West today. In narrating this saga, I have used Nkrumah as a fulcrum—a historical hub, if you will—to tell a larger story. Nkrumah, more than any other figure, transformed his era into a time when African leaders, unlike now, had entrée everywhere, a period when their continent floated high on the global agenda.

Alas, this is also the story of how this all came apart; of how, amid the triumph and exhilaration of continental liberation, the center once vested in the person of this man could not be maintained; of how the Cold War took Africa in its grip, and with Nkrumah's demise, the histories of Africa and African Americans entered a new and increasingly divergent phase, one with a less-than-happy ending.

Gone was the innocence of that turn of the decade from the 1950s to the 1960s, and for many, gone, too, and never fully recovered, was the period's immense hope. The connection between the self-belief and agency of that era and its optimism and achievement, which to me and to scholars of that time is abundantly apparent, needs to be strengthened for a younger generation, which has but a dim awareness of the relevance of African history in the world today.

AUTHOR'S NOTE

Throughout the colonial era and during Ghana's early independence period, the names of the major Akan subgroups that figure here were spelled as follows: Ashanti, Fanti, and Nzima. Indeed, Nkrumah used this spelling, Nzima, for his own ethnic group. In more recent decades, these newer spellings for these names have become standard: Asante, Fante, and Nzema.

When quoting archival materials, whether books or articles, that use them, I have preserved the older spellings. In all other instances, I have used the more modern forms.

THE SECOND EMANCIPATION

Introduction

AS A COLLEGE STUDENT IN THE LATE-1970S, I FOUND THAT THE SEMESters couldn't end quickly enough as I awaited the chance to board a flight on the now long-defunct Pan American Airways, with its big, blue, circular logo with curving white lines figuratively straddling the entire world. I was flying from New York's John F. Kennedy Airport to the romantic-sounding Côte d'Ivoire, which we know as the Ivory Coast, where I would spend my summers and winter breaks visiting members of my family who were then living in West Africa.

It was in that region that many of the most momentous discoveries of my life awaited me. It was in the country's economic capital, Abidjan, that I met Avouka, the woman I married; with her I founded a family and shared a long and exciting adventure of the world. And it was there, too, that I discovered my love of journalism, which would carry me, first to almost every country in Africa, and then onward to every continent.

In Abidjan, I became proficient enough in French to work as a translator, and this opened up a world that bore little resemblance to the depressing, Jimmy Carter–era America, with its high inflation and long gas lines, that I had left behind. In those halcyon days, Abidjan's central districts were almost as slick and postcard-ready as Miami, and well-functioning, too. It boasted clusters of high rises and fancy hotels, with swimming pools the size of small lakes, and even ice-skating rinks in the tropics.

What fascinated me more than those glittering pockets of rich world prosperity, though, was Treichville, the big and low-lying workers' district across the bridge from downtown, pungent with the aromas of cuisine being prepared in the open air and all the other smells of daily life. It was built on a modest spit of sandy ground; a grid locked in a vise between the city's large and murky lagoon and the roaring tides of the nearby Atlantic coast.

Treichville bulged and thrummed with migrants from neighboring countries who had fled subsistence farming or unemployment and flocked to a booming Ivory Coast in search of wage-paying jobs. It was there, in Treichville, that I experienced an enrapturing introduction to the culture of Ghana, the country located next door to the east.

I became a flaneur there on weekends, feasting on heavily peppered, charcoal-grilled fish with fried yams and plantains cooked right by my tableside at boisterous street restaurants—about as far as one gets, it seemed, from college cafeterias or fast food in America. Diners like me washed down these delicacies with beer or a fierce distilled spirit made from palm wine. This often led to sweaty all-night dancing in packed and smoky nightclubs. There I inevitably stood out with my light skin, six-foot-four-inch frame and billowing, sandy afro. On many other nights, food and drink fueled conversation with incidental friends—such as Sylla, a young dockworker from Guinea next door, or Mariam of Mali, who hustled in her own little import-export trade—about life in exile or politics back home. Like dreams, these diversions usually left little lasting mark.

What did stick with me were the frequent funeral celebrations held outdoors by members of Ghana's Fante ethnic group that I started getting drawn into on Friday nights. Their loud soundtracks bounced and swayed with guitars and horns and the cries of vocalists who belted out choruses in swooping, plaintive falsettos about life's unremitting struggles. It was music that somehow managed to be both mournful and rousing, and nothing like anything I had ever known before. And it drew ad hoc crowds of people, both intimates and strangers, to eat, drink, and dance the Highlife music of Ghana together deep into the night. It was in this way that I, game for discovery, began to learn some rudiments of the Fante language of southwestern Ghana and to build some of my first and ultimately indelible friendships in Africa.

Beginning with Kwamena, a voluble chauffeur and strutting rooster of a man, new acquaintances soon began inviting me to travel with them across the border to the country next door, an initiation into what I had all along imagined a Third World country would be like. It was precisely a decade after the overthrow of the country's first leader, Kwame Nkrumah, whose story I had first encountered while studying African politics in college. In Ghana by this time, love him or hate him, Nkrumah's life already seemed encased in legend. His Ghana, though, by my time, mostly offered up the specter of a shattered and rudderless land. The period that followed Nkrumah's tenure had been far harder on the country than his final, failing years as president.

The economy was prostrate, and everywhere I went, people, low on hope, were flattened by material need.

It's just a short distance from Abidjan to the border with Ghana, but on the other side of that frontier lay a world apart. To get to the nearest large towns in Ghana meant bounding over mercilessly rutted roads in overcrowded bush taxis, sometimes jostling in the back of jerry-rigged trucks whose flatbeds were made of lashed-together planks of wood. Most of these early trips culminated in Takoradi, the first city where functioning hotels could be found, albeit miserable and rundown ones. Because of the dire shortages of consumer goods, my new Ghanaian friends and I would load up on soap and cooking oil and tins of canned food in Abidjan to deliver as care packages to families and friends of theirs.

This corner of Ghana, I would quickly learn, was the true homeland of Nkrumah, someone who, even from a young age, as old photographs reveal, had a distinctive look. He was neither tall nor short; rather, ebony-dark skin, keen eyes, and a high-domed forehead were his hallmarks. More and more, people spoke reverentially of him then, in the years that I visited, following a period of scorn and derision that had accompanied his overthrow and exile in 1966. I would learn that Nkrumah was born on an uncertain date in September in 1909 at Nkroful, a tiny village near the coast in the far western corner of the country. It was a place as remote as could be from the cut and thrust of life in what was then a lucrative, cocoa-producing British colony known as the Gold Coast.

Such rural images are no longer. Today a stretch of excellent highway runs through Nkroful from the Ivory Coast border, and if you drive too fast or blink at the wrong time you could miss the town. While working on this book, I stopped there to visit the site where he was once buried in 1972 on the grounds of the home where he lived as an infant. Latterly, it has become a little-trafficked museum and loving shrine to Nkrumah's memory. A quote of his stenciled onto a crackling white wall there reads:

> Independence must never be considered as an end in itself but as a stage,
> the very first stage of the people's revolutionary struggle.

But just before I left on this detour, I walked down a cemented path past the village's "mud and wattle houses and bamboo compounds," as Nkrumah described them in his 1957 memoir: *Ghana: The Autobiography of Kwame Nkrumah*. Even now, these serve as dwellings for many of Nkroful's residents. I eventually reached the sloping embankment of the murky village creek that

Nkrumah remembered so fondly in telling his life's story. There I found schoolboys, looking not dissimilar to that child of future power and fame, casting for tiny fish with makeshift poles fashioned from tree branches and crude hooks made of bent wire. They hardly took notice of me, laughing as they competed in a sort of fishing adventure that could only be for fun, given that the creatures they pulled from the water were scarcely bigger than minnows.

AT THE AGE OF THREE, FRANCIS NKRUMAH, AS THE ONLY CHILD OF HIS MOTHER was then known, was sent to live with his father, who was a smalltime goldsmith, to attend a one-room, one-teacher school in a seafront town called Half Assini. It was hard by the frontier with the Ivory Coast and pinned to the seaboard by a peat-swamp forest that is prized today for some of the continent's richest biodiversity. The dense woods there harbor endangered species like leopards and slender-snouted crocodiles, spot-nosed monkeys and leatherback turtles. Half Assini was a considerably bigger town than Nkroful but still a place where little of note ever seemed to happen. That made the wreck of the SS *Bakana*, a British oil freighter that ran aground in 1913 on its way back to Liverpool from the Congo, drowning its English captain, almost epochal.

There is an often-told story from the opposite side of the continent about the 1979 visit of Kenneth Kaunda, Zambia's independence-era leader, to the village of Julius Nyerere, the founding leader of Tanzania, in East Africa. The dusty roads leading to the home of his fellow head of state in a place called Butiama, on the eastern shore of Lake Victoria, were so rutted that Kaunda became convinced the driver had lost his way.[1] An unfamiliar visitor might feel the same thing driving to Half Assini from Nkroful, a short distance but a long, jarring drive through wetlands and forest. Nkrumah and Nyerere both built one-party states that concentrated power in their own hands and deliberately ginned up reverence for themselves, which late in Nkrumah's rule, led to a near stifling cult of personality. Nkrumah and Nyerere differed on many things, but what united their stories, beyond pan-Africanism, is that both abhorred machinations of tribe and ethnicity. Both also eschewed building personal fortunes.

These traits plagued country after country in Africa in the 1960s and well beyond. Leaders such as the Ivory Coast's Félix Houphouët-Boigny and Mobutu Sese Seko of Zaïre (the former Belgian Congo), and many others among their peers would turn their natal villages into entrepots of luxury festooned with grandiose monuments. Mobutu's ancestral home in the far north of his country, Gbadolité, was mocked as Versailles in the Jungle for its exaggerated opulence, which included an extra-long runway built to accommodate Concorde supersonic jets that were used for shopping trips to Paris. In Houphouët-Boigny's case, he decreed his birthplace, Yamoussoukro, which would have otherwise ranked as a smallish, third-rate city, as the legal capital in 1983. Houphouët-Boigny ordered the construction there of what is often considered to be the world's largest church, the Basilica of Our Lady of Peace, at a cost estimated at $300 million. Nearby, as some medieval ruler might have done, the late Ivory Coast president built a vast palace protected by a moat filled with crocodiles, his totem. Nkrumah, by stark contrast, wore the relative neglect of his ethnic homeland as a badge of honor.

In Half Assini, I made my way through sandy, carless streets to visit the moldering shell of the simple two-story oceanfront family compound that Nkrumah built in the early 1960s as the leader of the first Black country in Africa to achieve independence from Europe. Its ruins, heavy with graffiti, are a hangout nowadays for young, dreadlock-sporting men who gather to idle there, smoking weed.

Later, I walked the misty, palm tree–lined shore at sunset, cutting a path through a fleet of roughly hewn wooden fishing boats, all adorned with talismanic quotes from scripture. There, I could just make out the blackened bones of the *Bakana*, now well over a century old, barely peeking out above the rising tide as it rusted away in the gathering darkness. Had it not been for that shipping disaster, which served as a kind of time stamp, even Nkrumah's birth year might have remained shrouded in uncertainty, as it was for most Africans of his era.

In his autobiography, Nkrumah would remark on a very different kind of accident that took place nearby: the drawing up of a border separating French and British claims in this part of coastal West Africa, the Ivory Coast and the Gold Coast. This would lay the basis for what would become nations, the latter renamed Ghana. Nkrumah happened to be born into a small ethnic group, the Nzima, who were a minority even in their native southwestern Ghana, where the much more numerous Fante predominate. "It is unfortunate for Nzimas that the Tano River and the Ayi Lagoon into which it drains were taken to form the boundary between the two countries, for the people had set up fishing villages all round the lake and are now divided. This has caused much discontent because of customs authorities, language and other barriers which they encounter when crossing from one side to another," wrote Nkrumah.[2]

As his words demonstrate, Nkrumah was keenly aware that being born barely a stone's throw to the east of the border was no minor biographical accident. It may have been written in the stars, but it had a profound legacy.

Invidious lines drawn up arbitrarily in cookie-cutter fashion by Europeans are one of the most consequential features of African life even now. They weigh especially heavily in relatively small countries, like Ghana, leaving ethnic groups cleaved, stranding blood relatives on opposite sides of what became international boundaries, and subjecting close kin and extended families alike to different legal systems and imperial languages that were completely unintelligible one from the other. Even Half Assini's name drives home the point. A narrow stretch of sand bar is all that separates it from Assinie, its sister beach town, in the Ivory Coast. In Nkrumah's Nzima language, the name for the area comprising the two Assinis rings poetic, Awiane, meaning the end of our land. Theirs, and yet sundered.

These fluky details of birth—both being from a negligible minority group and coming from such a liminal netherworld in Ghana—bred in young Nkrumah a sensibility that would help generate his profoundest insight. However urgent independence seemed in the 1930s and 1940s, and it truly did, Africans would not be freed by merely throwing off direct colonial rule, as the quote I had read at Nkroful affirmed. There remained an indispensable next step if one wished to break free from the fetters of foreign domination: the creation of a new world truly of one's own.

Nkrumah fervently believed that Africans could only achieve this by forging much larger states or at least federations that would remedy the curse of Balkanization, a tainted European portmanteau, that colonialism had inflicted upon them. This alone would give Africa's new nations, which were weak or puny as if by design, more of the scale and heft that they would need to prosper and to fend for themselves in the world of distant but constantly imposing powers, if not superpowers.

This conviction impelled Kwame Nkrumah on the road toward pan-Africanism, an ideal that obsessed him even during his intense and poverty-haunted years of university study in the Depression-weary United States, which he began in 1935 as a twenty-seven-year-old. During that time in America, he earned four degrees, in sociology, theology, education, and philosophy. And after a stint in Britain, where he worked alongside W. E. B. Du Bois in Manchester as an organizer of the Fifth Pan-African Conference, in 1945, he felt compelled to return to the Gold Coast after twelve years in the West. There, pan-Africanism remained Nkrumah's North Star as he quickly usurped the far more established figures who had recruited him to help run their fledgling political party. And so it remained during the audacious challenge he mounted to Britain, which was eager to continue milking the continent after emerging victorious but economically ravaged from the war. To foil their designs, Nkrumah campaigned on the clear and uncompromising slogan, "Freedom Now!"

What followed was an astonishing conquest of power via a landslide election won in 1951 from inside a prison cell, and then independence in 1957. Many in Ghana blamed Nkrumah's pan-Africanism for his very overthrow nine years later. But Nkrumah never second-guessed this bedrock conviction. Pan-Africanism continued to be his obsession down to the final period of his life, including the isolation he endured during his exile in Guinea, sometimes without so much as a reliably working telephone, until his lonely death of cancer in Bucharest at age 62.

Unexpectedly, my early cross-border forays connecting me with Ghana and to the story of Nkrumah brought me to understand my own country and the world of the last century in profoundly new ways. This was especially true of the twentieth century's early- to late-middle decades, which is to say from the late 1930s to 1970. These decades saw the powerful rise of a universal Black consciousness that tied peoples together politically and spiritually on all sides of the Atlantic. Ever more clearly, I came to see this time through a lens given a name by Du Bois, who, at Nkrumah's invitation, lived his final years in Ghana, where he was buried in 1963. Around the turn of the nineteenth century, in books such as *The Philadelphia Negro* and *The Souls of Black Folk*, Du Bois had begun to forcefully argue that the "color line" imposed on Black people was the central problem of the twentieth century. But to a degree that remains vastly underappreciated in the America of his birth, Du Bois understood the racial subjugation endured by Black people in fully global terms.[3] And as *The Second Emancipation* will demonstrate, he was far from alone.

Africans and members of the African diaspora alike had been advancing ideas about freedom for that continent since at least the mid-nineteenth century. The free-born Virginian journalist and physician, Martin Delany, for example, adopted the slogan "Africa for Africans" after traveling to Liberia in 1859 and then advocated for what he called the Black "return."[4] In Ghana, the progressive Fante lawyer, journalist, and educator Joseph Ephraim (J. E.) Casely Hayford, published a novel titled *Ethiopia Unbound* in 1911, and in 1917 he cofounded the National Congress of British West Africa (NCBWA), whose spirit of African nationalism anticipated Nkrumah's politics. For Africa and Africans, Casely Hayford's group repurposed the revolutionary American slogan of no taxation without representation. He also urged that a federation be created to unite Africans in British and French colonies in West Africa under the banner of self-rule. In 1922, the Jamaican Black nationalist and publisher, Marcus Garvey, founder of the Universal Negro Improvement

Association (UNIA) and African Communities (Imperial) League and a major influence on Malcolm X, wrote, "If you will but think down the future and compare the possibilities of that future with the happenings of the past you will come to the conclusion that there is no other salvation for the Negro but through a free and independent Africa."[5] Years later, Kwame Nkrumah would call Garvey the most important influence on his thought.

IN WESTERN CLASSROOMS, WORLD WAR I, WITH ITS DEPICTION OF TRENCH warfare, is seldom taught about in any African context, but this conflict was a crucial watershed in the long twentieth-century struggle against global white supremacy. Black soldiers from African colonies and African Americans, including both my maternal grandfather and great uncle, were recruited into Western armies and fought in France as so-called Buffalo Soldiers. There, they proved their mettle every bit as much as their white counterparts, despite inferior equipment and training. This contributed strongly to helping undermine widespread and deeply held notions in the West of a natural racial hierarchy in the world, one in which peoples of African descent sat permanently at the bottom. This hierarchy was not only challenged by valor on the battlefield, though. As relationships flourished between Black soldiers and French women, American authorities voiced fears of a resulting breakdown of white soldiers' morale.[6] For President Woodrow Wilson, an ardent segregationist, America's only recently emancipated Blacks were "unpracticed in liberty, unschooled in self-control, never sobered by the discipline of self-support, never established in any habit of prudence; excited by a freedom they did not understand."[7] After the war, Wilson warned that the welcome that African American soldiers had received in helping rescue European allies in WWI may have "gone to their heads." In a way, he was right.[8]

Black soldiers returned to the United States in that war's aftermath expecting steady movement in their society toward equality and full citizens' rights. Wilson had famously justified American entry into the war as a means of making the world "safe for democracy." What followed instead was an interwar period of rampant lynching and other extreme anti-Black violence. The era saw the rebirth of the Ku Klux Klan in America. No longer a mostly southern white racist phenomenon, the Klan made enormous inroads elsewhere in the country, including many northern cities. It burned crosses in New Jersey suburbs of New York City, and Anaheim, California, was sometimes referred to as "Klanaheim."[9]

Wilson's famous "Fourteen Points" of 1918 set out principles by which he said the world should be governed once the war was won. These included democracy, self-determination, and rights for small nations. Wholly left by the wayside, though, were the rights of Africans and other colonized peoples, whose destinies were consigned to Western powers under the self-serving guise of so-called trusteeships. Independence for Africans didn't even rank as an afterthought. Wilson's preoccupation with the rights of ethnic minorities also exempted America's Black population, to whom democracy had long been denied. To Wilson, willfully blind to this injustice, "America was an ethnically unique amalgam of enlightened democracy."[10]

For peoples of African descent, the Second World War was but a replay of the First, only this time with bigger stakes and many of the same disappointments in terms of dreams of equal treatment in America and around the world. As we will see, the Cold War played a complicating role in their struggle, but rather than becoming deterred or distracted, African Americans displayed renewed self-belief and determination in their push for full citizens' rights.

Even more than it had in America, the Second World War would play a central role in transforming the political landscape in Africa. Not only had much of Europe been reduced to ashes and rubble, Europe's longstanding pretensions of representing the summa of human civilization, already seriously undermined by the savagery of the First World War, now lay completely gutted. The genocidal politics of the Third Reich had seen to that, almost singlehandedly obliterating any notion of European moral superiority. As James Baldwin, with characteristic prescience, wrote, "death so calculated, so hideous, and so prolonged ... makes obsolete forever any question of Christian superiority, except in technological terms."[11] Although these were the sentiments of a revolted young Black American intellectual, they were fully consonant with feelings of many Africans who lived through the Second World War.

It is an under-credited fact that Africans had been called upon to rescue the Allied powers in their war against foreign domination and fascism. In truth, these were the same problems that the colonial subjects of Africa had been subjected to themselves at the hands of the very same Europeans they were called upon to defend. As the Black intellectual from Martinique, Aimé Césaire, wrote of fascism in his renowned 1950 essay, *Discourse on Colonialism*, before Europeans "were its victims, they were its accomplices," their eyes remaining shut to the moral implications of the racial domination of others so long as the subjugation was only being applied to non-Europeans.[12] For Black Americans, Langston Hughes gave voice to this same thought in a poem that referred to Hitler as a bad man, adding: "I guess he took lessons / From the ku klux klan."[13]

For Africans, the effects of seeing Europeans defeated by non-whites in Asia shattered whatever vestiges of the mystique of white invincibility remained. In Burma, for example, troops of the 82nd West African Division had constituted as much as a sixth of the British forces. In fact, these ninety thousand men had fought with great distinction, helping make for one of Britain's rare land campaign successes during the Second World War. It was a clear case in which peoples of color had in effect saved the colonizer's bacon.

The imperial powers were not only economically devastated by the war, they emerged from it dependent on revenues from agriculture and extractive industries in Africa—still often run by whites using forced Black labor. As Wilson had once done through his Fourteen Points, Franklin D. Roosevelt, with his Atlantic Charter, announced jointly with Winston Churchill in August 1941, also made stirring assurances of a coming new dispensation. It promised "the right of all peoples to choose the form of government under which they live," and vowed to "see sovereign rights and self-government" respected for those who had been forcibly deprived of them.[14] But principles like these were seldom applied outside of Europe, and when they were, it was with all deliberate speed.

Roosevelt, who died in April 1945, shortly before the war's end, didn't live long enough to make good on whatever sugar plum notions he might have had about independence. And his successor, Harry S. Truman, put enfranchisement for Africans and other colonized peoples on the very back burner. But over a million Africans had participated in the war both as soldiers in combat and support personnel working for their colonizers. They returned home with high expectations for better lives, including good wage-paying jobs, much better access to education, and self-government, but these were largely unfulfilled. Seeing the Philippines gain independence from the United States in 1946, and India pry itself from British rule the following year, Africans, like African Americans across the Atlantic, resolved to push for their rights.

In the immediate aftermath of the war, in many places, including Ghana and Nigeria and French colonies like Senegal and Guinea, strikes by workers and protests by returning war veterans paved the way for explicit calls and then surprisingly rapid agitation for outright independence. With his exquisite sense of timing, sharp organizational skills, a surplus of charisma, and years of constant thinking about how Africa could free itself, Nkrumah became the first Black African to fulfill this destiny.

Like few others, Nkrumah's life allows us to apprehend Du Bois's insight about the global color line—the categorical discrimination against dark-skinned people—afresh. It transports us to a mostly forgotten time of extraordinarily deep and fertile intellectual connections between Africans and members of the African diaspora in the Caribbean, in Europe, and in the interwar and postwar United States. In these years Blacks cast to the four corners of the Atlantic came to understand with unprecedented clarity how tightly intertwined were the questions of a lack of citizens' rights for Blacks in the Jim Crow United States and the enduring state of colonial rule over Black people elsewhere. Deepening reflections on this connectedness emerged on the campuses of historically Black American universities. Places like Lincoln University in Pennsylvania, where Nkrumah would accumulate several degrees, and Howard University in Washington, DC, became exciting intellectual loci for African and Caribbean students and intellectuals in the 1930s, '40s, and '50s.

The international population at Howard University alone rose to 706 in the final years of the 1950s, or 13 percent of the student body, "giving Howard the highest percentage of foreign students enrolled among American [institutions of higher education]."[15] What had been a trickle became a torrent, and this outpouring of African students came under the influence of the cream of the Black American and Caribbean intelligentsia—globally minded thinkers like Alain Locke, E. Franklin Frazier, Horace Mann Bond, William Leo Hansberry, Thurgood Marshall, Cyril Lionel Robert (C. L. R.) James, Eric Williams, Ralph Bunche, William Alphaeus Hunton, Rayford Logan, and many others. And as they did, this helped foster and catalyze a sense of deeply linked fortunes of Blacks throughout the Atlantic world.

This growing sense of connectedness was not merely an elite intellectual preoccupation, and outside of the academy the wave continued to grow. Mary McLeod Bethune mobilized African American women in this cause, too, and insisted they be heard out. She also pushed for groups of ordinary citizens to become involved. As a result, the liberation of Africa and the Caribbean, and the way their fates were linked to those of Black Americans, became a growing focus of local Black civic associations, church groups, and organizations around the country. This, too, is little recalled today.

By the 1950s, the African American press, long used to the erasure of Black issues in mainstream papers, had fully joined in these efforts, led by Black newspapers with large circulations like the *Chicago Defender* and the *Pittsburgh Courier*. They denounced the absence of Black diplomats in the State Department and cheered on the rise of Nkrumah, sharply elevating his profile in America. Their publicity helped win Nkrumah an invitation to the United States in 1951, as the so-called leader of government business at the time, with the Gold Coast still under colonial rule. And in 1957, lobbying by African Americans effectively obliged the White House to dispatch a reluctant, even fearful Richard Nixon to Ghana's independence ceremonies. That event drew a level of attention to Africa never before seen and rarely equaled since. Six hundred international journalists descended on Accra, which hosted scores of foreign dignitaries but also an unprecedented collection of leaders of pro-independence movements and civil rights groups, among which were the Harlem congressman, Adam Clayton Powell Jr., and Martin Luther King Jr., fresh on the heels of the Montgomery Bus Boycott.

For many, the times appeared robust, even heady, and in the end, it was the conjugated efforts of Africans and African Americans that spurred the birth of a new internationalist ethos. This occurred as representatives of communities on opposite sides of the ocean brainstormed together about tactics and provided each other with moral support and entrée to their networks. Each took inspiration and courage from the organizational advances and tactical victories of the other. For African Americans in particular, the ascension of Nkrumah in the 1950s took on unparalleled importance. As they built momentum for their own civil rights movement, Black Americans pointed to the Ghanaian's successes both in his own country and on the world stage with heartfelt pride. They held the West African country up as implicit proof that America had nothing to fear from granting full citizens' rights and political space to the descendants of Africans it had recently enslaved. Nkrumah's keen understanding of his symbolic power on the global stage can be felt in the words he spoke during his inauguration as prime minister, in 1957. "From now on there is a new African in the world. . . . That African is beginning to fight his own battles and show that after all the Black man is capable of managing his own affairs."[16]

Early in 1960, when James Baldwin visited Tallahassee, Florida, to report on a sit-in for civil rights by young African Americans, he wondered why they had not been cowed and frightened away by the threatening "baseball bats and knives" wielded by white mobs. To be sure, he told himself, there had been courageous resistance to racial subjugation among previous generations of Black people. This dated all the way back to antebellum slave revolts. What made this generation different, Baldwin concluded, was that they "were born at the very moment at which Europe's domination of Africa was ending." The example of bold and yet peaceful liberation from white domination given by Kwame Nkrumah, and the cascade of African colonies gaining independence that followed, had helped mold these American protestors into "the only people in this country now who really believe in freedom."[17]

SOME FIVE DECADES AFTER HIS DEATH, KWAME NKRUMAH LOOMS FOR MANY only as a historical wraith in the United States, and yet he remains the most compelling figure in an era that was the high-water mark of pan-Black politics in the world. While his reputation in Africa has ebbed and flowed, opinion polls on the continent nowadays often rank him as the greatest Black person of the last hundred years. He surpasses someone far more celebrated in the West, the antiapartheid hero, former South African president and Nobel Peace laureate, Nelson Mandela. Nkrumah's standing in these polls accords with some of the most astute assessments made of him in the years following his death. In 1974, the American historian John Henrik Clarke said of Nkrumah: "He was the first universal African hero of this century. He, more than any other person, figuratively, took Africa and its people for their 'walk in the sun'."[18] During Nkrumah's life, (C. L. R.) James, his decades-long mentor from Trinidad and author of the classic history of the Haitian Revolution, *The Black Jacobins*, had occasionally been sharply critical of the Ghanaian leader. As a scholar and activist with a Trotskyite background, James was notably impatient with the younger African's understanding of Marxist theory. During Nkrumah's final years in power, James also denounced the Ghanaian's increasingly sharp departure from the rule of law. In the year of Nkrumah's death, 1972, though, James stripped all racial qualifiers from his appraisal of the man, calling Nkrumah simply "one of the greatest political leaders of our century" and the sort of figure who only appears on the world stage "at long intervals."[19]

Through words like these, one can perceive the clear if unstated line that exists in the historian's mind between Nkrumah and Toussaint Louverture, the peerless progenitor of African emancipation at the beginning of the nineteenth century. The Ghanaian, James wrote, had "taught the people of the Gold Coast that political emancipation from imperialist domination was a way of existence and not something that they did in their spare time." Nkrumah had "set the people in motion, discovered and unleashed the immense powers latent in an apparently docile African people," showing the way for an entire continent. Perhaps most impressively, peacefully, James said, "Nkrumah had mobilized the people of the Gold Coast against British imperialism," and rendered London, the greatest colonial power the world had ever seen, "helpless before the new nation."[20] Whereas Toussaint in 1801 had laid the bases for the foundation of the world's first Black republic, Haiti, Nkrumah had not only led the first Black African colony of Europe into independence, but had also evangelized pan-Africanism as an ideological platform that countless others have spiritually embraced, if not politically implemented.

For decades, conventional Western views of the twentieth century have emphasized the centrality of events in the North Atlantic, focusing intently on the United States, Europe, and the Soviet Union. Firmly front and center in the US are the cherished American narrative of the Greatest Generation and the country's role in winning the Second World War. This was followed by the construction of a new world order and the tense and exorbitant, but ultimately triumphant political, economic, and arms competition with the Soviet Union during the Cold War. Convention holds the foundational events of this era to have been the announcement of the Truman Doctrine, the Marshall Plan, the secret blueprint for militarized competition with Moscow known as NSC 68, and the formation of the North Atlantic Treaty Organization (NATO).

The account that follows here takes a decidedly different approach to the history of the last century and is written very much in the mold of my last book, *Born in Blackness*, and with similar intent, that is, to place Africa and Africans on a centripetal path much nearer to the center of our history. This is not a matter of polemical willfulness. What is demonstrated here flows from the conviction that the end of colonial rule on the African continent deserves consideration as one of the most consequential events of our times, yet it remains widely undervalued.

Decolonization was, of course, a global phenomenon, affecting a large majority of humanity, which might seem like argument enough for taking it more seriously, including by the colonizers themselves. In his 1915 *Atlantic* magazine essay, "The African Roots of War," Du Bois blamed the murderous scourge of world war on the runaway ambitions of rival colonial powers unleashed by the Berlin Conference of 1884–1885, during which Europeans partitioned the continent to their south. There are far worse ways of understanding the great power competition and ideological struggles of the Cold War than this, or what one historian channeling Du Bois called "a reaction to the undoing of colonialism, which put a quarter of the globe into motion and drew the United States and the Soviet Union, by trying to manage the outcome, into repeated confrontations."[21] During this period, the Third World became the stage for most of the killing post-1945, producing a toll of roughly twenty million people in scores of ragged and, from the safe and comfortable perspective of the distant West, remote and obscure conflicts.

For Africa, though, this decolonization had an extra dimension all its own. Everywhere it occurred, Western subjugation of non-white peoples involved what an essayist from Barbados called "the full desecration of the human personality."[22] But only for Africans and for their diaspora in the plantation colonies of the Western hemisphere did this modern form of desecration follow centuries of sale into slavery and brutal and dehumanizing exploitation for their labor. As Lamine Senghor, a decorated French veteran of the First World War and Black internationalist, said of colonial rule in 1927, "Slavery is not abolished. On the contrary it has been modernized."[23] To the contemporary ear, this might seem like overkill, or a mere rhetorical flourish. But every European colonial power in Africa imposed forced labor programs on its subjects in the twentieth century, and Britain and France used their diplomatic influence to ensure that the 1926 international Slavery Convention left this practice untouched.[24]

It is conventionally held that the last major country to abolish slavery was Brazil in 1888, but this book contends that decolonization in Africa and the Caribbean should be understood as the true end of slavery, or better, as this book's title has it, a second emancipation. As Nkrumah and many of his peers knew, though, formal independence was not the end of the struggle. Far from it. Even the birth of African states, which proliferated in the late 1950s and '60s, along with bright new flags and anthems, was a mere waystation on the long road out of unfreedom. A more thorough liberation, pan-Africanists like him believed, awaited the banding together of nominally free new nations in novel federations or associations. This alone could lend them the heft they would need to fend for themselves in a world dominated by imposing powers.

That few remember how freedom for Africans was accompanied by and indeed became deeply entangled with the conquest by African Americans of their full political rights elevates its significance yet further. Consider that the main thrust of the civil rights movement in the United States, the period between the 1954 *Brown v. Board of Education* decision of the Supreme Court and the Voting Rights Act of 1965, aligns almost perfectly with the period from Nkrumah's rise to power to his overthrow. The parallels run deeper than this, though. Martin Luther King and other civil rights leaders quickly came to view triumphs over de jure segregation as a mere first step in their struggles for justice. The essential tasks that remained to them included greater equality of economic opportunity at home and peace and freedom for peoples dominated by great powers abroad. The same held true for African liberation.

As great as his achievement was, Kwame Nkrumah was an extremely complicated human being; flawed, to be sure, even deeply so, but above all "versatile." In the French usage of the word adopted here, this conveys a sense of multitudes of traits, many of which contain opposites or contradictions. In

Nkrumah's early life, some of this can be glimpsed in his religious trajectory. Raised a Roman Catholic, he seriously considered becoming a Jesuit priest before attending a Protestant university in the United States. There, he earned pocket money preaching to African American Baptist and Methodist congregations throughout the middle Atlantic region. It was in these settings that he honed his talent for oratory. As a politician, Nkrumah called himself a secular Christian socialist, but also sometimes a Marxist.

He possessed tremendous personal discipline, and he revered organization as one of the highest virtues in politics, and yet he had little passion for details and could be very impatient. With his deep and resonant voice, Nkrumah could easily rouse crowds and light up a room with his brilliant smile and humor, and yet he showed little interest in social life and loathed chitchat. He seemed to have an effortless effect on women, who were seduced by his charm and often proved devoted and willing to do his bidding. The most that can be said of his love life, though, is that it was a black box, whose truths remain impenetrable to others. On the available evidence, he formed few emotional connections and nothing resembling what in his era might have been called a conventional romance.

In some ways, Nkrumah was miscast for the role that he built his life around, but history is constructed from real lives, and not, as movies are, from casting. Nkrumah was a shy and introspective man, whose life played out on the most public of stages. He was a visionary whose genius lay in his dreams, and yet his political calling demanded endless concrete action and decision making. He achieved far more in life than anyone who knew him during his formative years might ever have expected, and yet he could be a clumsy, even obtuse, politician. His stubbornness, however, also contributed to success. Nkrumah was never able to realize the continental project of his aspirations, but his passion for pan-Africanism remained constant.

The Second Emancipation, then, aims to be much more than a telling of this one man's life. Extending its aperture well beyond a conventional biography of Nkrumah, this book's intention is to illuminate his age—a time of extraordinary possibility for Africa and for Black people the world over and also, ultimately, one of unrealized hopes. In the latter stages of his rule and in the early years after his overthrow, Nkrumah was decried for his government's growing authoritarianism and for the failure of his excessively ambitious domestic policies. Critics denounced what they saw as his improvisational and chaotic adoption of socialism, along with the distraction and expense of his precipitous drive for African unity. Even the historian John Henrik Clarke, quoted so favorably earlier, called him a "magnificent dreamer." With the benefit of decades of hindsight, though, the unravelling of Nkrumah's dreams deserves better. Seen in the fresh light of the still-early twenty-first century, those dreams appear to have been less the result of simple naivete or overreach than of something more common to his era, and indeed in that light, something more insidious. From the 1950s to 1970s, an astonishing variety of ideologies, political structures, and economic strategies for advancement competed on the continent. Africa's leaders in this era were willing to try pretty much anything on for size. The fact that their efforts to create prosperous nations all came to naught should tell us something important. The usual litany of explanations critics give for Africa's failure to emerge economically strong and politically stable after independence—corruption, incompetence, and a lack of democracy—is inadequate, and taken alone, I would even venture intellectually dishonest. As we will see, the West was often characteristically stingy and overbearing toward Africa in this era, as well as almost irrationally insecure. That is because the Soviet Union was inexperienced and lacking in financial resources, and for much of Nkrumah's political life, surprisingly lacking in serious geopolitical ambition toward Africa. With the exception of its one monumental showcase project, the Tazara Railway, China, which has become a leading partner of many African countries much more recently, was still a mere bit player economically and a political spoiler on the continent. Each of these powers, the West included, marshalled idealistic rhetoric in favor of its own system, but all demanded loyalty and imposed themselves in other ways, each promoting its own framework and interests, often cynically, as well. In the fractured international system of this era, the superpowers often behaved like "thieves on the same market" toward the weakest countries just then emerging onto the world scene.[25]

Seen in this way, Nkrumah's story is one replete with his flaws and weaknesses to be sure, but also one of pathos and tragedy, in that the world lost an opportunity to seize hope where there had been none. Yet through this necessary retelling of history, we are able to see not only the destiny of Africa more clearly in this decisive age, but also ourselves.

Part One

BRAIDED ROOTS

Kwame Nkrumah with fellow students, Lincoln University.

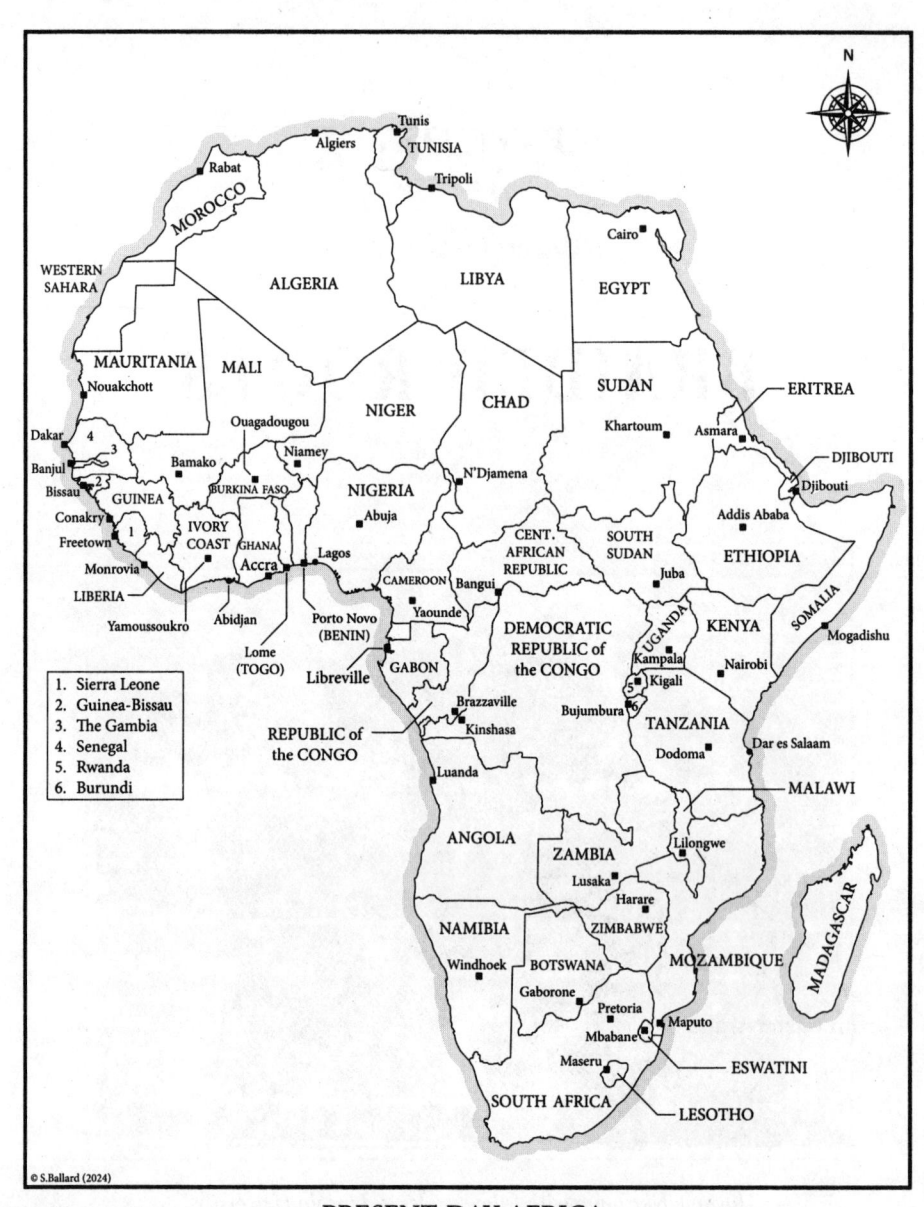

PRESENT-DAY AFRICA

CHAPTER ONE

Saturday's Child

OF ALL OF KWAME NKRUMAH'S ENDOWMENTS, THE FIRST WAS A KEEN sense of the sheer contingency that his own life story was woven from. "The only certain facts about my birth appear to be that I was born in the village of Nkroful in Nzima around mid-day on a Saturday in mid-September," he wrote, in the very opening passage of his first book, an autobiography.[1] Its publication was timed to appear in 1957, the year of his greatest triumph: leading Ghana into independence as the first Black prime minister of a former British colony. As simple as it appears, right away this statement nonetheless troubles. There are reasons to believe that the man who entered history under the name Nkrumah was born on a Tuesday, the twenty-first of September 1909. That was the day he was baptized by a Roman Catholic priest. To make things even fuzzier, Nkrumah's mother claimed this year was wrong; she insisted her only child was born in 1912. And these are not the only uncertainties that loom. Almost nothing is known about Nkrumah's father, a petty goldsmith in a territory just then transitioning from barter-trade to a cash economy. Some historians have even speculated that he came from Liberia, over five hundred miles to the west along the West African coast.[2]

Fussy details like these might seem like a strange place to begin a story about the origins of such a major figure, but they tell us something important about the man, and perhaps even something fundamental. Such a big error in recording Nkrumah's birth year seems quite unlikely, especially with news of the sinking of the cargo ship, the *Bakana*, serving as a convenient mnemonic. But in many of the crucial details of his life, Kwame Nkrumah was a persistent and imaginative self-inventor. To be born Black, restless, and so full of ambition in the British West Africa of his era, one almost had to be.

Under the naming conventions of the Nzima, Nkrumah's small,

southwestern Gold Coast ethnic group, as with the much larger linguistic cluster known as the Akan of which the Nzima form a tiny part, given names are assigned according to the day of the week the baby is born on, with a different set of day names used for boys and girls. For boys, Kwame matches Saturday, while Kablan is the day name traditionally associated with males born on Tuesdays.

Nkrumah left the land of his birth in 1935 at the age of twenty-six, spending a decade as a student in the United States and two years as a pan-African activist in Britain. But it was not until the eve of his return to Ghana in 1947, then still the British Gold Coast, that he began to consistently use the name familiar to us today, Kwame. Until then, he had been known as Francis Nwia Kofi Nkrumah. His mind had long been fixated on "resurrecting" Africa and independence for his country. This was a goal he already claimed for himself in his 1939 college yearbook. This, he believed, required unifying the continent's peoples, so Francis may simply have chosen Kwame because it had a more resonantly African sound to it.

From an early age, Nkrumah's life was peppered with chance encounters with people who helped propel his rise, many of them already remarkably well-established in the struggle to advance the interests and welfare of Black people throughout the Atlantic world. This began even before the young Nkrumah left Ghana for the United States. Shortly after arriving in Accra, the capital, from the near wilderness of his corner of the colony, he encountered and came under the influence of the future first president of Nigeria, Nnamdi Azikiwe, and a major reformist figure, educator, and nationalist, J. E. Kwegyir Aggrey. Both of them had spent long years studying in the United States and would shape his decision, still rare for a driven young colonial subject of this time, to study in that country rather than in the United Kingdom, preferably at Oxford or Cambridge.

Throughout Nkrumah's early life, history seems to have lain in wait for him. This happens dramatically, as he describes it, upon his arrival in Britain in 1935 on his way to school in the United States, where he would spend a decade accumulating degrees. The London of that era was incomparably whiter than the global city of today. Wandering its streets and feeling lost in the imposing and unfamiliar capital of an empire poised for decline, he says

> [I] heard an excited newspaper boy shouting something unintelligible as he grabbed the latest editions from a motor van, and on the placard I read: "Mussolini Invades Ethiopia".

That was all I needed.... For the next few minutes I could do nothing but glare at each impassive face wondering if those people could possibly realize the wickedness of colonialism, and praying that the day might come when I could play my part in bring[ing] about the downfall of such a system. My nationalism surged to the fore; I was ready and willing to go through hell itself, if need be, in order to achieve my object.[3]

These sorts of temporal accidents, being in the right place at the right time when the hinge of history swings loudly, are probably commonplace in the lives of major figures on the global stage. But their recurrence in Nkrumah's story is nonetheless remarkable.

Nkrumah, as we have seen, was not only born on the edge of a colonial border. He was also born at a moment of extraordinary transition in the life of the Gold Coast and West Africa. Just seven years earlier, after four wars during three quarters of a century of conflict, the British had finally consummated their conquest of the Asante, then one of the African continent's great empires. As one historian has written, Asante was "manifestly ... on its way toward becoming a nation-state with every attribute ascribed to a West European state," including a central government, borders, law and order, police and army, professional diplomats and even a precursor to a postal service.[4] The defeat of the Asante and the annexation of territories to its north snuffed out any sense of national self-determination and, in the process, paved the way for the carving out by Britain of a more or less definitive colony, and one whose early outline closely resembles the borders of modern Ghana.

Britain's imperial relationship with the Gold Coast had begun haltingly in the parts of the territory that fronted the Atlantic in piecemeal fashion in the 1820s. Then, in the aftermath of abolition, what became called "legitimate trade,"—meaning products like ivory, palm oil, and rubber—replaced an intense and longstanding commerce in enslaved human beings. A formal colony was declared in 1874, opening a period of remarkable policy inconsistency by London, whose pendulum swung sharply between different degrees of control and involvement as it experimented with forms of so-called direct and indirect rule.

Before the mid-nineteenth century, when British control along the coast was far more tenuous, nearly all of the senior members of the Colonial Service posted to the Gold Coast were men of mixed race, meaning of partial African descent, and often from the Caribbean.[5] In the second half of the century, though, Edwardian British attitudes began to harden and grow more draconian as a sense of the economic benefits of colonization and of the professional opportunities for Britons became clearer. All notions of opening up the colonial government to Africans were abandoned, and by 1915, all forty-nine of the district commissioners and assistant commissioners in the colony were white. "The African race stands today as it stood 3000 years ago; hopeless to a man and cursed by heaven," wrote one official. Another called Western-educated Africans "a worse evil than the primitive savage."[6]

During this rupture in more lenient colonial policies, British officials professed the belief that Africans had no capacity for self-rule, no knack for European-defined civilization, and nothing even worthy of a lowly rung on the ladder of world history. What is most remarkable about this is the degree to which it required the people who propagated such notions to close their eyes to the wealth of evidence that surrounded them. From their earliest contact in the fortress towns of Elmina and Cape Coast four centuries earlier, the local population of what would become Ghana had been extraordinarily resourceful when contending with the people who would become their colonizers.

The Asante, as we have just seen, had proven a stout challenge to London throughout much of a century when Britain's worldwide empire was rapidly expanding. Perhaps even more germane to questions of modern governance was the example of the colony's best established coastal people, the Fante. In 1868, this group, the sometime ally of the British and longstanding chief rival to the Asante in the region, had formalized a Confederacy led by a king-president. Three years later the Fante deepened their democratic experiment, drafting a sophisticated constitution that codified rules of governance. The British saw this Fante union not as a sign of modernization or progress, but as a serious threat to their control along the coast, and they worked hard to undo it.

The governance arrangements of the short-lived Fante Confederacy bore comfortable comparison to the political systems of many contemporary European polities. Its unraveling under foreign pressure was followed not by resignation or defeatism on the Gold Coast, though, but by a period of intense intellectual effervescence. It centered around the flowering of a first generation of cosmopolitan and highly articulate thinkers, including the pioneering pan-Africanist and political thinker, the aforementioned Casely Hayford. Its members devoted their lives to the search for ways forward toward true self-rule by Africans, if not always necessarily outright independence. In his 1903 work, *Gold Coast Native Institutions*, Casely Hayford, a federalist forerunner of Nkrumah's, wrote that Britain's persistent administrative problems in the colony were due to its refusal to accept an unavoidable fact, "that apart from the Natives of the soil any attempt at statesmanlike administration [here] is doomed to failure."[7]

Crediting African views like this would have required a sea change in European attitudes toward Africans in the late nineteenth and early twentieth centuries. In 1884, such superciliousness was hardly a possession of the British alone. Jules Ferry, an ardent promoter of French colonialism, for example, blankly asserted, "The higher races have a right over the lower races, they have a duty to civilize the inferior races."[8] The response among colonial officials to assertive self-confidence like Casely Hayford's was brittle and nervous. It was aimed at closing off paths to advancement in professions like law, education, and medicine to Africans, the obverse of enlightened colonial policy, effectively reserving such fields for whites, shielding them from competition with their subjects they convinced themselves were savages. Frederick John Lugard, a governor of Nigeria in the second decade of the twentieth century, was arguably the most influential colonial official in the history of British West Africa and the principal architect of London's policy of "indirect rule." In 1920, Lugard wrote:

> It is a cardinal principle of British Colonial policy that the interests of a large native population shall not be subject to the will ... of a small minority of educated and Europeanised natives who have nothing in common with them, and whose interests are often opposed to theirs.[9]

For a man often credited with great talent and perception, it is not the period racism inherent in his thinking that is so striking, but the utter failure of honesty. Lugard's formula, after all, asked people to believe that large majorities of people deliberately left "uneducated" under colonial rule had more in common with or were better understood and protected by their paternalist British overlords than by Western-educated Africans. Worse still, he pretended that imperial policy was principally driven by the interests of this so-called benighted African majority rather than by British interests themselves. In an ironic way, it was this closing of the ranks among the white administrator class, perhaps sensing that autocratic control was no longer in their grasp, that gave the most important boost to independence-minded thinking in the region in the pre-war era.

THE PRODIGAL-SOUNDING TALE OF KWAME NKRUMAH'S BIRTH AND EARLIEST years has an oracular quality to it. It resonates with notes common to the lyrics of certain Delta Blues classics, hinting at the preordained destiny of a man-child—a figure of dauntless resilience and of greatness foretold.

As his mother, Elizabeth Nyaniba, went into labor, there was great commotion in Nkroful, but it had nothing to do with the would-be Saturday's child. Save for the mother, the birth of her child was seemingly the least of anyone's concerns. The beating of drums and other musical celebration had been organized as part of the funeral rites to honor the passing of Nkrumah's grandmother. "My birth was of very little interest to the villagers," Nkrumah wrote, at least until the infant failed to show any signs of life; he was not breathing and appeared to be stillborn.[10] Female relatives who had dragged themselves away from the funeral resolved to jolt him to life; they banged cymbals while tugging at his limbs and spanking him. With his first uncertain breaths, they stuck a banana in his mouth in order to make him cough and fight, and with their mission accomplished, handed him bawling and kicking back to his mother.

Whatever reticence he showed in those first moments of life, from infancy, young Francis was unusually attached to his mother—even insisting, long after the ordinary age, that he sleep between his mother and father in their bed. Nyaniba would return this devotion. Nkrumah called her his "vigilant protector," and wrote, "she had a knack of knowing my wants without either of us speaking a word."[11] She was her husband's first, or senior, wife in a traditional family common for that time in Akan culture in which a man might have several spouses. By no means was Nkrumah's father wealthy, but making gold jewelry set him apart from other locals, nonetheless, placing him in the cash economy and giving him the wherewithal to sustain an immediate family that Nkrumah numbered at fourteen members. However, in an era when places in Western-style schools were rare, costly, and hard to come by, this modest well-being of his parents' household probably only sufficed for formal schooling for one member of the next generation. Nkrumah's mother, who had never been to school herself, did everything possible, starting with relocating to the larger frontier town of Half Assini and then selling loose cigarettes, sugar, and dry rice by the cup for long hours under the sun, in order to make sure that her son, who was not the oldest child in the family, became the one.

Nkrumah describes himself as a mischievous, even willful, child who was revered by his half-brothers as their "mascot and something sacred." Like the makeshift fishing rods I had seen still being used by boys on the banks of his village's creek, they made jerry-rigged toys for him from whatever materials were at hand. For all of their adulation of him, though, what Nkrumah said he cherished most was being alone—daydreaming, or catching birds and crabs and other small animals at forest's edge, or by the sea, and trying to raise them in captivity. To others, he wrote, "I must have appeared a strange and difficult child. Few would have believed that the small boy who kept himself in the background with his finger in his mouth or who would make himself scarce for hours on end, could, when roused, spit fire like a machine gun and use every limb and fingernail in defending his idea of justice."[12]

In Half Assini, when his mother secured a place for him in a one-room Roman Catholic mission school, Nkrumah writes that he ran away on his first day, resolving never to return. His mother, even more determined than Nkrumah, dragged her son back by the arm every morning those first few days and saw to it that he remained in class for his lessons. Later, the young boy bridled at his teacher, who frequently wielded the rod to keep the students in line, but he soon discovered that he enjoyed learning. Moreover, he was good at it; so good, in fact, that he came to the attention of George Fischer, a local priest, who became something of a guardian to Nkrumah. Fischer enlisted him as an altar boy during Mass, initiating a period when Nkrumah says he took Catholicism very seriously. The priest even helped cover some of the costs of the boy's schooling.

Strokes of fortune like this—finding a mentor or sponsor at crucial times—began to occur early in Nkrumah's life and would not soon let up. To fully appreciate their value, one must first understand just how scarce opportunities for formal education were, even at the primary level, under British rule in Ghana as late as the second decade of the twentieth century.

Since the founding of the Gold Coast as a crown colony in 1874, London had invested next to nothing in indigenous education, mostly leaving the provision of what scant schooling there was to religious orders and missionary associations. No wonder there was a benighted majority. In 1886, A. W. L. Hemming, the head of the Africa Department in the British Colonial Office stated that "the educated native is the curse of the West Coast."[13] Here one finds stark parallels to the experience of America's Black population in this same era, and for decades hence. In the Deep South, where African Americans were still heavily concentrated, even most cities did not yet have high schools for Blacks, for whom the prevailing ideology held that education so extensive was superfluous, if not dangerous. White extremist politicians, like James K. Vardaman, who became Mississippi's thirty-sixth governor in 1904, campaigned on platforms that explicitly called for excluding African Americans from *all* forms of education.

In 1881, five years before Hemming's statement, there were only roughly 139 elementary-level schools in the entire Gold Coast colony, with places for approximately five thousand students. And for reasons of cost, most of the lucky few Africans who entered elementary schools were unable to complete more than two or three years of primary education.

The Berlin Conference of 1884–85, which is popularly remembered as the founding event in the so-called Scramble for Africa, attempted to justify Europe's takeover of the continent in humanitarian terms, and especially by highlighting the need for education. The participating imperialist nations of Europe publicly vowed commitment to the "material well-being of [Africa's] native populations."[14] By the time of Nkrumah's birth in 1909, the number of students in the Gold Coast had roughly doubled from twenty years earlier, but it was still phenomenally small. A 1911 census estimated the colony's population to be 1.5 million, meaning that well under 1 percent of Britain's subjects there received any schooling at all. Experts nowadays regard this census count as a substantial understatement of the population.[15] By the middle of the 1910s, the number of primary students increased slightly to roughly twelve thousand. But the colonial government itself only maintained nineteen schools in this time period and had still not founded a single secondary school.[16]

For these reasons, it took a mere eight years of schooling to place Nkrumah among the relatively well-educated youth of the colony. This led to his being hired as a so-called pupil teacher at seventeen. It also set the stage for fate to make itself felt once again in his life. In 1926, during a routine inspection tour of schools along the coast, Nkrumah captured the interest of the head of the government training college in Accra, Alec Garden Fraser, who recruited him to be a student in the capital. Soon after his arrival at the college, in 1927, Nkrumah's father died, and he was unable to reach home before the burial. But soon, another auspicious event occurred. That same year, the training college that Fraser ran was absorbed into a new school that would immediately take on an enormously important role in the life of the colony as its most prestigious and powerful educational institution, Achimota College. Despite its name, Achimota was, in reality, an elite high school, and Nkrumah, who studied teacher training there, would go on to become one of its first graduates.

Although woefully insufficient when measured against the needs of a growing population, Achimota represented a dramatic departure in terms of commitments to education. Its creation was the inspiration of a remarkably progressive governor, the Canadian-born brigadier general, Gordon Guggisberg, who had worked extensively in the Gold Coast and Nigeria before serving in France and seeing action at the Battle of the Somme. Guggisberg's appointment came at a time when British governors of African colonies enjoyed extraordinary leeway in shaping policy toward their jurisdictions. In a book coauthored with Fraser, who would become Achimota's first principal,

Guggisberg took an unusually positive view of Africans compared to the imperial elite of the day: "My practical experience . . . during the last twenty-seven years has convinced me that what individuals have achieved, in spite of ill-selected systems of education, can be achieved by the race generally, provided we alter our educational methods."[17]

With this goal in mind, Guggisberg boldly carved out a coed campus originally named the Prince of Wales College and School, then located several miles to the north of Accra at Achimota, laying its foundation stone in 1924. The swelling capital of independent Ghana has long since brought Achimota into its precincts, but the campus, where I spent a day not long ago, remains insulated from Accra by a cordon of thick forest. The sensation one gets there of being in a world apart is reinforced not only by the prevailing quiet, but by the original design of the school itself; little changed since its creation. Large and stolid whitewashed buildings, replete with black roofs and trim, exude a colonial feeling. Each is set off from the next by resplendent expanses of lawn. The whole is dominated by a three-story administrative building with a soaring clock tower, double balustrade, and strikingly high ceilings. It was a design suited for an age well before the advent of air conditioning, or even electric fans. A mission statement posted on a sign at the entrance reads: "To be the best school both locally and internationally by training the Head and Hands and Heart, holistically."

The best way of measuring the impact of Achimota is by the distinctions achieved by its most celebrated Akora, as graduates are called. Including Nkrumah, there have been five heads of state of Ghana, each of very different class and political backgrounds. The presidents of two other African countries, Robert Mugabe of Zimbabwe and Dawda Jawara of Gambia, also studied there. At one point, no fewer than 126 out of Ghana's 140 sitting members of parliament were alumni of the school.[18]

Walking the grounds, I was shaken by the question of how different African history might have been if Britain had created good high schools and colleges on the continent from a much earlier time, or at least on a much wider scale. The same holds true for France, which provided sharply less access to education in the colonial era. But to dream about such things is to lose sight of what colonial rule in its long early decades was in fact really about: racial subordination for the purpose of economic benefit and the territorial aggrandizement that went with great power competition in that age.

After visiting classrooms with murmuring students bent over their lessons and then browsing the library during a private tour with a longtime alumnus, I located the residential hall where Nkrumah had lived during his time at Achimota. There, shaded by tall bamboo trees and squat palms, a crimson sign over the black wooden door read, "Aggrey House."

James Aggrey, a Gold Coast Fante, was the college's first African faculty member and vice-principal. He had been a member of the first substantial, albeit minuscule, wave of African students in the United States, where he graduated top of his class in 1902 with three academic degrees from Livingstone College in Salisbury, North Carolina. Aggrey then earned a master's degree in sociology from Columbia University. In 1927, Aggrey took an interest in the eighteen-year-old Nkrumah, becoming his role model and strongly influencing his decision years later to study in the United States. Aggrey may have also served as the originator of Nkrumah's initiation into nationalism and pan-Africanism. Aggrey died suddenly in the summer of 1927, shortly after returning to the United States to complete a PhD at Columbia at the age of 51. *The New York Age*, a leading Black newspaper of the day, compared Aggrey to Edward W. Blyden, Frederick Douglass, and Toussaint Louverture. In lumping him with figures like these, its obituary of Aggrey said, "The life and works of this coterie of intellectuals will outlive tablets of stone and bronze and continue to shine as the morning sun in the hearts of generations to come."[19]

Aggrey had begun to work for an influential American foundation, the Phelps Stokes Fund, which promoted educational initiatives in Africa. Aggrey had drawn inspiration from Booker T. Washington's Tuskegee Institute, and Phelps Stokes looked to him to help spread the Tuskegee model on the continent. But whereas Washington is generally remembered for favoring vocational school for Blacks over "pure" academic pursuits, Aggrey and even Achimota were never committed to such a limited agenda. Indeed, even Washington's enduring popular reputation may misrepresent him somewhat on this score.[20]

The British patronized Aggrey as "the good African," in part because of his undisputed intellectual excellence, but also because of his long record of maintaining cordial relations with whites. As a young man he taught missionaries Fante in exchange for lessons in French, Latin, and psychology. (He would go on to master ancient and modern Greek, German, and Japanese.) His most enduring quote, one associated with the founding of Achimota and still engraved on a plaque at the campus headquarters today, stated that, "You can play a tune of sorts on the black keys only; and you can play a tune of sorts on the white keys only; but for perfect harmony you must use both the black and white keys."[21] But to hold onto this thought of Aggrey's alone would be to misrepresent him. Aggrey was fiercely and unapologetically proud of his Blackness. He was equally fond of saying that if he went to heaven and

God offered to send him back to earth with a choice of skin color, he would opt to return "completely Black." Inevitably asked why, Aggrey would answer that he had work to do as a Black man that no white man could do. But the young Aggrey had also organized against the British administration in their attempts to control the sale of land in the Gold Coast. The New York University scholar, Pamela Newkirk, wrote of him and Washington, "There are indications that the two men may have merely appropriated the rhetoric of accommodation to secure resources while clandestinely advancing a counter-hegemonic education, political and economic strategy for Blacks."[22]

Aggrey's influence cannot be overstated. In 1926, he wrote that "there is a definite renaissance going on in Africa. A new Africa is being born. . . . I have talked with leading Natives all over. . . . I say this, that wise Governments and Mission bodies are those who will be willing to guide this spirit and not try to stop or curb it."[23] He also summoned the power of education to, as he put it, "stoop down and kiss the Sleeping Beauty of Africa back into life from her centuries of sleep."[24] Touring the continent, Aggrey spoke rousingly on themes of Black pride, revival, and self-determination, and he insisted that Africans never accept second-class standards. "Nothing but the best is good enough for Africa," was his motto.[25] Achimota didn't only exist to absorb knowledge from afar. Rather, Aggrey argued, it was a place where the best in African culture could be combined with the best in Western culture. This meant traditional academics, like science and mathematics, but also attention to indigenous art, to craft, and to African music.[26] And it was at his insistence that the college was made coed right from the start, with Aggrey saying that "If you educate a man you simply educate an individual, but if you educate a woman, you educate a family."[27]

In his autobiography, Nkrumah spoke of Aggrey's great powers of oratory, and of his vitality and "infectious laugh."[28] The older man cut an imposing figure on the campus of Achimota, where he was one of only two Black faculty members and served as the house master of the hall named for him that I visited. Nkrumah had resided there, holding Aggrey in some fear as a disciplinarian, notably about missing Sunday evening roll. He was impressed by the older man for many other reasons that may seem obvious given the background just laid out, such as Aggrey's rapid-fire accumulation of degrees, which Nkrumah would later emulate. But there was an added allure to Aggrey that particularly captured Nkrumah's imagination: the fact that this outstanding man had gone to the United States, rather than to Britain, to study.

Upon learning of Aggrey's unexpected death, Nkrumah cofounded a student society in his honor. "It was through him that my nationalism was first aroused," he would write. "He [Aggrey] was extremely proud of his color but was strongly opposed to racial segregation in any form and, although he could understand Marcus Garvey's principle of 'Africa for the Africans', he never hesitated to attack this principle. He believed conditions should be such that the Black and white races should work together." Adding to this encomium, Nkrumah opined, "I maintained that such harmony can only exist when the black race is treated as equal to the white race; that only a free and independent people—a people with a government of their own—can claim equality, racial or otherwise, with another people."[29]

IN THE OPENING YEARS OF THE TWENTIETH CENTURY, JUST INLAND FROM THE coast, independent African farmers in the colony began experimenting with the cultivation of a new cash crop, cocoa. With little input or support from the British, they made such rapid advances that by 1911, the Gold Coast became the world's leading producer of this crop, a position Ghana would retain until the 1970s. It quickly became clear that Africans could earn substantial cash incomes from this export. The resulting boom in cocoa farming set off a scramble for the fertile, semi-forested areas best suited to growing cocoa. And this, in turn, fueled largescale internal migration driven by unprecedented demand for farm labor.[30]

After a long boom cocoa prices collapsed in 1930, and this radicalized the Gold Coast farmers who complained that London-controlled oligopolies were rigging markets. They responded not only by withholding their beans from export markets, but also by boycotting imports from Britain. In these twinned actions, one can see early glimmerings of an African response to what, much later, Nkrumah would call "neocolonialism," by which he meant, in part, the structural nature of the West's economic domination of Africa. In reaction, alarmed colonial authorities proposed a vigorous strengthening of sedition laws that was finally approved in the face of strong resistance in the Gold Coast after a dramatic tightening of press restrictions. These measures were justified under the colonial administrators' pretense that the great majority of Africans were "backward folk of a primitive mind who ... can be easily misled," by "irresponsible" and "advanced," meaning educated, individuals.[31]

One of the main causes of British concern in its African colonies was Communist influence. A Trinidadian man named George Padmore had toured West Africa in 1930 as an agent of Comintern, aiming to recruit delegates for an International Trade Union Committee of Negro Workers (ITUCNW).[32]

Even as a near-coincidence, the presence of Padmore in Ghana at this crucial juncture is remarkable. There is no evidence that they met during Padmore's West African travels, but as we will see, Padmore would later become one of Nkrumah's most important and enduring influences in his turn to progressive politics and in the development of his pan-Africanism.

Long prior to meeting Padmore, Nkrumah came under another decisive influence at this early stage of his life, that of the Nigerian journalist, intellectual, and later first president of his country upon independence in 1960, Nnamdi Azikiwe. Azikiwe arrived in the Gold Coast in late 1934, at a time when British rule was becoming increasingly repressive as the colonial authorities pushed back on the economic demands of cocoa farmers, worried about rising labor union activism and a rising clamor for self-government. As the biographer of Nkrumah and historian of Africa, Basil Davidson, has written, "The coming of Azikiwe 'was like an electric shock' to the younger ranks of intellectuals in the Gold Coast, firing their imagination 'for emancipation from thralldom' by speeches, articles and private talks."[33]

In 1935, Azikiwe and a sometime politician and union activist from Sierra Leone named Isaac Theophilus Akunna (I. T. A.) Wallace-Johnson, collaborated closely in the Gold Coast in forming a group they named the West African Youth League, which advocated full rights for colonized Africans and successfully supported the election of Kojo Thompson, a progressive candidate, to the Gold Coast's Legislative Council in 1935.

What aroused the ire of the British and caught Nkrumah's attention far more, though, was this pair's crusading journalism. Following a stint in England after years of study in the United States, Azikiwe had moved to the Gold Coast to serve as founding editor of a new newspaper called the *African Morning Post*. Its owner was a Gold Coast native named Alfred Ocansey, who gave Azikiwe wide berth in running the publication. The Nigerian editor used the platform to boldly promote African pride and nationalist politics. Some of this he did using his own pen, writing a signed column he called "The Inside Stuff by Zik," and otherwise by pushing voices who shared his pro-independence views. The most famous of these was Wallace-Johnson. Although the most noteworthy, the *African Morning Post* was by no means the only publication in the colony that was agitating for freedom by this time. This prompted the British inspector general of the colony to rue the supposed lack of "a single editor of repute or sense of responsibility [at] any one of the local papers."[34]

On May 15, 1936, under Azikiwe's editorship, the *Post* published a willfully provocative article by Wallace-Johnson titled "Has the African a God?" Among other things, it stated:

> Personally, I believe the European has a god in whom he believes and whom he is representing in his churches all over Africa. He believes in the god whose name is spelt Deceit.[35]

What followed was a lengthy bill of charges. The god of Europeans, Wallace-Johnson wrote, commanded colonizers to use their strength to sap the vitality of the weak, to "civilize" them through barbarous methods, to employ labor and sedition laws to exploit Africans as slaves, to gag or exile them when they protest, to tax them into perpetual poverty, and to use the proceeds from countless levies to employ high-living Europeans to lord over them.[36]

Earlier that year, the British governor of the Gold Coast, Arnold Hodson, had requested "absolute power to suppress a paper at once, if, in his opinion, such action was warranted." Now, in keeping with the increasingly repressive atmosphere of British rule in the mid-1930s, Hodson felt justified in invoking the newly strengthened sedition law. It had been adopted on the alleged basis "that the people . . . in their present stage of development should be protected from disloyal intrigue and subversive propaganda." Of Azikiwe and Wallace-Johnson specifically, he wrote, they sought "to stir up trouble and break up the Empire."[37]

Azikiwe and Wallace-Johnson were arrested and charged with sedition, which the colonial government had a great deal of difficulty proving in court. This did not prevent it from legally harassing the two men until each chose to return to their native countries, leaving the Gold Coast permanently. The "African God" article was published a year after Nkrumah had departed the Gold Coast for school in the United States. Whether Nkrumah met Wallace-Johnson before then is unlikely, but he was certainly a reader of both him and of Azikiwe, whom Nkrumah heard speak and whom he eventually met at a decisive time in his life. In his autobiography, Nkrumah credits Azikiwe's influence for boosting his own nationalism, but also with providing him with another influential example, after Aggrey, of a West African who had chosen to study in the United States rather than Britain. Nkrumah even credited reading Azikiwe, hearing him deliver speeches in the Gold Coast, and meeting him with his abandonment of the idea of joining the Jesuit order and pursuing a vocation in the priesthood.[38]

Nkrumah's autobiography frustratingly provides the only source for much of his early life. There, it feels as if he has given short shrift to other important influences, especially in the case of others native to the Gold Coast. One of them, a man named Samuel R. Wood, had been active in a group called the Gold Coast Aborigines' Rights Protection Society (GCARPS) and later wrote a college entrance recommendation for Nkrumah. Wood was also a member of the African Friends of Abyssinia, which opposed Italy's imperial ambitions in Ethiopia, a cause that Nkrumah claimed completely galvanized him upon his arrival in Britain on his way to study at Lincoln College in Pennsylvania.[39] The Abyssinia group also included J. B. Danquah, an older, wellborn, University of London–trained Gold Coast lawyer whose age made him an intermediary between the generations of Casely Hayford and Nkrumah himself. Although more conservative, Danquah had beaten Nkrumah to the cause of independence by many years. As readers will soon see, their lives would later collide in unpredictable and eventually tragic ways.

The force that Azikiwe's ideas must have exerted on Nkrumah nonetheless seems abundantly clear. As a young man, Azikiwe had also met Nkrumah's mentor, Aggrey, and been profoundly influenced by him, to the point of adopting Aggrey's metaphor of the need to awaken a slumbering continent. In his 1937 book, *Renascent Africa*, Azikiwe called for the "mental emancipation" of Africans, writing boldly, "If there is any African who disbelieves his capacity to enjoy the fruits of liberty, mark him well, he is not sane, he is destined to be the footstool of his compeers, and his doom has been sealed."[40]

He also glorified "agitation," saying that Africans needed to be roused from their lethargy, and he spoke constantly of the need for people of the continent to overcome local and subregional chauvinisms based on ethnic, religious, and linguistic differences, many of them deliberately promoted by the colonizers. Early on, ideas like these would become hallmarks of what became known as Nkrumahism. Nkrumah wrote of Azikiwe and his newspaper crusading in Ghana, "it made Europeans aware that the Africans were not blind to all that was going on; it was the first warning puff of smoke that a fire had been lit, a fire that would prove impossible to extinguish."[41]

Although his letter does not survive in the archives of Lincoln University, where Azikiwe himself had recently studied, we have sufficient reason to believe that Azikiwe wrote a strong recommendation on Nkrumah's behalf, calling him "an enthusiastic teacher with great power of arousing interest." Samuel Wood, for his part, attested to the young man's "intellectual ability, his aptitude and ambition for learning."[42]

With little explanation, Nkrumah alludes to the fact that he had also sought acceptance to university in Britain, taking and failing the London Matriculation Examination, which would be the first of two academic setbacks suffered in a student career generally marked by strong performance. How seriously had he considered study in the United Kingdom at this time? It could be that his attempted application was more a matter of covering his bets in case his bid to follow in the footsteps of Azikiwe at the first degree-granting historically Black university in the United States fell through. In the essay that Nkrumah wrote as part of his Lincoln application, he quoted from, of all people, Cecil Rhodes, the devoted Anglo-South African imperialist and influential architect of a post-World War I global order, who legitimated new forms of white control over African territories under the rubric of "mandates." "So much to do so little done," the brief passage read.

This modesty was winning, but uncharacteristically, it was also excessively humble. For someone who might have easily died at birth, who was raised by an unschooled mother in a poor and forgotten corner of colonial West Africa, Nkrumah had traveled a very long distance already. The time would come for him to take on Rhodes and his intellectual and geopolitical progeny. More immediately, though, the still nearly penniless teacher had to figure out how he could possibly afford to make his dream of college in America come true.

CHAPTER TWO

Black Is a Country

THE ROOTS OF PAN-AFRICAN THOUGHT, THE BIG IDEAS THAT BEGAN TO tug at Nkrumah even before he left Ghana, are as numerous as they are tangled. Sometimes they bring people together who in no other sense could be considered sympathetic, never mind allies, and at other times they divide thinkers who might at first blush otherwise seem like soulmates.

Two of the first progenitors of pan-Africanism were active in Liberia and Sierra Leone, neighboring West African settler colonies. Liberia had been promoted by many elite American politicians, from James Monroe to Henry Clay to Abraham Lincoln, to accommodate formerly enslaved peoples, or "returnees from the United States." Following in the intellectual tradition of Thomas Jefferson, they believed that the United States could never successfully integrate Blacks with whites. Sierra Leone was also promoted in the early nineteenth century as a colony to absorb the "Black poor" of England. Soon, though, it became a resettlement center for trafficked Africans captured at sea off the continent's western bulge by British antislaving patrols established in the wake of formal abolition in 1807.

In terms of its genesis, the search for the origins of African nationalism is a complicated one. Among the most common responses of people who read modern histories of the transatlantic slave trade is to ask why Africans themselves sold "each other" to Europeans or to be shipped in chains to the Americas. Once relocated to the "New World" the captives, as is now common knowledge, were transformed into chattel and brutally put to work on plantations that generated wealth of an unimaginable scale for the West. But no understanding of the tragic uses to which these people were destined was available to the sellers at the time. Almost none of them had anything like the conventions of chattel in their own cultures. Slavery among West Africans was not tied to "race." It was seldom transgenerational, meaning that the children of Africans held in bondage by other Africans were usually not automatically enslaved, as they were in the Americas. Usually, in fact, they were rapidly and deliberately assimilated. Finally, although Africans had taken slaves among conquered neighbors from time immemorial, most of this was done in a spirit that John Locke would have recognized as a legitimate consequence of captivity in what he called "just wars."[1]

The question of why Africans sold "each other," though, runs even deeper than this. Compared to people in many other parts of the world, Africans came very late to the idea of seeing themselves in any unified or even racial sense that we would recognize today. Neighboring peoples, of course, had always known each other and maintained political and economic ties, as well as rivalries and warfare among themselves. But as the modern era unfolded, Africans were exposed to white people very gradually, in stages, and only very belatedly in large numbers. The first important contact that began in the late fifteenth century involved Europeans seeking to trade in gold along the West African coast. Although it had begun simultaneously to the gold trade, the European commerce in enslaved human beings started out as a mere trickle, only becoming a sustained, high-volume, transatlantic enterprise in the eighteenth century. Finally, in most regions of sub-Saharan Africa, Europeans only arrived as imperial masters, making sweeping territorial claims and imposing rudimentary administration beginning in the latter half of the nineteenth century. Prior to this, in a world where nearly everyone was Black, Blackness was not a politically, socially, or economically salient concept. The idea of Blackness as a coherent or synthetic identity only grew out of the European takeover of nearly all of the continent in the wake of the Berlin Conference, which took place in 1884–85 against a backdrop of intense pseudoscientific efforts in late-nineteenth-century Europe to classify the races in terms of their members' supposed relative physical and intellectual endowments, with Africans fixed at the bottom of a widely postulated hierarchy of races. Empire and imperial science, in other words, changed everything. As the economic historian Immanuel Wallerstein wrote, "All European empires in Africa were empires of race."[2]

The settler, or better put, resettlement colonies of Liberia and Sierra Leone were crucial to the emerging African response to these developments because they were cauldrons that threw together people who were unified by little other than their Blackness and the fact that they or their immediate ancestors had been enslaved by Europeans and Americans. The transplants from the Americas, whether in Liberia or in Sierra Leone, and the so-called recaptives freed from slaving vessels and returned by the British to these coastal enclaves, had no language or culture in common with the indigenous population. Together, as often in conflict as in concert, they forged new "creole" cultures as they invented what it meant to be "African" in the modern sense of the word. Simultaneously, they sought to work out how to fend for themselves in a world that had already long seen blackness as a coherent identity, and usually as a deeply devalued one, well before the Black people who had been cast together in places like this had begun to conceptualize any such identity for themselves.

AS GOOD A PLACE AS ANY TO BEGIN THE PAN-AFRICANISM GENESIS STORY would be with a Sierra Leonean man named James Beale Horton, a political and intellectual forebear of Nkrumah. Horton, who was born in 1835, was the seventh of eight children, and was the only one to survive infancy. He was born to Igbo parents from present-day eastern Nigeria who had been ensnared in the slave trade but freed by the British antislavery squadron and deposited hundreds of miles away at the aptly named Sierra Leone settlement called Freetown. Horton received an early education in Anglican missionary schools and showed great promise in Latin and other traditional subjects, eventually earning a place at the Fourah Bay Institution (later Fourah Bay College) in that city, where he studied Hebrew and Divinity. Although he had hoped to serve as a village pastor, he was steered away from this vocation by colonial church officers who felt that he spoke his own mind too freely.

Horton's life would change course in 1855, when instead of receiving religious training, the British army sent him to London to study medicine at King's College. This made Horton one of the first two Africans to acquire a medical commission from the Royal College of Surgeons. After three years in London, Horton pursued doctoral studies at the University of Edinburgh. During this time, he experienced an identity awakening, most likely in response to endemic racism in Britain. Instead of seeking to downplay his origins, Horton did the opposite, adopting the name Africanus, which he used for the rest of his short (he was only 48 when he died), but almost unimaginably full life.

A virtual polymath, Horton would build an astonishing scholarly legacy and record of publications. Beyond medicine, it included monographs and articles in scientific fields as varied as botany and geology. He dabbled in newspaper work and founded an African bank in Sierra Leone and a successful mining company in the Gold Coast. All the while, he was a tireless and lifelong advocate of the creation of a university intended to serve all of West Africa. He saw this both as a vital resource for self-rule and as a means of overcoming the fractured landscape of the region's countless tribal identities. He was one of the first African commissioned officers in the British army, later served as a magistrate, and in 1872 was appointed commandant of Sekondi, an important western port town in the Gold Coast. On the strength of that experience, he applied for the then-vacant position of administrator of the entire Gold Coast colony. If anything, he was over-qualified, but he was rejected out of hand as "unfit," purely on the basis of racial prejudice.[3]

In his published works, most famously, *West African Countries and Peoples, British and Native, with the Requirements Necessary for Establishing that Self-Government recommended by the Committee of the House of Commons, 1865; and a Vindication of the African Race*, Horton explicitly took on the racist pseudoscience of the age. He espoused a view of the African past as one not of barrenness, but of civilizational greatness, calling the continent "the nursery of science and literature" of Europe. And his vision of the future was equally confident, grand even. Africans "must live in the hope that in the process of time their turn will come, when they will occupy a prominent position in the world's history, and when they will command a voice in the council of nations."[4] To get there, Horton prescribed a wide array of unusually progressive measures for his time, from compulsory education, including for girls, to rational government planning, to state-backed investment finance and support for African businesses. It was in the arena of his political ideas, though, that Horton left the greatest mark. Pointing the way for others, including Nkrumah, who devoted himself to this goal, Africanus saw territorial amalgamation as the most important remedy for Africa's backwardness. As a first step, he proposed the creation of a supraterritorial legislative assembly that would gradually forge unity and prepare the way for self-government. Horton was the first known proponent of such an idea, earning him the description of "prophet of the new Africa" by one biographer.[5]

Although Horton deserves such exalted consideration, he was by no means the only person of African descent thinking along similar lines. Even before Horton, there was David Walker, not an African but a Black Boston abolitionist thinker, journalist, and activist. This son of an enslaved father, born in North Carolina 1785, had written that God's plan for the redemption of Blacks in America would not be fulfilled except through "the entire emancipation of [our] enslaved brethren all over the world."[6] Such sentiments were carried forward by the man who would become America's foremost pan-Africanist, W. E. B. Du Bois, who in 1904, relatively early in his intellectual development, wrote of establishing equality between the races, with whites recognizing Blacks as "co-workers" in the "kingdom of culture."[7]

Another early theorist was Martin Delany. He was born free to a free seamstress and an enslaved plantation laborer in 1812 in what is now West Virginia but grew up in Pennsylvania, where he founded two newspapers and cofounded a third, *The North Star*, which he edited with Frederick Douglass. All four of Delany's grandparents had been born in Africa. In his late twenties, he boldly undertook a tour of the South to study life under slavery for the region's Black population. Later, Delany became one of the first three Black people admitted to Harvard Medical School but was dismissed after large-scale protests by white students. These experiences radicalized Delany, who organized a secret convention in Canada to help John Brown incite a Black uprising. Delany led a wide-ranging life, serving in the Union Army; meeting with Abraham Lincoln; working briefly for the Freedmen's Bureau; and traveling to Liberia and to present-day Nigeria to research resettlement there; and later emigrating to Canada. Delany identified himself as a "Black nationalist," a term so strikingly modern that it seems to echo the 1960s. He also anticipated language more famously associated with Marcus Garvey, decades later, demanding sovereignty in "Africa for the African race, and Black men to rule them."[8] Finally, in a choice redolent of these politics, he named his son after the leader of the Haitian Revolution, Toussaint Louverture.

Delany wrote numerous influential books on the topic of Blackness, as well as a serialized novel, *Blake*, in 1859, which soon went largely forgotten. Scholars have belatedly come to regard *Blake* as one of the most important works of American fiction in the nineteenth century. At heart, it is a story built of early pan-Africanist dreams: an attempt by its eponymous hero, who flees a Southern plantation and travels throughout the United States, Canada, Africa, and Cuba, to foment rebellion and unite Black people scattered throughout the Atlantic world.[9]

On African soil, Horton's contemporary, Edward Wilmot Blyden, was working out a remarkably similar vision of pan-Atlantic Black identity and eventual self-determination for Africa. Blyden was born to free parents in the then–Dutch West Indian colony of Saint Thomas in 1832, where slavery would not be abolished for another sixteen years. After being educated on that island and in Venezuela, he sought, in 1850, to enroll in three American colleges, including Rutgers Theological College in New Jersey, only to be denied admission on the basis of his race. The following year, Blyden emigrated to Sierra Leone's neighbor, the American settler colony of Liberia. There, he began to espouse pride in Blackness and to describe the purpose of the Liberian experiment as "the redemption of Africa and the disenthrallment and elevation of the African race."[10]

Blyden's vision for the development of the continent emphasized the importance of unity among Black peoples, and openness to "return," meaning immigration from members of the American diaspora, like himself. A free Black maternal ancestor of mine, from whose line my middle name, Waring, is derived, felt this pull and emigrated to Liberia in the 1820s. After years of frustration over the feeble numbers of African Americans coming to Liberia, though, as the country's secretary of state, Blyden warned in 1864 that even the looming prospect of emancipation of American slaves would be a source of false hope to the country's Black population. Even if freedom was won, he wrote, the only sure protection against it being rolled back or infringed upon was having a "home and nationality of their own."[11]

Like Horton, Blyden also promoted the idea of creating a regional university and he, too, espoused territorial amalgamation, seeing Liberia "as the nucleus of a West African state" of the kind Nkrumah would later dream of.[12] And toward that end, he was willing to cooperate with Britain or the United States if that could help him incorporate new territories into what he hoped would become a new and expansive regional power.

An idea of Blyden's that both set him apart from other early pan-Africanist thinkers and persisted throughout his life was his insistence on the uniqueness of what he called the "African personality." He first developed this notion in *A Vindication of the African Race*, a book he published in 1857 at the age of twenty-five. What this formulation seems to have meant is that it was fine for Africans to pick and choose as they adopted ideas and institutions from Britain, Europe, the United States, or elsewhere, but that they should make no apologies for seeking the political arrangements that best suited Africa's own conditions and the traditions and history of its peoples. This too became a durable central theme in Nkrumah's politics. "We are going to demonstrate to the world, to the other nations, that we are prepared to lay our own foundation. . . . We are going to create our own African personality and identity. It is the only way we can show the world that we are ready for our own battles," Nkrumah hammered in his inaugural address.[13]

In the preceding pages we have already encountered the Gold Coast's preeminent pan-African thinker of the early twentieth century, J. E. Casely Hayford. Born in 1866, strictly speaking, this privileged son of a well-to-do mixed-race household was a peer of the pioneers from West Africa's settler colonies, Horton and Blyden. Given his intellectual indebtedness to them, and to Blyden in particular, Casely Hayford's place in history feels more like that of a successor. This impression is reinforced by the facts of Casely Hayford's political activism on behalf of African self-determination and the way that his politics up to his death in 1930 so clearly set the stage for Ghana's accession to independence under Nkrumah nearly three decades hence.

Casely Hayford, like Africanus Horton, had also studied at Fourah Bay College in Sierra Leone, where he came under the sway of Blyden. His civic life began immediately after returning home, working as a journalist at a newspaper, the *Western Echo*, founded by an uncle, where he started in 1885. Two years later, he became its editor, under the new name, the *Gold Coast Echo*. He then studied economics at Cambridge University for two years, beginning in 1893, and was later called to the bar in London. Once back in the Gold Coast, he joined a campaign by a pioneering anticolonial organization, the Gold Coast Aborigines' Rights Protection Society (GCARPS), to oppose the nearly new colonial regime's Land Bill, which took control over the land out of the hands of both ordinary people and traditional authorities.

The campaign by GCARPS won some important concessions from colonial authorities, but Casely Hayford and the small coterie of Gold Coast intellectuals he campaigned with had no illusions about what they were up against. In the years immediately following the Berlin Conference, imperial control over African colonies was still undergoing seismic consolidation. By 1915, Europe would add 10 million square miles to its imperial territories, with Britain alone accounting for 4 million square miles of that total, and France 3.5 million square miles.[14]

For the restless, seminal figures of the early era of pan-Africanism, including Casely Hayford, the quest to fulfil their ideals demanded so-called polyvalency—they lived their lives in multiple dimensions simultaneously. After his collaboration with GCARPS had begun, Casely Hayford entered a phase of intense writing, publishing his first book, *Gold Coast Native Institutions* in 1903. In this study of the political institutions of the Asante and Fante in Ghana, one finds a crystallization of one of his most important ideas. For the rest of his life, Casely Hayford would argue that West Africans in particular, but Africans in general, had all that they needed in terms of indigenous political traditions, which, contrary to Western tropes about their savagery, had been worked out over long generations of self-rule prior to the arrival of Europeans:

> Each of these important communities, in regard to the entire State, was a sort of imperium in imperio—in fact several native states federated together under the same laws, the same customs, the same faith and worship, the people speaking the same language, and all owning allegiance to a paramount king or president, who represented the sovereignty of the entire Union.[15]

What this called for wasn't overlordship by Europeans, whether it posed as benevolent or not, but rather, self-determination and an end to taxation without representation.

Casely Hayford envisaged the Gold Coast—most of whose people identified as Akan, a large and relatively homogenous cultural cluster—as a potential crystal seed for a new "imperial West Africa." If Britain would only get out of the way and let Africans perfect their own governance arrangements on the basis of this model, as he advocated, there would be no reason why its colonies could not remain within the empire and even fly the Union Jack.

To be sure, this glossed over boundless regional complexities in terms of ethnicity, religion, and custom. There is no refuting, though, that the Fante, the second largest people of the Gold Coast's large Akan cluster, had already proposed a formal constitution of their own in 1870. This would have established an executive council, a judiciary, and other modern institutions for orderly self-rule under a federal state based on indigenous principles. This notion was rejected out of hand, though, by a Britain intent instead on wiping the slate clean of indigenous traditions. Some described Casely Hayford as a nativist, but his reasoning was no mere chauvinism. He had studied the example of Japan's successful modernization during the Meiji Restoration beginning in 1868, and followed that country's victory over Russia, a major European power, in the Russo-Japanese War in 1904–05. The secret of Japan's success as a modernizing power, in his view, was that the country had preserved its cultural integrity, even as it had selectively imported ideas and technologies from the West. Africans could do this, too, if only they were allowed.

Casely Hayford best-known book, *Ethiopia Unbound*, was published in 1911, and beyond its clear pan-Africanist themes, it is an unusually difficult work to characterize.[16] On the one hand, it stands out as one of the first African novels. But on the other, it is also far more than that: it awkwardly incorporates a wide variety of other forms, an "unstable mix," as one writer has called it, of "varied genres of autobiography and novel, poetry and fiction, parable and realist narrative."[17] In this work, Casely Hayford conjures an Africa as a continent that will lead in the future.

By the time of *Ethiopia Unbound*'s publication, Casely Hayford's sights were high: to become the most influential figure in the Black intellectual world, and as such, a leader in terms of what he called "race emancipation." In this regard, the rivals Casely Hayford sought to overcome were Americans. The first of these was Booker T. Washington, who was born a slave and, as one critic has written, transformed the newborn school he took over in 1881, the Tuskegee Institute, "from a vacant lot with a two-thousand-dollar budget" into a world-famous center of vocationally focused education for Blacks. Tuskegee's remit was to produce skilled laborers, modern farmers, and industrial workers.[18] At the height of his influence, when he was a dinner guest of Theodore Roosevelt at the White House in 1901, Washington had become a powerful gatekeeper in the nation's capital; he was someone who held sway over what one historian called "political preferment," meaning deciding who won government jobs and appointments and who didn't.[19] But that was not all. Some even spoke of him with pride as the unofficial Black president of the United States.

Casely Hayford admired Washington enough to participate as a representative of the Gold Coast Aborigines' Rights Protection Society (GCARPS) at Washington's 1912 International Conference on the Negro, held at Tuskegee. Like many in Africa at the time, the Gold Coast's leading campaigner for self-determination saw great value in the practical emphasis of Washington's Tuskegee Institute, calling the school a "mighty uplifting force for the race."[20] For all of Casely Hayford's avant-garde postulation about new African forms of statehood, he and Washington shared a common sense of the importance of economic power as the foundation of any true and lasting political standing. "If we want to be really free, we must aim at financial and economic independence and here, as elsewhere, we ourselves must strike the blow that would loose our bonds," he wrote.[21]

Casely Hayford nonetheless bridled at the idea of American leadership of the pan-African cause, writing, "The African in America is in a worse plight than the Hebrew in Egypt. The one preserved his language, his manners and customs, his religion and household gods; the other has committed national suicide."[22] And in pushing this line, he singled out Du Bois, the most prominent thinker of the day on the place of Blacks in the world. In fact, one of Casely Hayford's main lines of criticism involved one of Du Bois's most celebrated notions, the idea of double consciousness, which the American formulated in 1903 in his most famous book, *The Souls of Black Folk*. In *Ethiopia Unbound*, Casely Hayford mockingly asked whether "Candace, Queen of Ethiopia, or Cephron, the Master of Egypt, [could be] troubled with a double consciousness." The Gold Coast native then all but answered his own question by stating, "to be a puzzle unto other is not to be a puzzle unto one's self."[23]

It is hardly surprising that the still tiny pool of West African intellectuals in the era of the Berlin Conference and its immediate aftermath became the focus of a withering campaign of marginalization by Britain. London viewed this nascent indigenous elite as first a nuisance, later a potential threat, and sought to discredit its members with the outrageous claim that their Western training had fundamentally denatured them. In other words, the very self-cultivation and learning that distinguished them disqualified them from representing their fellow Africans.

Casely Hayford's fault-finding toward Du Bois, meanwhile, operated on several levels. He wanted to refocus pan-African activism and shift its center of gravity away from the United States and other parts of the Atlantic diaspora and place it squarely in Africa, where he believed it rightfully belonged. The continent, Casely Hayford urged, should be upheld as "the treasure house of [every Black person's] nationality."[24] This foretold by several decades a coming shift in the global politics of Blackness that Du Bois himself would belatedly support, with a particular focus, as we will see, on Ghana and a new leader by the name of Kwame Nkrumah. For much of his public career, Du Bois had pushed for a leadership role for African Americans in determining the fate of Africa and in the wider Atlantic world. In 1959, late in his long life, though, Du Bois completely renounced the principle of a guiding role for Americans in the movement, writing this:

> Once I thought of you Africans as children, whom we educated African Americans would lead to liberty. I was wrong. We could not even lead ourselves, much less you. Today I see you rising under your own leadership, guided by your own brains.[25]

Bidding to gain more prominence for himself, Casely Hayford pluckily targeted the biggest figure in his field for criticism, Du Bois. Still, he took care to show occasional deference and not burn his bridges. In a handwritten 1904 letter addressed to "Dear Prof. Du Bois" that accompanied a signed copy of his own book, *Gold Coast Native Institutions*, for example, Casely Hayford wrote:

> I have recently had the pleasure of reading your great work "The Souls of Black Folk", and it occurred to me that if leading thinkers of the African race in America had the opportunity of exchanging thoughts with thinkers of the race in west Africa, this century would be likely to see the race problem solved.[26]

The least obvious of Casely Hayford's tactical goals might have been his most important. "There will be no deliverance for the Black man," he wrote "not so long as he turns away from the Father's house and elects to remain a slave in soul."[27] Posing as such an ardent defender of African authenticity was about more than upstaging his American rivals; it was above all a retort to British imperialists who sought to marginalize intellectuals like Casely Hayford as sons of the continent rendered illegitimate by virtue of their cosmopolitanism and their so-called distance from Africa's supposedly benighted millions.

The most ambitious project of a man who is relatively little remembered today came in the next chapter of his long public life. In the wake of *Ethiopia Unbound*, he turned his energies to forming a new regional polity aimed at overcoming the severe dismemberment of West Africa wrought by Britain and France. He promoted to regional elites a united West Africa, replete with a new, unified West African nationality. This campaign gathered steam with the creation in 1920 of a National Congress of British West Africa (NCBWA), of which Casely Hayford was the founding vice president and subsequently president. In 1927, when Nkrumah was just shy of his twenties, this group's goal was expanded beyond Britain's West African colonies. Casely Hayford and the NCBWA argued for a unified West Africa that would include brethren in French-speaking territories and, in time, incorporate "Africans . . . scattered all over the world."[28] It would be hard to find a more succinct statement in the interwar period of what would become Nkrumah's own eventual ambitions for pan-Africanism.

The NCBWA's most immediate aim reflected an elite urgency, albeit a solidly founded one: ending discrimination in appointments to colonial administration and employment generally, and more broadly still, convincing Britain to grant a greater role for educated Africans in the running of their own affairs. In 1915, all forty-nine district commissioners in the Gold Coast were nonnatives, and by 1919 only three of the high, or so-called European appointments in the colony, were held by Africans.[29] In 1920 Casely Hayford led a delegation to London with these goals in mind only to be refused an audience by the Colonial Secretary.[30] This earned him and his fellow petitioners disparagement by colonial officials as "trousered niggers."[31]

The NCBWA soon fizzled out. The reasons for its demise were filled with meaning and consequence. For all of his sniping at the American intellectual giant, Casely Hayford's and his allies' ideas shared a lot in common with those of early Du Bois, who had famously promulgated the idea that racial redemption would have to be a transgenerational project led by a "talented tenth," by which he meant a minority of highly cultivated individuals, presumably all men, who would prove themselves in contact and competition with elites of other races. Casely Hayford embraced a very similar core elitism, writing that "the future of the world is with the thinking few, be they black, white, brown or yellow."[32]

The NCBWA held a series of conferences in the 1920s, culminating with a final meeting in Lagos in 1930, the year of Casely Hayford's death, but it had been doomed by its elitism from the start. Not only did traditional chiefs in Britain's colonies distrust the intellectuals—with London's active backing and encouragement—but the fledgling regional formation never mobilized popular support among the masses in the four colonies where it was active. Its strategies and failures gesture toward the near future. Already, by the time of Casely Hayford's death, the baton was being picked up in the Gold Coast's political circles by a younger generation of men who would reproduce the NCBWA's elitism while discarding the regionalism.

The man who would emerge as the most important figure in the nationalist politics of the Gold Coast of this transitional era was J. B. Danquah, who was the leader of a group of British-trained barristers and wealthy merchants with conservative instincts. Danquah and his peers considered themselves to be and behaved as the natural rulers of the colony. They were not fixated on outright self-determination in the near term. Their chief grievance was centered instead on the social and economic exclusion of their class under the British, who practiced an undeclared brand of apartheid in the colony. It all but barred the way for Africans seeking entry into the professional world, however qualified.

It is not clear how closely Nkrumah studied the experience of Casely Hayford, who dominated nationalist politics in the Gold Coast throughout Nkrumah's childhood. But as we will see, when he returned home after twelve years overseas, Nkrumah dramatically outmaneuvered Danquah to spearhead a drive for independence that began in 1947. And this put Nkrumah in a position to become leader of a newborn nation ten years later. The magic key that made all this possible was rejecting the elitist elements in the politics of Casely Hayford and the NCBWA and concentrating his energies on popular mobilization.

IN BOTH IMAGE AND PEDIGREE, MARCUS MOSIAH GARVEY SITS UNEASILY, though significantly, in the mélange of visionary thinkers whose ideas Nkrumah drew from. Gaudy in personal style and given to bombast, Garvey had little of the educational background or refinement of predecessors such as Casely Hayford, Horton, and Blyden; his formal education was limited to church schooling, which ended at age fourteen. Garvey was not only more radical than these men, he was also a uniquely gifted performer who could assume the mantle of a Black Moses in an African Redemption movement and use his mastery of the language of the masses to rouse and inspire large crowds. His own wife called him "a showman, an opportunist and a propagandist of the first order."[33] A Black character in one of the most powerful works of twentieth-century American fiction, Ralph Ellison's novel *Invisible Man*, which depicts Harlem in the decade after Garvey, said it even better. "He must have had something to move all those people! Our people are *hell* to move. He must have had plenty!"[34]

The essence of the squat, dark-skinned Garvey's message was as important as any innate talent, though. It was redemption for his followers through overt pride in their Blackness; the through-line this created flowed down the generations. It could still be heard clearly, if uncredited to Garvey, in the "Black Is Beautiful" slogan and other popular language of the 1960s and '70s. Its spirit echoed in a faux naïve way in a 1971 interview with the American boxing champion Muhammad Ali who said he had challenged his mother with the question about why good things were so often presented as white, from Santa Claus to angel food cake to the White House. "The little ugly duckling was a black duck. And the black cat was bad luck. And if I threaten you, I'm going to blackmail you. I said Mama, why don't they call it whitemail? They lie too!"[35]

An orator, activist, publisher, and entrepreneur, Garvey, who was born in the small northern town of St. Anne's Bay, Jamaica, in 1887, was the son of a stonemason father and domestic servant mother. After apprenticing in the print trade and founding his own short-lived newspaper, *Garvey's Watchman*, Garvey left his native land as a twenty-three-year-old in 1910, worked briefly for the United Fruit Company in Costa Rica, and then, remarkably, established two newspapers successively there and in Panama. The high demand for Black laborers throughout the Caribbean basin fueled the creation of what the scholar Brent H. Edwards has called a "Black international" in the region.[36] Garvey's youthful wanderings situated him in a generation of West Indian intellectuals and other worldly figures who built richly transnational lives for themselves while helping to refashion both the narrative and politics of Blackness. After his stints in Central America, Garvey sailed off for the capital of the British empire.

Much as Lenin had in 1902, Garvey became a frequent visitor to the British Library, and to the famous Speakers' Corner in Hyde Park where he honed his oratory. Unlike the Russian, Garvey was not dreaming of Marxist revolution. Later, he would say, "those who unreasonably and wantonly fight against [capitalism] are enemies of human advancement."[37] Garvey was profoundly influenced, instead, by Blyden's *Christianity, Islam, and the Negro Race* and by Booker T. Washington's best-selling memoir *Up from Slavery*. These helped him lay the intellectual groundwork for a new and bolder form of global Black nationalism than had ever been seen before.[38] Garvey later wrote about the effect that the hours he spent in the library had on him:

> I saw before me then, as I do now, a new world of black men, not peons, serfs, dogs and slaves, but a nation of sturdy men making their impress upon civilization and causing a new light to dawn upon the human race. I could not remain in London any more. My brain was afire. There was a world of thought to conquer. I had to start ere it become too late and the work be not done.[39]

Garvey's borrowings from Blyden require little explanation. His attraction to Booker T. Washington, however, intrigues, helping lay bare the shifting valences of Black thought in this era. Its geometries could change dramatically depending on the personalities and dates involved. Garvey traveled to the United States in 1916 with the aim of meeting Washington, only to discover upon arrival at Tuskegee that the Wizard, as Alain Locke and other Black sophisticates had taken to sardonically calling Washington, had recently died.[40] That same year, Garvey settled in New York.

Washington has been remembered and sometimes reviled as the most conservative of leading African American figures of this era, someone who urged Blacks to "cast down your bucket where you are," meaning stay put in the rural South.[41] For the Wizard, racial agitation was "the extremest folly."[42] Garvey, in contrast, was nothing if not an agitator, and the program he gradually cobbled together called for the most thoroughgoing transformation of the position of Black people in the modern world of any of his prominent contemporaries.

One thing the two men clearly shared was the opprobrium of Du Bois, who was a direct rival and fierce critic of Washington, and who derided and ridiculed Garvey, with his gold-embroidered Hapsburg-style imperial getup, replete with scabbards and tassel-topped hats. Du Bois took delight in mocking Garvey's pretentious costume as a "military uniform of the gayest mid-Victorian type," and his oratorical flights, as those of a lunatic or buffoon. Sometimes, the elder Du Bois, who was of mixed-race ancestry, also stooped to ugly colorism toward the dark-skinned Jamaican. In 1923, for example, he derided him as "a little fat black man, ugly but with intelligent eyes and big head."[43]

Although pan-Africanism has no single line of paternity, Du Bois will be forever associated with its grand entry onto the world stage, beginning with a self-styled Pan-African Conference, held at the beginning of the century in

London in late July of 1900. This gave way, partially at Du Bois's impetus, to a series of Pan-African congresses that would play out over several decades. And his brand of activism (by no means limited to these conclaves) played a leading role in seeking to hold Western powers to account on several world-making occasions, from the formation of the League of Nations to the San Francisco Conference that helped launch the United Nations decades later.

Garvey's political activism operated in fundamental tension with that of Du Bois and yet on an altogether different plane. The elder American agitated almost entirely at an elite level, seeking the right for Black people to control the destinies of their own countries. From today's perspective, the Du Bois approach may seem vindicated by history, especially given that by the 1950s the world was moving squarely into a revolutionary age of nation-by-nation decolonization. By contrast, Garvey, as Nkrumah would decades later, worked from the bottom up. By 1920 he had built what would remain, despite his 1927 deportation, the largest Black organization in the United States into the late 1930s.[44] The contrast does not end there, though. At the level of ideas, Garvey rejected the conventional European-conceived nation state as a basis for political organization. His most famous slogan was "Africa for Africans," a phrase reflecting the general ideas of Horton, Blyden, and Casely Hayford.

Garvey insisted on Black control of Africa in its entirety, and he hoped to see this consolidated in such a way as to wipe away the borders and subdivisions that Europeans had drawn up at the Berlin Conference. His explicit goal was for the four hundred million "Negroes" of the world to possess their own unitary homeland. This, broadly speaking, was the objective later embraced by Nkrumah, who wrote that during his years of study in the United States, "of all the literature that I studied, the book that did more than any other to fire my enthusiasm was *Philosophy and Opinions of Marcus Garvey*."[45] In what were clear acts of homage, Nkrumah adopted the red, black, and green colors of Garvey's organization, the Universal Negro Improvement Association (UNIA), for independent Ghana's flag, and he would choose the name of Garvey's shipping company, the Black Star Line, for Ghana's maritime company. Years later, the American civil rights activist and Black Power militant, Kwame Ture (Stokely Carmichael) said of this homage that while they made fun of Garvey, but no one would make fun Kwame Nkrumah.

Garvey saw himself as a prophet of Black liberation and solidarity and spoke in almost eschatological terms about the special role that the people of the West Indies would play in the promised forthcoming reunification of a scattered Black race. "[B]efore the close of many centuries, [it] will found an Empire on which the sun shall shine as ceaselessly as it shines on the Empire of the North today," he wrote.[46] In time, he envisioned himself as the continent's provisional president.

Garvey led an intense, chaotic, and surprisingly mutable life, starting out as a supporter of British empire and even a would-be enlistee on its behalf in the First World War, even before a volunteer crisis forced the hitherto reluctant British War Office to embrace the recruitment of West Indians.[47] From defender of the Empire, he moved on to Black nationalism, pan-Africanism, and international business, with a publishing arm, factories, and a record company, among other interests.

Garvey's story is so critical in how it will reflect on Nkrumah's own political trajectory. Garvey launched the UNIA in obscurity in a Kingston hotel room in 1914 shortly after returning to Jamaica, destitute from London, where he worked as a docker and assistant to a pioneering Egyptian pan-Africanist and publisher of the *African and Orient Review* named Dusé Mohamed Ali. Two years later, Garvey moved to Harlem, where he frequented Black churches and enraptured crowds at Speakers' Corner on 135th Street. Almost immediately, he established a Harlem office for his UNIA, but the organization's takeoff wouldn't come until 1918, after he launched a weekly newspaper, the *Negro World*. His new publication's emphasis on pride in Blackness could be felt on every page and was reflected in the paper's advertising policy. *Negro World* promoted Black dolls for children well ahead of its time and refused to promote hair straightening products, for example, telling readers, "Take the kinks out of your mind, instead of out of your hair."[48]

The startlingly rapid rise of the UNIA, before Garvey's conviction of mail fraud, in 1923, involved far more than one man's personality or political talents, however great. It also reflected the ferment of the times. As we have seen, African Americans had fought in historic numbers in World War I. Although they were denied frontline action in France until late in the conflict, the so-called Buffalo Soldiers of the Black 92nd Infantry Division and its artillery regiment, of which my maternal grandfather, William James Howard, was a member, fought with distinction in the Meuse-Argonne campaign. Another group, the Black 367th Infantry, played a key role in the largest American action of the war, pushing the Germans into retreat at Metz. Still other American "Negro" troops were integrated into French brigades and were prized by their officers, who paid little heed to American commanders. These white officers, who hailed disproportionately from the American South, forbade Black soldiers from fraternizing with the local population and spread racist notions to their French allies about the risks Blacks allegedly posed in terms of crime and order. They placed special emphasis on the alleged threat that Black troops posed to the "honor" of French women.

Meanwhile, for many African American soldiers, the mere sight of Black French troops recruited widely from France's African empire to help overcome Germany's population advantage founded a novel sense of belonging to a large diaspora. Experiences like these doubtlessly helped prime some returning Black soldiers for the African-centered rhetoric of Garveyism, much as the Black experience of the next war would foster support for the pan-Africanism of Nkrumah.

Even for those who gave little thought to pan-Africanism, the Black contribution to America's victory in the war stirred expectations of an end to the brutally reactionary politics of the post-Reconstruction era. Many, in fact far too idealistically, dreamed of finally winning society's respect of their full rights as American citizens. As one historian has written, "Almost in spite of their strong sense of realism, Negroes were impressed by the wartime slogans calling for self-determination of all peoples in a world made safe for democracy."[49] Negroes believed, as had their forebears, that by taking part in the war they would have additional grounds for demanding better treatment after it was over. In a 1919 issue of *The Crisis* magazine, Du Bois expressed this conviction poetically.

We return.
We return from fighting.
We return fighting.

Make way for Democracy! We saved it in France, and by the Great Jehovah, we will save it in the United States of America, or know the reason*s why*.[50]

What followed instead were paroxysms of virulent racial violence that came to define the United States in the era around the end of the First World War. With the fighting in Europe not even over, this included the notorious anti-Black riots in East St. Louis in 1917, in which forty Black people and eight whites were killed, followed by the infamous Red Summer of 1919. Then, Blacks became targets in racial violence in twenty-six cities widely distributed around the country. But instead of being cowed into submission, many Black people mounted self-defense efforts and fought back. Indeed, the terror campaigns directed against them fed a growing determination among many Black Americans to intensify their political organizing not only against racial violence, but also against racial segregation and other forms of discrimination.

Some of this effort was poured into a law-based push for equality led by the National Association for the Advancement of Colored People (NAACP). Another channel of resistance focused its energies on literature and the arts, with Harlem emerging as the mecca for a New Negro movement and the center of the eponymous Harlem Renaissance.

Garvey's brand of Black nationalism, with its "Back to Africa" message aimed at African Americans and especially immigrants from the West Indies, was yet another major beneficiary of this restive climate, and for a time, perhaps the biggest. By 1919 Garvey rallies drew thronging crowds, including twenty-five thousand at Madison Square Garden the following year, where he declared, "If Europe is for the white man ... then surely Africa is for the black man ... and four hundred million Negroes shall shed, if needs be, the last drop of their blood for the redemption of Africa and the emancipation of the race everywhere."[51] By this time, his UNIA claimed as many as two million followers, including the Midwest-living parents of Malcolm X, who would be born in 1925.

This relatively well-known picture obscures for many Americans, even now, the depth of Garveyism's penetration of Africa itself. Garvey never managed to create a United States of Africa, but there is no refuting that he helped plant the germ of this idea firmly in the African imagination.

Just as World War I spurred African Americans into new forms of activism, it also transformed the political expectations and behavior of Africans in dramatic ways. Some of this derived from the revelation of just how dependent Europe's colonial powers were on their African possessions. Millions of Africans were ensnared in the production drives that European nations carried out to drum up the materials they required for making arms, other war goods, and food. Much of this involved forced labor. This dependence was also highlighted by the conscription of Africans as toilers and combatants in the all-too-often meaningless war efforts of Europe itself. For example, more than a million Africans were forced into pack animal–like roles to transport supplies.

The most important psychological shift, though, may have come from Blacks witnessing Europeans slaughtering each other in barbarous fashion. This profoundly undermined civilizational arguments long employed by the imperial powers to justify their rule over members of the darker races who were their colonial wards and minions.

In 1914, in Senegal, Paris's oldest West African colony, a politician named Blaise Diagne took keen notice of France's desperate need of African manpower and soldiers to replenish its deadly trenches and skillfully leveraged this to obtain full French citizen rights for recruits and their descendants from any of the territory's four urban "communes."[52]

Operating on the other side of the Atlantic, Garvey also keenly understood the potential that war held for forcing geopolitical and psychological paradigm shifts; he just didn't see Europe's so-called Great War as the decisive historical occasion Africa was waiting for. That would only arrive, he predicted, in another conflagration yet to come that would stem from unresolved imperial enmity between France and Germany.[53] In this prophetic mode, Garvey's oratory became increasingly eschatological and messianic and aimed at ensuring that the Black people of the world would be ready for their moment when it came. From the perspective of the present, especially knowing how important World War II would become in priming independence movements in Africa and beyond, he was remarkably prescient.

The penetration of Garveyism into Africa, which accelerated in the decade after his arrest in the United States in 1922, is even more striking when one appreciates that Garvey never visited the continent. Garveyism's inroads in Africa were organic. They resulted from determined, piecemeal activism to establish UNIA outposts peripatetically in a here-and-there fashion.

This occurred even in colonies like Kenya and South Africa that were quite distant from the currents of the Atlantic world. The spread was not limited, as one might imagine, to the English-speaking colonies, either. French authorities in Senegal grew alarmed by the penetration of Garveyite propaganda there, calling it "more dangerous than rifles," and saying there were "no walls thick enough" to stop it.[54]

Much of Garveyism's growth in Africa can be attributed to a kind of "common wind," to employ the phrase of the late scholar of Black enslavement in the West Indies, Julius Scott. Scott's term referred to the word-of-mouth transmission of news of resistance efforts that travelled over great distance and with remarkable speed during the era of plantation slavery in the Americas. With Garveyism in Africa, as in America, a new common wind spread through the passing around of third- or fourth- or even fifth-hand copies of the *Negro World*. This transmission vastly multiplied the number of readers and extended *Negro World*'s geographic distribution. In the Africa of the 1920s, ship workers, dockers, and others in maritime trades were an important vector, as were railway workers, church pastors, and students.

Nnamdi Azikiwe, a crusading progressive, future mentor of Nkrumah, and later president of Nigeria, avidly studied Garveyism as a young student in the provincial Nigerian port city of Calabar. Nkrumah's other great mentor during his school years at Achimota, its vice president, Kwegyir Aggrey, has often been regarded as something of an accommodationist conservative. But Aggrey, too, saw the appeal in Garveyism, writing:

Garvey's thought of the colored people's return to their native Africa is a dream, I think, but in time, as educated colored men come as missionaries and evangelists to their people in America, men may go back to the new Africa that we hope will arise.[55]

Examples like these reveal the impressive reach of Garvey's ideas. Although borne on this common wind, they quickly took root on African soil, where Garvey's influence far surpassed that of Du Bois or any other Black American intellectual. In the Jamaican transplant to New York, global Blackness had found its first great prophet.

CHAPTER THREE

So Much to Do, So Little Done

If the 1930s were hell in the depression-wracked West, they were hell's kitchen for colonial Africa, where Europe squeezed hard for revenue and spent little for the public good. As he would later tell it, the story of Kwame Nkrumah's journey to the United States to pursue his education there in 1935 is an odyssey in three parts, and for many of the details, his autobiography is virtually all we have to go by.

His account has a fated, nearly miraculous air about it. Like many political memoirs, it has been polished and streamlined in ways that seem intended to create the impression of an ineluctable ascent. The book turns Nkrumah into a man of destiny, and in doing so, it leaves a lot out. This, no doubt, was a matter of strategy because he published the story of his life in 1957, the very year that he became Ghana's leader, with copies handed out during the newly freed colony's independence ceremonies.

We learn of the influence of larger-than-life figures like Aggrey and Azikiwe. In an oddly glancing way, Nkrumah tells us that as an aspiring international student, he had taken the London Matriculation Examination in 1934, the year before he left the Gold Coast, without bringing himself to say that he had failed it.[1]

Then, early the following year, Nkrumah writes that he would have to take "more decisive efforts" if he was to ever get to the United States. From that point on, his life story acquires swift momentum.[2] Lacking money for the ocean passage to England, where he needed to transit in order to apply for an American visa, Nkrumah stowed away at the slave-trading-fort town of Axim, in the western Gold Coast, for Lagos. There he would solicit the financial help of an unnamed relative. "Mingling with the crew I slipped on board and stayed down with the firemen for the whole of the voyage, sharing their food and the extreme discomfort and heat of the boiler room." He was sick the entire time and arrived "unwashed, unshaven and with tattered clothing" but looking the part of a lowly crew member, so no one questioned him.[3]

After procuring a change of clothes in a local market, Nkrumah made his way to his relative's home where he stayed for a few days, eventually receiving £100 for his troubles, a paltry sounding sum, but worth roughly $10,000 today. Nkrumah said that he collected another £50 from a relative who was a minor chief back home, and this allowed him to pay for a third-class ticket from Takoradi to Liverpool.

One major obligation remained for him—sharing the news with his mother that her only child had decided to go abroad to study, and almost in the same breath, saying goodbye. As Nkrumah emphasized over and over, he had an unusually close relationship with Nyaniba, and this made accomplishing these final steps even more difficult. Before leaving the Gold Coast, Nkrumah traveled to his mother's village, with its mud-walled dwellings and kerosene lamps for lighting, to spend several days with her, waiting until the night before his departure to inform her. The two stayed up that whole night together, talking about family history and other matters. In the morning, Nyaniba looked so stricken as her Francis gathered his belongings that he told her that she only needed to say the word, and he would abandon his plans. She dismissed this thought, though, and gave his trip her blessings and waved goodbye.

Peopled by coconut farmers and fishermen, the land of the Nzima is distant from any urban center in Ghana, and even today, it still requires four or five hours of driving the bad roads from there to reach Takoradi, the only city of any size in the coastal west. Already feeling homesick, Nkrumah arrived in Takoradi just in time to board the *Apapa*, the ship that would bear him off in its lowest class cabin to England. There, he says, sitting on his bunk, his eyes welling with tears, he found a telegram waiting for him from his mentor-patron Azikiwe. It read: "Goodbye. Remember to trust in God and in yourself."[4]

In political terms, Nkrumah's passage to Britain was uneventful. It even lacked the seasickness that he had suffered on his way to Nigeria. But one incident is worth retelling, if only because it resonates within a larger theme of his life—he has an ambivalent, sometimes even fear-tinged attitude toward women. Near midway, when his ship stopped in Las Palmas, in the Canary Islands, passengers were given brief shore leave. A friendly Indian man roused the younger African to take a quick tour. Where this led the unsuspecting Nkrumah was to a hostess bar or brothel, and the story he tells of the experience has elements of both unintended humor and pathos.

Nkrumah asked for water but said that his new Indian friend insisted on beer, which he did not touch. Soon after they were seated, two young Spanish speaking women entered the room wearing negligées.

> [T]o my utter horror and embarrassment one of them came over, planted herself on my knee and began stroking my hair and generally enveloping me with her limbs. I had only seen white women from a distance and the fact that one of them should approach me at such uncomfortably close quarters completely unnerved me. I uttered a cry, jumped up, spilling both the woman and the beer on to the floor and ran as fast as my trembling legs would carry me back to the ship.[5]

In the years since I first encountered this story, I have had trouble not summoning images of the Cowardly Lion in *The Wizard of Oz*. This is not to say that Nkrumah should have gone along with the solicitation, but could he truly have had such a morbid fear of women? His autobiography does not reveal this, but Nkrumah was already a father by the time of this misadventure. Questions about his feelings toward women seem worth pondering because the writer himself often raised the subject.

Early in his autobiography, Nkrumah also recounts with unconcealed terror his experience of being the object of a neighborhood girl's crush when he was a teenager:

> If I happened to come out into the lane she used to approach me and try to start a conversation with me. When she saw that I simply stared at her like a frightened animal, she probably thought I was shy and so she bravely whispered to me that she loved me. I was horrified and abused her as if she had hurt me. I rushed in and told my mother of the wickedness of the girl. My mother laughed and said, 'You should be flattered, my boy. What is wrong with somebody being fond of you?[6]

If one knew nothing more of his life, most people would be inclined to write this off to common adolescent awkwardness. But Nkrumah's autobiography is interleaved with similar instances later in his life. This seems curious on a number of levels, not least because his first book was as much a political document as it was an exercise in literature or memory. Time after time, though, the adult Nkrumah encounters women only to flee from them at the first hint of sex or romance, or else he courts them as friends, leaving them disappointed whenever they show any interest in more.

Here, one cannot avoid getting slightly ahead of oneself in the narrative.

As a student in the US, he had worked briefly as a bellhop on a shipping line and was summoned to one of the cabins. There, Nkrumah "beheld a most attractive woman reclining on her bunk almost completely naked."[7] He wrote that he was so shocked that he rushed out of the room before she could even speak. More prosaic encounters with women in this period inevitably end with the female concluding that Nkrumah is a cold fish and finally abandoning romantic interest in him. Edith, a nurse at New York's Harlem Hospital, for example, wanted desperately to go dancing or to the movies with Nkrumah, who wrote that he was "quite happy" to spend his evenings at her apartment simply talking.[8]

Of another Black American woman, Portia, who fancied him, he writes, "I was really not worthy of such a devoted girl friend for, as usual, I neglected her shamefully. I was always pleased to see her but I never wanted anything permanent to develop from our friendship.... Probably she believed that with patience even the most stubborn of men will give in in the end."[9]

Both in his own words, and through the writings of others, one can see that somewhat later in life, Nkrumah formed powerful bonds with women who took attentive care of him in one capacity or another or provided company to a man with loner tendencies. But none of these ties ever left a trace of requited love. Even what is publicly known about Nkrumah's eventual marriage, which lies far ahead here, largely conforms to this pattern.

The first hint of this side of Nkrumah comes in the story he tells of a small circle of devoted young English women who volunteered to help produce reports and correspondence during his threadbare London days. He spent a two-year interlude of political activism there before he returned to the Gold Coast in 1947 to conquer power and win independence. They "used to come and type for hours on end in the evenings and they never asked a single penny for their work. The best we could do for them was either to put them in a taxi and pay their fare, if we happened to be in funds or, which was more often the case, to accompany them to the tube station and wave them goodbye."[10]

Later, both while in power and during his final years in exile, Nkrumah became extraordinarily close, sequentially, with two English women. In both cases, he enjoyed their company deeply without any hint, at least publicly, of sexual involvement. The near totalizing way he entrusted himself to them almost makes them sound maternal. In his writings, he sometimes comes across as self-conscious and defensive about his relations with women, protesting that he is a "normal man" with all the usual biological drives, and no eunuch or victim of impotence. He explains his dearth of physical relations with women as a matter of self-discipline: to sustain a conventional love life would distract him from his self-appointed world historical goals.

———

FORTUNE'S EMBRACE OF NKRUMAH DURING HIS FIRST TRIP AWAY FROM AFRICA was restored from the moment the *Apapa* docked at Liverpool in 1935. The city's location in the north of England, at once close to the country's industrial centers and astride favorable shipping lanes to the New World, made its port the epicenter of the British slave trade. Liverpool had, by itself, accounted for roughly 85 percent of the country's traffic of enchained Africans to the Americas. In the 1930s, like most of the Western world, the city was deep in the throes of the Great Depression. Unemployment rates were frightful. The city's housing stock was shabby and inadequate, and for many, food was even hard to come by.

Few Blacks lived in a city whose population was a little shy of a million then, but Nkrumah was greeted there by a successful timber merchant from his own Nzima ethnic group named George "Paa" Grant. Strangely, Nkrumah makes almost nothing of this, even though Grant's gesture was of far greater import than simply guiding Nkrumah to a hotel in an unfamiliar city, and then, along with his wife, hosting Nkrumah for a few days after he returned from London.

What explanation Nkrumah does provide is limited to a passing description of Paa Grant "the father of Gold Coast politics," and the "first president of the United Gold Coast Convention" (UGCC).[11] This was the somewhat elitist party, later led by the lawyer J. B. Danquah, that, twelve years hence, would invite the little-known Nkrumah to return home to become its secretary on the notion that Nkrumah was a good organizer and knew how to reach the masses. Just how well he could do so the UGCC leaders would later learn, to their great consternation.

Nkrumah says nothing about how he came to know Grant or who provided an introduction so compelling as to prompt such an impressive figure to turn out at the docks to welcome a virtual nobody. The conventional story of how the UGCC plucked Nkrumah out of obscurity says that he was recommended to what was then the colony's only political movement of any amplitude by a close friend and former fellow Lincoln University student in America, Ebenezer Ako Adjei, but only after Adjei had turned down the job himself. But Nkrumah's mysterious connection with Paa Grant, who remained influential in the UGCC until his death in 1956, predates Nkrumah's friendship with Adjei and may have been instrumental.

Nkrumah found himself lost and bewildered in London, where remarkably, getting a student's visa to the United States as a young African man of modest means was easily accomplished. Writing about the city in the 1930s, George Orwell called it "a sort of whirlpool which draws derelict people towards it." Extreme poverty was on far greater display in the vast capital than in industrial cities to its north like Liverpool and Manchester.[12] On the day of King George V's funeral, in 1936, Orwell describes being caught up in a crowd at Trafalgar Square. "It was impossible, looking about one then, not to be struck by the physical degeneracy of modern England. . . . Puny limbs, sickly faces, under the weeping London sky! Hardly a well-built man or a decent-looking woman, and not a fresh complexion anywhere."[13] This might help explain why Nkrumah felt so depressed under the smoky and dismal heavens of the great seat of empire that he says he considered abandoning the idea of going to the United States altogether and returning home. Then history struck him like a thunderbolt:

> I heard an excited newspaper boy shouting something unintelligible as he grabbed a bundle of the latest editions from a motor van, and on the placard I read: 'MUSSOLINI INVADES ETHIOPIA'. That was all I needed. At that moment it was almost as if the whole of London had suddenly declared war on me personally. . . . My nationalism surged to the fore; I was ready and willing to go through hell itself, if need be, in order to achieve my object.[14]

The year 1935 had opened with an agreement between the French prime minister and Benito Mussolini to respect each other's colonial claims. In February, Hitler ordered the reinstatement of the Luftwaffe and the launch of German rearmament. Italy's purpose in invading Ethiopia was belated catch-up in the imperial landgrab that Europe's powers had carried out in colonizing Africa over the preceding half century. Nkrumah's ambitious object, he says, was the diametrical opposite: to eradicate colonialism in Africa. Nkrumah presents his emotional response to headlines about Ethiopia as utterly spontaneous, an oracular flash. But that doesn't feel altogether convincing. Since the start of the previous decade, thanks in good part to Garvey, Ethiopia had occupied a special place in the thoughts of many people of African descent on both sides of the Atlantic. At Garvey rallies, this ancient kingdom in the East African highlands was celebrated as an unimpeachable symbol of Black sovereignty; unlike the rest of the continent, Ethiopia had never been colonized or settled by the West. For Black people, Ethiopia carried religious overtones, as well, and Nkrumah, with his church schooling and teaching had every reason to know this. Mention of the kingdom appears in the Bible, which says, "Princes shall come out of Egypt; Ethiopia shall soon stretch forth her hands unto God."[15] Garvey had often employed similar language in the 1920s, exhorting his followers to "Look to Africa when a Black king shall be crowned, for the day of deliverance is near."[16] Ethiopia seated a new emperor named Haile Selassie I in 1930. During the lavish event, he and his wife, Empress Menen Asfaw were swathed in crimson robes heavily bedecked in gold trimmings, and the emperor was graced with many new titles, none grander than King of Kings, Lord of Lords, Conquering Lion of the Tribe of Judah. The ceremonies drew diplomatic delegations and media coverage from numerous countries, and many in the African world and its diaspora celebrated the coronation as prophecy fulfilled.

Italy's invasion of Ethiopia also electrified African American public opinion, creating a surge of activism against Mussolini in defense of the kingdom. Under banner headlines in the months before the attack was launched, leading Black newspapers like the *Pittsburgh Courier* played up African American support for Selassie as volunteers, medical doctors from Harlem, and Black pilots traveled to the kingdom to offer help. J. A. Rogers, a *Courier* columnist, resorted to etymology to explain to readers why they should care about this distant land. "'Ethiopia' and 'Negro' have identical meanings," he wrote. "The first is Greek, the second is Latin, and both mean 'black.'"[17] After Italy's invasion was launched, the newspaper sustained heavy coverage of the war, often seeking to boost African American morale. "Italy May Take Decades and Then Not Subdue the Ethiopians," read one characteristic headline with an Addis Ababa dateline a month into the conflict.[18] This foreshadowed an even broader and more sustained campaign, almost entirely forgotten today, among Blacks in the United States in support of Ghana's independence and subsequently that of other African countries in the late 1950s.[19] But all that lay in the future, if only barely, at the time of Nkrumah's supposed epiphany with the newspaper boys flogging war in Ethiopia. It is what Nkrumah doesn't tell us about what was happening in the moment in London that is most interesting.

We know nothing about where he stayed in London during the two weeks he spent awaiting a visa, nor whom he met or spoke with. There was plenty of African activism in London then around Ethiopia. Did Nkrumah witness any of this? One activist group, the International African Friends of Abyssinia, counted Samuel R. Wood, an important mentor of Nkrumah back home, as a member. There were African student groups in the city. Was he aware of them, as seems likely? There was even a well-known hostel for African students in London, a vital resource for someone in Nkrumah's position at a time when finding a room for a Black person there could be very difficult. Even Nkrumah's conversations with his host, Paa Grant, after his return to Liverpool went unreported in any substantial way in the autobiography, except Nkrumah's mention that he was surprised to see the free-spoken ways of Grant's wife in replying to her husband. This was something the younger man made clear he was unaccustomed to back home.

Nkrumah seems to have wanted to use the story of his reaction to Italy's invasion of Ethiopia as a way to enhance his pedigree as an ardent nationalist and born leader of Africans. This guided his decision to try to appear as having committed himself to combating colonialism even if that meant he did so all alone. And yet there is no denying that even from his early days as a student in Pennsylvania, at Lincoln University, Nkrumah impressed peers and professors alike as being intensely preoccupied with Africa's future, with the colonial question, and with independence. In him, in other words, the self-conscious construction of an image and sincerity of purpose, even obsession, were joined as one.

Elizabeth Flower, a professor of philosophy who knew him in this period said of Nkrumah's work as a student, "no matter what a paper was supposed to be on, Nkrumah always twisted it around to write on African freedom and anticolonial struggle. Otherwise his papers were excellent. He could have been a brilliant scholar if he'd stuck to the topic."[20]

THE THIRD OF THE SEA VOYAGES THAT TRANSFORMED NKRUMAH'S LIFE AND thrust him onto the path of history was a decisive upgrade. "After a fortnight's stay in Liverpool I set sail for the United States in one of the boats of the Cunard White Star Line."[21]

Nkrumah had not embarked on this journey as Kwame, though. That was an identity that would not come into the world until more than a decade hence, after he had left the US for his two-year interlude in London. It was there that he would make his final acts of self-invention. Already, at this stage of Nkrumah's journey, though, signs of plasticity in his identity hinted at dramatic transformations. On the first line of his otherwise impeccably handwritten application from 1935 to Lincoln University, Nkrumah initially filled out his name as Francis Nya Kofi, only to scratch out the Nya boldly and replace it in superscript with Nwia-, hyphenated just so.

Nkrumah answers the stock question of "What do you plan as your life's work," with the succinct phrase: "Educational and social work." Beyond this, save for its first paragraph of the application's required short essay, Nkrumah adds little to the picture that we already have.

The essay's first paragraph, though, is quietly stunning.

> I neither know where to begin nor where to end; because I feel that the story of my life has not been one of achievements. Furthermore, I have not been anxious to tell people of what may have been accomplished by me. In truth, the burden of my life can be summarized into a single line in "The Memoriam" quoted by Cecil Rhodes. "So much to do so little done." Notwithstanding I shall endeavour to write few words to throw a dim light on the life that has hitherto been led by me.[22]

It is neither the hint of purpose nor the affectation of modesty from the twenty-six-year-old college applicant that stand out here. Rather, it is Nkrumah's invocation of Rhodes, a man who died in 1902 but whose complicated legacy is still debated today. Certain salient facts are nonetheless beyond debate. Rhodes was an early believer in the mission of unifying Africa, integrating as many of its territories as possible under British rule. This was to be achieved by lashing together London's many colonial claims with a railroad that he famously dreamed of building from the Cape to Cairo. But Rhodes's enthusiasm for empire did not stop there. It was married to an ardent belief in the racial superiority of whites in general and of the English in specific and to the importance of carefully limiting the franchise of Africans in the management of their own lives.

What was it that Nkrumah, the budding pan-Africanist, could have seen in such a figure, or what moved him to invoke Rhodes in this way? The key here may lie in the essay's penultimate line. There, Nkrumah wrote: "In all things, I have held myself to but one ambition and that is, to make necessary arrangements to continue my education in a university in the United States of America, that I may be better prepared, and still be of better use to my fellow man."[23]

Lincoln University, where Nkrumah was headed, had been founded as an institute of higher education for "colored men" with the support of Pennsylvania Presbyterians in 1854, the northern precursor of a nationwide push to create what have latterly been known as Historically Black Colleges and Universities (HBCUs). Du Bois called the flourishing of Black colleges in the South, that gathered pace in the 1860s and would include Fisk, Howard, Hampton, Talladega, Atlanta, and others, the "finest thing in American history."[24]

Lincoln's original focus was service, which in the early era mostly meant training young men for lives of religion and missionary activity. William Hallock Johnson, a white Princeton graduate who was president of Lincoln when Nkrumah applied, expanded the school's brief. Princeton's declared mission had been "in the nation's service." Johnson somewhat grandly said the motto of the school of which he now had charge would be, "Lincoln in the service of the world."[25]

Nkrumah's perceptive pitch for admission targeted just such a sensibility. From its very origins, the school, which had been carved out of rolling hills of farmland in southeastern Pennsylvania, had a special focus on Africa. On December 31, 1856, at the dedication of its first major building, Ashmun Hall, Cortlandt Van Rensselaer, scion of a wealthy Presbyterian family who had spent time ministering to enslaved people before the Civil War invoked both the "God of Ethiopia" and "our God," saying:

> The Ashmun Institute ... longs to rescue some noble Africans from their bark of slime and to train them for the statesmanship of a great and growing Republic.[26]

The slice of Africa the school's founders had in mind was the settler society founded for and by formerly enslaved Americans in Liberia. There, Van Rensselaer said, "in the set time of divine purposes," after being elevated intellectually, morally, and politically, Africans were "destined to demonstrate the equality of the races."[27] Even the naming of the institute's first hall spoke to this purpose. Jehudi Ashmun, for whom a street name still exists in downtown Monrovia, Liberia, had sailed to the territory in 1822 in charge of a party of fifty-three prospective Black colonists.[28] The dream of resettling former slaves in Africa, eventually incorporated as the American Colonization Society, was a project concocted at the highest levels of the American elite, with members and proponents such as James Monroe and Thomas Jefferson. At the time of Rensselaer's invocation, this project aimed at sending American Blacks to Africa to establish colonies there was still ongoing. Alongside it, though, had grown a realization that most of America's Black population was in the US to stay, and that some numbers of their men would need higher education, if only to gradually help improve the lot of their less fortunate fellows.

Nkrumah's successful application to Lincoln bears the mark of yet another of the many coincidences that filled the first decades of his life. Lincoln had begun gradually moving toward becoming more of a classical liberal arts institution, and a more selective one as well. But that is not all. The faculty had begun to diversify away from its heavy, original Presbyterian cast and slowly recruit people from other backgrounds. This still meant whites only, but that too was about to change. Most important was the arrival in 1928 of Nnamdi Azikiwe, who would exert a profound influence on the school, reenergizing and reshaping Lincoln's connections to Africa.

What Azikiwe told Nkrumah as he encouraged him to apply to Lincoln isn't known. We do know, however, who the young Gold Coaster stayed with briefly once he had disembarked from his Cunard ship in New York. That was with a 1933 Lincoln emeritus, known to and likely introduced to Nkrumah by Azikiwe. This was a man from Sierra Leone whose family roots lay in Nigeria named Thomas Dosumu-Johnson. He had been a transfer student at Lincoln during the brief time that Azikiwe taught there as a recent graduate instructor.[29]

Nkrumah listed Dosumu-Johnson as a reference on his application under the heading, "Who are your friends at Lincoln?"[30] Nkrumah and Dosumu-Johnson had engaged in only fragmentarily conserved correspondence before Nkrumah's arrival at Lincoln in 1935. In their exchanges, Nkrumah had spoken in fascination, though, about the National Congress of British West Africa, the organization aimed at uniting the region spearheaded by Casely Hayford. Not long before this time, according to other sources, Dosumu-Johnson and Azikiwe had gone to Philadelphia together to attend meetings of the Universal Negro Improvement Association (UNIA), founded by Marcus Garvey, with the aim of uniting "all the Negro peoples of the world into one great body."[31] By this time, Garvey had been deported from the US after his conviction and imprisonment for mail fraud. To these many threads in Black nationalism and pan-Africanist thought, we can add at least one or two more.

Dosumu-Johnson was fired by an ardent sense of pride in Blackness, which he had begun to publicly celebrate around the time of his acquaintance with Nkrumah. Although not quite fully formed, his thoughts contained clear elements of pan-Africanism. He once published a peeved sounding article in the *Philadelphia Tribune*, "in which he pointed out that Egypt was, contrary to the way Europeans usually wrote about it, very much a part of Africa. Further, the taunt that Africans were inferior because some had been enslaved should also be applied to the descendants of Angles and Saxons, who used to be sold in the slave markets of Rome."[32]

Dosumu-Johnson may therefore hold a key to understanding Nkrumah's sudden passion over the Ethiopian invasion while he was in London getting his student's visa to the United States. Their connection may also help explain Nkrumah's decision to draw on such an unlikely figure as Cecil Rhodes in his

Lincoln application essay and conclude with Nkrumah's humble message of devotion to service. Mussolini's forces undoubtedly invaded Ethiopia while Nkrumah was in London seeking his student visa to the US, but as we have seen, Ethiopia had already been a cause célèbre and spur to nationalist sentiment among Blacks throughout 1935. That year, there had been anti-Italian rallies by African Americans in many cities and efforts in Chicago and New York to raise Black volunteer brigades and money to help defend Ethiopia.

Support for Ethiopia was so broad, in fact, that both the NAACP of Du Bois and the UNIA of Garvey—starkly divided in most matters—each organized campaigns of their own. Never previously had African Americans shown such unity of interest and passion about foreign policy, and Blacks in Britain and the West Indies did much the same. Among other groups, the West African Students' Union (WASU), which was founded in 1925, organized protests against the invasion in London. African elites, for their part, had been rallying around Ethiopia for far longer—at least since Emperor Menelik II's defeat of an armed Italian takeover attempt in the wake of the Berlin Conference, at the Battle of Adwa, in 1896. This feat was widely celebrated among African intellectuals for having preserved a rare corner of the continent from European takeover.

Nkrumah's nationalism, in other words, had hardly been as fully formed from birth as he pretended. It took shape gradually, the fruit of a steady buildup, melding both ideology and feeling, as well as plenty of received thought. The dramatic presentation of his response to the attack on Ethiopia as a newcomer in the streets of London, therefore, is another reminder of just how profoundly political Nkrumah's autobiography was, and how unreliable the story it tells can be.

Written years earlier, Nkrumah's Lincoln application essay, an incomparably smaller document, is in some ways very similar. It created a strategically idealized version of him for public presentation. Under its specific circumstance, where Nkrumah felt the need to appeal to the administrators of a cautious American university with a history steeped in Presbyterianism, it would not have done to let on to any African sentiments that could be perceived as radical. For this purpose, the invocation of Cecil Rhodes seems to have been designed, above all, to signal safety. Nkrumah may not have been able to avoid mentioning Dosumu-Johnson, because he needed a recent reference at Lincoln, but he certainly didn't want to let on that they were political bedfellows.

For someone who goes unnamed in the autobiography, Dosumu-Johnson is alluded to with surprising frequency. In the first instance, Nkrumah wrote of his arrival in the United States on October 31, 1935, that he had been corresponding with a Sierra Leonean who had graduated from Lincoln University. "He was not expecting me so I called a taxi and directed the driver to the address in Harlem that he had given me in his last letter. Luckily, he was in and he made me very welcome."[33] As we will see, the "Sierra Leonean" would host Nkrumah in Harlem again the following summer, serving as an intimate guide to the city. Dosumu-Johnson and Azikiwe had frequented the large gatherings of Garvey's UNIA militants in the US in the past, and Nkrumah would later follow in their wake by attending their thunderous meetings in Harlem.

Seriously late for the start of school, though, Francis Nkrumah hurried onward for discoveries that awaited him at his new college in the Pennsylvania countryside. In New York, a twenty-year-old jazz vocalist named Billie Holiday had just recorded her first big hit, *What a Little Moonlight Can Do*, with Teddy Wilson's orchestra. The population of Harlem was still fast expanding then due to the continuing exodus of African Americans from the Deep South. "These were the poorest people of the South, who poured into New York City during the decade following the Great Depression . . . ," wrote the novelist, Claude Brown. "To them this was the 'promised land' that Mammy had been singing about in the cotton fields for many years."[34]

The storied Black slice of Manhattan offered up different faces to different eyes. To some, it was overcrowded and wicked, a world where families struggling to make it in the city doubled up in overpriced apartments by sleeping in shifts, a place of numbers runners, boisterous rent parties, and nodding, somnolent heroin addicts. Awed newcomers in every hue of brown and black poured in and out of its subways stations while streetcars plied the busy roads, watched over by police patrols on horseback.

Ralph Ellison arrived in Harlem as a sophomore from Tuskegee in 1936, just a year after Nkrumah's first experience of America's Black capital. He had dreams of playing trumpet and becoming a sculptor. With $75 to his name, Ellison lodged at the newly opened YMCA on 135th Street, the tenement-lined heart of the neighborhood. There, on his second day in Harlem, Ellison made the most of an astonishing chance encounter with Alain Locke and Langston Hughes, briefly engaging with both men. After Locke drifted off, Ellison discussed modernist poets like T. S. Eliot with the much older Hughes, who began suggesting books to read, sealing a friendship between them. Hughes later introduced Ellison to Richard Wright, who ushered him into the literary scene, allowing him to read his best-selling 1940 novel, *Native Son*, "as it came out of the typewriter."[35] These associations helped put Ellison on the path to become what many critics would call the greatest American novelist of the century.[36]

In a letter to his mother, Ellison described Harlem as a place of whores and pimps, ditch diggers and "likker heads," saying, "It makes me angry to think of the causes behind all the misery in the world, and the way it is concentrated here in Harlem."[37] But his encounters with Hughes and Wright and with other writers like Zora Neale Hurston and Chester Himes conjure another Harlem that existed on an entirely different plane: a world of literary salons, and of legendary shrines of music and performance, from the block-long Savoy Ballroom, with its enormous, glistening dancefloor and twin bandstands, to the Apollo Theater. It was a place of churches, too—not just the stately and famous ones like the Abyssinian Baptist Church on 138th Street, but every kind of house of worship imaginable, from hidden rooftop altars to narrow storefronts from which fervid prayer and song echoed onto the sidewalk.

To the perceptive, Ellison included, this Harlem could present itself as a dense but orderly realm of Black people who clothed themselves with "assertive dignity," in the apt phrase of David Levering Lewis.[38] Men wore fine hats and neckties and swung canes, the women long dresses, stylish coats, and fur stoles. This is the Black Mecca celebrated in paintings of the Harlem Renaissance by artists like Archibald Motley Jr. and William H. Johnson. Johnson's oil canvas, *Street Life, Harlem*, crystalizes this all with a foregrounded couple nattily dressed, the one with a hat festooned with a yellow feather, the other with matching flowers. The pair stand in mutual admiration set against a colorful background in which an orange crescent moon hangs languidly over an Expressionist-like Harlem skyline. Passing through this universe, Nkrumah said he had felt immediately at home.[39] What is certain is that in rural Pennsylvania, even at a Black school, that could not entirely have been the case.

CHAPTER FOUR

Ace Boy

As a student in the Gold Coast Nkrumah had dreamed of someday attending a prestigious school like the University of Oxford. And during his short London years, after departing the US but before returning home, years later, he was briefly registered as a student at other elite British institutions, such as the London School of Economics and University College London. By ironic happenstance, he found himself in Oxford, Pennsylvania, instead. This Oxford was, of course, not remotely as famous. Although secluded in a rusticated corner of the state, it was a storied place after its own fashion, nonetheless. Through the middle decades of the twentieth century, within the world of African American higher education, at least, Lincoln was known as the Black Princeton.

Having educated Nnamdi Azikiwe was but one notable distinction in Lincoln's cap. Other illustrious alumni included the eminent poet, novelist, and social activist Langston Hughes who, caught in the undertow of the ongoing Harlem Renaissance, transferred from Lincoln to Ivy League Columbia University. Thurgood Marshall, the pathbreaking civil rights lawyer who became the first African American justice of the US Supreme Court was another. These two men were classmates there in the late 1920s. Lincoln henceforth became an extraordinarily important institution for the promotion of African independence, and for the advancement of civil rights for African Americans. These proceeded not only in tandem, but much more hand in hand than has generally been recognized.

An early hint of this can be glimpsed in the experiences of Thurgood Marshall, who headed Lincoln's debate team as an undergrad. Meeting in a Harlem church, Marshall faced off against Britain's National Union of Students to debate the proposition that the United Kingdom's colonialism was "unethical and prejudicial to progress." The British team argued that the British empire had helped its colonies, a common enough theme in Western discourse, even today. But the young Marshall would have none of it. In unflinching rebuttal, he insisted that "the history of the Anglo-Saxon races has been one of imperialistic oppression for the sake of business advantages."[1]

This was a mere foretaste, though, of what would come out of Lincoln's verdant and rolling patch of Pennsylvania tilth and homesteads. During the leadership of Horace Mann Bond, who took over as Lincoln's first Black president in 1945, only Howard University rivalled Lincoln among historically Black centers of learning in its promotion of African independence. And through the leadership of Bond, the father of the future prominent civil rights leader, Julian Bond, it did more than any other American institution, Howard included, to help elevate Nkrumah's status in the United States during his drive to end British colonial rule over the Gold Coast in the 1950s.

I reached the Oxford of Lincoln after a dismal four-hour drive from New York City early one recent winter, spending the last quarter or so of the journey plunged into deep, almost timeless countryside. There, the curving, hilly roads I navigated under a chill rain cut through unbroken farmland. And the closer I got to my destination, the more frequently I found myself stuck on the road behind the black, horse-drawn carriages, prolific in Nkrumah's time, of the Amish community that still makes up a sizeable part of the local population.

Even calling this Oxford a town can feel like an exaggeration. It still lacks a hotel, however modest. Apple and grape orchards, Christmas tree plantations, and mushroom farms abound. Roadside signs advertise farm-raised rabbits for sale. Chester County leads the entire state in agricultural production, and the parts of that that surround Lincoln's campus are as rural as they would have been in Nkrumah's time.

Oxford, never much of a home for African Americans, still had segregated schools in the 1930s. And despite being the first establishment of higher education in the United States created "for the collegiate and theological education of Negro young men," Lincoln itself still had no Black faculty until early that decade. Frank Wilson, the university's second Black professor, joined the faculty in 1936, and taught Nkrumah in the seminary and a course in psychology.[2]

Nkrumah scarcely spoke about the adjustments that his arrival into such a world required of him. About his undergraduate years, he said that he had arrived at Lincoln with only about $90 to his name, and he threw himself on the mercy of the dean not only for arriving a month late, but for barely having a quarter of the money that he had scraped together and begged others for back home.

In his correspondence with the school from the Gold Coast, Nkrumah had been told that $250 was the strict minimum he would need to cover tuition and board. So now he pledged to the dean that he would work his way through school, and he was relieved to be told that if he sustained high grades, he would be eligible for a partial scholarship. Earning good grades proved little problem. Four years later, Nkrumah graduated magna cum laude with a bachelor's degree in sociology and ranked sixth in his class overall.[3] To whittle away at what he owed, he soon began working in the university library and engaging in the murky enterprise of writing school essays for other students for a fee. "In this way I raised quite a few dollars toward my out-of-pocket expenses."[4] It still wouldn't be enough.

Nkrumah speaks of joining the Phi Beta Sigma Fraternity, only to reveal his mortification over the initiation ritual. "My trousers were ripped off in front of everyone, when I was chased like a fox by the hounds across fields, captured, beaten and then pushed blind-folded through a hedge."[5] He also mentions becoming a Freemason—another patch in the unusually varied and changing quilt of his identity and personal development.

Nkrumah had been raised Catholic, and not long before coming to Lincoln, he seriously considered Jesuit priesthood. Now, enrolled in a Protestant university with a deep Presbyterian missionary culture, he was dabbling with the teachings of a group that purported to contain the essence of all religions. Nkrumah's eclecticism with religion would continue during his years in the United States and foreshadow a matching pliability in his politics. Was this because his nature resembled a vessel, able to accommodate whatever was poured into it? Was it the reflection of a restless, searching character, for whom dabbling and eclectic borrowing were the essence of learning? Or was Nkrumah at heart simply a dilettante incapable of achieving great depth in either faith or politics? Although Nkrumah's true North Star was African unity, questions like these would be asked about him again and again throughout his adult life.

In the 1930s, Lincoln was a "dry," male-only campus, with an almost exclusively Black student body lost in an overwhelmingly white countryside. Among other things, this meant that the opportunities for collegial social life were sharply limited. Being an African student presented additional challenges. Although there was little outright hostility, according to the recollections of many students from that era, both Africans and African Americans often favored their own kind. A classmate named Walter I. Johnson recalled, "at the time the few African students lived apart from the other students and unless they met us during course hours there was little socialization."[6] Lincoln had long been the American university with the largest proportion of African students—perhaps 15 or so during Nkrumah's time, out of a total student body of roughly 270. This freed young men from the continent from the extreme cultural isolation they might otherwise have faced. However, it may have paradoxically prevented others from making new, transnational friendships.

Nkrumah presents an intriguing and somewhat contradictory picture of his own adjustment. "I felt immediately at home in Harlem and sometimes found it difficult to believe that this was not Accra," he wrote not entirely plausibly of his first impressions of an African American world during his brief stopover in New York on his way to college.[7] And yet he also briefly recounts the alienation and apparent shame he experienced during a visit then to the Abyssinian Baptist Church in Harlem, then the world's largest Baptist congregation, where exuberant Black churchgoers wept at the story of Jesus carrying the cross to Calvary, and shouted, "It is Jesus! Have Mercy! Hallelujah!"[8] A white Dutchman who Nkrumah had met on the Cunard ship, then on his way to study at the Harvard Divinity School, had taken Nkrumah to the service at one of New York's biggest Black congregations.

> It was very embarrassing. Here was a European witnessing a most undignified Negro service. As we left the church I tried to apologise but he seemed surprised at this and said, with all sincerity, that it was the most beautiful thing he had seen so far in any church. If other denominations introduced something like it, he added, they might have a greater following. It was my turn to be astonished and I believe it was this young man who got me interested in theology.[9]

Even for a New York stopover so brief, the lack of any palpable sense of what was going on in Harlem at the time in Nkrumah's account is striking. Dosumu-Johnson's apartment was located at 271 West 117th Street, which was then a street of five- and six-story red brick walkup apartment buildings, each scaffolded with steel fire escapes. His building no longer exists, poetically replaced by a smart looking modern apartment building called The Douglass, after Frederick Douglass, which is now also the name of the avenue at the nearest corner. An enormous portrait of its namesake hangs in the lobby, just visible from the street. In a further twist, in recent years, this part of Harlem has become the favored residential area for a large community of West Africans, especially immigrants from Senegal. At the time of Nkrumah's visit,

125th Street, just a few blocks to the north, was the scene that March of New York's first modern race riot, in which three people were killed and $2 million in property was destroyed. It had been sparked by an unfounded rumor that a sixteen-year-old boy had been beaten to death by employees of a five-and-dime store after they caught him allegedly shoplifting a penknife.

The riot suffuses the concluding chapters of *Invisible Man*, in which several of the groups that competed for influence among urban Blacks during the early years of the Great Depression collided violently in Harlem. This meant members of Garvey's Ethiopianist movement organizers and sympathizers of the Communist Party of the United States, then thick on the ground; and holdovers of the older, conservative, stay-out-of-politics-keep-your-nose-to-the-grindstone tradition of Booker T. Washington. The New York City of the time was starkly segregated, and although it was only 5 percent Black, African Americans accounted for 15 percent of the city's unemployed and earned only half as much on average as white residents.

Harlem Hospital, which only grudgingly began making way for Black doctors in the 1920s and Black nurses thereafter, was the only place in the city for people of African descent to receive hospital care. Consequently, it was badly overrun. Back then, even a giant insurance company like Metropolitan Life sold separate policies for Blacks and whites, and did not hire "negroes."

As Wil Haygood has written:

> Jewish store owners in Harlem hired their own—other Jews—and not blacks. And blacks, who paid their electric and gas bills to Con Edison and the other big monopolies, could not get jobs at the utility companies, because the utility companies did not hire blacks either. Buses cruising through central Harlem, picking up black passengers, were driven by white Irishmen (to get a job driving a bus, you benefited from having a letter from your local parish priest).[10]

Circumstances like these in the 1930s drove residents of Harlem to mount a protest campaign directed at white-owned shops. For six days a week, through rain, snow, and shine, over a period of months, they carried signs urging residents: "Don't Buy Where You Can't Work."[11] That was until a court decision in early 1935 ruled that picketing efforts like these were illegal. This left no outlet for anger and frustration over soaring poverty and discrimination against Blacks and primed the city for an explosion. And yet Nkrumah conveys nothing but the most passing sense of the difficulties of life during the Great Depression, no hint of the politics roiling Harlem, or indeed any discussion of Black life in America overall. More broadly, even the New Deal escapes his mention. A Lincoln professor would say of him later that Nkrumah evinced no "particular interest in African American politics." But as we will see, here, too, he would soon demonstrate a striking capacity for changing directions personally, almost like a creature molting.

IN NKRUMAH'S DAY, THE CAMPUS OF LINCOLN WAS A TIDY COLLECTION OF stolid brick buildings with peaked roofs, each set off from the next by a stretch of green lawn. There, Nkrumah partook in the occasional extracurricular activity. He was a non-singing member of the glee club, for example. But his favorite way of passing time—something he'd done since his boyhood in Nkroful—seems to have been spending long hours by himself. In solitude, as a reputed page-a-glance reader, he devoured challenging books at an impressive rate, reading through the night as he plowed through Kant, Hegel, Descartes, Schopenhauer, Nietzsche, Freud, and others. One professor remembered him as a "quiet, introspective, serious student." Another spoke of him as a "loner," and yet someone "at times both open and reserved, reticent and jovial."[12] "To my way of thinking, unless I was busy pretty well the whole of the twenty-four hours of each day I was wasting my time," he wrote of himself.[13]

Deepening the paradox that surrounds his early character, W. Beverly Carter, a future US ambassador to Tanzania and Liberia, who arrived at Lincoln in 1939, called Nkrumah "one of the most liked foreign students on campus," saying "he mixed well in contrast to a number of others from Africa."[14] Nkrumah's historical timing in this was impeccable. Lincoln's vocation had begun shifting from forming missionaries for work in Africa to preparing African Americans for the professions. Nkrumah's arrival on the campus came, therefore, at a time when the concerns of Lincoln's students were becoming much more worldly.

This shift had not happened in isolation. It was a byproduct instead of a series of rebellions on Black campuses that had commenced in the early 1920s and were closely linked to the New Negro movement. As a matter of strategy, these uprisings were aimed sequentially at integrating university trustee boards, then subjecting decisions about whom to hire as president to alumni approval, and then finally, hiring Black presidents and faculty. Du Bois regarded all of this as a positive outgrowth of his struggle with Booker T. Washington over the role of higher education in Black life. And he played the instigator and cheerleader throughout. These struggles over governance and staffing decisions drove other transformations, too, notably through demands for efforts to recenter people of African descent in the teaching of history—a fight that is still being waged today.

"Knowledge of the world should focus at least in part on the black world in which most colored students live," Du Bois later wrote.[15] E. Franklin Frazier, a Howard University graduate and professor and leading Black intellectual of his era, captured the problem at the heart of this struggle with more pith. Whites, with their focus on Christianity, he said, wanted Black universities to "unlock the mysteries of the heaven," but resisted whenever faculty and students "unfolded the mysteries of this world."[16] This had to change, and it did.

Albeit a northern school, Lincoln was one of the last holdouts against this reformist wave. In 1926 it offered the presidency to a Philadelphia minister who defended the Ku Klux Klan's right to rally in that city.[17] The nomination was rescinded after a student uproar, but it would be two decades until Horace Mann Bond would become the university's first Black president in 1945. That was long after other historically Black colleges and universities had passed this milestone. Azikiwe played an important role in forging change at Lincoln before then, though, teaching courses on African history while he was obtaining a master's degree at the nearby University of Pennsylvania (Penn). He also invited William Leo Hansberry, of Howard University, then the leading African American scholar of the continent, into his classes as a guest speaker. By Nkrumah's time at Lincoln, African American interest in world affairs had exploded. The principal reason for this was Italy's invasion of Ethiopia, but there were other important causes, from the Spanish Civil War, in which some Blacks volunteered, to the rise of the Soviet Union. This was also a time when the mounting drumbeat of an impending new global conflict, Garvey's prophesy, was widely felt.

Nkrumah tapped into the globalizing of African American identity that was just then picking up momentum. With limited opportunities for social life, the school held nightly, after-dinner bull sessions just outside of the refectory. Their focus tended toward politics, both domestic—especially the shifting fortunes of African Americans during the Depression—and international. Nkrumah had studied oratory at Lincoln, winning a contest held by his fraternity in 1936, just a year after his arrival. His chosen theme was, "Africa, the burden of the Negro." That year he had also attended the Pennsylvania branch of the Oxford Union, the debate society. He also absorbed lessons in oratory from Black churches in Harlem and Philadelphia, and he worked hard at applying them. In the nightly gatherings at Lincoln, he measured his speaking prowess by gauging the attention of fellow students.

Even granting the changes that resulted from the university rebellions, this cannot have been easy. As one historian has written, "The ethos of the campus was one of competitive, middle-class striving"; one disenchanted student later recalled that the young men of Lincoln "thought of education exclusively in terms of prestige value. They wanted to be doctors and lawyers—doctors mostly—professions to which they referred as 'rackets.' There was money in them, and they were motivated by the desire to possess, as indeed they put it, yellow money, yellow cars, and yellow women."[18]

Another historian's account of Black campuses in this era held that "African students at black schools frequently reproved Afro-American peers for their apathy, frivolity, and naivete... [and] black American students remained oblivious to such admonitions."[19]

Even swimming against strong currents like these, Nkrumah made a vivid impression. According to Frank Wilson, the sole Black professor at the time, cheering students gathered around him would "egg him on as he stood there in oration slashing his hands in the air." Then, Nkrumah would get on his proverbial soapbox and "declaim about the coming independence of the African continent, of which he would become the leader."[20]

As 1939 opened, Emilia Earhart was declared dead, having disappeared eighteen months earlier during a bid to fly solo around the world. That spring, as Hitler's rearmament accelerated, the long dictatorship of Francisco Franco was established after his victory in the Spanish Civil War. In April, the Black American contralto Marian Anderson performed before a crowd of seventy-five thousand people at Washington's Lincoln Memorial, after having been denied use of Constitution Hall by the Daughters of the American Revolution. And the comic book character Batman and the mostly color feature film *The Wizard of Oz* both premiered. Two pictures of Nkrumah appear in his yearbook that year. In one, he is dressed somewhat jauntily outdoors in a dark, double-breasted jacket, light pants, and a Stetson hat. It is the second, more formal image that commands our attention, though. In it, Nkrumah is photographed shoulder up and neatly coiffed in a classic three-quarters pose, wearing a jacket and rep tie. His skin is so black it is radiant, and from behind rimless glasses he exudes cool confidence. The caption reads: "Africa's Nwia Kofi conditioned all his intellectual endeavours through his zeal for knowledge. As a freshman he easily and interestingly adjusted himself to Lincoln and the new environment and graduated a fine and polished gentleman intent on the economic resurrection of his bellowed native land."

Later, under a Who's Who entry closer to the back of the yearbook Nkrumah is described as the "most interesting" member of his class. Then finally, one finds this:

Africa is beloved of his dreams
Philosopher, thinker, with forceful schemes,
In aesthetics, politics, all he's "In the field,"
Nkrumah, "très intérresantes," radiates appeal.

FRANCIS NKRUMAH FAILED TO CONVEY ANY OF THE SENSE OF THE HARDSHIP and political turmoil and intrigue of Harlem in the 1930s that one finds indelibly depicted in works like *Invisible Man*. But his subsequent adventures in the United States, many of which were driven by an urgent need to earn money for school and to feed himself, feel worthy of a writer of Ellison's gift. For broad stretches, the section of his autobiography that covers his time in the country after his first academic year at Lincoln has the liveliness and color of a picaresque Bildungsroman.

At the end of that first school year, with campus housing closed, Nkrumah returned to New York, where he briefly lodged again with his "Sierra Leonean friend," Dosumu-Johnson and his American wife. Nkrumah explains that his host was also struggling to get by, leading the two into a desperate scheme to earn money. "We thought we had a brainwave and went to the fish and poultry market early each morning, bought fish at wholesale prices and spent the rest of the day trying sell it on a street corner."[21] He soon discovered that he had a fish allergy. A rash covered his entire body. But this wasn't his main problem. After a fortnight of this, he found that he had only lost money, causing a rift between him and his hosts and forcing Nkrumah out into the street. In one of his only direct comments about the impact of the Depression on African Americans, he wrote of Harlem, "Life was so hard on some people that sometimes I would see men and women picking scraps of food from out of the dustbins."[22]

Nkrumah was preserved from a similar fate by a West Indian family that took him in and deferred rent payment until he could find work. In Harlem, Ellison's unnamed Depression-era hero is hired into a miserable and dangerous job at a paint factory. Nkrumah next found work in a soap factory. In his naivete, he had imagined a delicately scented environment, one filled with aromas of honeysuckle and roses, but the reality he discovered was nauseating.

> It turned out to be by far the filthiest and most unsavory job that I ever had. All the rotting entrails and lumps of fat of animals were dumped by lorries into a yard. Armed with a fork I had to load as much as I could of this reeking and utterly repulsive cargo into a wheelbarrow and then transport it, load after load, to the processing plant.[23]

At someone's suggestion, Nkrumah next registers for membership in the National Maritime Union and from Philadelphia lands a job working aboard the *Shawnee*, a ship plying the route between New York and Veracruz, Mexico.

> When I first applied for the job, the official of the shipping line asked me brusquely, "Can you wait, boy?" At first I thought he was asking me to postpone my application and when I hesitated, he raised his voice and said: "Well, come on! Can you wait at table?" Terrified of being turned down, I assured him that I could wait. So I was sent to sea as a waiter.[24]

This job, too, commenced with comic misadventure. Nkrumah promptly confused dishes and place settings, drawing complaints from diners and the fury of the headwaiter, who shook him by the collar and demoted him to pot-washer for the remainder of that first trip. He called the work "soul-destroying." On subsequent journeys he was promoted to regular dish washer, and then to mess room waiter, and finally to bell-hop. It was in that role that Nkrumah had the mortifying encounter with the nearly naked female passenger ordering room service.

Nkrumah's other hardships during this period included being hospitalized with pneumonia while working the night shift at a Pennsylvania shipbuilding yard during the winter of 1943–44. This was an experience he said drove him "to the end of my tether," and sealed his decision to return to the Gold Coast. He also suffered bouts of homelessness, when he would spend nights in train stations and parks or riding the New York City subway system back and forth on a nickel's fare between Brooklyn and Harlem. He never frames experiences like these exactly in this way, but beneath the veneer of escapade they feel like stories of personal growth.

Nkrumah, the onetime ardent Catholic who spent his undergraduate years at a Presbyterian university and obtained a second bachelor's degree there in theology in 1942, filled in as a frequent for-fee guest preacher at a Black Baptist church in Philadelphia and in other congregations outside of Washington, DC. He was drawn, rapt, to the services of the famous Black preacher in the New York of the 1930s, Major Jealous Divine, who built a following of perhaps thirty thousand congregants and is said to be the inspiration for the Preacher character in *Invisible Man*. Divine was a fundamentally conservative charismatic who preached but did not practice abstinence—far from it—and foreswore both the Constitution and race. Black people, he said, bore much of the responsibility for the racism they faced in American society but could escape from its iniquities through positive attitude and faith. True believers took to calling him God, but many regarded the diminutive, extravagantly wealthy, and always impeccably turned-out Father Divine as a spectacularly enterprising cult leader.

In Salisbury, North Carolina, Nkrumah presided over a memorial service organized by African students to honor his first great mentor, Kwegyir Aggrey. There, in the presence of some of Aggrey's relatives, as well as members of two African student associations, Nkrumah followed his own African religious traditions and prayed for Aggrey's soul in the Fante language, ritually pouring three rounds of libations into the ground as he spoke. In doing so, Nkrumah "charged the spirit of Aggrey to leave the foreign soil in which it had been resting for years and go back home to Africa, to sleep with the spirits of his ancestors and have eternal rest."[25]

This act of supposed "animism" drew a sharp reproach from Dean Johnson, the head of the Lincoln seminary, who had learned about the event from coverage in a publication Nkrumah had helped launch, *The African Interpreter*. Johnson had been Nkrumah's most steadfast patron at Lincoln. He had loaned money to Nkrumah from his own personal funds and had once referred to his student from the Gold Coast almost boastfully in correspondence with another scholar, calling him his "ace boy." An aggrieved Johnson now reproached Nkrumah for leading prayers to "heathen gods." Nkrumah forthrightly rejected this alleged schism in a letter to his benefactor, saying, "the burden of my life is to live in such a way that I may become a living symbol of all that is best both in Christianity and the beliefs of my people. I am a Christian and will ever remain so, but never a blind Christian."[26]

What Aggrey's white British and American patrons relished most were his words about a piano needing its black and white keys. As this incident revealed, though, Nkrumah retained other lessons from his mentor, and none more so than Aggrey's admonition: "Let Africans remain good Africans, and not become a poor imitation of Europeans." Indeed, this later became the inspiration for one of Nkrumah's own most insistent thoughts, that when the continent's European colonies became independent, these newborn states must respect their "African personality."[27]

This concept became a touchstone of Nkrumah's politics, and something he would return to continuously throughout his political life. In 1963, late in his rule, he was still arguing that for Africans, a mastery of knowledge about their past was an essential and yet neglected bulwark against imperial domination:

> We were trained to be inferior copies of Englishmen, caricatures to be laughed at with our pretensions to British bourgeois gentility, our

grammatical faultiness and distorted standards betraying us at every turn. We were never fish nor fowl. We were denied knowledge of our African past and informed that we had no present. What future could there be for us? We were taught to regard our culture and traditions as barbarous and primitive. Our textbooks, telling us about English history, English geography, English ways of living, English customs, English ideas, English weather.[28]

Surely some of Nkrumah's defiance in the face of Johnson's rebuke also reflected his longstanding ambivalence toward religious doctrine. Speaking of his teenage years at Achimota College, in Accra, Nkrumah wrote:

I was already forming my own ideas on [religion] as against those set down by the Roman Catholic Church. I believed strongly that church-going should be a matter of conscience and should not be obligatory and I very soon began to cut the regular church services.[29]

In some measure, the defiant answer served up to Dean Johnson reflected Nkrumah's longstanding traits of iconoclasm and eclecticism, but it was also evidence of a more recent political maturation, which had allowed him to hold his own in person or publicly in a self-confident and articulate voice.

During this same period, meanwhile, in Philadelphia, Nkrumah, the erstwhile sociology student, was hired by the Presbyterian Church to perform what he would call "an intensive survey of the Negro from a religious, social and economic standpoint."[30] Philadelphia had been transformed by the Great Migration, at once becoming a much bigger city and a much more racially diverse one. In the 1920s alone, the Black population increased 61 percent, reaching 219,000. Nkrumah's survey covered over six hundred Black households in that city in neighborhoods like Poplar and Strawberry Mansion. Although it has not been preserved, here one finds an intriguing echo, unmentioned by Nkrumah, of the early accomplishments of W. E. B. Du Bois: an even more extensive survey of Black households that was commissioned by the University of Pennsylvania (Penn) and became one of the founding works of modern sociology when it was published in 1899 under the name, *The Philadelphia Negro*. Du Bois made groundbreaking use of statistics to demonstrate structural inequality that Black residents of the city faced in access to housing, employment, education, and other public services.

Any comparison would not be entirely fair. Nkrumah could never stick to anything long enough to become a scholar or an intellectual in such a grand or even conventional mode. But, nonetheless, Nkrumah was a prodigious and ambitious worker throughout this time. Late in his undergraduate years his hope had been to study at the Columbia University School of Journalism. Deciding this was too expensive, he began studying theology instead. He chose this in part because Lincoln had given him work as an instructor in introductory Greek, Negro Civilization and History, and Philosophy and Logic. This eventually earned him recognition by the *Lincolnian*, the school magazine, as "the most outstanding professor of the year."[31]

After admission to Lincoln's Theological Seminary, Nkrumah applied to Harvard University in hopes of pursuing a doctorate there with a full scholarship. Around that time, a professor of history at Penn wrote this appraisal of Nkrumah for his application to the PhD program in philosophy there: "He has, in my opinion, a distinguished mind. His essay on the political philosophy of John Locke, which he submitted for my graduate course, was far above the level of the average graduate performance.... Here is a man with an unusually fine mind who is or will be, in a position to do important work among his people."[32] In his recommendation to Harvard, George Johnson, the dean of students at Lincoln University was positive, if more reserved: "I take pleasure in [recommending him to you] because, in my opinion he is a worthy man, exceedingly interested in philosophy. He has a good mind and is preparing himself to return to West Africa to help in the college teaching in the Gold Coast."[33]

Nkrumah was rejected by Harvard and enrolled as a master's student at the University of Pennsylvania in the School of Education instead, compiling a record of two As, seven Bs, one C and one D. Like many compulsive overachievers, Nkrumah worked hard at cultivating his image, and he sounded a slightly defensive note about this performance. "In spite of the fact that, apart from teaching and studying, I was having to travel backwards and forwards three times a week from Lincoln University to the University of Pennsylvania, a distance of well over fifty miles, I managed within two years to complete the courses and the preliminary examinations for the doctorate" in philosophy, he wrote.[34] The historian, Marika Sherwood took a more reasonable view, when she wrote, "This is quite an achievement for someone 'carrying' 12 to 14 hours at the Lincoln Seminary and four hours at Pennsylvania in the first semester of 1940 and ten in the second."[35]

In fact, a complete account of all that Nkrumah was juggling during his graduate school years would be much fuller. His first master's degree, in education, came in 1941. Nkrumah's second master's at Penn, in philosophy, was awarded the following year. All the while, he was ceaselessly petitioning a miniature universe of organizations, from church groups to foundations, for the small increments he needed to cover his fees and stipend. All was not solicitation. Nkrumah did side jobs like teaching Fante during the summers, compiling a grammar of the language for the University of Pennsylvania Museum. He also audited classes at that university with an eye to an eventual law degree, wrote columns in a Lincoln University newspaper—signing his correspondence there "Yours Africanly, F.N. Nkrumah," and he was a driving force in the development of African student associations. It was in this capacity that he started to become a highly sought-after speaker in forums wherever the subject of Africa's future was on the agenda.

CHAPTER FIVE

Yours Africanly

Once he became a political leader, and from then on, Kwame Nkrumah affected the title Doctor, an honorific that all but his sworn opponents routinely appended to his name. Nkrumah was never awarded a PhD, though. It was a setback that he never directly addressed in his writing, but it was clearly a sore point. He wrote a thesis while working toward that degree in philosophy at the University of Pennsylvania and, in fact, produced a second, backup thesis.[1] The one he submitted for his doctorate was rejected. Although there is room for legitimate academic questions about why he was denied, the impression that political motives were also involved is practically unavoidable.

The academic problem involved something of a mismatch between the degree program and Nkrumah's chosen theme, well captured in his thesis's title, "The History and Philosophy of Imperialism, With Special Reference to Africa." Even to a non-philosopher or for that matter, to a nonacademic, this sounds like something that might be more appropriate for a history, political science, or international relations department. Moreso even than the title, it was probably the polemical content of Nkrumah's "History and Philosophy of Imperialism" that didn't just put off the philosophy faculty at Penn; it alarmed them. Nkrumah elaborated on a well-known critique of European imperialism that Du Bois had already made decades earlier: that the aim of establishing colonies was to hoard the natural resources of the undeveloped world, while simultaneously utilizing their imperial holdings as "dumping grounds" for their industrial goods. In this view, the Second World War could best be understood as a contest between two blocs, one of which, the Allied powers, had 1500 percent more colonial possessions around the world than the other, the Axis. The latter's sense of aggrievement essentially stemmed from the fact that it held so few. It was, in other words "a conflict between incumbent and insurgent imperialists," as one historian has recently argued.[2]

"The whole policy of the colonizer is to keep the native in his primitive state and make him economically dependent," Nkrumah wrote in his thesis draft. Whether they were traditional colonies or called protectorates or "mandate" territories, he argued, all of these imperial structures were founded on the basis of exploitation:

> The colonies gain no advantages whatsoever from being dependent; socially and technologically their progress is hindered; they pay for a nominal protection against aggression by providing troops for the mother country in time of war and their political freedom will never be automatically granted but won by their own endeavours.[3]

The first clause here strongly anticipates the thought of the man who would become the biggest influence on Nkrumah's politics in the very next phase of his life, the London-based Trinidadian journalist, intellectual, and global political organizer, George Padmore. Padmore not only rejected the idea that imperialism had anything to do with the needs of its dark-skinned subjects but asserted it was built on a clear, if unacknowledged, ideological foundation of white racial supremacy. It is the final clause in the preceding quote, though, that leads to the solution proposed by Nkrumah, and it was probably this, more than his diagnosis of the ills of colonial rule, that spelled trouble in the cautious and politically conservative precincts of American academia in the 1940s. Nkrumah called for a "complete revolutionary change of the colonial system." This should be attempted by moral suasion, but if that failed, it would have to be achieved through outright and righteous "physical force."[4] Such rhetoric is likely to have aroused concerns about possible communist influence on Nkrumah. Even short of that, these ideas would have raised hackles at a time when few in Western establishment circles had begun to challenge longstanding popular assumptions that Africans were not ready for, and were perhaps even incapable of, self-rule.

Even though it did not earn Nkrumah the degree he sought, this piece of writing, which would be later published as *Towards Colonial Freedom*, provides a valuable preview of what, a decade later, would be seen as the hallmarks of Nkrumah's political thought. African peoples, he argued, had been deliberately divided and subdivided and rendered economically dependent upon imperial powers under colonial rule. The only way forward for them rested in overcoming their fragmentation, both in ethnic terms and via the imposition of colonial borders. This is what made pan-Africanism imperative, and this explains what would later become one of Nkrumah's signature expressions, the exhortation: "Seek ye first the political kingdom." Lacking other weapons, Africans needed to wrest independence away from European control through persistent, concerted political action, mass mobilization, and unity.

In 1944, the dean of Penn's philosophy program wrote to Nkrumah to propose that he take another stab at the thesis he had submitted, but Nkrumah spurned the invitation. Years later, after he had become president of the first sub-Saharan African nation to achieve independence, the University of Pennsylvania reportedly sought to confer an honorary doctorate on Nkrumah in the midst of a tour of the United States. "Nkrumah refused it, saying why should he accept gratis that which they would not allow him to earn."[5]

Whether or not he had meaningfully come under communist influence by this time, almost from the start of his Lincoln days, Nkrumah sustained a remarkably consistent focus on African unity and independence. In 1938, two years after he had won a prize for oratory on the theme of "Africa, the burden of the Negro," he was also awarded something called the Robert Fleming Labaree Memorial Prize in Social Science for best dissertation on an assigned topic. Nkrumah's theme was "Imperialism: Its Political, Social and Economic Aspects."[6] In 1942, at Lincoln, Nkrumah was honored with an invitation to deliver a commencement speech. He recalled that it was titled, "Ethiopia Shall Stretch Forth Her Hands unto God."[7] Indeed, everything he turned out during his student years, or nearly everything, ended up somehow being about Africa. Even in his role as a guest preacher at Black American churches, those who recollected his sermons years later said they inevitably found their way to Africa.

By now, Nkrumah's compass was fixed on the liberation of his continent, and most of his intellectual pursuits were bound up in his busy search for answers to the challenges of ending colonial rule and economic dependence on the West. It was in this spirit that he devoured Marx and Lenin during his Lincoln years, but also the writings of Giuseppe Mazzini, a fervent nineteenth-century Italian nationalist and republican who fiercely opposed Marxism. And by the same token, this fixation on African emancipation inspired him to return over and over to Garvey, whose *Philosophy and Opinions* Nkrumah claimed affected him most of all. The tapping of Garvey as a source of insight or inspiration is unsurprising except for its timing, coming as it did at the end of Garvey's life and at a time when Garveyism was already in steep decline as a movement.

Nkrumah's personal growth did not stop there, though. His exposure to Harlem and his sociological work in Philadelphia, his frequenting of the Blyden Society there, and his regular preaching in Black churches all seem to have inspired a radical broadening of his conception of Blackness, and of the importance of the diaspora to the coming push for African independence. He alludes to this in his early writings, saying that in the course of his student activism in America, he had come to the position that, "unless territorial freedom was ultimately linked up with the Pan African movement for the liberation of the whole African continent, there would be no hope of freedom and equality for the African and for people of African descent in any part of the world."[8]

Nkrumah had become passionately interested in an early 1940s debate that played out around the publication of a book by the noted Northwestern University anthropologist, Melville J. Herskovits, called *The Myth of the Negro Past* (1941). In this landmark work, Herskovits took on the then widely held view that Black Americans had essentially been almost entirely shorn of their African ancestral cultures. This had supposedly happened by virtue of the Middle Passage, as well as through a deliberate strategy of mixing Africans of different origins on American slave plantations, where they were Christianized and forbidden from openly using their own languages and rituals. As it happened, Howard University was then a stronghold of the conventional wisdom on this question, led by the country's leading Black sociologist, E. Franklin Frazier, who had recently published *The Negro Family in the United States* (1939). Nkrumah wrote, "I supported, and still support, the [Herskovitz] view and I went on one occasion to Howard University to defend it."[9]

More important than this debate, were the ties that Nkrumah forged around this time at Howard. As America's most prestigious Black university, Howard was home to an unusually influential cluster of Black thinkers whose ideas would radiate far beyond academia in the middle of the twentieth century. Together, they would contribute to propelling both the American civil rights movement and the push for independence in Africa. What is more, members of this brain trust gradually came to see the two struggles as being inseparable, much as Nkrumah himself had just begun to say.

One of Nkrumah's most important contacts in this world was Ralph Bunche, who was born in 1903, six years before Nkrumah, in Detroit, and raised by a maternal grandmother in Albuquerque, New Mexico. A valedictorian in his graduating class at UCLA, the light-skinned Bunche continued to Harvard, where he became the first African American to earn a PhD in political science in the United States in 1934. Bunche chaired the Department of Political Science at Howard from 1928 to 1950 and went on to participate in the founding of the United Nations, where he became a high-profile peace negotiator and eventual under-secretary general for special political affairs. Bunche would go on to win a Nobel Prize in 1950 for his mediation in the Arab Israeli conflict, a role he reprised in the 1960 Congo Crisis, in which Nkrumah played an important part.

Bunche is mostly remembered today as a Black pioneer in the establishment mold. But his intellectual life had begun with an attraction to socialism almost equal to Nkrumah's. As one Bunche biographer has written, an early and consistent passion of his had been "the future of Africa and the rolling back of European empire."[10] In one of his last scholarly essays before entering government service, Bunche wrote the justifications used to defend colonialism in Africa were virtually identical to those "often employed to justify the enslavement of the Negro in America."[11]

By the early 1940s, Bunche and Nkrumah had established a close correspondence, and Nkrumah made a point of visiting him whenever he came to Washington, signing off in one letter, "many things we can talk over."[12] Next door to Bunche's office at Howard sat the office of one of the founders of African studies as an academic discipline, William Leo Hansberry, with whom Nkrumah also grew close. Howard was the host of other Black luminaries, including the Trinidadian, Eric Williams, a future prime minister of independent Trinidad and Tobago, and former student and protégé of the towering Marxist intellectual and historian from Trinidad, C. L. R. James.

By now, Nkrumah had cast off any remaining West African provincialism and not only enthusiastically embraced the idea of a shared past in racial domination between Africans and African Americans, but a closely paired future. In the Depression era Harlem of just a few years earlier, the "Don't Buy Where You Can't Work" placards that Black American protestors carried had been all but invisible to him. By 1942, though, Nkrumah found himself sharing the stage at an event held at Lincoln to discuss "decolonization at home and abroad" with one of the principal organizers of those protests.[13] This was none other than the slick-haired, glad-handing, cigar-smoking progressive Harlem congressman Adam Clayton Powell, Jr., who was one of the most prominent African Americans in politics. There were at least two ways one could look at someone like Powell: not only as a privileged, vain, and unctuous showboat and reputed lady's man, but as someone light skinned enough to "pass" as white, as Powell had selectively done as a college student. Or alternatively, one could see him as the grandson of an enslaved woman from Franklin County, Virginia, meaning, as with most African Americans of his generation, he was scarcely removed from America's "peculiar institution." By this time, Powell's credo had become "mass action is the most powerful force on earth," a belief strikingly shared by Nkrumah, and also by rapidly growing numbers of Blacks.[14]

Of all of the figures he met during this period, though, it was C. L. R. James, a man with a caramel complexion and high, chiseled cheek bones and hair that went white in middle age, who had the most decisive influence on Nkrumah. James, a wiry and urbane polymath from Trinidad who was a few years Nkrumah's senior, was equally and deeply versed in global history, political theory, and his beloved sport of cricket. A committed Marxist, but one who placed faith in the power of the masses much more than he did in the concept of proletarian dictatorship, James tutored the younger West African in radical politics and political organization. Nkrumah credited James with teaching him about Trotskyites and said, "through him I learned how an underground movement worked." In the 1970s, after Nkrumah's overthrow and death, James recalled that

> [I] got to know Nkrumah in the United States in 1943, and he and I and some of my friends were very close between 1943 and 1945. We went down to Pennsylvania or to Lincoln to see him—or he would come up to New York and spend a day or two with his friends and exchange ideas with us. Even in those years, Nkrumah was noted for his acute intelligence, his intellectual energy, the elegance of his person, the charm of his manners and his ability to establish easy relations with any company in which he found himself. We could observe that, behind his easy style, his primary concern was the independence and freedom of African people.[15]

There can be little doubt that the single most important act taken on Nkrumah's behalf by James was his introduction of Nkrumah to George Padmore in London. It is hard to square what James said to his London friend, though, with James's other recollections of Nkrumah. "George, this young man is coming to you," James wrote in his introduction. "He is not very bright, but nevertheless do what you can for him because he's determined to throw Europeans out of Africa."[16] Rather than a statement about Nkrumah's intelligence, it seems likely that James, who took his Marxism seriously, felt that Nkrumah's grasp of ideological matters was crude and approximate.

CHAPTER SIX

Euston Station

On the strength of C. L. R. James's missive, in May 1945, George Padmore met Francis Nkrumah at Euston Station, the rail hall that serviced trains to the London docks. Euston had been hit twice during the Blitz and remained badly damaged, but Nkrumah seems to have paid this no notice. The frequent "ack-ack" of antiaircraft fire had gone silent with the last Nazi attack on the city almost exactly a year prior. The British had seen to it that the streets of the capital were quickly cleared of detritus. But even this fastidiousness could not conceal what was deeply broken. London was a city of cracked roofs and windows that remained blacked out or shattered. The country was putting on a brave face as it staved off bankruptcy, and many of its people were barely getting by on the distributions of the Ministry of Food.

Nkrumah knew nothing about James's equivocal recommendation; his feelings were dominated, instead, by anxiety about whether or not he would be greeted at all in a city barely known to him.

> The only person I knew of in England was George Padmore, a West Indian journalist who lived in London and was the author of several articles which had aroused my interest and sympathy. I was so impressed by his writings that I wrote a letter to him from the States introducing myself and asking whether he would be able to meet me at Euston Station when I arrived. I heard nothing from him because I had left America too soon for a reply to have reached me, so I had no idea whether he would be at the station or not. I got out from the train and searched anxiously up and down the platform. We saw each other at about the same time and from the first moment I liked him.[1]

Padmore is not as widely remembered today as he deserves to be, but it is hard to imagine a better first contact in the capital of the world's largest empire than this unusually energetic and resourceful activist. Although he was not waiting for him alone on the train platform, as Nkrumah recounts, Padmore's welcome (witnessed by the uncredited presence of a fellow Gold Coast native, the London-based nationalist and student activist, member of the Asante aristocracy, soon to be close collaborator, and eventual opponent, Joe Appiah) was yet another one of those moments in which Nkrumah's rise can seem fated.

Nkrumah had sailed from New York City in May of 1945, and just one month after he arrived in London, he was named a co-secretary for the historically pivotal Pan-African Congress that would be held in Manchester in the middle of October. And largely on Padmore's account, Nkrumah would be named the rapporteur of this international gathering, which brought together Africans from many colonies, as well as elements of the Black diaspora from the West Indies and the United States. These included Du Bois, who was the event's international president. The American patriarch of pan-Africanism is revealed in formal portraits of the time taken by Carl Van Vechten, a white author and patron of the Harlem Renaissance. The images, which bear the painterly hallmarks of Kodachrome, burnished in the red-yellow-orange end of the spectrum and deep in shadow, reveal the so-called Wizard as a stoop-shouldered and mostly bald seventy-seven-year-old, but a twinkling-eyed and still elegant one, with his famous upturned moustache and goatee long gone gray.

By way of background, Padmore was a cofounder in 1936 of the London-based pan-Africanist organization, the International African Service Bureau (IASB), which was the leading anticolonial group in Britain. C. L. R. James and Amy Ashwood Garvey were among its cofounders. The IASB was a prolific publisher of antiimperialist books, pamphlets, and a newspaper, *International African Opinion*. Padmore had deep links to nearly every important base in the Black world. His West Indian identity politics placed him firmly within a proud and historically impactful regional tradition of nationalism and independence that stretched back nearly 150 years to the Haitian revolutionary, Toussaint Louverture. Louverture's uprising against the plantation slavery of the imperial powers created the second republic in the Western Hemisphere. It hastened the end of plantation slavery everywhere. And it constitutionally enshrined the most fundamental value of the Enlightenment for Haiti—legal equality for all, regardless of race—before any other nation had done so, white or Black.

Padmore was said to be the great-grandson of an Asante warrior from what became the Gold Coast who had been captured and sold into slavery in Barbados. His grandfather had been a slave on that island. And George himself, who was baptized as Malcolm Nurse, had been James's friend since their childhood in Trinidad. The nexus of their friendship and collaboration remained intact throughout their lives.

In 1924, Padmore had gone to the United States to study medicine at Fisk University, a historically Black institution in Nashville, Tennessee, but eventually he transferred to Howard University, already by then the center of gravity in African American higher education. At Howard, Padmore soon came under the influence of Alain Locke, a diminutive gay man inclined to full Victorian formality in dress, who had earned degrees in philosophy and English at Harvard in 1907 and then became the country's first African American Rhodes Scholar. The Howard don's tutelage of Padmore occurred during the cultural big bang of the Harlem Renaissance and the associated New Negro movement. Each of these had grown organically out of the deepening racial self-awareness and new assertive Black consciousness that followed in the wake of the First World War. And as it did so, it drew in novelists, painter, musicians, and poets, like my cousin, the war veteran Waring Cuney, who published and edited work together with his close friend, Langston Hughes.[2]

In an essay by Locke that announced the New Negro movement to the world, he wrote about "the wash and rush of this human tide on the beach line of the northern cit[ies]" that was bringing together large numbers of Africans and West Indians with American "Negroes" of the north and south for the first time in history. The resulting race-consciousness was one of pride and impatience "with being spoken of as a social ward or minor."[3]

Locke, who was born into a comfortable middle-class Philadelphia family, never joined in the protest movements and radical politics of many of the leading African American figures of his era. But in their own way, the cultural ideas he promoted posed equally stout challenges to the country's conventional values. He believed, for example, that Black people had created America's only arts of enduring distinction. Africa was the fountainhead for this, and a creative source of "almost limitless wealth," Locke believed, leading him to become a vigorous advocate of a kind of pan-Africanism.[4] As his biographer, Jeffrey C. Stuart wrote, it amounted to "a call on all of African descent, regardless of their origins within the Diaspora, to look upon Africa as their homeland."[5] This spirit ricocheted through the age, infusing innumerable writers and artists who picked up on Locke's notions. This would lead Ralph Ellison, for example, toward the belief that America's highest culture had come out of the experience of Blackness, creating a debt that could never be undone.[6]

While some of Padmore's Black nationalism seems to have taken root at Howard, blossoming under the influence of intellectual heavyweights like Locke, there was far more to it than this. Even before he left Trinidad, Padmore had named a daughter of his Blyden, after Edward Wilmot Blyden, the proto-pan-Africanist of Liberia, whom we met early in this book.

Malcolm Nurse adopted the name George Padmore after he became deeply involved in Communist Party activism in the late 1920s, a time when the party was rebounding from the fierce repression of its members during the First Red Scare, earlier in the decade. By then, the party had turned its attentions to fulminating against the repression of African Americans, and organizing Blacks, immigrants, and women in the progressive labor movement. Padmore's involvement began as a member of the American Negro Labor Congress, whose aim was to recruit Black Americans into the world of the party. Seen as an impressively effective organizer, the dark-skinned and high-browed Padmore was invited to Moscow as a rising star in 1929, and he took up residence there, where he was named leader of the Negro Bureau of the Red International of Labor Unions and member of the Moscow City Soviet. But Padmore's falling out with the Soviet Union and with communism came just as suddenly as had his falling in. The precipitating factor in this hostile divorce was Padmore's deeply held Black nationalism, which reflected the enduring influence of Garvey. The Communist Party of the Soviet Union and its affiliated offshoots frowned on race-based nationalism. Padmore's disenchantment with Marxism-Leninism as defined and policed by Moscow grew as he experienced racism in the communist circles he traveled in in Europe. According to the historian Leslie James, this came to a head after Padmore was blamed for a raid on offices of the International Trade Union Committee of Negro Workers, in Hamburg, in which he was arrested and deported, just two weeks after Hitler came to power in February 1933.[7]

Padmore was also dismayed over Moscow's abject strategic reversal after hostilities erupted with Hitler following Operation Barbarossa, Berlin's shock invasion of the Soviet Union in 1941. Until then, out of obedience to the Soviet line, the Communist Party of the United States and its Black members had opposed American involvement in the war. This was based in part on the pretense that the Axis powers were combating imperialism, which Lenin had famously held to be the highest stage of capitalism. After that point, Moscow cast aside its opposition to colonial dominion over others by Western powers in order to combat German fascism. For Padmore, as for Du Bois and for growing numbers of other Black intellectuals, the distinction between colonial rule premised on white supremacy and fascism was specious. It is worth noting that sentiments like this did not only emanate from Blacks. Earlier, Gandhi had written, "If there is a difference [between Britain and Nazi Germany] it is in degree."[8] Padmore experienced Moscow's deemphasis on combatting imperialism as a betrayal. It represented yet another instance of the reflexive historic subordination of the interests of Black people to those of whites.

The break with Moscow was by no means the end of radical politics for Padmore. On the contrary, now he was free to follow his own instincts and mount his own initiatives. And in order to do so, he moved to London, the belly of the beast in terms of colonial rule, or "the enemy's headquarters" in the words of one pan-African activist there at the time.[9] From London, Padmore set about building connections throughout the Black world, shaping debates about the place of Black people under empire and cultivating talent among people, such as Nkrumah, whom he saw as budding changemakers who could accelerate a global Black push for freedom. In time, Padmore would become the clear throughline between Lenin and Nkrumah, who would later author a book titled *Neo-Colonialism: The Last Stage of Imperialism*.

Throughout the period of his life that commenced with his move to London, Padmore was an unusually prolific author of both books and articles, with pieces published in newspapers and magazines all over the Atlantic world. This included the Gold Coast, where many of his writings about Ethiopia appeared in the *African Morning Post*. The quote from Nkrumah's autobiography that appeared earlier, which speaks to how impressed Nkrumah was by Padmore's writings, suggests that he had already come under the Trinidadian's strong influence even before leaving the United States in 1945. In fact, it is not unlikely that Nkrumah's response to the slaughter unleashed by the Italian invasion of Ethiopia, which he described in writing as sudden and emotional, was to some degree a byproduct of Padmore's extensive publication of outraged commentary about this event.

If so, one can chalk that up to a success for someone who was, at heart, an indefatigable old-school propagandist. Padmore's priority was ginning up the energy and will among Africans they needed to throw off European empires. This was not a goal to be pursued through the patient melioration that had begun mid-century, which London and Paris would have liked Africans to accept, but through urgent militancy and agitation.

Already in 1949, France's Charles de Gaulle had been unusually forthright about the leading imperial powers' desire to grant more autonomy to

Africans with all deliberate speed, meaning at an almost imperceptible pace, after the war.

> In French Africa, as in every land where men live under our flag, there can be no true progress unless men are able to benefit from it morally and materially on their native soil, unless they can raise themselves little by little to a level where they can partake in the management of their own affairs. It is the duty of France to bring this about.[10]

In its utter dependence on its colonies, Paris was no outlier. In an unusual moment of candor, a British delegate at the San Francisco Conference, which laid the foundation of the United Nations, stated baldly that their colonial empires had preserved the Allied powers in Europe from defeat. They had served as "one vast machine for the defense of liberty," and abandoning them now was out of the question.[11] The matter of exactly whose liberty was being defended was, of course, elided. The historian Tony Judt wrote of this as an "unseemly paradox" that existed at the close of the Second World War, in which "the peoples of Western Europe—who were hard put to govern or even feed themselves—continued to rule much of the non-European world." Judt continued, saying, "Without access to the far-flung territory, supplies and men that came with colonies, the British and French especially would have been at an even greater disadvantage in their struggle with Germany and Japan than they already were."[12]

Britain's colonial establishment was largely out of touch with all but the most assimilated, and therefore relatively accommodationist, elites of their African colonies. This favored the persistence of the illusion, pierced only briefly during the strike waves of the late 1930s, that colonial rule could continue for a very long time to come. It also left the British unprepared for the rise of a politician like Nkrumah, a peasant by background, even if an unusually fortunate one, and an inheritor of the traditions of Garvey and Padmore—people who saw the common folk, not as an inert mass, or rabble, but as the raw material or grist of political power.

Some African independence activists had celebrated the Labour Party's participation in the wartime coalition that governed Britain, seeing this as a possible harbinger of the continent's liberation on an expedited timetable. Labour's courting of the modest-sized Black vote in Britain had explicitly encouraged this. Such hopes were quickly disabused, though. In 1945, shortly after the closing ceremony of the San Francisco Conference in the grand, downtown Beaux-Arts hall of the city's Herbst Theater, Labour quietly backed South African plans to terminate the mandate that had allowed it to administer neighboring South West Africa (Namibia) and simply absorb that territory as part of South Africa, which was governed under a system of white supremacy. Then, in January 1946, with the Labour Party now fully in charge in Britain, Herbert Morrison, the party's deputy leader, bluntly declared to American journalists, "We are great friends of the jolly old Empire and are going to stick to it."[13]

The following month, another Labour leader, Aneurin Bevan doubled down, telling Parliament, "I am not prepared to sacrifice the British Empire because I know that if the British Empire fell, it would mean the standard of life of our own constituents would fall considerably."[14] This was functionally indistinguishable from the position Winston Churchill held during the War, as when he famously declared in late 1942 that "I have not become the King's First Minister to preside over the liquidation of the British Empire."[15] The country's political leaders were no outliers in this, either. Orwell said the entire population, from left to right, had bought into what he called "the empire-racket."

> In the last resort, the only important question is, Do you want the British Empire to hold together or do you want it to disintegrate? And at the bottom of his heart no Englishman . . . want[s] it to disintegrate. For, apart from any other consideration, the high standard of life we enjoy in England depends upon our keeping a tight hold on the Empire, particularly the tropical portions of it such as India and Africa.[16]

Beyond empire there was little else, Orwell wrote, that could preserve England from becoming "a cold and unimportant little island where we should all have to work very hard and live mainly on herrings and potatoes."[17] Home truths like these rarely leak into the public discourse of the nominally progressive elements of the British political establishment, and awareness of attitudes like these has almost entirely faded among the British public ever since, amid a hazy misremembering of empire as an extended exercise in benevolence. But on this topic, Padmore, characteristically well ahead of his time, had been making the case since the early 1930s that Britain could scarcely feed itself, never mind continue being a dominant global power, without the wealth and sustenance it extracted from its colonies and Africa in particular.

In his journalism and books, notably *How Britain Rules Africa*, Padmore returned over and over to this topic, and not with a once-over-easy argument that he merely repurposed time and again, but constantly, almost obsessively, gathering new details about Britain's imperial actions and drilling down on them. Padmore's writing documented how colonial control of African agriculture subsidized consumption in Britain while condemning farmers on the continent to penury. These were not the fevered imaginings of a revolutionary dreamer, either. In 1947, Stafford Cripps, the Labour minister for economic affairs, spoke candidly about his country's dependence on its African colonies, saying "the whole future of the sterling area and its ability to survive depends in my view upon a quick and extensive development of our African resources."[18] That same year, amid the decline of British power in Asia, Frederick Pedler, an influential colonial official, called Africa "the only continental space from which we can still hope to draw reserves of economic and military space."[19] By 1948, the Gold Coast trailed only Malaya as a source of imperial revenue for Britain. Cocoa from that single West African colony generated $47.5 million for Britain at a time when sterling was under severe balance of payments pressure and the Exchequer suffered from a $1.8 billion deficit.[20] Padmore spoke of the direct contributions of African colonies to the British war effort, making possible the purchase of airplanes and other armaments. And he documented the use of African manpower, first as a pack animal–like logistical force, and then, finally, in battle. A Padmore series that was published in colonial Trinidad in 1940 captured the flavor of many of his arguments with this title, *Colonial Aid to Britain in the Great War*.[21]

Padmore peppered the entire Atlantic periphery, filing endless dispatches to newspapers in the West Indies, Africa, and the United States. According to Leslie James's count, this included hundreds of articles for the *African Morning Post* and *The Ashanti Pioneer* in the Gold Coast, and a great many more for Azikiwe-owned papers in Nigeria like the *West African Pilot*. One must add to this the numerous articles he wrote for the African American press, such as influential and widely read papers like the *Pittsburgh Courier*, *Chicago Defender*, *Amsterdam News*, and *Baltimore Afro-American*.[22] Padmore's principal aim had nothing to do with reaching British "home" public opinion; it was "to prepare the ground for a post-war battle for independence."[23] And in the receptive Francis, soon to be Kwame Nkrumah, he found his most important target. The Trinidadian's ideas would not only infuse Nkrumah's writings about the nature of colonial rule and what he would call neocolonialism, they were foundational to his own political thought and strategies.

Padmore tweaked the famous saying of Du Bois about the color line being "the problem of the twentieth century," reformulating this idea into a much more potent and militant statement.

The Colonial problem is the central issue of world politics today. Africans and peoples of African descent are on the whole a "colonial people" that is, their destinies are not in their own hands.... They are told that they are being held in sacred trust for civilization.... We repudiate this imperial benevolence, because we are fully aware that behind it is masked ruthless and incessant exploitation. "International African Opinion" will aim always at breaking the economic, political and social chains which bind Africans and peoples of African descent.[24]

Here we find the very germination of Nkrumah's most ardent project, pan-Africanism, as well as the beginnings of another element that was key to his thought: the need to conquer power, and thereby, independence, quickly, for however weak, poor, and dependent Africa's colonies were, it was only by seizing the levers of government that one could begin to turn this situation around. And to his surprise and benefit, Nkrumah would discover the British to be more uncertain about their ability to hold onto African colonies such as the Gold Coast than they let on publicly.

CHAPTER SEVEN

The Dawn of Action

EVEN BEFORE LEARNING WHERE HE WOULD STAY OR DROPPING OFF HIS bags somewhere, Nkrumah went straight from Euston Station to a raucous labor union meeting. This wasn't the result of being taken under Padmore's wing, though. The new arrival's escort was his fellow Gold Coast native Joe Appiah, a descendant of the Asante aristocracy who had come to London in 1943 to study law at the Middle Temple and became active in emigre politics there. Appiah, who was Nkrumah's junior by nine years, delivered a fiery speech before an audience of railway union activists that day. Its militancy startled the freshly arrived Nkrumah, who tugged at the back of Appiah's coat mid-delivery, and asked in Twi, the near lingua franca of their homeland, "Won't these whites have you arrested?"[1]

After the speech, as Appiah (and presumably Padmore) accompanied Nkrumah to the West African Students' Union hostel where he would temporarily lodge, Nkrumah mused about the trouble that anything analogous to Appiah's remarks would have provoked in the United States. "Joe, in America, you and all of us would have been lynched or deported halfway through that speech."[2]

Nkrumah, adopted the name Kwame not long after his arrival in London in late May or early June of 1945. Germany had surrendered on May 7. The next morning, immortalized as VE-Day, it was as if the city's entire population had come out of hibernation all at once to fill the streets. People covered every square foot as they mobbed the great squares and Buckingham Palace. In their immensity, crowds seemed to swallow up passenger cars and double decker buses. Strangers kissed and locked arms and danced little jigs as they rejoiced.

That spring, Allied forces had taken control of concentration camps like Bergen-Belsen and Dachau, laying bare the exterminationist nature of the

Holocaust. The atomic bombing of Japan, unexpected, stood just weeks into the future. The writing of the United Nations Charter was proceeding in San Francisco, where thirty-five thousand delegates and staff—people from every continent—labored at a hectic pace. Africa, though, was represented only by Ethiopia and Liberia, along with a South Africa dominated by whites. This greatly enhanced the importance of the African American presence in San Francisco. There, progressive Blacks lobbied and pressured from the margins of the conference, and Ralph Bunche, the number two in the US delegation, did so from the inside, to insist that the urgent work of decolonization remain high on the agenda. Mary McLeod Bethune was another prominent Black attendee. She was the fifteenth of seventeen children born in South Carolina in 1875 to formerly enslaved parents. They encouraged pride toward the continent and maintained an oral tradition that said Bethune's maternal ancestors had been royalty in West Africa.[3] Dark-skinned and formidable, Bethune proclaimed, "Through this conference, the Negro becomes closely allied with all the darker races of the world, but more importantly he becomes integrated into the structure of the peace and freedom of all people everywhere."[4] Du Bois, ever prolific, published a book during the conference titled *Color and Democracy*, in which he decried European rule over people of color, calling colonies "the slums of the world."[5] Demands for freedom from foreign domination echoed now like clarion calls heralding the commencement of an entirely new era. In chemistry an abrupt shift like this to a new era would be called a phase change, as from solid to liquid, or liquid to gas. The dawning age should be seen as sharp a break from the past as, say, the birth of modern nation states in Europe was from the long era of religious wars on that continent that preceded it. This was not necessarily immediately apparent, but it would become so in remarkably little time. That is because of the great wave of emancipations from European colonial rule and births of legally sovereign nations that soon followed.

Black Africa, with Nkrumah and the Gold Coast at the forefront, would soon be at the very center of this era's great transformation. The continent had been virtually voiceless and without representation in San Francisco. But a mere two decades later, due to the wave of independence that followed in Ghana's wake, Africa would constitute the largest group of states of any continent in the world body.

During the early 1940s, like Marx's Soho flat in the previous century, the kitchen table in Padmore's modest northwest London apartment became the center of gravity for a unique global network of activists pushing for independence from colonial rule throughout the Black world. Frequent guests included not only Nkrumah and Appiah, but other future African presidents, such as Kenya's Johnstone (later known as Jomo) Kenyatta and Nyasaland's (now Malawi) Hastings Kamuzu Banda. There was Forbes Burnham, whose performance as British Guiana's top student won him a scholarship to the University of London and put him on the path to become a future prime minister of Guyana. There were progressive intellectuals and writers such as Richard Wright; C. L. R. James; the Black South African novelist, Peter Abrahams; and T. Ras Makonnen, a Guyanese author who claimed Ethiopian descent. Abrahams and Makonnen assisted Padmore in organizing the Manchester Conference, and Makonnen would go on to work with Padmore and Nkrumah in Ghana. It was the largely unsung Appiah, though, who provided Nkrumah's introduction to the African student world in London generally. And it was this milieu, above all, that would serve as the catapult for Nkrumah's rocket-like ascent on the London scene.

In those days, Britain's own citizens suspected it was finished as a power. It is striking to read the description—absent an explanation—in Appiah's autobiography of how, during his London days, Nkrumah transformed virtually overnight from an almost clueless Johnny-come-lately to a driven organizer and "very hard worker who enjoyed hard labor and needed very little or no rest."[6] These were traits that friend and foe would attribute to him for the rest of his life. Abrahams later wrote of Nkrumah during this time, referring to one of the myriad of small political organizations that Africans were forming in Britain:

> He had quickly become a part of our African colony in London and had joined our little group, the Pan-African Federation in our protests against colonialism. He was much less relaxed than most of us. His eyes mirrored a burning inner conflict and tension. He seemed consumed by a restlessness that led him to evolve some of the most fantastic schemes.[7]

For all of that, Nkrumah was soon being called "our man," and "our standard bearer," by people like Appiah. He and others in this tightly knit community of Gold Coast students would soon line up behind Nkrumah and buck him up as he made his way back home with the aim of conquering power barely two years after his arrival in Britain. It is just as striking, though, perhaps even more so, to think about how utterly undefined Nkrumah's fate remained nearly up to the moment he boarded a ship for his return journey to West Africa in the middle of November 1947.

In London, Nkrumah immediately immersed himself in pro-independence and pan-Africanist politics. Makonnen, for one, is said to have almost instantly discerned in Nkrumah the mien and stature of a natural-born leader and immediately thought of him as the perfect figure to lead the Gold Coast toward independence. Padmore, who reviled mere coffee-house revolutionaries, similarly seems to have seen Nkrumah right away as an exciting project; someone he could shape for leadership. Whatever James's early reservations, he also saw Nkrumah as an unusual talent who could be cultivated and molded for a big political role. But even as he became absorbed in this new world of international activism, Nkrumah's initial goals for himself remained much more down to earth.

Some accounts from the London of this era say the doors on rental units often bore signs saying, "No Coal," meaning people of color need not apply, and Nkrumah initially struggled to find suitable lodging. Black residents numbered well under twenty thousand, a firm color bar was still in place, and yet race seemed to him to work very differently than it did in America. There, the color line was shockingly overt and frequently de jure. What Nkrumah sensed about life in Britain was somehow stranger. Black people could go just about anywhere, but their presence was seldom wanted or welcomed.[8] With remarkable equanimity, he recounts his experience of being repeatedly turned away or having the door shut in his face as soon as landlords found themselves face to face with a Black man. In one instance, while he sat in a café, a small girl approached and apparently took him for a monkey, screaming to her mother, "Mummy! It talks!"[9] He finally found a white family that would take him in, renting a small room in a home without a bath in the Tufnell Park neighborhood of North London for 30 shillings a week, and there he would remain throughout his nearly two and a half years living in Britain.

While Britain was struggling to pull itself together after the war, Nkrumah spent that first summer working side by side with Padmore. Together they wrote hundreds of letters to groups in Africa and the Caribbean to drum up interest in Padmore's brainchild, the upcoming Pan-African Congress. The two proffered tactical advice to whoever would receive it on how militants in the colonies could advance toward independence. Nkrumah's enterprise and skill as an organizer impressed Padmore enough to share duties with him in the roles of political secretary and rapporteur of the sessions about West Africa at the Manchester Pan-African Congress that October.

The Manchester Conference, which brought together about ninety delegates at Chorlton-on-Medlock, the city's Doric-columned neoclassical town hall, was a watershed event in the dawning postwar era that received almost no notice in the Western press at the time. From the podium, Nkrumah delivered a declaration about the right of colonial peoples to be free, and on the need for "economic democracy" in the world, right alongside political democracy. This immediately deepened his credentials in progressive Black internationalist circles, sealing what would become a lifelong relationship with the elderly Du Bois, whom the conference honored with the largely ceremonial title of chairman. The two had met in the United States, but by Du Bois's own account, he had no recollections of Nkrumah prior to Manchester.

Despite Du Bois's nominal leadership, this was the first of these conferences at which Blacks from outside the United States and Europe, meaning West Indians and especially Africans, dominated the agenda. Gone was the gradualism of past conferences, which aimed at reducing the inequities of imperialism. Europe was on its knees, shattered and morally degraded by the charnel house slaughter and industrial-style genocide of the war. Although the gathering ended with no blueprint of how the continent would function under pan-Africanism, it nonetheless fostered an urgent new ethos centered on the responsibility of Blacks under colonial rule to promptly win their own independence outright.

In terms of Nkrumah's own trajectory, though, it was what was happening in the far less-glamorous setting of student and exile politics in Britain that played an even more important role both in his own immediate future and that of the Gold Coast. Reinvented as Kwame, he became active in an alphabet soup of student organizations and promptly rose to leadership positions in some of them. These roles, combined with the urgings and encouragement of Padmore and Makonnen, caused him to abandon his return to academic life and thoughts of publishing a PhD thesis in philosophy or obtaining a law degree. "Whenever they met they talked about little else but nationalist politics and colonial liberation movements," Nkrumah wrote of the student groups he was drawn to.[10] These included not only the Pan-African Federation mentioned by Abrahams, but also the West African Students' Union (WASU), of which he became the vice-president, and the much more militant West African National Secretariat (WANS), of which Nkrumah became the secretary general. It was in that role that Nkrumah had presented himself as an organizer of the Manchester Conference and founder of a short-lived magazine, *The New African*. Its first issue, in March 1946, announced the color with these words, "The Voice of the Awakened African," along with the motto "For Unity and Absolute Independence."[11]

Rubbing shoulders with luminaries like Du Bois had prestige value, but it was Nkrumah's involvement in the Gold Coast student circles in Britain that unexpectedly put him on the path to power. The story that Nkrumah tells of these events feels clipped and tended. As is the case with so many politicians, he has a just-so quality in his telling that lends the story a sense of predestination, and perhaps covers up other interpretive trails. While he is searching for an apartment in London, he explains, he is so exhausted he decided to take a bus. As if by providence, no sooner has he boarded it, then he sees Ako Adjei, the student who had worked on Azikiwe's newspaper in the Gold Coast, who had come to Lincoln University in 1939, and who had quickly fallen under Nkrumah's sway. Among other things, in those Lincoln days, Adjei had been Nkrumah's collaborator in putting out issues of the *African Interpreter*. "Nkrumah's room became a meeting point for Gold Coast and other students," Adjei wrote later. "We were the best of friends."[12]

Adjei had gone on from Lincoln University to study at the Hampton Institute and then to earn a master's degree at the Columbia Journalism School, where Nkrumah had also dreamed of studying. Since then, he had been in London reading law and had risen to become leader of the West African Students' Union. In 1945, it probably counted no more than one hundred full dues-paying members. When Adjei returned to the Gold Coast in April 1947, he immediately gravitated to the political scene there, where a network of Black lawyers and businessmen were in the advanced stages of planning to launch a political party. Their chief financial sponsor was none other than George "Paa" Grant, Nkrumah's host in Manchester on his way to the United States. The aim of these self-selected "natural leaders" was to begin the push for independence, something they imagined achieving at a stately pace, meaning in a matter of years, or perhaps even as long as a decade.

Nkrumah tells the story of his subsequent communications with Adjei as if they had arisen almost entirely out of the blue.

> One day I received a letter from Ako Adjei, who was then back in the Gold Coast, asking me if I would return and take on the job of general secretary of the United Gold Coast Convention. He explained that the U.G.C.C. was being faced with the problem of how to reconcile the leadership of the intelligentsia with the broad masses of the people and, knowing of my political activities in both the United States and in England, he had recommended to the Executive Committee that I should be invited to become general secretary.[13]

The natural leaders had offered him a car and £100 a month for his troubles, but Nkrumah brushed off these inducements as having little meaning to him, a man selflessly devoted to liberation. In the next breath, though, he said that the offer to become general secretary of a new party back home "most certainly" interested him. "I saw the opportunity that I had been waiting for, the chance to return home and actively help my people by the experience I had gained in party organisation abroad." Nonetheless, the whole thing "seemed too good to be true."[14]

Nkrumah then describes a round of consultations he undertook, first with a lecturer at Oxford who had just returned from a stay in the Gold Coast and who briefed him about the quickening political maneuvers there that were aimed at creating the colony's first political party. One imagines that man, Tony McLean, a member of the Communist Party, describing the leaders of the UGCC as reactionaries. "My revolutionary background and ideas would make it impossible for me to work with them," Nkrumah concluded.[15]

J. B. Danquah, the well-established lawyer who would soon rise to the leadership of the new party, then wrote to Nkrumah to urge him to take the job. His London friends equivocated, though. "They all seemed unwilling to persuade me one way or the other, for it was a tricky period. It might be our beginning, but it could also be the end," Nkrumah writes.[16] Finally, he called a meeting of the West African National Secretariat, the strongly pro-independence group that he led.

> After much serious discussion they decided that it was perhaps best for me to accept the offer. It was rather like the dawn of action at the end of a long and intensive training. However well equipped you may feel to meet any emergency during the training period, when you are faced with the prospect of the real thing, you suddenly feel like a raw recruit again. But I was very sure of the policy that I would pursue and fully prepared to come to loggerheads with the Executive of the U.G.C.C. if I found they were following a reactionary course.[17]

Unsurprisingly, this is precisely what happened. It is giving little away to say that Nkrumah returned home and soon found himself in conflict with the conservative, well-bred professionals who hired him. How Nkrumah came to accept the UGCC offer merits dwelling less on what would happen just down the road, and more on his tentativeness and doubt in this critical moment. He was so apprehensive that others had to talk him into taking the road that would lead him into history through the front door.

Beyond Nkrumah's own account, our other main description of his recruitment by the UGCC comes from Joe Appiah, and his take greatly complicates even the limited portrait of self-assurance that Nkrumah sketched in his autobiography. Appiah's telling also injects doses of pathos and humor that would be self-deprecating in the most winning way if they had been part of the tale told by Nkrumah himself.

According to Appiah, in early 1947, the hopes of the Gold Coast members of the West African Students' Union were focused on somehow getting Nkrumah appointed as editor of the *Ashanti Pioneer*, one of the leading newspapers of the colony. Nkrumah had been fascinated by newspapers ever since he read Azikiwe's editorials in the Gold Coast of his youth. Nkrumah had written columns for the Lincoln newspaper and had founded small, short-lived publications in the United States and Britain. More recently, he had witnessed the power of insurgent journalism as practiced by Padmore. Returning now to the Gold Coast to become a crusading editor with ulterior political ambitions might have seemed like a natural next step. Black war veterans were already creating a feeling of effervescence and mounting expectations of change there. In private letters, he had stated the desire, to lead a "politically fearless and militant newspaper," in the Gold Coast.[18] But an unexpected opportunity to rise faster and go much further suddenly knocked.

In Appiah's telling, Ako Adjei's letter arrived three weeks after Nkrumah's Lincoln friend's return to the Gold Coast. It was not addressed to Nkrumah at all, but rather to his "brethren" in the neighborhood called Primrose Garden, where Appiah and the other countrymen who formed a core of student activists resided. The letter not only announced that Adjei had met with Danquah, whom he described as the "doyen of Gold Coast politics," but that the formation of a political party "of the type we have discussed" was being planned. This twelve-page correspondence even included a draft constitution of the party-to-be. This was the boldest step taken by Danquah and his fellows so far, and their growing resolve can be seen in the invitation for comment from the overseas students. The historian Marika Sherwood has written that Nkrumah soon began consulting with Padmore and others outside of the West African Students' Union about how to respond in detail.[19]

Sometime shortly after the reception of Adjei's letter, Appiah writes that Nkrumah fell gravely ill and was bedridden with pneumonia, which had previously afflicted him while he was working in a Pennsylvania shipyard. Appiah credits Hastings Banda, the physician who would become the first president of Malawi, with reviving Nkrumah. Appiah's account of Nkrumah's health setback hints at the sharp political divisions that would accompany Nkrumah's rise to power in Ghana. Some of these were every bit as unanticipated as Nkrumah's abrupt emergence as a leader in London. They also point to a broader reality about Nkrumah that is little appreciated outside of Ghana. Although embraced as a nearly peerless continental hero in post-independence Africa, opinions about Nkrumah remain deeply divided in his own country to the present day. In recent years, Ghana has been ruled by a party whose leaders descend from the Gold Coast's conservative old guard. Some of their lingering dislike and even enmity dates from Nkrumah's precipitous break with the UGCC and his treatment of its leaders, including their repeated arrest and imprisonment. Other ambivalence grows out of the way that Nkrumah's personality came to dominate the country under his rule, and the enormous letdown people felt after many of the sky-high expectations that he fueled were never realized. All of this lies ahead in our narrative. For now, as Appiah attested:

> Some have wished that Kwame had never appeared on the political scene of Ghana and Africa; others have thanked God for his emergence on the political stage. Those readers who belong to the former category will, perhaps, find it difficult to thank Doc; those of the latter group will, of course, remain eternally grateful to him for saving Kwame's life in the nick of time. The decision is every reader's alone.[20]

During their London sojourns of the mid-1940s, Nkrumah and Appiah were so close that the older man handed over the £100 (worth roughly £2,000 today) that Danquah's new UGCC had sent for his use and entrusted his lieutenant with the arrangements for his return home. This makes what Appiah has to say about Nkrumah's frame of mind during this period, if accurate, especially noteworthy.

The Nkrumah that Appiah described on the eve of his sudden return to Ghana was a man wracked with anxiety and fear, words Appiah uses repeatedly. Just as they had greeted him on his arrival in London two years earlier, Appiah and Padmore accompanied Nkrumah to the Euston railway station for the first leg of his voyage home. Although London had come a long way in that time, many still lived on food rations and would continue to do so for another five years. "Kwame poured out his fears and doubts about the great task ahead that he was to execute without us—his trusted friends and comrades in the struggle. He felt very much alone even before we had parted, though [Kojo] Botsio was booked on the same voyage home. . . . It was necessary to reassure Kwame that from London—the enemy's headquarters—we would continue to watch over and protect him from all the attacks of the minions at home; that from London would come to him ammunition and support needed for the battles ahead."[21]

Anxiety over a change of life and circumstances so sudden and dramatic is not what is remarkable here. What is striking is how different this portrait is from Nkrumah's occasional self-mythologizing as someone who was ever ready to take up the hero's mantle. And the details of some of Nkrumah's activities outside of the West African Students' Union complicate the picture even further.

In December 1945, right on the heels of the Manchester Pan-African Congress, Nkrumah had helped found a group called the West African National Secretariat (WANS). To some extent it operated as a rival to the venerable West African Students' Union that Nkrumah had already helped lead as vice president, but WANS was unwavering in its militancy. Its declared aim was to forge a "front for a United West African National Independence," that would finally realize Casely Hayford's dream of undoing the colonial Balkanization of the region. "West Africans consider all West Africa as one united country (because) the existing territorial divisions are politically, socially and economically inimical to the interests of the people," the group declared in its first public meeting in London in 1946.[22]

With this grand ambition in mind, Nkrumah undertook a visit to Paris in May 1946, just one year after the rapture of liberation. The population of the French capital had rebounded from its wartime dispersal. But while it struggled through the same sorts of hardships as London, from old housing stock overwhelmed by demand and scarce food, it also lost its leader; de Gaulle resigned from the provisional government that year. Retreating to his home at Colombey-les-Deux-Églises, de Gaulle devoted his energies to writing his war memoirs. Their famous first line speaks volumes. "All my life, I have had a certain idea of France."[23]

Nkrumah's purpose in Paris ran in another direction entirely. He went there to meet the leading political figures of several French colonies. These included Félix Houphouët-Boigny of the Ivory Coast, and Léopold Senghor and Amadou Lamine-Guèye of Senegal, all of whom would occupy important positions in the French government and national assembly under France's Fourth Republic. The conversations with them were cordial, but unavailing. Partly at the urging of Africans like these, the French National Assembly had passed a law that same month that abolished the concept of colonial subjects and gave inhabitants of France's African colonies citizenship rights in that European country. Measures like these, which were part of ongoing, if ultimately unavailing, efforts to fuse French-speaking African countries with France itself, foreshadowed big problems Nkrumah would have with Houphouët-Boigny and other francophone leaders in the future. Senghor, a socialist, was the only one who displayed any sympathetic interest in Nkrumah's WANS platform.

Within WANS, meanwhile, Nkrumah created a secretive cell or "special service group," that he called The Circle. Its avowed purpose was to unite the most committed militants under Nkrumah's authority to "prepare ourselves for revolutionary work in any part of the African continent."[24] And its aim was to create "a Union of African Socialist Republics."[25] For obvious reasons, Nkrumah did not publicize this in his autobiography, which he wrote while he was still negotiating with Britain over the Gold Coast's accession to independence.

One should be wary of assuming that this wording reflected anything like a firm allegiance with the similarly named Soviet Union. Although Nkrumah even received criticism around this time from people like Padmore and Makonnen for his growing sympathies with Moscow, their concerns seems overblown. As best one can tell, this imagined union was nothing more than a fancy wordplay for the long-dreamed African federation, albeit one with progressive colorings.

As odd as the shadowy Circle might sound, its existence provides a strong counterpoint to the picture of a self-doubting and apprehensive Nkrumah during the year prior to his return home. The South African Peter Abrahams described Nkrumah as unrealistic and capable of "fantastic schemes." These involved Nkrumah's busy efforts to conjure a direct role for himself in the conquest of African independence.

But this is not the only window into the man that the Circle provides. Nkrumah swore the Circle's members to absolute secrecy and obliged them to participate in an almost juvenile-sounding blood rite, in which they ritually commingled a few drops in a bowl, before pronouncing an oath of loyalty to the "leadership of Kwame Nkrumah."[26] Ideologically insecure, the West seized on anything hinting of Marxism whenever such things cropped up in the record foreign ministries and intelligence agencies compiled on Nkrumah. But often, traces of Nkrumah's religious training trumped Marx, and they may cast more light on his identity and behavior. Tales of the Bible and its preeminent characters were imprinted on him from an early age and loom ever-present in Nkrumah's words and thought. A leading Ghanaian scholar wrote that Nkrumah's decision to study in the United States, unconventional for his time, was part of a Moses narrative of his own conception. Bringing home intimate knowledge of the globe's new leading power and especially of the world of the politically active Black diaspora there had set Nkrumah apart.[27] Along similar lines, what the Circle conjured for me is less a picture of Soviet influence than it is of a youthful seminarian's fantasy about Jesus and his disciples.

Jomo Kenyatta of Kenya, who had been in Britain since 1929 laboring to overcome his loose command of English due to the state of colonial education back home before emerging as one of Africa's leading anti-imperial activists, was known to walk around London with a leopard skin covering and a spear as a sign of his authenticity. But even Kenyatta scoffed at Nkrumah's blood rite as mere "juju."[28] Thus the Circle also strongly foretells what would become a key characteristic of Nkrumah's style once in power; it highlighted an urge for individual rule and the gradual blossoming of a strong personality cult.

CHAPTER EIGHT

The Darker Nations

THAT THERE WOULD BE A GLOBAL PHASE SHIFT AFTER THE SECOND World War was anything but obvious. Even the most astute Western observers failed to see it coming. With a powerful Security Council of five permanent members at its helm, the architecture of the United Nations had been designed to lock in the superior rights of the mighty and to mediate their competition. More than anything, it resembled a club of empires.

Well before 1955, the tenth anniversary of its founding, the UN, whose secretariat was housed in a sleek, new, modernist slab of glass overlooking New York's East River, had already become something else altogether, something of surprising influence and import: both the convening grounds and the central stage for a worldwide push by the colonized to end their formal subjugation by the old-line imperial powers.

In fairness to the Western observers who didn't foresee any of this, the starting phases of the new era all seemed to point in the opposite direction, toward the division of the world into blocs that would be ever more tightly corralled and ultimately bipolar, with just two dominant adversaries, the United States and the Soviet Union.

The UN's General Assembly was not designed with decisive power or agency in mind; it had no veto and could issue no commands. But with almost shocking speed, it nonetheless focused the energies of nationalists and anticolonial activists scattered across far-flung and once starkly divided geographies in Africa, Asia, the Arab world, and Caribbean, and to a slightly lesser extent, Latin America. And then it created synergies between them.

As the first newborn states began emerging from Western control and were quickly followed by others, their proliferation turned the General Assembly, which met in a large, domed concrete structure with a distinctive curved shape, into a potent vehicle for the otherwise uncounted people of the world.

For a time, Europe's lingering colonial powers were in denial about what this all meant. As it changed, white-ruled South Africa derided the UN altogether, calling it "The United Natives." But it was from the mantle of the General Assembly, as one historian has written, that peoples from these different regions "could articulate their Third World agenda." The struggle for independence was their first action item, but only slightly less urgent was their widely shared desire to push back against pressure to enlist with one side or the other in the deepening Cold War.[1]

Before any of this could happen, though, it was the fault lines of a global competition between the two newborn superpowers that would unfold with startling speed. With the collapse of Hitler's forces in the face of the Soviet Army's relentless westward advances late in the war, Moscow found itself in practical control of nearly all of central Europe. Moreover, in case of any direct confrontation, the Soviets possessed the troop strength and firepower to overwhelm anyone in the Atlantic reaches of the continent who dared oppose them. What prevented this was a new form of internationalism in the United States led by men who fought off the old reflex in America's political class and population toward isolation and made containment of the Soviet Union the centerpiece of virtually everything Washington would undertake in the world for years to come.

The main watersheds in the master narrative of postwar history are enshrined in legend. One of the first of them flowed from the pen of an American professional diplomat, George Kennan, who had been posted to Moscow in February 1946. Kennan was not of standard Establishment issue. He was born in 1904 in the Midwest to a Minneapolis tax attorney and a mother who died early in his infancy. Unlike so many of the Cold War managers who studied at Yale and became known as the Wise Men, Kennan attended Princeton. He affected a patrician manner, but after graduation he eschewed the more conventional routes to high offices of state of law and banking to become a diplomat. Kennan looked askance at much of American life, finding it hollow and lacking spirit. And he was reserved in his feelings about democracy, opposing majoritarian rule and looking with racism-fueled skepticism at the participation of Black people and other minorities.[2] His views of what became known as the Third World were even worse. It was an unreconstructed jungle. In his famous memo to the State Department, which became known as the Long Telegram, Kennan warned of the Soviet Union:

> We have here a political force committed fanatically to the belief that with the U.S. there can be no permanent modus vivendi, that it is desirable

and necessary that the internal harmony of our society be disrupted, our traditional way of life be destroyed, the international authority of our state be broken, if Soviet power is to be secure.[3]

Kennan's telegram was quickly followed by the sounding of a public alarm by Winston Churchill in a speech he gave at Westminster College in Fulton, Missouri, in March 1946:

> From Stetin in the Baltic to Trieste in the Adriatic, an iron curtain has descended across the Continent. Behind that line lie all the capitals of the ancient states of Central and Eastern Europe. Warsaw, Berlin, Prague, Vienna, Budapest, Belgrade, Bucharest, and Sophia, all these famous cities and the populations around them lie in what I must call the Soviet sphere, and all are subject in one form or another, not only to Soviet influence but to a very high and, in many cases, increasing measure of control from Moscow.[4]

One year later, Dean Acheson, Harry S. Truman's secretary of state, warned members of the United States Congress that, "Not since Athens and Sparta, not since Rome and Carthage, have we had such polarization of power."[5] And in this fast-emerging partitioning of the world, almost everything was subordinated to superpower competition.

Kennan had been unusually frank in his telegram in eschewing traditional American rhetoric about the importance of democracy. It was never intended as a public document. Speaking of the peoples of war-devastated Europe, he wrote, "[they] are less interested in abstract freedom than in security. They are seeking guidance rather than responsibilities. We should be better able than Russians to give them this. And unless we do, Russians certainly will."[6] It would be hard to find a more prophetic statement of the nature of the competition between Washington and Moscow as it unfolded not only in Europe, but throughout the broader world in the coming decades. A competition over "guidance" would certainly be forthcoming, and not only for Europe.

In what soon became known as the Cold War, both sides were driven by the reductive logic of a doctrine in international relations known as "realism." It saw the world as an essentially zero-sum contest between the two blocs, made more dangerous because each imagined itself incarnating universal values. One side enshrined private property, freedom from excessive government power, and (as long as it didn't get in the way) participatory democracy. And the other, a commitment to economic equality through the elimination of major class differences and highly centralized planning in the belief that only a strong state could fully rationalize economic development.[7]

According to realist theory, which drove moral considerations to the margins of discussions of strategy and tactics, every pursuit of gain by one's adversary had to be met or countered until it was checked, or at least until a balance of power was reached. Under these circumstances, as Hans Morgenthau, one of realism's leading proponents said, the rival superpowers "meet under an empty sky from which the gods have departed."[8]

That the Soviet Union imposed itself upon and dominated its European allies, allowing scant room for democracy or for deviation from Moscow's political line beginning in the late-1940s, will surprise few readers. Western memories of this period are dominated by heroic narratives about the Marshall Plan and the Berlin Airlift in 1948. But in the Global South, the power of the West was generally arrayed against those who were struggling for liberation. And early in the Cold War, in what became known as the Third World, it was above all the United States that saw neutrality as illegitimate. Washington, together with its European allies, sought to impose their political and economic preferences on the growing number of newly independent states in the world. As one historian of this period has written:

> The United States used its financial leverage to push American goods on foreign markets. It established military bases around the globe and intervened in the internal political affairs of other states, rigging elections, endorsing coups, enabling assassinations, and supporting the extermination of insurgents. A cold war rhetoric, much of it opportunistic and fear-mongering, was allowed to permeate public life. And the nation invested in a massive and expansive military buildup that was out of all proportion to any threat."[9]

At war's end, in 1945, France immediately moved to reassert its control over Indochina, over which Japan had exercised supreme authority during the conflict. As a first step toward what would end in disaster, not once but eventually twice, Paris dispatched thousands of troops into Vietnam's Red River Delta, determined to stop the rise of a nationalist movement that had already by then sunk deep roots. That same year, in a conflict that has gone almost entirely unremembered in the West, employing tactics of mass arrest and the deliberate fanning of interethnic violence, France also moved to suppress a nationalist uprising in Madagascar. Tens of thousands of people from that island were killed in that struggle.[10]

France was grimly determined to hold on to its empire, which was deemed crucial to both its economic recovery and to its status on the world stage. But beyond even these considerations, there was a deeper psychological dimension. Defeated and occupied by Germany and unable to liberate itself on its own, yet paradoxically haughty, France had been profoundly humiliated in the war, and regaining its perch atop a vast collection of colonies was seen as the best means for recovering a great nation's lost prestige. As the Martinican intellectual Frantz Fanon, the grand mid-century prophet of decolonization, wrote, the colonist derived his very "validity" from the colonial system.[11]

All in this era was not restoration, though; decolonization also had its avatars. In 1946, the Philippines, which today few Americans remember as having been their country's colony, won independence from the United States. This was followed the very next year by India, which gained its independence from Britain in 1947. Britain's former crown colony underwent an extremely violent breakup along religious lines, yielding the new Islamic nation of Pakistan. But even this did nothing to reduce the global resonance of this event. For peoples on every continent, India's new freedom was experienced as a sort of kickoff event of the independence era. This was due both to India's size and its nonaligned politics, which helped open space for others, like Indonesia, which became independent in 1949 after a bloody war to resist being corralled into the alliance systems of the Cold War.

Although the West initially treated it as an outright advance for the Soviet Union, the victory of the Chinese Communist Party under Mao Zedong in 1949, ending that country's internecine civil war, would also help bolster what came to be known as nonalignment. By the early 1960s, China under Mao had broken completely with Moscow, and in the following decade, in a characteristic statement of hostility for the era, a senior Chinese foreign policy official caustically dismissed the Soviets as "more imperialist than the worst imperialist."[12]

Often, it is the events long forgotten outside of the places where they occurred that best illustrate the ferocious tenacity of Western imperialism. In the immediate postwar era, as with France, Britain looked to its colonies to help restore its sense of identity and purpose in the world. Even as London made hasty preparations to relinquish control over India, it was laying plans to prolong its rule over other parts of the Empire.

Casting a bookkeeper's keen eye over the realm, it quickly identified some colonies as major cash cows. With its eponymous supply of precious metals, 40 percent of the world's cocoa supply, and rubber and timber, the Gold Coast, as we have seen, stood out as one of these. The bounty it presently offered was only surpassed, in fact, by London's sprawling Southeast Asian colony, Malaya (now Malaysia), which generated huge dollar surpluses for Britain through rubber and tin production. In 1948, when Britain was suffering a $1.8 billion deficit, these were worth $170 million.[13]

In the Second World War's aftermath, rather than making way for self-rule, the British forestalled Malay independence by imposing an ambitious but ill-inspired reconfiguration of the colony. In the process, indigenous Malay rulers had their authority usurped and subordinated to appointed governors. Historians point to efforts like these as a kind of second wave of colonialism imposed after the war by European powers who sought to renovate the institutions of imperial rule. In some cases, this even led to an increased investment in the colonies, but typically only from an extremely low base. The clear overall aim was to perpetuate control for decades longer.

In the case of Malaya, as with the Gold Coast, British policy reflected an abysmal reading of the political situation in the colonies. In a 1946 ceremony intended to celebrate the postwar restoration of colonial rule, Supreme Allied Commander Admiral Lord Louis Mountbatten, who also presided over Indian independence, bestowed medals on eight of the Chinese-Malayan resistance leaders. The ceremony called for them to kiss the ring of the representative of the British King. Instead, the resistance leaders defiantly hoisted clenched fists in the air, much as African American athletes would famously do from the medals podium at the Mexico City Olympics in 1968.

Malaya was soon plunged into what became a fierce dirty war in order to destroy the ethnic-Chinese-led resistance to colonial rule and sustain the flow of dollars into the British treasury. To weaken the imperial grip, the rebels began by launching stealthy attacks on British-owned rubber plantations, in which several Europeans were killed. One readily imagines tactics like these being labeled as terrorism today, but what of the British response? London assembled a force that outnumbered the rebels by nearly ten to one at its peak by drawing on soldiers from Africa and other parts of the empire to fight on its behalf and declared an Emergency. As the Harvard historian Caroline Elkins wrote in her book, *Legacy of Violence: A History of the British Empire*, opponents to British rule were subjected to collective punishment, rounded up by the hundreds of thousands and forced to live behind barbed wire in rudimentary camps, where torture was widely practiced. Individuals who were judged to be recalcitrant were banished from public life, and many others were simply deported to China.[14]

Year after year, the world over, during the following decade, rang in news of revolutionary bids for freedom and violent colonial pushbacks that aimed to hold the line on empire. In 1952, Kenyans, predominantly drawn from the large Kikuyu ethnic group whose original homeland was concentrated in the forests and foothills surrounding Mount Kenya, launched a prolonged and tenacious military struggle. The Kikuyu were traditionally cultivators and traders who had fiercely resisted the Arab slave trade, which peaked in East Africa in the late-eighteenth century. Their armed struggle against colonial rule was in response to decades of intensifying seizures of extraordinarily rich cropland in the country's central highlands by British farmers. The white farmers' hope was to re-create the kind of settler societies that existed in Southern Africa, where whites controlled a preponderance of the productive farmland, confining Blacks to the role of tenant farmers and cheap wage laborers, and subjecting them to civil codes that separated the races.

The Kenyan rebellion was a classic uprising of what Fanon immortalized in the title of his last book, *The Wretched of the Earth*. Britain deployed its army to put the rebellion down with unvarnished brutality, jailing people without trial by the thousands, employing mass torture, confining many to concentration camp–like detention centers, and killing more than two hundred thousand, according to some estimates. The British government and media branded the rebels with what they took to be a primitive, and to the white ear, terrifying-sounding colloquial, "Mau Mau," instead of the nationalists' own chosen name for their movement, the Kenya Land and Freedom Army, thus dismissing the fighters as African savages rather than people struggling for the freedom of their own land.

Such efforts by the British were hardly limited to Africa. In 1953, London intervened in the northernmost reaches of South America in order to overthrow the newly elected chief minister of British Guiana, a man named Cheddi Jagan. This was done on the basis of Winston Churchill's unfounded notion, in many ways echoing George Kennan's philosophy, that Jagan was a Marxist and would open up South America to Soviet penetration. That same year, Washington and London worked together to engineer the overthrow of the democratically elected government of Prime Minister Mohammad Mossadegh in Iran. Their enmity was prompted by the Iranian government's bid to inspect the books of the Anglo American Oil Company, which fed unsubstantiated claims that Mossadegh, like Jagan, was under communist influence.

In 1954, the imperial tide began to reverse more decisively in two historically momentous ways. One of them was crushing and immediate, the other far more gradual, but in the long run, just as telling. The first involved France's colonial war in Vietnam. Although they were already struggling perceptibly, the French expressed contempt for their adversaries, the Việt Minh. This included a haughty refusal to even refer to the rebel army's commander, Võ Nguyên Giáp, a sprite-sized lawyer turned brilliant, but largely self-taught, soldier, by his rank as general. Giáp had founded his fighting force just a decade earlier, starting off in the remote hill country of northern Vietnam with only thirty-one men and three women trainees armed with flintlock rifles.[15] They might never have seen action at all, except that after Japan's defeat after Hiroshima, the French insisted on resuming control of their erstwhile empire in Indochina. Vietnamese nationalists like Giáp and Hồ Chí Minh fatefully concluded that Paris would not agree to eventual independence.

In March 1954, on the eve of the monsoon season, the French moved to lure Giáp's rebels, the Việt Minh, into a set-piece battle on Vietnam's mountainous border with Laos. There, France had recently established an operational stronghold at an obscure and low-lying cluster of nearby villages called Điện Biên Phủ. Virtually undetected, the underestimated Việt Minh were able to position heavy weapons on the mountainsides surrounding the French garrison, eventually massing four times the firepower of the enemy's artillery. From the heights, over the next two months, the Việt Minh pressed this advantage, relentlessly pounding the isolated valley where French troops had taken cover in blood- and muck-filled trenches. One senior French war ministry official likened the situation to being cooked in a chamber pot.[16] One after another, French battalions of eight hundred men were reduced to companies of a dozen or fewer shell-shocked survivors. These included grizzled members of the Foreign Legion and also, notably, recruits from colonial Algeria. When all was told, ten thousand French soldiers were captured by the Vietnamese. Two thousand more were hastily buried there in unmarked graves. The French war correspondent Bernard Fall wrote:

> As a French colonel surveyed the battlefield from a slit trench near his command post, a small white flag, probably a handkerchief, appeared on top of a rifle hardly 50 feet away from him, followed by the flat-helmeted head of a Viet Minh soldier. And all around them, as on some gruesome Judgment Day, soldiers, French and enemy alike, began to crawl out of their trenches and stand erect for the first time in 54 days, as firing ceased everywhere.
>
> You're not going to shoot anymore? said the Viet Minh in French. No, I'm not going to shoot anymore, said the colonel. C'est fini? said the Viet Minh. Oui, c'est fini, said the colonel.[17]

Facing annihilation, Paris surrendered and then agreed to a humiliating withdrawal from all their colonies in Indochina. "The Asians, after centuries of subjugation, had beaten the white man at his own game," Fall wrote.[18] But another decade of America's Vietnam War and the full absorption by the West of the futile illusion of domination from afar still lay ahead.

AMERICAN POLICY DURING THE EISENHOWER PRESIDENCY WAS EVOLVING AT this time in favor of cutting the Pentagon's ballooning military expenditures. This was advocated for under the theory of massive retaliation. This held that nuclear weapons had great value even in supposedly limited war situations against regional foes or pesky leftist armies. Rather than fielding large, expensive armies, new generations of supposedly cost-effective thermonuclear bombs would ensure America's continual rapid economic growth while scaring off challengers.

This posture, which was called the New Look, was premised on the idea that the wave of uprisings against Western domination sweeping the Third World was inspired, underwritten, and fundamentally controlled by the Soviet Union. The thinking went that the mere threat of massive retaliation would call the bluff of the adversary who sat on the opposite side of the geopolitical checkerboard by forcing the USSR to stand down and freezing its hand in the game of undermining the West.

There are a number of reasons why things didn't play out this way. One of them was that the overwhelming majority of nationalist movements proliferating in almost every corner of the world were not Communist or even Communist-inclined. Truman's secretary of state, George C. Marshall, the son of a prosperous Pennsylvania coal-mine owner, enrolled at the Virginia Military Institute and rose from army company commander in the Philippine-American War to chief of staff in the Second World War, captured this reality as aptly as any American official would in this era when he said:

> We are in the middle of a world revolution—and I don't mean Communism. The Communists are ... just moving in on the crest of a wave. The revolution I'm talking about is that of the little people all over the world. They're beginning to learn what there is in life, and to learn what they are missing.[19]

The Eisenhower administration briefly considered using nuclear weapons to support the French in Vietnam, with Hiroshima and Nagasaki not even a decade in the rear-view mirror. This was rejected, though, and thankfully atomic weapons never became seen as a morally or tactically practical solution to any kind of war short of outright nuclear confrontation between the superpowers. Even then, all they would yield is mutually assured destruction. In the meantime, a thirst for freedom from imperial domination was mounting in the world of brown, black, and yellow peoples almost everywhere. Events were already moving too fast for this to be stopped by any kind of military strategy. Marshall was right.

Although it would not achieve its goal of independence quickly, the broad nationalist uprising that swept Algeria three weeks after the fall of Điện Biên Phủ delivered powerful proof of this. Once again, the United States helped underwrite the French, but already there were clear limits. Amid intensifying competition with Moscow, American geopolitical thinkers began to see that Washington could not simply stand shoulder to shoulder with Europe's colonizers everywhere that demands for freedom arose. Beyond North Africa, for now, much of that continent was quiescent, but at a minimum, an approach like this would turn all of Asia and the Middle East into enemies.

Part Two

WADING IN THE WATER

Kojo Botsio, Kwame Nkrumah, Komla Gbedemah, and Kofi Baako wear prison graduate caps following Nkrumah's release in 1951.

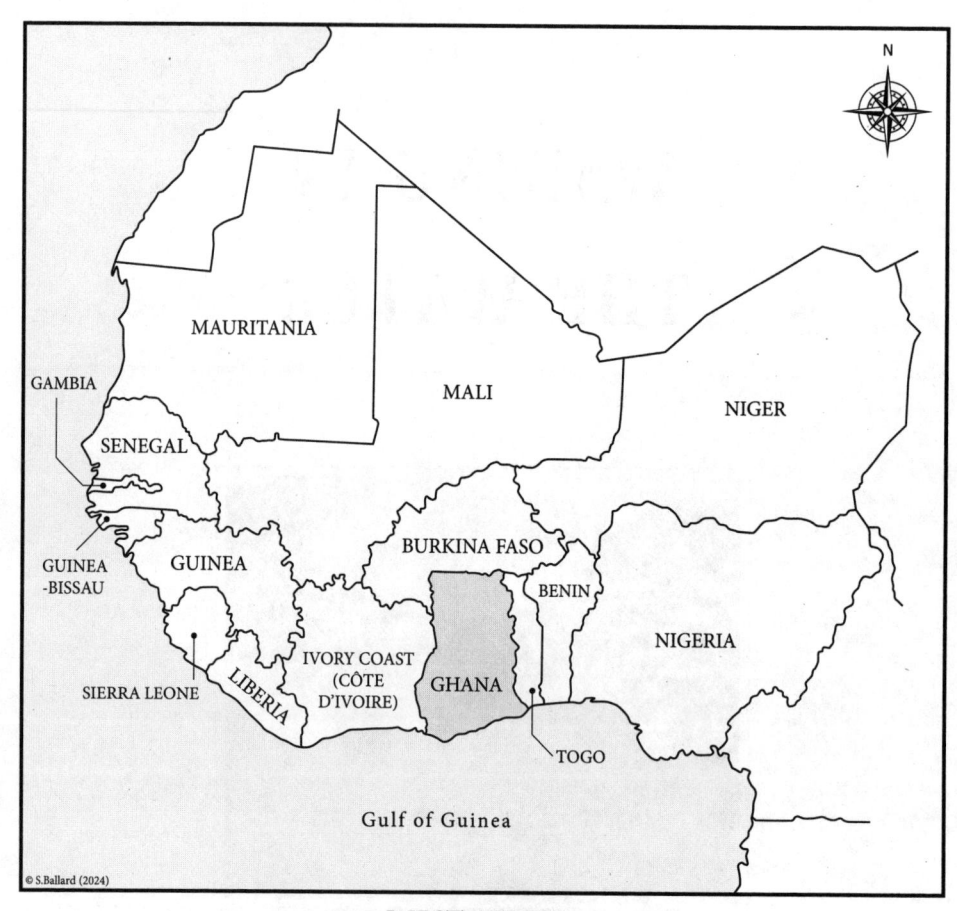

WEST AFRICA

CHAPTER NINE

Land and Freedom

SOUTH OF AFRICA'S SAHARA DESERT THE APPARENT CALM WAS DECEPtive. Colonized peoples there issued no loud outcry for political emancipation from Europe, and those who did enunciate the word *independence* usually envisaged it neither as immediate nor direct. Meanwhile, without exception, Europe's imperial powers busied themselves instead with plans to reinvigorate the systems they employed to rule the continent. Surprisingly, they launched new and substantial, if still wholly inadequate, investment programs to improve schooling and roads and other kinds of basic services. They did so, however, atop a very flimsy base built on decades of shoestring administration and neglect.

But Africa was no exception to the global political awakening seen throughout the colonized world. The people of the continent, especially in the cities, were increasingly alive to the injustice and humiliation of colonial rule. Because the new consciousness spreading across Africa was fueled by the Second World War, European masters who were mired within their own problems understood it only poorly. They thought the rising demands of Africans were merely economic in nature, not political. But in colony after colony, time would show that this assumption was an abysmal misreading of reality.

European imperialism had begun in the sixteenth century with the realization that states could gain enormous wealth and power by shipping millions of people across the Atlantic and exploiting their slave labor on plantations throughout the New World. This wholesale looting of Africa's human resources wouldn't end until well into the nineteenth century, but already by a hundred years before then, most of the energy that Europe committed to its global project of colonizing others had shifted to Asia.

The Second World War sparked a rediscovery of the importance of Africa to Europe's destiny and fortunes, and this caught the notice of Africans. Globally, the independence of India had come to be seen as inevitable, even well before Hitler's defeat. And with the fall of Europe's mineral- and commodity-rich colonies in Southeast Asia, including Indochina, Malaysia, the Philippines, North Borneo, and others to imperial Japan, Africa rose briskly up the ladder of Atlantic Europe's imperial priorities. And as the world war perdured, Africa once again became an indispensable source of manpower for its colonizers, and of crucial raw materials, as well.

Roughly one million Africans were impressed into battle or otherwise employed in Europe's war efforts. Britain alone raised hundreds of thousands of troops in separate drives in both East and West Africa. A small number of these African soldiers saw combat roles in Europe, while others were deployed to faraway places like Burma. Many more, however, were dispatched to fight in colonial wars in Africa, whether against Mussolini's armies in Ethiopia, or against Germany in Tanganyika or North Africa. More still were deployed to hold the line against provocation or attack by Germany's puppet government in French West Africa.

In a rare statement, the British Colonial Office acknowledged its war debt to the continent: "African soldiers beat the Italians out of Somaliland and Abyssinia, defeating the best Blackshirt battalions and native levies the Italians sent against them. They defended British West Africa from attack from Vichy territory, helped take Madagascar, and went to the Middle East as pioneers and to the Far East to fight Japan."[1] When first I learned of this acknowledgement, I remembered films like *Out of Africa* and *Mogambo*, and thought to myself, "*Someone please tell Hollywood.*"

African men were "levied," or conscripted en masse, into imperial forces, while others signed up without outright compulsion amid unceasing enlistment drives. For peasants, military enlistment was their only path into the wage economy, to health and retirement benefits, however rudimentary, and to elementary social status in colonies ruled by Europeans. Local chiefs, whose authority ultimately depended on their nomination or recognition by colonial governments, aided in the recruitment.

Mobilization this intensive served manifold ends. Some recruits dug trenches and ditches, or manually leveled the earth to create landing strips and airports, while others worked in mining, churning out critical supplies of gold, tin, bauxite, manganese, cobalt, and tungsten. Still others labored to cultivate rubber, sisal, coffee, cotton, and sugar; or for the production of specialty items like pyrethrum, a precious natural insecticide extracted from chrysanthemum plants in the age before more powerful synthetic compounds. Still other African labor, forced or unpaid, was deployed in food production schemes aimed at sustaining the consumption of Britons and other Europeans during the war. In this, edible fats from Africa, such as palm oil, were deemed indispensable. Speaking of these vital high-calorie rations, as Britain's wartime minister of food, Fredrik Marquis, Lord Woolton, told a colleague as he was leaving to take up his post as resident minister for the region, "It all depends on what you can do in West Africa whether we can maintain it or not."[2]

For commodities like these, as well as big cash crops like cocoa, Britain erected a variety of monopolistic agencies with names like the Board of Trade, the Ministry of Food, and the Ministry of Supply. These entities served as the sole purchasers of exports from its African colonies. They supported the war effort in another largely unaccounted for way by allowing London to maintain artificially low prices and thus cheat African colonies and their farmers of much of the value of their products. Other goods exported from Africa were taxed at steep rates to help finance the imperial war effort. Britain required that any dollars earned through the colonial trade be banked in London, where they could be used to help Britain service the debt of its sterling zone or finance its trade with other developed countries.[3]

All the while, London suppressed British exports to African colonies by a staggering 75 percent to keep their consumption low, thus finding yet another way to favor its citizenry at home at the expense of African subjects.[4] The constant production drives also diverted African peasants from working their own land and crops, imposing a kind of calculated administrative deprivation that increased hunger in rural areas even as it propped up consumption on the European "home front."

Even as colonial authorities drummed up conscripted African labor in settler colonies like Kenya, they also funneled workers to the white farmers who had carved out verdant plantations growing coffee, tea, wheat, and sisal on the seven million acres of appropriated land that included some of the richest topsoil in the world. The pipeline of uprooted African labor essentially subsidized the businesses of the settler farmers, and sustained their lavish and racially separate lifestyles, much as cotton slavery in the Mississippi Valley long underwrote the baronial comforts of antebellum plantation owners.

Only a few years after the war ended, the accumulated resentment brought about by exploitation on this scale lit an explosive fuse in Kenya. The British painted those who resisted as savages and extremists, hence its insistence on calling them the Mau Mau, a name that might be translated as "oath," as in those used by secret societies. The British favored this moniker because such nonsense words, like oogah-boogah, sounded primitive and threatening to European ears, In reality, these Kenyans had been rendered squatters on their own extraordinarily fertile land in the Kenyan highlands and who were now insisting on redress. Colonial forces employed terror tactics and the most appalling forms of physical torture to suppress the resistance of the Land and Freedom Army. At one point, Britain detained nearly the entire Kikuyu population of 1.5 million people in scantly provisioned camps and stockaded villages. London would never credit the struggles that these nationalists waged, but in 1963, just three years after its supposed victory over the Mau Mau, Kenya rang in its independence.

CHAPTER TEN

Nothing to Lose but Chains

EUROPE'S WARTIME FOCUS ON EXTRACTION FROM AFRICA, WHETHER through conscription, underpaid labor, or, essentially, the theft of farm products or minerals purchased cheaply through monopolies, drove urbanization in places like Lagos, Accra, Nairobi, and Dar es Salaam at a hitherto unseen pace on the continent. That is because cities and large towns were the only places where Africans could have any hope of entering the wage-paying economy.

Swelling cities fed the growth and consolidation of politically energized local intelligentsias. African urbanites came together in vibrant literary clubs, debate societies, and civic groups, where Africans flaunted a new cosmopolitanism by adopting the latest styles in dress, manner, and speech. In the Gold Coast, a rich tradition of literary societies and other self-styled highbrow associations dated back to the mid-nineteenth century. In the 1930s, though, in place after place, such groups exhibited a direct interest in both international affairs and domestic politics, which helped lay the foundation for a nonviolent push for independence.[1] Members of these new elite clusters had been excited by the rhetoric of Franklin Roosevelt and Winston Churchill in the Atlantic Charter of 1941, when the two leaders of the West had declared, "the right of all peoples to choose the form of government under which they will live."[2] On the continent and abroad, the Atlantic Charter fired the hopes of educated Africans like Nkrumah, who was then still a student in Pennsylvania. It also fed their determination to hold the West to account.

Churchill soon distanced himself from this statement, saying that these freedoms were essentially reserved for Europeans and did not apply to the non-white subjects of their overseas colonies. After Roosevelt's death in 1945, the Truman and Eisenhower administrations also walked back this commitment, offering financial and even military backing for European colonizers, as in Washington's aerial bombing of Việt Minh positions in support of the French during the 1954 Battle of Điện Biên Phủ.

During World War II, as many as fifteen thousand Africans had died on the battlefield in defense of the interests and personal liberties of Europeans. After so much sacrifice, whether of blood or their wealth, Africans now openly wondered when their own freedom would come. The universal principle of self-determination had been raised as a raison d'être of the war and its many hardships, and Africans were determined to be treated the same as others. They would use the newly created UN General Assembly, as well as gatherings of newly proclaimed nonaligned nations, to remind Europeans of their rhetorical commitments to equality and to parade the West's hypocrisy before the world.

Africa's largely involuntary contributions to Europe's war had cost the continent enormously in terms of lost income, lower standards of living, and deferral of even minimum investments needed to meet the continent's own parlous needs. On top of this, high demand throughout the war had created inflation. On the continent, the years from the onset of the Great Depression through the end of the war were utterly lost to meaningful progress on the continent.

City dwellers were treated as good enough to fight, but not good enough to gain anything from risking their lives. By the conflict's end, they were desperate to claw their way back to real wage levels that had peaked as far back as the end of the 1920s. After the return of veterans, labor unions became the second grand vehicle of social and political change in the era. Strikes suddenly proliferated in an unusually large number of cities on the continent as workers walked off their jobs or threw down their tools. They came alternately in bunches or in rapid succession. In less than five years after 1945, walkouts hit Senegal, the headquarters of French West Africa, Tanganyika, Kenya, Nigeria, Sudan, Tunisia, Zanzibar, and the Gold Coast.

Europeans, characteristically ham-handed, were slow to grasp the political implications of all of this. In January 1944, de Gaulle traveled to the French Congo, France's small Central African colony, to attend the Brazzaville Conference that would initiate gradual preparations to transform France's African imperial holdings into a federation. De Gaulle's Free French ally, René Pleven, formally presided over the conference, announcing "In the Great French Empire, there are neither people to liberate nor racial discrimination to abolish."[3] The declarations captured the unique mixture of progressive idealism, denial, and naivete toward Africa that one could find in this era's French liberal thought. Only two African representatives were participants at

Brazzaville, little more than a neat array of fading, manila-colored colonial administrative buildings that projected inland from the bank of the broad and powerful Congo River. The conference issued a concluding statement: "The eventual creation, even in the distant future, of *self-governments* in the colonies, is to be rejected."[4]

In fact, the French and other Europeans had long been blinded by their own ideology. This began with the beliefs that Africans were innately inferior to whites and that Africans welcomed Western tutelage as the best thing for themselves. Had they been attentive, they would have grasped much sooner that behind each strike lay urgent, if not yet fully articulated, demands for fundamental political change.

Irrespective of their colonizer, African political thinkers in this period were still groping for the right formula for their demands, and the appropriate dispensations for their peoples. In the era of Casely Hayford, remaining part of a European empire still seemed acceptable, so long as Africans enjoyed broad local autonomy over their own affairs. What might once have been considered progressive thinking like this, though, was already becoming a relic of the past. The coming push would be for nothing less than full citizens' rights. Within a surprisingly short period of time Africans across the continent would regard this demand as their bottom line and the first step toward outright independence. The struggle to get there, though, would follow many different paths.

The complexity of this political landscape is best seen through the experience of French West Africa, which Paris was so determined to hold onto that it declared its collection of African colonies to be an integral part of France. In theory, this would eventually have to mean that Africans who were newly declared members of the so-called French Union would have equal rights and benefits not only with the French people who were sent to trade among them or administer them in Africa, but ultimately with French people in metropolitan France, as well.

French maneuvers to sustain the idea of a grand union between France and its African empire ultimately faced insurmountable obstacles at home. They also struggled to keep up with the rapidly evolving political situation in French West Africa.

At the 1944 Brazzaville Conference, the sense grew that forced labor could not be able to survive long in the postwar world, especially after the pronouncements of the Atlantic Charter. And as de Gaulle's government in exile met under the high, pitched roofs of the city's balconied colonial buildings, it belatedly provided for the phase-out of this form of exploitation within five years. But conservative French *colons* (plantation owners), merchants, and many colonial administrators even resisted this reform. As one historian has written, noting the scornful reaction to reforms from this quarter, "the Brazzaville declarations were for external, 'American' benefit ... the African bush would not see any benefit from them for a long time."[5]

In December 1944, an event in Dakar, Senegal, the capital of France's West African empire, became a watershed for Paris's colonies. With Hitler's armies collapsing and Allied forces advancing toward Berlin, France's liberation loomed. For many Africans, a prisoner-of-war swap that November and its violent aftermath highlighted both the utterly racial nature of empire and the hollowness of union.[6] Over twelve hundred Africans, from among the more than two hundred thousand who had fought for France were included in the swap. But they were housed separately and in much worse conditions than their French counterparts. When the African POWs were shipped back to Senegal that November, they were denied their allowances and arrears, and when they grumbled, they were transported to Thiaroye, a dusty assemblage of tents that served as a camp outside of Dakar, from which they were to be sent back to villages scattered about the region.

When demands for their pay were not met, the former prisoners of war took the French commander at Thiaroye hostage. On the morning of December 1, French forces responded by opening fire on the demobilized African troops, killing at least thirty-five of them and as many as four hundred, and this number does not include the wounded. Although the incident did not immediately lead to any broader political organization in the colony, historians have noted that some of the survivors of Camp Thiaroye soon formed a group called the Mouvement Nationaliste Africain and began producing a militant newspaper called *La Communauté*.[7]

FORCED LABOR DID NOT SURVIVE THE FIVE YEARS THAT THE FRENCH HAD mandated at Brazzaville. In 1946 newly liberated France formally abolished it, as a result of legislative action led by a wealthy plantation owner from Côte d'Ivoire, Félix Houphouët-Boigny, who sat in the French National Assembly and served as a minister in government. Houphouët-Boigny, an ardent conservative who aspired to leadership of the Ivory Coast within the French Union, was briefly allied at this time with the French Communist Party, giving a sense of how fluid the political scene was both in France and between France and its empire.

The next phase of dramatic change would not be initiated by politicians in

Paris, though, whether Black or white. The intelligentsia in France's African holding was pushing for drastic improvements in colonial education, especially in Dakar, where, as the seat of West African empire, most of the few schools created by France for Africans were located. In 1946, as the historian Tony Chafer has noted, only 5 percent of children in France's African colonies were even eligible to attend French primary schools; secondary schools were almost entirely closed to them. In the rural areas where colonial subjects overwhelmingly lived, even after forced labor was abolished, the few schools that France created in the Senegalese countryside pursued a kind of practical training for students that was so focused on farming that many Africans took them to be labor camps.

Léopold Senghor, a politician from Senegal who sat in the French National Assembly, gamely challenged France's pretenses to welcome Africans into the embrace of French civilization on the basis of equality. "While we are very happy to praise the work that France has done in the field of education in its old colonies [Martinique and Guadeloupe]," Senghor commented, "we cannot but deplore the fact that the local authorities in [French West Africa] have not been equal to their mission in this field. . . . In sum," he added, "the intention is to limit education to the primary level, even if it is called 'upper primary' and to keep it practical."[8]

Although they differed in crucial ways and would later become open rivals, neither Senghor nor Houphouët-Boigny was pushing for outright independence. They grasped France's need of a strong connection with Africa in order to hold its own against a reconstructed Germany. And as astute readers of France's psychology, they understood the power that lay in flattering French self-regard and prestige by celebrating the rhetoric of the French Enlightenment about the innate equality of human beings. Both of these men saw membership in a union with France, a Eurafrica, as it was fancied, as a means of pressing material demands for capital from France (and through France, from Europe) for the modernization of the continent. As the historian Frederick Cooper has written, "Europe's claim to exploit African resources would become Africa's claim for resources it needed to develop."[9]

The struggle around the nature of a French Union with Africa, and ultimately around independence itself, though, would turn instead on a challenge from labor. In October 1947, amid this wave of African strikes, the eighteen thousand members of the Railway Workers' Federation of French West Africa who ran the imperial railroad network in French West Africa that linked big port cities like Dakar and Abidjan with the agricultural hinterland went on strike. They had two demands. One was ending widespread abuse of temporary employee status, which not only drew low pay, but no housing or benefits. Nine out of ten African rail workers were treated as temps, including longtime veterans. The second was creating a *cadre unique*, or a single and equal pay and benefits system for both African and French employees.

French West Africa was only lightly and unevenly industrialized, but the strike commanded broad popular support, nonetheless. Enormous credit for this was due to the African women who ran markets in every city. Easily discounted as a mere colorful presence due to their lively palaver and the brightly patterned print cloths they favored for clothing, they mobilized fundraising efforts, provided food for strikers, and helped sustain public morale through song writing and performance. In March 1948, after five months of industrial action, an agreement was reached between the French parastatal that operated the railroads and wharfs in the region and the Railway Workers' Federation. The workers gained nearly all of what they had demanded.

Houphouët-Boigny, who hoped to rule his country in independence within the French Union, had sought to undermine the strike, withholding support from the Ivory Coast, the most prosperous colony in French West Africa. It's relative wealth, due to the booming production of cocoa, coffee, and other commodities, made Houphouët-Boigny wary of any kind of political arrangement that would put the Ivory Coast in the position of having to share its wealth with much poorer colonies. His "my country first" politics prevented the region-wide railway strike from becoming a launching pad for independence, antagonizing Senghor, who had hoped to create a strong-enough federation of French-speaking African states to hold their own in union with France. They would soon also lead Houphouët-Boigny into a conflict with Nkrumah because of the Ghanaian leader's famous aim of bringing African countries together in something even broader, a federation that looked beyond colonial affiliations and could serve as the basis for an eventual United States of Africa.

For a whole decade after the strike, politicians in both France and Africa continued to wrangle over plans for a French Union. But the railway workers' demands had served up an important signal to Paris that any kind of union with its African colonies would generate irresistible African demands for equality across the board, and in the end, this would prove insurmountable. Whether it was the intelligentsia, through the voice of people like Senghor, or ex-soldiers, or African teachers, rail workers, or others, a union with France would have to mean being paid just like French people, having schools as good as those in France, enjoying unrestricted access to metropolitan France and, crucially, to the job market there. Paris wanted to hold on to its colonies for the grandeur that this offered and for the economic support that Africa provided it. Some even still clung to the ultimate colonial fantasy of assimilation, which meant the long-term project of transforming Africans into French people. But guaranteeing Africans the same pay as French people and opening France to unlimited migration was a bridge too far. Lofty ideals were fine to a point. But that, some groused, would be to turn the old metropole into the colony of the erstwhile colonized, and this could never be countenanced.

CHAPTER ELEVEN

Saltpond

THE DOCKS OF LIVERPOOL HAVE SUPPLIED THE WORLD WITH PRODUCTS of all kinds. The city's name alone conjures the Industrial Revolution and endless reams of exported textiles. By the early nineteenth century, Liverpool was processing about 40 percent of all the world's traded goods. In the 1740s, though, when it overtook Bristol, its commerce had been altogether more specialized and savage, centered on a trade in enslaved Africans. Now, what it was re-exporting was a man on a mission, albeit self-appointed and largely unheralded, to free his country, and all of Africa, from colonial rule.

In November 1947, Kwame Nkrumah sailed third class from Liverpool on his fateful return trip to the Gold Coast. A dozen years earlier, on his first passage through this grimy shipping metropolis, he had been very much a project in the making, a young man still in search of himself.

Sailing with Nkrumah was Kojo Botsio, a powerfully built and broad-featured man of trust who had attended the Fifth Pan-African Conference with him and studied at Oxford and who would rank among Nkrumah's closest advisors throughout the next phase of his political life.

Somehow, Nkrumah had imagined that his homebound ship would amble down the West African coast, making leisurely stops at major ports of call, where he could go ashore to preach the gospel of pan-Africanism. But his steamer, the *Accra*, never called at Bathurst, the steamy, tin-roofed British administrative outpost at the mouth of the Gambia River and the first stop he expected, sailing onward to Freetown, Sierra Leone, instead. There, on a lark, Nkrumah, impatient to toe the African soil, entrusted most of his sparse belongings to Botsio, and disembarked for a two-week stay.

Freetown, a major port city that drapes seaward in palisades from its red-clay hills, was the birthplace of the early pan-Africanist, James Beale Horton, and of the labor organizer and audaciously pro-independence journalist,

I. T. A. Wallace-Johnson, who had labored with Nkrumah in the West African National Secretariat in London. In Nkrumah's telling, Wallace-Johnson had no space to put him up. Undaunted, he said grandiosely that he busied himself making "important political contacts" and advising the colony's badly divided political leaders on how they could "form a united front and work together for West African unity."[1]

This accomplished, Nkrumah sailed onward to Monrovia, the capital of Liberia, the old African American settler colony, in effect a giant rubber plantation and one of only two Black-ruled, independent countries on the continent. "That was the first time I had ever seen Africans who were heads of state and I was greatly impressed and encouraged," Nkrumah wrote, even though the president, William V. S. Tubman was out of town during his stopover. Nkrumah did what he could to meet people, hoping to talk up the idea of a regional gathering to discuss pan-Africanism, but with little luck. Why would Africans in an unfamiliar country line up to confer over something like this with someone as unknown as Kwame Nkrumah? It is a sign of his unusual self-confidence, or perhaps naivete, that Nkrumah doesn't seem to have asked himself this. At thirty-eight years old, he represented no political party and had no movement behind him. His worldly belongings easily fit into two flimsy cardboard suitcases.

Nkrumah says that during the onward journey from Monrovia to the Gold Coast's major port city, Takoradi, whose busy rail terminus and small factories lent it an early hint of industrialization, he traveled as a deck passenger. Determined to remain incognito, he took care not to disclose his name as he mixed with crew boys and other passengers. This was because British authorities had grilled him extensively about what he called "my alleged Communist associations" when he shipped out from Liverpool, making him fear that he would be arrested upon arrival.[2] What is remarkable about this story is that the colonial authorities, so often clueless about the shifting political landscape on the ground in West Africa, were better informed about Nkrumah than the nascent political party that had recruited him from abroad to be its secretary general.

Nkrumah had not joined the Communist Party while in Britain. And although he would later be arrested back home and found to be in possession of an unsigned party membership card, he was never seriously considered a Marxist. Responding candidly in his own defense, Nkrumah said that he had associated with all kinds of political movements in Britain as he shopped around for ideas and tactics that could help advance his project of pan-Africanism. Not joining the Communist Party was about more than eclecticism, though. Nkrumah already possessed the mindset of an aspiring leader, not that of a joiner. This was evident in the charter of The Circle, the evanescent secret society he had formed in London. He was far more inclined toward demanding loyalty than maintaining allegiance to forces beyond his control.

Someone as sophisticated as J. B. Danquah, who had personally summoned Nkrumah home to help lead what became the United Gold Coast Convention (UGCC), had only himself to blame for not knowing what he was getting himself into. Danquah was the first West African to earn a doctorate in Philosophy in Britain. He then entered London's Inner Temple and was called to the bar in 1926. By the early 1930s, he was prosperous, well-established, and so much the veteran of debates about self-determination that he already ranked as the leading critic of Casely Hayford's attempts to pull all of West Africa's colonies together in a regional federation.

Unfortunately, being headman in a group whose members took themselves for the natural leaders of Ghana bred smugness. Danquah and his associates were certain that the group they were pulling together would become the ruling party of their model British colony. In their minds, it was just a matter of time, and their sense of destiny came at the expense of urgency.

The UGCC had been forged out of the fusion of two bickering associations of Accra city lawyers whose rivalry was at least partly centered on ethnic identity. Their new political machine of puffed up "convention" was not quite stillborn, but it was lugubrious from the start, and some of its members had the good sense to know it. This is precisely what led them to Nkrumah. Ako Adjei, his friend from London and Lincoln days, told them that Nkrumah had a verve for speaking to the regular folk. And Danquah and his fellow doyens of the UGCC had the foresight to know that pressuring the colonial authorities on independence, and eventually winning elections—even elections that were formalities—would require some kind of purchase with the masses. They were so pleased with themselves and certain of their superiority, though, that they didn't need to think any harder about their recruit. In the language of Ghana, then and now, Nkrumah was a "small boy," and it was therefore inconceivable that the impressive men of the UGCC couldn't keep him well in hand.

Back in 1935, when Nkrumah had embarked for Britain on his way to America, his thoughts were filled with hope. But on December 10, 1947, when he returned to his point of departure at Takoradi, his heart raced less from excitement than trepidation. There, ships were lined up for loading and unloading along a narrow pier crammed with warehouses that projected far into the still waters of a shielded bay. The wood and spice aroma of cocoa stockpiled for export hung thickly in the air as Nkrumah approached the first native immigration officer he spotted on the dock. His nervous eyes were cast downward. He fully expected that the mere sight of papers with his name on them would draw the interest of the police. After a long pause, though, the agent who inspected his documents looked up at the man who had just disembarked with "his eyes protruding from his head" and whispered in tones of awe, "So you are Kwame Nkrumah!"[3] Nkrumah's account in his autobiography has an unmistakably messianic quality to it. One senses the influences of parables about Jesus in the Bible, which Nkrumah had studied deeply from a young age. With his political life now beginning in earnest, the gospels spilled over into the way he thought and spoke about himself, at least in his ipso facto storytelling.

On the day of his arrival back home after twelve years abroad, no one in the world save for Nkrumah himself would have bet on him leading the Gold Coast into independence, much less galvanizing a continental movement of pan-Africanism that would both inspire and frustrate Africans and members of the diaspora for the next century. But Nkrumah, by this point, seems to have already convinced himself that he was a chosen one: a prodigal son who had returned home to make good on his ambition to launch his continent's rebirth. In Nkrumah's account, the reverential immigration agent said not only that he had heard a great deal about him, but that people "had been waiting anxiously for my arrival day after day."[4]

After the agent expedited his formalities, Nkrumah made some phone calls and was eventually collected by a UGCC member sent to welcome him. But instead of immediately heading to meet with the group, he traveled to Tarkwa, the venerable western mining town, whose clustered workers' bungalows, smokestacks, and rock crushing works clung to the apron of old pits. There he would be put up with a friend while he plotted his next moves. In Tarkwa, Nkrumah also immediately sent for his beloved mother and was guilt-stricken to find her so frail and gray. Nyaniba was probably seventy-one years old and physically diminished, as much by a life of hard use and modest fare as by her advanced age. She squinted fiercely when she first laid eyes on her son, not recognizing him because as part of Nkrumah's preparation for the public stage, he had had his two front teeth pulled so as to correct a conspicuous gap between them. In their place sat two gleaming white and perfectly aligned artificial ones. By his own account, it was Nkrumah's hands, delicate for a man's, with fingers whose thickness scarcely tapered from the base to their tips, he wrote, that confirmed for his mother that this was indeed her son.

During the fortnight that he spent in Tarkwa, Nkrumah says he spent long hours in conversation with his mother. He regaled her with his student days and life in London, and he explained some of the dramatic changes afoot in the world. Liberation movements were making gains in a growing number of places, from China, India, Burma, and Ceylon, to Palestine, Indochina, the Philippines, and Indonesia, which was fighting off Dutch rule. As Nkrumah spoke of all of these transformations, however, he said nothing to her about the role he saw for himself in Africa.

In late December, after taking stock of the situation in the Gold Coast in numerous conversations with friends in Tarkwa, Nkrumah organized his first political meeting back home. It was a modest rally held discreetly in a Roman Catholic schoolroom. There he again told of his experiences abroad and revealed to a sympathetic audience that he had returned home to help lead the UGCC. "From their absorbed interest and their acclamation I sensed that they, a representative gathering of the working class of the country, were indeed ready to support any cause that would better their conditions," he wrote.[5]

At a prearranged date, Nkrumah then traveled the nearly 120 miles by bumpy road from Tarkwa to a tiny, backwater hamlet that hugged a gorgeous stretch of beach, not far from Cape Coast. Decades earlier, Saltpond, as it was called, had become the site of the first paved road in all of the Gold Coast. Now it was fast becoming an improbable political hub of the colony. It was here that the UGCC had been founded in August 1947 under the sponsorship of George "Paa" Grant, the timber merchant who had hosted Nkrumah on his way to the United States in 1935.

In these early days, the UGCC still took care not to call itself a political party, not yet willing to fall afoul of the colonial administration. The Working Committee of the convention had summoned Nkrumah to meet their newly hired secretary, and this first encounter of theirs, although devoid of overt conflict, would foreshadow much of the distrust and difference in style and philosophy that was to come. At this meeting, Nkrumah quickly learned that the inducements promised him to bring him home from London were just that—more lure, than substance.

> The hundred pounds a month and the car had obviously, I realized, been used only as a bait for I soon discovered that the Convention (which itself lacked any kind of programme or mass organization) had no funds at all and had not even attempted to open a banking account.[6]

The lawyers and other professionals who made up the new party's leadership all earned more-than-comfortable livings for themselves, but all they were willing to put up for Nkrumah's services now was a mere £25 a month. This was a quarter of the decent but not exorbitant sum they had originally promised. Nkrumah suppressed his disappointment and countered saying that he was willing to work for nothing, as long as the group paid his office and lodging expenses. This in turn produced looks of astonishment and suspicion, followed by an insistence that Nkrumah receive some kind of regular payment, however modest. "They must have thought that I was either a pretty queer character or that in a shrewd way I was trying on something too clever for them to see," Nkrumah wrote.[7] What he said at the time, after the contretemps over payment, though, as recorded in the group's minutes, was more conciliatory. "I am happy to be with you at last. At the moment I can't say anything more than to affirm that if you need me I am at your service."[8]

An exchange with Danquah proved that Nkrumah's labors at securing the trust of his new patrons were not over. By this time, Danquah had done more homework on Nkrumah and asked him how he could "reconcile his active interests in West African unity (through the West African National Secretariat) with the rather parochial aims of the United Gold Coast Convention?" By this, Danquah was signaling that his convention had no interest in pushing for any regional federation. Having to be fast on his feet, Nkrumah told the committee members that he "believed in TERRITORIAL BEFORE INTERNATIONAL solidarity." Others challenged him about his use of phrases like "comrade," which they warned, "might arouse the suspicion of the public as well as officialdom regarding the political connections of the Convention with certain unpopular foreign forms of government."[9]

These first wrinkles were quickly overcome, though, and on the basis of the Working Committee's offer, plus the use of a driver and car, or balky jalopy as it turned out. Nkrumah quickly got to work, setting up a modest office in a mixed-use building with a warehouse, showroom, and sales office, part owned by the United Africa Company, an old-line trading firm that was one of the biggest British companies in the region.

Little has changed in Saltpond since those days. During a visit I made there in 2022, the town, which is located just off the narrow coastal highway that traverses the breadth of Ghana, felt like a fossil specimen trapped in amber. On Zongo Road, a gently sloping stretch of asphalt that was entirely free of automobile traffic, I found the landmark I was looking for, the Canaan Lodge, a simple, two-story building, freshly tricked up in hues of slate gray and orange-brown. There, on an upper floor, was where the UGCC had first gathered. In an internal courtyard, a handful of children were playing hide and seek in the sharply slanting afternoon sun and its pooled shadows. One of them pointed me toward a slate plaque that read: "This is the house that served as the meeting place and lodgings of the founding members of the United Gold Coast Convention."

A short distance away, its colors withered by the decades, stood the building where Nkrumah opened a party office in December 1947. High above its louvered wooden windows, now badly warped, I could barely make out the faded stenciled imprint, set off by three stylized ionic columns, announcing "United Gold Coast Convention National Headquarters."

From there, the road out of the town took me to the foot of a steep hill dominated by Fort Amsterdam, the slave-trading "castle," in local parlance, that Holland built in the early seventeenth century, a time when England and the Dutch Republic repeatedly fought each other over control of the enormous traffic in human beings from this stretch of the West African coast.

On this day, with hand-hewn local fishing boats pulled up onto a banked and sweeping curve of beach just beyond the reach of the surf, a lone Chinese engineer led local workers in erecting a small bridge. As I rejoined the highway, my last sight before leaving the town was the only other discernable new construction in the area. There, at the small roundabout, sat a simple monument made of three conjoined pillars atop which sat rough, silvered busts of three men who had driven independence politics in the years just after the war, all in jacket and tie. On the left was Nkrumah, whom the inscription noted was first prime minister (1957–1960) and then first president of Ghana (1960–1966), described as "teacher, philosopher and astute politician." On the right sat J. B. Danquah, founding member of the UGCC, and "lawyer, scholar, author and patriot," and "doyen" of Ghana's politics. And in the middle, elevated slightly above the others, George Alfred "Paa" Grant, "the Father of the liberation struggle and the 'Moses' of Ghana's independence."

When they dispersed from Saltpond, leaving by the same road that bore me back to Accra, a semblance of agreement seemed to unite these three men, but a fitful struggle pitting Nkrumah against the old guard lay ahead. Years later, they could all claim an important role in the independence of Ghana, but there would only be one founder, and despite his recent return from years overseas and his inexperience in local politics, his name was Nkrumah.

CHAPTER TWELVE

The Mongoose

MANY YEARS LATER, AN ASSOCIATE OF NKRUMAH'S FROM THIS ERA, Michael Dei-Anang, a member of the clan of farmers whose successes turned cocoa into a global commodity, would remark that Nkrumah's desire for innovation and his fundamental impatience had created in him an enormous capacity for work. In fact, this was a quality people had been observing in him at least since his days as a student at Lincoln. Dei-Anang, an Achimota graduate who would become Nkrumah's leading advisor on African affairs and who spent two months in prison when Nkrumah was overthrown, said that work under Nkrumah was like being employed in "a non-stop factory," and that he had "a deep longing to have all his tomorrows today."[1] But it didn't take friendship or allegiance for people to note qualities like this. A fierce critic of Nkrumah's whom he had expelled from the country after he became prime minister wrote:

> He has reserves of energy so immense that he lives on a minimum of food and sleep. To accompany him on a tour is always an exhausting experience for his colleagues . . . he can sleep anywhere and at any time, even on two hard chairs for a quarter of an hour.[2]

Soon after his return from overseas, Nkrumah convened a second major gathering for the UGCC's hitherto lightly scheduled Working Committee for January 20, less than a month after his first meeting with them; there had been no time for ideological divisions to drive them apart. Such a fast pace came as a shock to their stately rhythms.

A year earlier, in 1946, the British had created a new charter for what they regarded as their model African colony, the so-called Burns constitution, named after Alan Burns, the governor of the Gold Coast from 1941 to 1947.

Its biggest innovation was to provide for an African majority on the legislative council, a largely toothless body that a string of nearly all-powerful governors had dominated. The select members of the council would be chosen from among African chiefs, a distant analog of the British aristocracy. Naturally, these chiefs would be carefully vetted to include only those most likely to readily support the governor's agenda.

The British were congratulating themselves on what they saw as the liberal nature of the Burns constitution. In London's view, it was so progressive that colonial authorities expected it would remain in place for a couple of decades or more. But the members of the UGCC, albeit mostly conservative, quickly saw the charter as an obstacle not just to meaningful self-government, but to their own rise as their country's legitimate new modernizing establishment and predestined rulers.

Traditional rulers were permitted to elect nonchiefs to the legislative council, but in 1946, only two nonchiefs were elected, suggesting that the traditional rulers long favored by London were not ready to relinquish their place in politics. One of the commoners chosen for the council was Danquah. This composition stung of betrayal for members of the intelligentsia, who felt strongly that the beneficiaries of amended rules governing the legislative council should be the "right people," individuals who should be chosen for their education and competence, and not for their inherited titles.

For a brief time, it was this class frustration, an echo of earlier times when London had stymied the advancement of African medical doctors and the entry of educated Blacks into the colonial administrators, that propelled history in the Gold Coast. Disappointment over the paltry Black representation on the legislative council had driven Paa Grant and his allies to found the UGCC. When its members came together at Saltpond, they announced that its goal was "to ensure that by all legitimate and constitutional means the control and direction of the Government shall within the shortest time possible pass into the hands of the people and their Chiefs."[3] The word "chiefs" seems like a sop thrown in to avoid alarming the British and the traditional rulers about the wholesale change they had in mind. The phrase "shortest possible time" was similarly chosen to sound innocuous, or at least nonthreatening. But in the UGCC's deference to British sensibilities, it fatally misread the historical moment in West Africa. The pace or timetable for independence was about to acquire an enormous weight in driving the fortunes of conservative and progressive forces in Ghana. Nkrumah's sense of urgency and Danquah's patience would drive them apart, pushing the former toward political triumph and the latter toward his unimagined eclipse.

True to his distaste for temporizing, Nkrumah opened his very first meeting of the party's Working Committee with Lincolnian urgency, announcing a program of action like nothing members of the native elite had ever contemplated. He called for the prompt establishment of a shadow cabinet to begin studying the functions of the various ministries in the colonial government and their decision making. This was to "forestall any unpreparedness on our part in the exigency of Self-Government being thrust upon us before the expected time."[4] Nkrumah also urged that the nascent party immediately begin coordinating with all the major civil society groups in the colony, from farmers' and women's organizations to trade unions, ethnic organizations, and cooperatives. And hinting at what he had learned from revolutionary spirits like Padmore, he urged the creation of party-affiliated weekend schools that would undertake "the political mass education of the country for Self-Government."[5]

Finally, in implicit criticism of the hitherto sluggish leadership of the convention, he said that it should begin opening local offices and organizing sections in the whole of the country—meaning Ashanti, the Northern Territories, and Togoland—instead of confining itself to the coastal band traditionally known as the Colony.[6]

Immediately after the meeting, Nkrumah took his whirlwind energy on the road, touring the country, from clamorous cities to the small towns of cement shacks with zinc roofs that grew like cataracts every few miles along the colony's dusty roads. He even insisted on making stops in villages that were only reachable by foot. With each appearance he gave speeches and launched local party offices.

> Things might have been a bit better if I had had a more reliable car, but the ancient model that was supplied to me rarely finished a journey. It usually meant that I had to leave it with the driver while I continued my trek on foot. Sometimes if a "mammy" lorry happened to be rattling past I managed to get a lift, but I was not always lucky in this respect. Most time I managed to arrange things so that I spent the night in one of these villages but on several occasions, when I had got stuck too far out in the bush by nightfall, I was obliged to sleep on the roadside.[7]

As he surmounted difficulties like these, Nkrumah issued membership cards and collected party dues, for which purpose he had also opened the party's first bank account. Sometimes he appeared with Danquah or other leading members of the UGCC, but most of the time, Nkrumah ran a tireless, one-man road show.

We have often spoken about the role of chance, or rather, of timing and providence in Nkrumah's life. With uncanny consistency, it had accompanied his every step. The weeks immediately following Nkrumah's inaugural tour as the party's secretary, though, brought him one of the biggest shifts in circumstances imaginable. And for the first time in Nkrumah's life, the fissures that it would open offered him a glimpse of a path that might lead to power. It would also have him test the famous dictum of the nineteenth century French scientist Louis Pasteur who is said to have remarked about luck: "Chance only favors the mind which is prepared."

Until this historical juncture, the British had been so self-satisfied in their stewardship of the Gold Coast that they thought of their subjects as contented residents of a model colony. But this was based on a gulf in perceptions and needs between colonizer and subject so profound that it was unbridgeable. As a perceptive critic wrote in 1961:

> The heritage of Ghana from the British is not one of bitterness, exploitation and misery as such. It is a heritage of a certain sort of economy, one which worked passably well according to the standards set for it: the earning of sufficient revenue to run a government to provide for order and promote the exports necessary to pay for imports for the metropolis.[8]

Passably well here meant in service of British, not African, needs. As the writer went on to observe, colonial governments were always shoestring operations that were inadequately staffed, especially with Africans. "These were simply not administrations in any way designed for the job even of assessing national economic development prospects, much less for their implementation." This pattern held fast until it didn't. That was in the opening months of 1948, when the illusion of satisfied calm gave way to chaos.[9]

Even before the cascading drama that follows here, the ambient contentment that supposedly reigned in the Gold Coast was already being rendered hollow by the sudden outbreak of an epidemic of a swollen shoot disease. Appearing out of nowhere, this deadly crop virus began to ravage the plantations operated by hundreds of African farmers whose labors supplied two-thirds of the world's cocoa. With no other means of controlling its spread, the British inspected plantations and ordered contaminated plants to be destroyed. Because cacao plants take about five years to mature, this instantly affected the income of the farmers for the years that followed.

To be charitable, the imperial establishment worthies who boasted about a model colony were being forgetful. Gold Coast cocoa farmers had already been politically active for decades, and they had always been quick to fight for their interests. In 1937 this had led to a dramatic cocoa holdup, or strike, in which they refused to sell their crop to the major British trading firms that controlled the market, while boycotting colonial imports, to obtain better prices.

Disgruntlement over the fight against swollen shoot disease fed an even broader anger about uncontrolled inflation in the colony, which made imported goods unaffordable, a basic element in how people judged their standard of living and status, especially in the colony's growing cities. Whether it was sugar, flour, printed cloth, or basic tools like machetes, many necessities had tripled in cost compared to their prewar levels. What is more, imports grew scarce as Britain, like the French, favored its own consumers as its devastated economy underwent recovery from the war. As a result, even an ongoing spike in international cocoa prices, a nominal bright spot, turned into something of a liability, because amid declining harvests due to the shoot virus, this meant more money sloshing around in the pursuit of an inadequate supply of goods.

This cauldron of discontent was brought to a boil by the fact that roughly sixty-three thousand war veterans had recently returned to Ghana after supporting British campaigns in places like Burma and the Middle East. Once home, they discovered that the upward mobility they expected from their sacrifice was blocked, and that their "gratuities," as the package they were given after being decommissioned was called, were far too small to shield them from the fast-rising prices. London had only budgeted a miserly £1.2 million in total for this purpose. This amounted to less than £20 per serviceman.[10] Veterans who expected to be able to launch themselves in business or enter professions were instead reduced to driving trucks and other kinds of work performed by commoners.

Inflation had become a major bone of contention as did the grip that foreign actors, whether they were powerful British firms like the United Africa Company or merchants from the Levant, had over most commerce. Foreign firms furnished an irresistible target for the mounting discontent, and toward the end of 1948, a modestly successful Accra businessman named Nii Kwabena Bonne stepped forward to take aim.

Bonne was not exactly a member of the intelligentsia, but he had a history of civic activism. "The white men and the Syrians are tricking you out of your money," he preached in small meetings with fellow African business people in market gatherings, and then, finally, in large rallies early in January 1948.[11] Emboldened by the fervent support this won, Bonne then announced that a monthlong boycott of goods sold by the Association of West African Merchants (AWAM), a trade group dominated by European-owned companies, would commence on January 24. Only basic necessities, things like soap and medicines, would be spared.

Nkrumah learned about Bonne's boycott drive while he was still in Tarkwa, where he was reunited with his mother. Bonne even visited Tarkwa, Nkrumah claimed, saying he was unable to attend the meeting. "Here at least was an attempt to give voice to the dominant political wishes of the people," he wrote.[12]

Bonne's call for a boycott also seized the attention of the colonial administration. Alarmed by the prospect of unrest, the administration brokered an agreement between Bonne and AWAM and the Chamber of Commerce to relieve inflation by cutting the merchants' profit margins between 50 and 75 percent. This might have seemed like a remarkable victory, but promising to reduce commercial profit going forward did little to relieve baseline inflation or the crisis in purchasing power that the administration had already created. The relief measures were also misunderstood by the ordinary people whether they bought their provisions in packed, open-air markets or made their purchases in foreign-owned shops. They believed something that had never been promised—that prices would be slashed outright.

Nkrumah and Danquah, who were traveling together on the stump during much of the monthlong boycott, did not fail to notice the ferment. They sought to draw Bonne into some sort of alliance with the UGCC, but he rejected the convention's advances. Despite the vast differences between them in politics and style, the two UGCC leaders also saw the discontent of the colony's returned veterans as a strong potential source of energy and support for their proto party, and together they addressed a packed meeting of the Ex-Servicemen's Union at the Palladium Cinema in Accra on February 20, 1948. This was a Friday, eight days before the merchants' boycott was scheduled to end. No record survives of his words that day, but for the first speech Nkrumah ever gave in the capital, he chose the title, "The Ideological Battles of Our Time."

"After I had finished," he later wrote, "I realized more fully than ever before, from the reaction of the crowd, that the political consciousness of the people of the Gold Coast had awakened to a point where the time had come for them to unite and strike out for their freedom and independence." Carried along by the enthusiasm of the audience, Danquah, in follow-up remarks after Nkrumah's speech told the crowd, "If all the leaders of the UGCC failed them, Kwame Nkrumah would never fail them."[13]

By this time, the servicemen had resolved to march on the old, whitewashed seaside fort, Christianborg Castle, which was built by the Danish in 1659 for the trade in slaves. Remarkably, under the British, it was made the seat of the colonial administration. There, the servicemen vowed to deliver a petition to the governor. The original plan had been to do so the following Monday, but the march was postponed until February 28, and by fateful coincidence, this was the same day the merchants' boycott ended.

By midday, hundreds of ex-servicemen and their supporters had assembled at Accra's polo ground, an enormous open space near the sea, in preparation for their march, and around 3 p.m., roughly two thousand of them set off in orderly fashion down Christianborg Road. As they neared the Castle, they took a minor detour from the route that had been authorized by the police, and trouble quickly broke out. When the police blocked them, the protesters insisted that their demonstration was peaceful and should be allowed to proceed. In the ensuing standoff, what had been an orderly protest turned angry, and then, in a flash, deadly. According to some accounts, marchers showered verbal abuse on the colonial police, African men commanded by white officers, who gave no ground, and some of the people in the crowd then began to hurl rocks.

In response, the British commanding officer ordered his Black policemen to open fire. When they balked, he grabbed a rifle from one of his men and fired into the scattering crowd. By one account, this left two dead and four or five others wounded.[14] With these cracks of gunfire, what was intended to be a loyal request for relief from the governor became something else altogether. This was a Saturday, and because the boycott had just ended, the streets of nearby central Accra were pulsing with shoppers and others who were merely out and about in the revivified city. Word of the shootings spread instantly through the heart of town, triggering looting that targeted foreign merchants. Prices had not been slashed, as many had mistakenly thought they would be because of the boycott, and therefore city dwellers believed that the foreign store owners who had come from afar to profiteer on the backs of a defenseless people had earned their wrath.

In the ensuing riot, angry crowds attacked the offices and shops of the Unilever subsidiary, the United Africa Company, the regionally dominant British trading firm, as well as storefronts owned by Syrian merchants, who were often viewed as predatory. As looters dashed about, parked cars were overturned and set ablaze, and one business after another was stripped of whatever goods or equipment could be carried away. When the stores were emptied, crowds converged on another of the monumental relics of the Middle Passage that dot Accra, Ussher Fort, the high, white-walled Dutch slave trading base that served as the city's main prison. There they breached the gates and freed its inmates. As news of the unrest spread through the colony, looting quickly spread to major cities and provincial towns alike. According to the official toll, by the end of the weekend, twenty-nine people lay dead and over two hundred others were injured. Goods valued at some £2 million had also been lost or destroyed.

These were not the only casualties of the shooting of the ex-servicemen and the rioting that it set off. In the space of a weekend, the myth of the contented model colony had been exploded. Invoking a phrase popularized by Edgar Rice Burroughs, creator of the Tarzan series, colonial authorities lamented how the unrest had stripped away "the thin veneer of civilization" in the Gold Coast. Others quickly singled out Nkrumah, characterizing him as a dangerous troublemaker. They speculated that he had the backing of communist organizations in the UK and would soon make common cause to destabilize the region with other West African political movements.

The colony's shiny image in London was not the only thing that was destroyed. Although it would take nearly a year and a half for a complete rupture between Nkrumah and the establishment core of the UGCC to play out, the fault lines were now plain and clear. It had been barely two months since its leaders had paid Nkrumah's fare for the sea passage that delivered him from London to be their instrument. They had recruited Nkrumah to galvanize ordinary folks, and especially the colony's so-called youngmen and verandah boys, as graduates of the recently and belatedly expanded elementary schools were variously called. Nkrumah's sponsors were now aggrieved, blaming him for inflaming passions and arousing the hostility of the British. Henceforth, the questions would be about whether Nkrumah had what it took to lead in his own right and about the strategic matter of when the best moment would be to consummate his divorce from the people who had lured him back home.

Kwame Nkrumah and J. B. Danquah, who had both returned to Saltpond after their appearance before the veterans a week before the riots, now rushed back to Accra, where they prepared separate responses to the crisis. Danquah sent a one-thousand-word telegram to the British secretary of state in London. "Civil government ... broken down.... Working Committee ... prepared ... to take over interim government," it read in part. He demanded that London send a "special Commissioner ... to hand over Government to interim government of chiefs and people and to witness immediate call of Constituency Assembly." He signed his message with these notable words: "God Save the King and Floreat United Gold Coast."[15]

For once, it was Nkrumah, who was known for his prolixity, who was more concise. His message, however, was addressed to the United Nations and to a grab-bag of media, including *Pan-Africa* magazine, in Manchester, the *New York Times*, the London-based *Daily Worker*, and the *Moscow New Times*. It called for the immediate recall of the inexperienced, just-appointed, and now thoroughly discredited governor, Gerald Creasy, and for the appointment of a commission to "supervise the formation of a constituent assembly."[16]

Unsurprisingly, the colonial government's instincts immediately pushed things in the opposite direction. After meeting with police officials, Creasy concluded that the riots were the culmination of a carefully laid plot to destabilize the Gold Coast. In doing so, he seized on what would become the one-size-fits-all Western explanation for political unrest in the colonial world in this era, communist influence. To put things right, Creasy invoked the riot act and ordered that the main leaders of the UGCC, a group already known as the Big Six, including Danquah and Nkrumah, be arrested.

The notion that any of them had directly encouraged the rioting in any way was baseless. The theory that they had lent themselves to some communist conspiracy, though, was worse. It smacked of heads buried in sand and utter delusion. Five of the Big Six had been steady-as-she-goes advocates of a stately progression toward some kind of eventual independence that would be led by conservatives who were imbued with a love of Britain. And the sixth, Nkrumah, was neither a communist, nor as we will see, someone who had the power to impose his more militant politics on other much more conservative members of this group.

As word quickly spread of impending arrests, Nkrumah hid out for a few days near Accra, where he says he was housed by "two women supporters" who gave him shelter. From there, he returned without incident to Saltpond, only to discover that the United Africa Company had shuttered his office. Nkrumah then traveled onward to Cape Coast, where he was roused from sleep one night by two European police officers and two other menacing plainclothes men. They meticulously searched his belongings. It was here that Nkrumah's famous unsigned Communist Party card from Britain was discovered, along with the charter of The Circle.

Nkrumah was intensely grilled about whether he was a member of the Communist Party, which he denied. But as one might expect, the seized items were treated as proof of Nkrumah's incitement of the Accra riots and of the grave danger he represented to public order.

To justify carting him off, the agents then produced a copy of the legal paperwork the administration had prepared providing for Nkrumah's arrest and detention under colonial law. For reasons explained in a moment, it is worth citing at some length.

> WHEREAS I am satisfied with respect to FRANCIS NWIA KOFIE NKRUMAH, alias F.N. KWAME NNKRUMAH, that it is expedient for securing the public safety and the maintenance of public order to make a Removal Order against him under the provisions of regulation 29 of the Emergency (General) Regulations, 1948 (inserted in such Regulations by the Emergency General Regulations, 1948) . . . I do hereby make this order, and direct that the said FRANCIS NWIA KOFFIE NKRUMAH, alias, F.N. KWAME NKRUMAH shall be apprehended and detained and that he shall be removed in custody, as soon as may be, to such a place in the Gold Coast as I shall hereafter appoint by directions under my hand.
> AND I DO HEREBY FURTHER ORDER and require that the said FRANCIS NWIA KOFFIE NKRUMAH, alias, F.N. KWAME NKRUMAH, from the time of his removal to the place to be appointed by me, and so long as this Order continues in operation, shall at all times—
>
> a. Remain and live in, and not leave or be absent from, the place to be so appointed by me;
> b. Comply in all respects with such directions and requirements as I may issue at any time.
>
> This order may be cited as the Removal (F.N.K. Nkrumah) Order, 1948, and shall come into operation on the 12th day of March 1948.[17]

The procedural details here bear relevance to much more than the immediate circumstances of Nkrumah's arrest that day. In this incident, in the Gold Coast, as in most British colonies, London used legal codes to arrogate extraordinarily broad authority over speech and political behavior. It basically rendered opposition activity illegal at its own whim. As a careful reading of his "removal order" shows, Governor Creasy exercised unchecked personal power over when Nkrumah would be arrested, where he would be detained, and how long he would be held. And this would be done without the filing of charges of any kind or the granting of habeas corpus, a pillar of English jurisprudence that predates even the Magna Carta.

The policemen who arrested Nkrumah taunted him and then shoved him into the back of a windowless vehicle for a long drive to an undisclosed location. When they arrived, he found himself on a tarmac at Accra's airport, where he was reunited with the other members of the UGCC Big Six

(J. B. Danquah, Edward Akufo-Addo, William Ofori Atta, Ako Adjei, and Emmanuel Obetsebi-Lamptey). Together, they were then bundled off on a flight to Kumasi, the old capital of the Asante kingdom. There, the six were held for three days, a time they spent in deep and often acrimonious conversation. The others blamed Nkrumah for their unpleasant circumstances, having never dreamed that their involvement in politics might lead to their arrest. Nkrumah wrote that their detention in close quarters had provided him with his first inkling of the gulf that separated him from the others. "I became painfully aware that they were losing interest in me because whenever we entered into a discussion, the five of them would always make a point of supporting the opposite point of view to mine and nothing I proposed was acceptable to them."[18] For the first time, he said they also openly blamed Ako Adjei for having suggested Nkrumah's services to them.

After three days in a Kumasi jail, the authorities roused the prisoners in the middle of the night, transferring them to the provincial capital of Tamale, far to the north. The reason they invoked was that one of Nkrumah's closest associates, an ethnic Asante named Krobo Edusei, had alerted some of the youngmen of the city about the Big Six's detention in Kumasi, and the administration feared the prison might come under attack. After three more days of detention in Tamale, the group was broken up and dispersed to separate locations. Nkrumah was sent to the tiny town of Lawra, in the colony's remote northwest, near the border with French-ruled Upper Volta. There, he was held largely incommunicado in a small, guarded bungalow for six weeks, able to receive letters but not to write them, and allowed to read books, but not newspapers. The only company he enjoyed during this time, he said, was a mongoose, a creature with thick, banded fur and a long snout roughly the size of a squirrel, that would creep into his lodging after dusk and spend the night by his side.

After weeks of solitary detention in the north, Nkrumah was once again reunited with the other members of the UGCC leaders and flown to Accra, where they learned that a commission of inquiry consisting of people pulled together in Britain had been empaneled and was ready to interview each of them separately. For this purpose, they were all freed from detention. June 1948 was a month that saw fighting between Jews and Arabs in Palestine, the outbreak of the Malayan Emergency, the start of the Berlin Airlift, and the formal start of apartheid rule in South Africa. In the Gold Coast, the new panel, the Watson Commission, finally released its conclusions. The surprising findings were an open rebuke of the colonial government's handling of the social pressures that had been rising in the Gold Coast since the combined outbreak of the swollen shoot infestation, the discontent among ex-servicemen, and the anger of inflation. The administration of Governor Creasy was seen as hopelessly remote and ill-informed, and even irresponsible in the way it had played up a theory of the case that leaned on communist conspiracy.

But even for a commission that seemed more open minded, Nkrumah was a separate matter. It quoted him as testifying that The Circle was little more than a dream from his London days. "Mr. Nkrumah appears to be a mass orator among Africans of no mean attainments..." the committee found.[19] "Suffice it to say we are satisfied, having seen and heard Nkrumah, that given the smallest opportunity, he would quickly translate his dream into reality."[20] Citing seized documents, the committee also concluded that while in London, through the West African National Secretariat, "a body which still exists," Nkrumah had "openly campaigned for a Union of West African Soviet Socialist Republics." Here, though, the commission was gilding the lily. As Nkrumah later wrote, "No doubt the authorities were so bent on labelling me as a 'man to be watched,' that they thought the introduction of the word 'Soviet' in itself was all that was needed to imply a threat of Communism in its most extreme form to the Gold Coast and to Africa as a whole."[21]

The commission also cited the action plan that Nkrumah had delivered to the UGCC in his first working meeting with them, calling it "all too familiar to those who have studied the technique of countries which have fallen the victims of Communist enslavement."[22] The other members of the Big Six rose to this bait and disavowed Nkrumah's program, even though they had largely assented to it weeks earlier.

On a more progressive note, the commission declared the Burns constitution of just two years prior, which had been trumpeted as a charter of durable value, to be "outmoded at birth."[23] It would have to be replaced with a new constitution that could consider broader social forces in the colony, from the growing trade unions to farmers, miners, and even market women. Most of the UGCC's leadership was invited to take part in this process under a new committee named for a judge on the Gold Coast Supreme Court, James Henley Coussey. Over the ensuing years Nkrumah's critics and some historians have faulted him for his haste and impatience for change. But if anything, by leaning on the bogeyman of communism at this stage to exclude him, the British compelled him to push for change even harder.

CHAPTER THIRTEEN

Positive Action

BEFORE ANYONE IN THE GOLD COAST HAD TIME TO PREPARE FOR IT, HIStory began to lurch in great, spasmodic leaps. Confident in its ability to control the scale and pace of change intact, London's Colonial Office accepted the creation of a new local committee to propose further constitutional reform for the Gold Coast. Why refuse something so innocuous sounding? Such thought was validated when the colony's traditional rulers hewed closely to what they imagined were Britain's priorities after the recent unrest. This meant calling for the strict enforcement of law and order and even threatening politically active youth with arrest if they incited any further boycotts. The Colonial Office in London knew enough to also yield some ground, though, and so it rejiggered the formula for representation on what became officially known as the Committee on Constitutional Reform. Of its forty members, henceforth thirty-one would be mostly prosperous and well-educated "commoners," leaving only nine traditional chiefs. Six United Gold Coast Convention (UGCC) members played a central role in the deliberations. Surprising nobody, neither Nkrumah nor any of his allies were invited.

The composition of the constitutional reform body introduced a complicated new dynamic to the colony's fast-evolving politics. The lawyers and property owners of the UGCC were now all-but-official political insiders. Moreover, as masters of rulemaking and process, they were seemingly well placed to fashion a new dispensation for the colony that would favor their emergence as its eventual leaders.

At a first glance, Nkrumah appeared to be more of an outsider than ever. But to understand things this way, as many in the UGCC leadership and the colonial administration did, was to misread Nkrumah's resourcefulness. In 1948 and '49, he would nimbly operate with a foot in both worlds. He did so both as a member of the convention, but one who was not tainted by its coziness with the next governor, and as the driver of increasingly militant activism among the partially educated youngmen and the urban poor.

The UGCC searched for ways to rid itself of Nkrumah but never quite managed, in large part because it had never developed its own way of speaking to the excluded—the verandah boys. Unable to connect effectively with what would inevitably become a large and crucial part of the electorate, the convention feared the popular backlash that purging Nkrumah would generate.

By articulating terms for eventual self-rule, the Coussey Committee was expected to calm the waters in the Gold Coast. Nkrumah, though, saw the kind of stately change it proposed as favoring conservatives in Ghana and the colonial establishment, and therefore he pushed hard on his advantage as someone who could speak to the young. Furthermore, Labour was in power in London, and although that didn't mean anything like outright support for his politics, Nkrumah knew that whenever the Conservatives returned to office, there would be much less sympathy toward African independence.

After the release of the Big Six in April 1948, Nkrumah repaired to Cape Coast, a three-hour drive to the west. There, in July, in one of West Africa's oldest cities, dominated by a forbidding, chalk-white slave trading fort that dates to the seventeenth century, he opened a small school he called the Ghana National College. He staffed it with teachers who volunteered after being dismissed for demonstrating against the recent political arrests. The UGCC accused Nkrumah of indiscipline for launching a college without the convention's backing and denied him financial support. In response, Nkrumah paid for basic supplies out of his own small salary. Just a year later, the school boasted 230 students and a long waiting list, and Nkrumah began talking up the possibility of opening campuses around the country.

Some of the UGCC leaders secretly arranged to have Nkrumah's offices searched and confronted him that August with new claims of disloyalty to the convention. Some argued for his dismissal as secretary, others that he be moved to a lesser job, such as honorary treasurer.

Undaunted, Nkrumah proposed that the UGCC open a newspaper to drum up more popular backing for independence, which they rejected, perhaps fearing Britain's disapproval. He then followed in the mold of so many of the pan-Africanist figures he had studied, from Africanus Horton and Casely Hayford in the nineteenth century to Marcus Garvey and Nnamdi Azikiwe in the twentieth, opening a new paper, the *Accra Evening News*, on his own. For weeks, Nkrumah slept on an ordinary mat on the floor in the newspaper's office as he supervised its rollout.[1] The paper took a bold and unmistakable stance against colonial rule and the gradualist recommendations of the

Coussey Committee. Its ink may have bled copiously through the atrocious newsprint, but the *Evening News* quickly built a large readership with columns signed under pen names that were redolent of the Harlem streetcorner speakers that had dazzled Nkrumah in the 1930s with monikers like "Rambler" and "Agitator," and they gave hell to the establishment.

In December 1948, Nkrumah followed this up with his biggest move yet, overseeing the formation of a nationwide association of young people, which became the Committee on Youth Organization (CYO). At its first meeting in Accra that month, the CYO officially adopted the potent slogan, "Self-Government Now," language conceived to undercut the far-less-urgent-sounding "shortest possible time" formulation of the UGCC. Nkrumah would urge its members to "wake to organize for redemption, to make the Gold Coast a paradise . . . so that when the gates are opened by Peter, we sit in heaven to see our children driving their own airplanes, commanding their own armies."[2] The police responded to this ginning up of militant fervor by banning a conference the youth group planned to hold in Kumasi. This was just one of many severe colonial infringements on the rights of free speech and assembly in this period. The UGCC, meanwhile, declared that membership in both the convention and the CYO were incompatible, but by this time, Nkrumah and his backers were already rapidly digging the ground out from under the party's feet.

Nkrumah had recently been stripped of his position of secretary of the convention. Months of vacillation, both by Nkrumah and the UGCC, over his possible participation in the leadership in some lesser capacity followed. In a series of clamorous meetings, some in Nkrumah's camp argued for a clean break with the convention, while others said the CYO should press ahead to "capture the UGCC from within."[3] The UGCC leaders suffered from even graver doubts, wondering if a complete rupture with Nkrumah would fatally wound their organization. Remarkably, this eventually led to an offer to reinstate Nkrumah as secretary, which he tentatively, albeit briefly, accepted.

Against this backdrop, youth elements among Nkrumah's followers, many of them former students with a few years of school under their belts, moved to form a breakaway entity that they tentatively called the Convention People's Party (CPP), and they drew up a six-point program that's stated purpose was to "fight relentlessly by all constitutional means for the achievement of full Self-Government Now."[4] This was the objective Nkrumah had sought all along, but he had wavered over matters of timing. The tail was now wagging the dog.

Things finally came to a head at a raucous public meeting at the Accra

Arena on June 12, 1949. Sixty thousand people turned out that day, drawn by the unfamiliar spectacle of politics being played out openly in their society. But the mood was dominated by newly enlisted members of the CYO, young and zealous advocates of independence, whose cheers for self-government were echoed by the excited crowd. What the militants and uninitiated yearned for most, though, was to hear from Nkrumah himself, and when he finally took the stage, he began with a cool articulation of the logic for pushing for independence, and by implication, for breaking with the UGCC. "Backstairs" methods of pressure for freedom such as those endorsed by the convention, he said, were doomed to failure. Only "frankness and firmness" could deliver rapid self-government.[5]

As a theoretical matter this was all well and good, but the crowd thirsted for more, and sensing this, Nkrumah then gave himself over to the kind of call and response he had witnessed so many times in America, from his visit to a Baptist church in Harlem during his first days in America, to the Black churches he visited in Philadelphia and then guest-preached in himself as a penniless divinity student.

If he should lead the Gold Coast down the path toward independence, would they follow him, Nkrumah asked the crowd, or should he simply "leave this dear Ghana of ours?" It was a leading question and an instant winner, and when the crowd roared its approval, he reformulated it for emphasis. "May I remain here and keep my mouth shut?" To this came a thunderous "Noooo!" With many shouting "stay and open your mouth," Nkrumah finally announced his intentions. The CYO, he said, would "transform itself into a fully-fledged political party with the object of Self-Government NOW!"[6]

In those giddy and tense moments Nkrumah announced a definitive break with the group that had brought him back to Ghana and the creation of a political formation of his own. Ironically, in addressing the rally, Nkrumah adopted a new name for the Gold Coast first promoted by the rival he was breaking with, J. B. Danquah. Drawing energy from the pulsating crowd that had come to hear him speak at the Arena in Accra, Nkrumah proclaimed the founding of his new party invoking:

> the CYO, in the name of the chiefs, the people, the rank and file of the Convention, the Labor movement, our valiant ex-servicemen, the youth movement throughout the country, the man in the street, our children and those as yet unborn, the new Ghana that is to be, Sergeant Adjety and his comrades who died at the crossroads of Christiansborg during the 1948 riots, and in the name of God Almighty.[7]

The party's forthright purpose, Nkrumah said, would be to achieve "immediate self-government, that is, for full Dominion status within the Commonwealth of Nations." To eliminate all ambiguity, he added that this meant Ghana would seek the same dispensation as the "old white Dominions," meaning settler colonies like Canada, Australia, New Zealand, and South Africa. They had become self-governed and legally autonomous from Britain following the Balfour Declaration of 1926.[8] Under Nkrumah's program, in other words, the first Black country in Africa to ever be freed from colonial rule would only accept equal standing with the white lands that Britain had once also ruled. No intermediate or second-class status would do.

The vehicle that Nkrumah summoned into being there was to be called the Convention People's Party (CPP). The usurpation of the word "convention," introduced by the UGCC, was, of course, a final dig at his rivals and antagonists, but it also reflected an astute practical consideration. The future electorate would inevitably be dominated by people with little or no schooling. As a tactical matter, too many of these people already associated the word "convention" with independence politics to concede it.

During the uncertain months ahead, as he pushed hard for self-government, Nkrumah's biggest challenges would no longer come from the old guard of the UGCC, but from the colonial administration itself, especially in the person of its tough new governor. Charles Arden-Clarke had previously served not only in Nigeria and Bechuanaland (later Botswana), but in the Kingdom of Sarawak, in northwestern Borneo. For generations Sarawak had been ruled by a line of so-called White Rajahs, descendants and relatives of a British sailor named James Brooke, who had helped a local ruler quash a rebellion in the 1850s and had thereby become the territory's governor. A constitution written under the Brooke rajahs in 1941 had called for the gradual establishment of local rule there, but Japan occupied Sarawak during the war. In what has been called an "against the grain" expansion of colonial rule, Britain maneuvered to take control of Sarawak after Japan's defeat just as the curtain was falling on empire in Asia.[9]

Toward that end, Britain imposed an unpopular cession agreement that would eventually allow this territory of dense tropical forests, rich in oil, rubber, and tin—exports that earned coveted dollars—to be incorporated into British Malaya. In 1947, Arden-Clarke was appointed as the first governor of the new crown colony. During his brief stay there, he employed aggressive psychological warfare and punitive methods, such as firing civil servants and denying access to schools for children of people who opposed British control.

In August 1949, Arden-Clarke was transferred from Sarawak to the Gold Coast. Four months later, Duncan Stewart, his successor as governor in Southeast Asia, was killed in a stabbing attack for implementing Britain's recolonization plan. Arden-Clarke had been the original target.

Ensconced in his new post in Accra, Arden-Clarke promptly embraced the roadmap established by the Coussey Committee as the only legitimate path forward for Ghana. Its gradualist framework called for eventual elections in the Gold Coast and the constitution of a bicameral government with an upper house constituted of chiefs and the lower house of commoners. Under this plan, the colony's governor would retain strong powers, including veto power and the ability to appoint expatriate ministers in key portfolios.

Right from the outset, Nkrumah had declared that his new party's political leverage would stem from what he called positive action, meaning carefully calibrated nonviolent civil disobedience resistance. This was inspired by the example of India's Gandhi, who had a profound realization as a forty-year-old living in South Africa in 1909. Britain had only been able to dominate other countries through the active cooperation of their people. In a world awash in violence, Ghandi believed the best strategy for undoing foreign control was not force of arms or bloody confrontation, but rather nonviolence. Distilled to its essence, this meant peacefully refusing to acquiesce or cooperate. If applied with discipline, here lay the means to bring the imposing superstructure of imperial rule to a grinding halt and then allow it to collapse of its own weight.

Nkrumah's campaign of refusing to acquiesce, or positive action, would begin with localized party activism, including frequent public meetings to gin up support among ordinary people along with the use of propaganda slogans. Power, they were told, resided within them, and not with the British, whom people had long been taught to regard as their masters. The opening of a party-controlled newspaper, the *Accra Evening News*, and in its wake a slew of other CPP publications, gave a strong boost to this effort. From the outset, though, positive action also held on to the possibility of more muscular means of applying pressure on Britain. These included work slowdowns and other forms of passive resistance and civil disobedience. The ultimate card to play was consumer boycotts in the mold of the one held in Accra in January 1947.

Nkrumah had begun brainstorming on the strategies that became known as positive action with other intellectuals from Africa and the diaspora during the Pan-African Congress of 1945 in Manchester. The Black activists from around the world gathered there were already keenly focused on using nonviolence as seen in India's ongoing independence struggle. In the second half of the 1950s, the African American civil rights movement led by Dr. Martin

Luther King Jr. would famously draw on this same ethos. Well into the next decade, the independence movement in sub-Saharan Africa that Nkrumah initiated and led and the African American struggle for civil rights would be linked and intertwined like a double helix. And as each fought for change, Black people on each side of the Atlantic studied each other's experiences and drew on each other's energies and accomplishments in vital and surprising ways. All the while, the spirit of pan-Africanism was their bedfellow.

At this moment, Nkrumah's political calculus was based on a sense that even though Britain had been gravely weakened by the Second World War, it retained formidable strengths and advantages over the unarmed and, for the most part, poorly organized pro-independence movements of his continent. In his Accra speech, Nkrumah revealed the logic that underpinned the adoption of positive action by warning that when the Conservatives eventually returned to power in Britain, they would not look favorably on colonial independence struggles. Winston Churchill, he pointed out, had vowed to preserve the realm: "I did not become the Prime Minister of His Majesty's Government in order to preside over the liquidation of the British Empire."[10]

A struggle for independence that failed to occupy the moral high ground by disavowing violence, he believed, would not only alienate British Labour, but also eventually invite a crushing riposte from Churchill's Conservatives. As Nkrumah would quickly discover, though, not even an explicit commitment to nonviolence would spare his movement from a muscular effort to limit its advances by Arden-Clarke and the Labour Party that appointed him governor.

After working out its preliminary notions about how the Gold Coast's political system should be reformed to lead the colony toward what a historian called "responsible self-government within the British Commonwealth," the Coussey Committee began an extended round of consultations within the Gold Coast. These involved traditional leaders, members of the small African business and professional class, and others. Most notable of all, though, were those it excluded: Nkrumah and his fellow leaders of the newly formed CPP.

The committee's final recommendations were released after eight months in October 1949, and predictably they drew a swift rebuke from Nkrumah. This set the stage for a new high-stakes struggle between the man who had swiftly emerged as the principal advocate of independence and the new governor, Arden-Clarke. The latter was deeply suspicious of Nkrumah and what he called his "communist methods," and still imagined that he could preside instead over the creation of a political system that would favor the old-line politicians.[11]

Nkrumah recognized the Coussey Report's recommendations as a gilded but nonetheless custom-made cage—one that would impose serious, even crippling, constraints on any new leader who harbored ambitions for real independence. Worse, they left no room whatsoever for a pan-Africanist agenda. In addition to a powerful governor endowed with a veto, the report called for a National Assembly of seventy-five members, as well as eight African ministers who would serve as members of the Governor's Executive. Under the hood, though, this architecture still allowed the traditional chiefs, who had long served Britain as pliable allies, to appoint thirty-seven of the assembly members. This left thirty-three others to be elected in an indirect fashion via an electoral college system in which the chiefs would also notably play a role. Only five members of the proposed new assembly remained to be chosen by direct vote.

Some have professed to see the proposed constitution as "a revolutionary document which totally changed the role of the Governor," as one historian wrote.[12] For Nkrumah, who was keenly aware of the hold that his party had on the population, it was a mere gift horse designed to frustrate and constrain the CPP.

To push back against the Coussey Report, Nkrumah organized what he called a Gold Coast Representative Assembly, which met for the first time in late November 1949. Even though the traditional leaders and UGCC bosses refused to acknowledge it, the assembly managed to bring together dozens of civil society organizations, lending a veneer of popular legitimacy to his alternative vision for constitutional reform and near-term elections.

In the last month of the 1940s, facing defeat by the armies of Mao Zedong, Nationalist forces fled western China to reestablish themselves in Taiwan. Indonesian sovereignty was recognized by the Netherlands and Sukarno was elected president. A forty-meter-high monument was inaugurated to honor the Boer settlers whose exodus to the interior by wagon train from Britain's Cape Colony in 1836 inspired the founding of the apartheid state of South Africa. And the future revolutionary leader, Thomas Sankara, was born in the northern village of Yako, in a French colonial backwater named Upper Volta. That December 15, Nkrumah warned the colonial administration that if it refused to work with his assembly or consider its recommendations, he would launch a civil disobedience campaign. Arden-Clarke had spent his first weeks in the colony touting the benefits of the Coussey Report's supposedly moderate approach toward "responsible self-government" and of the rewards of cooperation with London that it would yield. By embracing it, he said, residents of the Gold Coast would soon see

Africans occupying ministerial-level portfolios, with administrative assistants from Britain helping guide their work during a time of transitional government under his direction.[13] Steeled by the successes he had enjoyed by taking a hard line toward Sarawak independence, Arden-Clarke also warned that he would not hesitate to arrest anyone who fomented trouble or resisted his agenda.

Nkrumah responded by stepping up the pressure, signing an article in the *Evening News* that same day under the headline, "The Era of Positive Action Draws Nigh." At another large rally at the West Accra Arena that night, Nkrumah announced that the CPP would give Britain two weeks to meet its demand that a new constituent assembly be formed to replace the Coussey Committee from whose consultations Nkrumah's party, by all evidence the most popular in the country, had been completely excluded.

Arden-Clarke relished the challenge. Under his direction, police and security forces had already devoted considerable energy to monitoring the CPP leaders, and they were braced for a crackdown. On both sides, though, there was a wariness about how events would be perceived; neither wished to be seen as the initiator of violence, which could easily spiral.

In Sarawak, Arden-Clarke had baited nationalist opponents of absorbing the territory into the British empire by issuing an edict forbidding any employee of the local government from criticizing incorporation and by banning pro-independence posters and other propaganda. This pushed some activists over the edge into more aggressive forms of resistance to the British, including violence. All along, restricting peaceful means of protest had been intended as a trap, meant to justify widespread arrest of those who continued to resist British policy.

In the Gold Coast, Arden-Clarke looked to devise a similar strategy. Toward that end, he first ordered his colonial secretary, Reginald Saloway, a newly arrived veteran of British negotiations over Indian independence, to meet with Nkrumah to ask that he avert a crisis by abandoning positive action. British accounts of these discussions claim that Saloway repeated Arden-Clarke's warning that Nkrumah would be held responsible for any breakdown of order or violence under a civil disobedience campaign. Saloway also urged Nkrumah to accept the Coussey recommendations saying, among other things, that when they came, the elections would be clean and fair, and Nkrumah's party would be strongly favored to win.

Nkrumah wrote later that he had objected to Saloway, saying that "order, as far as your government officials are concerned, means suppressing the rank and file, having them where you want them, to be told what is best for them and what they have to do."[14] He then quoted the colonial secretary as issuing this patronizing reply about weak African mettle:

> You must think seriously before you take this step. Now take India, for instance.... The Indian was used to suffering pains and deprivations, but the African has not had that spirit of endurance. Mark my words, my good man: within three days the people here will let you down—they'll never stick it. Now had this been India... [15]

Nkrumah cut Saloway off in the midst of these patronizing remarks, insisting that his party's demand for a constituent assembly was the only proper way forward under the circumstances and that the government had proposed nothing that could alter his public commitment to launching positive action.

It is often remarked that Nkrumah's accounts of the politics during the Gold Coast's transition to self-rule were framed with an eye to conserving sympathy toward Ghana in the West where anticommunism utterly suffused views of the world. Much less often noted is how British authors, by the same token, typically wrote with an eye to casting London's management of decolonization in Africa in the most sympathetic possible light. And on the topic of the Gold Coast, none benefited more from this kind of press than people like Arden-Clarke and Saloway.

Nkrumah held a second meeting with Saloway shortly thereafter, and on that day, he gained a new understanding of the secretary's supercilious judgment about the lack of tenacity in Africans. Radio stations in the Gold Coast had begun broadcasting the news that plans for a positive action campaign had been abandoned. This was just the start of an intense psychological warfare the government waged to sap the public's will.

Nkrumah responded by holding the latest of several of his rallies at his preferred protest ground, Accra's West Arena, where the CPP's birth had been proclaimed. There, lacking access to the airwaves, he told another large crowd to ignore what the government was saying about positive action; it would not be abandoned.

As Nkrumah's deadline drew nearer, forces outside of both his and of the governor's control impinged. The colony's tiny Union of Meteorological Workers might seem like an unlikely catalyst for events that would decide the fate of the Gold Coast and very quickly acquire continental significance, but when it went on strike in late December and saw its members dismissed, the union appealed for support to the nationwide Trade Union Council (TUC), a militant nationwide umbrella labor organization, which called a general strike on January 8, 1950, a Friday.

Nkrumah's CPP had momentarily lost the initiative, but as a friend of labor and especially of its rank and file, the CPP saw the TUC strike call as something that could give a boost to its efforts to put pressure on the governor. On Saturday, the CPP leadership met in an all-night session, in which it fatefully decided to launch the positive action campaign at midnight on Sunday. Nkrumah announced this to the public at yet another rally that day at West Arena, urging everyone but essential workers, like hospital staff, to stay at home.

Nkrumah left Accra Monday morning for rallies in Cape Coast, Sekondi, and Tarkwa, all economically important southern cities, where he hoped that positive action would quickly take hold, but when he returned to the capital two days later, he was dismayed to find that life in Accra had changed little. The radio airwaves had been saturated with messages calling on people to return to their jobs. They sapped morale with reports claiming that people here and there across the colony were ignoring the call to strike. Arden-Clarke had also employed strike-breakers to keep buses and trains running, and Europeans and Syrian and Lebanese merchants were deputized to supplement the security forces in keeping order in the streets.

Still stewing over Saloway's insulting comparison of Africans to Indians, Nkrumah took to walking about the city dressed in what would become known as revolutionary chic as Ghana moved toward independence: a rough-textured, blue cotton smock traditionally worn by commoners from the north. As he went, he exhorted people to resist the governor's imposition of a colonially approved constitution without considering the views of ordinary people. Crowds swelled around Nkrumah and began to follow him on these wanderings through the city. At one point, the crush was such that Nkrumah had to escape in a taxi and headed one last time to the West Arena for an impromptu rally. "The whole of Accra appeared to be assembled there," he later wrote.[16] Positive action was now in motion.

Nkrumah's public recommitment to civil disobedience set off a rapid-fire chain of events. The streets filled with protesters and their sympathizers, and the next day, the governor called an emergency meeting of his own to denounce what he called "hooligans." Arden-Clarke fumed before the legislative council that among the CPP leadership and its growing crowds of followers "there is not one responsible person.... No chief has asked for self-government, no responsible person in this country has asked for self-government and self-government is not attained overnight"[17]

Arden-Clarke spoke contemptuously of Nkrumah as "our little Hitler" and of positive action as "his putsch."[18] In his defiant speech to the Legislative

Council, he foreswore the creation of any kind of commission to investigate the unrest or reconsider his plans for constitutional reform, saying, "I know of nothing that has occurred that cannot be dealt with justly and effectively by the Courts of this country and established disciplinary procedure."[19]

True to his promise of a vigorous response to "lawlessness," whether that meant striking workers or general civil disobedience, security forces under Arden-Clarke had already deployed mobile policing units and began arresting people on a large scale. Next, a state of emergency was declared, followed by a nighttime curfew.

Beginning with the *Evening News*, the colonial government began raiding papers that were affiliated or even merely sympathetic with the CPP, arresting their editors on sedition charges and closing them down. The traditional chiefs, closely allied to the government, invited leaders of the TUC and of the ex-serviceman's association to meetings that it said were aimed at reaching a peaceful settlement. The TUC sensed a trap and stayed away, but when ex-servicemen showed up, they, too, were arrested. As the streets were cleared over the next few days, the police also began arresting most of Nkrumah's senior CPP colleagues. Amid this campaign of lawfare by the colonial state, they were charged and convicted expeditiously, variously, of promoting an illegal strike, of attempting to coerce the government, or of sedition. For the time being, though, Nkrumah had been spared arrest, even during a visit to his party headquarters. As it had following the Accra riots after the shooting of repatriated veterans in 1948, the slowness of the authorities to arrest Nkrumah fed popular myths about his occult powers and possible invincibility. Some said that Nkrumah's secret consort was Mami Wata, a sea goddess of legend throughout West Africa, and that she had conferred upon him the power to disappear, and to anticipate the moves of the white man one or two steps in advance.

That changed on the morning of January 22, 1950, when Nkrumah once again approached his headquarters, seeing from a distance that it had been thoroughly ransacked. He would later learn that his lifelong personal assistant, Nyamekeh, had been arrested there and beaten by police, along with some of his other associates, after they refused to disclose Nkrumah's whereabouts. Police agents rushed Nkrumah as he drew closer to his trashed office on foot. From there, he was bundled off in a van to the James Fort Prison, a slave dungeon and gold entrepot built by the Royal African Company of England in 1673. There, Nkrumah was jailed in a row of dank cells hidden away behind the fort's thick, black-striped walls until his trial, which ended quickly. Nkrumah was convicted, like his peers, of inciting an illegal strike and coercion and sentenced to two consecutive years in prison. In a separate trial in Cape Coast, Nkrumah was defended by Archibald Casely Hayford, son of the famous pan-Africanist thinker. He was swiftly convicted of sedition over comments printed in a newspaper there and sentenced to a third year in prison. It would take Arden-Clarke, who had frustrated Sarawak's push for independence, some time to realize it, but now, from behind bars, where his reputation and popularity soared, it was Nkrumah who had the governor trapped.

CHAPTER FOURTEEN

Seek the Political Kingdom

O N HIS WAY TO BEING LOCKED UP IN JANUARY 1950, NKRUMAH CROSSED paths with one of his top lieutenants, Komla Gbedemah, who was simultaneously being released from jail. With this encounter's distant Biblical echoes of Jesus encountering Peter after his arrest in the Garden of Gethsemane, this must count as another of the extraordinary coincidences that marked Nkrumah's life. The younger Gbedemah, a balding, sharp-eyed, and supremely confident-looking man, had met Nkrumah in their days boarding at Achimota. The two had then fallen out of touch for two decades, during which time Gbedemah had made a living as a building subcontractor with the Seventh Day Adventists. He would soon become one of Nkrumah's most capable and trusted associates, but much later in their lives, Gbedemah would become a rival and source of great intrigue.

Gbedemah had reunited with his old acquaintance during the Watson Commission investigation of the unrest that had ensued after the police shooting of the ex-servicemen who marched on Christianborg Castle. Like police officials in the United States who reflexively claim that people who die in their custody violently resisted arrest, even when they didn't, the colonial authorities concocted a cover story for the shooting incident.

In a statement titled "Here Is the Truth," the colonial administration claimed that the rioting in downtown Accra had preceded the shooting of the marching war veterans, thus explaining why the police guarding the castle were on edge. By this time, the African American press was keenly following events in the Gold Coast and poured scorn on the official justifications for the use of force against protesters and the loss of life. In a dispatch from London that appeared under the headline "British Rulers Whitewashed in African Riots," the *Chicago Daily Tribune* decried what it called "the old refrain that the police were right and the natives are Communist." The newspaper also pointedly reminded its readers why they should care about such a faraway event, noting that under Britain, the colony had once been a rich source of slaves for North America.[1]

Gbedemah powerfully undermined the British disinformation, testifying convincingly that he had arrived from out of town and was completely unaware of the ex-servicemen's march. He said he drove through central Accra at 2:35 pm that afternoon—just before the shooting—and all was still calm in the streets. "I was not only angry about it, I was depressed that these foreigners could rule [over] us in our own land with lies and untruth[s]," he recalled years later. "And that is why, in fact, I decided to join the political fighting."[2]

In October 1949, Gbedemah was convicted of publishing false news and sentenced to six months of hard labor, later shortened by six weeks. This reflected the sharp escalation in the colonial government's efforts to muzzle Nkrumah's movement. A few months earlier, Nkrumah, too, had been arrested on contempt charges related to articles published in the *Accra Evening News*, but when large crowds formed daily outside of the courtroom for his trial, the authorities thought better of jailing him.

In their furtive conversation at the courthouse, Nkrumah directed Gbedemah in hushed tones to take charge of the *Evening News* and to oversee party organization in his absence. Nkrumah later wrote that he told Gbedemah, "I'll do my utmost to keep in touch with you somehow, though goodness knows how."[3] In his own, slightly lengthier account, Gbedemah said that when they crossed paths in the courthouse, an iron gate between them, Nkrumah inquired blandly, "How are you, how are things? . . . How is your wife and how are the children?" before asking Gbedemah, "So what are you going to do?"

> [Nkrumah] kept quiet for a moment and then he raised his face and I saw tears streaming down his eyes. I said, "Kwame, if I tell you some things are in God's hands, is that cause for you to cry? Everything is in God's hands," I said. Then he understood my meaning and after a while he said, "O.K. Goodbye. Good luck to you." And he told the warder, "Let's go."[4]

Nkrumah's account shows himself to be resolute. Gbedemah's reveals Nkrumah to have been more vulnerable. Whichever the case, history would show there could hardly have been a better choice to manage the affairs of the Convention People's Party while its leader was behind bars.

With Nkrumah on ice, the old UGCC, long favored by the governor, sat on its hands; it was lulled into complacency by the belief that, as J. B. Danquah said, the "wolf had been driven away."[5] But the energetic Gbedemah wasted no time making rounds throughout much of the colony in order to establish new party branches and to begin identifying potential candidates in the legislative elections that Arden-Clarke had scheduled for February 9, 1951, which was just shy of a year in the future.

Nkrumah soon found himself treated as a common criminal, confined to a cell stuffed with ten other recently convicted members of his party. To humiliate them, they were forced to share a single latrine bucket, with no curtain or divider for privacy. Their bland food rations consisted of paltry servings of watery porridge and boiled corn or cassava-based dishes. And in an effort to neutralize them politically, they were not allowed to receive newspapers or send more than one letter a month, which had to be to an immediate family member and was written under the watchful eyes of a censor.

Nkrumah, who had always been particular about both hygiene and privacy, grew a full beard because he couldn't abide the idea of sharing a razor blade with his cellmates. As some of the shock of the rude conditions he faced in jail wore off, though, he busily made plans. From the start, the CPP had ardently opposed the Coussey Report. The decision that loomed now was whether it should participate in elections under the Coussey arrangement. Nkrumah later wrote that after weighing this at length, he decided that campaigning offered the best chance to accelerate the end of colonial rule. For politicians who were still novices, this was an important lesson in pragmatism.

Nkrumah's pragmatism involved something more, though. If he could get himself elected to the assembly, he believed, the government would probably feel obliged to shorten his sentence. The influential old-line British weekly *West Africa* had been founded toward the end of the First World War with a self-described mission to document how "the commercial and food products of [the region] are vitally necessary to the Empire in war, and scarcely less so in peace."[6] In December 1950, even it saw the need for the Colonial Office to bend with the suddenly changing times. "Mr. Nkrumah, whether you agree with him or not, is much the most capable leader of the party, and is the most popular individual in the Gold Coast. Clearly, if he remains in gaol, the new government [that would be formed after the February elections] will be like Hamlet without the prince," it editorialized.[7] Ironically, the Coussey Report had included a narrow loophole that would allow Nkrumah to run. Convicts serving sentences of more than one year were banned from seeking office, but Nkrumah's three sentences, for incitement of an illegal strike, coercion of the government, and in a separate case, sedition related to a newspaper article, were limited to a year apiece.

The CPP prisoners launched themselves into all kinds of post-prison planning, forming committees and subcommittees for all the various functions of government, which they now aimed to conquer via the ballot box. Writing materials were banned in the jail, forcing Nkrumah to come up with a clandestine method of composing his thoughts and communicating with Gbedemah on the outside. He got hold of a pencil stub, which he hid in his pants waist, and wrote on squares of toilet paper, for which he bartered away rationed food with fellow prisoners. Anticipating the methods of the imprisoned Nelson Mandela a decade and a half later, Nkrumah used these materials to scrawl an entirely new CPP manifesto during the nights, working under the pale flicker of the nearest streetlamp.

Early on, Gbedemah had registered as a candidate for Accra Central, one of the capital's two legislative seats, and the most prominent in the country. But once Nkrumah's right to be a candidate had been confirmed, Gbedemah switched his own registration to another town, allowing the imprisoned party leader to run in the capital in his place. The CPP lacked the financial resources of the UGCC and its wealthy patrons, but under Gbedemah's leadership, it settled upon an ingenious campaign to rally public support by making a virtue of one of its biggest liabilities.

Nearly all of the party's leaders had been locked up during the crackdown on Public Action, but as they were released, one by one, the party took to publicly celebrating them as "prison graduates." Thus, the CPP ably turned serving time into a badge of virtue, and a series of rituals was organized around the release of detainees, including "graduation" ceremonies and press coverage to fête them. Most famously, this came to involve crowning those who were let out of jail in distinctive white headgear that resembled a Muslim prayer cap, with the letters PG (for prison graduate) prominently woven on them in florid cursive.

Before long, Arden-Clarke, too, sensed what was coming. The CPP was building a popular following quite unlike any other party, and this created a dilemma for him that mirrored the one Nkrumah had recently faced in deciding whether or not to contest the elections. If the governor aborted a voting exercise that he himself had set in motion, or he otherwise changed its rules mid-course, the CPP would probably grow even stronger, and the colony might very well become ungovernable. But if he stood back and observed as a neutral enforcer of the rules, Nkrumah and the CPP, which Arden-Clarke had worked so hard to defang, would surely triumph. As Arden-Clarke wrote:

Nkrumah and his party had the mass of the people behind them and there was no other party with appreciable public support to which we could turn. Without Nkrumah, the Constitution would be still-born and if nothing came of all the hopes, aspirations and concrete proposals for a greater measure of self-government, there would no longer be any faith in the good intentions of the British Government . . . the Gold Coast would be plunged into disorders, violence and bloodshed.[8]

But the governor's clarity was belated. During the long months of campaigning in 1950, Arden-Clarke's government often seemed incapable of getting out of its own way; even actions intended to show Britain's goodwill backfired. The governor announced a list of new permanent secretaries appointed to administer a colony supposedly headed for self-rule. In the British tradition, civil servants like these perform most of the hands-on work that makes government ministries run. Yet all the new secretaries were white, despite years of dissatisfaction over the trickling pace of "Africanization," since the relatively accommodating UGCC first expressed that grievance.

Late in the year, the administration tried to remedy the negative political impact of its staffing announcement by naming a Gold Coast native to the newly created post of Commissioner for Africanization, to be "responsible for . . . ensuring that the maximum of suitably qualified African candidates became available for appointment to the higher grades of the public service."[9] This was akin to a modern-day Western corporation waking from a deep slumber to the need for diversity, and merely appointing members of minority groups to DEI (diversity, equity, and inclusion) positions. What is worse, this curiously rear-guard action, which reflected the weakest possible form of affirmative action, was being taken in a country now fairly speeding toward self-rule.

While the government dutifully went about the business of drawing constituency boundaries and encouraging people to register in a country that had never held a popular vote, the CPP, under Gbedemah's leadership, quickly demonstrated its verve at campaigning. It mounted loudspeakers on party vehicles and screened short public-service films outdoors. A CPP flag of red, white, and green was designed, and the colors were painted on the ubiquitous vans that drove through market areas and populous neighborhoods blasting campaign slogans. With their every passage, these drew lusty roadside cheers and the honking of horns from drivers of taxis and the battered fleet of collective transport small trucks and buses locally known as mammy wagons and *tro tro*. Red, white, and green swag, too, could now be found everywhere. A distinctive party salute was rolled out, perhaps the fruit of Nkrumah's revolutionary mentoring by Padmore in London. It called for the raising of one hand with an open palm while shouting "Freedom!" To attract big crowds, dances were held, and theatrical performances staged. Perhaps the most effective campaign tactic of all centered on the use of Nkrumah's portrait, in Lenin-like fashion, which appeared everywhere.

"One of the tools I used was to have a full, life-sized photograph of Nkrumah made into three parts so that it made a decent small parcel," the fervently religious Gbedemah later wrote. "And this I carried around . . . for the campaign. Nkrumah's body is in jail but his spirit is going on. Now how can we not vote for such a man?"[10] Christianity had very deep roots in much of the Gold Coast, and the religious overtones in the messaging, which positioned Nkrumah as a kind of martyr or spiritual warrior, were anything but accidental. Such things would sometimes spill into Nkrumah's characterizations of himself, as well, even years later, as a personality cult exploded around him. Describing the public adoration he received, Nkrumah could sound like he was talking about John the Baptist or of Jesus himself.

Even though its barons had helped draft the rules of the Coussey Committee, the UGCC invested itself much less in campaigning. Having expected power to fall into its lap for so long, it showed little of the spirit needed to successfully fight for it. As if anticipating a drubbing, in November 1950, Paa Grant, the timber merchant who had housed Nkrumah in England and later sponsored the UGCC, said of his party, "Our aim is not just to present candidates; we must really get first class people into the Assembly." This was a party inescapably attuned to what it fancied as a better class of people, and this was not just a matter of education. The UGCC was not an ethnic party, but many of the leading figures were descendants of the Gold Coast's various hereditary aristocracies.

With its appeal to the broad proletariat—people who worked in artisanal jobs, or part-time or semi-skilled laborers, market women, and verandah boys, the CPP was focused on turnout. In rewriting the CPP manifesto, Nkrumah had deployed what would become one of the most famous phrases of his political life, also vaguely biblical: "Seek Ye first the Political Kingdom and All Things will be added unto it." Simply put, this meant, as he would write later, "The people of the country needed political power to manage their own affairs."[11] Only by daring to insist on control over their own lives, rather than living under colonial servitude, would Africans be able to begin addressing their most fundamental challenges of economic development and self-defined democracy.

Ably and steadily, Gbedemah's campaign played on this theme, promising the people of the Gold Coast that their destiny was in their own hands; it only awaited unlocking by the act of registering to vote and going to the polls. As one editorial in the *Evening News* starkly intoned:

> Should anybody fail to register his or her name today then that body forfeits his or her own liberty. This is the hour calling all real and dutiful citizens of this country to their duty.... It is this registration that will prove that we should have our S.G. [Self Government] now or wait in further squalor and discontent for the next hundred years.[12]

In keeping with this spirit, campaigning by the CPP never slackened—not even on election day, February 9, 1951. That month, France had bowed to the inevitable and recognized the sovereignty of the State of Vietnam. In the United States, credit cards, a harbinger of the country's dominant financial power, were introduced and used for the first time, and the American senator Joseph McCarthy claimed possession of a list of 205 communist infiltrators in the State Department, thus launching what became known as McCarthyism. Although the government had forbidden partisan sloganeering on the day of the vote, Gbedemah ordered the party's vans to go about blasting the message: "Today is election day, protest, don't forget to go and vote, but vote wisely." This drew complaints from the outmaneuvered UGCC, but the colony's electoral commissioner ruled in in the CPP's favor.[13] Beyond even the dreams of Nkrumah and Gbedemah, when the election finally came, urgent messages like these had carried the day.

That evening, already certain that the CPP would receive the most support, but less sure that ballots would be transparently and accurately counted, Gbedemah went to the commission's headquarters to witness the tallying of the vote. Reginald Saloway, the colonial secretary who had fenced with Nkrumah just months earlier, eventually called Gbedemah into his office to tell him, "Mr. Gbedemah, you are the winner, you have to make a speech."[14]

"At long last the battle is over," Gbedemah improvised before a crowd gathered outside. "Our Convention People's Party has won by an overwhelming majority. The people have spoken the language imperialists understand, the language of the ballot box. From now on we are carrying out another duty—to prove that we could do it."[15]

From behind bars, Nkrumah received hourly updates from his warders on the night of the election. The reports became more and more positive as they poured in, but he felt too anxious to sleep. Finally, at four in the morning came news that he had been elected by landslide to his Accra Central constituency, with 22,780 votes. This was ten times more than his opponent. And by morning, it was becoming increasingly clear that the victory was not Nkrumah's alone. The other CPP candidate up for election in Accra had also outpolled Ako Adjei, Nkrumah's good friend from Lincoln and London. It was Adjei who had recommended Nkrumah to the UGCC, and he had remained loyal to that party. Now, the CPP was winning almost across the board countrywide. When the smoke had cleared, the CPP had captured a rousing thirty-four of the thirty-eight seats that were popularly contested in the colony even though, just a few months earlier, the government appeared to have handily defeated positive action, and with it, the insurgent nationalist, Nkrumah.

Arden-Clarke had both underestimated his foe and the historical forces that were carrying him along. In the following decade, as was the case with Martin Luther King Jr., another disciple of Gandhi who was buoyed by his jailing in Birmingham, Alabama, the crackdown against the peaceful resistance of positive action had turned Nkrumah and his fellow leaders of the CPP into true national heroes, martyrs even, at least while they were imprisoned, and alumni of jail afterward, celebrated upon their release and distinguished forever by their PG caps.

Enormous crowds began to form around James Fort Prison early on the morning after the vote, converging before its heavy black gates. That evening, the British chief of police called in Gbedemah to express his concern that a bid to spring Nkrumah from jail might be in the works. "You should stop it; don't let them do this, otherwise you will spoil everything you have worked for," the chief told him. Following his advice, Gbedemah rushed to the prison and told the crowd, "We have won a victory. Let's enjoy the benefits of it. Don't spoil it. Go home all of you, we will meet tomorrow."[16] Remarkably, the excited crowd promptly complied.

Three days later, Arden-Clarke summoned Gbedemah and other members of the CPP executive to tell them that Nkrumah would be released at 1 p.m. that afternoon. As with the message of the police chief, the news came with an implicit threat. "I am giving you advanced notice so that you will organize. There is no disorder in the country—otherwise you will forfeit the election you have won."[17]

No sooner had he left the meeting, then Gbedemah dispatched party vans around Accra to spread the electrifying news of Nkrumah's imminent release, and to simultaneously warn the people "no violence and no disturbances."[18] Within half an hour, he said, the whole area surrounding James Fort was thronging with jubilant party supporters. When Nkrumah walked out, beaming into the harsh daylight, a prison graduate cap was placed on his head. "I was too bewildered to do anything but stand and stare. I don't think I have ever seen such a thickly packed crowd in the whole of my life," he would write.[19] Then he was hoisted aloft.

For fear of being trapped in the crowd, Gbedemah nudged the group carrying Nkrumah toward an open car waiting nearby. Inching their way forward they drove to the West Accra Arena, the CPP's ceremonial birthplace and a favored rallying spot during the independence struggle's most difficult moments. At the party's founding event there in 1949, in deference to local traditions like those that had gotten him into trouble at Lincoln, a sheep had been sacrificed and Nkrumah had trod in its blood seven times. A free man now in the fullest sense, he addressed another large crowd as ecstatic women dressed in flowing white robes danced in the front rows and the cheering and stomping of partisans raised clouds of dust all around. When he had finished, a knot of his closest aides surrounded Nkrumah and escorted him to the party headquarters where he had been arrested the year before. A second crowd greeted him there chanting the slogan, "there is victory for us!" Once indoors, overcome by emotion, Nkrumah collapsed on the nearest chair.[20]

The next day, Nkrumah was summoned to his first face-to-face meeting with Arden-Clarke. It was a signal moment in history, not just for the Gold Coast, but for the entire African continent, where the election news had spread far and wide, stoking dreams of freedom for others. The London *Observer* said that it had been bold of the government to allow Nkrumah to take office and dolefully predicted that the man from the Gold Coast would become "an African Perón, but with less discretion and a touch of Marxism."[21] A scornful and bigoted item in the international section of *Newsweek* labeled Nkrumah as "openly pro-Communist," and a "tomcat triumphant," who maintained a hold on his followers through "voodoo." It went on to denigrate his supporters as illiterates who substituted his name for Christ's in familiar English hymns.[22] The Black-owned *Philadelphia Tribune* reported this watershed of emancipation in a completely different spirit, connecting African liberation with African American freedom. It did so by noting that Nkrumah's prison release following his electoral victory had coincided with Abraham Lincoln's birthday.[23] Never had there been a meeting between an urgent advocate of independence who had just won a ringing victory at the polls and the colonial governor of an empire not quite resigned to relinquishing its hold on a subjugated people, and both men faced the encounter with anxiousness and doubts.

That their sit-down together in Christianborg Castle would become a foundational set piece in the country's path to independence was obvious. Less famously, Nkrumah gave a press conference that same day that helps frame the serious compromises he had to face. In it, he called the constitution that resulted from the Coussey Report "bogus and fraudulent," because it would create the false appearance of giving power to Africans, when in fact, Arden-Clarke, as governor, would continue to enjoy veto power over a new cabinet dominated by African faces. Even this was deceptive, though.[24] Nkrumah would not become prime minister. He would instead carry the awkward and distinctly more diminutive title of leader of government business. The most powerful ministerial functions, the attorney general, finance, foreign policy, and security, would all remain under British control. Even the staffing of the civil service remained under London's purview. "There is great risk in accepting office under this new constitution, which still makes us half slaves and half free," Nkrumah told his party colleagues. And still, he accepted the bargain with the devil, however reluctantly, branding this new phase of his struggle "Tactical Action," a phrasing that signaled the replacement of insurgency with pragmatism.

> It was felt that had we not accepted office by virtue of our majority in the Assembly, but had we embarked on non-cooperation and remained in the Opposition, we would merely have been pursuing a negative course of action. It was moreover the opinion of the Party Executive that by taking part in the new government, we were at least preventing the "stooges and reactionaries" from taking advantage of the position. Governmental positions could also help us to obtain the initiative in the continuing struggle for full self-government.[25]

As big as the challenges their first meeting presented to the two men, Nkrumah and Arden-Clarke, each brimming with suspicion of the other, seem to have gotten on well. This can be deduced from things they each wrote later, but it can also be seen in the record of the next three-plus years of their unusual power-sharing arrangement. Nkrumah had reason to feel aggrieved, but he knew that nursing his frustrations openly would ill-serve him. He was too keenly aware of the ways he needed the cooperation of a governor who still held so many cards. What Arden-Clarke was seeking, for his part, was to submit Nkrumah to a probationary period of British tutelage. The tacit bargain he was willing to extend went something like this: accept the Westminster model that we proudly bequeath to you, behave prudently while exercising your limited powers, and if things go well, we will eventually grant your desire for fuller autonomy. As recently as a few months earlier, British officials had imagined preserving their authority in the Gold Coast for another generation.[26] Arden-Clarke understood now that his power and control were limited. Winds were already blowing in an unmistakable direction around the world that made clear that one way or another, the colonial era would soon have to end. The game for the governor was all about preserving British interests, including its global image, and in controlling the pace at which it inevitably relaxed its grip.

Arden-Clarke had one more thing going for him. With his plumed helmet, braided gold epaulettes, and the constellation of medals that sparkled on his red-sashed chest, representing not one, but three saints—Michael, George, and James—he was the perfect embodiment of British cosmological bluster. Nkrumah had been denouncing imperialism for years, but now he was to meet with its incarnation in an actual castle. It was a slave trading fort by origin, to be sure, but it was universally known simply as "The Castle." And with its long rows of canons facing outward toward the ceaseless rollers of the Atlantic, and its stark white walls and high tower with a flowing flag on top, it looked like one. It was there, in Arden-Clarke's redoubt that Nkrumah was to stand eye to eye and shake hands with a doubly knighted representative of the king. After having traveled this far, it is hard to think of Nkrumah as being intimidated, but he seems, nonetheless, to have been somewhat disarmed.

> Had I known this man before, I should not have doubted the courtesy that would be shown me. A tall, broad-shouldered man, sun-tanned, with an expression of firmness and discipline, but with a twinkle of kindness in his eyes came towards me with his hand outstretched ... a man with a strong sense of justice and fair play, with whom I could easily be friends.[27]

Soon after they met for the first time, Arden-Clarke recorded his impressions of Nkrumah in a letter to his family, and one can't help but feel a certain symmetry in the tentative but open-minded way the two now spoke of each other:

> I do not know what to make of Nkrumah. My first impressions, for what they are worth, are that he is an idealist, ready to live up to his ideals, but I have yet to learn what those ideals really are. Unlike most of his colleagues he seems quite genuinely to bear no ill-will for his imprisonment and is not venal. He has little sense of humor but has considerable personal charm. He is as slow to laugh as he is quick to grasp the political

implications of anything he discusses. His approach to questions is more that of a psychologist than a realist. He has proved he can give inspiration and I find him susceptible of receiving it but I fear there is a streak of weakness that might be his undoing. A skillful politician, he has, I think, the makings of a real statesman and this he may become if he has the strength to resist the bad counsels of the scallywags by whom he is surrounded.[28]

Much of this was prescient. One cannot dismiss the psychological quite so easily, though. Arden-Clarke's framing reflected the common mindset of the powerful in a relationship of domination. Anger, for them, is the burden of the persecuted; something they alone must overcome. In one regard, though, the governor quickly extended his good offices. This was in response to the anger of the election's biggest losers, the barons of the UGCC. Paa Grant lashed out at Nkrumah, accusing him of "filching" the UGCC's program, and even most of its name. J. B. Danquah went further, saying:

Ruthlessly [Nkrumah] split the national front, then made a filthy deal with the British.... One day he said he wanted national freedom, and the next day he compromised with the British.[29]

The hypocrisy was evident. Before Nkrumah's rise to the fore, the approach of the UGCC, largely founded on gradualism, had scarcely budged the needle toward independence. Now they were implausibly accusing him of selling out to the British. This bit of bad faith augured especially poorly for the prospects of a colony approaching independence at last. How would its politicians be able to smoothly adopt a Westminster model, with its functional prerequisite of a loyal opposition? Set in his political convictions and sense of rightness about British ways, Arden-Clarke was poorly positioned to understand this. To his credit, though, he was able to see when his natural allies in the UGCC had gone too far, which they soon did. In addition to their bitter complaints about Nkrumah during the first days after the election, the men who had considered themselves the natural leaders of the colony made an outlandish demand: Nkrumah had the right to name Africans to eight of the incoming cabinet's ministerial posts. They said he should concede four of them to his old partners. It fell to Arden-Clarke to inform the UGCC that this was not the result that resounding electoral defeat had earned them; party politics didn't work that way. Showing greater maturity and conciliation than his rivals, Nkrumah nonetheless named Emmanuel Quist, a conservative baron of the old political class, as speaker.

Twelve days after Nkrumah's release from prison, the legislature met for the first time and, in near unanimity, approved his proposed cabinet. It contained figures like Gbedemah and Kojo Botsio, his most important allies during this phase of his political career. History offers many instances of politicians who have served time in prison only to go on to become statesmen, but examples of transitions this abrupt are exceedingly rare. As they sat in the hall, all his appointees wore prison graduate caps, save for one of them, Archibald Casely Hayford, more barrister for the party than man of the field. He wore a special cap, its initials reading, DVB, or defender of the verandah boys.

Three weeks later, on March 29, 1951, the new era was formally inaugurated as the parliament opened its first working session under an oil painting of the British monarch. The small and simple hall, with its tiers of long benches, filled quickly that morning with a combination of the well-connected and curious onlookers—all aware of the moment's import. Many Africans came draped in ceremonial kente cloth, with its bright hues of gold and green, or in the flowing white robes of Muslims from the north. Judges were there in formal white wigs. Crowding the visitor's gallery, a few of Nkrumah's friends from his years overseas had come to bear witness, and in the case of George Padmore, to proffer advice. A handful of reporters staked out positions here and there in the crowd.

At the appointed hour, Nkrumah entered the hall, striding down the red carpet, surrounded by his ministers, and finally everyone took their seats. Harsh midday light shone in from the windows at the sides. As people fidgeted in those tense moments, Nkrumah sat stoically, with a sheen playing on his black forehead. Then, telling sounds began to reverberate in the hall from the outside. The governor's delegation had saved its entry for last and had pulled up with police outriders and a full honor guard to gather in formal assembly by the entranceway. Arden-Clarke strode into the hall, tall and relaxed looking, even in his majestic white uniform and ever-present helmet.

A flurry of trumpet blasts was followed by the reading of a message from King George VI, whose reign was almost at an end. Then came a seventeen-gun salute. After a few other brief interventions, the governor read a speech on behalf of his government. And then, at last, it was Nkrumah's turn.

There was a hush in the hall as he gathered himself before announcing his project. It was firm and unambiguous, even pointedly redundant, but with no hint of bitterness or of well-earned defiance. If the Gold Coast would not have independence now, independence could not be deferred long:

> The Gold Coast people are determined to achieve self-government. They have been patient for a long time, but they have now reached the end of their tether. They are no longer prepared to be treated as second-class citizens in their own country. They are determined to have self-government, and they will not be satisfied with anything less. . . . They are determined to build a better future for themselves and for their children.[30]

As he brought his peroration to a close, Nkrumah strove for magnanimity. "I am confident that the British Government will grant the Gold Coast self-government. I believe that the British Government is a just and fair government, and that it will not deny the Gold Coast people their right to self-government."[31]

Beyond these grace notes, though, there was no mistaking what had just occurred. The first Black country in Africa was bound for independence, however uncertain the path ahead, and there had been very little granting at all. What had been achieved by Nkrumah and his movement was won, not bestowed. And although the bemedaled Arden-Clarke and the government and king that he represented were scarcely reduced to irrelevance, never again would they be in the driver's seat. Now, for the first time, without bloodshed, that would have to be vacated for Africans. It was only a question of how.

CHAPTER FIFTEEN

After the Ball (The Drums Are Heavy)

NKRUMAH'S MORNING AFTER OFFERED NO HONEYMOON. ON FEBRUARY 26, 1951, in a nearly unanimous vote, the National Assembly approved the eight ministers whose names Nkrumah put forth to man his cabinet.

Still a democracy only in name, the country's new system was actually an awkward halfway house between the outright dictatorship of colonial rule and a new regime of government genuinely by and for the people. The country's new nominal leader would be able to assert his authority freely, so long as the assembly on the one side, and the all-powerful governor, on the other, consented to his actions.[1]

Even Nkrumah's initial title reflected this. It reflected London's calculation before the vote and, indeed, its hope that no party would emerge with an outright majority. Having badly underestimated Nkrumah and his CPP, the hale and self-possessed Arden-Clarke, ever the projection of self-confidence, had prepared for the colony to be led by a British attorney general for an interim after the elections rather than by an African.

The strange new political contraption that Nkrumah was given to lead was burdened by yet another consideration. It came with a rusty old sidecar with a brake of its own in the form of the chieftaincy, whose feudal power the British had long favored and made sure to safeguard in the new assembly.

These were all big, structural problems that Nkrumah would spend the next six years and beyond struggling with. In the meantime, much more urgent and immovable constraints loomed. The party Nkrumah led was barely two years old, and although by now he had spent years theorizing about independence and working as a political organizer in the United States and especially in Britain, he had no hands-on experience of running anything.

What is more, however talented Gbedemah and certain others among his key allies were, none of them had any experience in government or anything even remotely analogous. This was not because the CPP was an insurgent party, as might be imagined. Colonial rule had hitherto given almost no opportunity for Africans to participate in the administrative lives of their countries, and that was by design.

Under the new, post-election dispensation, not only did the governor wield veto power and British appointees control the key portfolios, but the colonial secretary who had organized Nkrumah's arrest, Saloway, the commissioner of police who had executed it, and the crown counsel who had prosecuted him all still occupied their old positions.

Even more constraints came from the old civil service. Africans occupied about 20 percent of its jobs, but most of them had been very recent appointees who dwelled in the lowest ranks of the bureaucracy. Among those few who had risen a bit higher, the majority had been hastily promoted late during the period of Nkrumah's rise. African demands that the colony be endowed with a university dated back three-quarters of a century and now Britain's parsimony and political hesitations about more education for Africans weighed heavily. British power now resided, in the first instance, in the new government's dependence. How could things be sped up? The government offices that Nkrumah's cabinet would occupy had been emptied out. Knowledge of the day-to-day workings of the state resided with the whites who occupied the bureaus next door held by permanent secretaries, as these senior technical advisors and administrators were called.

Some of them were not only highly capable but often eager to contribute to the colony's success under the new regime. Even for those of good will, though, shifting gears did not come easily. Most felt that the colony in which they were ceding limited authority to Africans was basically already run sufficiently well. The job of the colonial government had never been to develop the country or bring it up to the level of more affluent nations. The longstanding spirit of tutelage that existed before Nkrumah burst onto the scene had only aimed at preparing for an independence that would come far in the future, and therefore existed only in theory. The task at hand was to keep things on their present course. Training Africans to run the place or occupy posts of policy formulation or administration could be pursued with all deliberate speed. In the meantime, the main hope was to keep the place quiet, avoid "trouble," and keep generating dollar surpluses for London through cocoa and gold exports.

Other expatriate advisors, however, could not abide seeing Blacks in jobs beyond near-menial responsibilities. "Instead of leaving the country as their conscience dictated, [they] chose for one reason or another to stay and battle on, making life miserable for themselves and objectionable for those with whom they came in contact," Nkrumah later wrote. "For instance it did not escape my notice that where the administrative service was concerned, if a policy was laid down for the officials by the Government with which they disagreed, means were adopted, by subterfuge or otherwise, to wreck that policy."[2] Others adopted a more insidious passive resistance, simply dragging their feet.

Nkrumah chose not to be more explicit, but it is not hard to understand the motivations of these hangers-on and the sources of their resentment toward Africans. In her memoir, Erica Powell, the British woman who went directly from being Arden-Clarke's personal secretary to working in that same role with Nkrumah for a decade, wrote:

> For whatever reasons we [white members of the colonial establishment] were in the country, it seemed that to mix freely with the African people was not one of them. The European Club, for instance, would admit no African, however high in rank, not even as a guest. The enclosed community of Europeans in which I now found myself seemed to be trying to cut themselves off from reality, while remaining blind to the existence of the black masses without. Their lives centred around the polo club, the tennis club, the golf club, the dining club and the European Club, which was simply called The Club. They might have been anywhere in the world.[3]

During her first weeks in the colony, in 1952, long before she had become acquainted with Nkrumah, Powell wrote that in nearly every conversation with fellow whites in which his name came up, Nkrumah was spoken of as a "rabble rouser," a "radical verging on communist," or dismissed as a "flash in the pan."[4]

The bind that he was in was obvious to Nkrumah. Africans rightly yearned for what became called Africanization, meaning the appointment of nationals throughout the civil service and administration. This was not just a matter of political symbolism, although that was certainly important. In an economy that still had little in the way of an African private sector, government jobs were prized, offering security, abundant pay, and basic benefits. But the best of these jobs—nearly eight hundred positions in all, down to the level of district commissioners in outlying areas—remained in the possession of whites, and this remained the case for years to come. This, Nkrumah noted, stood in stark contrast to the administrative capacity inherited by newly independent governments in India and Sri Lanka, where the British had made considerable investments in building a native civil service.

During that first year as leader of government business, Nkrumah delivered an address to the assembly in which he sought to allay the anxieties of European functionaries. Some of them openly bridled at his push for further constitutional changes to give more meaning to self-government. Others had difficulty accepting the idea of seeing Africans doing anything more mentally demanding than the work of a clerk. Toward this end, he had had to increase the compensation paid to the expatriate civil servants:

> We seek to avoid any sudden exodus of overseas officers and by safeguarding their future induce them to remain. While appreciating the need for accelerated Africanization, Government do not propose that this should be achieved at the expense of efficiency, or that promotion in the service should be on the basis of color.[5]

This was largely unavoidable, but to publicly express such thoughts showed considerable pragmatism and graciousness, given the strong pressure on Nkrumah to hire and promote Africans, and given what he knew about the attitudes of a considerable fringe of the remaining colonial civil servants.

Nkrumah had an ambitious political agenda that aimed for "full internal self-government" and an intensive, five-year development program, and these fed the high expectations of the public. The solitary Nkrumah responded to the vacuum around him by establishing a personal work regimen that few could match and which he would maintain nearly uninterrupted for the rest of his life. He was almost always up and busy by 4 a.m., using the predawn hours to sift through government reports, draft speeches, attend to correspondence, monitor news of the world, or simply read. In his desperation for solutions and impatience with delays, he began taking a personal hand in nearly everything that mattered to him. One acquaintance who knew him well in this period recalled that Nkrumah became obsessed with attending "to official business with care and concern above the ordinary. He was a stickler for discipline and hated lazy, slipshod or slovenly work of any kind."[6]

Most mornings, by the time of the first cock's crow, visitors gathered themselves in lines in his courtyard. These groups were composed of an accustomed mix of the humble and the prosperous. Their needs were all and sundry and in no way limited to matters before the government. Some sought patronage of various kinds, such as help in winning a civil service job or gaining access to school for a child or relative, others wanted his support in disputes over property, help with medical costs, or to appeal decisions by traditional chiefs to a higher authority. He felt that he couldn't let people down and took "trying to sort out the hundred-and-one problems they brought to place before me" as an inescapable duty.[7]

IT TOOK SOME SEARCHING, BUT I FINALLY FOUND THE HOUSE WHERE NKRUMAH lived during the early 1950s. It is on a quiet, unpaved side road just around the corner from a busy commercial street that crests one of Accra's shambling hills. There, in what used to be called Lagos Town, I discovered a large, flat-roofed, two-story, red brick building with white trimmings in a state of creeping desuetude. The neat, white rectangular sign that made no note of its history bore a curious address, 14 Elephant Walk Street. It sat behind a high, white wall with a red metal gate.

First, I knocked, then shouted, and then finally banged on the gate with my fist, before a man, who was naked to the waist, leaned out of the upper floor window bearing a look of annoyance to confirm that yes, this had once been Nkrumah's residence, and that no, I could not come inside. Further pleas from me were of no avail. Back in the day, instead of the cramped lot that I found, a fence or outer retaining wall offset the building from a generous yard. It was there that authorized visitors' cars parked and others were given chairs or simple stools to sit in the shade of trees, often for many hours, while they waited for a hoped-for audience. In the open air nearby, food was cooked throughout the day and portions shared with those who were patient.

By 8 a.m. Nkrumah, the onetime seminarian, was at the small, makeshift office provided to him in the main ministry building, just down the hall from the colonial secretary. There, many others lined up to speak with him, usually with more explicitly government- or business-related matters. From there, he would repair to his party's headquarters where yet more meetings and petitioners inevitably awaited him. Nkrumah seldom broke for a proper lunch, remaining at his desk and eating sparely on the fly while dealing with people into the evening. Powell, the tall and handsome large-boned woman who served as his English secretary, later wrote that Nkrumah displayed a "complete lack of concern for food—not only what he ate, but if and when he ate."[8]

He would return home for more rounds of meetings, some of them with people who had been waiting since the morning. Dinners inevitably came late, with him sitting at a table crowded with his cabinet ministers or party advisers for yet more discussions. Throughout, Nkrumah was cared for after a fashion by two people. There was his mother, Nyaniba, who still had her high, round cheeks but was slowing. And there was Nyamekeh, a nephew who would be his trusted manservant or majordomo until the end of his life. This was Nkrumah's inner world, his realm of comfort, a sanctum composed exclusively of his own people, Nzima like himself. And beyond them was Powell, whom Nkrumah could also not do without.

Nkrumah's work naturally brought him into constant contact with others, from the fellow party leaders and government ministers he worked with, to glad-handers and favor seekers, to diplomats and businessmen who ran the gamut from straight shooters to high-grade crooks and hustlers in expensive suits. Then there were the crowds he stirred; people who hung on his every word. As someone who knew him well wrote, he could "switch their emotions like a radio set."[9]

Still, Nkrumah was never truly at ease outside of the tiny, intimate circle he kept close by. When things needed doing, he didn't easily delegate, and in any event, there were few to whom he could reliably do so. The cost of all of this was not only a steep and insidious tax posed on Nkrumah's health. It was in the administrative and political vacuum Nkrumah inherited and in the nature of his desperate response to it that lay the foundations of a system of personalized rule that would powerfully shape both his own future and that of Ghana.

CHAPTER SIXTEEN

The Race Men

MAY 1951 SAW THE ESTABLISHMENT OF REGULARLY SCHEDULED DIRECT flights between New York and London. In another breakthrough that spring, hotels and restaurants in Washington, DC, were legally integrated. Willie Mays won rookie of the year that season, his first in the Major Leagues. And that award sunk a final nail into the coffin of segregation in America's most popular sport, and with it, hastened the doom of the Negro Leagues.

That May, amid what he called "the hurly-burly which seemed to be the pattern of my new life—an unworkable constitution, a disgruntled Opposition, an embryo office and a suspicious civil service," Nkrumah received an invitation to Lincoln University. The news that his alma mater had plans to confer upon him an honorary doctorate the very next month landed with total surprise. As Nkrumah wrote:

> It was just over six years since I had left America and I could not believe that such an honour could be bestowed upon me in so short a space of time. I felt that I had not done enough to merit it and my first inclination was to decline it.[1]

The Lincoln invitation had been the doing of Horace Mann Bond, the first Black man to lead the university and its president since 1949. Bond, a precocious African American student from Nashville, had graduated with honors from Lincoln in 1923 at nineteen and then earned advanced degrees from the University of Chicago. He had made his academic reputation with original research on the education of Blacks in the American South. In his first book, *The Education of the Negro in the American Social Order*, he questioned the use of IQ tests by the army to assess the intelligence of African American recruits.

This anticipated by decades a scholarly consensus that that would eventually find that standardized tests were anything but culturally neutral.

Subsequent work by Bond reappraised the history of the American Reconstruction Era and refuted the idea long held dear to champions of the myth of the "Lost Cause" and of the so-called Redemption, the period of resumed white supremacy across the South that followed Reconstruction. It held that profligacy caused by the entry of Blacks into government after the Civil War had driven the South into economic ruin.

In addition to being an original thinker, influential scholar, and part of what was still a very small cohort of academically trained Black historians in the United States, Bond was also a classic "race man." This once-common term was used for African Americans who wore pride in their identity openly and believed that their social duty was to do whatever they could to advance the prospects of Black Americans as a group. In many of the black and white photographs of Bond from this era, there's a hint of a scowl, and in that expression, I have often been tempted to read not just the flinty combativeness he was known for, but also smoldering resentment over the wages that racism in his society exacted from him and from Black people in general.

Although descended from enslaved great-grandparents, Bond was born into the Black middle class as the son of two college-going parents, a mother who became a schoolteacher, and a father who was a Congregational minister who preached throughout the South. As a boy, he was regaled with memories of Africa by his aunt Mamie, who had worked as a medical missionary on the continent. Then, as a young man, he had avidly read stories about Africa in the pages of Du Bois's NAACP journal, *The Crisis*, which often emphasized the existence of kingdoms and accounts of African achievement.[2] Du Bois wrote much of this content himself, beginning with the story of his first voyage to the continent, in 1923, when he visited Liberia, one of only two Black-ruled countries in the world at the time (although Haiti was then under American military occupation). Du Bois often lapsed into what one historian has called "a hyper-lyricism brought on by the sheer euphoria of having slipped the surly bonds of American racism."[3] "Africa is vegetation. It is the riotous, unbridled bursting life of lead and limb," Du Bois gushed in one typical column. It was also "sunlight in great gold globules," and "soft, heavy-scented heat," that produced a "divine, eternal languor."[4]

In 1949, Bond took the first of his own eventual ten trips to Africa, and it utterly reshaped his life. It wouldn't be an exaggeration to say that it also powerfully altered the historical trajectory of Black people on both sides of the Atlantic for the next two decades. Bond's interest in Nkrumah, and the bridge he helped build for him with African Americans, threw a precious lifeline to the emerging Gold Coast leader at a time when he had few other cards at his disposal. And it pointed to a possible future of deep and mutually strengthening ties between two parallel movements, one for civil rights in America, and the other for independence for Africa's colonies. Both were in dire need of allies as the world entered the Cold War.

Bond's early trips to Africa placed him at the forefront of an ideologically diverse group of African American intellectuals and political activists that would swell dramatically throughout this period—all of them fired up with the idea that the liberation of Africa and the battle for full citizenship rights for Black Americans were so fundamentally linked that if they were to advance at all, they would have to proceed in tandem.

In its first phase, this group included African Americans who had become familiar to the broad public: the novelist Richard Wright, the diplomat Ralph Bunche, the nationally prominent labor leader and elder statesman, A. Philip Randolph, and, just slightly later, a young Baptist minister named Martin Luther King Jr. Behind big names like these stood a panoply of others who also played crucial roles in building bonds between Black America and Africa but who mostly labored in relative anonymity. These included people such as William Alphaeus Hunton, a professor of English, and the historians Rayford Logan and William Leo Hansberry, all of whom taught at Howard University. The latter, uncle of the playwright, Lorraine Hansberry, had begun teaching African history at Howard in 1922. Four years later, with the appointment of Mordecai Wyatt Johnson, Howard got its first Black president, but it wasn't until two decades after that, in 1954, at Hansberry's initiative, that the university introduced the nation's first African Studies curriculum.[5]

As the example of Du Bois and others who have appeared prominently in this narrative illustrates, the dream of uniting Africans, African Americans, and other members of Africa's diaspora in a common struggle for political rights, full citizenship, and respect is a venerable one. The Second World War and its aftermath saw a recentering of pan-Africanist energy in Africa itself. After following the example of Lincoln's leadership by educating more and more students from Africa and the Caribbean, Black colleges and universities in the United States became a catalyst for this, spurring the development of a global Black consciousness movement. Not only did thinkers from different continents come together on these campuses, but with a critical mass came much more militantism. Here, although Lincoln had been the undeniable pathbreaker, it was Howard University that, starting even before the Second World War had ended, surged ahead to become the most important locus of ideas and activism linking Blacks from Africa and the diaspora in profound new ways.

Nnamdi Azikiwe of Nigeria has been called a "student zero" of African nationalism on American campuses for the way he had helped recruit African students, including Nkrumah, to historically Black colleges in the United States.[6] Although Azikiwe eventually graduated from Lincoln, he had transferred there from Howard, where he had been unable to pay the bills for his studies. It was at Howard, he later wrote, where "the idea of a new Negro evolved into the crusade for a new Africa."[7] This resulted from the intense stimulation he experienced on a campus that had been assembling a deepening bench of intellectual stars since Alain Locke, a Rhodes Scholar, was hired in the 1920s. In Azikiwe's case, it came from studying there under people like Leo Hansberry and Ralph Bunche.

At Howard, and wherever else a critical mass of students from Africa and the Black diaspora outside of the United States gathered, something else important began to occur: a sharing of experiences of exploitation and suffering under imperial rule. This also juiced campus progressivism. Learning from each other bred a bolder self-confidence, and as it did so, colonized and recently emancipated peoples began to lose whatever lingering patience they had with the temporizing of Western nations based on the supposed need for tutelage and gradual preparation for the responsibilities of self-government.

ON THE EVE OF THE PARIS EXHIBITION OF 1900 A PAN-AFRICAN CONFERENCE was convened in London for the first time. It grew out of the organizational efforts of a Trinidadian lawyer named Henry Sylvester Williams. Three years earlier, he had founded a group in London he called the African Association "to promote and protect the interests of all subjects claiming African descent, wholly or in part, in British colonies and other place[s], especially African, by circulating accurate information on all subjects affecting their rights and privileges as subjects of the British empire, by direct appeals to the Imperial and local Governments."[8]

This London conference attracted the interest of Booker T. Washington and the direct participation of his rival, Du Bois. It also drew on the active and remarkably prominent participation of numerous women, from the Black South African activist Alice Victoria Kinloch to Anna Julia Cooper. The latter, born into slavery in North Carolina, was the Oberlin- and Sorbonne-trained principal of the segregated M Street High School (formally the Preparatory High School for Colored Youth) that my maternal grandmother attended in

Washington, DC. She was also the founder there of a group called the Colored Women's League.

This first pan-African conference received widespread notice in the British press and sought to engender political change, mainly by influencing public opinion. At its conclusion, the signatories issued a letter to Queen Victoria, only a year before her death, inviting "your august and energetic attention to the fact that the situation of the native races in South Africa is causing us and our friends alarm." Among the conditions it cited were indentured labor and racial segregation imposed through a strictly enforced pass system.[9]

By the time of the second major gathering of this type—then-styled a Pan-African Congress—in Paris in 1919, even Du Bois still espoused gradualism. Du Bois sailed to Europe shortly after writing a "Memorandum on the Future of Africa," which proposed the creation of an "independent Negro Central African State," which would be run as a trusteeship to be overseen by "the thinking classes of the future Negro world," a kind of talented tenth of the diaspora, which he said included "the twelve million civilized Negroes of the United States."[10]

In Paris, Du Bois enjoyed a meeting of minds with Blaise Diagne of Senegal, then a deputy in the parliament and high commissioner of African troops for the French government. Both men agreed on the idea that the valorous wartime service of Blacks, whether Africans or Americans, should open the pathway toward true democratic citizenship rights wherever they lived.[11] Diagne convinced an initially skeptical prime minister Georges Clemenceau to allow Du Bois to convene his congress on French soil, but only after Du Bois promised him that he would not criticize French colonial rule.[12] True to this commitment, the delegates modestly resolved: "The natives of Africa must have the right to participate in the government as fast as their development permits."[13]

Before the end of the next world war, though, the pan-Africanism of Africans (and Blacks from the Caribbean) began to eclipse that of Black Americans both in terms of energy and initiative. A new urgency was felt across a variety of venues, from the campus of Howard University in Washington, DC, to the Fifth Pan-African Conference in Manchester, England, in October 1945, and increasingly on West Indian and African soil, as well. Instead of the old gradualism, these activists now openly yearned for what Nkrumah would turn into his rallying cry in 1947, "Freedom Now!"

Here arises an unavoidable irony. With the notable exception of Du Bois, whose politics grew steadily more radical as mid-century approached, along with a few others, many African American intellectuals during the war and its early aftermath still tended to be conservative in their internationalism.

Their caution flowed from multiple sources, starting with the fact that African Americans constituted but a small minority—12 percent—of the country's population. But that was not all. Jim Crow, with all its menace and violence, had shown no sign of easing in the South, while Blacks in the North faced boiling hostility to even modest gestures toward legal and social equality and integration. All the while, the Cold War sharply increased pressure for political conformity and narrowed the political space for dissent.

Where the experience of African Americans most closely mirrored that of Africans (and of others in the Black diaspora) was in their treatment during and immediately after World War II. Soldiers of color of disparate origins were deployed in theaters of combat whose citizens also came in a wide variety of skin hues and were often as dark as they were. This was true in the US Pacific campaign and in Burma, where Black Americans, laboring in jungles under extreme duress, built the second Burma Road. This alone made it possible for Allied armies to resupply their troops overland in the East. These were eye-opening experiences for African Americans, much as they had been for African troops, and they deepened their standing conviction in the innate equality of Black soldiers with their white counterparts.

What is more, after African soldiers were shipped back to their colonial homelands, they bridled at the evident unwillingness of Europeans to accept them as equals and initiate moves to end their imperial domination. At the same time, African Americans were returning home from the war with heightened expectations of a new dispensation. This meant breaking America's legalized inequality and discrimination and being treated with equality and respect. Alas, they would become as disenchanted as their transatlantic peers.

By and large, the Western reading public, including most Europeans, has never learned of the service record or wartime experiences of Africans. With African Americans, though, a different sort of erasure is at work. The self-mythologizing common to all nations, the U.S. need to construct a postwar ideology to rival the Soviet Union, and the deeply segregated American news and entertainment media combined to create a monochrome fable of a noble Greatest Generation. And from this legend, the experiences of Blacks and other Americans of color were etiolated, almost entirely written out.

In 1944, *Life* magazine, the country's most powerful framer of popular memory, published a handsomely bound pictorial history of World War II. Its 368 pages contained more than one thousand photographs, but as the historian Matthew Delmont deftly observed, only *one* of them showed a Black American. And even this image did not highlight Black Americans' actual contribution; rather it depicted a uniformed US Navy accordion player weeping at the passage of Franklin Roosevelt's funeral train—an image that fit snugly within the tradition of minstrelsy.[14]

African Americans, like Africans, imagined that the sacrifices in blood and hardships of every other kind brought on by the war would help usher in a new era for them—of equal citizenship rights, democracy, and vastly expanded economic opportunity. Given America's racial history, though, Black intellectuals and ordinary folk alike were wary. In fact, an intellectual tradition dating back to 1899 and to the most famous formulation of Du Bois's life, stated that *the* problem of the twentieth century is the problem of the color line. This predisposed no small number of African Americans to look skeptically upon America's possible involvement there as Hitler unleashed war on Europe. George Schuyler, a kind of Black H. L. Mencken and nationally famous columnist for the *Pittsburgh Courier*, who turned sharply conservative in the late 1930s after leaning left early in his career, bluntly called the conflict a "white man's war." In a 1939 column, he wrote:

> So far as the colored peoples of the earth are concerned it is a toss-up between the "democracies" and the dictatorships. . . . [W]hat is there to choose between the rule of the British in Africa and the rule of the Germans in Austria?[15]

Much later in this account, a man named Malcolm Little, who came to be universally known as Malcolm X, would come to play an important role in the unfolding history of relations between Black Americans and Africans. In 1943, though, when he went by his street name, Detroit Red, Little approached the race-line problems posed by the war from another angle altogether. Hauled before the army's Selective Service System, he objected that he had nothing against another non-white race like the Japanese and told his interviewer that he couldn't wait to "get sent down South. Organize them nigger soldiers, you dig? Steal us some guns, and kill us crackers!"[16] To be sure, this was mostly a ploy to avoid being drafted, but it was also a potent restatement of Du Bois's color line.

Large numbers of African Americans, in contrast to Malcolm Little, were eager to support the war and to fight for their country, but they, too, were confronted with the stark limitations imposed by their society's racism and hostility toward Blacks. The United States Army was a rigidly segregated force at the outbreak of the conflict and remained so long afterward. Initially, it did not recruit Black men at all, and even after opening the door a crack, actively discouraged Black enlistment. Late in the war, it imposed a formal quota ceiling on Blacks, limiting their enrollment to their overall weight in the American population.

Segregation was so zealous that American officers drew pushback from their British counterparts when they asked for bars and nightclubs near Allied bases in the country to be segregated to keep Black soldiers out and away from white women. This prompted George Orwell to write that "[t]he general consensus of opinion is that the only American soldiers with decent manners are the negroes."[17]

The military's obsession with racial separatism extended down to the costly and painstaking separation of blood collected and stored for the treatment of wounded soldiers. Blacks were excluded from the marines and, initially, from the Army Air Force, as well. In the navy, they were limited to steward duty. Everywhere Blacks received notoriously inferior training and equipment. Ultimately, more than one million African Americans served during the war, including my father, then a medical doctor in training at Howard University who narrowly missed deployment near the conflict's end but was served a long draught of humiliation, instead, forced to pick cotton at Camp Barkeley, in Texas, in plain view of Nazi prisoners.

Space doesn't allow a fuller airing of the range of indignities like these that African Americans suffered during the war, but even the most convincing candidates for celebration as war heroes, men like Doris "Dorie" Miller, were spurned. A Black cook second class in the navy, Miller had rescued wounded fellow shipmates aboard the USS *West Virginia* during the Japanese attack on Pearl Harbor. Despite his complete lack of combat training, Miller manned an antiaircraft gun and shot down several attacking aircraft, firing until he ran out of ammunition. In January of 1942, the navy merely issued a commendation for a *nameless* Black man. Coverage of this slight of Miller in the *Pittsburgh Courier* prompted a campaign of letter writing to demand that he be honored. As a result, that May, Chester W. Nimitz, the Commander in Chief of the US Pacific Fleet, finally decorated Miller with the Navy Cross for his gallantry, making him one of the first American heroes of the war.

The Dorie Miller story served as an object lesson for African Americans proving that there were two fights underway. One of them was a battle to integrate the armed services. The other aimed to win full political rights and end segregation in the United States overall, while obtaining a fair share of the economic benefits from the enormous war spending during the Roosevelt years. At the same time, of course, there was a war against fascism overseas. These struggles were explicitly twinned in what came to be known as the

Double V (Victory) campaign, meaning triumph over white supremacy in America as well as Europe.

Double V had multiple progenitors. Rayford Logan, the Howard University political scientist, had pushed a similar idea under a different name. It was the *Courier*, though, that popularized the slogan that stuck, following the Dorie Miller affair, when it published the letter of a twenty-six-year-old African American from Wichita named James Thompson, in January 1942. Crystalizing the widespread feeling that liberation for Blacks from segregation and racism at home could not be separated from the war effort to liberate Europe from fascism, he wrote:

> I suggest that while we keep defense and victory in the forefront that we don't lose sight of our fight for true democracy at home. The V for victory sign is being displayed prominently in all so-called democratic countries which are fighting for victory over aggression, slavery and tyranny. If this V sign means that to those now engaged in this great conflict then let we colored Americans adopt the double VV for a double victory. The first V for victory over our enemies from without, the second V for victory over our enemies from within. For surely those who perpetrate these ugly prejudices here are seeking to destroy our democratic form of government just as surely as the Axis forces.[18]

The Pittsburgh weekly ran editorials, articles, and political cartoons in every issue until 1943, demanding that the patriotic sacrifices of African Americans serve both ends: freedom at home and overseas. The campaign captured the Black popular imagination so thoroughly that men wearing "VV" tattoos or simply Vs burned into their skin became a common sight.

Historians have long remarked on how the Double V campaign drew upon deep traditions within the Black struggle for emancipation in the United States. Even as he urged Blacks to enlist in the Civil War, Frederick Douglass, nearly a century earlier, spoke of a "double battle, against slavery in the South and prejudice and proscription in the North."[19] Du Bois carried this principle yet further at the close of the First World War. Understanding that Black veterans would return to the United States with an enhanced sense of their rights and eager to see movement toward racial justice at home, he wrote in the May 1919 issue of *The Crisis*, "Make way for Democracy! We saved it in France, and by the Great Jehovah, we will save it in the United States of America, or know the reason why."[20]

More than any other individual in the immediate post–Second World War period, though, A. Philip Randolph, whose formidable gravity and resolve come across in photographs of him from this era, would come to be most associated with the campaign for equal treatment of Blacks. He almost always appears straight-faced, slightly dyspeptic, and forbidding in a white shirt and black-knit tie. Randolph's neck seemed permanently cocked, as if welded to keep his head held high. In 1925, Randolph, a socialist political activist and labor leader, rose to unparalleled national influence for an African American man of his generation as president of the Brotherhood of Sleeping Car Porters (BSCP), the country's first major predominantly Black labor union. Although not as well remembered today as some other giants of the twentieth-century American civil rights struggles who came after him, Randolph's life as an activist was so long and eventful that it served as a bridge connecting others not only across a huge expanse of time, but also in a range of political directions.

Born in 1889 in Crescent City, Florida, Randolph, the son of a tailor and itinerant African Methodist Episcopal Church minister and a seamstress, was educated at the Cookman Institute, in the lone academic high school for Black students in Jacksonville, Florida. There, he became a standout student and dramatist.

Randolph credited his reading of Du Bois's *The Souls of Black Folk* with sparking his desire to push for African American equality and rights. In 1911, he moved to Harlem, where he took classes at City College, became a member of the Socialist Party, and made frequent appearances on Harlem's Black soapbox scene. A migrant from Florida, he spoke in a sui generis accent that has been described as a "mating of the Bostonian and West Indian."[21] In 1916, already a veteran public crier, Randolph claimed to have momentarily surrendered his soapbox on 135th Street and Lenox Avenue to Garvey. This gave the freshly arrived and unknown Jamaican, a man possessed of a voice as resounding as an artillery piece, his first introduction to the American public. Although the two would eventually become antagonists, there was a reason why this setting drew one remarkable Black figure after another, like them, in this era. As the critic Jervis Anderson wrote, politically, Harlem, "for all its limits and all the aspirations it imprisoned [was] a somewhat freer place to operate, to articulate the demand for Black freedom, than any other oppressed Black community or any colonized Black country in the world."[22]

Du Bois had famously urged African Americans to get behind America's contribution to World War I, and he even applied for a commission as a captain of military intelligence. "Let us, while this war lasts, forget our special grievances and close our ranks shoulder to shoulder with our own white fellow citizens and the allied nations that are fighting for democracy," he wrote in an editorial in *The Crisis*, in July 1918.[23] Randolph took the opposite tack and joined many other prominent African American leaders in excoriating Du Bois. In the pages of *The Messenger*, the monthly magazine he founded in Harlem in 1917, Randolph cowrote a letter to President Woodrow Wilson saying, "Lynching, Jim Crow, segregation, discrimination in the armed forces and out, disenfranchisement of millions of Black souls in the South—all these things make your cry of making the world safe for democracy a sham, a mockery, a rape of decency and a travesty on common justice."[24] The famously racist Wilson, who had approvingly screened *Birth of a Nation* in the White House and actively reversed the limited integration of the Federal government achieved during Reconstruction, rebuked him, branding Randolph "the most dangerous Negro in America."[25]

In 1920 Eugene V. Debs, who was then in prison for his antiwar activism, ran for US president as a Socialist candidate. Randolph supported his campaign, generating a wariness toward him in more conservative African American political circles. Later, though, organizing sleeping car porters, who were overwhelmingly Black, turned out to be the master stroke in his rise to national influence. In the 1930s, the Pullman Company, a railroad service enterprise, was the largest single employer of Black men in the country. After dispatching club-wielding thugs to attack members of Randolph's union during sign-up drives, in 1937, the BSCP won a contract from Pullman and major concessions on working hours, wages, and overtime.

With the outbreak of the Second World War in Europe, Randolph was initially as reticent about backing the cause of American involvement on behalf of democracies there as he had been two decades earlier, but his criticism this time pointed forward, toward a coming period of anti-imperialism shared across the Black world. London and Paris did not deserve American support, he wrote in 1940 because of the "long, tragic history of the fingers of England and France dripping with the blood of black, yellow and brown colonials."[26]

In time, Hitler's rabid Aryan supremacy tempered this view, but Randolph could also see that Franklin Delano Roosevelt's call for the United States to become the "arsenal of democracy" implicated issues of labor and economic justice for Blacks as much as it did war and peace. The push to arm Britain and America's decision to enter the war after Pearl Harbor turbocharged the American economy, ending the Depression and strongly boosting employment. Longstanding patterns of discrimination, though, meant this new economy heavily favored white workers. Between April and October 1940 alone, overall unemployment dropped from 18 percent to 13 percent for white workers, while remaining frozen at 22 percent for Black workers.[27] The defense companies that feasted on government largesse, moreover, were unapologetic in their racial bias.

"Negroes are not getting anywhere with National Defense," Randolph complained in the pages of the *Courier*. "The whole National Defense Setup reeks with race prejudice, hatred, and discrimination."[28] The solution he devised was to call for a march on the nation's capital by African Americans to protest their exclusion from defense manufacturing jobs that initially envisioned ten thousand participants. This sent alarm waves through the Roosevelt administration and, in December 1940, won Randolph a meeting with the president, together with the head of the NAACP, Walter White.[29] Randolph's forthright message at the White House was that Black people demanded the right both "to work *and* fight for our country."[30] Thus began a string of consequential meetings Randolph had with American presidents that would continue through the Kennedy Administration.

Roosevelt sought to placate these rare African American visitors with the vague offer to place personal calls to defense contractors, but Randolph flatly rejected this. "We want you to do more than that. We want something concrete, something tangible, definite, positive, and affirmative."[31]

Since the idea of the march had first been mooted, the number of hoped-for marchers had been raised ten-fold to one-hundred thousand, which reflected widespread support among the Black civil rights community. This placed FDR in a jam, having to navigate between the demands of African Americans for equal treatment and the Southern Democrats who were key to his governing coalition. To sniff out whether Randolph's audacious gambit was in reality a feint, the president turned to White of the NAACP and pointedly asked him, "Walter, how many people will really march?" White, who often projected optimism, replied stone-faced, "One hundred thousand, Mr. President."[32]

After the White House meeting, to drive their point home, Randolph issued a public letter as a leading member of the March on Washington committee, in which he wrote:

> Dear Fellow Negro Americans: Be not dismayed in these terrible times. You possess power. Great power. Our problem is to harness and hitch it up for action on the broadest, daring, and most gigantic scale.[33]

From the beginning, Randolph had been determined to establish the viability of his approach to fighting for Black rights. It couldn't have been more distinct from the more elitist, lawyerly approach to the fight for Black rights of the NAACP. It was based on mobilizing the Black masses, and it succeeded.

At some other time or under different circumstances, Randolph's appeals for a march might have been called as a bluff, but on June 25, Roosevelt issued Executive Order 8802, which declared, "There shall be no discrimination in the employment of workers in defense industries or government because of race, creed, color or national origin." It also established the Fair Employment Practices Committee to investigate violations, albeit without any direct power of enforcement. Executive Order 8802 also notably failed to include any measures to desegregate the armed forces.

Despite this crucial omission, African Americans saw Roosevelt's executive order as a major victory at the time—a Second Emancipation, some even called it. Although the Washington march was cancelled, the forces that had been so powerfully galvanized by the showdown with the White House did not stand down. The ceaseless activism in the months that followed seems now like a workshopping of tactics that became central to the classic civil rights movement of the 1950s and '60s: sit-ins, boycotts, protest rallies, sustained Black press coverage, and letter writing campaigns. As much as these focused on integration of the armed forces, which Truman finally conceded under pressure in July 1948, they were also aimed at political justice for Black people at home. This activism extracted a promise from Roosevelt to address Black voter disenfranchisement through polls taxes, literacy tests, and even patently absurd challenges to their right to vote, such as being asked to state the number of jellybeans in a jar. In 1940, hurdles like these, combined with rampant anti-Black violence and intimidation, resulted in only 3 percent of Black people in the South registering to vote.[34]

Randolph's mark on this era by no means ended there. As early as 1953, with places like the Gold Coast in mind, he lent his voice to pressuring President Eisenhower for American support for African independence.[35] Domestically, meanwhile, his personal and tactical influence could be felt throughout the world of African American activism. Malcolm X followed in his tradition as someone who rose to prominence as a streetcorner speaker in Harlem and Hartford and who, in 1959, may have modeled his first publication for the Nation of Islam (NOI), the *Messenger Magazine*, after Randolph's similarly named magazine of decades earlier.[36] Randolph's 1941 March on Washington never came off, but the idea was revived when he inspired one of the most famous and important protests of the civil rights era, the March on Washington for Jobs and Freedom, on August 28, 1963.

As head of the BSCP, Randolph had hired the brilliant young organizer Bayard Rustin, who was born in West Chester, Pennsylvania, in 1912, less than twenty miles from Lincoln University. Decades later, Rustin would emerge from the Quaker pacifism he was first exposed to in his youth, and the Gandhiism he studied in India in the late-1940s, to became a key civil rights organizer, handling logistics for the 1963 March on Washington and acting as a close advisor to King. King would say of Randolph, whose counsel he often sought, that he was one of the ten most important people among all Black Americans. And Rustin would say of King, that "Martin, in a sense, had a deeper affection and respect for A. Philip Randolph than he had for his own father."[37]

It is unlikely that Randolph and Rustin would have known of Nkrumah in the early 1940s, but each of them was keenly interested in Black internationalism and in putting an end to colonial rule, just as surely as they were devoted to ending Jim Crow at home. Already though, slowly but surely, their lives and causes were beginning to converge.

CHAPTER SEVENTEEN

The Rape of Decency

THE ROOTS OF SHARED STRUGGLE LINKING AFRICANS AND AFRICAN Americans had been deeply commingled for decades, even if for most people on either side of the Atlantic this was still hardly self-evident. It was only during World War II, and especially in that conflict's peaceful aftermath, that the synergies between them could be powerfully felt.

African Americans' letdown of expectations after the war mirrored that of Africans and registered just as sharply. The political class in the South expressed a bold resolve to hold the line on the American flavor of apartheid that ruled in the region. In the North, meanwhile, discrimination in housing, schools, and jobs, although often less formal or explicit, remained pervasive. Even many labor unions resisted opening up factory floors to African Americans as millions of migrants seeking to build new lives for themselves flooded northward.

Black troops returning from the war found themselves consigned to segregated bases on American soil, where German prisoners of war fraternized with their white American vanquishers.[1] Similarly, Black nurses were assigned to care for former Nazi soldiers, but not white American troops, for fear of offending their own countrymen's racist sensibilities.

As demobilization proceeded, insults were followed by more overt and violent expressions of racism. Only beginning in February 1945, for the first time since the American Revolution, had Black troops been permitted to fight side by side with white troops. And this was only after action surveys conducted among white officers showed that 84 percent of them found that Black troops had performed "very well" on the field. Speaking on the floor of the United States Senate that June, however, Mississippi's eager champion of Jim Crow James O. Eastland declared "the Negro soldier was an utter and dismal failure in combat in Europe," who had "disgraced the flag of their country." Fresh on the heels of the Nazi surrender, Eastland went on to assert:

> I say frankly that I am proud of the white race. I am proud that the purest form of white blood flows in my veins. I know the white race is the superior race. It has ruled the world. It has given us civilization. It is responsible for all the progress on earth.[2]

In many parts of the country, but especially in the South, hate speech like this from unreconstructed bigots fueled attacks on returning African American veterans. In Georgia, Mississippi, Texas, and elsewhere, Black ex-soldiers were savagely murdered for daring to cast a vote or for merely trying to register. In industrial Bessemer, Alabama, on the outskirts of Birmingham, Timothy Hood, a demobilized marine, was shot and wounded by a white streetcar operator after removing a Jim Crow sign and then shot in the head and killed by the police after his arrest.

As a *New York Amsterdam News* correspondent later wrote:

> The veteran from Okinawa may well be lynched on the streets of a Georgia town if he does not step off the sidewalk when a white woman or man passes. He had better not wear his uniform or battle ribbons in certain towns in Mississippi. He will be patted on the back in large cities in the North by victory-flushed white Americans and then knifed for the job of his desire by the same whites who are seeking to continue the age-old policy of "last to be hired, first to be fired" where the Negro is concerned.[3]

For the United States, the war had been a game changer for its role in the world both economically and geopolitically. Its economy surged to a position of unprecedented global dominance. New wealth generated during America's postwar boom years created a vastly more prosperous standard of living for millions of families. But racially speaking, the fruits of this new abundance were distributed in the most unequal of terms.

As a result of the GI Bill, American cities were rapidly endowed with freshly conjured suburbs to which whites flocked. Blacks remained unwelcome and were kept out. Between 1950 and 1980, eighteen of America's twenty-five largest cities lost population, while these new suburbs gained sixty million new residents, and accounted for 83 percent of the nation's growth.[4] A pioneer in all of this was William Levitt, who created the suburb Levittown in Hempstead, Long Island, by building seventeen thousand cookie-cutter two-bedroom homes, then selling them for $7,990, starting in 1949. Early on, veterans who wanted to buy one needed to provide only a $100 deposit. But there was a catch. As Levitt himself would later say, using language that was almost identical to that of the military brass who had pushed back against calls for racial equity during the war:

> I have come to know that if we sell one house to a Negro family, then 90 or 95 percent of our white customers will not buy into the community. That is their attitude, not ours.... As a company our position is simply this: We can solve a housing problem, or we can try to solve a racial problem but we cannot combine the two.[5]

Lending for all the new housing required by the postwar baby boom was, in theory, available to all, but in both absolute and proportional terms, Blacks received far less of it. Very often, their business was simply not welcome in banks. In 1947, in Mississippi, to take an extreme example, Black borrowers were only granted two home loans out of more than thirty-two hundred by the Veterans Administration.[6]

The bold truth about the GI Bill, which provided another cornerstone of the happy myth of the Greatest Generation, is that its design was largely shaped by Southern politicians who saw it as a way of sidestepping Roosevelt's initial inclination to create a massive new antipoverty program at war's end. These Southerners, like the in-your-face racist John E. Rankin of Mississippi, chairman of the Committee on World War Veterans' Legislation of the House of Representatives, were ideologically opposed to virtually any kind of new federal authority, such as those the New Deal had already spawned. They were even more hostile to anything that could challenge Jim Crow in their home region by generating greater equality of opportunity for Blacks.

The GI Bill enjoyed an unearned reputation as a uniquely color-blind program that equally lifted the prospects of a whole generation of American men and their families. After participating in combat during the war, Jews and recent Catholic immigrants were able to take advantage of the Bill in order to join the fold of mainstream America. Its effects were remarkable. But politicians like Rankin were wildly successful in making sure that when it came to the disbursement of the Bill's funds—greater in total than the Marshall Plan that revived postwar Europe—local, not federal, officials would sit firmly in the driver's seat.[7] As such, the Bill, in the words of one historian, became a

Wreck of the SS Bakana, *Half Assini, Ghana.*

Traditional fishing boats, Half Assini.

House where Nkrumah was born, Nkroful, Ghana.

Boys fishing in the creek where Nkrumah played as a child, Nkroful.

Achimota College, Accra.

Aggrey House, where Nkrumah lodged while attending Achimota College.

Yearbook photo, Lincoln University, 1937.

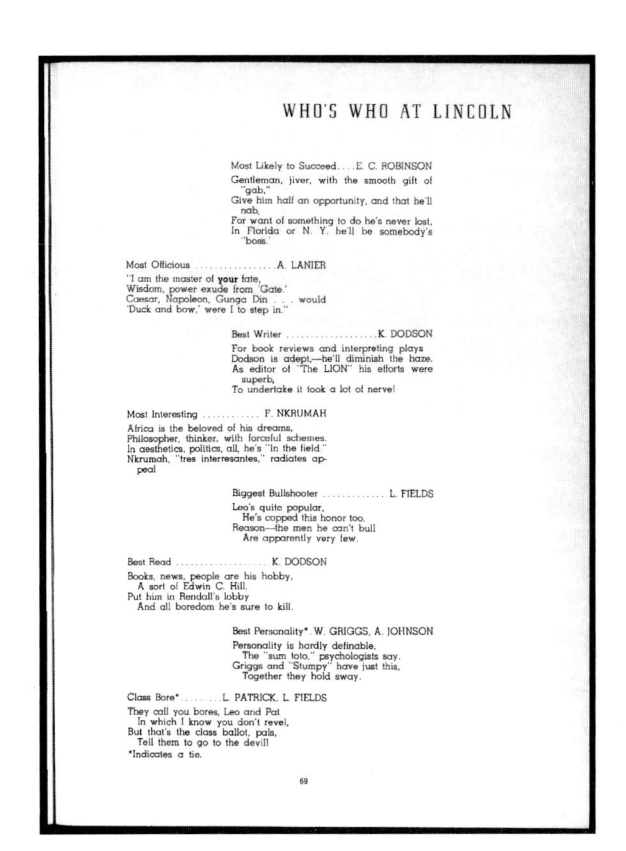

Who's Who at Lincoln.

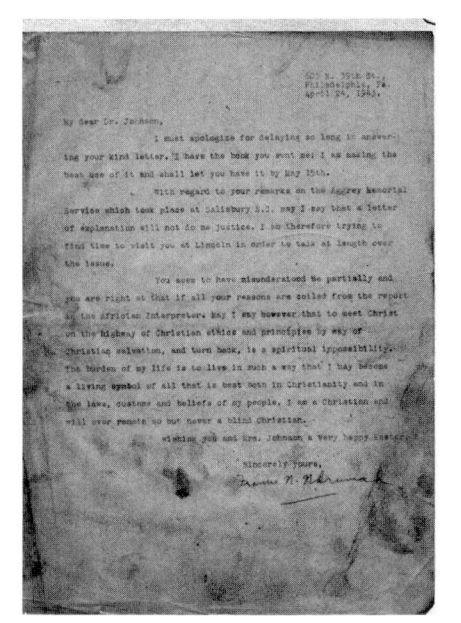

Nkrumah's letter rejecting the dean's objection to African religious content in a ceremony in remembrance of J. E. Kwegyir Aggrey.

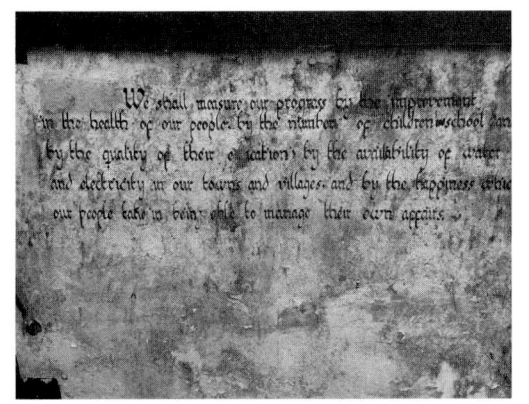

Guide at the Kwame Nkrumah Mausoleum, Museum and Memorial, Nkroful, Ghana.

United Gold Coast Convention National Headquarters, Saltpond, Ghana.

Canaan Lodge, Saltpond.

Monument to Kwame Nkrumah, George Alfred "Paa" Grant, and J. B. Danquah, Saltpond.

Nkrumah's home during his conquest of power in the 1950s.

Nkrumah with his wife, Fathia Rizk, presenting a gift to W. E. B. Du Bois on his ninety-fifth birthday, Accra, Ghana, February 23, 1963.

Nkrumah at Ghana's independence ceremonies, Accra, March 5, 1967.

Nkrumah at the All-African People's Conference, Accra, December 1958.

Nkrumah and Ralph Bunche, Harlem Lawyers' Association, 1958.

Nkrumah dances with Queen Elizabeth, Accra, November 18, 1961.

Lake Akosombo, site of the Akosombo Dam.

George Padmore Research Library on African Affairs, Accra.

George Padmore's tomb.

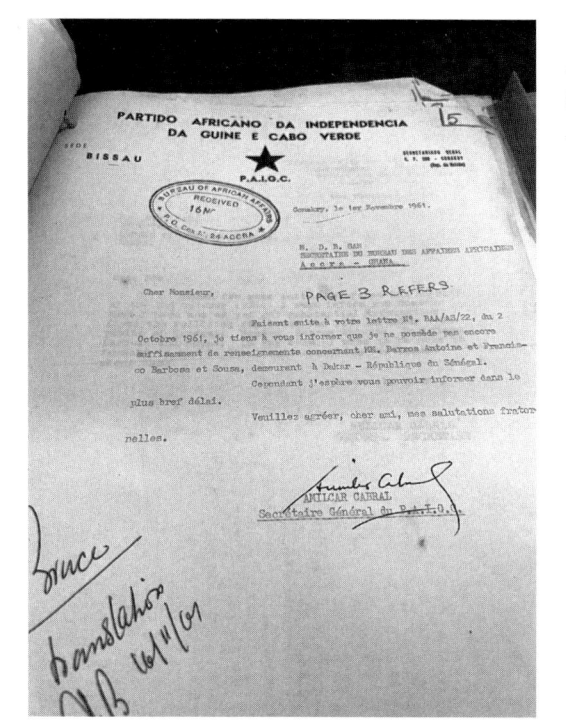

Letter from Amílcar Cabral to Ghana's Bureau of African Affairs, November 1, 1961.

Nkrumah greets Patrice Lumumba (right), Accra, August 1960.

Nkrumah with John F. Kennedy, the White House, March 8, 1961.

W. E. B. Du Bois's former home and Du Bois Memorial Centre for Pan-African Culture, Accra.

The grounds of Du Bois's childhood home, Great Barrington, Massachusetts.

Foundation ruins of Du Bois's home.

Nkrumah visits Harlem, October 6, 1960.

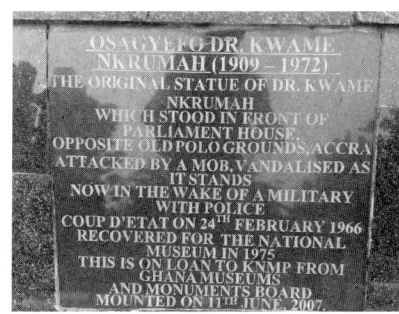

Statue of Nkrumah decapitated during the coup d'état against him, and plaque that now accompanies it.

The mausoleum at Kwame Nkrumah Memorial Park, Accra.

Nkrumah's final tomb.

massive "affirmative action [program] for whites" that measurably widened the country's already vast racial gap.[8]

This is also born out in the statistics associated with the program's other main propellant of upward mobility, education. Alongside housing finance, its effect on education is what the bill is best remembered for today. Taken in the aggregate, the effects of spending on education were utterly transformative, propelling the American economy rapidly toward knowledge- and service-based jobs. Just prior to the start of the war, roughly one hundred and sixty thousand Americans graduated from college each year. By the end of the 1940s, there were five hundred thousand graduates per year, and these numbers continued to increase rapidly. By 1955 the United States had gained more than ninety thousand new scientists, four hundred thousand engineers, two hundred thousand teachers, and sixty thousand doctors.[9]

Traditionally white universities were the overwhelming beneficiaries of this and grew explosively based on a combination of government-funded tuition for veterans and new investments in the sciences and technology. Only slowly and quite reluctantly, though, did they open their doors more widely to aspiring African American students. A poll taken at Princeton during the war, for example, showed that two-thirds of students opposed admitting Blacks at all, and even those who were open to some form of integration called for Blacks to face higher admissions standards than whites. In 1946, at the University of Pennsylvania, the least racially restrictive Ivy League university, out of nine thousand students only forty-six were Black. This is where the story of Horace Mann Bond resumes.

From the moment of his appointment as the first Black president of Lincoln University in 1945, Bond faced persistent pressure from trustees and others to change the school's vocation. For decades, its official mission had been "the education of Colored youth." Bond acceded to the removal of that phrase from Lincoln's charter, but he pushed back against demands that the university actively recruit white students in order to significantly dilute its Black student body. These calls became even more insistent in the early 1950s when desegregation cases were working their way through the federal courts, making it seem increasingly likely that racial separation in American schools was doomed to fade.

True race man that he was, Bond was furious over the board's pressure and responded defiantly. At most northern colleges and universities, Black students and faculty still numbered few to none. Lincoln, by contrast, had long welcomed white students and even recruited small numbers of them from nearby communities. "Having done this have we not done enough?" Bond asked. "Our self-respect will not permit us to do more."[10] In 1949, the Lincoln alumnus Thurgood Marshall, then legal counsel of the NAACP, gave a speech on campus in favor of integrating his alma mater. But Bond, who had personally led the desegregation of local schools in the community surrounding Lincoln by suing to force them to accept Black students, pushed back. According to a biographer, he criticized Marshall and the NAACP for praising white colleges that had two or three Black undergrads while maintaining all white boards and faculties. "Let those white colleges with token Black students hire Black faculty and choose Black board members; then they might merit being called interracial, as Lincoln did."[11]

Resentment over such double standards fueled Bond's determination to intensify his school's relations with Africa, both in terms of supporting applicants from the continent, as it had long done, and through a new kind of personal diplomacy toward Africa. Through Bond, the politics of these two issues—integration at home and the pull of Africa abroad—on the surface, seemingly unrelated, would become increasingly and explicitly joined. As they did so, they set him at odds with Lincoln's board and ultimately contributed to his firing in 1957, ironically the year that Nkrumah led Ghana to independence.

Bond's first visit to Africa in 1949 was on a trip partially paid for by a Lincoln alumnus from Nigeria. His first inkling of what Africa could mean for Lincoln and what Lincoln could mean for the continent had likely occurred two years earlier. That was when Nnamdi Azikiwe had returned to the campus to receive an honorary degree. Around that time, Bond began to argue that his university's longstanding connections to the continent constituted a major competitive advantage that Lincoln had done little to exploit. Africa was clearly moving into a new age of eventual independence, and with alumni like Azikiwe and Nkrumah, the school had a special role to play. Bond even wrote that these two had "learned Democracy-with a capital D" at Lincoln, where they were made "good Americans—with an immense admiration for American inventiveness, enterprise and industry."[12]

By the time of his 1949 tour of West Africa, Bond's thinking had evolved from vague and boosterish notions about the public relations gains to be won by Lincoln to a political vision about synergies to be developed between currents of Black nationalism on opposing sides of the Atlantic. Writing from Africa to the editor of the *Baltimore Afro-American*, then a leading Black newspaper, Bond affirmed: "Here is Black nationalism—the more astonishing to an American because of the low esteem in which the African American is held. But the American Negro enjoys that same tremendous prestige here that

America does." This was the germ of a robust and sophisticated later argument that the exercise of sovereignty and self-rule by new African leaders could serve as powerful sources of pride and inspiration for African Americans, while also helping to undermine the worst sorts of racist stereotypes held by whites against them.

"The key point for realizing the aspirations of the American Negro, lie[s] in Africa, and not in the United States," Bond remarked in a "Letter from Africa" column dated October 17, 1949. "It is the African who, I think, will dissipate forever the theories of racial inferiority that now prejudice the position of the American Negro."[13] Of all the colonies in sub-Saharan Africa, the Gold Coast seemed closest to achieving independence from a European power peacefully. Bond became one the first African American thinkers to seize on its importance as a lodestar for African American liberation as well. If the Gold Coast, soon Ghana, could bring to vivid life images of Black people successfully conducting their affairs in a reasoned and orderly manner, he believed, it would deliver a serious blow to white supremacy everywhere.

The acerbic, chip-on-his shoulder Bond may have been among the first to think this way, but he was by no means alone. Indeed, one of the most remarkable things about this forgotten epiphanic moment is how widespread such thinking became across the African American political spectrum. According to the standards of the early Cold War, Bond stripped of his pan-Africanism was a run-of-the-mill, pro-business, anticommunist figure. Thoughts like his about the importance of Ghana's example to African Americans found their neat echo, though, in 1950 in the words of Alphaeus Hunton. This Harvard educated grandson of Virginia slaves, Howard University English professor, and Communist Party member, became a leader of a pioneering anti-imperialist group called the Council on African Affairs (CAA). The CAA's members were fiercely hounded by the McCarthy-era's hysterically anticommunist House Un-American Activities Committee. In 1951, Hunton was imprisoned for his refusal to testify before the committee. He emigrated to Africa in 1960, first to Ahmed Sékou Touré's Guinea, then to Nkrumah's Ghana, and finally to Zambia, where he died of cancer in 1970. In one letter, he wrote:

> It is not a matter of helping the African people achieve freedom simply out of a spirit of humanitarian concern for their welfare. It is a matter of helping the African people because in doing this we further the possibility of their being able to help us in our struggles here in the United States. Can you not envision what a powerful influence a free West Indies or a free West Africa would be upon American democracy?[14]

Bond's writings and conversations from this time reveal still more complexity about the ways in which racial identity questions for Black Americans were evolving in relation to a changing Africa. From that first trip to the continent, at a time when "Negro" or "colored" were the standard appellations for Blacks, Bond had already begun to anticipate the shift, still at least a quarter century away, toward the term African American. "Sincerely—(and with a great new pride that I am an American of African descent . . .)" he wrote at the close of one letter.[15]

This was not a casual detail for him. An explicit embrace of the term *African American*, following the pattern of *Irish*, *Greek*, and *Italian American*, was as much a way of valorizing the continent as it was a statement of pride aimed at breaking with longstanding associations of Africa with shame. Even late in the war, the often-crusading *Pittsburgh Courier*, in protesting the ill and unequal treatment of "Negro" soldiers, had bowed to this convention emphasizing, "We're not Africans."[16]

For Bond such things had always formed part of a two-sided coin. Just as Black Americans needed Africa's help to regenerate themselves and assume a better place in American society, Africa needed Black Americans' assistance in its own rebirth and rise to a worthy station in the world. African Americans could play a special role in strengthening education on the continent, especially at the woefully inadequate college level, and this was a vocation that seemed to be waiting to be fulfilled by Black universities like his, in particular. And this would involve more than training visiting students or providing teaching materials.

In Bond's view, the lingering colonial mold of the higher education that was available in places like Nigeria and Ghana was harmfully mute on questions of identity and historical exploitation. In another letter he wrote to an African American intellectual from that trip, he decried the lack of "race consciousness" that the British system conveyed to students, whether in England or in the colonies. Remedying this lacuna was a task for which African Americans were ideally suited. Bond insisted that reinforcing a common sense of identity would help both Africans and Black Americans.[17]

CHAPTER EIGHTEEN

The Negro Circuit

IN 1951, ON THE LAST DAY OF MAY, KWAME NKRUMAH AND KOJO BOTSIO, HIS close associate and education minister, boarded a long-haul flight, the first of Nkrumah's life. He was on his way from Accra to London, where he would land eighteen hours later, after refueling stops along the way. Later, in his written musing, Nkrumah wondered whether the man who embarked on this trip was the same person who had left Africa for Britain sixteen year earlier.[1] On that occasion he had sailed in steerage aboard an uncomfortable steamer, with few belongings and insufficient funds to pay his tuition at the American university that was holding a place for him. But this trip differed even more notably. On that first voyage, he had not been Kwame Nkrumah. Neither this name, which was about to become known on every continent, nor the political persona that went with it, had yet been dreamed up.

One year earlier, London had been hit by the Great Smog, whose coal haze killed as many as four thousand people. On the eve of Nkrumah's arrival, the rationing of sweets that was introduced during the war was finally lifted, and Ian Fleming published the first of his James Bond novels, *Casino Royale*. These were empire-nostalgic adventure tales that Fleming would roll out on an annual basis over the next fourteen years. By the time of *You Only Live Twice*, which appeared in 1964, Fleming voiced open contempt for the independence movements sweeping the Global South with lines like these:

> I'd add that the U.N. are going to reap the father and mother of a whirlwind by quote liberating unquote colonial peoples. Give 'em a thousand years, yes. But give 'em ten, no. You are only taking away their blow-pipes and giving them machine guns.[2]

George Padmore, ever the master in London of Nkrumah's comings and goings, was there in the welcome hall at the airport to greet him, and straight away they repaired to the mentor's apartment for lengthy discussions across the old kitchen table. Padmore had doubtlessly been busy, but only one of them, Nkrumah, had assumed control of the day-to-day activities of a country that now seemed to be striding toward independence.

On his next day in the capital of what remained the world's largest empire, Nkrumah said he put the "problems and perplexities" of his homeland out of his mind and gaily engaged in the most ordinary kind of tourism. This led him to the Tower of London, Kensington and Buckingham palaces, and St. James' Palace—all places he later wrote that he had once attacked in "fiery speeches as monuments of imperialism."[3]

Two days later, Nkrumah was aloft once again with Botsio, this time aboard a silver, triple-tail British Overseas Airways Corporation Lockheed Constellation crossing the Atlantic to New York. He was unaccustomed to the big, international stage, and butterflies must have filled his stomach throughout the flight. The tone was set for what would become an unexpectedly triumphal whirlwind visit to the United States, though, from the moment they touched down at Idlewild Airport. "What are all these people doing?" he asked Botsio as a crush of onlookers awaiting his arrival engulfed the two of them.[4]

The answer lay in the fanfare that Nkrumah's visit to America had engendered despite the sudden arrangements. In the *New York Times*, a dispatch from Accra compared Nkrumah to Gandhi. It claimed that hymns were sung to him as if he were a saint in the Gold Coast and that he was gaining large followings in other colonies nearby. "Nkrumah could become the leader of all the African peoples," a European source said.[5]

Instead of an old comrade in arms in the transatlantic struggle for Black emancipation like George Padmore, the greeting party in New York was led by a protocol officer sent by the State Department. The man was trailed by a mixture of Gold Coast overseas students and a delegation from Lincoln University that included members of the alumni association headed by Horace Bond. The entire time, the flashbulbs of the press that turned out to cover Nkrumah's arrival popped blindingly from every conceivable angle.

The African man who stood before them was sullenly handsome, his face full and unlined. Nkrumah explained to them that while he had returned to the United States to receive an honorary degree from his alma mater, his trip had a higher purpose: soliciting American assistance to help develop his country. At a meeting with the Gold Coast students later that day, he intoned the same theme. They should devote themselves to obtaining the most advanced possible qualifications in their fields of study, Nkrumah implored them, and then return home to help make up for the desperate shortfall the country faced of expertise in the countless fields that a new nation would need to draw upon.

On his second day in the country, Nkrumah visited Philadelphia, where policemen had molested him years earlier for sleeping overnight in Union Station. Pinch me again, he must have felt that morning, when he was presented with the keys to the city by the mayor, Joseph S. Clark Jr., a reformist Democrat. That same day, Lincoln University and the World Affairs Council hosted a lunch for him downtown at the Bellevue-Stratford Hotel, a landmark tower grandly built in the French Renaissance style. But when Nkrumah repaired to his room beforehand to freshen up, he discovered that his suitcase was missing. Later he would relate with a light touch how unnamed friends suggested to him that this might have been the handiwork of the FBI. The truth of the matter will never be known, but as we have seen, J. Edgar Hoover's all-powerful agency had been keeping files on Nkrumah since his student days, and in the deepening Cold War, the FBI and CIA would retain an active interest in Nkrumah—and possibly much more than simply that—until his overthrow in 1966.[6]

At the luncheon, Nkrumah returned to the most urgent matter on his agenda, breaking with the stately colonial timetable for developing his country by attracting talented people of goodwill from overseas to help build the new country to come that he was already calling Ghana. Then, that evening, after drafting the commencement address that he was to deliver at Lincoln the next day, Nkrumah roused Botsio and asked him to accompany him on a search for old friends from his Philadelphia days whom he felt obliged to visit.

First he visited his old landlady, a Mrs. Borum. He had never once written to her but still called her his surrogate mother in America for having generously taken him in years earlier. It was well past eleven o'clock in the evening when he knocked at her door, and in her grogginess, she didn't immediately recognize him there in the dark. Then, as he spoke, she teared up. Nkrumah pressed a $100 bill in her hand and poured forth his gratitude for her kindness.

Next came a visit to Portia, the woman who might be called Nkrumah's surrogate girlfriend in the city during those years. He had gone Dutch during meals with her but slipped her clutches each time the prospect of a meaningful embrace seemed near. True to that pattern, after Portia offered seats to her unannounced guests in her living room, Nkrumah said that he worked to conceal the true interest of his visit, steadily averting his eyes from the collection of books that he had entrusted to her. She quickly caught on, though, and assured him that they had been kept in good condition.

Nkrumah needn't have bothered about leading Portia on, though. She was married now, her husband merely away for night-shift work, so they ended the evening very late with a middle-of-the-night meal somewhere nearby, and for once it was on him.

For his commencement address, Nkrumah had to borrow a shirt from Bond, whom he had never met before. Before the speech, there were other occasions for wonderment. The air of excitement, he said, was so intense "I could not believe it came only from me." Here, after all, was a man who, in 1935, "had not even enough to pay for one semester ... but had the nerve to persuade the Dean to give him a try." Finally, "the little village schoolteacher with his precious library of three books—the Bible, Shakespeare and Alcock's Grammar" reared himself at the rostrum ready to speak.[7]

As he summoned his thoughts before a hushed audience, Nkrumah recalled the last sermon he had given in America during his student years, at a Presbyterian Church in Philadelphia. Its title, he still recalled, was "I Saw a New Heaven and a New Earth." Here one finds his unusual belief in himself as chosen one, which could be a source of great strength but also of obstinacy and blindness:

> I reminded the people of how history repeated itself. Just as in the days of the Egyptians, so today God had ordained that certain among the African race should journey westwards to equip themselves with knowledge and experience for the day when they would be called upon to return to their motherland and to use the learning they had acquired to help improve the lot of their brethren. I impressed upon the people that they should not be despondent or impatient, for their turn would come any day now. "Be prepared," I warned them "so that you are ready when the call comes, for that time is near at hand." I had not realised at the time that I would contribute so much towards the fulfillment of this prophecy.[8]

Nkrumah made no mention of this sermon to his big audience but opened instead with stories aimed to impress of his studiousness and abnegation in America. He then regaled them with anecdotes about his political activities in London as Padmore's understudy and the fevered debates over independence among African student groups. He told them of his return to the Gold Coast at the invitation of the UGCC, of the hardship of arrest and detention. And he told a tailored and abridged account of his falling out with the UGCC's old-line politicians, and his decision to "seek first the political kingdom," as head of the new Convention People's Party. Finally, Nkrumah came to what had been his intended destination all along. It was time now for help "from all sources especially that of American Universities and especially Negro personnel who shared an interest in making the new Gold Coast Government a success."[9] He spoke of the Gold Coast's need for technicians and machinery and capital to help develop its resources and lift its people out of underdevelopment. If this was not forthcoming from the rich West, he would have to turn elsewhere to seek help wherever it could be found. This was a struggle for freedom, though, he insisted, not wanting to lose his audience. It was "a test case for Africa and for the peoples of African descent all over the world," and "therefore incumbent upon the Negro-world, upon all lovers of democracy and liberty irrespective of race ... to give every moral and physical support to the struggling millions of Ghana."[10]

Bond would have been hard-pressed to compose an itinerary on Nkrumah's behalf more to his own liking. From the pasture and orchard terroir of rural Pennsylvania, Nkrumah traveled to New York, where he conducted television and press interviews, met with Trygve Lie, the Norwegian Secretary General of the United Nations, and with Ralph Bunche, director of its Trustee Division. With them he talked up his dream of building a massive hydropower dam on the Volta River to smelt aluminum from the Gold Coast's abundant reserves of bauxite. This was to become a core objective of Nkrumah's presidency.

The next day it was on to Washington, for a meeting with congressmen, a State Department luncheon, and back-to-back receptions at the British Embassy and at the State Department. Before these stops, though, Nkrumah laid a wreath at the memorial to Abraham Lincoln and paid visit to the Jefferson Memorial, a mile to the southeast on the National Mall. For an aspiring leader of a Third World country, especially one known for his leftist bent like Nkrumah, this was an astute nod to the political culture of the United States at a time of mounting anticommunist hysteria.

Throughout his visit, Nkrumah and his delegation were given prominent coverage in almost all of America's Black newspapers, which hailed him effusively. The word "honor" became de rigueur as they chronicled each of the many banquets, receptions, and audiences with politicians that Nkrumah received, and the leader of the Gold Coast was lauded as a "high dignitary." To understand the outpouring of Black pride and enthusiasm, one must comprehend the endless and ubiquitous ways in which African Americans were demeaned in their daily lives in the United States. In a regular feature titled "On the Town," *The Philadelphia Tribune*, in the very next paragraph after it mentioned Nkrumah's honorary doctorate at Lincoln, lamented that the racist minstrel show "Amos 'n Andy" was moving to television that spring. It had been one of the most popular radio programs in the nation since the 1920s. And its use of white actors to fill the airwaves with their base caricatures of Black speech had engendered large letter-writing protest campaigns by African Americans. Now, Black actors, all but invisible as three-dimensional characters in the newish medium of television would be employed to make fools of themselves.

Nkrumah's last evening in America was spent back in New York, where the white, Catholic mayor, Vincent R. Impellitteri, extended what the *Amsterdam News* called a "royal welcome." The irony of this is that Impellitteri was often considered a mere puppet of his powerful commissioner, Robert Moses, who was busily transforming New York through road, park, and housing projects designed to segregate Black people. Impellitteri, though, may have seen the red carpet for the leader of the Gold Coast as a sop to garner support from Black voters. He received Nkrumah for breakfast and then hosted a large dinner party for him, about which Nkrumah wrote "all the leading Negro dignitaries and officials were present." There, amid fulsome thanks for the hospitality shown to him throughout his tour, Nkrumah expressed a final plea for the help of people of goodwill in the development of his country. He had already confided to a New York audience his plans to abandon the name Gold Coast, "because it brings back to mind the old slave days," and replace it with Ghana, which he said was redolent of a time "when we had emperors, large cities and a high level of culture."[11] Now he summoned African Americans to help build a cultural bridge to his continent and said Africans throughout the continent vitally needed their help to gain their freedom.

Never before had the West seen personal diplomacy such as this from a Black politician from Africa, though, and more than the Black press took notice. In its coverage of his visit, the *New York Times* quoted from speeches of Nkrumah's that had invoked Marcus Garvey in calling for a new "back-to-Africa movement," and touting hydroelectric power. It speculated that Ghana might soon create the equivalent of a Tennessee Valley Authority. "A new day is dawning in Africa," the *Times* quoted Nkrumah as saying at a reception at Columbia University's International House. "A gigantic movement is now underway in all West Africa. The old Africa is gone forever and I hope it never comes back again."[12]

Kwame Nkrumah may never have learned the extent of Bond's efforts to bring these events about, and Lincoln's president was left feeling somewhat jilted by Nkrumah. With very brief notice, Nkrumah had shortened his American tour from an originally planned sixteen to just six days. Bond's outreach had led to invitations from many more places than Nkrumah ended up accepting. These included Northwestern University, Atlanta University, and the University of Michigan, as well as churches and numerous newspaper interviews. In New York State, Buffalo even offered to give Nkrumah a parade.[13] "This has greatly embarrassed me," Bond wrote in response to one of the many requests for newspaper interviews of Nkrumah he had to decline.[14]

Despite this, Bond was nonetheless fully aware of the extraordinary feat that he had accomplished. In a letter afterward, he wrote:

> Considering the fact that the man was in jail in January, and that the British at that time were filling the world press and radio with accounts of his savagery and Communism, you will be interested to know that the British Embassy in Washington and our own American State Department, is leaving no stone unturned to provide him with a lavish reception.[15]

These days, African countries pay small fortunes to Washington lobbying and public relations firms hoping to win the tiniest fraction of the attention that Nkrumah drew. Bond had first notified the State Department of plans to invite Nkrumah to Lincoln in late March 1951, writing, "We respectfully call this event to your attention and solicit any suggestions you may wish to make so that we may give more significance to the attainment of this purpose," which was to "cement the relations existing between the people of the United States and the people of the Gold Coast."[16]

At the time, foreign policy minders, and Washington generally, held very mixed views of both Nkrumah's and Bond's agenda, such as they understood it. But after consulting with his superiors, State's director of the Office of African Affairs, E. M. Bourgerie, soon responded, thanking Bond for "bringing this matter to [our] attention," and ultimately agreed to organize a luncheon for an unaccustomedly prominent African visitor.[17]

Under Harry S. Truman's administration, America's top priority was competing with the Soviet Union. Toward this end, Washington focused on keeping its imperial allies in Europe happy; American diplomats knew that their economic recoveries were substantially dependent on the windfall rents they received from their colonies. For the United States, as Richard Wright, the most prominent African American novelist of the period, would soon write, this meant actively accepting that Europe's "hunger for raw materials and the opportunity to sell merchandise at high prices constituted the crux of British imperialism."[18] Customary and unexamined racism and fervent anticommunism among the Americans charged with remaking the world order inclined them toward a skeptical view of African independence. However, their calculations were complicated by the increasingly assertive ways in which African Americans were now connecting their own struggle for emancipation with the issue of African freedom.

In fact, this had begun before the war's end. In July 1944, during discussions about a new international monetary system at the Bretton Woods conference, John Maynard Keynes, the British economist who was the leading fount of Western ideas about postwar order, fumed over the involvement of delegations from what would become known as the Third World.[19] Their presence, he said, had turned the great gathering into "the most monstrous monkey-house assembled for years."[20] During the San Francisco conference just a few weeks earlier, Black intellectuals like Mary McLeod Bethune, Roy Wilkins, Rayford Logan, and Alphaeus Hunton had already begun denouncing the exclusion of people of color from the big questions of postwar order.

In an article in the *Pittsburgh Courier* titled "The Little Man Just Isn't Here," Logan lamented that the conference delegates designing rules for a new international system were almost all white, while the people who would be governed by it were mostly Asian, Black, or Brown. "The People's Peace will be white, male and middle-class if the other conferences at the end of the war are similarly constituted," Logan wrote.[21]

Du Bois, to whom the State Department had grudgingly conceded observer status as a "consultant" in San Francisco, went further still. He directly linked the decisions being made about colonized peoples to the fortunes of African Americans:

> We are particularly concerned with what is done about colonial empires and the well-being of colonial peoples around the world. Most of these colonial peoples are colored. What happens to even the most exploited of these has direct bearing on the future of Negroes in the United States.[22]

With a remarkable freedom from inhibition, George McGhee, assistant secretary of state for Near Eastern, South Asian, and African Affairs, the seniormost American official with responsibility for relations with Africa, gave a speech at Northwestern University that laid bare Washington's orientation toward the continent. This came just one month after Nkrumah's visit to the country. It was titled "Africa's Role in the Free World Today." (Africa wouldn't have an assistant secretary of state devoted to it until 1958.) McGhee's speech called the continent a "fertile field for communism," and warned against "premature independence for primitive, uneducated peoples." For the foreseeable future, he said that continued European "tutelage" was best advised. Around this time, Bourgerie, another American diplomat with oversight of Africa, said: "Our main objective in the Gold Coast is to secure the maximum use of its resources and keep the territory firmly within the political orbit of the Free World."[23]

Postwar Washington was deeply wary of conceding influence to Blacks in foreign policy. Yet, it was also aware that America's hard-earned reputation for persistent racial injustice at home was a serious liability in its competition with Moscow. In 1947, when Robert K. Carr, the executive director of Truman's President's Committee on Civil Rights (PCCR) wrote to Secretary of State George C. Marshall on this topic, Marshall initially ignored his letter. When the persistent Carr wrote again, he received a reply from Dean Rusk, then director of the Office of Political Affairs. Rusk tentatively conceded that "the conduct of our foreign policy is handicapped by our record in the field of civil rights and racial discrimination." But after the PCCR pushed for more engagement on the topic, Marshall stepped in, stating that "much of the adverse publicity abroad given to our civil rights record" was caused by followers of "a political philosophy," ostensibly meaning communism or anti-imperialism, who were cynically exploiting the issue of civil rights.[24]

Ideological bluster was easy to come by. But Washington was about to discover how difficult it was to shake America's bleak reputation on race. Over the next few years, reports streamed in from nearly every region of the world stating that America's treatment of its Black population involved more than cosmetics and revealed a deep-seated hypocrisy about democracy. In 1951, for example, one visitor to Europe wrote his congressman saying questions about the "Negro problem" were "the most frequent" themes of his encounters there, and that Europeans considered this "a permanent blot on our character." A State Department report from Latin America reached much the same conclusion. And an American embassy dispatch from India damningly summarized local press reports that concluded "segregation is a national practice" and constituted "the most realistic measuring rod of [American] democracy."[25]

If anything, the Eisenhower administration was far less attuned to questions of racial justice in the United States than the Truman administration had been, even as one civil rights issue after another took on tremendous prominence in the news. Nothing short of a judicial revolution had been brought on by the *Brown v. Board of Education* case of 1954 and the school integration confrontations that ensued, as in Little Rock, Arkansas, in 1957. Driven to revolt by discrimination, African Americans mounted their own positive action in the Montgomery Bus Boycott of 1956–57. Racist whites determined to hold the line against change launched a white bombing and terror campaign in Alabama over the next two years. Fighting reaction with action, Black Americans brought their protest movement to Washington, DC, holding two large Youth Marches for Integrated Schools in the nation's capital in 1958 and 1959.

A famous comment by Eisenhower distilled his seeming indifference. At a White House dinner in 1954, while a *Brown v. Board of Education* decision was pending, the president turned to Earl Warren, the new chief justice of the Supreme Court, and asked him to consider the feelings of white parents in the Deep South. "These are not bad people. All they are concerned about is to see that their sweet little girls are not required to sit in school alongside some big Black bucks."[26]

A few years later, Eisenhower would express very similar sentiments about South Africa. On March 30, 1960, in telephone conversation with his then-Secretary of State Christian Herter, the president voiced his reluctance to criticize that country's apartheid system. "He said the South Africans have a right to say they want to make progress any way they want to do it," Herter noted. Moreover, the president declared, "If we vote for a tough resolution, we may find ourselves red-faced—in other words concerning our own Negro problem."[27] Remarkably, this was just nine days after the Sharpeville massacre, in which South African police opened fire on protestors demonstrating against the pass laws used to restrict the movements of Blacks in the country. The monochrome photos taken that day and immediately transmitted around the world show thick crowds of Black people fleeing the hail of bullets, and stragglers being beaten viciously by white police swinging truncheons. As many as two hundred people were killed, 70 percent of them women and children shot in the back.

Internationally minded Black activists during this time complained bitterly about the appalling lack of African Americans in the State Department and in the circle of men in proximity to the president. This near total lack of diversity contributed to administration policies that took little heed of Black interests both domestically and abroad and contributed to the president's tone-deafness on race. In 1947, by one count, there were only four Blacks among the twelve hundred people who held the rank of foreign service officer in the diplomatic corps, and they were largely confined to what was called the Negro circuit, meaning small countries with brown-skinned majorities that were traditionally deemed of scant global importance.

In this regard, the story of E. Frederic Morrow, who became the first Black special assistant to work at the White House in 1955, is instructive. Morrow, or Uncle Fred to my family, was married to a family cousin and lived on the same block in northeastern Washington, DC, that my siblings and I grew up on. A rare Black Republican, he had been a field secretary for the NAACP, had worked in public relations for CBS, and had served as the Eisenhower campaign's liaison to Black voters. His campaign job "was to be visible at certain times and invisible at others." In government he was frequently treated as a token, and used as "a kind of pacifier for Black people" who were aggrieved over the president's unwillingness to meet with even moderate Black leaders.[28] Although Morrow experienced endless humiliations—from being mistaken for the menial help by white officials, being forced to use separate accommodations during trips, and once even being urged to be the briefcase carrier at the Supreme Court for the solicitor general during the Little Rock school case—he was determined to do more than this.

On those infrequent occasions when he could be sure of getting the president's ear, Morrow tried to sensitize Eisenhower to the problems of race in the United States and in the world. Sitting with Eisenhower during a train ride back from West Point, Morrow, a war veteran, told the president of his and other Blacks' bitterness at having had to serve in segregated units. Eisenhower had publicly defended segregation on the eve of the American invasion of Japan and said that was no time for social experiments, especially with field commanders who were disproportionately Southern.[29]

By mid-1957, Morrow had concluded, "I can state categorically that the rank and file of Negroes in the country feel that the president has deserted them in their current fight to achieve first-class citizenship via Civil Rights legislation, etc."[30] Any appraisal of his commitment to emancipation overseas for colonized people of color would have been equally dismal. A year later, partly because of Morrow's urging, Eisenhower finally acceded to his sole meeting in the White House with the so-called Big Four of the civil rights movement, receiving Randolph, King, Wilkins, and Lester Granger, the head of the National Urban League.

Eisenhower and his guests somehow managed to produce beaming smiles at the conclusion of their encounter, but this was completely belied by the tense nature of their discussions. According to White House notes on the meeting, Wilkins told Eisenhower that it was normal for African Americans to turn to Washington for help in achieving social justice and said that enforcing equal voting rights for disenfranchised Black citizens was the "most effective and bloodless way" to solve the country's race problems. But when Eisenhower characteristically said there was only so much a president could do, Granger warned that he had not known a period when the bitterness of the "Negro" had showed "more signs of congealing than today." All this produced was the equivalent of a shrug from the man who led America through the evening of the postwar era, the shiny-domed, avuncular man still often remembered as a steadying and comforting presence. The president wondered aloud if further constructive action on his part would only bring about more bitterness.[31]

CHAPTER NINETEEN

Land of My Fathers

IN AT LEAST ONE SENSE, EISENHOWER'S LACK OF INTEREST IN EITHER AFRIcan American equality or African emancipation from colonization may have served as a blessing for both Nkrumah and his continent. As the Cold War reached an early peak in the 1950s, his administration orchestrated a hit parade of coups d'état and covert actions against governments throughout much of the Global South. They were ordered at the merest hint of affinity with communism and, often enough, on groundless suspicion. A sense of their geographic spread is conveyed by this small sample: coups against the elected governments of Mohammad Mossadegh in Iran in 1953 and Jacobo Árbenz in Guatemala in 1954, along with a failed US-backed military rebellion against Sukarno in Indonesia.

The overthrow of Árbenz, in particular, gives a flavor for how little political room to maneuver many small states were afforded. Eisenhower's Secretary of State John Foster Dulles (whose ideologically similar brother Allen was head of the CIA), even viewed nonalignment by newly independent countries as "immoral."[1] That neutrality had been a recurrent posture in America's foreign relations throughout the country's history seems never to have occurred to him.

In his inaugural address, in 1951, Árbenz, more moderately progressive than revolutionary, declared his government had two fundamental objectives: to end the colonial-style domination long enjoyed by the United States and to simultaneously end the feudal domination of the country's indigenous peasantry. From the start, though, Árbenz also made it clear that his aim was to build a modern capitalist state that would always welcome foreign investment. Moreover, he wanted to achieve this transformation through democratic means and the rule of law.[2] In other words, there was nothing remotely Bolshevik about his program. Sentiments like these were the common stock of people like Nkrumah and emerging nationalists in every corner of the postwar world. The trigger that set into motion the overthrow of the Árbenz government was its announced plans for land reform. Specifically, the Guatemala City government expropriated nearly four-hundred thousand acres of unworked farmland held by the American banana giant, the United Fruit Company, offering to pay whatever value the company had declared for the land. This drew sharp objection not from United Fruit, but from a belligerent State Department, which demanded ten times more in compensation on the company's behalf.[3]

Nkrumah, in this regard, can be said to have escaped a bullet, at least at that point in time. Amid the Western ideological paranoia and extremism of the 1950s, his personal and political history had enough hints of his interest in Marxism as to have Western anticommunists add him to their ever-growing hit list. These hints ranged from his friendship with Padmore (albeit Padmore was someone who had broken publicly and sharply with the Soviet Union), to his unsigned membership card for the Communist Party, to his formation of the shadowy and ephemeral group known as The Circle. At Lincoln in 1951, he took care to say that "[t]he Convention People's Party is not a communist organization as some of our detractors have tried to label us."[4] But in his acceptance speech for his honorary law degree there, Nkrumah nonetheless pointedly borrowed a choice Mao Zedong phrase whose vintage dated to the Chinese revolution: "the liberation movement at home today is a crusade and is spreading like a Prairie fire."[5]

The maneuvering room that Nkrumah briefly enjoyed was much more than happenstance. At mid-century, with the exception of white settler colonies in Kenya and South Africa, Africa below the Sahara was far afield from the core zones of traditional Western geopolitical interests. Although heated communists-hiding-under-every-bed rhetoric held the day in Washington, while Stalin was alive, the Soviet Union displayed no inclination to invest in what became known as the Third World. Moscow showed even less interest in the cause of African independence. This would change with Stalin's death in 1953, but only very slowly. The leadership group around Khrushchev wanted to lower both the costs of armament and risks of confrontation with the United States in Europe and only began to eye the Global South as a fruitful theater for competition with the West around 1955. And even this change of direction in Moscow only began to have teeth after Khrushchev consolidated his power in 1957.

Two events help explain Moscow's shift. First was the enthusiasm exhibited for Mao's China at the 1955 Afro-Asian gathering in Bandung, Indonesia.

Although China's influence was less direct than widely remembered, this watershed event is credited with helping lay the foundation of the Non-Aligned Movement. Bandung unleashed a wave of alarmism and paranoia in the West about the perceived threat posed by yellow- and brown-skinned peoples joining forces against the prosperous, majority-white nations of the First World. In one memo, Nelson Rockefeller, then a special assistant to the president for foreign affairs who advised Eisenhower on psychological warfare, wrote of the necessity of "prevent[ing] Africans and Asians from ganging up on the United States." In an essay in the *New York Times Magazine*, Arnold J. Toynbee, a Briton and one of the most prominent historians of the era, warned of the prospect of a war between the white race and a "coalition of all the other races."[6]

The second watershed was the Suez Crisis in July 1956. Beforehand, Britain had already begun to oppose the assertive nationalism of the Egyptian leader, Gamal Abdel Nasser on this general basis. On top of this, it feared that his plans to nationalize the Suez Canal would threaten its position in the Middle East, cutting its maritime trade link with Asia. France also opposed Nasser and joined in the ill-conceived seizure of the canal with an additional motive of its own. Paris feared Nasser's influence on its North African colonies, where Paris was already struggling to hold on. For good measure, Israel joined in on the canal seizure, igniting one of the biggest global crises of the era.

The Soviet Union declared its support for Egypt's nationalization of the canal and warned darkly of a third world war. Eisenhower responded by forcing the powers that had seized the canal to back down, humiliating them. Among other things, he had feared that supporting America's old-line imperialist allies would backfire against the United States because Nasser "personified the emotional demands of the people in the area . . . for slapping the white man down."[7] In the wake of this geopolitical drama, almost all of what the superpowers had hitherto regarded as "periphery"—meaning far-flung regions of Africa, Asia, and Latin America—became stages of continuous and intensifying competition.

In January 1956, even before Suez, Khrushchev issued the watchword to his Eastern European allies to "take action and develop their own economic and diplomatic relations" with the hitherto peripheral parts of the world, making Ghana an important early place of focus for Moscow in Africa. As Khrushchev broke with Stalinism, the Soviet Union revived a concept called "noncapitalist development," which held that Third World countries could peacefully forge their own legitimate paths toward socialism through a combination of economic statism and trade and support from Moscow.[8] As we will see, though, in addition to whatever shortcomings were displayed by Africa's new, independence-era leaders, from the very outset, the Soviet Union's own economic weaknesses rendered such an outcome highly unlikely.

Nkrumah's prestige was also boosted in an indirect and entirely unplanned way by the extreme violence of Britain's campaign to put down the native uprising against the takeover of Kenya's best farmland by white settlers. In an act of projection worthy of a dictionary definition, the British demonized the so-called Mau Mau as terrorists, covering up their own brutal methods and the use of concentration camps and apartheid-like pass books to subdue Kenyan opposition. It is not that the British were especially fond of Nkrumah, but his adoption of a form of Gandhian nonviolent resistance—Positive Action—gave London a useful counterexample to Kenya and even something to briefly cheer for: an example of gradual, negotiated, constitutional change they hoped could be a model for other colonies in Africa.

The least understood of Nkrumah's advantages, however, was the entree created by Horace Mann Bond's invitation for him to speak at Lincoln in 1951 and the steadily deeper embrace of Nkrumah by African American society that ensued. Support from Black Americans played a surprisingly powerful but historically overlooked role in creating space for Nkrumah amid the stark and hostile East-West competition of the early Cold War. It was African American interest that drove American momentum toward engaging with Nkrumah's government and that would lead to another Washington visit a few years hence. In the meantime, this interest even forced a reluctant Richard Nixon to represent the United States at Ghana's independence ceremonies. Popular interest in Africa had been on the wane since the highwater mark of Garveyism in the early 1920s. Friends of Ghana associations now began to sprout up among Black Americans in the United States, such as the one my parents were to join early in my childhood in Washington, DC. And the African American press as well as nationally famous authors, led by Richard Wright, began to visit the Gold Coast and to write about it.

This helped put Africa on the radar of the American media in a much more visible way than it had ever been before. In 1953, *Life* magazine, for example, published a special issue titled "A Continent in Ferment," and placed a Maasai warrior on the cover. It was a cliché, to be sure, but *Life*'s cover was also a stage that Africa had never occupied, save for a portrait of South Africa's white prime minister, Jan Smuts, in 1943, and a feature about travel on the Nile River, in 1950.[9]

If anything, the prominent new interest in Africa in the Black press was even more remarkable. As one historian has put it, during its first few years after its launch, the Johnson Publishing Company's *Ebony*, a Black-owned *Life* magazine copycat created in 1947 for a "colored" national audience, was determinedly provincial. Above all, it strove "to emphasize Black people's Americanness—their political loyalty, their material progress, their role in making 'the United States the glorious democracy that it is.' Within that framework Africa represented, at best, a distraction and, at worst, an impediment, evoking all the associations of 'backwardness' and 'savagery' that *Ebony* was designed to expunge."[10]

With Nkrumah's rise in the Gold Coast, and the continent seemingly poised to march toward independence, the magazine pivoted sharply, embracing African sovereignty and self-rule as powerful new motifs of pride for Black Americans. For its large and loyal Black readership, the company's publications, which later included the weekly, *Jet*, became a major source of news about the continent. One poorly remembered reporter, in particular, played an outsized role in this. Era Bell Thompson had grown up in North Dakota, where her family constituted the entire Black population of their small town. Later, she made her way to Chicago, where she began working for Johnson Publishing in 1947, rising to comanaging editor, and then became one of the first Black American foreign correspondents, male or female. Richard Wright, who also wrote on Africa for *Ebony*, was immeasurably more famous, but it was Thompson, who traveled widely on the continent in the 1950s and beyond, and her large output that drove the magazine's new Africa coverage.

Wright had been urged to visit the Gold Coast by George Padmore, who provided him with introductions there, including to Nkrumah, whom Wright had already met briefly once during Nkrumah's American years. After traveling there by sea, the novelist stayed on in the Gold Coast for months. At Nkrumah's invitation Wright addressed a CPP rally, saying:

> I'm one of the lost sons of Africa who has come back to look upon the land of his forefathers. In a superficial sense it may be said that I'm a stranger to most of you, but, in terms of common heritage of suffering and hunger for freedom, your heart and my heart beat as one.[11]

Wright eventually produced a book called *Black Power*, which evinced a great deal of puzzlement about Africa and Africans, as well as disenchantment with Nkrumah. Wright seems to have arrived with many preconceptions about the differences between Africans and Black Americans, which he never got over, and much of *Black Power* is steeped in his own identity struggles. Langston Hughes, the Lincoln University graduate and Wright's immediate predecessor as the leading Black American literary figure and bard of the Harlem Renaissance, embraced racial pride and cultural nationalism wholeheartedly. This included Africa, which he came to know after traveling by ship to the Gold Coast three decades ahead of Wright. In his autobiography, *The Big Sea*, an enchanted Hughes wrote:

> People, black and beautiful as the night. The bare, pointing breasts of women in the market places. The rippling muscles of men loading palm oil and cocoa beans and mahogany on ships from the white man's world, for that was why our ship was there—to carry away the treasures of Africa. We brought machinery and tools, canned goods and Hollywood films. We took away riches out of the earth, loaded by human hands.[12]

Wright's impressions, though, could hardly have been more different, down to his revulsion at the sight of bare breasts "flopping loosely and grotesquely in the sun." He felt constantly oppressed by the "strangeness of a completely different order of life," and "absolute otherness," contrary to the common heritage that he had once claimed. He had little regard for either the elite Black project of Du Bois, talented tenth, or a mass program like Garvey's.[13] By this time, he was already moving toward a view that regarded race thinking as a form of unscientific delusion.[14] To Wright's dismay, but not surprisingly given his alienation, *Black Power* did not win a large audience.

Era Thompson coincidentally published a book about Africa the same year as Wright titled *Africa: Land of My Fathers*. Even though she had arrived on assignment for what had begun as a very staid and conventional magazine like *Ebony*, Thompson was far more open minded and, in the end, incomparably more upbeat about her topic. Where Wright was repelled or, in his better moods, confused by Africa, Thompson was charmed by the continent she discovered, and with no forced feeling, she naturally gravitated toward topics that could instill pride back home: indigenous Black business tycoons, the pomp of African statesmen and their meetings, and high cultural achievement, such as was apparent in her depiction of Ife, the ancient Yoruba capital in Nigeria, about which a feature of hers appeared under the title, "Is the Garden of Eden in Africa?"[15]

And then there was her sit-down interview with Nkrumah, who seems to have had a strong effect on her. In a chapter titled "Gold Coast Glamor Boy," Thompson wrote of Nkrumah's "brooding look" and "sculptured lips" and said of the prime minister, as if also speaking for herself, that he was "so admired by women." Her Nkrumah was "handsome, dreamy-eyed, and wistful," but also alluringly full of fiber and self-control. She wrote that he possessed a "cold, calculating calmness that lay close beneath his boyish charm."

"I have been called a 'Show Boy,' a 'histrionic radical,' and a 'Communist,'" Nkrumah once answered in reply to Thompson's questions. "I have been hounded by police on two continents and three times I have been thrown into jail, but I have never once lost sight of my vision of a free Africa."[16]

CHAPTER TWENTY

The Motion of Destiny

IN JULY OF 1953, AFTER YEARS OF SLAUGHTER, THE WAR ON THE KOREAN Peninsula that had pitted the United States and China and their respective allies in the north and south ended in a stalemate, leaving Korea permanently divided. That month, Fidel and Raúl Castro led a failed attack on the Moncada Barracks, in Santiago, Cuba, foretelling the coming start of the Cuban Revolution. And in a sign of the quickening pace of de-Stalinization in Moscow, Lavrentiy Beria, the Soviet Union's longtime head of secret police, was arrested, charged with high treason, and later executed.

On July 10, 1953, Kwame Nkrumah stood before the National Assembly and delivered what was up to that point the greatest speech of his life. By demanding the Gold Coast's independence from the United Kingdom—a matter of destiny, he called it over and over—it was certainly the most momentous.

Nkrumah was the kind of speaker whose thoughts could be delivered with fluidity, even when his remarks were peppered with ideas drawn from a life of study and learning. But he belonged firmly to the era before the teleprompter, and when making formal addresses, his delivery could be halting and slightly awkward, marked by odd little quirks of cadence, sometimes even giving the fleeting impression that he might have lost his train of thought.

The speech he delivered in Accra that day, however, was a work of both lofty ideas and high polish. The man who had not long ago been the target of near constant demonization by the British was keenly aware of just how narrow the needle was that he had to thread. Only his immediate audience sat in silence before him. At least as important, other intended recipients resided in London, some three thousand miles away, where a text of his remarks would soon be handed up to the imperial government.

The portions of his speech that were aimed primarily at his countrymen were focused on history, and on reminding the people of the Gold Coast of the long and sophisticated native experience of politics, of self-government, and of their history's powerful, if bygone realms. Nkrumah's embrace of the name Ghana, a bygone empire that had existed in another part of West Africa, both nodded at pan-Africanism and allowed him to sidestep the delicate fact that the remnants of another great empire, Asante, albeit not as old, existed within the Gold Coast's borders. Asante was problematic for a host of reasons. People from other ethnic groups, rivals and vassals, would have bridled at naming their country after the Asante. And moreover, there was a lively nationalism specific to the Asante themselves, with whose leaders Nkrumah had an antagonistic relationship.

> "In the very early days of the Christian era, long before England had assumed any importance...," he said, "our ancestors had attained a great empire, which lasted until the eleventh century.... At its height that empire stretched from Timbuktu to Bamako, and even as far as to the Atlantic.... Thus we take pride in the name of Ghana, not out of romanticism, but as an inspiration for the future.... What our ancestors achieved in the context of their contemporary society gives us confidence that we can create, out of that past, a glorious future, not in terms of war and military pomp, but in terms of social progress and of peace."[1]

Nkrumah's look back in time did not end with the crepuscle of the Ghana Empire in the twelfth century, though. That was merely part of his ongoing push to remove and replace the name Gold Coast as it hurtled toward independence. There were many modern feats to catalog that he wanted his listeners to be equally proud of. "When the Gold Coast Africans demand self-government today they are, in consequence, merely asserting their birthright which they never really surrendered to the British who, disregarding their treaty obligations of 1844, gradually usurped full sovereignty over the country," he said, referring to a treaty governing trade negotiated between the Fanti and British, and quoting his friend, George Padmore.[2]

The modern history lesson that he strung together began with accomplishments like Asante's successes in war against the British and the 1897 founding in Cape Coast of the territory's first anticolonial movement, the Aborigines' Rights Protection Society. It continued with the creation of the proto-pan-African National Congress of British West Africa, cofounded by J. E. Casely Hayford in 1917. It's slogan, Nkrumah reminded his audience, had been "We fight for freedom."

He then went over the glacial evolution of various colonial constitutions and the governing councils they authorized, on which Africans were either absent or merely a nominal presence. "Were not our ancestors ruling themselves before the white man came to these our shores?" he asked rhetorically, while skillfully segueing to his CPP as part of the answer. "With its uncompromising principles [it had] led the awakened masses to effectively demand their long lost heritage."[3]

To the British who would study his words in faraway Westminster and Whitehall, Nkrumah offered irresistible chestnuts, culled from their own political culture—phrases drawn from Edmund Burke, an Aristotle quote, and echoes of American Enlightenment thinkers. And there was enough poetry in the text to overcome whatever stodginess might have crept into his delivery as he spoke of reclaiming the Gold Coast's ancient heritage and restoring the rights of its citizens as "free men in the world."

"Mr. Speaker," Nkrumah began:

> we have frequent examples to show that there comes a time in the history of all colonial peoples when they must, because of their will to throw off the hampering shackles of colonialism, boldly assert their God-given right to be free of a foreign ruler. Today we are here to claim this right to our independence . . .
>
> The right of a people to decide their own destiny, to make their way in freedom, is not to be measured by the yardstick of color or degree of social development. It is an inalienable right of peoples which they are powerless to exercise when forces, stronger than they themselves, by whatever means, for whatever reasons, take this right away from them.[4]

Nkrumah then moved far beyond the chiefs and the commoners of Ghana, on whose behalf he had initially claimed to speak, to put global Britain in the klieg lights. "The eyes and ears of the world are upon you; yea, our oppressed brothers throughout this vast continent of Africa and the New World are looking to you with desperate hope. . . . At this time, history is being made; a colonial people has put forward the first definitive claim for independence." Then, as he closed his speech, to ensure that the bottom line could never be lost amid these flourishes, he hammered, "Mr. Speaker, we can only meet the challenge of our age as a free people."

The power of his rhetoric was unassailable, but Nkrumah's abrupt shift from Ghana to the world stage foreshadowed what would become the biggest contradiction of his presidency. Save for a few rare moments of national unity, the international ambitions of the visionary, who in so little time would push to the forefront of global pan-Africanism, always outpaced his ability to sustain a governing consensus domestically.

In his Motion of Destiny speech, the aspiring president claimed to speak in the name of the chiefs, but as Nkrumah would soon learn, even something as seemingly basic as this was fraught and full of danger. The Ghana that he hoped to lead into independence was still far more a collection of piecemeal colonies and ethnic and regional protectorates than a unified nation awaiting proclamation. Far from being wooed by visions of African unity, even the traditional chiefs remained intensely jealous of their lingering prerogatives and were hostile to central authority.

THE THREE YEARS SINCE NKRUMAH AND HIS NEW PARTY HAD FIRST TRIumphed in colonial elections had already been a very strange time, one full of unhappy compromises. As we have seen, the constitution that Nkrumah reluctantly accepted prevented him from taking charge of the civil service or even effectively stamping it with his priorities. Almost everything vital, from foreign relations to managing the economy, remained in Britain's hands. The colony's sterling zone currency was under the British treasury's control, sharply limiting access to dollars. Its commodity exports were run by an imperial-era marketing board and foreign trading houses that reaped most of the profits from its cocoa. Even the power to reassign functionaries from one post to another or oversee the police remained vested in the governor.

Frustrations and limitations of this sort were the inspiration for one of Nkrumah's most famous sayings: "Seek ye first the political kingdom, and all other things shall be added unto you." Adopted and modified from a popular catechism in the Gospel of Matthew, Nkrumah's intended meaning was that only true and effective sovereignty could furnish his nation with the means to pursue its own development and welfare. For the masses, this held the promise of more and better jobs and education. It was not long before rival and more cynical interpretations began to circulate widely, though. Here, the "other things" in his famous formula meant patronage jobs for party loyalists.

In March 1951, London upgraded Nkrumah's title to prime minister, but this changed little in the political life of the colony. Suspicious of his populist style and socialist ideology, the British were determined to keep their apprentice hand-tied for as long as possible. Maybe in time, some hoped, Nkrumah would warm to the political views of the vanquished old guard and become London's star pupil. And to a surprising extent, Nkrumah seems to have felt the need to play along, even tweaking his slogan from Positive Action to the far tamer and more pragmatic phrase of "tactical action." Faced with criticism from the left by progressives who had hoped for sweeping changes in the country that would do more to empower and uplift its citizens, Nkrumah sheepishly joked that his approach might also be called "tactful action." And around the same time, he made a show of purging a few conspicuous leftists in his midst, in what was publicly branded a campaign against "communist ideas."[5]

Nkrumah's predicament was like that of a man sitting astride two horses, as one historian put it:

> The first horse was the fiery steed of popular demand for change and progress, a creature best ridden at a gallop, ill-suited to a trot, and hopeless at a walk. The second horse was the comfortable beast of everyday negotiation with the British authorities... a gentle amble was its only reliable pace, while its head was turned most usually towards its stable and its sack of oats. If the first horse was held back too much it would lose interest in disgust; if the second was spurred it was likely to stop dead in its tracks.[6]

Mastering the game of playing nice with his erstwhile adversary, Governor Arden-Clarke, did nothing to burnish Nkrumah's credentials as a socialist or yield popular dividends. Nor, though, did it win him the cooperation or respect of the old guard conservatives. In defeat, J. B. Danquah, the erstwhile leader of the UGCC, accused Nkrumah of cynically campaigning on a platform of prompt independence in collusion with the British who had no intention of granting it. Incongruously, Danquah even claimed that London sought to install Nkrumah as a dictator. Danquah also complained that Nkrumah had raised taxes too high, ignoring the fact that as yet he had no control over such matters.

None of this is to say that Nkrumah and the CPP went into the 1954 elections with nothing to campaign on. Even working within the tight constraints of colonial oversight, Nkrumah had presided over large budgetary increases from Britain. These reflected the very belated recognition by London that it had vastly underspent on human development in its African colonies, which were now suddenly poised for independence. For London, finally allowing for greater outlays was something of an image operation aimed at being able to say—come what may in the future—that it had put colonies like the Gold Coast on a firm path to success.

As prime minister, Nkrumah cut the timeline of the British plan that he inherited by half, from ten years to five. To propel the country's development further, he introduced free primary schools, doubling enrolment in a mere two years. University education was expanded, and a new College of Technology was opened in the Asante capital, Kumasi. The government showed yet more political initiative by sending community development teams into villages and townships to mount low-cost but high-impact projects. Large numbers of secondary roads were graded and improved. Hundreds of schools were built. Wells were dug. Public latrines were established.

All the while, there was still no one who could credibly outflank Nkrumah on his biggest issue: independence. This could be freely observed in the response Nkrumah drew at rallies and political meetings. His mere appearance unleashed thundering cries of "Freedom!" his party's totemic slogan. In fact, with its jigsaw identity politics, the CPP's most important rivals were campaigning for things that could just as soon tear the colony apart as hasten the birth of a self-governing state. A formation called the Northern People's Party (NPP), for example, which represented a sparsely populated Muslim hinterland, campaigned under the slogan, "The North for the Northerners." The colony's east was dominated by a large, non-Akan minority group called the Ewe. Its leaders sought their own homeland along the border with French-ruled Togo, which some Ewe wished to join outright. This would have snuffed out Nkrumah's ambition of building a major hydroelectric dam on the Volta River, which ran through the Ewe region, and with it any prospect for Ghana of industrialization. In what would become the biggest challenge of all, from Asante, source of most of the cocoa in a colony that produced 40 percent of the world's supply as well as most of the Gold Coast's gold and timber, came near simultaneous demands both for more seats in the assembly *and* for a federal constitution.

Here lies tremendous irony. For years, Nkrumah had dreamed of creating a federation of African states; one that would reposition Africa in the world, building a stronger continent by bringing its smallish, cookie-cutter fragments together under some degree of central authority. The Asante project, by contrast, flung open the door to fragmentation. It would guarantee self-rule for a region that was long accustomed to governing itself (and ruling over others), but at the likely expense of a hollowed-out Ghana. And if it had succeeded, this would have strengthened demands from the north and east, and perhaps even other areas, for yet more political fissures just as a new country was coming into being.

One month before Nkrumah's Motion of Destiny speech, his CPP had won what seemed like a decisive triumph at the polls, taking 72 out of 104 seats, and producing a healthy representation almost everywhere in the colony. The only region the CPP had showed poorly in was the remote, largely Muslim Northern Territories, where the NPP won 15 seats. With deeper poverty and far higher illiteracy rates than elsewhere, the north, a distant afterthought of British colonizers, feared domination or further marginalization by southerners in a unified, independent country. This, indeed, mirrored the divisive politics of regionalism in much larger Nigeria nearby, whose north-south cleavage produced a devastating civil war in the 1960s.

Nkrumah's party, which ran under the banner of a red cockerel, herald of dawn, won victory in Asante and in the east by satisfying, if not huge, margins. The ponderous old intelligentsia, called the Ghana Congress Party, which chose the symbol of a blue elephant for its formation, was thoroughly drubbed. Even Danquah, its most prominent figure, had been unable to win a seat. Richard Wright had paraphrased Danquah, explaining his inability to communicate with ordinary folk in this way: "One did not speak *for* the masses; one *told* them what to do."[7] With rivals like these, never before had CPP rule seemed so inevitable, and taking the appropriate cue, Arden-Clarke announced that he would be the last governor the colony would ever know.

Seen against the backdrop of this electoral triumph, the confidence Nkrumah displayed during his Motion of Destiny speech looks well-earned. His party now turned to emphasizing its pan-African agenda, and to strengthening the leadership cult that had been forming around him since his prison days. Campaigning in 1954, the CPP hitched its reputation to Nkrumah's growing worldwide fame; he was already its chairman for life. The new party manifesto announced Ghana's continental ambitions. "Our victory in the forthcoming election is Africa's hope. We . . . are determined to be FREE and to use our position as a free independent sovereign state to help in the redemption of all Africa."[8]

The party-controlled newspaper, the *Accra Evening News*, extolled the country's leader as "Man of Destiny, Star of Africa, Hope of Millions of downtrodden Blacks, Deliverer of Ghana, Iron Boy, Great Leader of Street Boys, personable and handsome Boy from Nzima." More improbably still, he was called generalissimo. The piece of flattery and aggrandizement that would endure longest, though, was a traditional Akan title, Osagyefo, or "victor in war," but it would cut both ways. Nkrumah quickly embraced the honorific, and use of Osagyefo became de rigueur as the CPP moved toward authoritarianism. But for the opposition, and especially for conservative Western media, it became proof of Nkrumah's dictatorial nature. And this was aided by a willful and persistent mistranslation in the Western press as "redeemer," making Nkrumahism sound like a millenarian cult.

Even before the CPP had given in to verbal excesses like these, the opposition had begun attacking Nkrumah with a rhetorical violence it had never applied to their colonizer, which had long wielded near absolute power over their lives. With a consuming relish and no hint of irony, it denounced Nkrumah as a dictator and totalitarian. Opposition critics called him a communist, and one newspaper even called him an incipient Fuhrer.

Even though the 1954 election that September delivered a CPP victory over multiple subnational challenges, opposition in Asante flared anew, this time hinting at armed revolt. As this air of menace gathered, the quick final dash to independence that many awaited suddenly turned immensely more complicated. The initial spark for a renewed Asante challenge was a bit of policy clumsiness by the government in failing to boost cocoa prices for farmers following its electoral triumph.

Nkrumah and his advisors aimed to use the gap between the international market price for cocoa and the amount they paid to farmers to fund the programs they hoped would accelerate economic development. The mechanism they relied upon to capture this capital—buying low domestically and selling high abroad—was the same that the British had employed for decades as a routine matter of colonial policy. The difference was that the British channeled all of the surpluses into their own economy. Nkrumah wanted to invest the money in Ghana. There were two problems with Nkrumah's approach. International cocoa prices were near an all-time high, and this gave opposition forces in the Asante region ammunition to claim unfair treatment—exploitation even—at the hands of politicians in Accra. Opposition was strengthened further by the blatant patronage practiced by the Nkrumah appointee—subsequently forced out—who ran the new Cocoa Purchasing Company, which was created to compete with European brokers. Only marginally competent himself, this director freely handed out jobs to unqualified relatives.

In reality, the vexed economics of cocoa masked even deeper grievances. The British had provided subsidies to the Asante royalty and largely deferred to it in the management of local affairs, even allowing Asante's king and his coddled chiefs to raise certain taxes independently of the state. Now, the feudal institutions of the Ashanti Confederacy were coming under steady pressure from the central government and from social mobility, as more and more people migrated from one part of the colony to another for work. This caused traditionalist Asante elites to view the prospect of independence with deep alarm. Unless they could wring major structural concessions out of Britain, they saw doom ahead for their remaining autonomy, as well as for a hierarchical traditional culture, whose rites of protocol and deference bore a faint resemblance to Chinese Confucianism. Nkrumah, by sharp contrast, had built his movement on the inimical idea of involving the "verandah boys," "youngmen," and "school leavers"—code words for rootless strivers and forgotten commoners—in power.

On September 19, 1954, a new group burst onto the scene in Asante and its very name, the National Liberation Movement (NLM), announced the tune. For its coming-out event, over forty thousand people gathered at the source of the Subin River, a sacred location in the kingdom, all symbolically dressed in traditional funeral cloth, to signal protest. As the crowd shouted traditional war cries to the sound of drums under a blazing midday sun, organizers unfurled newly designed flags. A green stripe at the bottom symbolized the region's heavy forests and the resources they harbored. A yellow stripe across the top represented Asante's wealth in gold. And in the middle stood a black stripe, representing the ancestors. A cocoa tree fixed at the center symbolized the most important source of income of all, and the motif of their political disenchantment.

It had been a mere eight years since Asante was brought together under one unified legislative body with the broad strip of coastal territory that was traditionally known as the Colony, home to ethnic groups like the Fanti that had long resisted Asante hegemony. Now arose a faction willing to shed blood to press the region's separate claims. Soon afterward, the Ashanti Royal Council pledged its support and that of the king to the NLM and began to raise money on its behalf. The council also passed a unanimous resolution asking Queen Elizabeth, who was two-and-a-half years into her reign, to appoint a royal commission to devise a federal constitution for the Gold Coast.[9]

The CPP cried that the NLM was undermining a government that was seeking to achieve rapid independence. But disgruntled Asante offered an aggrieved historical rejoinder based on the bitter experience of Ashanti's defeat after nearly a century of resisting foreign takeover: "If in 1900 we had the support of all sections of the country we could have fought the British Empire and driven the British away and it would have been unnecessary for us today to agitate for self-government," B. F. Kusi, a politician who had stepped down from the CPP told the Assembly.[10]

Almost overnight, Kumasi became the scene of persistent unrest as the political contest between the CPP and Asante nationalists turned violent. Shadowy gangs that supported the monarchy or the NLM prowled the red clay hills and gardens of the city, attacking partisans of Nkrumah and the CPP. This drove most of the partisans out of the city, but not before Nkrumah's camp had landed some equally vicious blows. The new prime minister wisely judged it unsafe for him to visit the Ashanti heartland. Even Arden-Clarke, the governor, thought it prudent to lie down on the back seat of his Rolls Royce, hiding, in effect, as it pushed through angry crowds under a hail of rocks on his way to a meeting in the palace of the Asantehene, or traditional monarch.

The violence in Ashanti never reached the level of pitched battles or produced mass casualties, but amid killings on both sides, the British wrung their hands about another "Mau Mau," the denigrating new code language they applied to just about any political violence by Africans. And with yet more exaggeration, the tabloids compared the tit-for-tat incidents to gangland Chicago in the 1930s. In short order, in the mind of officials in Britain, the image of the Gold Coast as a largely placid model colony that was smartly mastering the routines of parliamentary democracy was shattered. Whitehall did nothing to satisfy Asante demands, and in fact, as reflected in the writing of a colonial official, it gave quiet backing to Nkrumah.

> He is intelligent, cooperative, courteous and friendly to Europeans, willing to listen to advice and (I believe) sincere.... In all the circumstances I feel that the right course now is to do what is possible to strengthen and consolidate his position in the Gold Coast, and by doing this, we should incidentally, make it clear beyond doubt that to a very large extent the responsibility for the conduct of internal affairs in the territory is firmly on African shoulders.[11]

Britain still enjoyed exclusive control of the security forces in the Gold Coast. For as long as anyone could remember, in fact, it had held all of the strong cards. This new stance nearly amounted to washing one's hands and hoping for the best and came closer to producing a disaster than is commonly appreciated. Not only could the Ashanti revolt itself have easily spiraled out of control, but in the rising ferment, the threat of violence reached Nkrumah's own doorstep.

CHAPTER TWENTY-ONE

Imagined Communities

IT WAS IN THIS SEASON OF TURMOIL AND UNCERTAINTY, WITH BRITISH CONtrol beginning to wobble prior to the 1954 election, that Nkrumah began to show the depths of his skill as a politician. It is impossible to say how much calculation was involved, but in a signature display of both unpredictability and audacity, in one of his first moves that season, Nkrumah poached ArdenClarke's secretary to become his own personal assistant.

As a new prime minister, Nkrumah had been coming to Christianborg Castle two or three times a week to see the governor. Very often he arrived without having made a prior appointment and sat quietly outside ArdenClarke's office across from his white secretary, Erica Powell, who had constantly heard repellant things about Nkrumah, such as his reputed deep hatred of white people. Yet, in fact, she had had few exchanges with the man. Sometimes, she said, Nkrumah seemed secretly amused. Usually, though, he just sat as if meditating as he clutched his bulging files and waited silently to be received by the representative of the Queen.

Quietly and carefully Powell studied him, from the stark black sheen of his complexion—dark even for a West African—to his prominent forehead, made even bigger by a deeply receding hairline, and his frank and open face. In one of their few conversations, Powell said Nkrumah leaned forward over her desk one day to point out a blemish, and to offer a common patent remedy, Mentholatum, which he swore by and offered to supply her with on a future visit. He even gave a little demonstration, pretending to massage the ointment onto his lip with his pinky, and added, "Sometimes I rub my neck with it when it aches."

The next conversation she recalled came a few months later. After Nkrumah's meeting with the governor had ended that morning, he made to descend the staircase that led out of the building, only to turn around and approach her. "Which night can you have dinner with me?" he asked. Powell stood but was too stupefied for words, so Nkrumah pressed his request. "Thursday OK?"[1]

This caused puzzlement and even consternation from Arden-Clarke, who eventually gave Powell permission to have dinner, at Nkrumah's home, no less. Months later, she quit her job with the colonial government and, after a short hiatus back home, began working as Nkrumah's personal secretary instead.

In short order, Erica Powell, a smart, perceptive, and single Englishwoman who had come to the Gold Coast on a lark in 1952 after her career had dead-ended in postwar Britain, became Nkrumah's closest confidant. Their relationship remains one of the essential mysteries of his life. It bears a surface resemblance to almost all of the other known ties with women that Nkrumah established in adulthood. But it ran far deeper.

The idea that Nkrumah was driven by hatred of white people was one of the slurs that circulated most widely among colonials. "The fact that I was white meant nothing to Kwame Nkrumah, for he seemed blind to race, colour and creed," Powell wrote in a remembrance after Nkrumah's death. "That I was British did not worry him either. 'I am fighting against a system—the system of colonialism, imperialism and racialism—not against peoples,' he declared, and the truth of that statement was demonstrated many times."[2]

Often sounding enchanted, Powell spoke of Nkrumah's "lithe figure," his "smooth and quick" movements, his gentle, fine-boned hands, the glow from his eyes, "soft and brown," "sometimes friendly and amused, sometimes sad, always expressive," and about his "magnetism," but she always insisted their ties were platonic. Many people, however, remained unconvinced. Almost from the start of their acquaintance, Powell became the one person Nkrumah, a man rendered increasingly lonely and intensely overworked, felt he could confide in. He would invite her over on short notice or call her late at night, purring in his deep voice about just wanting to talk and then dozing off midsentence. "If I suggested hanging up he would immediately come to life like a dud battery that gets a boost from a warm oven."[3]

One evening in November 1954, two months after the start of the revolt in Asante, Nkrumah summoned Powell to his home over some urgent work matter. The scene she discovered in the courtyard of the brick walkup building in Lagos Town where he still lived in a modest rental apartment was typical. Ducks quacked. Dogs barked. Hot cooking oil bubbled and cracked in the massive pots suspended over open fires that would serve up plantain fritters to feed the stream of petitioners and hangers on who endlessly sought him out. Dull thuds resounded from the fresh yams being pounded with enormous wooden pestles into fufu. And under this din, one could make out all manner of conversations, from politics and business to pitched woo from wherever pools of dark and shadow gathered. Then, from the second story level, where Nkrumah resided, Powell suddenly smelled something unusual. It reminded her of fireworks:

> A brilliant light pierced the smoke in the back yard. Kwame Nkrumah was standing by the edge of the verandah looking straight at it. Then came a violent explosion and the sound of breaking glass. The Prime Minister was still standing there. Were we dead? . . . Then, like another explosion, life began again. Children screamed, the women wept and moaned, the men rushed to the scene of the explosion, yelling, abusing, laughing. Kwame Nkrumah was walking down the steps.
> Where are you going, P.M., I asked anxiously?
> To see if my mother's all right.[4]

The police arrived within minutes and reported that Nkrumah and everyone else present at the time of the blast had been extremely fortunate. The device that went off had been heavily packed with explosives, but it was poorly assembled. No one was ever caught.

SOME OF THE MOST ELOQUENT ARTICULATIONS OF ASANTE GRIEVANCES WERE given by defectors from the CPP, including by some of Nkrumah's earliest political associates. The most prominent of these was Joe Appiah, who had done so much to help Nkrumah settle into the London exile scene years earlier and who had seen him off at the dock when he sailed home to accept the offer of the secretary general's job for the UGCC. Appiah turned coat and joined the NLM, accusing Nkrumah of arrogance, dishonesty, and a kind of soft corruption through patronage, citing the cocoa board as exhibit number one. In power, he said, the CPP was following "the doctrine of 'jobs for the boys.'"[5]

The breakdown in Nkrumah's relations with Appiah seems to have been driven by a combination of factors. There was genuine Asante anger over the government's appropriation of income from cocoa farming, which was dominated by the Asante. And more speculatively, Appiah, an Asante aristocrat, may have resented Nkrumah for his more humble origins (or vice versa).

The ruling party's growing reputation for corruption, like its leader's personality cult, created serious liabilities for Nkrumah. This was merely the beginning, though, and the corrosive effects would take their time. The irony here was that thus far, the corruption was generally quite petty. Beyond party patronage, it involved a kind of grubby opportunism in which office holders reflexively used their positions for low-grade self-enrichment. This was a far cry from the gross pillage that would later gut many African states within a decade or two of independence—the salting away of millions, or even billions, through systematic and far-reaching graft. And it did not convincingly directly implicate Nkrumah. Some took issue with his purchase of a long, black Cadillac, but for the most part, Nkrumah was remarkably frugal, bordering on ascetic. He couldn't even be bothered to feed himself well. Although many tried, even after his overthrow, he would never been shown to be venal. But people around him were already building impressive brick homes, becoming landlords, and collecting fancy cars. While some people admired or even openly envied the nouveau riche, more and more people grumbled.

Instead of definitively settling the colony's political landscape or opening the way for immediate independence, the 1954 election exposed something insidious about the country's inherited political system. Nkrumah had not only faced quasi-separatist opposition from different regions of the country, but he had also faced a crisis within the CPP itself. It had little to do with ideology. The problem was that the party leadership could not control its own list of candidates. Without any central authorization, scores of ambitious people declared themselves as CPP candidates. Most often, these were people who had no history with the party, nor even buy-in to Nkrumah's socialist ideas or pan-Africanism. They had merely understood that being an elected representative offered the chance of personal reward in a land where little opportunity for wealth had existed for Africans. Representing a district in the assembly or, even better, becoming a high state official or member of the cabinet offered the irresistible prospect of economic spoils, whether fat or slim, a slice of what Nigerians would later call "the national cake."

This problem would quickly proliferate throughout the continent as one European colony after another won independence, and it raised profound questions about the suitability of Western-style parliamentary democracy for brand-new polities that were all being invented on the fly. This was not because, as some Europeans and Americans commonly assumed, often taking a starkly racialist view of things, Africans were political primitives and therefore constitutionally incapable of democracy as a matter of form and procedure. Personal gain was a powerful lure, especially in countries that lacked economic substance and had scant tradition under colonization of the state working primarily for the benefit the people. But there was also the fact that, whether one speaks of the Gold Coast or Nigeria or any number of other possible examples, these were not real countries yet. Africa's decolonizing territories were, instead, nations awaiting invention, and this necessitated the conjuring from scratch, in Benedict Anderson's famous phrase, of newly "imagined communities."

Unless and until that work could be done, Africans in the Gold Coast and elsewhere were doomed to lean reflexively on the types of association that they knew best. These involved smaller-scale identities like language, kindship, and ethnicity, or what Westerners have long preferred to speak of, with an unerringly patronizing ring—tribe. This left scarcely any space for a new kind of mindset to emerge, that of a loyal opposition. This, at bottom, was the reality that Nkrumah was quickly confronted with during the transitional years prior to independence, and he was not alone in this; it would pose profound challenges to one new African country after another in the decades to come.

Nkrumah's primary ambition, perhaps linked to his background as a member of a marginal subgroup of the Akan from the colony's western borderlands, was to build a genuinely national party, without ethnic or regionalist associations, and then to move beyond this to dissolve Ghana into larger regional or even continental states or federations. This would prove to be a bit like the Marxist dream of the state that withers away and disappears. Meanwhile, everywhere around him, subnational groupings rose to challenge the center, as we have seen, in Asante, in the north, and with the Ewe. And as this happened, political debate, and even politics itself, broke down, giving way to pure identity questions and to violence. As in politics everywhere, his opposition never had a shortage of substantive reasons to disagree with this or that initiative or action that Nkrumah undertook. Just as often, though, objections to Nkrumah's policies arose on purely partisan terms. For his opponents, it was enough to say that the CPP is not "ours" or Nkrumah himself is not "one of us."

"People refer to them as the Opposition, but they aren't an official Opposition," a frustrated Nkrumah once told Powell. "If the Government went out of office tomorrow they could not successfully take over. All they do is oppose, oppose, oppose. Sometimes I wonder if they even bother to listen to what is being proposed by Government?"[6]

When unrest began to sweep through Asante, some diehard imperialists or sentimentalists in Britain's colonial establishment fantasized briefly about ways in which they could sideline Nkrumah altogether. Many of them had long loathed and distrusted him, believing him to be a closet communist. But Britain's humiliating failure to seize back control of the Suez Canal from Egypt in 1956, in which Washington forced its retreat, all but ruled out any new muscular assertiveness toward its African colonies. A somewhat chastened London now did what it considered the safest thing instead, postponing the transition. To Nkrumah's deep dismay, colonial authorities informed him that there had to be yet another election—the third in five years with Nkrumah at the fore. He was told he would have to produce "a reasonable majority" in his favor, all in all a subjective standard, before his Gold Coast could become independent Ghana. Never mind that Nkrumah had already done so twice. Even the nominally progressive Labour Party, then in opposition, agreed.

NKRUMAH DIDN'T SO MUCH FEAR LOSING YET ANOTHER VOTE AS HE DID THE idea that an atmosphere of continued violence would make it difficult to hold a successful nationwide election and would therefore produce continual delays.

As the campaign season barreled toward a July vote, the vitriol was unbridled, but violence itself gradually waned. The CPP once again leaned heavily on Nkrumah's international prestige. To the relief of both Britain and France, which feared any amplification of demands for independence in Africa, the election prevented Nkrumah from attending the Bandung Conference of newly emerging states in April 1955. Nkrumah sent surrogates in his place. Sukarno, the Indonesian president, opened this unprecedented event—a gathering of leaders of countries he boasted totaled 1.6 billion inhabitants—with these remarks, "How terrifically dynamic is our time! We can mobilize all the spiritual, all the moral, all the political strength of Africa and Asia on the side of peace. Yes, we! We, the people of Asia and Africa!"[7]

The CPP now fairly boasted that Nkrumah "is talked about with surprise in Johannesburg, in Nairobi, Uganda, Alabama."[8] The party called its rivals "devils and brutes," and accused them of being stooges of imperialism and colonialism, as well as agents of what it called "feudalism." The Asante-dominated NLM retorted by calling Nkrumah and his associates liars and thieves and exponents of "democratic socialism." One sinister joke that made the rounds held that the governing party's acronym really stood for Communist People's Party.

In reality, much of the campaign boiled down to elementary matters of platform. The CPP's couldn't have been simpler. Nkrumah's party hammered away at its brand, the primacy of independence: "This is the end of the road. Whether we go through the golden gate to freedom or whether we remain behind, is now a matter for you to decide." By dismal contrast, the NLM produced a thirty-point program under its parochial main slogan, "Why you should vote for cocoa." It was an amateurish act of political malpractice.[9]

Nkrumah felt the CPP's prospects were strong on the eve of the election but wanted to leave nothing to chance. He had urged party supporters who had fled Kumasi at the height of the violence to return home to vote and announced plans to appear there at a major rally. He decided against going at the last minute, though, sending a passel of well-known party leaders in his place to an event scheduled before sunset in keeping with the curfew. The opposition ridiculed Nkrumah for not daring to show his face in Ashantiland. Despite his absence, and the late arrival of the CPP's featured speakers, the rally was heavily attended. And this seemed a very bullish omen for the ruling party.

For Nkrumah, the election evening suspense was unbearable. On at least two occasions late in the campaign he went forty-eight hours without sleeping. On one of them, Nkrumah called Powell, telling her that he didn't know what to do with himself, and asking her to come over. She brought food, which he scarcely touched. And then he told her:

> You know sometimes I would give anything to be an ordinary person again. Wouldn't it be fun to go down to the polo ground and mix with the crowds, to be one of them, to feel the throb of excitement.[10]

Together they devised a plan to disguise Nkrumah, and especially his most distinctive feature, what he often called, his "big fat forehead," by pulling a red beret low down over his brow. He then sat still as a waxwork while Powell nosed her car, a second-hand Fiat she called Fifi forward through the thick crowds that had massed at the city's polo ground to cheer the announcement of results as they rolled in. No one got wise to the presence of the prime minister, who was delighted by the positive mood of the crowd in anticipation of a CPP victory. And by the time they returned to his place, party cars had arrived to return him to the sports field so he could speak about what they had just learned was a resounding victory.

The CPP's triumph was nearly identical to that of the previous election—a majority of 71 seats out of 104 in the assembly, or more than two-thirds of the seats. The NLM and its allies had won 13 out of 21 seats in Asante, but 8 seats for the ruling party was a healthy showing considering the extreme divisions over the last year. It also did better than it had before in the north, winning 11 seats compared to the NPP's 15. And in Ewe Togoland, the CPP won an outright majority, with 8 out of 13 seats. The center had held rather well, and from this point onward, Nkrumah could no longer be denied.

Soon there came more unexpectedly good news from Togoland, the ethnic Ewe region in the east; it voted in a United Nations–organized referendum in May 1956 about whether to remain part of Ghana or fuse with the French colony called Togo to the east. Sixty-one percent preferred to remain.

Stubbornly, with persistence and resourcefulness, a unitary state held together within the boundaries left behind by colonial rule—which, ironically, undermined Nkrumah's dreams of federation and pan-Africanism. Many other new African states would face similar centrifugal tensions, as large kingdoms or whole regions sought to cleave themselves off via war or secession into ever smaller new states. But the example of Nkrumah and of Ghana became the rule. Meanwhile the hegemony of the new nation-state born of colonialism, though often hard won, made the elites, who had inherited structures as vehicles for power and privilege, unwilling to give them up.

CHAPTER TWENTY-TWO

Birthday Party

IN MOST HUMAN ENDEAVORS, EFFORTS TO AVOID THE UNAVOIDABLE EVENtually end in the same way, resignation to the inevitable. And so it turned out with Britain's effort to hold on to the Gold Coast. After the general election of 1956 produced a third triumph for the CPP, Arden-Clarke did the only thing that remained for him to do—accept the results and invite Kwame Nkrumah to form a new government. The very next day, a humiliated Britain completed the pullout of its troops from the Suez Canal. At virtually the same moment, a crippling wave of strikes, protesting continuing domination by Paris, swept the French colony of Algeria.

As the new assembly met in the Gold Coast for the first time, with an independence motion now widely anticipated, dismay and confusion broke out in the hall when the NLM opposition members failed to show up at the appointed hour. It turned out not to be a feared boycott, though. After arriving late, they showered apologies on the governor, explaining that they had had to abandon their cars well short of the hall out of fear of the jubilant crowds that had massed outside. Although the opposition was now open to the same sort of ridicule it had dealt Nkrumah for failing to appear in Kumasi, the motion for independence passed quickly and with a large majority.

The predominantly Asante NLM had still not quite thrown in the towel, though. It organized a massive rally of its own in Kumasi to continue pressing for a federal constitution. Opposition militants pushed on other fronts, as well. This included sending figures from the old intelligentsia, connoisseurs in defeat, to Britain, where they pushed the idea of partitioning the colony and getting the Colonial Office to recognize Asante and the Northern Territories as separate states.

London received the petitioners, but this was only in service of decorum. Even with its sympathies for the conservative opposition and longstanding ideological reservations about Nkrumah, it was far too late for Britain to intervene in such a way. By now, Arden-Clarke had come to see the ushering of the Gold Coast across the finish line to independence with Nkrumah as its legitimate leader—under circumstances of substantial continuity with a Westminster model at least superficially intact—as his crowning achievement as governor. In a letter to his wife on Sunday, September 16, 1956, he wrote of the hectic times he had experienced during the last several months, with Nkrumah "ready to do foolish things," and of the British Secretary of State "doing a wobble and wanting to defer announcing a firm date for independence, while I was insisting that the announcement must be made before the Assembly rises on Tuesday next."[1]

After a beach picnic later that day, Arden-Clarke received an urgent telegram from London authorizing him to invite Nkrumah to announce the date it had selected for the birth of a new nation. "I shall have to see to it that my children do not smirch the record or throw their 'freedom' away between now and Independence Day," he wrote.[2] The following morning, he called Nkrumah, who was one day shy of forty-seven years old. "I just wanted to tell you that I have received some good news for you. I wondered if you could come up and see me for a few minutes when you are free."[3]

Nkrumah replied that he had a fully scheduled morning but could arrive at the Castle at three o'clock. Was this a little show of diffidence or gamesmanship in what had always been a complicated relationship? It is hard to know, but Arden-Clarke's recollection of the meeting that ensued unselfconsciously blends touching sentiments of warmth with a hint of condescension. When Nkrumah arrived in his office, he allowed the prime minister a moment to read the momentous dispatch from London. After a moment's pause, Arden-Clarke said Nkrumah spoke in an awed voice, only to say, "H.E. that's nice." The governor then reminisced fondly about their first meeting alone, after Nkrumah had been released from prison, and said there were only two people who could "break this experiment," which had been five years in the making, and they were standing face to face. According to Arden-Clarke, Nkrumah said, "We must have a party to celebrate this," to which the governor soberly replied, "Not yet. We have got to plan how this situation is to be handled."[4] In Arden-Clarke's telling, this entailed his dictating of an outline of what Nkrumah should say in announcing the news to the assembly.

Nkrumah related these same events in his autobiography and in much the same positive spirit. He tried to race through several of the telegram's thick paragraphs as his eyes blurred with the welling tears. When Arden-Clarke congratulated him for having finally won what he been struggling so long for, Nkrumah found his voice and corrected him. "It is the end of what WE have been struggling for, Sir Charles," Nkrumah replied, striking a magnanimous tone. "You have contributed a great deal towards this; in fact, I might not have succeeded without your help and co-operation. This is a very happy day for us both."[5]

After Nkrumah took his seat in the assembly and then rose to address the body the next morning, on his birthday, no one in the hall had the least inkling of what was coming. It was the rare kind of announcement where history pivots as if swinging on a hinge. Nkrumah announced gravely that the queen had decreed that full independence should come about on March 6, 1957. As no one needed reminding, this would mark the first time that a Black nation in Africa south of the Sahara had achieved emancipation from colonial rule or been admitted to the Commonwealth.

"The whole of the Assembly was for a few seconds dumbfounded," Nkrumah wrote. "Then all at once the almost sacred silence was broken by an ear-splitting cheer.... Some were too deeply moved to control their tears, among them some of my closest associates, those who had really felt the brunt of the battle and who perhaps realised more forcibly the true meaning of the word 'Victory.'"[6]

According to many accounts, even members of the opposition NLM were overcome by the moment. After completing his remarks, Nkrumah was hoisted on the shoulders of his supporters and carried outside, where a boisterous crowd that was already in the know giddily awaited. For several long minutes, as Nkrumah was paraded aloft, they chanted "Victory is ours." He then traveled with his cabinet to pay a visit to Arden-Clarke in the Castle for a toast together. First, libations were poured from a freshly opened bottle of Scotch onto the uneven stone grounds of the fort that served as the seat of colonial government. At Lincoln, many years earlier, the dean who was Nkrumah's main benefactor had severely reprimanded him for the supposedly heathen act of paying respect to African ancestors. In that case, it was for his early mentor, the Achimota vice principal and pan-Africanist, Kwegyir Aggrey. This time there would be no reproaching him. Instead, Arden-Clarke followed with a traditional European ritual, a champagne toast.

As happy as he was, Nkrumah was scarcely in a mood to pause. As he wrote in the final passage of his autobiography, "I have never regarded the struggle for independence of the Gold Coast as an isolated objective but always as a part of a general world historical pattern."[7]

Without African freedom, the independence of Ghana would mean little.

Part Three

ELBOWS AT THE HIGH TABLE

Kwame Nkrumah with John F. Kennedy, Washington, DC, March 8, 1961.

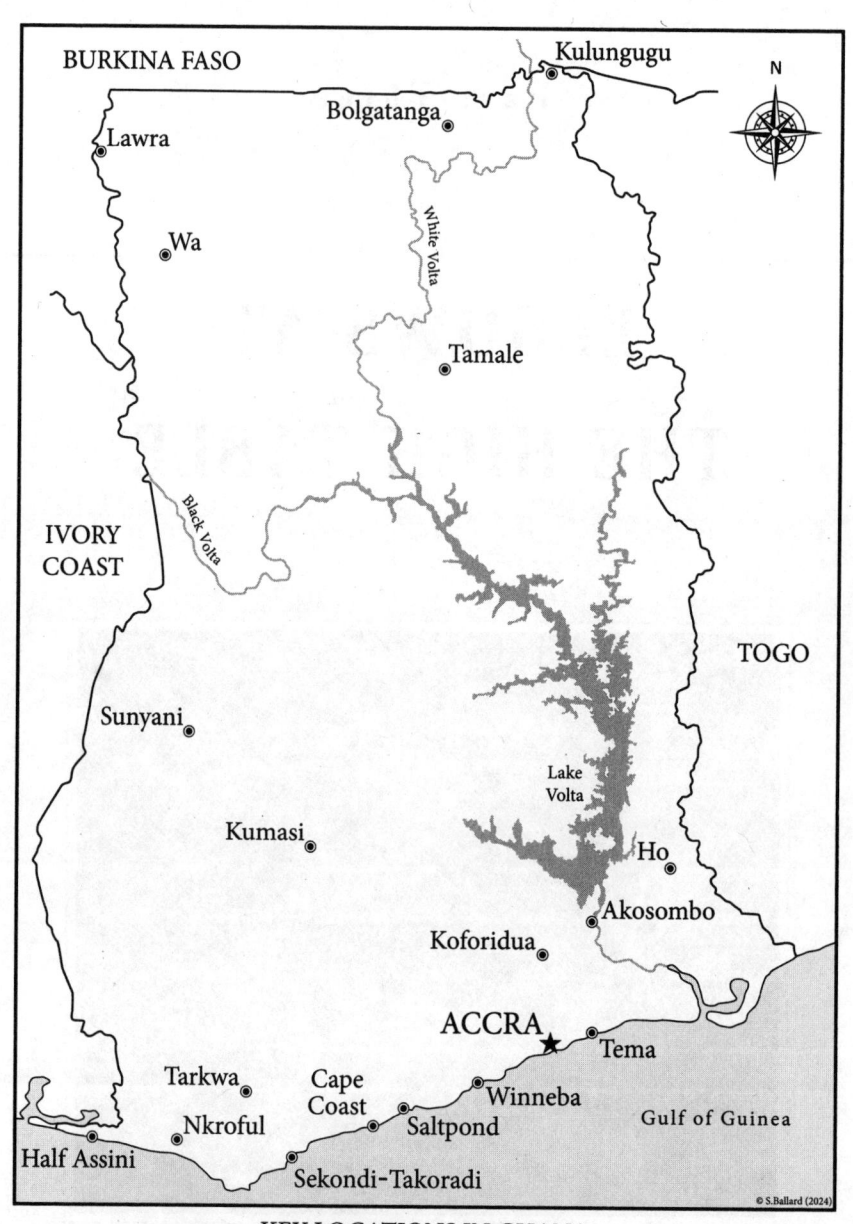

KEY LOCATIONS IN GHANA

CHAPTER TWENTY-THREE

New Africans

As midnight approached on Tuesday, March 5, 1957, Kwame Nkrumah delivered his final address to the colonial assembly of the Gold Coast before a crowd of about five hundred people. He had come dressed for the occasion not in a business suit, but in the traditional attire of the lowly peasant, a rough-hewn cotton smock favored in the country's poor far north called a *fugu*. His domed head, brilliant and black, was adorned with the white skullcap that he and his fellow political detainees had adopted upon their release from jail a decade earlier. The letters PG, for prison graduate, stitched in cursive, figured prominently on its front.

Once he had finished, Nkrumah strode out of the building and awaited the precise moment. The minutes passed quickly. Something very old was passing away: his people's overt domination by another country, another race. With the tolling of the hour, the Union Jack fluttered down the flagpole that loomed high over the nearby field where a throng of untold size had assembled, and as one the people seemed to hold their breath. Then, up went the British standard's permanent replacement. It was emblazoned with the earth tones of Africa, red, gold, and green, and embossed with a black star in the middle, symbol of an entire continent and of its peoples. The colors were an inversion of the flag of Ethiopia, the nation whose invasion by Italy in 1935 had galvanized Black thinkers and activists all over the world, and the five-cornered star in black, an iconic echo of Marcus Garvey. Ghana had been first, but here was the belief made manifest that all Africans were destined to free themselves. In this moment, with faith filling the air like a living spirit, Africa's march into the future could no more be stopped than the motion of the celestial objects in the sky above.

For the second time that glorious night, Nkrumah was lofted onto the shoulders of his supporters and transported to the old polo grounds, where a crowd of many tens of thousands of his stunned compatriots had gathered. There they had assembled peaceably and in utter delight to await both the man and the hour, and in this grand moment, the two were inseparable.

Followed by a handful of his closest CPP associates, all dressed in rough African smocks just as he was, Nkrumah climbed atop a simple scaffolding draped in the country's new colors. Fireworks streaked and whirligigged overhead. The new national anthem resounded. Those who had been present in the immense crowd later recalled that tears flowed from every eye. Even after the music had stopped, Nkrumah continued to spring up and down on the balls of his feet, punching skyward with one arm. The grin of a lifetime occupied his face. Then, with his eyes as wet as anyone else's, he finally announced what everyone had anticipated. "At long last, the battle has ended! And thus Ghana, your beloved country is free forever," Nkrumah said, daubing his visage with a white kerchief as he summoned those first words slowly. As he drew on the crowd, his comments became ever more forceful, his vision clearer:

> Seeing you in this ... it doesn't matter how far my eye goes, I can see that you are here in your millions, and my last warning to you is that you are to stand firm behind us so that we can prove to the world that when the African is given a chance, he can show the world that he is somebody! We have awakened. We will not sleep anymore. Today, from now on, there is a new African in the world! That new African is ready to fight his own battles and show that after all, the Black man is capable of managing his own affairs. We are going to demonstrate to the world, to the other nations, that we are prepared to lay our own foundation. Our own African identity.[1]

As emotive a message as this was, the words with the greatest significance, came later, at the close of the speech: "Our independence is meaningless unless it is linked up with the total liberation of the African continent."[2] It could not be fully appreciated at the time, but in this succinct statement one finds a veritable manifesto for the new government. What these words meant was that as long as colonialism and neocolonialism persisted, the potential of Ghana's own independence would be stunted and its survival would remain at risk.

When Nkrumah had finished speaking, the new national anthem resounded yet again. Then, hard as it was to imagine, something even more buoyant washed over the crowd, sealing the unforgettable mood. It was the sound of Highlife, the Gold Coast's cascading popular band music, an original blend of uplifting African beats and melodies inflected with horn stylings borrowed from American jazz and Cuban clave and guitar chords. Their rhythms had originated in Africa and had been borne to the Caribbean by the slave trade. Now, they played in testimony to the way that modernity had killed distance, they had come ricocheting back to their origin. Hidden away somewhere, a deejay reeled off a string of lilting hits by E. T. Mensah and other giants of this style. And as they played, the people danced and swayed as one compressed mass. A great many had never been to school and lacked a firm grasp of English, but there was one word that they all knew, and it was poised on every lip. Like news of Dido's love spreading like fire in Virgil, it reverberated from distant rooftops, too. No spelling or punctuation can adequately convey the feeling of joy and hope that it carried. That word was F-R-E-E-D-O-M!

Two days earlier, in New York, Miles Davis released the debut album from what came to be known as his first great quintet and the first of a series of recordings for Columbia Records that seemed to announce a new creative epoch. Here, Davis often played his trumpet muted, making it seem shrouded, as if in velvet smoke. Yet paired with John Coltrane's pealing saxophone, the music always remained angular, incisive, and above all, thrusting. With the birth of Ghana at the passing of midnight came the realization of something Nkrumah had begun yearning for far longer than the decade he had spent in the political struggle since returning home from Britain. His yearning had begun when he was a pupil and understudy of role models in the Gold Coast such as Aggrey and Azikiwe and continued with the concretization of ideas he absorbed from an expansive pantheon of other thinkers and organizers around ideas of universal freedom, of Black dignity, and of self-determination. It was a circle large enough even to encompass virtual enemies from the far shores of the Atlantic, people such as Marcus Garvey and W. E. B. Du Bois, as well as the even older forebears who had emerged earlier on his own continent—people such as Casely Hayford and Africanus Horton. But there was another sense, of course, in which Nkrumah knew his work had just begun. As he wrote in a passage at the end of his autobiography, officially published that same day, "I have never regarded the struggle for independence of the Gold Coast as an isolated objective but always as part of a general world historical pattern."[3] Ghana, in other words, could never be completely free until all of Africa was. In the spirit of a Portuguese phrase not yet made popular, *a luta continua*, he knew that the struggle would have to continue.

THE HUGE CROWDS OF NKRUMAH'S EXUBERANT FELLOW CITIZENS IN THIS newborn nation were not the only people drawn to the scene. Ghana's emancipation attracted attention to the continent on a scale Africa had never known before, and one that has perhaps never been matched since. Six hundred reporters and photographers flew into Accra, most of them no doubt visiting Africa for the first time. The celebrations would last for six full days, and envoys of seventy-two nations poured into the city from nearly every corner of the world. Princess Marina, the Duchess of Kent, represented Britain and its queen, and in a scene whose delight was captured in photographs published worldwide, she danced with Nkrumah at a formal ball. He had been personally instructed in the waltz and slow foxtrot by Lucille Armstrong, the spouse of jazz royalty, the trumpeter, Louis Armstrong. The year before, her husband had come to the country and dedicated a public rendition of *What Did I Do to Be So Black and Blue* to Nkrumah and to the cause of freedom, saying "After all, my ancestors came from here and I still have African blood in me."[4] That Armstrong performance drew the largest crowd Accra had ever seen until the independence ceremonies.

Leaders and their envoys flocked in from the Arab world. The Soviet Union sent a junior minister, who promptly invited Nkrumah to visit Moscow. China dispatched a general who dressed in a head-turning turquoise-blue uniform. At the official independence ball, Nkrumah's secretary, Erica Powell, said, "Every other face seemed to be a famous one and every single one of them, famous or not, was radiant." Nkrumah, who was a lifelong teetotaler, whispered to her that evening that "every damned steward is plastered." Among the other celebrations that week, there was a Miss Ghana beauty contest, a horse racing derby, a sailing boat regatta, a Pontifical High Mass, the opening of a new national museum, a convocation at the national university, and the unveiling of a new national monument. Perhaps most touching of all, amid the constant juggling he had to do to play host to so many dignitaries, Nkrumah threw a tea party for hundreds of Accra children, who frolicked to his delight on the lawns his prime ministerial office.[5]

Of all of the encounters that the celebrations produced, the one that would have the greatest global resonance, both in these moments and well beyond, may have involved Eisenhower's envoy, Vice President Richard Nixon. Nixon stubbornly resisted traveling to Ghana; he resented having to attend independence ceremonies like this, thinking them a prime example of the kind of dreary duties of marginal importance that he was assigned by a president who didn't particularly care for him. On top of this, there was race. It was not so long beforehand that Nixon had actually uttered the following in a White House conversation, "But those Africans, you know, are only 50 to 75 years out of the trees, some of 'em."[6]

The State Department had come under heavy and persistent pressure from prominent African Americans like A. Philip Randolph and Horace Bond to send a high-level delegation, and John Foster Dulles and other senior officials at State repeatedly wrote to Nixon urging him to lead the American delegation to Accra. Nixon said he would do so only if personally directed by his boss, and that is what eventually happened.[7] Once he was on African soil, though, Nixon somehow got into the spirit and even showed enthusiasm for his mission, which included making several other African stops after Ghana. With each successive visit, his appreciation of the importance of Africa, especially as a stage for Cold War competition, deepened.

Nixon's presence at the independence ceremonies had begun most inauspiciously. At one event, as he gladhanded with a crowd of Ghanaians, he turned to the nearest Black man, slapped him on the shoulder, and asked what it felt like to be free. "I wouldn't know, sir," the man replied. "I'm from Alabama."[8] Competing versions of this story survive, which suggests the possibility that it may be apocryphal. But Alabama hung over these events in a way that couldn't have been more resonant.

That is because Richard Nixon was not the only eminently noteworthy American undertaking his first trip to the African continent. Martin Luther King Jr. had also just arrived in Ghana, via stops in Senegal and Liberia. The Kings, Martin and Coretta, were lodged as guests on the campus of Nkrumah's alma mater, Achimota College. Two things still surprised people when they met Martin. It was natural to imagine a larger man, but he stood at only 5"7'. His grand stature was illusory, borne of his famously deep and resonant voice. Moreover, despite the carefully etched moustache, he still bore a hint of the cherub in his striking baby-face.

King was the most prominent member of a high-powered group of African American civil rights leaders who had come to bear witness to Ghana's moment of freedom. Flying on the plane from America with him had been Randolph, then vice-president of the AFL-CIO; the Harlem congressman, Adam Clayton Powell Jr.; Ralph Bunche; Roy Wilkins; and Lucille Armstrong (Louis couldn't make it).[9] Other movement people who made their way to Ghana separately included Horace Mann Bond; Detroit Congressman Charles C. Diggs Jr.; Lester Granger, director of the National Urban League; and James Robinson, the New York minister who would found Operation Crossroads Africa, an African American–led forerunner to the Peace Corps; and several influential figures from Howard University, starting with its president, Mordecai Johnson.

Members of the late Marcus Garvey's Universal Negro Improvement Association were also present, as was Norman Manley, the future prime minister of

Jamaica. Powell marveled, "Nothing in my public life of 27 years has attracted the attention and attendance of colored American leadership as has Ghana."[10] There were two highly noteworthy absences, however: Paul Robeson and W. E. B. Du Bois, both of whom had been refused passports by the US State Department on the pretext of their procommunist beliefs. A year earlier, in 1956, Du Bois had also been blocked from traveling to Paris to attend the Congress of Black Writers and Artists, whose organizer, Alioune Diop, editor of the important journal, *Présence Africaine*, spoke of it as a "second Bandung."[11] Du Bois presented his excuses to the congress in a searing telegram in which he wrote: "Any Negro-American who travels abroad today must either not discuss race conditions in the United States or say the sort of thing which our State Department wishes the world to believe."[12]

The twenty-seven-year-old Martin Luther King Jr., who had recently been appointed pastor of the Dexter Avenue Baptist Church, was a brand-new father. He had come straight out of the cauldron of anti-Black terror in Alabama as a leader of the Montgomery Bus Boycott. The struggle that had just unfolded there against racial segregation in public transportation fixed King, his philosophy of nonviolent resistance, and together with them, the country's accelerating civil rights struggle, front and center in the minds of the American public. On February 18, 1957, four years to the month after Nkrumah's image had made its appearance there, a portrait of King stared out resolutely from the cover of *Time* magazine, with a text noting that he had "risen from nowhere to become one of the nation's remarkable leaders of men."[13] All of this was before the man who would become renowned for his oratory had even given his first national speech.

The historic bus boycott had ended in December 1956, but the racist backlash against African Americans pushing for their rights in Alabama was still very much underway. Days after the boycott was called off, forty carloads of Ku Klux Klan members made a show of force on the streets of downtown Montgomery. In Birmingham, ninety miles to the northwest, after Fred Shuttlesworth announced that he would organize a similar strike there, terrorists exploded fifteen sticks of dynamite outside of his home on Christmas Eve. There had also been a spate sniper attacks, and earlier in the year, while the boycott was underway, the homes of King and of his closest ally, Ralph Abernathy, were also firebombed. The following year, after receiving numerous death threats, Rosa Parks, whose brave defiance of a driver's command to sit in the Black section had launched the bus strike, abandoned Montgomery for Detroit.

Nkrumah's invitation to King and to other African American leaders represented his astute but somewhat belated attempt to actively cultivate deeper connections between the fight for rights by American "negroes" and the incipient African liberation struggle that was still in its incipient stages. As we have seen, Nkrumah's response to the racism he experienced during his years in the United States often seemed surprising studied and less than visceral. It was as if he had not quite reached any deep form of identification either with American Blacks in racial terms or with their struggles in political ones. Now that was clearly beginning to change.

King had recently extended an important invitation of his own, only to be snubbed. Not long before his trip to Ghana he had written to Nixon to invite him to tour Alabama with him to witness firsthand the denial of rights to Black people and the continuing reign of terror there. "We are convinced that you will be better able to represent America's defense of justice and freedom at the celebration, if prior to your leaving for Africa on March 6th, you arrange for the fact-finding trip we have proposed. Into the South."[14]

Nixon never replied, but Ghana managed to bring the two men together, nevertheless. "You're Dr. King," the vice president said when they came face to face at an event in Accra, just prior to the independence ceremonies. "I recognized you from the cover of *Time*."[15] With that, King relaunched the invitation to join him in Alabama. "We are seeking the same kind of freedom that Ghana is celebrating."[16] Nixon told King vaguely that they could arrange a meeting in the United States. The African American press, which was heavily represented at Ghana's ceremonies, quickly got wind of the encounter, though, and carped that King had had to travel all the way to Africa to get Nixon to engage with him.

Toward King, Nkrumah played the opposite of hard to get, inviting his younger guest and his wife, Coretta, to a private lunch, a remarkable gesture of interest and respect given the presence of so many visiting foreign statesmen and officials in the country. But well beyond King's newly minted celebrity their backgrounds were very similar. King had first begun to give prominent emphasis to Gandhian ideas during the Montgomery bus boycott and had occasionally dropped the Indian's name into his sermons. In a speech before a Brooklyn congregation, he had explained how Gandhi's strategy of nonviolence, or what King called "passive resistance," had been used "to break loose from the British and brought the British Empire to its knees. . . . Let us now use this method in the United States."[17]

King's leadership during the bus boycott at such a young age had lifted him almost out of nowhere to the status of America's most famous and esteemed Black man. Many African Americans called him their president. Across the

African continent, millions of people now similarly revered Nkrumah and invested him with enormous hopes.

Both men had also been divinity students. King now was a famous preacher, but Nkrumah, too, had worked the pulpit, not just in a generic sense, but in the African American tradition before congregations in Philadelphia, New York, and the Washington, DC, region. Both men were far more widely read than most of the well-educated people they encountered, and both had studied and were influenced by Marx without ever becoming Marxists. Both had been prison graduates, secreting out of jail epistles scrawled on pilfered scraps of paper that would later inspire and guide a social or political revolution. Both rejected hatred of whites, or indeed of any "other," and embraced love as a core element of their philosophies.

Both, finally, had been the object of his own careful self-reinvention. First, Francis Nwia had jettisoned his birth name to take on the more African and alchemically more urgent- and political-sounding name Kwame Nkrumah. For his part, Michael King, who was universally known as Little Mike in boyhood, then as ML, finally, as a student at Boston University, embraced his father's chosen name—itself only adopted in adulthood—Martin Luther. "It linked the King men to a fearless religious reformer who held fast to his beliefs despite excommunication and threats of death," wrote one King biographer.[18] It is difficult to imagine either man's career developed quite as it did without these changes.

It is easy to conjure a sense of how deeply King registered the vulnerability and danger of life for American Blacks as he came to Africa, fresh from the white terror of Montgomery and the reticence of the Eisenhower government to side with justice. These risks only increased for those who were now standing up for their rights more and more in public throughout the South. This reality helps us to imagine the pride, awe, and exhilaration that King experienced through the scenes of fresh emancipation and newfound freedom he witnessed in Ghana. His own Georgia family was a mere four generations removed from the horrors of the American racial prison labor complex known as plantation slavery. As he sat in the assembly to witness Nkrumah's final address, just before his midnight declaration of independence, tears welled in King's eyes and spilled down his cheeks.

In his turn, Nkrumah told King of the inspiration he had drawn from the courage of Montgomery's Black protesters and said that he "would never be able to accept the American ideology of freedom and democracy fully until America settles its own internal racial strife."[19] This was followed by a pitch. Measured in 2023 dollars, Ghana's per capita income of $490 was roughly equivalent to that of Singapore, and far ahead of other Asian economies like South Korea and Taiwan—countries that would famously emerge as powerhouses in the future. But despite statistics like these and any surface appearances of modest prosperity, Nkrumah told his guests, his country was dangerously overdependent on an unreliable source of income, cocoa. If it were to achieve prosperity, Ghana would urgently need to industrialize. This was the idea behind Nkrumah's centerpiece aspiration, the Volta Dam project, which he called "[my] baby and my ambition."[20] And he desperately wanted African American help in drawing attention to his country's needs and in generating investment and lending expertise.[21]

CHAPTER TWENTY-FOUR

Keep On Keeping On

RICHARD NIXON AND MARTIN LUTHER KING JR. WERE FINALLY BROUGHT together by the entangled convergence or interleaving of two great historical movements: Ghana's precedent-setting independence and the accelerating struggle for full Black citizenship rights in Alabama and throughout the American South. Freedom in Ghana resonated far beyond the pews of King's Dexter Avenue Baptist Church in Montgomery, and indeed, much more widely among African Americans than is remembered today. The primary agent for this was America's Black press, which displayed an extraordinary level of interest in the topic.

The most insistent but by no means the only chronicler of the emancipation moment was the *Pittsburgh Courier*. Writing near mid-century, James Baldwin had extolled the paper, saying that it "reflects with great accuracy the state of mind and the ambitions of the professional, well-to-do Negro who has found a place to stand."[1] One month before the independence ceremonies, a journalist wrote in the *Courier*, "The liberation of Ghana is more than the achieving of self-rule by a small country; it will become the symbol for the liberation of an entire continent and a breakthrough of the color bar to the Western European white world which has maintained colonialism."[2]

Articles and columns in other Black publications were prompt to emphasize a relevance far closer to home for American readers. "When Ghana is accepted into the UN, it is quite possible that the spokesmen for the land of our fathers may be the ones to rise on the floor and challenge the U.S. about its racial problems and so in effect, history will have turned a complete circle," opined Ethel Payne, a *Chicago Defender* writer dispatched to Ghana. "For it was from these shores that the slaves in chains were brought to America. Now, the free people of Ghana may be able to strike the last of the shackles from their brothers in America. It's an exciting idea to say the least."[3]

On March 9, the *Courier* ran a special edition consisting solely of articles about Ghana's independence. One column asked, "Are American Negroes an inferior people? Can they meet the full challenge of modern, Western civilization? We American Negroes look to Ghana to furnish the answers to these questions." Another column in the special edition concluded,

> When we, American Negroes, shake hands with Ghana today, we say not only "Welcome!" but also, "Your opportunity to prove yourself is our opportunity to prove ourselves." . . . It is our hope that the brilliant example of Ghana will spur us to close ranks similarly and pool talents and resources so that we in the great American democracy may attain a larger measure of independence.[4]

Letter writers to Black publications like these expressed even more ardor for the topic. Never had identification between Africans and African Americans seemed so complete.[5]

Newspapers were not the only venues for such sentiments and were possibly not even the most influential ones. On March 3, while Adam Clayton Powell Jr. was in Ghana, the minister who presided in his absence at Harlem's famous Abyssinian Baptist Church, David Licorish, offered up this interpretation of the significance of Ghana's independence for African Americans.

> At long last American Negroes are beginning to understand the ties of kinship which bind together the African people and American colored citizens. We sincerely hope and trust that this new nation in Africa will serve as a symbol to all colored peoples everywhere that freedom is possible for all. Ghana means that peoples everywhere must throw off the yoke of colonialism, servitude and second-class citizenship and enter into the full ranks of the rights of freedom and equality. It means that a people though downtrodden and held down by the shackles of servitude can rise and throw off the yoke of bondage. . . . It means that no people are permanent pawns in the hands of their masters.[6]

But it was through King, speaking from the pulpit of his Dexter Avenue Baptist Church soon after returning from his trip, who gave the message of Africa's transcendent importance for Black Americans its sharpest articulation. Montgomery has long been justly regarded as the crucible that turned King into the era's preeminent American civil rights leader. But his African travel shaped him no less profoundly. What King observed in Ghana solidified the strains of Gandhian nonviolence that were already building in him. It forged the birth in King of genuine pan-Africanist thought, and it deepened his awareness of the universal righteousness and fundamental connection between anticolonial and anti-imperial campaigns around the world. From this was born a sense of fellow feeling not only with Africans, but with the plight and struggles of all the brown- and yellow-skinned people that Sukarno had spoken to at Bandung. Years later, the fruit of this change in King, its seed planted in Ghana, ripened in his strong and vocal opposition to the American war in Vietnam, a position shared by Nkrumah.

King's firmly middle-class Montgomery congregation was well-informed, and it had enthusiastically helped fund his African trip. This guaranteed a rapt audience after he returned home, and he duly preached about the experience for the first time on April 7. King titled his sermon "The Birth of a New Nation," a play on the name of the notoriously racist film that was American cinema's first national blockbuster.[7] He did not patronize the people in the filled pews but assumed a degree of unfamiliarity with Africa, which remains in force today, and worked his way patiently into his topic by delivering some general history and background. First, he told them it was a continent composed of many countries, something that even today some reasonably educated people don't know or feign to ignore. "Egypt is in Africa," he announced, offering that many people would not realize this.[8] This was far from gratuitous, though. Egypt was much more than geography. Through the Book of Exodus, it was one of the central metaphors in the Bible, and this day, King was to make pointed use of it.

Before doing so, he told the congregation, seated in his red-brick, Gothic Revival church, that the Gold Coast had been "exploited and dominated and trampled over" since the first Europeans arrived there in the fifteenth century in a search of gold, which later gave way to a high-volume commerce in the Africans they enslaved.[9] Portugal, Holland, England, and even Denmark and tiny Brandenburg-Prussia had vied for this wealth measured in human flesh. But over time, their cruelty and avarice were no match for the human urge to live freely. "There seems to be a throbbing desire, there seems to be an internal desire for freedom within the soul of every man. And it's there; it might not break forth in the beginning, but eventually it breaks out." This, King argued as he warmed to his topic, was the lesson of Ghana.

Britain, he explained, had only come to rule over the whole of what became the Gold Coast in 1850. Even before then, the exploited peoples of the land had begun to organize themselves for the reconquest of their freedom. King alluded to the best-known example of this, the Fanti resistance to the so-called Bond of 1844. This notorious act was coincidentally signed on the same day, March 6, that Ghana obtained its independence. It had accorded Britain local trading rights but was slyly used to assert political control over the territory. Although countless setbacks awaited the denizens of the Gold Coast, what was key was that they never abandoned their struggle.

King then told his listeners that he had read Nkrumah's autobiography during his stay in Ghana and he drew on it to relate the key moments of Nkrumah's life. First he spoke of Nkrumah's humble birth to illiterate parents from a marginal ethnic group. He then spoke of his decade in America, his study of theology, his London days and engagement with pan-Africanism, and finally his return home.

As King forged deeper into his sermon, it was impossible to miss how much he had begun to identify his own struggle with Nkrumah's, and some of his words now feel like eerie prophecy. Nkrumah had started writing and was finally "placed in jail for several years because he was a seditious man. He was an agitator. He was imprisoned on the basis of sedition." But once the fixation on freedom and justice had taken hold of him, he could not be turned back.

A staid congregation like King's would have had mixed feelings about sedition, but this was nothing peculiar. One can assume the same was true for a great many African Americans. Labeling people who pushed publicly for ending segregation, for full citizens' rights and greater equality, as troublemakers, as rabble-rousers or as radicals and communists, was a time-honored tactic of forces that were opposed to change. King warned his listeners of this. He then explained how the Ghanaian had studied "Gandhi and his techniques." Nkrumah called his adoption of Gandhi's thought "positive action," which King described as "a beautiful thing," that would result in the creation of a "beloved community." He then picked up his biblical metaphor of Egypt to steel his listeners. "This new nation was now out of Egypt and had crossed the Red Sea," King said. "There is a great day ahead. The future is on its side. It's now going through the wilderness. But the Promised Land is ahead."

The word "wilderness" meant all of the political uncertainty and resistance from the West that Ghana would encounter. But it also signified Ghana's extreme reliance on raw commodities, and especially cocoa, whose prices fluctuated wildly, and which the Gold Coast had had no ability to transform under British rule. Overcoming this "wilderness" called for a new and enlarged beloved community, one that would draw African Americans to Ghana to contribute to the building of a new nation. "There will be hundreds and thousands of people, I'm sure, going over to make for the growth of this new nation," he said. "And Nkrumah made it very clear to me that he would welcome any persons coming there as immigrants and to live there."

Ghana held many lessons for his listeners, King concluded. Its freedom was part of a "new order of justice and freedom and good will" coming to the world, one that included "the whole Asian-African bloc." Here was another clear echo of Bandung. But King wanted his listeners to believe that this new order included African Americans, as much as any other people of color, stepping into emancipation from colonial rule. Ghana had taught that "you can break aloose from evil and nonviolence, through a lack of bitterness," but "the road to freedom is a difficult, hard road," mined with hardships and setbacks.

Completing the difficult task that lay before his congregation and before fellow African Americans would require "persistent revolt," "persistent agitation," and persistently rising up against the system of evil. "The bus protest is just the beginning." Then invoking the cap stitched with the letters PG that Nkrumah had worn at his country's birth, King said, "Ghana reminds us of that. You better get ready to go to prison." The unavoidable sacrifices and even suffering that awaited Black Americans would ultimately be worth it, because "Ghana tells me that the forces of the universe are on the side of justice." Parishioners would not have missed that this phrase was a virtually identical phrase to one he had used after the triumph of the Montgomery bus boycott.[10]

CHAPTER TWENTY-FIVE

Frenemies

THIRTY DAYS AFTER LEADING HIS COUNTRY INTO INDEPENDENCE, KWAME Nkrumah boarded a plane for his first trip as prime minister. It sped 320 miles westward, lofting him above the blinding white cumulus clouds that coalesce and explode like enormous popcorn kernels so near the equator. Steadily, its loud twin propellers powered the craft over the canopy of thick tropical forests and narrow coastal lagoons that seemed to scroll by along the Atlantic seaboard far below. Nkrumah's destination was Abidjan, the rapidly modernizing capital of the neighboring Ivory Coast, where he had arranged to meet with Félix Houphouët-Boigny, the leader of a land that had very contentedly remained a French colony, at least officially speaking.

Houphouët-Boigny turned out at the Abidjan airport that morning to welcome his guest as he descended from his stubby, two-propeller DC-3. Protocol seemed to demand it. But others who were present greeted Nkrumah as well, with an enthusiasm that was not on the program. "Freedom! Ghana! Nkrumah!" the crowd of onlookers shouted from behind a red cordon as the two men shook hands and exchanged routine niceties. Houphouët-Boigny was short in stature, with dark skin and eyebrows that arched over animate, black marble irises. His expressions tended toward the kindly, his manner was courtly but he was every bit as confident as Nkrumah. And as he led his guest to their waiting motorcade, with both men still smiling, girls dressed in Ghana's national colors danced in the path of the two men, their enthusiasm getting the better of them, slowing the men's progress.[1]

The Ivory Coast visit marked the start of an extraordinary burst of African and international diplomacy for Nkrumah, whom some critics soon came to believe was already placing more emphasis on pan-Africanism than he was in successfully steering his new nation into the future. For Nkrumah, though, the two notions were inseparable.

Nkrumah's early encounters with Houphouët-Boigny receive little attention in most accounts of his political life, but the ties between the men, mutually suspicious, if superficially cordial, quickly turned to fierce rivalry. To a degree that is rarely emphasized, their relations would profoundly shape Nkrumah's pan-Africanist project and his hold on power.

In many ways, neighboring Ghana and the Ivory Coast were and remain twins. Although the latter is marginally bigger in territorial size, the former came into independence with a substantially larger and more urbanized population. The borders of both had been determined by the whims of Europeans in the wake of the Berlin Conference of 1884. The curious product was two generically rectangular territories sitting adjacent to each other. Each was somewhat longer on its north-south axis than east to west. The one was ruled over by Britain, the other by France.

By the middle of the twentieth century, the superficial resemblances had even extended to their leaders. Houphouët-Boigny was just four years older than Nkrumah, and early on, he had forged his path into politics as something of a radical. Under French rule, the people of the Ivory Coast had always enjoyed far less political space than Ghanaians, not even holding a local election until 1946. French colonial authorities frequently worried about the arrival of subversive influences from next door. People of the Ivory Coast, the French imagined, might emulate the people of the Gold Coast by demanding to sit on local governance boards of various kinds. Or more troublingly, the French imagined, the Ivory Coast intellectuals might fall under the sway of proto-pan-Africanists like Casely Hayford, or dabble in Garveyism, or somewhat later, embrace the aggressively pro-independence politics of the Gold Coast's crusading newspapers, like Azikiwe's *African Morning Post*. That paper had heavily promoted writings by George Padmore, including a book with the title, *Africa: Britain's Third Empire*.

Early in his political career, Houphouët-Boigny formally allied himself with the French Communist Party, but this was mostly a reflection of the stark conservatism that prevailed in France's international politics; even France's Communist Party hoped that empire would survive in Africa. "Can it be said that I, Houphoët-Boigny, a traditional chief, a doctor of medicine, a big property owner, a Catholic ... am a Communist?" Houphouët-Boigny asked, after breaking with the communists.[2] Nkrumah, for his part, was frequently attacked by the British press, by critics in Ghana, and ultimately by Houphouët-Boigny, too, for his reputed communist leanings. But although he routinely made vague allusions to scientific socialism as an element in what became known as Nkrumahism, he never identified himself as a communist nor even aligned Ghana with a communist power.

As his quote about landholding hinted, Houphouët-Boigny descended from traditional royalty in the largest ethnic group in the Ivory Coast, the Baoulé. He inherited large land holdings and obtained an elite education in Senegal, where Dakar was the administrative center for all of France's West African colonies. There, he attended medical school, qualifying as a so-called African doctor, which implies something short of the full French medical *cursus*. For all of the tactical opportunism that had once pulled him to the left, Houphouët-Boigny governed the Ivory Coast as an archconservative. He rose to power partly based on the fortune he had built as an owner of cocoa and coffee plantations at Yamoussoukro, near the colony's geographical center. But there was more to his success than wealth and privilege. He had cleverly found a way to marry the interests of the small class of indigenous "planters," like himself, with the aspirations of the masses.

For most of France's subjects in the colony, the main way to enter the wage economy was through a hellish form of near slavery known as *travail forcé*: planting, weeding, and harvesting on lands owned by the powerful and fiercely conservative French settler community. Every year peasants would be rounded up to perform this grueling labor: Houphouët-Boigny made the ending of travail forcé the centerpiece of his political activism and in May 1946, he rose to immense popularity locally on the basis of its abolition.

As Houphouët-Boigny, a deputy representing the colony, said in a crusading speech just prior to the abolition vote in the French National Assembly:

> One has to have read the eyes of planters forced to abandon their own land to work for starvation wages; one has to have seen the long lines of men, women and children, brows furrowed, march silently along the road to the fields; one has to have seen the recruiting agents, the modern slave traders, crowd people heedlessly in trucks, exposed to all climes, or lock them into baggage cars like animals; one must have lived, as chief, through the poignant, heartrending scenes, when old women demand their sons, orphans ask for their fathers, women weighed down by children for their husbands, their only providers, to understand the drama of forced labor in the Ivory Coast.[3]

For a cosmic instant, political opportunism and justice were perfectly aligned. Beyond this elemental question of human and labor rights, though,

Houphouët-Boigny's politics were hitched tightly to France. Paris's policies toward its colonies underwent repeated shifts in the mid-1950s, as the country's leaders slowly came to terms with the reality that as the French empire began to crumble in other parts of the world, holding onto colonies in the sub-Saharan reaches of Africa was probably untenable. Houphouët-Boigny became a minister in various French cabinets beginning in 1956 under the arrangements of the French Union, which gave Paris's African colonies modest representation in the French National Assembly. There, his ardent attachment to France made him more conservative on this issue even than the imperial-minded de Gaulle, who returned to power as president in June 1958.

Houphouët-Boigny's singular political history presented a thorny political backdrop for Nkrumah's first diplomatic foray after achieving independence. As we have seen, Nkrumah was a lifelong anticolonial activist who aspired to building a federation of West African states. Moreover, he conceived of this as a mere steppingstone to his even grander vision of creating a continent-wide government. Houphouët-Boigny, whose territory had recently begun generating more wealth through plantation agriculture than any of France's other African colonies, was unabashedly in favor of putting off independence. An opportunist, Houphouët-Boigny was also chary of any scheme that could cause his country's income to be used to underwrite poorer countries. The ideal arrangement for the Ivory Coast, as far as he was concerned, would be to remain hitched to France but only loosely connected with his neighbors.

Houphouët-Boigny had not deigned to attend Ghana's independence ceremonies. This was perhaps his way to avoid fueling hopes for independence among more progressive elements in the colony he presided over, including a fringe within his own party, the Rassemblement Démocratique Africain (RDA). Just a year earlier, Pierre-Henri Teitgen, then French minister for the colonies in a center-right government and later champion of the European Convention on Human Rights, had warned, "nothing is more contagious than the thirst for independence.... It will spread successively to the Anglophone and Francophone territories."[4] And if contagion was the worry, Nkrumah was the most likely vector.

Raymond Aron, a grand French political thinker in the mid-twentieth century liberal tradition who obsessed over individual and collective liberties in the Western context, posed very different questions about how France should relate to each of its colonies: "What is it worth? What does it cost? What does it bring in?"[5] Having just been routed in Indochina and now facing a war to hold onto to Algeria, France had decided that the Ivory Coast stood out as a place that still offered very good value. And a man with Houphouët-Boigny's politics made him an ideal partner and beneficiary.

Houphouët-Boigny rode with Nkrumah in a limousine to show off some of the impressive infrastructure that France had inaugurated in 1950. These included Port-Bouët and its adjacent Vridi Canal, which connected the sheltered shipping terminal with the Atlantic. To reach the new modern port, they had crossed a major bridge, which spanned the city's lagoon, freshly built by the French and named for de Gaulle. Monumental recent projects like these clearly announced Paris's resolve to turn the Ivory Coast into its regional showcase and to promote export agriculture there hard in order to make the colony pay off big.

The two men, host and guest, were twinned in two other ways not yet mentioned. Whereas Nkrumah had adopted the Osagyefo honorific, Houphouët-Boigny had appended the word Boigny to his surname. This was said to be a family totem signifying the ram, whose powerful horns could batter down any obstacle. Houphouët-Boigny's Baoulé and Nkrumah's Nzima ethnic groups were both also members of the Akan peoples, a large linguistic and cultural cluster that straddles Ghana and the Ivory Coast, and of which the Ashanti were the largest component. Their two vernaculars were similar enough to be mutually comprehensible. So even though the one spoke French and little English, and the other the opposite, they dispensed with translators and had little trouble making themselves understood. After ensuring that his guest had taken in an eyeful of the various recent construction projects, from which his political career would benefit, Houphouët-Boigny pointedly remarked: "All of these were gifts of the French. Without the generous participation of the metropole, how could Africa develop?" In his enthusiasm toward France, Houphouët-Boigny was overestimating Paris's economic potential. It's largesse toward this favored colony had been made possible by American support for France under the Marshall Plan.[6]

That evening, Nkrumah was given an opportunity to reply. Generous cheers greeted him when he addressed local dignitaries at the new National Assembly building, yet another French creation. Winning yet more applause, Nkrumah told his audience that independence should be the goal of all African countries, and that there should be no differentiation in their principles on this subject. But Houphouët-Boigny rose then to respond to this perceived challenge and criticized his guest's ideology with unusual directness. "Your example has not ceased interesting us," he said, before rejecting Nkrumah's notions of federation and pan-Africanism. "Because of the human relations that exist between the French and Africans, and given the imperative of the century, the interdependence of peoples—we felt that it was perhaps of greater interest to attempt a different kind of experiment from yours, the only one of its kind: a Franco-African Community based on equality and fraternity."[7]

Houphouët-Boigny went on to dramatically announce that a wager has been made between the leaders of the two territories, "one having chosen independence, the other preferring the difficult road to the construction, with the metropole, of a community of men equal in rights and duties. . . . Let each of us undertake his experiment, in absolute respect of the experiment of his neighbor, and in ten years we shall compare the results."[8]

The Ivory Coast leader's words and manner had the veneer of congeniality, with perhaps a small trace of condescension, but this could scarcely conceal the colder reality beneath. Besting Nkrumah, or better, clipping his wings, was a deadly serious matter. France saw the Ghanaian as a serious threat to its interests in the region, and in addition to wanting to build up the Ivory Coast as a dominant economic player in the region, it sought to bolster Houphouët-Boigny politically as well, turning him into a kingpin of French West Africa.

CHAPTER TWENTY-SIX

Quand On Refuse On Dit Non

FINDING HOUPHOUËT-BOIGNY IMMUTABLE, NKRUMAH IMMEDIATELY SET about working around him, forging strong ties with the Ivory Coast's three French speaking neighbors. His very next visit was to Guinea, the country that, of the three, would become the most important on the African stage. Houphouët-Boigny's neighbor to the northwest was far less developed than the Ivory Coast, but it had a glorious history. Four centuries earlier, it had been part of the Mali Empire, which was prodigiously wealthy in gold and had ruled for centuries over a vast stretch of West Africa south of the Sahara.[1] More recently, the highlands of Guinea had also been the homeland of a formidable Islamic leader named Samori Ture. For sixteen years, toward the close of the nineteenth century, the tactical brilliance of Ture's armies had frustrated French efforts to extend colonial control over the region. Ture was finally captured by French troops in 1898 and exiled to Gabon, where he met a lonely death. Now, with Ghana having just gained independence, the French colony was presided over by a direct descendant of Ture, which set the stage for another showdown with Paris.

Houphouët-Boigny's counterpart in Guinea, Ahmed Sékou Touré, reputedly Samori's great-grandson, had begun his public life in labor activism as an organizer in the colony's Post and Telecommunications Office but had risen quickly to lead the Guinea branch of the Confederation Générale du Travail, the communist-affiliated umbrella French labor union. He became a national figure in Guinea by leading a seventy-one-day general strike in 1953, the longest ever in French West Africa. The previous year, Touré had founded the Parti Démocratique de Guinée (PDG), which became a local affiliate of Houphouët-Boigny's regional umbrella organization, the RDA. The spotlight on him from these activities earned Touré a seat representing Guinea in Paris in the French Assembly, right alongside Houphouët-Boigny.

Unlike Houphouët-Boigny, though, Touré's politics were tilted decidedly leftward. A legendarily energetic man, with handsome, sculpted features, he was endowed with a fierce trait of defiance toward France that some imagined was passed down from his famous ancestor. By the time Nkrumah came calling, Touré was working out the rudiments of his own version of pan-Africanism. His ideology possessed little of the internationalist pedigree of Nkrumah's, and almost none of its transatlantic history. It was profoundly rooted, instead, in a proud regional history and local notions of African identity. By 1956, Touré had renounced his ties with the French left and with Communist Party–affiliated unions. Instead of class struggle, he now insisted that Africans needed to forge a new politics of solidarity that would unite workers and peasants in a common mission of national construction and the recovery of African dignity. Among other things, this meant that labor unions should not strike in pursuit of their own narrow, albeit collective, interests. Touré insisted on putting the national interest first, requiring labor to submit to a central political authority. In the final analysis, this would come to mean him.

Not much is known about the content of Touré's conversations with the visiting Nkrumah. But the two men clearly forged a bond right from the start. Their relationship would remain a pillar of Nkrumah's political life all the way to his death in 1972. Nkrumah had recently come through his own major showdown with organized labor on the eve of independence. Unions had played a vital role in Nkrumah's rise, but in 1955, gold miners went on strike demanding higher wages at a time when the new leader's government was desperate for foreign exchange needed to finance its ambitious development programs. This presented Nkrumah with an excruciating tradeoff, and one that powerfully exemplifies a dilemma that nearly all of Africa's new independent states would soon face. If he supported the big foreign companies that operated Ghana's mines, some of the richest in the world, he risked losing the support of his base. If he backed the striking workers, on the other hand, this would be seen in the capitalist West as hostility to foreign investment in a country that badly needed to attract capital.

Ultimately, a wage rise so small as to be symbolic—a single shilling—was agreed upon and this ended the strike. Soon after independence, though, understanding the threat that Western-style organized labor could pose to his program in the future, Nkrumah moved swiftly to bring Ghana's unions under the control of a party-dominated umbrella organization, the Trade Union Council. At the same time, Nkrumah coopted some of his country's most militant labor leaders. This was the very path that Touré had chosen in Guinea, only even less compromisingly.

Touré, for his part, was about to make an entrance into African history nearly as grand as Nkrumah's breakthrough to independence had been, if completely different in nature. On June 1, 1958, Charles de Gaulle was returned to office in France as a president with strong executive powers in a France that had spent much of that decade politically adrift. De Gaulle's mandate included salvaging what remained of French empire in the face of its recent defeat in Indochina and a costly and divisive new war in Algeria.

In sub-Saharan Africa, this placed de Gaulle and Nkrumah on a collision course, with Houphouët-Boigny cast alongside the Frenchman as his eager surrogate if not sycophant. From the first moments of independence, Nkrumah, as we have seen, acted with determination to place his vision of a federated Africa at the heart of state policy. To promote the idea, Ghana hosted what was called the first Conference of Independent African States (CIAS), in April 1958. It was attended by Ethiopia, Ghana, Liberia, Libya, Morocco, Sudan, Tunisia, and the United Arab Republic. Among the conference's published priorities, "assisting dependent African territories in their efforts toward the attainment of self-government" was listed fourth. But this was clearly the heart of the matter for Nkrumah, who presided. In his opening remarks, which were addressed not only to participants but to attentive international observers, as well as his neighbors. Nkrumah noted that this was the first time that representatives of independent African states had met together to forge closer relations, and he urged great powers to "let the African states work out their own destinies."[2]

The most obvious targets for such a message aimed at helping to keep the Cold War out of Africa were the world's two big emerging blocs. Western governments and communist powers were all working up assessments of what Ghana's independence could portend for the continent. Nkrumah's commitment to nonalignment was clear. In a National Assembly speech in 1958, he stated, "Our attitude . . . is very much that of America looking at the disputes of Europe in the nineteenth century. We do not wish to be involved." By the same token, he said, Ghana believed that "the peace of the world in general is served, not harmed by keeping one great continent free from the strife."[3]

The CIAS had other, less obvious non-African audiences in mind, as well. The Ghanaian leader had opted not to attend the Asian-African Conference in Bandung, Indonesia, in 1955, sending Kojo Botsio, one of his most trusted lieutenants, in his place. The Bandung Conference brought together twenty-nine participating countries in a movement aimed at hastening the end of colonial rule around the world and loosely banding countries of the newly decolonized world together to allow them to escape domination by the superpowers. This was done through political solidarity, refusing to choose sides, and through economic cooperation. As such, Bandung had widely been seen as a major first step toward the creation of what became known as the Non-Aligned Movement.

Nkrumah had strong ideas of his own in this realm, though. His aim was to somehow unite Africa politically, and as the triumphant leader of the first sub-Saharan country to free itself from European control, he was equally fixated on playing a leadership role on the continental level. This fed in him a resentment of what he perceived to be a patronizing attitude toward Africa from leaders in Asia, including Jawaharlal Nehru and Sukarno of Indonesia, whose countries had enjoyed a head start in gaining independence. Nkrumah was also wary of Nasser, who enjoyed a star turn at Bandung. Egypt had traditionally turned its back to Europe's Black colonies in Africa, but after the Indonesian gathering, Nasser—long inclined to considering Egypt superior to sub-Saharan Africa—became fixated on the idea of building influence to Egypt's south.

Nkrumah saw the CIAS as a steppingstone toward creating a grand, Bandung-style conference for Africans. He had studied Sukarno carefully and sought to emulate his achievements, proving that African countries could come together just as Bandung had shown more broadly how non-Western nations could strike a common cause. He also wished to use the Accra gathering as a "global megaphone," as one writer has called Sukarno's Bandung, to trumpet Ghana's independence.[4] At the CIAS, following Nkrumah's lead, delegates from participating countries spoke openly about the need to limit the direct involvement of outsiders on the continent, European or Asian, explicitly likening this idea to a Monroe Doctrine for Africa.[5]

De Gaulle's vision could scarcely have been more different. For him, finding a way to somehow hold on to France's Black colonies in a world increasingly hostile to old-fashioned European imperialism became a central preoccupation. The same day he was returned to power, de Gaulle announced a plan before the French National Assembly to refashion the old French Union into what it called a community, with the president of France as its head. This was a significant new step in postwar efforts to remodel French imperialism that had been proceeding in fits and starts. The previous year, for example, had seen the passage of the so-called Loi Cadre, or enabling act. This measure set in motion the fragmentation of France's African empire, which had hitherto been administered as two immense zones, French West Africa and French Equatorial (meaning central) Africa. Prior to the Loi Cadre, each of these regional blocks had been overseen by a governor general, with one seated in

Dakar and the other in Brazzaville, the capital of French Congo. This arrangement only allowed a minimal role for local administration of what were only nominally distinct colonies. With the new law, however, each colony belatedly became the custodian of its own internal affairs.

Houphouët-Boigny was a French minister of state as Paris pursued this scheme of deliberate division. Under the rubric of "territorial services," the Loi Cadre devolved responsibility for the civil service and for programs that addressed localized economic and social development—and the heavy costs that went with them—to each of France's colonies. Paris, however, retained control of areas that were considered vital to its own economic interests and standing in the world. These so-called state services included foreign relations, the police, defense, monetary matters, and the customs service, as well as media and communications. Paris adjudged all of these areas necessary for "maintaining the solidarity of the elements comprising the Republic."[6] From the perspective of France, this meant the best of both worlds, allowing it to shoulder minimal costs, while enjoying maximal benefits. It would be wrong to characterize the debate about a French Union as entirely reactionary and devoid of ideas about the expansion of rights for Africans and power sharing with them. Although never resolved because of division in France and, indeed between African leaders like Senghor and Houphouët-Boigny, these included the possibility of full citizenship and representation in the French National Assembly.[7]

On August 21, 1958, with many of the fine points of his grand design still in flux, de Gaulle, a man renowned for a haughtiness that had little to do with his tall and thin stature, set off on a tour of France's Black colonies to sell the idea of this new community. In each capital, he rode into town standing in the back of an open-roofed car, waving in full uniform to crowds that had been turned out to cheer him by colonial authorities who declared public holidays to ensure a turnout. In a would-be show of supposed magnanimity, he pledged that Africans would be allowed to vote to endorse or reject his plan, but France, he warned, would construe any rejection to mean secession "with all its consequences."[8] By clear implication, this meant the rejecting country would lose French economic support.

At six-foot-three, as one early acquaintance described him, de Gaulle "stood out not so much because of his size but because of his ego, which glowed from afar."[9] A measure of this can be heard in a famous declaration of his after he returned to power months earlier: "Great circumstances bring forth great men. Only during crises do nations throw up giants." At one stop after another de Gaulle drew large, approving crowds that seemed to signal strong backing for the community scheme. But when de Gaulle arrived in Conakry, the seaside capital of Guinea, like a mirror falling from a wall, the pattern was suddenly shattered. From the platform, as de Gaulle looked on, Sékou Touré, as stockily built as a boxer and dressed in his trademark white robes and fez, calmly delivered a defiant speech. "We do not and never shall renounce our legitimate right to independence," he vowed, without explicitly recommending a yes or no vote. He was a progressive, although not the radical ideologue he was made out to be. As a *New York Times* profile of him held a few years later, "For Touré the test appears to be whether something is good for Africa or bad for Africa."[10] He had long preferred the idea of a federation of French-speaking African countries that could subsequently join in association with France, but the rank and file of his party had nudged him somewhat to the left.[11] He certainly did not see himself as calling for a complete rupture with France that day, though. Indeed, he explicitly stated that his country still desired cooperation with France. This is not how things would be remembered, though, least of all by a frothing de Gaulle, whose paternalistic manner and gallant sense of droit de seigneur had been questioned.

In reply, the French leader curtly warned from the podium that his country would "draw the necessary consequences." These began that very evening when de Gaulle skipped a scheduled official dinner with Touré. He also abruptly canceled an offer to allow the Guinean to fly with him aboard his plane to Dakar, Senegal.[12] After a cold handshake with Touré at the Conakry airport, an airfield really, with hangars and a rudimentary tower, de Gaulle reportedly uttered the words, "*Adieu, Guinea*," and boarded his plane, never to return. Few remember that during his next stop in Senegal, voices in the crowds there also shouted down de Gaulle, and speeches by some local politicians also called for independence, but in terms that sounded less blunt.

On September 28, it was the people of Guinea, not Touré per se, who delivered an overwhelming "no" to de Gaulle's proposal for a devolved community under French tutelage. Just over 95 percent of voters in Guinea opposed it. In reverse fashion, this figure mirrored the overwhelmingly "yes" vote registered in several colonies. And in no other French territory did "no" even reach 25 percent. Once again, de Gaulle's most enthusiastic partner was Houphouët-Boigny of Côte d'Ivoire, who told his people that to refuse France's offer would be to "exit from History." Houphouët-Boigny's backing and his party's fingers on the scales had seen to an implausible 99.98 percent "yes" result, and this sealed support for his rule from Paris that would endure for decades.[13]

Acting out of a mixture of embarrassment and pique, de Gaulle made good on his word and granted Guinea independence on October 2. France was long accustomed to patronizing its Black colonies. This was an inherent attraction of imperialism, perhaps even as important to the French as the income that empire generated. Grandeur necessitated it. Touré's Guinea, though, had broken this principle by delivering an unpardonable injury to France's self-regard, and to de Gaulle's, as well. To deal with this unaccustomed humiliation, Paris quickly set about punishing its wayward colony, following the same pattern seen when Toussaint Louverture defied Napoleon a century-and-a-half earlier. Then, even in victory, Haiti had "been made to kneel and crawl into the community of nations."[14] The acts of pettiness and retribution that ensued are legendary, but nonetheless true. French work on a major dam over the Konkouré River, albeit then still at an early stage, was abandoned. A French rice shipment was turned around at sea. French teachers working in Guinea were called home. French colonials destroyed everything from administrative files and office furniture to medical equipment and official vehicles. They destroyed prison records, requiring Guinea authorities later to ask detainees what they had been incarcerated for. Not even light bulbs and their fixtures were spared.

But Touré's remark, "We prefer poverty in freedom to riches in slavery," made him a legend almost overnight across the continent. He was lionized as the man who dared tell arrogant whites to their face what Africans believed in private. Going by his country's actions, France's leader seemed committed to the first half of Touré's formula. In good part as a result of the pressure created by the example of Ghana's independence, the French scheme of a grand community would not survive for two years, as, in domino fashion, one of its colonies after another emulated Ghana and sought at least a kind of flag sovereignty of its own. Nkrumah, in the meantime, busied himself seeing to it that a defiant Sékou Touré would not be isolated and left alone.

CHAPTER TWENTY-SEVEN

Keep Your Juice

IN THE MIDST OF GHANA'S INDEPENDENCE CEREMONIES, KWAME NKRUMAH put out word that he would soon be visiting the United States as his sovereign country's new leader, which is slightly puzzling because there is no record of any invitation or even any serious official planning for such a trip up to this point.

Whether this remark was pure aspiration, a bit of boastfulness, or intuition, or whether Nkrumah knew of the scattered efforts afoot to bring him to the country where he had received his education for a victory tour, one cannot say. What is certain is that his celebrity and reputation in the United States were at a peak, and even before he was sworn in, African Americans had been nudging the State Department to make plans to host him. Here, a little-known figure, Albert Ceres, the director of public relations for the Veterans of Foreign Wars (VFW), took the lead. Beginning in early 1957, Ceres took it upon himself to contact Lincoln University, the University of Pennsylvania, and the Hershey Chocolate Corporation, whose confections were made from Ghanaian cacao, to enlist their help in organizing a return visit by Nkrumah to address an annual meeting of the VFW that July. Soon thereafter, Ceres reached out to the State Department. "Hundreds of our members are Negroes," Ceres noted, adding that Nkrumah's presence "would have domestic and international significance," given the strong Black interest in the man and in Ghana's pending independence both in the United States and around the world.[1]

At first, the State Department was slow to pick up the ball. Diplomats told Ceres that Washington could not provide support for a visit unless it was made under official auspices, and the planning for foreign dignitary visits for that year was already complete. It was not until that August that foreign service bureaucrats began casting around internally for names of Africans to invite to the United States during the following year. African specialists at State argued that not only had Nkrumah been the first politician in sub-Saharan Africa to lead his country into independence, but he had received an American education, and even in power he had maintained close ties with a network of African Americans in academia. Nkrumah's name then rose to the top of the list.

Months of preparation went into putting together the official invitation and program. But even before this work could be finished, another high-level visit from Ghana to the United States seriously threatened relations between the two countries. This was the visit of Komla Gbedemah, the finance minister who had almost singlehandedly managed the CPP's victorious electoral campaign in 1951 while Nkrumah was in a colonial jail. Seven months after Ghana's independence, Gbedemah traveled to the US for meetings with the World Bank and International Monetary Fund and also to seek American support for the overwhelming priority of Nkrumah's economic development program. Its linchpin was a project to build the large hydroelectric dam on the Volta River that would allow Ghana to smelt bauxite into aluminum and thereby enter the industrial age.

On an October evening in 1957, Gbedemah set off from New York City by car for Washington, DC, to pursue his official program there. He was accompanied by Bill Sutherland, a Black American pan-Africanist and pacifist whom Gbedemah had previously engaged as an aide. In his time, few other people lived a life more intricately connected to the workings of the Black Atlantic than Sutherland. A lifelong political activist, Sutherland had joined the NAACP as a New Jersey teenager. Upon graduating from college in 1940, he began an enduring relationship with the Quaker-affiliated American Friends Service Committee. His involvement in a Congregational Church in his hometown had also planted a seed of devoted nonviolence in him. This involved joining movements to save the Scottsboro Boys at the end of the 1930s, as well as a Gandhian commune in Newark that was opposed to the Second World War. From there, Sutherland moved to Greenwich Village, where Richard Wright and C. L. R. James were his neighbors. After Pearl Harbor, Sutherland's conscientious objection to America's entry into the war and outspokenness against racial discrimination in the United States earned him a four-year sentence in federal prison in Pennsylvania, double the penalty imposed on anyone else up to that time, for refusing induction into the military. Incarcerated under segregated conditions, Sutherland, a light-skinned Black man with frazzled hair and goatee when he was free, fasted to protest the violence and Jim Crow conditions he was subjected to.

After his release, Sutherland demonstrated at home against the Korean

War and then, in 1951, traveled with three others by bicycle from Paris to Moscow. As members of a group called the War Resisters League, they took this action to protest the proliferation of nuclear weapons. After rubbing shoulders with many Africans in Europe, Sutherland then became a supporter of the Defiance Campaign, an early anti-apartheid movement led by Nelson Mandela, Walter Sisulu, and Oliver Tambo. It was amid these efforts that he became acquainted in turn with Bayard Rustin and George Padmore, each in his own sphere, as we have seen, an early and enormous force in Black political activism. In 1953, Sutherland pulled up stakes in the United States to move to newly self-governed Ghana. This made him one of the earliest members of what would grow to become a historic wave of hundreds of African Americans drawn by Nkrumah's rise and by the bright promise of Black emancipation under pan-Africanism. Padmore had furnished a letter of introduction to Nkrumah, and Marguerite Cartwright, a columnist at the *Pittsburgh Courier* who had known Nkrumah since his student days in the United States, had suggested Sutherland to Gbedemah as a personal aide.[2] In Ghana, Sutherland married Efua Morgue, a Junoesque dramatist and cultural activist whose life work and writings inspired the creation of a biennial continental festival of theater arts called PANAFEST. As Sutherland explained years later:

> I thought that America, in the height of the McCarthy period—I didn't foresee Martin Luther King, I didn't foresee the women's movement or all these other things—I thought things were going to just go down, down, down in America. And I decided that I wanted to put my lot in with the African liberation movement.[3]

As Gbedemah's aide, Sutherland had personally arranged for King to be invited to Ghana's independence ceremonies and while King was there, he introduced him to both Nkrumah to Julius Nyerere, soon-to-be leader of independent Tanzania, where Sutherland would relocate in 1961. Sutherland would also later play a role in hosting Malcolm X during his 1964 visits to both Ghana and Tanzania. Beginning in the 1970s, Sutherland helped lead the campaign that would culminate with South African anti-apartheid activist Bishop Desmond Tutu being named a Nobel Peace laureate in 1984.

Because they had a scheduled speaking engagement in Maryland, both Sutherland and Gbedemah dressed in sober business suits for their 1957 drive from New York City to Washington. At Dover, Delaware, they pulled off the highway for a rest. There, they ordered two 30¢ orange juices at an orange, brick-roofed Howard Johnson's, which was then the nation's largest restaurant chain. A waitress there exposed the Ghanaian to a grim central truth of American society, one that Sutherland had probably already briefed him about in depth.

Segregation was still the rule in much of the United States, including in the North. The lived Black experience of being turned away from a public accommodation was one that James Baldwin had likened to "some dread, chronic disease, the unfailing symptom of which is a kind of blind fever, a pounding in the skull and fire in the bowels."[4]

What the waitress said when she returned with the refreshments could scarcely have conveyed America's dark truth more starkly. Gbedemah would have to enjoy his cold drink outside, she told him. The visitor protested by presenting a business card that displayed his high official position back home and demanding to see the manager. But this made no difference. "Colored people are not allowed to eat in here," she stated flatly. When the manager appeared, Gbedemah told him, "If the vice president of the US can have a meal in my house when he is in Ghana, then I cannot understand why I must receive this treatment at a roadside restaurant in America."[5]

Gbedemah then told the stalwart manager to keep his juice and warned him that he had not heard the last of this, and he was true to his word. News of the way he had been refused service quickly spread both in America and in Ghana, along with Gbedemah's vow that he would demand an apology from the US ambassador in Ghana upon his return home.[6] "Gbedemah Meets Colour Bar in the United States," read a headline in the *Ghana Evening News*. The *New York Times* was more oblique. Its headline read, "Restaurant Bars African Leader."[7]

Coming at the height of the Cold War, the Gbedemah incident flirted with becoming a public diplomacy disaster of the first order. Barely a month earlier, the United States had received harsh unwanted worldwide attention over the school desegregation crisis in Little Rock, Arkansas. There, the governor, Orval Faubus, had called out the state national guard to thwart a courageous attempt by nine Black students to integrate the city's Central High School. Years later, the Black Harvard Law School scholar Derek Bell wrote that the 1954 Supreme Court desegregation ruling in *Brown v. Board of Education* could not be fully understood in terms of majority American concerns about the "immorality of racial inequality." The need to abandon segregation was almost equally about the search for "credibility [in] America's struggle with Communist countries to win the hearts and minds of emerging third world peoples."[8] In Arkansas, in the highest-profile way imaginable, that credibility was put to a stiff test. This forced Eisenhower's hand in federalizing the

National Guard to shield the Black students who became known as the Little Rock Nine from howling white mobs, captured in what are now historic photographs, so that they could attend classes. Eisenhower had a well-earned reputation for shunning involvement in the country's now rapidly escalating civil rights struggle, but his advisors prevailed upon him that a continued hands-off approach would inflict prohibitive damage to America's image overseas.

Two years earlier, fourteen-year-old Emmett Till had been brutally murdered near Money, Mississippi, for supposedly making a pass at a white woman. This drew expressions of shocked disapproval of America's grim racial realities, even from some of the closest US allies. "The Life of a Negro Isn't Worth a Whistle," read one German headline.[9] During Little Rock, the president had been shamed into action by one of the country's best known African Americans, Louis Armstrong. The jazz trumpeter and vocalist had become one of America's most widely revered performers, in part because of his jovial—that is, nonthreatening—image, but also because of the political circumspection that he usually displayed. Outraged over the government's reluctance to enforce school integration, Armstrong was moved to call Eisenhower "two-faced" and said, "It's getting almost so bad a colored man hasn't got a country."[10]

Not long after returning from his tour of Africa that included Ghana's independence ceremonies, Richard Nixon warned Eisenhower, "Every instance of racial prejudice in this country is blown up in such a manner as to create a completely false impression of the attitudes and practices of the great majority of the American people. The result is irreparable damage to the cause of freedom which is at stake."[11] In this spirit, the State Department rushed to apologize over Gbedemah's treatment, calling it "an exceptional and isolated incident."[12] Nixon received Gbedemah in his home the next morning, and shortly afterward, Eisenhower issued a breakfast invitation for the Ghanaian, not at the offending Howard Johnson restaurant, but in the White House, for the following day.

Eisenhower's lone Black White House advisor, E. Frederic Morrow, gamely attempted to spin all of this, saying: "The President was incensed," and had decided on the gesture "without any prompting from his aides." Morrow called this "an eloquent rebuttal to the Delaware treatment."[13] But that the initial apology alone was deemed insufficient reflected the fear in Washington of losing yet more ground in a fast-emerging theater of the raging Cold War, a propaganda competition in Africa with Moscow. Regular reports of racial discrimination and violence against Blacks in the United States had become common fodder for Soviet propaganda.

The discussions in Washington about how to handle Gbedemah were hardly free of casual prejudice. Christian Herter, the under-secretary of state and former Republican governor of Massachusetts, said of the breakfast invitation, for example, "It's a very nice idea—he is an *uncouth fellow* but a nice idea."[14] If the somnolent Eisenhower White House still lacked the will to decisively support the struggle for civil rights in America, here at least it did not fall hopelessly behind on an evolving story.

Gbedemah, a proud Achimota alumnus, made the most of his breakfast with Eisenhower. He showed up at the White House that morning dressed in a traditional outfit of bright, ceremonial Kente cloth slung over his left shoulder and wasted no time putting the unanticipated meeting with the American president to another use—pressing the case for Ghana's dam-building ambitions.

Nkrumah exhibited some pique over Gbedemah's reception by Eisenhower, upstaging him as the first official from Ghana to visit the White House. The finance minister's entrée at the highest levels in Washington presaged trouble between the two men much later. It also signaled a closing of space in the Ghanaian state press for anything that criticized Nkrumah or otherwise displeased him. Likely in response to his orders, news of the meeting was not broadcast in the country.[15] Gbedemah had nonetheless been able to put Ghana's case for the Volta Dam before Eisenhower, and, spurred in part by the Howard Johnson incident, a president who had little history of interest in Africa had proven receptive. No promises were made, but Eisenhower said he would try to interest American industry in assessing the viability of the project, and this led to a breakthrough, albeit a long, drawn-out one, that bore many new bitter fruits. At the White House's encouragement, the Kaiser Aluminum Corporation soon entered preliminary talks with the Nkrumah government, and the company's chief and founder, Henry J. Kaiser, was about to become an important figure in Nkrumah's diplomatic life and economic program.

CHAPTER TWENTY-EIGHT

High Water

AFRICAN AMERICAN ATTENTION IN THE UNITED STATES TO NKRUMAH'S Ghana crested again in the spring of 1958, around the time of the first anniversary of independence. A Black-owned newspaper, the *Chicago Defender*, even sent its United Nations correspondent to cover the celebration. "The Africans have two vital things we need badly," Marguerite Cartwright reported. "The Africans have a sense of destiny, of inescapable achievement and glory while we are being smothered by a gnawing cynicism. They are reaching for a massive all embracing unity through which to express a new idea of African personality, while we fester in our insularity behind the borders of the United States."[1]

That same March, the State Department extended a formal invitation to Nkrumah to make the first visit to Washington of a Black leader of an African state. This represented something of a turnabout, influenced by Nixon, who had been reluctant to attend Ghana's independence ceremonies, and who, before that, had likened Africans to "tree-dwelling apes." The vice president was a paranoid and ambitious climber whose politics were as pliable as his features—adored, if only by cartoonists—all leonine jowls and ski slope nose. His support for engaging with Nkrumah clearly grew out of Cold War considerations. In a report issued to Eisenhower following his Africa tour, the vice president wrote that the United States must "follow most closely the evolution of [Ghana], realizing that its success or failure is going to have profound effects upon the future of this part of Africa."[2]

By this time, Nixon's sights were set firmly on succeeding Eisenhower as president, and clearly the Cold War already figured to be at the center of the 1960 general election. In 1956, Eisenhower had won nearly 40 percent of the Black vote. In response, at least in part as a way of appealing to African American voters who were wary of the Democratic Party's hostility toward civil rights (as well as his own tepid record), John F. Kennedy had begun inserting messaging about support for African independence into his speeches and campaign statements. By one tally, Kennedy spoke about Africa 479 times during the campaign and, unimaginable today, made the continent a main focus of thirteen speeches while running for president.[3]

The most important and consistent impetus behind the high-level engagement with Ghana and Nkrumah, though, was lobbying by African Americans, whose demands for a visit had begun with Albert Ceres of the Veterans of Foreign Wars. In fact, as it began to come together, the Nkrumah visit marked a high point in relations between African Americans and Africa, a Golden Age that has not been matched since. The details reveal a tantalizing moment of almost unbridled optimism about the future of the continent. This was still a time of awed pride in Nkrumah's emergence as a confident and elegant Black statesman on the world stage, when intellectuals and civil rights activists who spanned almost the entire political spectrum of Black America saw Ghana's independence and the rise of a free Africa as a source of redemption and empowerment for African Americans. And this sentiment was hardly limited to Black American elites.

By definition, though, every high-water mark gives way to receding tides, and as we will see, although the causes were varied and the circumstances complex, the unprecedentedly broad interest in Africa would recede remarkably quickly. For starters, two factors stand out, each the seeming reflection of progress, and therefore dosed with irony. As the American civil rights movement gained strong momentum and began to regularly claim national attention, African Americans increasingly turned their focus inward, and the recent reliance on Africa as a source of inspiration or uplift ebbed. In a similar vein, beginning with a virtual cascade in 1960, one African country after another gained independence from European rule, sapping the theme of anticolonialism, hitherto so effectively linked with the cause of Black American emancipation, of much of its urgency.

As word spread of Nkrumah's pending visit to the United States, mostly by way of the African American press, the State Department and the Embassy of Ghana in Washington were inundated with invitations for Nkrumah to add stops and participation in local events in his itinerary. Harlem wanted in. Chicago wanted in. And besides these two citadels of African American life, both of which were incorporated into the program, many other places had to be turned down.

First up, though, Nkrumah had to be formally received, and for this, official Washington spared little effort. Here was another feature of this high-water moment. In the annals of American relations with sub-Saharan African countries, one can find few parallels for the quality of the protocol extended to Nkrumah. Richard Nixon, wearing a dark suit, white shirt, and striped tie, turned out to greet Nkrumah's plane as it landed at Washington's National Airport, accompanied for this purpose by General Maxwell Taylor, who would later become chairman of the Joint Chiefs of Staff and a leading advocate of America's escalation in the Vietnam War. Despite a scant record of interest in Africa, Eisenhower met with Nkrumah not once but twice, which included hosting him at a luncheon. Nixon and John Foster Dulles, the conservative American secretary of state, each held meetings with Nkrumah and hosted separate dinners for him. Nkrumah also addressed each house of Congress and was feted here and there by nationally prominent local politicians. Nkrumah also made an appearance at the National Press Club, and appearances elsewhere were as numerous as one might have expected for the leader of a major allied nation.

Averill Harriman, the patrician governor of New York, organized a luncheon in Nkrumah's honor at the city's most prestigious hotel, the Waldorf-Astoria. In Chicago, Mayor Richard J. Daley, one of the last old-time big-city bosses, whose relations with the city's Black population were often troubled, greeted Nkrumah at the airport and then paraded him around the city like a returning war hero. This all led W. E. B. Du Bois, not easily given to a favorable impression of white American attitudes toward Africa, to effuse that Nkrumah was "treated as never a Negro had been treated by the government."[4] In fact, it almost felt as if it was a fad, with each politician trying to outdo the last in impressing the Ghanaian.

Over Sunday morning breakfast, American television viewers were also greeted with the unusual spectacle of a Black guest in the role of leader of an independent country. During that appearance on NBC's *Face the Nation*, Nkrumah was pressed on two topics: nonalignment and the recent preventive detention law. The panel of reporters repeatedly grilled him about his policy of nonalignment, treating his stance with skepticism verging on hostility. If he was bothered, viewers would not have known it; Nkrumah sustained an even tone and an almost subdued demeanor. In one reply, he stated flatly, "we have to watch how we align ourselves to any particular group, but that does not mean a sort of negative neutralism, or rather, the suspension of any judgement. If any situation were to arise, I think we can take the view which we think is the right view to take."[5]

Turning to real cases, one of the interviewers pressed Nkrumah to explain why the Egyptian president, Gamal Abdel Nasser, had recently turned to the Soviet Union for the construction of the Suez Dam. This had more relevance to Ghana's future than the journalist could have known, as did Nkrumah's answer. "At the time when he needed help, he didn't get it, and in order to survive, he had to go somewhere else, and that is why he took that step he took," he replied reasonably. As for his view of pan-Africanism, after explaining that Egypt was part of Africa, Nkrumah said, "All that we are trying to achieve is some sort of united outlook to solve our common problems. As I have made quite clear, we are not ganging up on anybody."

The other subject that came into focus, albeit much more briefly, was the recent passage in Ghana of a preventive detention law by the legislature, which allowed for the jailing of people who threatened the stability of the state, or as critics said correctly, were merely inconvenient. "Do you intend to get rid of your opponents?" Nkrumah was asked. "That is not true," came Nkrumah's reply, only to spur the TV host to reformulate his question:

"Do you have a law of preventative detention?"

"Yes, I was responsible for introducing that bill myself."

"Could you explain this?

"We have to adopt certain temporary measures. We have an independent judiciary. An independent civil service," Nkrumah can be heard to say in the poorly preserved recording. " . . . Some temporary measures [are needed] until everything can go the right way."

Nkrumah's answer was not particularly vigorous or even coherent. Still, his 1958 visit was a moment to celebrate a rare source of inspiration for African Americans on the world stage. Nkrumah embodied a modulated, fastidious cool. It came across in his Rat Pack look of sleek business suits in classic colors, his crisp dress shirts, and narrow ties, and the indigenous, hand-woven kente cloth—Ghanaian *ntoma*, or togas with their explosions of gold, green, black, and crimson patterns—that he slung regally over his shoulder. Nkrumah exerted an archetypal power on audiences in the West. In this, he was like the Miles Davis of the same era, only something even rarer: a Black head of state and international statesman instead of jazz nobility. Once again, James Baldwin captured the flavor when he wrote about the feelings of pride that came from the simple act of seeing Nkrumah after a lifetime of being exposed to degrading images of Black people: "The shot of Nkrumah getting off his plane has an effect on all the other images. It takes a certain sting out of the African savage."[6] He was Obama before Obama floated down the Air Force One staircase—Blacker, cooler, and seeming more unselfconscious, and because he was the first, he was a breathtaking sight for most eyes, almost irrespective of their politics.

The fullest measure of Nkrumah's American moment can be seen in the range and depth of the responses he drew from his African American hosts, from the crowds that gathered to take a peek at him, from ordinary people, and from the press coverage given his US tour.

Nkrumah's appearance in America sent Ralph Bunche spiraling into an unaccustomed rapture. This was all the more remarkable because by then Bunche was already a Nobel Peace laureate for his mediating the 1949 armistice in the Arab-Israeli conflict over Palestine. More to the point, he was already well along in his personal evolution from a left-leaning, globally minded progressive, and for an American, a precocious and forthright advocate of decolonization, to a moderate and establishment-oriented United Nations bureaucrat.

Bunche introduced Nkrumah to a crowd of ten thousand people at the 369th Regiment Armory, a massive brick office and meeting space that had been built earlier in the century as the home of the Harlem Hellfighters, soldiers who were drawn from an all-Black National Guard unit. The renowned diplomat opened by calling Ghana's independence ceremonies "an event more impressive than any in my long experience." As he spoke, the normally buttoned-down Bunche became increasingly swept up in the enthusiasm of the loudly cheering crowd. Addressing himself to Nkrumah, Bunche said:

> You were more, much more, than the leader and liberator of the people of Ghana; much more, indeed, than the spokesman for African Africa.... You as a consequence of the successful upward climb of the people of Ghana under your dedicated leadership ... represent spiritually and symbolically, all of us whose skins are pigmented, all the people the world over who have suffered from prejudice and discrimination because of color or race, all who know the subjection of colonialism, all of the depressed and underprivileged, the scorned and deprived. .

Then, to close his ringing peroration, Bunche added, "But above all, Mr. Prime Minister, we embrace you because you and your people and we are brothers—brothers of the skin and beneath the skin."[7]

The following day, the elite of Black New York traveled to midtown Manhattan for a $1,000-plate dinner in Nkrumah's honor. There, in the enormous, tiered Waldorf Ballroom, amid gilded tables, thick red and gold carpets, and chandeliered balconies, the chieftains of American business, including heads of banks, and airlines, and oil and steel companies, were matched up with the elite of African American civil society. Rarely did these twain meet. A. Philip Randolph, the old lion of Black labor was there, as was the NAACP chief counsel and future Supreme Court Justice, Thurgood Marshall. Mordecai Johnson, the Howard University president, traveled from DC to attend. Other sports celebrities and political stars included Jackie Robinson, Adam Clayton Powell Jr., Charlie Diggs, and once more, Ralph Bunche.

Lester Granger of the Urban League proclaimed there was "no more than the whisper of a bird's breath between the hopes and aspirations of the Black citizens in Arkansas in the Deep south and the triumph of and expectations of the Black men and women of Ghana who walk the streets of Accra proud and tall."[8]

Roy Wilkins, the executive secretary of the NAACP, spoke to the role that Ghana could play in repairing some of the loss that African Americans had suffered via their violent severance from Africa during the transatlantic slave trade. During that era, plantation owners had deliberately mixed enslaved Blacks from disparate regions of Africa together to render communication between them, and hence resistance, more difficult. As a result, direct connections with ancestral history were almost entirely lost. "As other loyal Americans look back upon their European homelands with affection and pride, so we look upon Ghana and the emerging nations of Africa. Your struggles and your successes have aided us in our trials and tribulations here."[9]

The euphoria that greeted the African leader was unprecedented. Never had the minds of Black America and Africa been so completely in sympathy or in sync. This was reflected well beyond the fancy dinners in brightly lit ballrooms. If anything, Nkrumah's rise fired the imaginations of African Americans at the popular level even more deeply than it inspired the Black elite. Their responses to his visit revealed a Black grassroots that was primed to renew and deepen its bonds to the continent where their ancestors had come from. And this speaks to the tragedy of the opportunity that was ultimately lost in this period: to carry the momentum of this transatlantic pan-Africanism forward.

One letter writer said, for example, "The reason we blacks are held in universal contempt by whites and suffer from self contempt ourselves is not so much blackness as weakness. We Negroes are not a strong people. Yet our race is a race of tremendous potential wealth and power. Many American Negro and African leaders have spoken of a closer bond between them. Yet no organization has been created among us to extend aid to Africa." The writer went on to criticize blind consumerism among Black Americans, who, he said, wasted money on "cars, cigarettes, skin whitening 'processes' etc." And he said that money squandered like this should be marshaled for direct help to Ghana, to aid in the construction of the Volta Dam and basic development needs. "If our race is to be strong and win the respect of the world and gain back our own self respect, as a race, then we Negroes ought to do all we can to help our brethen [sic] in Africa to become strong, free and united." In fact, as we will see later, waves of African American migration to Ghana began to swell around this time, spurred by Nkrumah's high profile.[10]

In a letter to the *Chicago Defender*, another letter writer, Peter Mosely, hammered, "I believe strongly that the time has come when we American Negroes do something to help Africa attain her freedom. We should offer our technical, educational and financial aid to our mother country. . . . If we have any pride left, we should waste no time in bringing to formation a society of interested Negroes with the aim of deliberating [sic] the rest of African from the yoke of colonialism."[11]

To be fair, one could find echoes of these views in elite Black American commentary, too. Roy Wilkins's observation that the deepening feelings of "Negroes" toward Africa mirrored Italian American feelings toward their "mother country." But both Nkrumah and the pan-African tradition called for something much deeper and more consequential than rustic nostalgia. And for this, the American Jewish community's allegiance toward and support for the young Israeli state was perhaps the best model, albeit one that would remain a distant and unrealized dream, as we will see.

Isolationism and self-absorption have a way of recurring in American history, and for all of the unique elements in their story, African Americans have never been truly exempt from this. As the movements of civil rights and then Black Power grew and crested, these struggles would return to being mostly American ones, and that has been the loss of peoples on both sides of the Atlantic.

CHAPTER TWENTY-NINE

The Bureau of African Affairs

On a June morning not long ago, I stood collecting myself on the driveway of a villa near the center of Accra that was eerily sheltered from the bustle of the Ghanaian capital. The driveway sloped downward into a depression, revealing a courtyard fringed by a passing tropical imitation of an English garden. There, shielded by tree-sized fiddle leaf figs, sat a red-roofed, two-story structure built on concrete pillars. For anyone who had wandered this way by accident and wondered about the nature or origin of this small sanctuary, their question would be answered at the end of the driveway. There sits a small, tiled plaza that bears a horizontal tombstone in light-colored slate that reads "George Padmore—1903–1959." Inlaid in black at the tablet's center is the figure of the African continent, above which looms a bold black star.

At a practical level, no one influenced the public life and politics of Kwame Nkrumah more than Padmore. His photographs reveal him as intense and formal-looking, his head held high, and often smoking a pipe, exuding a cultivated and insistent dignity. As we have seen, Padmore, who was Trinidadian by birth, entered Nkrumah's life the moment Nkrumah arrived in Britain after a decade of study in the United States. In countless meetings, Padmore schooled the younger Nkrumah on revolutionary theory, and on the ideas of Trotsky.[1] He also steadily imparted his disdain for the Soviet Union and for its style of communism. Most fundamentally, though, he intellectually ushered Nkrumah more deeply into the world of pan-Africanist thought and activism. At the very outset of their relationship, Padmore positioned Nkrumah in the inner councils of the Manchester Conference of 1945. There, Nkrumah not only met Du Bois, but enjoyed his first cameo on the international stage.

If America had its "race men," Padmore was a rare figure in his undeviating all-business-all-the-time dedication to global Black liberation. To those who knew him, he often gave the impression that he thought about little else. By never taking his eyes off his ideological priorities, he developed a crusty, suffer-no-fools-gladly manner. In 1957, he flew to Ghana for its independence ceremonies aboard a VIP plane packed with dignitaries who were all of very different stripes than him, including British former governors and numerous parliamentarians. Padmore would later lament that most of the invitees to the various balls and festivities he attended had either been outright opponents of Ghana's emancipation or were mere opportunists and profiteers. Meanwhile, the masses in whose name the country's nearly revolutionary change had been brought about languished outside in the darkness, drinking cheap beer or palm spirits.

After the ceremonies, at Nkrumah's request, the older Padmore agreed to move to Ghana with his wife, Dorothy Pizer, to serve as a special advisor to the prime minister on African affairs. The Nkrumah government created a successor institution called the Bureau of African Affairs (BAA) in 1959, which had its headquarters near the villa I had come to visit that humid morning. The BAA was given statutory approval the following year. In the meantime, Padmore, who was Trinidadian by birth but naturalized as a Ghanaian, died suddenly and unexpectedly in London in late 1959. His ashes were returned to Accra where he was given a funeral, presided over by Nkrumah, in the former "Castle" that served as the headquarters of government. There, in the stifling heat and damp air, the mourners crowded together on a parapet overlooking the dank and miserable pens where Africans were held awaiting their shipment to the Americas in chains. Some tossed small bouquets into the dark, others murmured prayers. "Who knows, but from this very spot, [Padmore's] ancestors were carried out across the ocean there, while the kinsmen stood weeping here as silent sentinel," Nkrumah managed to utter, before he choked up and began to cry. "We've brought his ashes home to rest."[2]

For the space of three years at the end of the 1950s, Ghana was not only the jewel in the eye of an impressive number of Black Americans, it was also easily the most talked-about, and indeed the most influential, country in the Third World, with the possible exception of vastly larger India. During this time, Nkrumah threw nearly all his energies into generating momentum for African independence, and just as importantly, from his perspective, creating a common agenda for the continent of pan-African unity. At the moment, he was arguably the most compelling and important statesman in what we now call the Global South.

By this time, Nkrumah's capacity for work was already legendary, but during this period he outdid himself. In Nkrumah's challenge—to achieve three hundred years of progress for Ghana in a single lifetime—one finds both the spirit of the day and a source of many of the problems that would ultimately undo his rule. Much of his sense of urgency was inspired by economics—the need he felt to break out of dependency from Britain after six years of "tactful action," in which he played along with London. He felt that Ghana needed to control much more of the wealth generated by cocoa, and that more broadly, his country needed to somehow reduce its domination by the rich West. With the Cold War growing more intense by the season, a good deal of this exigency was geopolitical, as well.

Nkrumah was as aware as could be of France's agenda, with its opposite impulses that aimed to maintain or even strengthen its control over a collection of new flag states, whose levers Paris pulled from barely behind the curtain. For starters, France created and governed the currency shared by most of its former colonies, and therefore controlled their wealth. It effectively dictated their foreign policies. And it established security pacts with many of them, maintaining or deploying its troops willy-nilly to install, unseat, or defend governments as it saw fit.

But Nkrumah was worried about Nigeria, too. That nearby British colony was not only far larger in territory, but even more so in population, counting forty-two million people in 1957, nearly seven times Ghana's size; Nkrumah was keenly aware of the importance this gave it. These circumstances allowed Nkrumah little time to stamp West Africa, and the continent beyond, with his mark, especially given that Nigeria's politics were generally far more conservative and more inwardly turned. What was worse, it was already clear that Nigeria, an immensely complex place, suffered deep regional divisions, and these would eventually lead to a devastating war of secession and near-breakup.

Another factor in his foreign policy was the gravitational field of the Cold War. Almost inexplicably, Ghana had somehow been exempted from its sharpest pressures, but now the United States and the Soviet Union were working harder than ever to box other countries in and force them to choose sides. As their contest spread more and more deeply into Africa, Nkrumah worried, quite sensibly as it turned out, that this would make the already fiendishly difficult challenge of achieving continental unity much harder.

From the moment Nkrumah stepped out of jail in April 1948 until his triumphant hour at independence, the colonial governor, Charles Arden-Clarke, had been the most important political figure in his life. At its outset, their relationship had been frankly adversarial before gradually turning to merely deeply suspicious. Over time, though, and somewhat paradoxically given their sharp ideological differences, Nkrumah the populist and socialist came to depend heavily on the flinty British peer and defender of empire that was Arden-Clarke. According to the governor, at the height of his struggles with the NLM opposition in Ashanti, Nkrumah said to him in a conversation on the balcony of the Castle, "H.E. I am worried about the future. Now I can come and talk to you about these things, but what is to happen when you have gone?"[3] Although we don't have Nkrumah's account of this exchange, if indeed it occurred, the prime minister would speak later of Ghana's independence as having been the joint project of the two men. He showed his appreciation to Arden-Clarke afterward, too, by granting the Briton's desire to serve briefly in the career-capping ceremonial role of governor-general.

Nkrumah had shown almost latex suppleness at other points in his life, and in the immediate aftermath of independence, this quality shone through more than ever. George Padmore followed on the heels of Arden-Clarke, becoming Nkrumah's most trusted advisor in most every matter that defined Ghana's new politics and its position in the world. C. L. R. James said of him, "It is impossible to understand the development of the revolution in the Gold Coast that brought Ghana unless you realized from the start, the man behind [it] was Padmore."[4]

THE ORIGINAL BAA, THE NERVE CENTER OF PADMORE'S FORMIDABLE ACTIVISM and strategizing in Ghana, has long disappeared. The pan-African research library that I visited that morning that sits nearby is the surviving monument to Padmore and archival custodian of his work in Accra. Nkrumah extolled his friend lovingly at its opening on June 30, 1961, in what felt in moments like a second eulogy. Padmore had devoted his life to "break[ing] the myth of white supremacy," he said.

> "He was a pearl of priceless value, a real and deep-loving elder brother... loyal to me because he believe implicitly that what I stand for is the only thing that can lead to the total emancipation of the African continent, and as a West Indian he also felt that the emancipation of Africa would have its repercussions on every person of African descent throughout the world. No matter what hour of the day or night I called upon him, he was there at my side, ready to help me."[5]

As he went on to announce an ambitious vocation for the library, Nkrumah deplored what he saw as the weak reading culture in his young country. "I wish particularly to call upon the youth and workers of the nation who have hitherto become victims of passive amusements and purposeless hobbies to desist from unprofitable activities which clog their aspirations and sap their energies to take up reading as their hobby and to make the fullest possible use of this library." It was to become the cornerstone of a new national library system, stocked with books and up-to-date periodicals and abstracts and indexes, together with "the most modern devices for the preservation and storage of knowledge." There was to be microfilm and photocopy machines, and climate-controlled underground archives that would provide "the raw material of scholarship on the whole of Africa." But visiting the place today, there was no getting around the fact that this all-but-hidden villa and burial site has become a strange and even sad symbol of the waning spirit of its era, and of the pan-African ideals that Padmore lived for.[6]

I spent a few days in its enveloping quiet and dim light, making my way through folders containing poorly organized and often mold-eaten files. There, I read faded, hopeful letters addressed to the BAA from Conakry by Amílcar Cabral, perhaps the greatest revolutionary theorist of Africa's independence era. There were telegrams from Kenneth Kaunda, the leading Black politician of Northern Rhodesia. There were endless pleas for assistance from political refugees stranded here and there by the widespread colonial violence of the time, from war in Algeria and rampaging settlers in Kenya to the vice grip of apartheid and the schemes it inspired to extend white rule up the spine of southern Africa. And there were the travel plans of the innumerable delegations who passed through Accra to receive aid and political guidance from Nkrumah's government.

I cannot know for sure, but during the days I visited, appearances suggested that I was the only person who had come to research the pan-Africanism of the Padmore era. I was surely the only one calling up folders from the lone librarian on duty. In any case, there were never more than a handful of other people present in the long, rectangular, bookshelf-lined reading room, and that included the clerks who worked there. Some visitors slumbered. Others remained bent over their tables taking refuge in the cool air assured by the large, open windows and slowly spinning ceiling fans as they scrolled their phones. A voracious learner, Padmore had left his books to be preserved in Ghana. But inexplicably, few of the remaining tomes in the collection had anything to do with him, and there seemed to be no rhyme or reason to their organization. Among the arbitrary themes I noted as I browsed the musty stacks were numerous works on Christian theology, on high school geography, and on practical science, and then, finally, these two, typical in their sheer randomness: *Talking Trees and Singing Whales* and *Prosperity Made Simple*.

Here there seemed to stand vivid proof that the retreat from pan-Africanism had not just been on the other side of the ocean. The loss of so much of the documented history of the Nkrumah era was not just a loss to Ghana. It was not even merely, if such a word can be used, a loss for history. Despite the neat and orderly appearance of the setting, I stood as if amid ill-tended archaeological ruins, and the loss I experienced was to a coherent sense of the Black self, the loss of some of the most important threads in a story that we have traced here to the mid-nineteenth century, but one that surely has roots yet deeper than that. It was a loss to civilization itself.

CHAPTER THIRTY

Slogans and Manifestos

WELL BEFORE THE MANCHESTER CONFERENCE IN 1945, WHEN THE whole world was remaking itself amid the wreckage of war, Nkrumah had already dreamt of sweepingly transforming his continent. What this meant, as he saw it, was necessarily positioning himself at the center of pan-Africanism, which throughout its history, as movements go, had often been as diffuse as a dust cloud. One can date Nkrumah's focus on this goal at least as far back as March and April 1945, the eve of his departure from the United States, when he spoke from the stage at conferences in New York about the future of Africa; that was the month of FDR's death by stroke, of the Battle of Okinawa, and of Hitler's move into his Berlin bunker.

Now, upon hearing the news of Sékou Touré's rupture with France in 1958, Nkrumah, prime minister of an independent African state, at last had an opportunity to move his pan-African ambitions out of the realm of aspiration and into the real world.

Guinea became independent on October 2 of that year, but de Gaulle's abrupt and spiteful divorce left the newborn nation facing near-term bankruptcy and desperate for partners. Nkrumah was alert to its problem, and behind the scenes, the deeply networked Padmore labored to launch talks between Nkrumah and Touré.

On the surface, at least, the Guinean seemed to share similar notions about the need for a fragmented continent to come together in new and paradigm-breaking ways. By late October, Touré was hinting publicly that he was interested in exploring some kind of association with Ghana. And on November 20, he arrived in Accra on a De Havilland aircraft embossed in the colors and black star of the new national character, Ghana Airways, to begin formal talks with his neighbor.

Even at this early date, many of the people around Nkrumah were leery of the idea that a continent-wide government or representation of any kind could be forged in the imaginable future. Padmore, despite his revolutionary credentials, believed it would be more practical to begin by building regional associations, a strategy that his boss rejected. But a Guinea joining Ghana in independence so soon after its own emancipation, especially a Guinea led by a socialist-inclined pan-Africanist, and moreover, a Guinea in need, created an opening for Nkrumah and Padmore to initiate an experiment.

Right from the start, Nkrumah's experience with Touré highlighted many of the devilish complications that made the practice of pan-Africanism so difficult. As both skeptics and champions of pan-Africanism immediately pointed out, Ghana and Guinea lacked a common language. They didn't even share a border. Between them lay six hundred miles of territory—the antagonistic Houphouët-Boigny's Ivory Coast. And they were just as deeply separated by the disparate administrative practices and customs inherited from two very different colonizers.

Something was even more challenging than all of this, though: an impediment to progress toward unity that Guinea, and Ghana, and a host of other African countries that were soon to become independent would soon discover. This was the irresistible traction of the European invention that they had all inherited or were emerging into—the nation state. This, ultimately, was the paradigm that Nkrumah had sworn to explode in order to create a federated, continent-sized nation. But even before he could take conversations about such a vast and novel enterprise very far, he would run into one of the nation state's stickiest features. The leaders and ruling classes that quickly gelled around them in each newborn state were as disinclined to surrender their power and privilege to a larger and untested entity as they were to remain under colonial domination. Maybe even more so. Nkrumah was different by upbringing, by temperament, by vision and conviction. George Padmore had helped mold the latter elements, likening Ghana's vocation under Nkrumah in a world of enduring imperialism and colonization to "a lighthouse in a dark continent [to show] Blacks the way safely into port."[1] None of this would have mattered, though, had he not come first.

Nkrumah evinced no discouragement, and may not even have registered the fact, but the first hints of difficulties of this sort began to surface right away in Ghana's experiences with Touré's Guinea. Touré arrived in Accra on a Thursday, a day ahead of his first scheduled meeting with Nkrumah. By the next day, high-level working delegations had already produced a draft agreement for unifying the two countries, and a session to finalize things between the two leaders was planned for Friday evening. Inexplicably, Touré arrived so late to the meeting that Nkrumah thought he had been stood up and had retired for the night. The next day, when their meeting finally occurred, as Touré looked over the draft, he behaved almost as if the details didn't concern him. He announced that he was willing to defer to his host and "big brother." "I give you Ghanaians a blank check to write a constitution for an organic union," two of Nkrumah's aides who participated in the talks remembered Touré saying.[2]

No account of the talks from Touré's perspective survives, but Guinea's leader was like some mendicant figure in history—an African Diogenes—whose ability to hold to his values depended on the charity of a patron, and he eagerly awaited a check. His apparent detachment from the nitty gritty details behind the birth of their novel union between Ghana and Guinea is perhaps best explained by this quality. Touré was desperate to avoid having to crawl back in humiliation to the French, or worse, see his new government collapse. What overrode other considerations for him was Nkrumah's magnanimity in ordering up a loan for £10,000,000—no mean feat for a fraternal African state, even one whose cocoa and gold had been bankrolling Britain.

It was out of Nkrumah's extraordinary largesse that a new, experimental state conceived as a first step toward some broader pan-African project was born: the Ghana and Guinea union. Thus, on November 23, 1958, the two leaders announced grandly:

> Inspired by the example of the thirteen American colonies, the tendencies of the countries of Europe, Asia, and the Middle East to organize in a rational manner, and the declaration of the Accra conference, we ... have agreed to constitute our two States as the nucleus of a Union of West African States.[3]

The reference to the American colonies that came together to form the independent United States reflected ideas about pan-Africanism that Nkrumah had forged in his years of study in America, and perhaps especially in Pennsylvania, near Philadelphia, the birthplace of the nation. America's lesson for Africa was therefore clear. In order to avoid domination by powerful outside forces, particularly the rich West, through a process that Nkrumah had begun calling "neocolonialism," the continent needed to bulk itself up by building strong economic circuits between its states. Many different forms of political authority could emerge from this scenario, Nkrumah felt, but unless Africa took its economic destiny into its own hands, independence in Africa would be rendered meaningless and its new states would forever remain empty vessels.

For all of Nkrumah's economic ideals, during the talks with Guinea, political considerations nonetheless had a stubborn way of staying in the forefront. During his talks with Guinea, even the most basic questions remained to be resolved, and out of them grew ever more new, nettlesome problems. How would a state as nebulous as this function? Who would make decisions? How would sovereignty be shared or divided? As the two sides stepped up their contacts back and forth, Nkrumah began to push for a maximal integration between the two countries—a true political fusion. Touré was never especially known for his practical mindedness. He was also the descendant of a legendary emperor who was jealous of his own power. So for starters, Touré pressed for a monetary union instead. Padmore supported this idea seeing a common currency as a good platform upon which the nations (and eventually others) could begin sharing sovereignty, but Gbedemah, Ghana's cautious finance minister and number two after Nkrumah, suspected this would merely lead to a further drain on his country's resources and so he held out.

For the time being, each government agreed to dispatch a resident minister to sit in on the other's cabinet meetings, while Touré worked behind the scenes to restore a working relationship with the French. In the meantime, while Nkrumah came under stout criticism from the opposition for showering money on Guinea, he had little choice but to tout his still unsteady venture. Standing before Ghana's National Assembly, he proclaimed

> [I have a] deep sense of pride... that I have been instrumental in this move.... This new Africa of ours is emerging into a world of great combinations—a world where the weak and the small are pushed aside unless they unite their forces.... Our African edifice, though we still have to draw up the plans for it, must have solid foundations... whether we like it or not, history has assigned us a great responsibility.[4]

ON THE HEELS OF HIS FUSION WITH GUINEA, NKRUMAH'S PAN-AFRICAN agenda shifted onto an even higher plane. On December 8, 1958, his government convened a weeklong gathering at the Accra Community Centre billed as the All-African People's Conference (AAPC). The meeting fired a glowing nimbus around Nkrumah, and it created for Ghana a degree of continental goodwill that endured for months afterward and gave Accra something of a reputation as the virtual capital of the Third World. Amid this hope-filled ambience of new pan-Africanist camaraderie and idealism, the practical difficulties of working with Guinea began to fade in significance. But like the "Era of Good Feelings" in the United States of the early 1820s, and like outbreaks of optimism in general, it was bound not to last.

Formally speaking, planning for the AAPC had occupied most of 1958. In a deeper sense, it was the realization of a much older dream, one long shared by Nkrumah and Padmore and, at least notionally, by the entire lineage of pan-African thinkers and activists whom we have met over the course of this narrative. Nkrumah had insisted on using the phrase "All-African" for the gathering, instead of pan-African, to impart a ring of originality. But both he and Padmore understood the meeting to be a lineal descendant of the Manchester Pan-African Congress in 1945, where they had worked together. But in 1945 few beyond the participants had taken note. Soon after Nkrumah became leader of government business in 1951, Padmore had urged him to organize a successor conference in the Gold Coast.

By design, the AAPC was completely unlike the staider Conference of Independent African States (CIAS) that Nkrumah had convened the previous April. The CIAS had hosted a small number of established governments, all different in politics and geography. Five of the eight countries that participated in the earlier gathering were Arabic-speaking, and one of them, the United Arab Republic—a short-lived fusion in the mode of Ghana and Guinea between Egypt and Syria—was only partially located in Africa. By contrast, the AAPC welcomed individuals and movements dedicated to the emancipation of their countries, and on strategies for cooperation across borders to hasten the independence of Africa's remaining colonies. The invitation's title announced the ambitious tone: "Plan of the Liberation of Africa by Gandhian Non-Violence." The invitation was sent to three hundred delegates on the four corners of the continent. The text contained this message, in all caps:

THIS CONFERENCE WILL FORMULATE AND PROCLAIM THE PHILOSOPHY OF PAN AFRICANISM AS THE IDEOLOGY OF THE AFRICAN NON-VIOLENT REVOLUTION. HENCEFORTH OUR SLOGAN SHALL BE: PEOPLES OF AFRICA UNITE!

YOU HAVE NOTHING TO LOSE BUT YOUR CHAINS!! YOU HAVE A CONTINENT TO REGAIN! YOU HAVE FREEDOM AND HUMAN DIGNITY TO ATTAIN!

HANDS OFF AFRICA!!

AFRICA MUST BE FREE!!![5]

During most of the proceedings, Nkrumah remained astutely out of view as he helped nascent liberation movement leaders strategize or engaged in one-on-one meetings with leaders of national delegations. This turned his public scarcity into a currency, as attendees exchanged excited words of sightings of him or poured over his statements, and helped ensure that Ghana's leader remained the star of the show. Nkrumah's exultant opening remarks left no doubt that he strove for this effect, as he harkened back explicitly to Manchester and paid generous tribute to Padmore, while also claiming that the conference represented "the opening of a new epoch in our Continent's history":

> Never before has it been possible for so representative a gathering of African Freedom Fighters not only to come together, but to assemble in a free independent African State for the purpose of planning for a final assault upon Imperialism and Colonialism.[6]

For some time already, Nkrumah had been calling for a union of African States, but at the end of his opening speech, he now urged the creation of what he called, a "United States of Africa." The meeting was historically remarkable given the fact that many of the delegates would come to play prominent roles in the coming independence of their own countries, with some becoming presidents and prime ministers. The emergent figures included Tom Mboya, the Kenyan founding father and labor leader, and Félix-Roland Moumié, who was exiled from the Cameroon for campaigning against colonialism there (and later assassinated by France).[7] There was Joshua Nkomo of Southern Rhodesia. This was a land that whites still advertised in British newspapers as "An English Country away from England," and "an empty paradise," in order to attract settlers. And there was Holden Roberto of Angola, who may have already been on the CIA payroll and would soon become America's proxy early in his country's long civil war.

Also present were Kenneth Kaunda of Northern Rhodesia (later Zambia) and Julius Nyerere of Tanganyika (later Tanzania). Within six years, each of them would lead his country into independence and espouse new forms of what they called African socialism. Kaunda was deeply influenced by Nkrumah and remained loyal to him after he was overthrown and even in death. For a time, Nyerere stood as more of an ideological rival of Nkrumah's. This may be due, in part, to the fact that their personal stories bore such uncanny similarities. Nyerere, too, was recognized for his keen intelligence by a Roman Catholic priest. He, too, became a schoolteacher at a young age. Sent to Edinburgh on scholarship, he was one of the first people from his land to study overseas.

While he was there, he read about Nkrumah's rise to power and it convinced him to become an independence activist.[8]

> When Kwame Nkrumah was released from prison this produced a transformation. I was in Britain and oh you could see it in the Ghanaian! They became different human beings, different from all the rest of us! This thing of freedom began growing in all of us.[9]

Much later, Julius Nyerere would unquestionably become Nkrumah's most important successor as an avatar of a pan-Africanist-style progressivism on the continent. He became East Africa's greatest independence-era statesman. But it would take him another ten years after their Accra meeting to fully understand Nkrumah, he would later reflect. After the Ghanaian's death, his public reappraisals of Nkrumah tended in an ever-more-generous and positive direction. He would eventually call him the greatest African ever.

Both in terms of what their appearances in Accra presaged for the future, and their impact on the proceedings, two other figures stood out: Frantz Fanon and Patrice Lumumba. Although Ghana did not yet support him, Lumumba, a cofounder of an emergent political party, the Mouvement National Congolais (MNC), had been recommended to the conference organizers by the Israeli ambassador to Ghana, Ehud Avriel (as had Roberto of Angola). Tel Aviv even paid Lumumba's transportation to Accra.[10] This reflects the little-remembered fact that Israel enjoyed tremendous influence in Ghana at the time. This was due to a confluence of factors. Israeli diplomacy in Africa was fantastically energetic as it aimed to avoid isolation during the Nasser years. Moreover, as an ideology that worked to bind people together across numerous international boundaries via a powerful, shared identity, Zionism in that bygone era resonated deeply with many pan-Africanists. When Du Bois organized the first major Pan-African Conference in Paris in 1919, he drew direct parallels between the gathering's efforts to unite the Black world with Zionism.[11] Finally, some of Nkrumah's most important deputies, including Kojo Botsio, had also toured Israel and returned, deeply impressed by the kibbutz movement and the Hidastrut. This Zionist labor organization played a crucial role in Israeli nation building, helping found a wide range of new institutions, from finance and industry to culture and sports. The cooperative ethos on display in these Israeli institutions appealed to progressives around Nkrumah for their potential in creating alternatives to capitalism.

As of late 1958, Lumumba was unknown outside of the Congo. He had just freshly surged to the fore in Belgium's giant central African colony, where his entire political career, and indeed his life, would play out in less than four years. Until then, he had been a provincial postal worker, a beer salesman in the slums of the capital, Kinshasa, autodidact with ambition, boundless energy, and mesmerizing rhetorical skills. The main representative for Belgium's colony at Nkrumah's confab was expected to be Joseph Kasa-Vubu, the country's future president and one of Lumumba's main rivals during Congo's first year of independence. Colonial authorities denied Kasa-Vubu permission to travel, however, fearing the experience could render him much more militant.

The Belgians allowed Lumumba, hitherto thought to be much more moderate than Kasa-Vubu, to travel, instead, but only "in a personal capacity and as a mere observer."[12] The colonists' confusion is understandable. Lumumba's writings from the previous year had almost made him sound like a conservative accommodationist. "It is easy enough to shout slogans, to sign manifestos, but it is quite a different matter to build, manage, command, spend days and nights seeking the solution to problems."[13] In lieu of immediate independence and complete sovereignty, what he foresaw then was a federation with Belgium under a political system in which only Congo's tiny educated elite would be granted political rights, and not "dull-witted illiterates."[14]

However, in Accra, Lumumba was completely transfixed by the force and conviction conveyed by Nkrumah's speech, and his participation in the AAPC radicalized his politics even more than the Belgians had dreaded might happen with Kasa-Vubu. Lumumba's speech to the conference bore the unmistakable imprint of Nkrumahism and of his rhetoric about the "African personality." "In spite of the frontiers that separate us, in spite of our ethnic differences, we have the same conscience, the same soul that bathes day and night in anguish, the same wish to make the African continent independent," Lumumba declared, freshly reborn as a pan-Africanist.[15]

This was a mere beginning. From this conference would arise one of the most dramatic episodes of the early independence era and a signal event of the Cold War in Africa, as well. Soon after his return to Kinshasa, Lumumba organized the first political rally in the history of the capital. At a time when Belgium was still planning to extend its dominion over the Congo for another decade or more, Lumumba vowed to "wipe out the colonialist regime" by the end of 1960. Fortified by the rhetoric of the AAPC, he announced that "Africa is irrevocably engaged in a merciless struggle against the colonizer for its liberation."[16]

With his truncated political career, Lumumba was, to use an apt astronomical image, akin to a streaking meteorite. He seemingly came out of nowhere and bolted to the center of the global stage before crashing violently. Practically unknown just two years earlier, he became the first elected prime minister of Congo in June 1960, leaving Belgium, the United States, the Soviet Union, and the entire African continent staggered by his rise. Barely six months after taking office, Lumumba was made to disappear in the grisliest of ways, assassinated with the deep connivance from Belgium and the CIA. During much of Lumumba's brief tenure, Nkrumah would provide the Congolese with surprisingly sober advice, while Ghana's armed forces and diplomats would play frontline roles in resisting Belgian efforts to unseat him. The stories of these two men are usually told separately, with only incidental mention of their ties. But as we will see, the demise and death of Lumumba at thirty-five had formidable and perverse effects on Nkrumah's own political life, tragically foreshortening it and helping bring to an irremediable end the first and most hopeful phase of Africa's independence era.

FRANTZ FANON, THE FRENCH-MARTINICAN WHO HAD JOINED THE ALGERIAN revolutionary movement, the Front de Libération National (FLN), after working as a psychiatrist in that French North African settler colony, made a very different impression on the AAPC. He would die of leukemia in December 1961, outliving Lumumba by less than a year. Fanon barely survived long enough to see the publication of the books that would establish his name in the firmament of anti-imperialist thinkers, *Black Skin, White Masks*, and *The Wretched of the Earth*. But in Accra, where Lumumba mostly went with the flow, Fanon took sharp exception to the conference's officially proclaimed pacificism and issued a searing tirade against the violence inherent in colonialism. His voice strained as he spoke from behind dark sunglasses and gripped the podium: "Africa is at war with colonialism, and she is impatient."[17]

Fanon's rhetorical fire reflected far more than mere intellectual fervor. In 1943, as a teenager, he had made his way clandestinely to France from Martinique to fight against the Nazis with the Free French. His combat there earned him a medal, along with a serious chest wound. But the treatment he had received in France as a Black man damaged him more. As his older brother Joby wrote later, it left him "torn, quartered" and "wounded to the core of his being."[18]

"African countries must be on the way to a partnership of combat, for the enemy is powerful, strong, and its abilities to maneuver remain important," Fanon prophesied at the APPC, practically scolding moderates in the audience.[19] And he did not stop there. "In our fight for freedom, we should embark on plans effective enough to touch the pulse of the imperialists—by force of action and, indeed, violence," Fanon declared.[20] This brought the house down, requiring Mboya of Kenya, the session chair, to hastily schedule a press conference afterward in which he struggled to harmonize Fanon's rousing speech with the conference's nonviolent platform. "The actions of the colonial powers, especially in Algeria, will eventually determine whether we should use force, and when that time comes, we should not be blamed," Mboya said.[21] Later, in his keynote speech, the Kenyan strained for a yet more radical cred, saying that it was time for Western imperialist nations to reverse their Scramble for Africa, and "scram from Africa."[22]

When he is remembered nowadays, Fanon is both fervently adored and dismissed as a troubled and troubling thinker. But the lucidity of his charged words in Accra stands out now, ratified by the known historical facts: in most of Africa, European imperialism was thoroughly unmoved by African pacifism as a form of resistance and was intent on holding on as long as possible. This inevitably produced armed struggle, and sometimes, as in each of Portugal's colonies, devastating and protracted wars. Another key idea of Fanon's is more historically contestable but resonates strongly nonetheless when one looks back at the history of this era from the perspective of decades hence. Fanon believed that only revolution, meaning the use of violence, could produce a "tabula rasa" or break with the past of colonialism sharp enough to place Africa's new nations on a meaningfully new footing. "What is singularly important is that [decolonization] starts from the very first day with the basic claims of the colonized," Fanon wrote on the first page of his *The Wretched of the Earth*, which was published on the eve of his death at age thirty-six in 1961. "In actual fact, proof of success lies in a social fabric that has been changed inside out."[23] Later, in the same book, he continued in this lustral vein:

> Violence alone, perpetrated by the people, violence organized and guided by the leadership, provides the key for the masses to decipher social reality. Without this struggle, without this praxis there is nothing but a carnival parade and lot of hot air. All that is left is a slight readaptation, a few reforms at the top, a flag, and down at the bottom a shapeless, writhing mass, still mired in the Dark Ages.[24]

Nkrumah and Ghana certainly never achieved a clean break from the colonial era, as the awkward dance of cohabitation of his government with the British governor between 1951 and 1957 attests. During these years, old officials, favoring continuity and caution, maintained old policies and many old priorities. Nkrumah's party took his path, in part, because it lacked the power—and despite its occasional bravado—the confidence, to throw off British rule sooner and more thoroughly. London also steadily encouraged the view that an extended period of apprenticeship of statehood would serve Ghana best, preparing it to walk more surely on its own feet later, once independence did come.

In retrospect, all of this remains highly debatable. The years of British supervision certainly cost Nkrumah dearly in the political momentum he needed to create a program to meet the urgent basic needs of Ghanaians. Honesty should compel us to recognize that colonization had never been designed to meet the people's needs, yet even today some persist in pretending that it was. Now, as the 1950s drew toward its close, Nkrumah's attentions were drawn to the world outside Ghana. Its problems and challenges seemed more attractive to him. Perhaps this was because diplomatic dramas create illusions, and the electrical storms of flashbulbs and prominent headlines in the international press wherever he went diverted him from the challenges within Ghana. He also used the attention that he drew on the world stage to bolster his image and power at home. Increasingly, he was a global celebrity, which became a major feature of a personality cult that was by now trending toward oppressive. All the while, the real problems of Ghana remained as intractable as ever—and just beneath the surface, signs of serious trouble were multiplying.

For the time being, while Nkrumah still basked in the glow of his African American supporters, the United States was still willing to resist its most rigid of its Cold War instincts and more or less continue extending the benefit of the doubt to Nkrumah, despite his increasingly socialist-inflected pan-Africanism.

The United States had worried that Nkrumah's All-African People's Conference would be hijacked by delegates of the United Arab Republic and by Nasserism. An intelligence briefing prepared for Eisenhower took satisfaction in noting that this had not happened, which it credited Nkrumah for averting. Moreover, the CIA had had an American labor leader named Irving Brown present throughout the AAPC, where he worked as an asset. Two days after the conference, American diplomats reported to Washington, "Embassy Accra has expressed the tentative view that conference which ended December 13 was better from U.S. viewpoint than had been expected; it exhibited some degree of moderation and responsibility despite the expected attacks on European metropolitan powers and white settlers."[25] But Nkrumah's support for Lumumba would test Washington's forbearance toward him, and it would ultimately crumble in the face of American paranoia and exaggeration over Soviet inroads in Africa.

CHAPTER THIRTY-ONE

Imitation Is the Sincerest Form

EARLY ON NEW YEAR'S EVE IN 1957, AN OVERNIGHT FLIGHT ARRIVED IN Accra from Cairo after stopovers in Khartoum, Sudan, and Kano, Nigeria. The flight had proceeded from the seat of the great dynasties that built Egypt's ancient pyramids to the home of Black desert kingdoms on the distant inland banks of the Nile, and onward to the heartlands of vast and populous West African empires and centers of Islamic learning on the southern fringes of the Sahara. In other words, bound up in this single long-haul itinerary was an unusual amount of African history.

Still unknown to the world, one traveler stands out on the passenger list, a twenty-six-year-old Egyptian Coptic Christian woman. Fathia Halim Rizk was the daughter of a Cairo telephone company clerk who had died when she was a girl. Her mother had raised her, in modest circumstances, with her four younger siblings. She had worked briefly as a French teacher, then taken a job at a local bank. The flight southward and across the Sahara under acetylene stars was her first big adventure. When she boarded the plane, she had little idea what to expect, outside of the knowledge that this journey would define her life. On the day of her arrival in Ghana's capital for the first time, Rizk would wed Kwame Nkrumah, sight unseen, and in a stroke become the first-ever first lady of a newly independent sub-Saharan African nation.

Nkrumah's political associates knew nothing of his plans. When he showed up to work that morning at the Castle at his usual time, the only thing remarkable was his formal clothing. A surprised colleague called out to him and asked him if he was planning to attend a wedding that was not on his official calendar. Nkrumah said nothing, merely smiling in reply.

Rizk was a solidly built woman of medium height and sharp features. She possessed lively eyes, a warm and generous smile, and a great, bouffant head of hair. Just before their marriage, Nkrumah presented Rizk to his aged mother, who had recently gone blind. By way of getting to know her, she then ran her fingers through the Egyptian's long, jet-black curls, only to dismiss the bride-to-be as not African enough.

As devoted as he had always been to his mother, Nkrumah was not deterred; it was far too late for that. There would be no walking down an aisle, or priest presiding, only a quick ceremony with a few guests who were given scant notice. The bride eschewed a veil of any kind, but she glittered with royal jewels and the Grand Cordon of the Order of the Nile. This was proof that she had come with the blessing of the powerful Egyptian president, Gamal Abdel Nasser.[1]

The accounts of how this unusual coupling came about are legion, but even today, facts remain scarce. Many are the stories that tell of how Nkrumah's mother had begun to complain that he had never married. Some accounts have presented this as a budding political problem for the man who was the most eligible bachelor in Ghana. The conservative mores of the time held that a national leader must have a wife. Remaining single fed a prurient rumor mill about the imagined serial heterosexual dalliances of a man who many women described as attractive, even irresistible. Alternatively, some might wonder if there was something about Nkrumah that was even less socially acceptable in that place and time. Any hint of a lack of interest in women could be weaponized into stories about an interest in men.

The standard account of how Nkrumah and Rizk came together starts with some nagging by his live-in mother to find a spouse. Once he resolved to do so, Nkrumah is said to have assigned the task to a trusted personal aide and fixer named Ambrose Yankey, who was a fellow ethnic Nzima from the same remote southwest region as the prime minister. Yankey, in turn, engaged the services of a practitioner of traditional religion and reputed soothsayer named Kankan Nyame. This person is said to have advised that a woman from far to the north would best suit the prime minister, which ultimately came to mean Egypt.[2]

How such a great leap was arranged is the subject of myriad versions. One of them has Nkrumah meeting a woman he was attracted to during a visit with Egypt's Nasser, only to be informed that she was already married. Upon return to Ghana, word came that she had an eligible younger sister, who turned out to be Fathia Rizk. Another version holds that Nasser introduced Rizk to Nkrumah in Cairo. Still another says that Nkrumah was involved with an Egyptian woman in Accra, and that she was sent back home after she became pregnant in order to sidestep a scandal. Later, Nkrumah allegedly told people that he wanted to find someone who resembled this lover, and that led to

Fathia. The version that I find most persuasive, and there are others, is that Nkrumah dispatched an associate, Alhaji Saleh Said Sinare, a Ghanaian Muslim who was married to an Egyptian woman, to find him a Christian bride in Egypt. A coupling like this seems to have offered to Nkrumah the possibility of a rich political payoff, symbolically uniting halves of the continent so routinely divided by the Sahara. Sinare returned with a yield of five candidates for Nkrumah to choose from. In this telling, Nkrumah is said to have selected Fathia in part because Copts were reputed to be of "the most ancient and purest Egyptian stock."[3]

Fathia, who spoke Arabic and French but little English at the time of her wedding would bear Nkrumah three children, but by most accounts, their marriage remained emotionally vacant. Years later, Nkrumah would write to his English secretary Erica Powell, whose closeness with Nkrumah made her the subject of frequent rumors, saying:

> Have you noticed over the years that I have known you that I am a very lonely man?... I am friendless and companionless.... I suffer from intense loneliness which makes me sometime burst into tears. I am an isolated man—isolated from life itself. You only know and understand that, Erica—few people know this.[4]

Nkrumah's sparse comments about his relationship with Rizk make clear that he fiercely protected the privacy of his marriage. They also help cast light on the challenge of understanding the man himself. Throughout adulthood he exhibited extraordinary self-control in limiting what others could see or know about his inner life. This is all the more remarkable since for nearly two decades, his most famous attribute was his mastery of mass politics. Powell, in fact, is one of the rare people—well fewer than a handful—to whom Nkrumah bared his innermost thoughts. Another of them was Shirley Du Bois. In a 1964, the freshly widowed Du Bois, who ran Ghana's television service, requested permission for a visiting crew to film Nkrumah and his family in his state residence. He answered:

> It has always been my strong conviction that my domestic affairs—my home and my family—are purely private matters which should not be "mixed up" with my official and public life. I see no reason why I should exhibit my wife and children in order to satisfy public curiosity.
>
> My view—and this may jolt you a little!—is that marriage does not exist in nature and does not warrant the importance that has come to be

attached to it.... I am most anxious that no one should tamper with my own liberty within my family.[5]

Whatever his other motives, Nkrumah does seem to have been attracted to the idea of wedding an Egyptian for purposes of state—namely, to help fulfil his loftiest political ambition, gaining purchase from every corner of the continent for his vision of pan-Africanism. If that is the case, this made Nkrumah's pairing with Fathia an old-fashioned diplomatic marriage in the mode of Europe's grand imperial houses, if not a love match. Nkrumah would not only be the first person to lead a Black African country into independence, but he would also narrow the wide identity gulf that often served to separate the continent's Arabic-speaking north from so-called Black Africa.

In most matters, Nkrumah's personal life was consistently enigmatic, and his marriage was no exception. Fathia learned English quickly and threw herself dutifully into her first-lady role. She came to relish Ghana's culture and food, and she connected especially well with the country's women, including some who had initially taken Nkrumah's choice of an Arab bride badly. But after his overthrow in 1966, while Nkrumah was in exile in Guinea and had no great means at his disposal, Fathia moved with their children back to her native Cairo, where they got by on what must have been modest support from her husband. The correspondence back and forth between them during these years was regular but altogether cursory. Nkrumah usually contented himself with brief and bland inquiries about her well-being, the happiness of the children, and little more. The couple never met again.

After his death in 1972, however, once she was allowed to return to the country, Fathia expressed the desire to be buried alongside her husband, and that is where I found her tomb, housed next to his in a dusty mausoleum situated behind a gleaming, giant bronze-colored statue of Nkrumah in a memorial complex that sits off Accra's monumental Black Star Square.

To close the circle, after studying in Britain, their daughter, Samia Nkrumah, returned to Ghana in 2007, and after working her way into public life, she was elected to the assembly as the leader of a political party: her father's CPP.

JUST OUTSIDE OF THE CONFERENCE VENUE OF ONE OF NKRUMAH'S GREAT early symbolic triumphs as the leader of an independent state, anyone taking note could find unmistakable signs of trouble to come. Like the ominous afternoon massing of storm clouds in the tropics, hints of trouble were gathering over Ghana. All around the perimeter of the Accra Community Centre where the All-African People's Conference was playing out, police and other security forces were posted. Their numbers alone signaled that this was no routine precaution.

By 1958, Ghana had become a beacon of hope for most of the continent, as well as for a great many African Americans and West Indians. To celebrate its freedom, immigrants to Britain from the Caribbean had even begun to identify as Ghanaians. For a shining moment toward the close of this decade, Ghana's stock soared throughout the Third World.

But with independence ceremonies barely over, the country also entered into a new escalatory spiral between Nkrumah and an ever more determined opposition. In fact, as early as April 1956 some leading members of rival parties were already vowing to battle any new government under Nkrumah hammer and tong. If Britain granted the Gold Coast independence under the authority of the CPP, one group warned, "this would make for a 'country of riot, rebellion, revolution,' the road long ago taken by those unhappy countries where one can change only the Head of State or the people who govern by armed insurrection after underground conspiracy and sabotage."[6] This was strangely grim language for a country that was poised to peacefully burst the dam of colonial rule in Africa and achieve self-government, but many took it seriously.

During the independence year, Nkrumah was confronted in the capital with a disquieting new source of hostility. In fact, it was centered in his own electoral district and came from members of the Ga ethnic group, who claim most of Accra as their ancestral homeland. Ethnic groups in the north also manifested continued vigorous opposition to the popular prime minister, as did many Ewe, another large minority group clustered in the southeast of the country along Ghana's border with French-governed Togo.

In the year of emancipation, aggrieved leaders of these constituencies huddled together and mobilized against Nkrumah with hard-edged determination. To meet this mounting specter, Nkrumah's party, the CPP, began parliamentary discussion of a bill, which eventually passed, that bore the name, the Avoidance of Discrimination Act. Its ostensible aim was to create a more responsible, nationally minded opposition. Toward that end, it outlawed political parties that were formed along ethnic, regional, or religious lines.

Before the law passed, though, members of these disparate identity groups came together to form a major new opposition organization, the United Party (UP). And it was joined by members of the historic old guard of Nkrumah rivals and nemeses led by J. B. Danquah, the London-trained lawyer, and Kofi Busia, Ghana's first student at Oxford. The surprising timing of the UP's launch gave it the feeling of a potentially decisive gambit in a winner-take-all game of chess.

Nkrumah's honeymoon with the political class was perennially expected, and yet it had not materialized, at least not so far. To the frustration of the opposition, he retained rousing national popularity, and CPP membership was still swelling. Yet despite seemingly having built considerable momentum for his programs, he began to exhibit ever more personal insecurity and brittleness. Was this all paranoia? Certainly not. Reflexively, the newly configured opposition rejected nearly every idea his government put forward and opposed every action it undertook. In seeking to undermine him, Nkrumah's rivals employed varied motives. Some, like Danquah, had always believed themselves to be the rightful rulers of the land. Others simply thought themselves more knowledgeable than Nkrumah and the plebian advisors and followers he attracted. Others knew that control of the state could bring opportunity and rewards that were unknown under colonial rule, and for all their complaints about corruption, this was an irresistible lure. In unison, Nkrumah's opponents adopted a scathingly personal tone in lambasting him. He was either a new African Hitler, as one Kumasi newspaper pretended, or he was secretly bent on delivering the country to communism.[7]

Threats and attacks against Nkrumah would soon follow one after another in rapid succession, but his innate suspiciousness also fed his own worst political instincts. The first of these was the Deportation Act that Nkrumah signed in August 1957 after the CPP pushed it through the assembly. It was employed almost immediately to expel Bankole Timothy, a writer from Sierra Leone who had once been close to Nkrumah and who published a newspaper column that denounced the personality cult building around the prime minister. Several months later, speaking before the assembly, Nkrumah defended his government's use of the act, saying that a small number of foreigners were interfering in Ghana's domestic politics.

Following the government's use of this act to shrink the political space for criticism and opposition activism, Nkrumah's parliamentary allies passed, and he signed into law, another, even more sweeping bill, the Preventive Detention Act of July 1958. Its proximate justification had been the November 1957 arrest of two Ewe leaders, S. G. Antor and Kodzo Ayeke, on charges of plotting Nkrumah's assassination. The legislation, which authorized detention for five years, was put before the National Assembly the following month.

Rather than calming things, the government's actions fueled even more determined resistance from its opposition. As a result, more turbulence began to roil the newborn country. Suddenly, the emancipation that had been so widely and fervently dreamed of was delivering people into a world of deepening uncertainty. Nkrumah's government wielded the Preventive Detention Act vigorously against enemies of the state both real and perceived. By the time of his overthrow eight years later, Ghana counted some eight hundred detainees, of which roughly half were being held for political reasons.[8] Preventive detention became one of the most important motifs of opposition grievance against Nkrumah, and eventually of Western criticism of him, as well. It would be invoked more than any other single cause to justify Nkrumah's eventual overthrow. But certain objective truths were almost always left unmentioned or glossed over by those who bridled most about Ghana's turn to authoritarianism, both domestically and abroad.

Any law that allows a government to lock up its opponents based on mere suspicion, even spurious, has oppressive potential. But what was preventive detention if not a staple of colonial rule? In fact, Africa's new political classes, including Nkrumah and the CPP, had just emerged under that very tradition. Nkrumah himself had been jailed preventively, and even briefly banished to the northern hinterlands, where the colonial government held him incommunicado. In a slightly earlier era, the British had run I. T. A. Wallace-Johnson and Nnamdi Azikiwe out of the Gold Coast, deeming their newspaper criticism intolerable. Until the very eve of the 1951 election that brought Nkrumah into government, the colonial authorities routinely attacked and muzzled the opposition press. Many persistent critics of British colonial rule were made into political prisoners.

By comparison, Nkrumah and his CPP faced far stiffer and more violent challenges than the British colonial authorities had ever faced. In 1956, in the runup to independence, a bomb attempt had been made against his home. A near insurrection against Nkrumah had been mounted in Kumasi and the surrounding Asante heartland. Nkrumah, even as the incipient national leader, was declared persona non grata in that region and opposition partisans threatened secession. Almost immediately after the Preventive Detention Act was passed, police foiled a conspiracy to overthrow the government.

From 1960 repeated close-call attempts were made on Nkrumah's life. In 1964 *The New York Times* counted five bids to assassinate Nkrumah.[9] In 1962, a year before Birmingham, Alabama, became known as "Bombingham" due to the bombings targeting Black people there, Nkrumah had to declare a state of emergency in Accra. This was prompted by a series of acts of political terror in Accra—bombings in stadiums, along motorcade routes, and in the nearby port city of Tema. These attacks killed numerous people and left hundreds injured. Yet, in all of the reported attempts on his life, and indeed generally,

Nkrumah's government suspended the sentences of people who were condemned to death for their crimes.

More comparisons with Great Britain are instructive. Since the early 1920s, London had used its so-called Special Powers Act, passed in Northern Ireland's Parliament, which provided for detention without trial and other forms of legal exception to contain sectarian violence in Ireland, which is to say in Britain itself. Moreover, when these powers were introduced in Ghana, British colonial authorities were simultaneously employing similar powers, and even harsher measures, to suppress the revolt of the Kenya Land and Freedom Army. This included the execution of hundreds of African prisoners.

Other governments of the day, like India and Pakistan, commonly resorted to forms of preventive detention. In 1957, in Singapore, when the government detained thirty-two members of the opposition without trial, *The Times* (London) opined that "Democracy sometimes has to resort to undemocratic means to defend itself."[10] Much more recently, Western countries have reprised the use of measures like these in the fight against Islamist extremists, who have been arrested preventively or held without trial in places like Guantanamo Bay for years.

This is not to make light of the fact that Nkrumah's government wielded the law in increasingly bareknuckle ways. But rather than paying off, as the prime minister might have expected or hoped, this usage would bear strongly negative consequences for Nkrumah over time. Western governments, and perhaps most of all the United States, saw Nkrumah, the leader of the first Black African country to emerge from colonial rule, and feared that he would tilt his continent in the direction of the Soviets.

In this regard, his authoritarian drift was never the real issue. In the 1950s, even before Ghana's independence, Vice President Richard Nixon proposed that as African countries became independent and flirted—inevitably in his view—with socialism, Washington should cultivate military strongmen to hold the line ideologically.[11] Indeed, this stance became a mainstay of American policy toward the continent. If Nkrumah was becoming a dictator, the only real problem was that he couldn't be reliably counted upon to be Washington's dictator.

Violence was far from the only challenge posed by Nkrumah's most determined opponents. It is hard to overstate the many other difficulties inherent to adopting parliamentary democracy on the fly. Nkrumah largely avoided one of the biggest scourges of African politics in the independence era: the capture of the state by a dominant ethnic group or cluster and the resultant perpetual tribal contestation that followed. Even the opposition of the Asante never fully gelled along these lines, and that is because no one could credibly point to a tribalist basis for Nkrumah's appointments.

This does not mean that other grave problems didn't await him, for they clearly did. Although not on a rigid or predictable tribal basis, public affairs often played out with the fierceness of a zero-sum dispute. For every criticism one could wield toward Nkrumah over a weak or faltering commitment to Western-style democracy, one would also have to say that those who faced off against him rarely did so with anything resembling the spirit of a loyal opposition. This was an essential feature of any Westminster-inspired system, but in Ghana, as in so much of the continent in the first decade or more of independence and very often well beyond, this never developed. Instead, what politics remained was a grimly predictable, give-no-quarter affair based on charges of corruption, apocalyptic innuendo, and scandal mongering.

Some of the reasons for this now seem abundantly clear. Compared to the minuscule amounts of private economic activity in African hands at the time of independence, in country after country, the state loomed as more than a simple leviathan; it was effectively the only game in town. Under these circumstances, for most, getting ahead meant landing jobs for oneself or members of one's clan in the civil service or securing contracts with the government of one kind or another. This fueled unquenchable nepotism and self-seeking. Even the most scrupulous individuals came under constant pressure from family members to share in the spoils. Therefore, for members of any political party, the conflation of holding office with the opportunity for personal advancement and even enrichment became nearly absolute. In the early years of independence in Ghana, a concise popular expression captured this beautifully. "Power sweet," people said as they admired the new villas, new automobiles, and new mistresses accumulated by members of the government. Alternatively, the phrase was used with bitter sarcasm to denounce anyone in office who acquired anything, honestly or not.

This pattern emerged first in Ghana and would be repeated in country after country as the tidal wave of independence washed over Africa. It scarcely mattered whether the state was pro-Western, left leaning, or later, staunchly Marxist. In the East African nation of Tanzania, after independence in 1961, Julius Nyerere pulled off the rare feat of establishing a determinedly socialist government that maintained generally strong support from the West. Nyerere was able to achieve this, in part, because of his reputation for asceticism and incorruptibility. Still, Nyerere's ruling party, the Tanganyika African National Union (TANU), remained a vehicle for personal benefit and enrichment. In January 1967, this prompted Nyerere to announce a virtual relaunching of TANU with a major speech known as the Arusha Declaration. In it he announced a doubling down on self-reliance as a national development strategy. Nyerere identified corruption as a major impediment to progress and introduced a stern code of conduct for party members. Henceforth, they could not manage private companies or own shares in them, receive more than one salary, or rent property to others. Plots to kill Nyerere followed. Fortunately, they were unsuccessful. Corruption, though, continued much as before.

This situation also applied almost equally whether one considers civilian governments or the military juntas that became commonplace as some of the first independent governments began to be overthrown shortly after the first blush of independence. Lurid tales of spoliation became a major motif in Nkrumah's overthrow in 1966. Krobo Edusei, one of his closest longtime associates, was even said to have imported a gold-plated bed from Europe. Nepotism, bribery, the featherbedding of contracts, and other forms of corruption remained rampant in Ghana after Nkrumah's overthrow. In fact, if anything, the historical consensus today is that scourges like these worsened under post-Nkrumah regimes when governments succeeded each other rapidly, coup after coup. With almost every change, corruption was the common justification. But the rare ambition for the future and optimism that Nkrumah had unleashed made the grubby official rent seeking of some of those who surrounded him harder to swallow.

As the Ghanaian novelist Ayi Kwei Armah wrote, "How horribly rapid everything has been, from the days when men were not afraid to talk of souls and of suffering and of hope, to these low days of smiles that will never again be sly enough to hide the knowledge of betrayal and deceit."[12]

IN 1958, JUST A YEAR AFTER NKRUMAH TOOK POWER, MANY OF THE KEY FIGURES around the prime minister responded to the disloyal, petty, and often tribally inclined opposition by trying to build up the image of the ruling party and of its leader. "The Convention People's Party is Ghana," John Tettegah, the man that Nkrumah had coopted to lead the Trades Union Council proclaimed grandiosely. "The CPP is Ghana and Ghana is the CPP . . . those who sit outside the ranks of the CPP forfeit their right to citizenship in the country."[13] Officially driven adulation for Nkrumah, meanwhile, became more and more stultifying. From its tentative introduction in the 1950s, Nkrumah's first glorified honorific, Osagyefo—or victor in war, brave one, or simply leader—gradually became his de rigueur title, with his clear acquiescence. But like a medicine whose effects require higher and higher doses, Osagyefo steadily required further boosting and supplementation. The party officials who managed Nkrumah's image turned to the most powerful model of proselytization they knew, the Church. The language soon became wildly excessive, as when some spoke of Nkrumah as Ghana's savior. But even this was not enough. Soon, school children were taught to sing:

> *If you follow him*
> *Osagyefo, he will make you*
> *Fishers of men . . . , if you*
> *follow him . . .*
> Nkrumah is our Messiah! Nkrumah is our Leader. Nkrumah never dies![14]

Like preventive detention, this kind of official exaltation delivered negative returns. What Ghana needed was an opposition that would work to hold the government to account on a reasoned basis. Such an opposition would demand transparency in budgets and contracts and participate in policy debate. Nkrumah's near deification fed the opposite impulse. Every excessively fawning blandishment inspired new extremes in scathing denunciation.

Here again, history invites us to carefully examine the problems that Africa's new rulers faced and reflect on the solutions they grasped for. Contrary to the conventional wisdom that European imperial rule had been a healthy finishing school for democracy and good governance, it had in fact been an academy of authoritarianism. At all times, empires had had far more resources at their disposal to impose their rule than did Africa's post-1957 governments. Empires could deploy not only money and military force as needed, but also the soft power of education, information, and popular culture. Monarchies wielded cosmological bluster through the ceremony and pomp organized around royals. Over generations, European rulers carefully ginned up respect and awe and drilled them into Africans and imperial subjects on other continents. They kept on display in public spaces official portraits that emphasized the majesty of European emperors. They richly celebrated royal birthdays, and organized holidays for a kind of secular worship of imperial rulers. Classroom instruction and especially textbooks, which were almost always supplied by the colonizer, emphasized the wisdom and benevolence of the monarch.

Soon after they took office, independence leaders in Africa sought to mobilize some of that symbolic power for their own use. Here too Kwame Nkrumah was a pioneer. These many years later, the postage stamp albums that I once avidly kept as a boy in Washington are long lost. For unknown reasons I have vivid memories of stamps from Nyasaland and Sudan. But with parents who were enthusiastic supporters of Ghana's independence, I imagine my collection included samples from early in the country's new era. Under the rules of the Commonwealth, newly independent countries still retained the sitting British monarch as their head of state. In ordering the redesign of Ghana's new postage stamps, Nkrumah quickly broke with protocol. Out went images of the Queen, which were replaced with Nkrumah's likeness in the upper righthand corner. The design also included a sketch of the African continent, which highlighted Ghana's place in West Africa. To top it off, a newly adopted national symbol, an eagle, flew in the foreground, seemingly headed in Nkrumah's direction.

During my stays in Ghana while researching this book, I visited Accra's neat and well-lit, if modest, National Museum. There, in a series of dioramas showing the country's monetary history, I saw pound and shilling coins issued in 1958 that were dominated by Nkrumah wearing kente cloth on one side and Ghana's five-pointed black star on the other. Above the leader's bust, just inside the coins' rim, read the Latin legend: *Civitatis Ghaniensis Conditor*, "Founder of the State of Ghana," sounding like a scientific classification of a newly identified species. Lest anyone not recognize him, beneath his bust appeared Nkrumah's full name. Here was a subtle yet powerful use of iconography and appropriation. In a stroke, Nkrumah had not only usurped the British crown, but he had effaced J. B. Danquah and all his other erstwhile allies and peers. Breaking with the old guard, he stood alone.[15]

One after another, new African regimes in the 1960s and beyond would come in for ridicule for their early resort to personality cults. Around the continent, honorifics like Osagyefo became more rule than exception. When I moved to the Ivory Coast out of college, one of the first things I remarked on, was the little box that appeared in bold above the fold every day in *Fraternité Matin*, then the sole national newspaper. It was called the "Thought of the Day" and was dedicated to the paternalistic wisdom of the president, Félix Houphouët-Boigny. Schoolchildren memorized them.

In Tanzania, through careful image cultivation, the frugal and disciplined Julius Nyerere was elevated to become that new nation's Mwalimu, or teacher. Jomo Kenyatta of Kenya, who ceremonially wore leopard skins and colorful beaded headgear, adopted the persona of the nation's Mzee, or revered elder. Hastings Banda of Malawi affected black, pinstriped English-tailored suits and heavy homburgs, together with African symbols like carved walking sticks and whisked flyswatters. Banda named himself President for Life, and because they were not legally married, he bestowed upon his much younger companion, Cecilia Kadzamira, the title of the new nation's "official hostess."

These early instances of political glorification look tame in light of the later degeneracy of leaders like Idi Amin of Uganda and Jean-Bédel Bokassa of the Central African Republic. Amin took to appearing in full military dress uniform with his chest even more heavily festooned with medals than a North Korean general. Bokassa, whom I interviewed after he was overthrown in 1979, took the self-ridicule through aggrandizement yet further, proclaiming himself "emperor" of Central Africa. Mobutu Sese Seko was an abbreviated version for the name of the longtime Congolese (Zaïre) leader who was the United States' most important client in Africa for three decades. The full name he adopted as ruler, after the overthrow and assassination of Patrice Lumumba, was Mobutu Sese Seko Kuku Ngbendu wa za Banga. "The all-powerful warrior who, because of his endurance and inflexible will to win, goes from conquest to conquest, leaving fire in his wake."

Most of Africa's new nation-states were weak as well as ethnically, religiously, or geographically incoherent. Their leaders required the display of their official portraits first in every government office, then in every business, and finally, in some countries, in every home. It was a small step from there to demanding ever more elaborate and unswerving forms of celebration to prove the loyalty of their people.

But what were all these new leaders compared to the European royals they had clearly emulated to one degree or another, with their endless titles, bemedaled dress uniforms, fussy ceremonies and protocols, and indecipherable pedigrees? Africans inherited ersatz nations whose wealth—like cocoa and tea, rubber and palm oil, and whose people's energies, wielding shovels and pickaxes in gold and diamond mines—had all been diverted abroad for many decades. With independence, rulers had to suddenly invent traditions from scratch and gin up the prestige needed to enforce them on the fly. To a much greater degree than most people recognize, not least their European critics, they did so by studying the habits of their erstwhile masters.

CHAPTER THIRTY-TWO

Forward to Independence

IN LATE MAY OF 1960, THE ADULT MALE POPULATION OF THE BELGIAN Congo turned out to vote for the first time in an exercise that, stretched out over a two-week period, was designed to lead to independence barely one month hence. Congo's path toward independence had come with such little preparation that many of the colony's people had no real sense of what difference it was supposed to make in their lives.

The confusion was such that in the capital, Kinshasa, a city of green and breezy hills, on which only Europeans lived, and fetid African quarters that stretched inland from the banks of the great Congo River, streetcorner hustlers were able to sell elaborately wrapped boxes to the gullible after taking care to scrawl the word "independence" on them. Like children advised not to peek at Christmas gifts beforehand, the unfortunates who forked over 50 francs for them were warned not to open the boxes before June 30, when the Congo would emerge from seven decades of Belgian rule.

When that date finally rolled around, as Stuart A. Reid wrote in his biography of Lumumba, the credulous were surprised to discover that the fancy boxes were full of dirt. For the new nation of Congo, independence would be filled with surprises, too: time bombs that would plunge the country into one of the biggest early crises of the postwar international system. The biggest victim of this catastrophe in the making was not the election's winner, Patrice Lumumba, who was famously murdered after only a few short weeks in effective command of his country. It was any future hope of democracy, peace and order, and improvements in the living conditions of one of the continent's largest nations for the coming decades.

The Congo Crisis, as it came to be called, was a tragedy that involved some of the worst bad faith imaginable both on the part of the colonial power, Belgium, and the leader of the West, the United States. Right from the start,

Washington was deeply engaged in unseemly efforts to undermine and ultimately eliminate Lumumba. As the wrapped independence box scam indicates, the crisis also involved a population that Belgium had done precious little to ready for self-government, while hoping, all the while, disastrously, that the day for such a thing could be postponed indefinitely. Lumumba was a tall, rail-thin thirty-four-year-old leader with an unslakable thirst for any idea or notion that could help him modernize his nation. This was evident even in the studious look he affected—his carefully parted hair, his double-breasted suits with pocket squares, and his half-rim glasses that screamed intellectual. He was brilliant, but largely unschooled because, effectively, Congo had almost no higher education outside of training for the priesthood. In addition to Lumumba's inexperience, he was also mercurial and deeply imbued with paranoia, somewhat like Nkrumah. Here, though, as is so often the case, his paranoia was fueled by the antagonistic and cynical behavior of outside powers so extreme that it is hard to credit, and yet it is completely true.

Washington readily imagined the USSR to be ten feet tall. But the Congo Crisis came early enough in the Cold War that the Soviet Union scarcely had an Africa policy, nor the means to project much power or influence on the continent even if it had wanted to. The best Moscow could do was posture in trying to buttress the Lumumba government, after Belgium, the United States, and even the United Nations had begun to betray it. All that the Congo was left with was Nkrumah's Ghana, one of Lumumba's earliest sources of inspiration and support, as well as his final rampart. After the arrest of Lumumba by Congolese forces that were allied with Belgium, and with the connivance of Washington, which obsessed irrationally about a Soviet takeover of the country, Nkrumah became the clear target of cold warriors in the American capital. Lumumba's elimination was a powerful tocsin, a warning call to Nkrumah who was unable to fully grasp its meaning. Although it would take some time for the West to muster plans to try to get rid of him, the bell of Nkrumah's fate began to toll from the moment Lumumba was carried off into the forests of southern Congo for an extrajudicial execution of the most gruesome sort. There, he was murdered by firing squad and dismembered, his remains dissolved in powerful chemicals by Belgian agents.

The parallels between the early personal histories of Patrice Lumumba and Kwame Nkrumah and the late colonial histories of their homelands, the Belgian Congo and the Gold Coast, are striking. But where they arise, the differences are sharp and telling. Lumumba, like Nkrumah, who was sixteen years his elder, was born in 1925 in a remote village, Onalua, just southwest of the Congo's geographical center in a colony that was seventy-seven times larger than Belgium. Being from the middle of a territory as vast as all of Western Europe was the opposite of hailing from a border zone. But Onalua managed to be just as liminal. It was the inner frontier, far from any of the giant colony's handful of major cities, and indeed so small—like Nkrumah's Nkroful—that it doesn't even appear on most maps. During the Scramble for Africa, tiny Belgium successfully staked its claims to the Congo with other Europeans through an audacious and obscenely mendacious ruse. It posed as a benevolent force in the world. Its King Leopold II emphasized his new country's commitment to eradicating vestiges of African slavery and uplifting the people of the continent through Christian missionary work and education.

It is true that the rolling savannas of Lumumba's native Kasaï Province had long been a zone of predation for the Indian Ocean slave trade as well as for a rich commerce in ivory obtained through the decimation of roaming elephant troops. But Leopold, grim of face, frightfully long-bearded, and more weighed down with gilded epaulettes, thick sashes, and heavy medals than any of the African dictators who would eventually follow him, obtained the Congo as a royal property and not as a possession of Belgium itself. It generated enormous revenue for the crown through an economic model based on lucrative cash crops—rubber and cotton. De jure slavery was officially done away with, but forced labor with production quotas for villagers promptly took its place. This applied in Lumumba's native region and throughout much of central Congo. In the late 1880s and early 1900s, output was maintained through systematic violence and terror. Villagers deemed to be laggards had their wives held hostage as one form of punishment. Large numbers of men, meanwhile, had their hands amputated for failing to meet quotas, or in some cases, they were summarily shot.[1]

For all its remoteness, the district that contained Onalua was endowed with two Christian missions, one Catholic, the other American Methodist. Lumumba, almost famished-looking then, learned how to read and write at the latter but never completed grade school. Like Nkrumah, he had illiterate parents and a father who was not a large presence in his life. Like Nkrumah, too, his true birthdate is uncertain, and he invented new names for himself. First, he changed his given name from Isaïe to Patrice, and then, for unknown reasons, he abandoned Tolenga for Lumumba.

In 1942 or 1943, after briefly attending a second missionary school, Lumumba stole away from Kasai to Stanleyville, named after Henry Morton Stanley, the American journalist and adventurer who would become Leopold II's agent in the Congo. Stanley, who gained a reputation for extraordinary brutality in driving rubber production through forced labor once wrote:

Only by proving that we are superior to the savages, not only through our power to kill them but through our entire way of life, can we control them as they are now, in their present stage; it is necessary for their own well-being, even more than ours.[2]

Lumumba's bid for life under a new dispensation as far away from a world like this as possible echoes the movements of penniless cotton pickers who abandoned indentured plantation life in the Mississippi Delta in this same era by jumping freight trains bound for Chicago. Lumumba made his way north with forged travel papers and only 3 francs in his pocket. It was in Stanleyville (later renamed Kisangani), at the navigable end of the great Congo River, that he would seek his future. And there, with far less preparation than Nkrumah, he began his spectacular rise. In little more than a decade, Lumumba arrived into the front ranks of African society in Congo, then saw setbacks involving petty criminality, and finally, political prominence, international travel, evanescent power, world fame, and martyrdom.

However extraordinary, a trajectory like this was facilitated by the vacuum of the Congo, where Belgium had done so little to train and educate the population. The colonizers openly touted their belief in the maxim that no elites meant no troubles, and they confined Blacks to menial or infantilized roles by design.[3] Lumumba broke through with a rare combination of individual drive, force of personality, an appetite for learning fed through obsessive self-study, daringness, and not least, his quicksilver tongue.

Some of what drove him was entirely intrinsic. Other elements were responses to the radically stratified colony the Belgians built in the Congo. Given their dread of tropical diseases, Europeans tended to avoid equatorial settings. But because Congo was so wildly endowed in minerals, from copper and cobalt to uranium, gold, and diamonds, Belgians were undaunted. Pestilence be damned, they built a settler society there that became home to one hundred thousand Europeans. Like most colonies on the continent, segregation was enforced through strict rules. The Belgians created a tiny escape valve for the inevitable social tensions this produced, though. A minuscule number of Africans were eligible to become so-called *évolués*, meaning officially civilized. This status was granted very selectively, through careful examination of the degree of assimilation of Belgian speech, dress, manners, and even domestic lifestyle. An extensive credentialing process governed this social elevation. It involved intrusive inspections of the African postulate's home and the solicitation of detailed reports from people in his social and work circles.

Lumumba's first important job in Stanleyville was as an entry-level clerk in a provincial government office. That meant completing menial tasks and running errands for whites. Bent toward uplift, he took night classes and correspondence courses, and in 1947, like untold thousands of other Congolese in this era, he made his way to the capital, Leopoldville, distant, pulsating, and hubristically named for the Belgium king. There he attended a new government-run postal school, and after nine months, returned to Stanleyville to a job as a third-class mail clerk. This was a big step up in life, but the driven Lumumba was only getting started. He got a bank loan to build a house and proceeded to marry for the first of several times. His real passion, though, remained self-cultivation. Like Nkrumah at Lincoln, Lumumba stayed up for long hours every night to read books that he took out from the library. He devoured French classics—Hugo, Molière, Rousseau, and Voltaire, among them. When his marriage prevented him from enrolling in the university, he became a librarian in the city's underused library instead.

By this point, the tall and lanky Lumumba spoke polished French and the studious look he affected, along with his thirst for self-improvement, his distinctive parted hair, brow-line eyeglasses, and taste for bow ties elevated him in the eyes of the Belgians. He was issued a "civic merit card" effectively admitting him into the ranks of the *évolués*, and he became one of the first applicants for an even more rarified station when he sought a newly introduced "registration card" that theoretically granted its holders the same legal status as Europeans.[4]

The impassioned advocate of liberation and of pan-Africanism that Lumumba eventually became was largely born from his exposure to Kwame Nkrumah during his visit to Ghana in 1958. For the time being, though, Lumumba still sounded surprisingly conservative. In this era, he spoke of the need for Belgium to grant full access to education, but he did so almost apologetically, expressing appreciation for Brussels' civilizing mission. "We promise docility, loyal and sincere collaboration," he wrote.[5]

These early political thoughts came at a time when Belgium had begun to discuss independence for its colony, but only in the most attenuated of ways. In 1955, a furor erupted when A. A. J. Van Bilsen, a professor in Antwerp, suggested a thirty-year timeline for Congolese independence, which would have placed it in the 1980s. "Our domination of this half-century is definitely outmoded and whoever considers that this method has succeeded until now ought recognize that this cannot apply to the future without risk. The period of political emancipation of the Congo . . . is opening before us."[6] Van Bilsen's gradualism recalls certain Southern American thinkers, timid modernizers whose notions about the slow acceptance of change were widely denounced by others as wildly precipitous. Even among Belgium relative reformists, discussion was limited to conjuring some symbolic means of participation in government for the Congolese while retaining Belgian control of all the important levers of power. This also echoed Ghana's experience early in the decade when British administrators retained almost all of the key positions when Nkrumah was named chief of government business.

It was in the very next year, 1956, that the first Congolese student graduated from the University of Louvain in Belgium. Almost simultaneously, Congo's Catholic University of Lovanium opened its doors. Lumumba had been unable to enroll there because it lacked housing for married students. By the time of independence in 1960, the newborn country of fifteen million people had produced a total of thirty university graduates.

Congo's educated class was still microscopic, but one would not know that from the torrent of the discussions about independence that the Van Bilsen recommendations had unleashed, and its pace would never relent. In 1957 Brussels, under pressure from this, allowed the colony to hold its first local elections—far later than even France allowed its colonies. That year, the head of the ethnically based political party Abako, one Joseph Kasa-Vubu, won a seat representing a district of the capital.

The two men would soon become direct rivals, with Kasa-Vubu promoted by Washington and Belgium and pitted against Lumumba. By 1956, Lumumba had risen to the status of a first-class clerk at the Stanleyville post office. From that prominent perch and because of his early writings, he was invited that year on a study tour of Belgium. Soon after his return, though, he was arrested on charges of embezzlement of 125,000 francs, or the equivalent of two years' salary. By this time, Lumumba's pride had swollen because he had been distinguished as an *évolué*. His trial and conviction, though, degraded him in ways that went well beyond the narrow terms of his punishment. Speaking in court, the Belgian prosecutor asked rhetorically, "Without our presence in Congo, what would Lumumba be?" Answering his own question, the prosecutor said, Lumumba "owes it to the state that he is not a slave." As a supposedly mitigating factor, the judge added insult to injury, condescending that Lumumba "is still not that far away from the most primitive natives."[7]

It was while serving a two-year sentence that some of the strongest biographical parallels with Nkrumah emerged. Lumumba sustained a constant output of writings, which were smuggled out of the Stanleyville prison. He also produced an autobiography of sorts that he addressed to the Belgian public and titled *The Congo, Land of the Future. Is It Threatened?* Then, on the recommendation of the Belgian minister for the colonies, after fourteen months,

Lumumba was granted a royal pardon, and he left Stanleyville for the much more lively and politically connected world of the capital.[8] There, by 1957, open debates among Africans about independence were all the rage.

In August 1958, during his tour of French colonies to sell his program of a French community, Charles de Gaulle spoke in puny and quiescent Brazzaville, the capital of French Central Africa. After boasting that France had never been prouder of "the work in Africa it has accomplished, of the effort of its administrators, its soldiers, its builders, its professors, and its missionaries," de Gaulle finally came to the choice Paris was putting before its colonies.

> It is Community that I propose to each and every [colonial subject], wherever they may be. Some say: "We have a right to independence." You certainly do. In fact, whoever wishes to take it can do so right away. [France] will not object.[9]

In the Belgian Congo, words like these had a stunning, if unintended, effect, not least on Lumumba himself. No two world capitals sit as close to each other as Kinshasa and Brazzaville, divided only by the immense Congo River. With the cities not quite three miles apart, radio broadcasts from each were avidly listened to in the other. But in Belgian-controlled Kinshasa, subjects were neither eligible for membership in a French community nor for what de Gaulle claimed could be immediate independence. Two days later, a group of *évolués*, including Lumumba, signed a petition they sent to the Belgian colonial minister denouncing what they called Congo's "anachronistic political regime," and demanding a date for "total independence."[10]

In December 1958, as we have seen, Lumumba traveled to Accra to attend the All-Africa People's Conference. There, he listened raptly as Nkrumah invoked Gandhian nonviolence and delivered a powerful articulation of his pan-Africanist vision. "This decade is the decade of African independence," the Ghanaian prime minister proclaimed in his stirring opening address. "Forward then to independence. To independence now. Tomorrow, the United States of Africa. I salute you!"[11]

Later, in the final speech of the conference, Lumumba heard Nkrumah dramatically broaden his vision of pan-Africanism to embrace the Black diaspora in America and throughout the Atlantic world:

> We must never forget that they are part of us. These sons and daughters of Africa were taken away from our shores and despite all the centuries which have separated us, they have not forgotten their ancestral

links. Many of them have made no small contribution to the struggle for African freedom.[12]

Nkrumah's words and those of the other conference speakers, all clamoring for independence, had an incalculable impact in the thirty-three-year-old Lumumba. In his own speech, more forthrightly than in his recent writings, he condemned the injustice inherent in Belgium's baby steps toward allowing the Congolese a degree of democratic participation. He also denounced the threats he perceived of fragmentation and tribalism that Nkrumah had also faced. But while speaking proudly as an African, Lumumba also invoked universal values.

> We wish to see a modern democratic state established in our country, which will grant its citizens freedom, justice, social peace, tolerance, well-being, and equality, with no discrimination whatsoever.... In our actions aimed at winning the independence of the Congo, we have repeatedly proclaimed that we are against no one, but rather are simply against domination, injustices and abuses, and merely want to free ourselves of the shackles of colonialism and all its consequences.[13]

On December 28, 1958, two weeks after his return to the Congo, Lumumba told a rally in the capital of his newly formed party, the Mouvement National Congolais (MNC) that the Accra conference had "marked a decisive step toward the self-realization of the African personality, and toward the total unity of all the peoples of the African continent." He then vowed that the MNC would carry out the conference's resolutions.[14]

Joseph Kasa-Vubu had been involved in pro-independence activism much longer than Lumumba. Worried now about losing ground to an upstart, he scheduled a rally in January 1959 for his Abako party, but authorities forbade its gathering. This led to widespread rioting in Leopoldville, in which hundreds of Africans were killed or injured by the colonial police, the Force Publique. In the wake of this full-blown crisis, Brussels arrested Kasa-Vubu and temporarily banned his political party. Just days later, in an intended gesture of appeasement, Baudouin, Belgium's twenty-eight-year-old king, the great-nephew of Leopold II, announced that the government would soon begin work to pave the way for Congo's eventual independence. "Our resolve today is to lead the Congolese peoples to independence in prosperity and peace without delay, but also without irresponsible rashness."[15] Baudouin said nothing, though, about how Africans would be consulted in the matter or what timetable this would follow. In those moments, almost no one could have imagined the blinding speed with which events would unfold.

During 1959, political parties proliferated like mushrooms spawning on a forest floor. Most of them were narrow ethnic affairs or like Abako, of regional composition. Lumumba and his MNC were virtually alone in rejecting this approach and building a national following. Washington monitored developments in the Congo closely, partly out of reflexive Cold War anxieties, but also because the Congo possessed some of the richest uranium deposits in the world. These had been tapped to develop America's first atomic weapons. Eisenhower betrayed his characteristically low estimation of Africans when he told aides that he hadn't realized there were as many people who could read and write in the Congo as there were new political parties.[16] By this time, in fact, the Belgians and Christian missionaries had seen to it that a little more than half of the population could read. For Belgium, primary schooling for Congolese had a compelling utility. It allowed its subjects to follow basic instructions in servile roles. Anything much beyond this, as we have seen, higher education in particular, was exceedingly scarce.

Lumumba stayed in close touch with Nkrumah from Stanleyville in 1959, leaning on him often for advice about the Americans, the Soviets, and the United Nations. Nkrumah was eager to have, in Lumumba, a much younger understudy, someone more impressionable than his Guinean near-peer Touré. The time would soon come when Nkrumah would propose to Congo another of his political unions, which was as eccentric in geography, insofar as the involved countries were not neighbors and employed different colonial tongues. Lumumba accepted the idea, but the whirlpool of foreign destabilization and violence that took hold of the Congo at independence afforded him no time to put meat on the bones of this scheme. Lumumba's political rhetoric nonetheless bore unmistakable echoes of Nkrumah. In his speeches, he now routinely called for immediate independence and voiced ideas that sounded strikingly similar to Nkrumah's promotion of what he called the "African personality." Visiting Ibadan, Nigeria, for example, Lumumba told a seminar that Africans needed to "free our peoples psychologically."[17] Finally, that November, the Belgians arrested him for incitement, provoking rioting first in Stanleyville, and then in the capital. Lumumba's arrest came just before Brussels hosted the first major consultative event that included Congolese in discussions about their own country's future. It was billed as the Table Ronde, and scores of Africans belonging to seventy-nine separate delegations were flown in to participate and put up in downtown hotels.

Just as the conclave began came something unexpected. A strong clamor arose from the delegates to include Lumumba, who at that very moment was being flown to a prison in Jadotville, in the southeast of the Congo. Eight years earlier, the British had been lucid enough to understand that the elections it had approved for the Gold Coast would have little legitimacy if Kwame Nkrumah, the colony's leading politician, continued to be imprisoned, so it released him in 1951. With Lumumba, Belgium now made the same calculation, releasing him from prison and flying him to Brussels. There to greet him at the airport was one Mobutu Sese Seko, a novice journalist and aspiring political operator who had previously ingratiated himself with Lumumba. By this time, the young Mobutu was almost certainly a Belgian intelligence asset, and he would eventually play a central role in Lumumba's overthrow and murder.

With his prestige enhanced by his recent persecution and his unrivalled speaking skills, Lumumba almost completely dominated the Table Ronde. Although Congo's politicians were divided on many fundamentals, with some notably demanding a federal state as many Asante had in Ghana, Lumumba was able to line up most of the delegates behind his demand for independence on June 1, 1960, just four months hence. To the astonishment of nearly everyone, Belgium agreed to a June 30 date.

FOLLOWING HIS RELEASE IN 1957 FROM HIS FIRST INCARCERATION, LUMUMBA had moved to Kinshasa, where he found work as an accountant for Polar, one of the two major breweries that served the colony. He quickly transitioned from this office job to a salesman's role with the company, which he excelled at. Lumumba had little difficulty mastering Lingala, the lingua franca of western Congo, and he was tireless in his efforts to match the sales of an older, better established beer brand called Primus. He addressed gatherings of people in boisterous neighborhood bars and noisy nightclubs and delivered his pitches before crowds at sporting events and commercial sponsorships of all kinds, a perfect training course in campaigning for a man who would soon formally launch himself into politics.

The first of the Table Ronde's two big gatherings had only ended in February 1960, leaving a second set of meetings to discuss fine points of the constitution and economic matters in the nascent country in April and May. This left little time for campaigning, but here Lumumba, excelled. It would be easy to skip over the political and economic discussions with Belgium during this period, but that would be a mistake. For months, the political debate in Belgium had been about how to preserve what Baudouin himself called his nation's "imperishable rights" in Congo. Brussels, meanwhile, distrusted Lumumba, and funneled money to a collection of minor political parties that it hoped could form a coalition government, just as had happened in the Gold Coast. Meanwhile, Belgian officials and corporate figures tried to impress upon their Congolese counterparts that given the intricate governance challenges that would come with independence, they should leave Belgians in charge of as many things as possible. They even proposed that the new country retain Belgium's king as its sovereign. Without prior consultations, the Belgians deployed three army companies to strengthen Belgium's position in the Congo even as it stood poised to formally cease being a colony. The commander of Belgian forces, Émile Janssens, then sought to gain acquiescence for the idea of having his European officers remain in charge of Congo's army indefinitely. Nkrumah already knew a thing or two about this sort of thing, another manifestation of what he called neocolonialism. He had been persuaded to accept something similar, if more limited, with British generals commanding Ghana's armed forces from independence until the eve of Nkrumah's overthrow, in 1966.

All the while, corporate registrations were being revised to shift the legal domiciles of lucrative colonial businesses back to Belgium, instantly stripping the Congo of vital tax revenue and income.

When the election came in May 1960, Lumumba and his party emerged with a creditable plurality, although one complicated by the large numbers of contestants for office. The MNC enjoyed the most widely distributed support of any party, and its affiliates won 41 out of 137 seats in the inaugural Chamber of Representatives. In the Senate, though, the MNC won just 19 of 84 seats.

This lack of an unassailable mandate set off another round of manipulation by the government of Belgian prime minister, Gaston Eyskens, as his counselors tried to cobble together coalitions that could deny Lumumba leadership of the country. All of these failed, but through no choice of his own, Lumumba, the incoming prime minister and head of government, was saddled with the phlegmatic and more conservative Kasa-Vubu as his partner and largely ceremonial president.

In the final runup to June 30, independence day, Lumumba searched for a gesture that could bring the country together and that would give its leadership, with so few means at its disposal, political momentum. Lumumba's position was further weakened, though, by Belgian acts of sabotage and wanton destruction of colonial records, office equipment, and other items, mirroring the spiteful French departure from Guinea. Outgoing Belgian officials and settlers alike seethed over their sudden change of circumstances, going almost overnight from lordly masters to disempowered foreign guests who were now made to suffer the indignity of being subjected to the laws of Black people. The idea Lumumba seized upon on the day before the ceremony was a broad commutation of sentences for prisoners. As Reid relates in his biography, the original idea had been an across-the-board reduction in prison terms by ten years, but Lumumba was persuaded that this would nearly empty the jails and so the commutation proposal was reduced to three years.

When King Baudouin arrived that day to preside over independence ceremonies, there was no skimping on pomp and circumstance. Like de Gaulle, the king stood waving tall and stiff from the back of a convertible limousine for a ceremonial ride through streets lined with throngs of Africans turned out to cheer him. Uniformed schoolchildren bearing large flags performed carefully rehearsed marches. Women dressed in colorful tribal gowns danced and sang the king's praises. In all, Belgium had spent sixty-two million francs on the independence ceremonies, or more than three times what it spent each year for education in the Congo. The outgoing colonial governor proposed that the king be allowed to announce the lenience decree. "Thus the last act of the king will be an act of generosity," Lumumba agreed generously. "That will make an excellent impression."[18] That evening, on the very eve of independence, though, Belgium's minister for the colonies, August De Schryver, informed Lumumba that his amnesty plan, already whittled down once, would now be restricted to prisoners who were serving sentences of six months or less. Having already endured multiple forms of resistance and sabotage from the Belgians since his electoral triumph, Lumumba was outraged, but his attempts at pushback went nowhere.

This is what set the stage for Lumumba's remarks the next day, in what would become the most important speech in modern African history—more important than Sékou Touré's defiant retort to de Gaulle, or even Nkrumah's spine-tingling declaration at independence about the arrival of "a new African in the world." The events that marked Congo's independence ceremony plunged that country, a large and scarcely cohesive newborn nation, into a vicious cyclone and created a pall of doom and dysfunction that still hangs over Central Africa. In its own indirect and unforeseeable way, it also greatly hastened the demise of Nkrumah in faraway Ghana.

THE CELEBRATION OF INDEPENDENCE BEGAN IN LEOPOLDVILLE ON JUNE 30, A Thursday, with the solemn and ancient rites of an early Te Deum chanted at the Catholic Cathedral. Like Accra, the city bulged with foreign dignitaries who had converged there to witness the still-novel spectacle of the birthing of an African nation. The dawn of independence on the continent had become a central theme of global diplomacy in 1960, and Congo was poised to become the fifth African country to win its freedom that year, beating out Somalia by just one day.

After mass, the invited guests, elegantly clothed and coifed, streamed into the site of the formal independence ceremony, the House of Parliament near the banks of the Congo River. Construction of this neoclassical building, with its clean lines, unadorned decorative columns, and grand entranceway, had only recently been completed. African self-rule was still unimagined when its architectural plan was drawn up; the grand building's original purpose was to host Belgian royals during visits to the colony. Before the official program began, the people seated inside were treated to musical performances by some of the Congo's most popular bands. This was virtually the only concession to local content, and the most famous song, "Indépendence Cha Cha" was delivered by Joseph Kabasele, who was then widely known by his performer's name Le Grand Kallé, Lingala for the great communicator. The song was first performed by Kallé's group, Africa Jazz, during the Table Ronde and would be danced and sung all over the continent during the Year of Africa. Its popularity was such that when neighboring Zambia achieved independence from Britain in 1964, the new government renamed a main street after the song. Le Grand Kallé's hit was sung in a bright falsetto and matching guitar lines played over a medium tempo rumba beat that few could resist dancing to. The sound was unmistakably jubilant, but it contained a slyly defiant message in Lingala, meaning that few Belgians and probably none of the visiting dignitaries grasped it. To them, it was just happy-sounding African entertainment. Hidden in its bouncy cheerfulness, though, was a firm political statement of African agency and deep pride; a message with a defiant spirit much like that of the speech Lumumba was about to deliver in that very space.

> *Independence, cha-cha, we've won it.*
> *Oh! Independence, cha-cha, we've achieved it.*
> *Oh! The table ronde cha-cha. We've pulled it off.*
> *Oh! Independence, cha-cha, we've won it.*

Apart from members of the new parliament, few Congolese were admitted into the semicircular, heavily curtained grand hall, but they could hear echoes of Kallé's hit from without. Thick crowds surrounded the palace and hung from an enormous, pedestal-mounted bronze statue of a horsebound Leopold II that faced the entrance.

Lumumba, smarting from the patronizing and deceptive treatment he had just received from the Belgians, stayed awake late into the previous night writing a speech to deliver during the independence ceremony. The problem was that the protocol for the event with the twenty-nine-year-old king, an unproven and untested tin idol, only called for words from Congo's incoming president, not its prime minister. In the morning, Lumumba shared his hasty draft with one of his most trusted associates, Thomas Kanza, asking him to edit his remarks for concision and form and to tone down its most "explosive" elements. Kanza expressed alarm over the content but could do nothing to talk his boss out of giving his speech. The time had finally come, Lumumba had decided, for the Belgians to hear some straight talk from the Africans they had lorded over for so long.

Tall, thin, and dressed in a ceremonial white uniform and sheathed and belted sword, young Baudouin cut a striking figure. Standing stiffly erect, he delivered his prepared remarks before a freestanding microphone. They contained a brazenly unselfconscious remembrance of Leopold II, the monarch who had sold Belgium's colonial ambitions at the Berlin Conference on the basis of a supposedly civilizing mission. It was as if the year 1885 had never ended. The great fortune that Leopold had reaped while carrying out a genocide of starvation and amputations in the Congo was not even hinted at. Baudouin had little inkling of what Lumumba was planning, and through his ill-chosen words, the king was pouring oil onto already smoldering embers. From the poorly preserved newsreel that survives, Lumumba can be seen sitting off to the side, scribbling last minute changes to his text on the sheafs of paper he held in his lap. The king's words are both shocking and ludicrous to twenty-first century ears:

> The independence of the Congo represents the culmination of the work conceived by the genius of King Leopold II, undertaken by him with tenacious courage and continued with perseverance by Belgium. For eighty years, Belgium sent to your soil the best of its sons—first to deliver the Congo Basin from the odious slave trade that was decimating its population, and then to bring together the various ethnic groups that were once enemies.[19]

Even as potted history goes, this was a grotesque travesty, considering the thick record of violence and appropriation accumulated under Leopold II's colonial regime. The willful amnesia here reflects everything heinous about the colonial period. To take but one example in an 1883 letter to colonial missionaries Leopold II wrote:

> Always convert the blacks by using the whip. Keep their women in nine months of submission to work freely for us. Force them to pay you in sign of recognition goats, chicken or eggs every time you visit their villages. And make sure that niggers never become rich. Sing every day that it's impossible for the rich to enter heaven. Make them pay tax each week at Sunday mass. Use the money supposed for the poor to build flourishing business centers. Institute a confession system, which allows you to be good detectives denouncing any black that has a different consciousness contrary to that of the decision-maker. Teach niggers to forget their heroes and to adore only ours. Never present a chair to a black that comes to visit you. Don't give him more than one cigarette. Never invite him for dinner even if he gives you a chicken every time you arrive at his house.[20]

In his coverage of the day's events, even the *New York Times* correspondent, Harry Gilroy, understood that something was grossly amiss. "Today, barely half of the Congolese can read and write, and only sixteen Congolese are university or college graduates. There are no Congolese doctors, lawyers or engineers, and African officers in the 25,000-man Congolese Army."[21] But despite having completely glossed over the true historical record in distilling the myth of the White Man's Burden, the independence day speech Baudouin delivered was an improvement over the nausea-inducing hypocrisy of earlier drafts. In those, he called his great grand uncle, Leopold II, the "liberator" of Congo, which had been "formed by freely concluded treaties between its leaders and the king's envoys."[22] Perhaps most offensive of all, though, was Baudouin's smug peroration. "It is now up to you, gentlemen, to show that we were right to trust you." Independence, Baudouin warned, "is not achieved through the immediate satisfaction of simple pleasures but hard work ... do not jeopardize the future with hasty reforms, and do not replace the structures that Belgium has given you until you are sure you can do better."[23]

Kasa-Vubu, like a pipsqueak, then spoke briefly and struck a meek and humble tone in expressing his gratitude to the king and to his country. Then, Lumumba, looking as austere and intense as ever in a dark, thinly tailored suit and white shirt, black bow tie, and thick, half-frame eyeglasses that were his trademark, sprung from his seat and strode to the front of the hall to deliver his unscheduled address. This set the hall astir, but the scene had unfolded with such suddenness that no one could object before he had implanted himself behind a stout wooden podium. Across his chest, Lumumba still wore the maroon sash of the Order of the Crown, Belgium's highest decoration, which had been bestowed upon him the night before.

Far beyond the hall where he stood before king and dignitaries, even well beyond the crowds that thronged outside, millions of soon-to-be citizens across the vast territory of the Congo bent to their radios following the events of that morning. Lumumba implored them "to make this day, June 30, 1960, an illustrious date that you keep indelibly engraved in your heart, a date whose meaning you will proudly teach your children so that they, in turn, can tell their sons and their grandsons the glorious history of our struggle for freedom." Thus, one might say, began his Independence Cha Cha. We, the Congolese people have achieved this. Our freedom wasn't granted to us. By itself, this message would have generated scarcely more of a frisson than Lumumba's surprising break in protocol, but Lumumba was just getting started. His speech will not be quoted in full here, but like few other politicians' speeches, its emotional and political truths have not diminished even decades later:

> Although the Independence of the Congo is being proclaimed today in agreement with Belgium, a friendly country we treat as an equal, no Congolese worthy of the name can ever forget that it was obtained through a fight—a daily fight, an intense and idealistic fight, a fight in which we spared no force, hardship, suffering, or blood. It was a fight made of tears, fire and blood. We are deeply proud of it, because it was a just and noble fight, indispensable for putting an end to the humiliating slavery that had been forced upon us.
>
> That was our lot for eighty years of colonial rule, and our wounds are still too fresh and painful to erase from our memories. We have known backbreaking work, demanded in exchange for wages that allowed us neither to feed, nor dress, nor house ourselves decently, nor to raise our children as loved ones.
>
> We have suffered contempt, insults, and blows morning, noon, and evening because we were Negroes. Who can forget that a Black was addressed by the familiar *tu*, certainly not as a friend, but because the formal *vous* was reserved for whites alone.
>
> We have known that our lands were seized in the name of supposedly legal texts that recognized only the rights of the strongest....
>
> We have known that in the cities, there were magnificent houses for whites and decrepit huts for Blacks, that Blacks could not enter so-called

European movie theaters, restaurants, and stores, and that Blacks would travel in the holds of a riverboat, underneath the whites in their luxury cabins....

All that, my brothers, has brought us deep suffering. But we who have been voted by your elected representatives to lead our beloved country, we who suffered in our bodies and hearts from colonialist oppression, we say too out loud: from now on, all that is over.[24]

As he listened to Lumumba, Baudouin could do nothing but squirm and cast his eyes downward. For the duration of the speech, Africa was for once in charge, and this was as unfamiliar an experience for Baudouin as if he had been stranded on an island with no one to rescue him. In the immediate press coverage of the day's events and for most of the time since, Lumumba's actions have been treated as a show of untamed impertinence. The same *New York Times* correspondent wrote that in the Congo, "The Belgian Government set out to substitute the carpenter's hammer for the tribal drum, introducing the twentieth century overnight to a primitive people divided into many warring tribes." Lumumba's "attack on colonialism," though, had "marred the ceremonies."[25]

CHAPTER THIRTY-THREE

Nei Luan Wai Huan

BY A STRIKING COINCIDENCE OF TIMING, THE VERY DAY AFTER CONGO gained its independence, Friday, July 1, 1960, Ghana became a republic, and Kwame Nkrumah its president. Nkrumah had twinned motives for engineering this fundamental change in the country's constitutional system, which had recently been ratified in a national referendum. One of them was strongly guided by geopolitics and especially by his ardent pan-Africanism. The other was firmly aimed at strengthening his own hand as national leader and containing what had long been an obstreperous and often threatening opposition. Both motives were heavy with portent.

In foreign affairs, as in so many other things, Nkrumah was able to hold fast to seemingly conflicting sentiments. Those who knew him well say that he was a genuine Anglophile. One glimpses this in the effort he invested in trying to bring the young Queen Elizabeth to Ghana in 1959, and in the heartfelt disappointment he exhibited when the visit was cancelled due to her pregnancy with her third child, Prince Andrew. Britain made up for it by inviting Nkrumah, that August, to be the queen's guest at Balmoral castle. While he was there, Elizabeth invited Nkrumah to join Britain's prestigious Privy Council, a distinction that clearly delighted him. He said upon returning home:

> As the first African to be admitted into the great Council of State, I consider it an honor not only to myself, but also to the people of Ghana and to peoples of Africa and African descent everywhere.[1]

For all of Nkrumah's pan-Africanism, closeness to Britain and to the West remained a vital gauge of Ghana's standing in the world, even in his own eyes. This powerful and enduring legacy is something that Richard Wright wrote about, saying that "Asians and Africans had been subjugated on the assumption that they were in some way biologically inferior and unfit to govern themselves."[2] Even as they rebelled against this canard, they yearned for acceptance. By 1960, there was already no way to reconcile a program centered on African sovereignty, on anti-imperialism, and on firm nonalignment with the idea of remaining subjects of the British crown. As Nkrumah told a peace conference in Accra in 1960, "We face neither East nor West: we face forward."[3]

The breadth of Nkrumah's pan-African ambitions can be seen in many of the initiatives he took during this period. Unwilling to concede the ideological field to the international radio broadcasts of the great powers, such as the Voice of America, Radio Moscow, or the BBC, Nkrumah funded a continental broadcast service of Ghana's own, the Voice of Africa. Its programming grew rapidly and came to include numerous colonial and African languages. Ghana also deployed intelligence agents in several African countries, and Padmore's Bureau of African Affairs built close ties with independence movements around the continent, constantly fielding their requests for help and contributing funding or training assistance to a handful of them.

Nkrumah took the lead in rallying African countries against French atomic tests planned for the southern Algerian desert, not far from that country's border with French-controlled Mali. This he did in close collaboration with Bayard Rustin, the unapologetically gay master strategist behind Martin Luther King Jr., and Bill Sutherland. Both Black men were longstanding progressive internationalists and tactical disciples of Gandhi who had cut their teeth early in the mid-century civil rights struggle in the United States. Rustin published books bearing titles such as *The Negro and Non-Violence* and *Non-Violence vs. Jim Crow*. And both men had been arrested and beaten in 1942 for refusing to surrender a second-row seat, nominally reserved for whites, on a bus from Louisville, Kentucky, to Nashville, Tennessee. This was more than a decade before Rosa Parks's iconic bus boycott in Montgomery. Nkrumah's party, the CPP, leaned on these veteran makers of "useful trouble," to paraphrase John Lewis, another American civil rights movement giant, to help organize a bold pacifist protest against the French atomic tests.

In the first of several forays, an international team of protestors, which included Ghanaians, Africans from other countries, at least one French person, and the African Americans, was detained at the first French outpost in Upper Volta (now Burkina Faso) on December 7, 1959. Nonviolent resistance could only carry them so far. At one point, when Bayard Rustin ordered his small caravan to start their engines and make a run for it, French troops drew their automatic weapons, forcing the protesters to stop. The Sahara Protest

Team, as it became known, made at least two other attempts to traverse colonial Upper Volta and reach the Algerian test zone, but each met with a similar fate.

Shortly after dawn on February 13, 1960, France, which treated African soil like something of a junkyard for its nuclear experiment, detonated the first of an eventual seventeen atomic devices in Algeria. "Hurray for France," exulted Charles de Gaulle. "As of this morning, she is stronger and prouder."[4] Nkrumah's government immediately froze the assets of French companies in Ghana. After a second French test, on April 1, Nkrumah suspended diplomatic relations with France and stopped issuing visas to that country's citizens. These tests continued unabated, even after Algeria's independence in 1962, ending in 1966.

The Positive Action Conference for Peace and Security in Africa opened on April 7, with the United States represented by Ralph Abernathy, a Baptist preacher who was the son of an Alabama farmer, and Martin Luther King Jr.'s number two in the Southern Christian Leadership Council. The *Ghana Evening News* celebrated this wedding of pan-Africanism with American sit-in protest tactics, saying that only one incident in living memory compared with it in terms of energizing a global Black protest movement: "Mussolini's rape of Abyssinia with the gas bombs and mass slaughter that eventually sounded the death-knell of the League of Nations. . . . Then as now, certain nations, loud in their profession of humanity, fraternity, justice and democracy sat complaisantly as Ethiopia, nailed to the wall, stretched her bleeding hands for succor."[5]

Nkrumah was angered but hardly chastened by France's continuation of the test blasts. What had mattered, said Nkrumah, was "the effect of hundreds of people from every corner of Africa and from outside it crossing the artificial barriers that divide Africa to risk imprisonment and arrest." They had made this "a protest that the people of France . . . could not ignore."[6]

There were yet other ways in which this peaceful confrontation could not be ignored. In 1959, at a time when few African countries had yet reached independence, Ghana made common cause with an emerging Afro-Asiatic block at the United Nations in support of a nonbinding resolution against atomic testing on African soil. Accra was supported in this by Guinea, Morocco, Libya, Liberia, Ethiopia, and Tunisia, as well as India and Iran.

Arrayed against this group were the United States, the United Kingdom, Portugal, Belgium, Spain, Israel, and white-ruled South Africa. One concern for the United States and Britain was preempting a Nkrumah-led effort to ban foreign military bases in Africa. Beyond that, all the opposing nations were either imperial powers, nuclear aspirants, or both. South Africa had the added distinction of being an explicitly white-supremacist state.

The statement against nuclear testing, which ultimately passed, was also backed by the Soviet Union, itself in the vanguard of nuclear armament, and Cuba, in addition to typical nonaligned countries. This lent a Cold War veneer to a motion that, for Africans at least, had little ideological basis. Herein lay an element in the docket being steadily assembled against Nkrumah in the West: he was a stalking horse of global communism. It was a lazy, even specious notion, but an unsurprising one given the stark ideological lines drawn in the diplomacy of this era. And Nkrumah never did enough, or perhaps even cared enough, to spare himself the trouble this was destined to bring.

THROUGHOUT RECORDED HISTORY, AMBITIOUS STATES HAVE LINKED THEIR domestic legitimacy and power to the influence and prestige they enjoy beyond their borders. In ancient China, this principle was expressed in the form of a classic maxim: *nei luan, wai huan*.[7] When the situation is chaotic and confused domestically, influence dissipates abroad, and vice versa. Nkrumah's preoccupations with the external world were no different.

In the decade or two that followed his overthrow, it was commonplace for critics to dismiss his foreign policy and the pan-Africanism that underpinned it as little more than a diplomatic vanity project, or worse, the reflection of his megalomania. Nkrumah's desire to play a leading role in the history of this era was real, but judged from the vantage of time, his personal ambitions seem to be the least of it. His aim was to infuse as much substance and African agency as possible into the coming wave of formal independence. Once this began, in 1960, colonial rule would end in one country after another with a clatter of falling dominoes. Nkrumah understood that this would require something much more meaningful and lasting than the changing of flags or the publication of new constitutions. Genuine self-determination would require growing economic strength and less dependence on the old colonizers, something that only cooperation among Africans could bring about, at hitherto unseen levels.

The West lampooned Nkrumah over his pretensions of blazing the trail of independence and solidarity for other African countries. Its hypocrisy was scarcely concealed, though, not least because Britain had itself only recently placed enormous stock in the Gold Coast as a "model" for its other African colonies, an implicit advertisement for Britain. What was unfamiliar and uncomfortable was the notion of self-assured Black people in charge of their own destinies.

In seeking to rule as president—that is, as the executive leader in a republic—Nkrumah saw his main challenge as much more than reconciling his habitual stance of anti-imperialism while remaining a member of the Commonwealth. He needed to do much more than simply push back against a disloyal and even seditious opposition. In a world so unpredictable and full of peril, Ghana needed, above all, to consolidate its economic takeoff and rise up the ranks of middle-income nations. To be sure, the Nkrumahist program for Ghana itself was already premised on this. But securing Africa's rise demanded more. Only the building up of synergies between new progressive governments and like-minded liberation movements could enable the continent to escape the extractive patterns of colonial rule.

Nkrumah expressed this heartfelt urgency with unusual directness in his 1957 autobiography:

> What other countries have taken three hundred years or more to achieve, a once dependent territory must try to accomplish in a generation if it is to survive. Unless it is, as it were, "jet-propelled," it will lag behind and thus risk everything for which it has fought.[8]

THE BEGINNINGS OF WHAT WOULD BECOME NKRUMAH'S GOVERNMENT'S BIG push for economic transformation can be traced back to his first months in power. In 1951, as the newly named leader of government business, he revived, as mentioned earlier, a long-dormant British plan to develop a major hydroelectric dam on the Volta River. In theory, it would power the smelters that he hoped would allow Ghana to transform its large bauxite reserves into aluminum for use in local building and construction and for export. This would allow the colony to escape its dangerous overreliance on one major commodity export, cocoa. It would lay a foundation for future industrialization. It would power homes for Ghana's fast-growing population, bringing new generations out of a darkness that British rule had done little to lift. And it would allow Ghana to export electricity to many of its neighbors, showing by way of example how a pan-Africanist vision goes beyond narrow self-interest to unlock the strength of a region.

It would take years for Nkrumah to find the investment he needed to bring the Volta River power project to fruition, and the story behind this, which lies ahead, is an ill-fated tale of desperate and credulous dealmaking in which the best of intentions went badly awry. As it happened, the Akosombo Dam was finally inaugurated in 1966, just one month before Nkrumah's overthrow.

Even governing as an inexperienced executive with sharply limited powers, Nkrumah had done anything but sit on his hands. The British government had recently committed a meager £1,000,000 toward the Gold Coast's internal "development" needs, but once in office, with cocoa prices booming, Nkrumah immediately boosted this tenfold.[9]

Much of this money was invested in education. The approximate literacy rate in the Gold Coast was a mere 10 percent in the early 1950s. In focusing on its own economic recovery after the Second World War, Britain was unwilling to bear the financial responsibility for developing its African colonies. As a result, even basic education was effectively rationed. "Parents want to send their children to school but cannot get admission for them," read one editorial in Accra's *Evening News*. "Children cry to go to school but cry in vain, for there is no accommodation for them."[10] As one historian has written, "between 1951 and Ghana's independence . . . enrollments at the primary and middle school levels soared in the colony from approximately 220,000 students to more than 570,000." Secondary enrollments grew similarly, more than tripling to just under 10,000 in 1957.[11]

Nkrumah hoped to unleash development by providing basic education, but almost from the start of his premiership, he also pushed for scientific, technological, and agronomic training. A keystone of this effort was the opening, in 1952, of the Kumasi College of Technology, which Nkrumah created in the Asante capital, heartland of the most powerful and determined regional and ethnic opposition to his rule. Soon, a school of engineering and departments of commerce and pharmacy were added to the college, which would grow into a full-fledged university in 1961. Nkrumah intended this, too, as an example for all of Africa, believing it could fulfill its potential only by boosting the local production of knowledge, lessening intellectual dependence on others, and thereby playing a leading role in the abolition of disease and poverty. Alas, few African countries followed Nkrumah down this path.

Around the world, emerging national leaders exhibited an almost boundless belief in the ability of science and technology to deliver economic growth and improve human life. Modernization ideology, common to the age, embraced as a universal verity the proposition that freshly decolonized peoples had to retrace, "in double time, the phases of European civilization," and move in a straight line from peasant-based agriculture to urbanization and industrialization, from polytheism to monotheism and then to secularism, and from kinship-based politics to models based on parties and on participation.[12] In the early 1950s, intellectuals like Walt Rostow and Lucian Pye, who were staunchly American protagonists of the Cold War, propounded modernization theory. Modernization and development quickly came to be seen as indivisible and were embraced by both left and right. The Soviet Union and even China just as eagerly sold their visions of what modernization should look like.

Few leaders were more enamored of modernization through development than Nkrumah. He dreamed of smokestacks and heavy industry, assembly lines and shipping lines and airline fleets embossed with black stars. Another totem almost universally worshipped in modernization theory's heyday was nuclear power, and unwilling for Africa to be left out, Nkrumah pursued this, as well. Britain came close to providing a research reactor to Ghana, and when it declined, Moscow stepped in. By 1966, construction of the reactor stood 90 percent complete. (It was never finished.)[13]

For Nkrumah, one of the most important facets of modernization was urban planning and developing a new national iconography of public spaces. Traveling through northern Italy while working on this book, I was impressed by the plethora of buildings that have survived from the fascist Mussolini era. They were statements, conceived to project boldness and strength through their use of long, clean lines, and classical Roman elements distilled to the point of starkness. Much as the attachment of George Washington (via his appointee Pierre Charles L'Enfant) and Thomas Jefferson to the layout and architecture of their nation's new capital and many other examples attest, the connection between urban planning and design and power is as old as politics.

In Accra, even with the limited means at his disposal, Nkrumah moved immediately to usher in a novel tropical modernism on Accra to signal the commencement of a self-confident new era. That modernism drew on the innovative late-colonial designs of the British architects Maxwell Fry and Jane Drew, who were devotees of Le Corbusier and Walter Gropius. But Nkrumah insisted that every public project that his government built incorporate the Bauhaus-inflected designs of Ghanaian architects like John Owusu Addo and Victor Adegbite. In 1958, this led to the opening of an ambitious department of architecture at the sumptuously designed Kumasi College of Science and Technology. Even before independence, Nkrumah had pushed to have smart new roads in service, along with a set of iconic new public buildings, from a new State House and national library to the Ambassador, an international hotel worthy of hosting dignitaries. Today, Accra's National Museum, one of the fruits of this push, sits under a white dome that resembles a spaceship. Another of the impressive modernist buildings, the Accra Community Centre, was delivered just in time to host the All-African People's Conference in

1958. There, above a tiled mural that depicts peasants and common people, reads the slogan written in Twi, "Together We Are Strong."

For all the changes in Accra, though, Nkrumah's modernizing experiments came together in their fullest form in the town of Tema. Less than twenty miles east of Accra, Tema became the scene of an enormous set of projects that reflected a faith in the budding developmentalist ideology. It rose from a sparsely populated area of traditional Ga villages to become a major new port city with modern neighborhoods replete with standardized housing, new roads and schools, and infrastructure. With its "ordered, disciplined, and methodically planned urban center through which not only the nation's industrial development could flow, but also its civic productivity," Tema was Nkrumah's modernist vision of the new Ghana made manifest.[14]

Tema, whose construction began in 1952, was intended as a symbol of the "new African" that Nkrumah would speak of in his independence address. And its capacious new harbor, which began operations ten years later, was the foundation upon which Ghana's hopes for industrialization reposed. The surrounding region was slated for the manufacture of simple consumables like soap and cigarettes, and for goods of greater complexity that would require bigger investments: tanneries and textile factories, assembly plants for electronics and automobiles, and most importantly of all, in the ordering of Nkrumah's dreams, mills that would churn out finished aluminum sheeting, from Ghana's own bauxite reserves, as well as steel.

The city was drawn on a blank slate by planners who saw its docks and the goods they shipped in an out as motors of regional integration in both economic and political terms. All of this, functioning in concert, was to make Tema a potent emblem of pan-Africanism. Once other Africans witnessed what Ghana had accomplished, and once they had benefitted from transshipment of goods through its efficient port, or benefited from the surplus electricity produced by damming the Volta River, who would be able to resist Nkrumah's visions of unity or his leadership?

In many other respects, though, Nkrumah's hands were tightly bound both before and after Ghana won its independence in 1957. However much Nkrumah may have wanted to accelerate economic development and push a pan-Africanist policy, commodity trading was controlled by foreign cartels, the major companies that operated there were foreign owned, and Ghana remained overwhelmingly reliant on Western investment.

As someone whose political ideas had steadily evolved under the influence of leftist Black thinkers like C. L. R. James and George Padmore, Nkrumah ardently hoped to slip the controlling reins of Western capitalism. But as a modestly sized, under-developed country of no real strategic importance, Ghana desperately needed investment, and Nkrumah could scarcely afford to alienate foreign capital. Adding to his dilemma, under the tightening grip of the Cold War, much of the British press and foreign policy establishment held Nkrumah in constant suspicion for his progressive anti-imperialism and pan-Africanist language. As another historian has written about Nkrumah's government leadership in the pre-independence years of the 1950s, he had "collaborated with the British in every way, except perhaps in taming the anti-colonial enthusiasm of the press," and yet, "Nkrumah came to be seen in Whitehall as the black sheep who could do no right. No way could be found of denying his independence, but there was an element of grudge against his success."[15] No matter how accommodating Nkrumah was, he could never be subservient enough, or sufficiently obsequious, to be the first heir to an African colony. Abject groveling was not in his nature. As the historian David Birmingham has written, "he even committed the heinous crime of talking about neocolonialism."[16] The historian Jeffrey Ahlman reached a similar conclusion: "As a radical, African-led government ultimately operating within the British-run colonial state, Nkrumah and the CPP had to balance their own anti-colonial desires with their need to be seen as responsible political actors by a colonial apparatus that, prior to the CPP's electoral victory, had—among other things—portrayed the Nkrumah-led party as an 'extreme Nationalist group' prone to acts of 'lawlessness.'"[17] Ultimately, his path was a tightrope performance that would have doomed even the most talented funambulist.

A longstanding reflex in Western writing about Africa emphasizes so-called tribal differences to explain political problems. Nkrumah, though, faced serious ideological and policy opposition to his development agenda. The aristocratic pioneer of Ghanaian nationalism, J. B. Danquah, denounced Nkrumah as a communist and as a budding dictator, even during the period when Nkrumah's behavior was still irreproachably democratic. Danquah's overheated rhetoric, partly aimed at Western Cold War audiences, obscured the serious class interests at stake in any new national development strategy. Moreover, since most of Ghana's cocoa crop grew in the Asante heartland, some argued that those regions should be the primary financial beneficiaries of cocoa exports.

This position received sophisticated ideological articulation from Danquah, who served on the colonial Cocoa Marketing Board. His arguments on the role of cocoa in national development echoed classic Western arguments for laissez faire, small government, and low taxes. In the political debates of this era, he staked out a position as a doctrinaire free marketeer.

During the postwar years as consumer demand exploded, international prices for cocoa soared, creating a classic commodity boom for the Gold Coast. By 1955, the peak of the cocoa market, revenues had doubled from levels of just seven years earlier, reaching an impressive £77.5 million (roughly £3.2 billion in today's money). Even as cocoa surpluses grew rapidly, though, Danquah firmly opposed government spending on "long-term projects having the development of the country as their object." He accused the government of wishing to milk the Cocoa Board for mere public works, rather than simply returning all the profits to the growers. The state, he complained, was placing "too much emphasis on development."[18]

During the pre-independence years, Nkrumah had inherited as finance minister an underqualified British civil servant. Kenneth Tours, upon whom the prime minister relied heavily for development strategy advice, had strong ideas of his own about taking maximal advantage of the ongoing commodity boom to launch industrialization in the Gold Coast. In his eagerness to take advantage of that window of opportunity, Tours helped steer Nkrumah into one of the great political blunders of the decade: he advised against raising the price paid to cocoa farmers at a time when international prices were soaring. Far more than Danquah's ideologically based opposition to activist government, this mistake lastingly inflamed opinion against Nkrumah and the CPP in Asante and other cocoa growing areas. If Nkrumah's government had allowed for steady, modest local price increases, it would probably have averted most of this trouble and still left sufficient budget surpluses for the state to finance its development plans.

In 1958, Nkrumah balanced this major blunder with making an inspired choice for his development planner: W. Arthur Lewis, an economist from Saint Lucia, who was one of the most gifted economists of his generation. Lewis had finished high school at fourteen, initially hoping to become an engineer, but it soon "seemed pointless since neither the government nor the white firms would employ [one]," he later said.[19] A future Nobel Prize winner, in 1937 this Black West Indian graduated with first-class honors from the London School of Economics. His advisor called him "the most brilliant of all graduates whose work I have seen."[20]

Lewis had had plentiful, direct experience of racism in Britain—being turned down from prestigious appointments or subjected to extra scrutiny because of his blackness. And although roughly a decade Nkrumah's junior, he had already rubbed shoulders in London with C. L. R. James, George Padmore, Eric Williams, and Paul Robeson. As Lewis's biographer wrote, Nkrumah and members of his circle admired Lewis for "his independence and his suspicion of imperialist motives lying behind even the most altruistic-sounding British proposals."[21]

Despite this Black Atlantic pedigree, Lewis was no economic radical. He was a firm believer in capitalism and a disciple of Keynes, with impeccable scholarly credentials, including early studies such as *The Theory of Economic Growth* and *The Principles of Economic Planning* that would cause some to identify him as the father of development economics.

Nkrumah may have been attracted to Lewis by the scholar's Keynesian rejection of laissez faire and conviction in a legitimately strong role for the state. But the true brilliance of the choice of Lewis for this advisory role lay in Lewis's credibility within the British policy establishment coming at a time when Nkrumah was frequently dismissed as a dangerous leftist. For everyone concerned, a rich mixture of unexpected consequences would soon flow from this appointment.

Lewis, then a tenured professor at the University of Manchester, accepted the Nkrumah government invitation, spurning one from Singapore, and traveled widely in the Gold Coast over the course of three weeks beginning in mid-December 1952. Five months later, he delivered an extensive report on industrialization. In some ways its findings validated the hopes of Nkrumah and his inner team of advisors, supporting, for example, the principle of capturing some of the profits from rising cocoa income to finance development projects. In many other respects, though, Lewis's cautious advice about industrialization must have felt like cold water.

Briefly, he outlined three paths to industrialization. Developing countries could achieve this by beginning to process their existing primary products, whether farm commodities or minerals. Alternately, they could begin to industrialize by manufacturing basic goods for their own growing domestic markets. Finally, they could attempt to export their output from new light industries of their own. Usually, he cautioned, this would still require the importation of raw materials sourced from other places.

The problem for the Gold Coast was that it was a small country with a very modest domestic market that also lacked sufficient investment capital of its own, as well as lacking the kinds of skilled human resources—from engineers and technicians to managers—that would be required to run competitive new industries.

Rather than seek rapid industrialization, Lewis urged the new government to focus heavily on less glamourous pursuits, like raising the productivity of its agriculture and improving public services. "Very many years will have elapsed before it becomes economical for the government to transfer any large part of its resources towards industrialization," he wrote.[22]

Nkrumah had yearned to persuade the timid and skeptical West, starting with Britain, that making a big push toward early industrialization in soon-to-be-independent Ghana made sound economic sense. In the end, though, Lewis's findings were considerably more guarded and less sanguine than even the suggestions of Kenneth Tour, the British civil servant Nkrumah had inherited as finance minister.

Nkrumah was courteous but tepid in receiving Lewis's conclusions. His report would be adopted in parliament, but not for another year. In the meantime, the ideas of Tours and of other advisors who shared Nkrumah's sense of urgency about the Gold Coast's window of opportunity steadily gained traction. Still, Lewis's involvement with the Gold Coast was far from over.

CHAPTER THIRTY-FOUR

Dam(n) Volta

IN 1915, AFTER TRAVELING A LENGTH OF THE VOLTA, THE GOLD COAST'S largest river, by canoe, the British geologist and longtime public servant Albert Kitson, a towheaded and short-of-stature teetotaler who was driven by work, conceived of a project to dam the waterway at a place named Akosombo, a site well inland from the coast, in order to produce hydroelectric power. Kitson's scheme had little to do with making electricity available for the African population of the colony. Rather, it was about generating the abundant current necessary to process bauxite into aluminum. Largely forgotten today, Kitson was a major figure in helping organize Britain's rapacious extraction from its African colonies in the early twentieth century. This was a program not only to make empire on that continent pay for its own meager administration, but also to generate handsome profits for London while doing so.

Working in Nigeria during the previous decade, Kitson had discovered substantial reserves of bituminous coal in the east of that colony. After this triumph, moving westward to conduct mineral surveys in the Gold Coast, he quickly located important deposits of manganese and diamonds. The first of these became vital to Britain's production of munitions during the First World War. The latter, diamonds, peaked at nearly 40 percent of the world's supply in 1934. Despite these impressive results, it was bauxite that retained most of Kitson's attention. In 1914, the year before his canoe voyage, Kitson had also discovered important reserves of this mineral in the mountains of the Atewa Range in the southeastern Gold Coast. His calculations about the hydroelectric potential of the nearby Volta River sparked a Eureka moment. Putting the two together, bauxite and cheap electricity, would make Britain a force in the production of aluminum, one of the most important industrial metals in a rapidly industrializing world.

The idea of turning the Gold Coast into an aluminum-producing powerhouse for Britain's benefit did not die with Kitson, even though the intervening world wars made the kinds of investments that would have been necessary unfeasible for London. In the wake of the century's second great global conflict, though, a Britain starved of hard currency warmed again to the idea. Its renewed appeal grew out of an economic priority discussed previously: the need to shore up the United Kingdom's sterling zone by avoiding the draining away of precious dollars through the purchase of essentials that London could source from its own colonies.

The plans for a dam-powered aluminum industry had long sat on the shelves of the Colonial Office gathering dust. In July 1950, with the sterling zone's imperatives in mind, the plans were revived when a British surveyor was hired to carry out a new study of the idea and issue a report. It quickly confirmed the great hydroelectric potential of the Volta River but said that a major dam would not be attractive "without an aluminum producing industry as the main outlet for [its] power. [Hence], it should be developed in close collaboration with an aluminum company with suitable guarantees on both sides."[1] Many journalists and politicians in the Gold Coast criticized a November 1952 British white paper titled "The Volta River Aluminum Scheme," however, for its failure to say anything about the revenue to be gained by the colony or even the numbers of Africans who would be employed and trained.[2]

At virtually the same time, Kwame Nkrumah's CPP's sweeping electoral victory and mandate for emancipation from colonial rule under the banner "Freedom Now!" had begun to turn expectations upside down in London. Colonial officials who had been on the verge of establishing a mixed, public-private administrative body to move forward on the dam idea developed cold feet. Private companies, they warned, would be reluctant to invest "in a country where the political position offered so uncertain a future."[3]

Even as London began to show its ambivalence toward a Gold Coast under pan-Africanist leadership, some British officials still clung to upbeat visions for the project. Norton Jones, the colonial minister of defense and external affairs, likened the then-projected £130 million cost of the project to a tale from the Arabian Nights, so cheap the figure seemed compared to the benefits that the colony and Britain stood to reap from its construction. "The door stands open, and at our bidding prosperity will cross its threshold into this country," Jones declared in 1952.[4]

By this time, Nkrumah already had become thoroughly seized with the idea of building a dam on the Volta for the purposes of smelting aluminum and thrusting his country into the ranks of industrialized nations in the space of a generation. This, in fact, became a matter of almost obsessive focus for him, rivaled only by his pan-Africanist visions of promoting independence throughout the continent and then stitching Africa's newborn nations together under some kind of supranational government.

During a Legislative Assembly debate in 1952, Nkrumah called the dam "a gigantic project for the industrial development of our country—a scheme which can change the face of our land and bring wealth and a higher standard of living to our people."[5] Other CPP members were even more exuberant, saying the dam scheme would turn Ghana into "a miniature paradise." However, the white paper gave a rare opening to the conservative opposition to paint Nkrumah as insufficiently nationalist and naïve about the schemes of the British. It claimed that London sought to use the dam to engineer a return to "economic enslavement" or to "the old imperialism."[6]

Despite such skepticism, Nkrumah won approval from a closely divided legislature for establishing a preparatory commission to lay the groundwork for the project. Moving to rally yet more support, he then deftly named one of the most outspoken critics of the white paper, William Ofori Atta, to what became a national committee to promote the dam.

Ghana's political old guard, however, was the least of the Volta River dam idea's problems. As time passed, British interest in the scheme continued to flag, partly due to Nkrumah's socialist-tinged pan-Africanism. In 1952, hoping to overcome this, Nkrumah leaned once again on the economist Arthur Lewis. The Black St. Lucian was a firmly established and committed capitalist, but one who used Keynesianism to argue in favor of vigorous government intervention in the weak and fragile economies of developing states. The more time Lewis spent trying to assess the dam project, though, the less enthusiastic he was about it. And as the economist became overtly pessimistic, Nkrumah's determination to push ahead with the scheme put the two men on an increasingly direct collision course.

One of Lewis's first findings highlighted a stark reality that would hinder the economic development of African countries for decades, remaining true even now: the companies of rich countries are rarely willing to invest in poor ones, especially in Africa, unless they feel sure that they will win outsized returns for themselves. Lewis spelled this out to Nkrumah's government, saying that a British aluminum company would "not put money into this sort of enterprise unless it expects to make a profit of 25 per cent per annum; not necessarily in the first 3 or 4 years; but it expects to get all of its capital back in the first 10 years and thereafter to make 100 per cent every 4 years."[7] This was far from Lewis's greatest concern, though. Rather, it was his prescient fear that in its enthusiasm for a big push toward industrialization, the Gold Coast's inexperienced government and the preparatory commission it had named to promote the dam and aluminum complex would fail to drive a hard enough bargain with the tough-minded bankers and corporate executives it would have to come to terms with.

Even before the dam's preparatory commission had completed its work, Nkrumah's department of information launched an elaborate campaign to rally public opinion behind the scheme. This was multimedia long before the popularization of the term in recent decades. Vans and buses were outfitted with maps, charts, and dioramas to illustrate the projected layout and benefits of the new dam and aluminum smelting infrastructure, with translations provided in the main indigenous languages. At this stage, the Canadian company, Alcan, was the Gold Coast's keystone partner, and the traveling exhibitions showed promotional films derived from Alcan's work in other parts of the world with titles such as *Packaged Power* and *A River Creates an Industry*. The latter tied representative democracy together with physical accoutrements of modernization like factories and electrification. It promised that the people of the Gold Coast would be able to "discuss the project fully through their elected representatives in the Assembly" before any contract was signed or executed. The film ended on this boosterish note nonetheless, "Here is a project that will tax the imagination of the world, a great plan that will match the emergence of the Gold Coast as a free and independent nation."[8]

Unfortunately for Nkrumah, by the time his preparatory commission finished its work in July 1956, world aluminum prices had dramatically softened. That year, still clinging to aspirations for a deal that was seemingly close to being lined up, Nkrumah again sought Lewis's council, hoping for a final seal of approval. After visiting the Gold Coast that February, though, Lewis had cautioned Nkrumah that "the price [of a package deal for a major dam and bauxite to aluminum plant] was too high" and warned the prime minister against signing any agreements.[9] When Lewis visited Ghana again that July, he told Nkrumah Alcan's interest had dwindled further. The Canadian corporation would only be willing to proceed, he warned, if Ghana were willing to lower the price Alcan would be charged for electricity and switch to the use of imported alumina rather than invest in transforming its own bauxite reserves.[10]

Lewis was subsequently alarmed to read in the Gold Coast press a dated statement of his, in which he had spoken positively about the dam project. He had issued those words well before the outlines of Alcan's position had become known. Lewis expressed his shock at still being used to promote the dam despite altered terms that he felt greatly disfavored the colony in a blunt letter to Nkrumah. The pending arrangements, he wrote, were an "act of treachery to your government and to your people."[11]

In the back and forth between them, Lewis then worked to impart some hard-nosed realism to Nkrumah, warning him of the folly of investing too much capital, or for that matter, too much faith in what had been the cornerstone of his economic vision. Williams warned that contrary to Nkrumah's deeply held beliefs, cheap electricity was not key to the Gold Coast's future, and neither was the kind of heavy industry that a shiny new aluminum smelter symbolized. "While Ghana resists appointing a first-class commissioner for industrial production, it is risky to pour millions into providing cheap electrical power, which will be of crucial interest only to bauxite and chemicals," Lewis wrote.[12] These commodities, he argued, would employ few Ghanaians and would have few other downstream linkages with the economic life of the country. In other words, big foreign corporations would profit largely at Ghana's expense, the seeming opposite of Nkrumah's nationalist vision.

Nkrumah responded crisply to Lewis, writing, "My mind is finally made up, and irrespective of *anybody's advice to the contrary*, I am determined to see that at all costs the dams at Bui and Ajena are built in the shortest possible time."[13] (At the time, Ajena was the name of the proposed site for the main dam, which would eventually be built at Akosombo, in accordance with Kitson's original proposal. Bui was the site of a proposed smaller, sister dam whose construction far to the northwest had also been long envisioned as part of Kitson's master scheme for aluminum production.) This, already, was remarkably blunt, but Nkrumah had more to say in reply to Lewis. "The advice you have given me, sound though it may be, is essentially from the economic point of view, and I have told you, on many occasions, that I cannot always follow this advice as I am a politician and must gamble on the future."[14] Although Lewis would attend the independence ceremonies in 1957, this exchange effectively put an end to his role as Nkrumah's economic advisor.

By the cusp of independence, immense political hope had been bound up in the prospect of industrialization via electricity and aluminum. And yet during the five years from Nkrumah's initial conquest of power in 1951 until mid-1956—the period during which the politics, technical details, and financing of this scheme were being worked out—the economic circumstances of the colony had shifted radically. The first half of the decade had been a classic commodity boom, a time of unprecedentedly high international prices for cocoa, whose production the Gold Coast dominated. By the eve of independence, though, cocoa prices were in sharp and persistent retreat. On top of that, during the years of study, parliamentary debate, project design, and stop-and-start negotiations, cheap aluminum had also flooded onto world markets. What had once looked like a tale of easy riches worthy of the Arabian Nights now looked more like a mirage created in the poof of a mischievous magician's trick.

On July 28, 1956, the big news in the Gold Coast press was word that the dam scheme's preparatory commission had issued its final report. That same day in London *The Economist* declared that the project had been put on hold. The causes it invoked recalled Britain's earliest reservations: with a nationalist, pan-Africanist party about to lead the colony into independence, Alcan was concerned about political risk, and London felt growing ambivalence about financing the project. This all meant new rounds of studies, led by the World Bank, whose financial support would now be needed, and the cancellation of the elaborate promotional campaign. As it happened, it would be another five years before Nkrumah's Volta River dream would begin to take shape.

During this time, one thing alone kept the idea alive: the Cold War. And paradoxically, it also bedeviled its consummation. As we have seen, the publicity around a Howard Johnson's waiter's refusal to allow Ghana's minister of finance, Komla Gbedemah, to enjoy an orange juice in an all-white dining establishment produced an unanticipated invitation to breakfast with Eisenhower. And this audience led, in its own unexpected way, to an introduction to the president's acquaintance, aluminum magnate, Edgar Kaiser.

Kaiser met Nkrumah during the latter's official visit to Washington at Eisenhower's invitation in July 1958, and the two immediately hit it off. Nkrumah had always been susceptible to influence by powerful and driven outsiders who took the time to develop personal ties with him, but this bond with Kaiser would open a critical new phase in Nkrumah's development as a leader and statesman.

The first of his decisive relations with outsiders, *contre-nature* in ideological terms, had been with Charles Arden-Clarke, the British colonial governor who had jailed Nkrumah only to then gain his trust during the Gold Coast's final transition to independence. Under Arden-Clarke's influence, Nkrumah postponed moves to break cleanly with London's gradualist development policies and pursue his own transformational economic vision, and this incurred huge opportunity costs on Ghana.

Nkrumah's second great influence had been George Padmore, a mentor whose ideology was largely in sync with Nkrumah's own, but who was a complete outsider from the perspective of Ghana's domestic politics. Nkrumah installed Padmore in a bureau right next door to his own as head of the Office of the Advisor to the Prime Minister on African Affairs. Thereafter he relied on Padmore not just as his "ideological engineer," in the apt phrase of the historian Ama Biney, but also for his tirelessness in the essential tedium of networking, organization, and propaganda.[15] Padmore had years of diverse experience in this last area as a contributor to the *Moscow Daily News* during his Soviet period, and afterward, he enjoyed frequent bylines in Black-run publications throughout Africa, the Caribbean, and the United States, where he wrote for the *Pittsburgh Courier* and the *Chicago Defender*. Nkrumah's reliance came at the expense of the badly needed strengthening of professionalism in the ruling party, as well as in the cabinet and civil service. As close as the two men became, few in Nkrumah's CPP ever saw Padmore as anything more than an outsider, and despite his unambiguous blackness and lifelong pan-Africanism, many resented Padmore's influence. What is worse, Nkrumah's trust in and reliance on the Trinidadian left a huge and never-filled void after his sudden death.

As an influence on the socialist Nkrumah, Edgar Kaiser, a charismatic midcentury American industrialist, was nearly as far against type as Arden-Clarke had been. This didn't prevent the two men from drawing close, though, and they sustained a strong bond that survived seven years of jolting geopolitical events and constant negotiating ups and downs. This began after Kaiser's firm, the Kaiser Aluminum and Chemical Corporation, stepped forward in 1959 with a proposal to carry out the dam project at a price that seemed alluringly cheaper than anything Ghana had been offered before.

At the time, Ghana's economy was slumping after years of high flying, and Nkrumah saw few other levers beyond a major dam project to pull to sustain its growth. That the tenth anniversary of his arrival in power stood less than two years away heightened the urgency. Kaiser's plan not only offered a chance to salvage the scheme, but shave £12 million off the total cost, reducing the project's headline value to £55 million. And just as Arthur Lewis had feared, for an increasingly desperate Nkrumah, the interest of a spellbinding white knight proved thoroughly irresistible. For the West Indian economist, the details behind the £12 million saved made all the difference in the world in what needed to be assessed with cool, calculating eyes as a pure business transaction. But for Ghana's leader, priority was given to the appearance of momentum, and ultimately political survival.

Eisenhower's interest in bringing Nkrumah and Kaiser together was not driven by mortification over the Gbedemah incident alone. In Washington, the question of "who lost China?" to a hostile communism still resonated, and however innately indifferent the American president was to Africa, "losing" another continent, according to Eisenhower's way of understanding world politics, had to be avoided. Toward that end, he played the attentive and smiling host in greeting Nkrumah at the White House in July 1958, but he stopped short of promising any financial backing for a Ghanaian dam scheme. Kaiser's desire to push forward with the project, though, all but forced the White House's hand. This turnabout came after the World Bank let it be known that it would only provide funding if the administration gave its unconditional backing. This led the previously cautious Eisenhower to pledge $30 million in financing in an August 1960 letter addressed to Nkrumah.[16]

Kaiser's plans for a cheaper industrial complex involved moving the proposed dam construction back to Akosombo, the site originally envisaged by Kitson. It was objectively superior to Ajena from a hydraulic perspective, he argued. More crucially, Kaiser proposed building a smelter near the Tema port, while jettisoning the idea of building an integrated aluminum industry. Bauxite would be supplied to the smelter not from Ghana, but from Jamaica, which in a dark irony had been one of the largest destinations for enslaved people from the Gold Coast during the eighteenth century. There would be no aluminum industry per se, only the export of untransformed ingots. This was akin to the way cocoa had always been exploited in Ghana, with the crop's oozing raw pods or crude paste being exported to Europe untransformed, which meant little value added was earned locally. Ghana's lone plum would be a dependable national electricity supply.

Kaiser and Washington shared convergent motives in this fundamental revision of Nkrumah's scheme, which reality constrained him to accept. Kaiser was protecting himself from the risk of nationalization (which Nkrumah had always foresworn), while the other sought to limit the Ghanaian leader's political options, tying him to the West by making approval of the package an elaborate new form of dependence.

Even after getting Nkrumah to swallow such large concessions, negotiations remained difficult. Kaiser pushed, and eventually won for himself and his smelter a concessionary rate on electricity from the dam that was far below what Arthur Lewis had deemed acceptable. The charge had seemed fanciful when Ghana's opposition politicians had once used Akosombo to flay Nkrumah for opening up the country to renewed economic colonization. The reality now was somehow even more baleful. Early in the African independence era, in places like Egypt, Northern Rhodesia, and Mozambique, dams were one of the most important sites of competition between east and west. The projects to build them involved immense complexity. Like most African countries in this era, Ghana had little formal technical or economic expertise of its own, and taken alone, its financial resources were vastly inadequate. This caused Nkrumah to agree to what might be considered a prime example of his own most important ideological concept: neocolonialism. This was Nkrumah's favored term for situations where distant powers could pull the strings economically and politically, profiting off of weak developing nations where they no longer maintained the formal political control—or obligations—that they held during the colonial era. Famously, Nkrumah called this kind of domination the last form of imperialism.

The interlocking equities and compromises at play were stunning in their complexity and intrigue. Eisenhower's interests were driven by the Cold War generally, and most particularly by the then fast-unfolding Congo Crisis. Kaiser spied a low-risk opportunity to make a killing in Africa. Meanwhile, Nkrumah, who dreamed of keeping the Cold War out of Africa, was desperate to salvage his economic program and leap into the ranks of the middle-income countries. The Volta River dam scheme was never just about Ghana. Nkrumah saw its success as fundamental to his ambition to lead a continental pan-African movement. To do so, he felt that Ghana, a modest-sized nation dwarfed by the likes of Nigeria, Sudan, and his momentary ally, the Congo, had to show the way in delivering modernity and development to its people. Factors like these led both the American president and the Ghanaian head of state to override some of their own deepest instincts, and it set the stage for what has been called one of the first Western corporate raids in independent Africa.[17]

CHAPTER THIRTY-FIVE

Hard Places

On an incandescent July day not long ago, I set out early by car from Accra to visit the site of the Akosombo Dam. After the driver had navigated through the heavy traffic of the city's busy center, the scenery opened but did not exactly beautify, revealing a landscape of warehouses, truck stops, and auto parts stores. Finally, though, the city faded and gave way to pure countryside. There, the narrow, nearly traffic-free highway cut a path nearly due north, with green hills and broken mountains visible in the distance on either side. As we sped along, alarmed baboon mothers collected their young from the shoulder of the road where they were foraging for fruit and retreated into the distance.

After a little more than two hours of this, we began a climb into the cooling air of forested hills, and within minutes, arrived at an administrative station at the gates of the town. The high hills just beyond revealed a somnolent district of bungalows—no metropolis, but a neatly manicured, planned city built for the staff that would administer Nkrumah's birthchild, which was visible from these heights. There a broad and mirror-smooth body of water—once the largest manmade lake in the world—stretched far into the distance.

American support for Ghana's Volta River project (VRP), which had created all of this, played out between Nkrumah and Eisenhower against the doomed fate of Patrice Lumumba, Nkrumah's main protégé on the continent. Less than two weeks after Lumumba was sworn in as prime minister, Belgium dispatched troops to Congo to derail its independence. The following day, on July 11, 1960, Katanga Province, the country's storehouse of copper and cobalt, and its richest province, unilaterally declared its secession from Congo. A headline in the *Los Angeles Times* that week described Congo as a country "suffering a national nervous breakdown."[1] Two days later, Ghana announced its eagerness to send troops as part of a United Nations force there. On July 14, for the time being acting in close concert with Kasa-Vubu, Lumumba severed diplomatic relations with Belgium. This measure was taken after Brussels denied an airplane carrying the two landing rights at Congo's second largest city, Elisabethville (Lubumbashi), which Belgian troops controlled, as they did much of the capital. As all of this was happening, the United Nations passed a resolution calling for Belgium to withdraw its forces from Congo and promised to provide military assistance to the Republic of Congo "as may be necessary."[2]

When Western countries temporized in the face of Nkrumah's request that they fly Ghanaian soldiers to Congo under the UN's authority, Nkrumah turned to Moscow, which offered the services of three Ilyushin ll-18 aircraft. Soon thereafter, two more airliners were added, allowing Ghana to quickly constitute the largest contingent in the entire 15,700-member UN force, at 2340 soldiers and 370 policemen. This amounted to a large portion of the Ghanaian armed forces and stoked alarm in Washington, where a consensus was already hardening on the need to eliminate Lumumba. It also bolstered a growing assessment that Nkrumah was becoming a Soviet pawn.

Nkrumah's rhetoric on Congo played strongly to his pan-Africanist image. He asked for the UN to allow African troops to restore order in the Congo and warned that the countries of the continent "would not tolerate the construction in the centre of Africa of a puppet state maintained by Belgian troops and designed to fit the needs of an international mining concern."[3] Nkrumah also spoke of forming a joint command between the army of Ghana and the Congolese government to expel the Belgians from Congo or, alternately, of forming a joint command with other African nations for this purpose.

On his return home from an emergency visit to New York and Washington, Lumumba, looking overwrought, landed in Accra where, together with Nkrumah, he was buoyed by large, cheering crowds. Speaking on August 8 in the presence of his guest before the Ghana National Assembly, Nkrumah said of the Congo crisis, "This is a turning point in the history of Africa. If we allow the independence of the Congo to be compromised in any way by the imperialist and capitalist forces, we shall expose the sovereignty and independence of all of Africa to grave risk."[4]

Meeting privately, the two men signed a secretive union between their two countries, much as Nkrumah had done with Guinea. It called for a federal parliament and head of state and allowed for any other African state to join in their union. Unlike the pact with Guinea, though, out of deference to Congo, a far larger country than Ghana, this new pact called for Leopoldville (Kinshasa) to become the federation's capital. The Congo's disintegration continued apace, as if in mockery of Nkrumah's vision. The very next day, conditions on the ground there weakened further for Lumumba, when a second mineral-rich province also declared its secession and alliance with breakaway Katanga.

Even before the Congo reached independence, Nkrumah had been forewarned about committing his support to Lumumba and overinvesting in that country, and from a most surprising quarter. Frantz Fanon's revolutionary credentials were impeccable. He had singlehandedly shifted the course of the most important debate at Nkrumah's All-African People's Conference in December 1958. In his keynote, Nkrumah had pledged Ghana's unequivocal "support [for Africans involved in] every form of non-violent action" against colonial rule. "As long as we remain true to that Cause," he continued, "we have nothing to fear but fear itself."[5] On the second day of the conference, however, wearing dark sunglasses and gripping the wooden podium tightly as he leaned into his delivery of a blistering speech, Fanon singlehandedly forced changes to conference resolutions. After describing the horrors of the war for independence in Algeria, he said it was time for African countries to prepare for violent conflict.

Although they were on good terms personally, Fanon reproached Lumumba for "his exaggerated confidence in the people," by which he meant the ability to win effective power at the ballot box.[6] He considered Lumumba too raw and unprepared for the challenge to Belgian imperialism that he left the Accra conference vowing to rush into, and he shared his reservations with Nkrumah, but to little effect:

> I talked with him through the night, but Nkrumah promised [Lumumba] mountains and marvels and even to "go to Congo and install him by force" if necessary.... [H]e was very reserved with regard to my counsel for prudence. But [Lumumba] is a demagogue.... Kasavubu for his part asked me not to help out Lumumba any more, since he had "sold out to the Ghanaians and Guineans."[7]

Nkrumah's support for Lumumba and his engagement in the Congo crisis more generally would cost him dearly. Until that point, Ghana had barely rated a footnote in the competition between East and West. The Congo, with its vastly larger size, its mineral holdings, its central position on the continent, and its direct involvement with the Soviet military, which was dramatic for its novelty even if quite limited in scope, was a different matter. For all of that, on Congo, Nkrumah's actions cannot be plotted with a straight edge.

Lumumba's turn to Moscow for support, though, was in desperation. That even some international news dispatches, including stories from the Associated Press, persisted in describing his country as the "Belgian Congo Republic" can only have spiked his anxiety. "We need the fastest and most efficacious help," he told reporters. "We are willing to accept anybody ready to bring that help, the United States or Russia or anybody."[8] Historically, in fact, Lumumba had shown a strong preference for engaging with the United States, but the antipathy he faced from the Eisenhower administration, which regarded him as a dangerous radical, was fierce. Aware of this perception of him, Lumumba frequently sought to assuage Washington's anxieties, publicly declaring during his visit to the United States in July 1960, for example, that "We want democracy, the sort of genuine democracy we see here in the United States, for instance, where every sort of philosophy is respected, where the dignity and the rights of each and all are respected." But his own erratic behavior on this trip, which included meeting with a high-ranked Soviet diplomat and allegedly requesting that the State Department aide assigned to his visit furnish him with a blonde female escort, only worsened things.[9]

For all of Washington's fear that the Congo was "turning red," Moscow did not consider the Congo to be a place of vital self-interest, nor did it even view Lumumba as a promising stalking horse. When Washington turned down the embattled Congolese leader's requests for aid, Moscow was befuddled. "Why? Explain to me why," a disbelieving Khrushchev asked in the Kremlin.[10]

In public, Nkrumah remained Lumumba's staunchest defender, but he had begun to modulate his diplomacy with considerable nuance. In doing so, he once again displayed the quality of versatility so evident during his youth. Nkrumah urged Lumumba to place any Soviet assistance he might receive firmly under United Nations authority. In fact, Nkrumah had quickly understood that decisive help for Lumumba from Moscow would not be forthcoming. In this era, the Soviet Union still had surprisingly few means to project power so far afield. It even lacked an embassy in Leopoldville until several weeks into the Congo crisis.

Nkrumah was laboring to reconcile several of his own competing objectives. He sought to assuage Lumumba over his abandonment by the international community even as Ghanaian peacekeepers were contributing to reining Lumumba in. And he spoke loudly, even boldly, in defense of principles of pan-Africanism and nonalignment while creating some distance between himself and Moscow. He even defended the behavior of the United Nations, which was widely seen as heavily favoring the West. In August 1960, Dag Hammarskjöld, the Swedish secretary-general of the United Nations and a bookish, confirmed bachelor, given to studies of poetry and philosophy in his private time, had told American diplomats that "Lumumba must be broken," and explained his own actions by saying that all "he was trying to do was to get rid of Lumumba without compromising the UN position and himself through extra-constitutional actions."[11]

After strong prompting by the CIA, on September 5, 1960, Joseph Kasa-Vubu, the phlegmatic president of the Congo, went on the radio in Leopoldville to announce the dismissal of Lumumba as prime minister. This prompted Lumumba to follow him on the air to announce the removal of Kasa-Vubu. Subsequently, UN Secretary-General Hammarskjöld's representative in Leopoldville, an American named Andrew Cordier, ordered UN troops to take Lumumba off the air. This order was carried out by Ghanaian troops, enraging Lumumba, who wrote to Nkrumah, complaining: "I hasten to express to you my indignation regarding the aggressive and hostile attitude of Ghanaian soldiers towards me and my Government.... Instead of helping us in our difficulties, your soldiers are openly siding with the enemy to fight us."[12]

Nkrumah's ambivalent actions toward the Congo continued even after Lumumba's overthrow. In late 1960, he reneged on a secret agreement between Ghana and the Soviet Union to help the Soviets deliver weapons to the forces loyal to Lumumba who were based in Stanleyville (Kisangani) under the leadership of Antoine Gizenga.[13]

Some of the parting of ways between Nkrumah and Lumumba here can be explained by the fact that Ghana's troops were under the command of a British major general, Henry Templer (H. T.) Alexander. A product of English public schools and of Sandhurst with bushy eyebrows, a brush mustache, and a plummy accent, Alexander had a look and sound from central casting, in the mold of a Peter Sellers character. The Briton had been behind the disarming of the Congolese military and other gestures of outright support for the Belgians. Here was yet another example of the politically costly legacy of Nkrumah's protracted transition from British oversight spanning what was now nearly an entire decade. Ghana's ambassador to Congo, Andrew Djin, complained bitterly about this to Nkrumah, urging the Briton's dismissal. "If you would allow me, I would say that this is the culminating point of Gen. Alexander's intrigue and subversive action which I have time and again pointed out and which was also confirmed by all the delegations which paid a visit to the Congo."[14] Alexander's instincts, which were conspicuously conservative, pro-Western, and ferociously anticommunist, only explain Ghana's actions during the Congo crisis to a point, though.

On September 14, after the Congolese army chief of staff Joseph-Desiré Mobutu (who later changed his name to Mobutu Sese Seko) seized power and arrested Lumumba, both actions taken after strong CIA urging, the Soviet Union denounced the behavior of the UN in Congo and attacked Hammarskjöld in unusually harsh terms for not protecting Lumumba as he did the bidding of the West. The Ghanaian representative to the United Nations, Alex Quaison-Sackey, then strongly defended the UN's behavior. "The Government of Ghana is convinced that the United Nations has a decisive role to play in assisting the Government and people of the Congo to safeguard their independence, unity and territorial integrity," Quaison-Sackey said.[15] A statement like this could only have been made with Nkrumah's approval.

To understand why Nkrumah would have staked out such a clear position in support of the UN Secretary General in Congo, despite his actual deep frustration with the UN's failure to protect Lumumba, one must consider discussions over American backing for the Akosombo Dam. Just two weeks earlier, the State Department had signaled to Accra that it had decided to provide the $30 million in bilateral backing that Nkrumah needed in order for the World Bank to fund the dam, and Nkrumah's eyes were fixed firmly on this prize, even at Lumumba's expense.

Looming in the background as these events played out were preparations for the upcoming fifteenth General Assembly of the United Nations in the fall of 1960, one of the most momentous gatherings in the body's history. It would culminate in the passage of a major watershed in international relations, the Declaration on the Granting of Independence of Colonial Countries and Peoples.[16] The declaration's momentous first article read, "that subjection of peoples to alien subjugation, domination and exploitation constitutes a denial of fundamental human rights." That year, the world organization's New York headquarters also brought together not just the leaders of the United States and Soviet Union, but outsized non-Western figures of the moment such as Jawaharlal Nehru of India, Josip Broz Tito of Yugoslavia, and Gamal Abdel Nasser of Egypt. This General Assembly would also be a kind of global coming-out party for a young, bearded figure who had taken power the previous year in Cuba, Fidel Castro.

Castro had initially stayed at a midtown hotel called the Shelburne but had stormed out after it demanded a huge cash deposit. The Cuban then theatrically threatened to camp out in Central Park, saying, "We are mountain people. We are used to sleeping in open air." Malcolm X persuaded Castro and his delegation to relocate to the Hotel Theresa at Seventh Avenue and 125th Street in Harlem, where Malcolm became one of the first people to meet with him. As one of his biographers, Manning Marable relates, "thousands of Harlemites thronged to the hotel to witness the coming and goings of the delegation and the various visits by international dignitaries. These included "black nationalists who promoted the cause of deposed Congolese premier Patrice Lumumba, civil rights activists favoring desegregation, pro-Castro demonstrators, and even beatniks from Greenwich Village."[17]

Nikita Khrushchev, bald, portly, and garrulous, was also one of the visitors to the Theresa, where he embraced the tall, youthful, and full-bearded Castro for the first time. It was at this session of the General Assembly that an indignant Khrushchev took off his shoe and banged it during a famous speech. And it was here, also, that Nkrumah would give an address that he thought would reconcile his competing foreign policy objectives. In the end it only proved that where the soon-to-depart Eisenhower team members were concerned, only near-total obeisance to the West would make them happy.

Knowing how narrow and strewn with perils his path was, Nkrumah had taken care to meet with Eisenhower the day before his UN address, and from all evidence, in deference, quite deliberately prior to meeting with Khrushchev in New York. Eisenhower came away from their meeting sounding positive.

> Mr. Nkrumah professed, to my surprise, considerable optimism regarding the situation in the Congo. He said the situation was not insoluble, and that the solution had to be worked out through the United Nations. Indicating his respect for the United States, he said he had taken special steps to arrange a visit to me before going to see Mr. Khrushchev, upon whom he had been invited to call.[18]

For his part, Nkrumah notably thanked Eisenhower for "all the assistance he had given Ghana toward the realization of the Volta project" but he also requested an additional loan of £10 million to help compensate for the unfavorable concessions he had been obliged to grant Kaiser on electricity rates. Eisenhower was noncommittal.[19]

The next day, Nkrumah's address before the General Assembly followed that of Khrushchev. The blustery Soviet leader had railed against Hammarskjöld and said that the United Nations' failure to protect the sovereignty and independence of the Congo justified the wholesale reorganization of the UN Security Council. The body's present membership was dominated by the United States and its allies, Britain and France, both still colonial warlords. Khrushchev argued this structure should be replaced by a troika that would be composed of "members of the military blocs of the Western powers, socialist states and neutralist countries."[20]

After Nkrumah's address, Khrushchev made a florid show of congratulating him. But on these two points, Hammarskjöld's record and a radical reorganization of the Security Council, Nkrumah could hardly have set himself further apart. "It would be entirely wrong to blame either the Security Council or any senior officials of the United Nations for what has taken place" in Congo, Nkrumah said. He even expressed personal appreciation for the Secretary General and put whatever shortcomings the United Nations had displayed there down to the still-young organization's "growing pains."[21]

Nkrumah, working both ends, did not stop there, though. His multiple political priorities and diverse constituencies obliged him to promote pan-Africanism and nonalignment, while also denouncing European imperialism and South African apartheid. Belgium's actions in Congo, Nkrumah said, reflected "a system of calculated political castration in the hope that it would be completely impossible for African nationalists to fight for emancipation." He decried the fragmentation of Africa and urged the UN to "delegate its functions in the Congo to independent African states." These, he said, should take the lead as a unified force under responsibility to the United Nations in restoring Lumumba's authority and safeguarding the badly imperiled territorial integrity of the Congo.[22] And he spoke to what by then had become a trademark theme for him, denouncing neocolonialism as "the process of handing independence over to the African people with one hand only to take it away with the other."[23] Finally, although Nkrumah did not back the Soviet leader's ideas about the Security Council, he offered a proposal of his own—something built on the foundation of W. E. B. Du Bois's teachings about the global color line. The UN's executive body, Nkrumah said, needed to be opened up to people of color, meaning the nations of Africa, Asia, and the Middle East. For good measure, he added that the People's Republic of China should be admitted to the UN, from which it had thus far been excluded in favor of Taiwan.

Nkrumah may have thought that he had successfully negotiated the most perilous shoals of the Cold War contest between Washington and Moscow, all the while upholding his own fundamental principles. But the Eisenhower administration wasted no time in upbraiding him. American Secretary of State Christian Herter held a hastily organized news conference that afternoon to denounce Khrushchev's General Assembly speech, and when questioned about Nkrumah, made it clear that the Ghanaian's attempts at subtlety and balance were lost on Washington:

> As much as I heard of it, it sounded to me as though he were very definitely making a big push for the leadership of what you would call a Left-wing

group of African states. He, I think, went out of his way from the point of view of showing a very close relationship to what Mr. Khrushchev said.[24]

On Herter's orders, an American diplomat lodged a formal protest with the Ghanaian government over Nkrumah's speech and his supposed sympathy for communists. "The content of the Nkrumah and Khrushchev speeches and the display attached to the reception by the eastern bloc delegates of the Nkrumah speech gave us every reason to believe there had been collusion between the two," wrote the official, Joseph C. Satterthwaite. Washington was also aggrieved by Ghana's decision to open diplomatic relations with China. It took this as further evidence that Nkrumah was now under the Soviet imprint. In fact, Beijing and Moscow were in the midst of an irreparable breach in their erstwhile alliance.

American deafness to the substance of Nkrumah's statements before the United Nations are vividly revealed in the nearly hallucinogenic recollections of President Eisenhower. In his memoir, he wrote, "Mr. Nkrumah went directly from my room to the United Nations General Assembly and within forty-five minutes cut loose with a speech following the Khrushchev line in strong criticism of Secretary-General Hammarskjöld."[25]

From this point onward, Ghana dwelled in Washington's doghouse, placing Nkrumah on a slow and wending path toward his own eventual overthrow. Things were aggravated further when Nkrumah stood with other leaders of the nonaligned world—Sukarno, Nehru, Nasser, and Tito—to propose that Eisenhower and Khrushchev meet in order to lower Cold War tensions. The American president described Nkrumah's support for the idea an "effrontery."[26] There would be a reprieve under Eisenhower's Democratic successor John F. Kennedy, but even that would be fragile and subject to constant reversals. The invocation of Nkrumah's supposed communist leanings was characteristic of the era. During the Eisenhower years reflexive judgment like this had often been used to subvert or overthrow Third World leaders. But this was not Washington's main problem with Nkrumah. Nor was the principal issue what the White House almost surely saw as the outlandish spectacle of Nkrumah, a Black man from Africa, presuming to issue solemn proposals about how the world should be run. The proximate cause for the crackup between Ghana and the United States was the Congo.

As one historian of the period has written, on the same day as Nkrumah's General Assembly speech, "the State Department claimed that 'It has unfortunately become clear' that Guinea, Ghana and Egypt were 'deliberately intervening in internal affairs of Congo in violation [of] repeated S[ecurity]

C[ouncil] and G[eneral] A[sssembly] resolution.'" The interference, according to the department, was in the form of "refusal [to permit the arrest of Lumumba] and the attempts to persuade Kasavubu and his camp to embrace a power-sharing formula which accommodated Lumumba."[27]

Strategically speaking, Ghana was but a flyspeck. Congo, at the heart of the continent and as large as all of Western Europe, was an altogether different matter. Washington was as deluded about Soviet influence in the Congo as it was about Ghana, but in this paranoid era, delusions often carried great weight. The United States could easily bear Nkrumah so long as his stage remained small—say, limited to his immediate confines in West Africa. But Nkrumah's pan-Africanism, mixed with Washington's unfounded fear of his susceptibility to communist control, made his involvement in the Congo intolerable.

In fact, the mistrust would cut both ways, presaging nothing but ill will. Nkrumah had worked long and hard to sustain close relations with the West and with the United States in particular, but America's betrayals of Lumumba and of democratic ideals and respect for Africa in the Congo were about to feed a deep and irreparable distrust in him toward Washington.

CHAPTER THIRTY-SIX

A Way in the World

THE GRAY AND STEADY-AS-SHE-GOES STYLE OF LEADERSHIP THAT AMERicans had become accustomed to under Dwight Eisenhower ended instantly with the inauguration of his successor, John F. Kennedy, on January 20, 1961. In fact, harbingers of its end had already been in the air for years. In September 1955, Eisenhower had a cardiac event during a Friday golf outing in Denver. It was confirmed overnight that he had had a significant heart attack. This was in an era before effective treatments were known. Two days later, the stock market suffered the worst crash since 1929 due to the shock and uncertainty brought on by news of the president's health. Eisenhower's heart attack was not the end of his health woes, though. In his second term, at the age of sixty-seven, in 1957, he suffered a stroke which noticeably affected his speech.[1]

Whatever one felt politically after what had been an extraordinarily close election, everything about Kennedy commanded attention—the fresh and handsome face, the startlingly thick hair, the high-voltage rhetoric, the stylish, attractive wife. And from the outset of his sole, uncompleted term, the world's demands on his attention would seldom pause, either. Kennedy had been in office as the thirty-fifth American president for all of three days when disturbing news from Africa came to him in a call from Adlai Stevenson, his ambassador to the United Nations. Stevenson informed him that Patrice Lumumba, Nkrumah's thirty-five-year-old understudy in pan-Africanism, had been murdered. Kennedy had taken the call in the Oval Office where portraits were being taken of him by his family photographer. In that instant, he lifted his right hand to his head, his face seized in an anguished grimace.[2]

Word of Lumumba's assassination was greeted with incomprehension and fury as it spread almost instantaneously across Africa, where most people learned of his murder bent over their radios. Nkrumah took the news as badly as anyone. Certainly, no one had invested more heavily in Lumumba's success. Nkrumah had sent a trusted personal envoy to Leopoldville to ensure constant contact with Lumumba, and the two leaders had also spoken frequently by telephone. As we have seen, Ghana had been among the first nations to dispatch peacekeeping forces to Congo and constituted the largest single contingent in the UN's blue-helmeted army.

But it was all for naught. Smarting from the impertinence of Lumumba's prideful independence speech, distrustful of his nationalism, eager to safeguard the Belgian settler community there, and above all determined to hold onto Congo's fabled mineral wealth, Belgium fanned rebellion against Lumumba from his first days in office. In its most destabilizing action of all, it encouraged secession of Katanga Province, the incredible storehouse of copper reserves in the country's south. The Soviet Union had no roots and scant influence in the Congo, but haunted by an irrational phobia of communist takeovers wherever nationalism reared its head during the final half year of the Eisenhower administration, the United States did nearly as much as Brussels to encourage the destabilization of the Congo and eventually, the murder of Lumumba. In the words of Eisenhower's CIA chief, Allen Dulles, unseating Lumumba quickly became Washington's "urgent and prime objective."[3]

Nkrumah had other, more personal reasons to be alarmed by Lumumba's elimination. The assassination fed a lively fear in his mind that he was witnessing the beginnings of an open season on progressive rulers in Africa by Western powers. And he readily imagined himself to be next.

In an angry statement broadcast on Ghanaian radio that betrayed this worry, Nkrumah denounced Kennedy by name, calling him a "murderer." With Ghana's press devoting nonstop coverage and feverish editorials on Lumumba's assassination, anti-American rioting broke out in Accra. According to *Time* magazine, as large crowds of demonstrators formed, people hoisted signs saying, "UNITED STATES MURDERS LUMUMBA" and then they "besieged the U.S. embassy, ripped the emblem from over the door and smashed an outdoor light with rifle shots."[4] In this, however, Ghana was hardly alone. Lumumba's murder was a global event, and throughout Africa and beyond, many immediately suspected CIA involvement. Angry crowds protested in much the same way in Lagos, Nigeria, which had never become swept up in Nkrumah's pan-Africanism. Demonstrators expressed similar outrage over the assassination in cities as distant from the Congo and as far-flung as Colombo in Sri Lanka, Dublin, Rome, Tehran, Melbourne, and Delhi.[5]

The destabilization of Lumumba by Western powers had already caused a sharp decline in Nkrumah's relations with Washington well before

Lumumba's murder. Even though Washington had often wavered, especially during Eisenhower's eight years in office, the United States had cut a figure as a fundamentally anticolonial power. The Congo crisis forced Nkrumah to conclude bitterly that wherever the specter of competition with Moscow arose, however credibly, the United States would align tactically with its European colonizer allies against the interests of pro-independence forces in Africa.

The Ghanaian leader traveled to the United States in September 1960, two months before Kennedy's nail-biter election victory, and four months before the transition from Republican to Democratic administrations. Nkrumah's sharp criticism of the West for its failure to back Lumumba against Belgian aggression had clearly begun to sour Eisenhower toward him. Neither the president, the vice president, nor even Christian Herter, the secretary of state, greeted Nkrumah on his arrival in Washington, as ordinary protocol might have suggested. Things went downhill from there over the next few days. Eisenhower received Nkrumah in New York at his suite at the Waldorf on September 22, and American accounts of their conversation suggest that it went well. Press photos afterward showed the two men smiling broadly.[6]

But Ghana's ambassador to the United States, W. M. Q. Halm, who was present during this meeting, remembered things differently. He noted that Nkrumah had been "heartily dissatisfied" over how little interest Eisenhower had shown in engaging on what was at the top of Nkrumah's mind: the Congo Crisis.[7] That very morning, in fact, the American president had delivered a speech at the United Nations in which he said, "nowhere is the challenge to the international community and to peace and orderly progress more evident than in Africa." He went on to announce a five-point plan to assure African countries a chance "at the freedom, domestic tranquility and progress they deserve." Nowhere, though, did he express any criticism of colonial rule.[8]

Nkrumah had no substantive basis for knowing this, but at this moment, discussions were already advancing in Washington about how to get rid of Lumumba. Barely a month before Nkrumah's arrival in Washington, for example, a telegram from the American embassy in Belgium to the Department of State cited Lumumba's "opposition to the West," and his "increasing dependence on [the] Soviet Union." It bluntly concluded, "A principal objective of our political and diplomatic action must therefore be to destroy [the] Lumumba government as now constituted."[9]

When Nkrumah addressed the General Assembly the day after Eisenhower had, he did anything but avoid the topic of European dominion over his continent:

> For years and years, Africa has been the foot-stool of colonialism and imperialism, exploitation and degradation. From the North to South, from the East to West, her sons languished in the chains of slavery and humiliation, and Africa's exploiters and self-appointed controllers of her destiny strode across our land with incredible inhumanity—without mercy, without shame, and without honour. But those days are gone, and gone forever, and now I, an African, stand before the General Assembly of the United Nations and speak with the voice of peace and freedom, proclaiming to the world the dawn of a new era.[10]

The previous day, taking his cue from the administration's disengaged tone on Congo, Nkrumah had done little to press the idea of his cherished Volta River dam project with Eisenhower. Soon afterward, though, the administration reversed its previous pledge to provide the financial backing needed to make the dam possible. In his public assessment of Nkrumah after his unflinching General Assembly speech, Herter said the Ghanaian had "marked himself as very definitely leaning toward the Soviet bloc."[11]

Nkrumah had always been alive to this kind of risk, but he also seemed to have a genuine preference for building strong economic ties with the West before looking elsewhere to diversify his sources of foreign aid and investment. Reflections of this instinct could be seen throughout most of the 1950s. "I want for the Gold Coast Dominion status within the British Commonwealth. I am no communist and never have been," Nkrumah said shortly after being released from prison by the British, who had branded him then for supposedly communist leanings. In 1953, Nkrumah's government limited travel to countries that belonged to what it called the "communist bloc," and he threated to fire the editor of his own party's daily, the *Accra Evening News*, if it published "pro communist material." In a remarkable moral compromise, at the 1957 meeting of Commonwealth leaders, Nkrumah even abstained from confrontation over the issue of apartheid, saying that the organization was "big enough for both Ghana and South Africa."[12]

Nkrumah's prioritization of engagement with the West continued well after independence and the departure of the colonial governor, Arden-Clarke. This was demonstrated most vividly in the deliberate way that he slow-walked relations with Moscow until the turn of the decade, partly on the advice of his famously anti-Soviet mentor, George Padmore, whose death in September 1959 Nkrumah had grieved deeply. As C. L. R. James wrote, "I who knew both of them cannot think of Padmore without Nkrumah and Nkrumah without Padmore."[13]

Nkrumah had relegated Moscow's representatives to the sidelines at Ghana's independence ceremonies, leaving the Soviets to grumble that they had been excluded from the "high table."[14] Ghana then delayed the reciprocal opening of embassies, which the government feebly rationalized, insisting that it didn't have the necessary funds. A few months later, Moscow invited Nkrumah's government to send its minister of agriculture to the USSR to study that country's experience with state farms. Ghana expressed polite gratitude for the invitation but turned it and other solicitations like these down. In August of 1957, a Soviet diplomat, Yakov Alexandrovich Malik, interpreted these signs to characterize Accra's attitude as hostile.[15] Even after the two countries finally exchanged ambassadors in 1959, Ghana, acting at the behest of the United States and Britain, enforced a strict limit of eighteen on the number of people who could work at the Soviet embassy in Accra.[16] Ghana's cabinet also approved a bill that required that any government agency "receiving any request for information emanating from a Communist country should be required to pass it to the Ministry of Defense . . . for scrutiny and consideration."[17]

At various points, Washington would claim that Nkrumah and the two African political leaders closest to him in this period, Touré and Lumumba, were outright Soviet pawns. And ideological typecasting like this was by no means limited to Africa. In Guiana, after Cheddi Jagan's People's Progressive Party triumphed at the polls in 1953, Britain suspended the colony's constitution and removed Jagan from office because of his supposedly pro-Soviet politics. I came to know Jagan in the early 1990s as a reporter after voters returned him to power decades after he was ousted. He was in his mid-seventies then, and governed not as a communist, but as a social democrat and humanist, who appealed to the rich countries for a restructuring of the international economic order to reduce poverty and inequality. Kennedy's onetime confidant and biographer, the historian Arthur M. Schlesinger Jr., called him a "London School of Economics Marxist filled with charm."[18]

For Lumumba, though, the unjustified tag of being Moscow's plaything become a literal death sentence. After being brutally punished by France, Sékou Touré, Guinea's president, openly lobbied for good relations with Washington but was kept at arm's length by the Eisenhower administration for the same ideological reasons: Paris warned the State Department that he was a communist. In the longer run, this would scarcely matter. In the post-Eisenhower years, even though he enforced blanket-style one-party rule in which he held nearly total power, Guinea's leader maintained smooth relations with Washington. In bad health after twenty-six years as president, Touré opted to travel overseas for emergency cardiac surgery. Instead of Moscow (or even Paris) Touré travelled to the United States, where he died on the operating table at the Cleveland Clinic in 1984.

For all three of these fiercely independent-minded men—Nkrumah, Touré, Jagan—and for a fourth, Modibo Keïta of Mali, whose country also briefly joined in union with Ghana and Guinea on Christmas Day in 1961, the idea of lining up on one side or the other of the Cold War's sharp ideological divide was an anathema. Each believed deeply that what the continent needed most of all was to find its own way in the world. They all understood this to mean some kind of "third way," meaning being able to maneuver free of pressure from outside powers, whether from the old colonizers of Europe or the dominant new rival powers, Washington and Moscow, or even China. They believed in pan-Africanism as the answer. For each of them this was defined by nonalignment, by some form of socialism, and by close intra-African cooperation.

In December 1961, Touré demonstrated just this sort of independence by expelling Daniel Solod, the Soviet ambassador to his country, in the very year that Moscow had awarded the Guinean its Lenin Peace Prize. Less often recalled is that within a few weeks, Touré also kicked out a French Archbishop and closed Koranic schools in the capital. Some said the ambassador's expulsion was over unhappiness attributed to Moscow's unfulfilled aid promises and the abysmal quality of equipment provided by the Soviets. The favorite example to illustrate Guinea's complaint involves the supposed delivery of Russian snowblowers to tropical Guinea in place of badly needed tractors, but this is an apocryphal legend.

Although a much less colorful story, what really happened tells us far more about the travails of independent-minded pan-Africanists in an era of relentless superpower jousting. Moscow had pinned big hopes on Touré as its first prospective client in Black Africa, but it soon grew disenchanted with the Guinea government's failure to implement what the Soviets regarded as a sufficiently socialist three-year plan. As he had with the French, Touré insisted that Guinea would follow its own ideological blueprint. He was as indifferent to Soviet aims in Africa as he had been to French ones, and openly skeptical of Moscow's dogmas. He regarded things like class warfare, for example, as having little relevance in Africa. His country was one of the poorest and least developed in the world, a place where average life expectancy for babies born in the year of independence was a mere thirty-four years.[19] Push came to shove when Touré's government accused Solod of meddling in the country's internal affairs by sponsoring Marxist-Leninist reading groups and fomenting a coup plot. "Had I organized it [the plot], it would have succeeded," Solod later sulked to a French diplomat.[20]

THE YEAR 1960 HAD OPENED WITH A RHETORICAL THROWING IN OF THE towel by the British government on colonial rule. In a speech made in Accra that January, the Conservative prime minister, Harold Macmillan, said that London would no longer stand in the way of African governments seeking independence. For such a dramatic change of posture, though, the address, known as the Wind of Change speech, made little impression on the world. It would only draw wide notice after Macmillan repeated his pronouncements before the South African parliament the following month. Cameroon had won its independence from France that January 1, opening that year's floodgate of decolonization. Over the next twelve months, seventeen new African countries were born, but fundamental change in the economic life of the continent or even its political relations with the West was much slower in coming.

This left Nkrumah, who had felt strung along by the West for much of the 1950s, more anxious than ever to demonstrate to the world what African independence could mean, beyond the mere acquisition of new flags and passports, country names and national anthems. For Ghana's independence to have any true significance, he had always said, all of Africa would have to be independent and much more united, and this, too, had a premise: the economic transformation of Ghana, which would show the way, spurring the development ambitions of others.

Toward this end, Nkrumah only reached out to Moscow belatedly for help with his dam project ambitions. This began in late 1960, roughly a year after Padmore's death. At the time, bilateral trade between Ghana and the Soviet Union amounted to a paltry $16 million.[21] During a visit to Sunyani, in northwestern Ghana that December, Nkrumah announced that a Soviet hydroelectric dam would be built at Bui and boasted that it would supply electricity and water "to every town, village and cottage for miles and miles."[22] The idea for a secondary dam at Bui had been part of Kitson's original plan. But in scaling back Nkrumah's industrial vision, the Kaiser Corporation had stripped Bui from the overall scheme.

Nkrumah's speech about the Soviet Union's willingness to build at Bui was about much more than an attempt to resurrect the smaller dam. He aimed to spur the United States to stop wavering over the Akosombo project, knowing that the CIA would closely monitor any Ghanaian cooperation with the

Russians.[23] In January 1961, Ghana confirmed to the Soviet Union that in the following month it would send a delegation to Moscow to discuss the construction of a civilian nuclear reactor in Ghana.[24] Soon thereafter, Nkrumah gave confirmation to Ghana's National Assembly that Moscow had offered to build a secondary dam at Bui.

This was bold statecraft by Nkrumah, who was certainly aware that his diplomatic communications had all along been carefully monitored by Washington. He may even have seen this as an advantage. That is because he was counting on leveraging American anxieties. That was the kind of risk-taking that survival as a progressive pan-Africanist required in this era. We have just seen how, to affirm his independence, Touré ejected the Soviet ambassador despite being strangled by France and receiving scant assistance from any other quarter besides Ghana. Nkrumah's moves with the Bui dam should be read in a similar light. As one Western historian who is generally unsympathetic toward Nkrumah has written about this episode, the Ghanaian leader "saw nothing contradictory in what he was doing. He was genuinely trying to work out a new system of African socialism applicable to the problems of Africa ... and to work this out on a pragmatic and eclectic basis ... helped only by those who would subscribe to his philosophy." The author continued, saying, "This incident explains the real core of Nkrumah's philosophy—to get help from East and West for the benefit of Ghana—and he could see no reason for anyone to object to the idea."[25]

Nkrumah didn't simply want to play one great power off against another in order to reap dividends for Ghana, though. That ageless game would be played by plenty of others in the years ahead, as most of Africa became independent. Think of Mobutu Sese Seko, the army colonel who engineered Lumumba's overthrow and then held onto power for three decades by playing a constant balancing game that came to involve the United States, China, North Korea, Belgium, and France. Nkrumah wanted assistance from the powerful countries of the world, to be sure, but his ultimate aim was altogether different. It amounted to a rebellion against a hostile world order. Nkrumah wanted to make Ghana economically powerful, and to use Ghana's wealth and its expertise and example to thereby galvanize the continent into being both prosperous and self-sufficient. This was nothing less than a project of worldmaking, in the language of the political scientist Adom Getachew.[26] Its objective was a redistribution of global wealth and power in ways more favorable to Africa in the wake of world war and colonial rule. And Nkrumah merits credit for this, even if it is against these ambitious standards that his failures must ultimately be understood, and indeed judged.

IN 2012, WHILE RESEARCHING A PREVIOUS BOOK, *CHINA'S SECOND CONTINENT*, I set out by car from a coastal town in western Ghana to Sunyani and beyond, to Bui. There, I was to be received by the king of a local ethnic group, a man named Nana Kojo Wuo. After traversing the sea-hugging heart of Fante territory, the route jutted northward into the ancestral heartland of the Asante, finally reaching Kumasi, where I slumbered through a raging downpour that lasted all night. In the morning, the crisp daylight revealed a dew-sparkled panorama of open, rolling countryside, broken now and again by the sloping shoulders of an old and fragmented mountain chain. The king's teenage son awaited me in Sunyani, where he attended boarding school, and it was a good thing that he knew the way. It consisted of nothing but wending dirt roads that were all but indistinguishable to me.

The Bui dam had finally been commissioned during the presidency of John Kufuor, who had left office in 2009 after two elected terms. In the end, it was not the Soviets who built the massive hydroelectric infrastructure there, which was then two weeks away from entering into service. By this time, the Soviet empire had fallen, giving way to the Russian Federation. The patron that had made this fragment of Kitson's dream come true was a rising China. There seemed to be a lesson in this. The interest of great powers in what they often regard as their periphery comes and goes. The needs of the countries that constitute this world remain.

Just as Nkrumah had done before him, Kufuor had felt obliged to sell the dam project to the local populations who would be displaced by the construction and subsequent formation of a large, inland lake. To do so for the Akosombo Dam, Nkrumah had even invoked the then-voguish gadget of modernization, nuclear power. Kufuor instead pledged a new, hypermodern city to be built in this remote part of Ghana. Here and there, promotional posters could still be seen displaying visions of tall apartment buildings, a gleaming regional airport, and a promised new university.

The ensuing reality, revealed to me after a few minutes driving through access gates to the dam zone thrown up by its Chinese builders, was rather more mundane. They had built something, yes: a new village of neat and simple concrete compounds on the crest of a hill. But it was nothing like a city, never mind the fantastic new one that had been dangled as a prospect—no, promise—before the locals. "The houses are finished, and they've laid the foundation of a new high school," the local king, Nana Kojo Wuo, told me, with a residue of letdown playing on his face. "We're supposed to get a church, a clinic, a market, a community center, and a police station." "We have not achieved perfection," he added. "But there is electricity, and potable water, and latrines."[27]

There was a lesson here, I thought, and not a small one. No outside power or force would come and build Africa. Friends may come and go, but this struggle remained as complete as it had in the times of Nkrumah. When the struggle is finally met, whenever that should occur, what is achieved will have to reflect the labor of its peoples.

CHAPTER THIRTY-SEVEN

Southern Strategies

AFRICA OCCUPIED AN IMMENSE SPACE IN THE AMERICAN IMAGINATION around the middle of the twentieth century, but that has been almost completely forgotten today. And in the short term, when judged in a narrowly pragmatic sense, the election of John F. Kennedy—a man intensely focused on the continent—can almost seem like a lucky break for Nkrumah. This is especially true insofar as Nkrumah's Volta River dam ambitions were concerned.

As a young, nominally liberal senator from Massachusetts, Kennedy had been no real friend of the African American civil rights movement. What might charitably be called his caution toward this cause was the fruit of several factors. These ranged from Kennedy's lack of exposure to Black life, to the fact that by this point in his political career, the scion from Massachusetts had few deeply held ideological positions of any kind. Mostly, though, it reflected a conundrum faced by any northern Democrat who harbored presidential ambitions: one could strengthen one's base in relatively liberal northern states by speaking up on civil rights, then an issue of rising national urgency, but at clear risk of losing the large, white supremacist Southern vote that Democrats traditionally needed to win. Alternatively, one could strike an indifferent stance toward equal rights for Black people to curry favor with Southern power at risk of losing Northern support, Black and white alike. Complicating matters further, there was also a tradition among urban Irish Americans at the time of not supporting Black advancement.

Kennedy affected slim-cut Brooks Brothers suits and shirts and skinny neckties in plain colors and patterns to make the most of his nearly gaunt figure. And when he dressed casually, it was in faded chinos and button-down Oxford shirts, often complimented with dark Polaroid sunglasses. His aim seems to have been projecting both effortless style and robust health, even athleticism. In fact, he was a sickly man who suffered from Addison's disease and was often in great pain.

As an ambitious senator, Kennedy took the latter of these two possible paths, joining with Southerners on two important votes over the 1957 Civil Rights Act. At one point, this caused Eleanor Roosevelt, an early supporter of Kennedy, to call him out for what she saw as his rank political cynicism. Kennedy was the author of a bestselling political memoir titled *Profiles in Courage*, so the former first lady ridiculed him as "someone who understands what courage is and admires it, but [who] has not quite the independence to have it."[1]

Roosevelt had rightly identified the Kennedy campaign strategy's cynicism, but it worked, albeit barely. The Massachusetts senator squeaked through to triumph with a 112,827 margin in the popular vote, and Black voters were crucial to his victory in five states—New Jersey, Michigan, Illinois, Texas, and South Carolina. The last two of them were Southern. In his inaugural address, where he famously said, "Ask not what your country can do for you," Kennedy made but one nod to the great struggle for equal rights for Black people then unfolding. It was a vague promise to respect "those human rights to which this nation has always been committed, and to which we are committed today at home and around the world." As the critic Louis Menand has noted, "at home" were the only words that referenced domestic affairs at all.[2]

As a matter of political strategy, the Kennedy campaign's cautiousness toward civil rights was compensated for to some extent by Kennedy's growing ardor during this period in championing African liberation. As Nkrumah's visits to the United States and the large African American presence at Ghana's independence ceremonies had both powerfully demonstrated, African emancipation was a topic that mattered deeply to Black voters in the United States. Ironically, for someone who would lead the United States into war in Vietnam, Kennedy's appreciation for the historical importance of nationalism in the Third World, which fed his interest in Africa, began to take root after a 1951 tour of Southeast Asia, when he criticized what he called American "toadying" in support of Europe's listing empires.[3]

By 1957, Kennedy's views on this topic had become both stronger and more coherent. "The most powerful single force in the world today is neither Communism nor Capitalism, neither the H-bomb nor the guided missile—it is man's eternal desire to be free and independent," the Massachusetts senator hammered on the floor of the Senate.[4] He uttered these words in criticism of France's war to beat back Algerian demands for independence, a topic Kennedy returned to often. But thinking like this, which was pilloried by

Republicans and some fellow Democrats alike, was soon extended to include the entire African continent. As one historian of Kennedy's foreign policy has written, "In 1960, for the first (and perhaps last) time in history, Africa figured prominently in an American presidential election. Kennedy repeatedly attacked the Eisenhower-Nixon administration's record on Africa, making 479 references to the continent during his 1959–60 campaign speeches."[5] No other modern American campaign featured Africa in a prominent way. In one speech, Kennedy argued that "we have lost ground in Africa because we have neglected and ignored the needs and the aspirations of the African people—because we failed to foresee the emergence of Africa and ally ourselves with the cause of independence."[6] The legacy this has left is one of tremendous lost opportunity. For both Africa and for Black Americans, the United States' failure to pursue and deepen connections with the continent after each had initiated a rediscovery of the other in the 1950s and '60s is one of the era's great tragedies.

Early on, one of the sharpest ways that Kennedy began to distinguish his world view from those of Eisenhower and Nixon was to express much more tolerance toward nonalignment in the Third World, a Republican bugbear, and especially in Africa.

Kennedy's feelings about the urgency of winding down European imperialism and supporting Africans' push for independence were fueled by his prescient sense of the continent's potential for becoming a more central stage in a coming round of competition with Moscow. This fed a feeling of alarm that the United States was woefully unengaged in Africa. It is scarcely less apparent, though, that Kennedy also saw his outspokenness in the cause of African liberation as a card to be played to retain the support of influential Black American voices who had bridled at his pusillanimity on civil rights.

One of the Kennedy campaign's highest profile nods to the promise of a much deeper engagement with Africa should he win the presidency, came after Guinea's president, Sékou Touré requested a meeting with the Democratic candidate during a visit by Touré to California in October 1959. Touré, whose country was being punished and humiliated by de Gaulle for seeking early independence, was copresident of the nominal Ghana-Guinea union. Encouraged by Paris, the Eisenhower administration dragged its feet in recognizing the Touré government and then refused to send aid to Guinea. Officials in the State Department predictably dismissed Touré as an irremediable communist and a lost cause, despite the Guinean leader's clear and repeated statements that he was a committed nationalist who had no use for Marxism-Leninism.

This had the ironic effect of pushing Touré closer to the Soviet Union, but only briefly. Kennedy responded favorably to Touré's outreach during his 1959 visit to the United States, flying him to Disneyland, then a glimmering icon of American modernity, where the two men flashed warm smiles together in a highly publicized encounter. Late the following month, Touré would become the first sub-Saharan African head of state to visit Moscow, where nearly all the members of the CPSU Presidium feted him. Khrushchev, who was absent from Moscow at the time, received Touré privately at his luxurious Black Sea vacation home at Gagra. But Kennedy's persistence and flair for personal diplomacy allowed him to sustain warm communications with Touré, despite Washington's insecurity and jumpiness over ideological competition with Moscow. And this sort of thing would pay many dividends. During the Cuban Missile Crisis in 1962, for instance, Guinea declined an overflight request by Moscow to ferry supplies to the Caribbean nation. The following year, during the founding meeting of the Organization of African Unity in Addis Ababa, the French press mischievously reported that the Guinea delegation was planning to introduce a motion to denounce the Kennedy administration over racial violence then exploding across Alabama. At Touré's instruction, Guinea issued a statement saying that it supported Kennedy's handling of the anti-Black crisis in Alabama "without any reservations."[7]

ONE OF KENNEDY'S FIRST MAJOR FOREIGN POLICY MOVES AFTER THE LOFTY hopefulness and tuxedoed fanfare of the inauguration was to back the construction of Ghana's Akosombo Dam. It was a decision taken despite great internal opposition, with many officials in Kennedy's national security apparatus warning, as Eisenhower's advisors had, that Nkrumah was a lost cause, someone too closely aligned with Moscow. In the end, Kennedy mostly kept his own counsel. A rare exception to this was Barbara Ward, a progressive British woman who was an early advocate of sustainable development. Ward had deep connections both to Nkrumah's Ghana and to Harvard, where she had become friends with the new president. And Ward's husband, Robert Jackson, was a paid advisor of Nkrumah's over the dam project. Despite this major conflict of interest, Ward helped Kennedy overcome whatever reservations he held, arguing that rejecting the project would be tantamount to abandoning Nkrumah, whose prestige was near its peak on the continent, to the Soviet Union.

When Nkrumah learned of Lumumba's assassination, he extended an impromptu invitation to Leonid Brezhnev to travel to Accra from Guinea, where the Soviet president and number two in the Soviet nomenclature, then found himself on an official visit. The two men lavished praise on each other, with Nkrumah, whose blood was aboil over Congo, saying that the views held by the Soviet Union and Ghana on world affairs were in essential harmony. During his hastily arranged stop in Accra, Brezhnev issued Moscow's first public acknowledgment that it would build the dam at Bui. Here, one must understand the psychology of both superpowers in this era. For all of Nkrumah's newfound warmth toward the Soviets, Moscow's principal motivation was its fear that if it did not match American backing for the Akosombo project, Ghana would be irredeemably "lost" to the West. It scarcely bears stating that much of the behavior of the West was driven by the exact opposite impulse.

Nkrumah employed private communications to signal very different sentiments to Kennedy during the transition between administrations and in the early days of what was an ill-fated relationship after Kennedy's inauguration. In one long letter to the new American president, with Congo top of mind, Nkrumah encouraged Kennedy to show the "same courage and realism" toward Black Africa that he had displayed in supporting Algerian independence. For Africans, this had been the most important early signal that a Kennedy presidency could mark a real shift from the American coziness toward European colonial rule seen under Eisenhower.

> The reputation of the US could be irretrievably damaged if it sits by and watches the crumpling up of democracy in Africa by one of your close military allies—Belgium—in flagrant disregard of the unanimous opinion and sentiment of all those African people who are free to express their views.[8]

Nkrumah stressed that he looked forward to a new start in relations with the United States and would not blame the incoming president for any wrongs he imputed to Eisenhower. The Ghanaian leader still clung to his suspicion that Washington was behind Lumumba's assassination. The CIA had not killed Lumumba, though. Or, not quite. That had been accomplished by Belgian henchmen at Brussels' behest. After he was deposed as prime minister, Lumumba lost out in an internal power struggle in the Congo that pitted him against the president, Joseph Kasa-Vubu. By this time, though, the West had turned hard against Lumumba. Moscow's modest provision of aircraft to ferry troops loyal to the Lumumba government into battle against Katangan separatists had been the final straw. From then on, even the theoretically neutral United Nations and its large peacekeeping operation in the country openly worked to undermine him. Under a diluvian rain, Lumumba pulled off a nighttime escape from house arrest in his home on Boulevard Albert I in the heart of the capital, mounting a longshot bid to reach Stanleyville. It lay twelve-hundred miles away by road. From there he hoped to somehow rally his supporters and reclaim power. He was captured due to the actions of the CIA station chief in Leopoldville (Kinshasa), who dispatched a small plane to spot the Peugeot carrying Lumumba on the road wending north from the capital.

After he was brought back to Leopoldville in the hold of a truck, at which point he was savagely beaten, Lumumba was flown to Katanga Province in the south and pummeled again remorselessly by local separatists. Afterward, he was tied to a tree by his Katangan enemies and cut down by a firing squad, along with two associates. To eliminate evidence of the murder, a team led by a Belgian gendarme recovered the corpses from a shallow grave and, the next day, hacked them into pieces and dissolved the remains in drums filled with powerful alkalis.

One cannot say how Nkrumah might have responded had he known these details. Lumumba's murder had contributed strongly to the radicalization of Nkrumah's politics, then well underway, but many factors pushed him in this direction. The death of Padmore toward the end of 1959 had been one key event. As we have seen, no one had more influence on Nkrumah than his longtime mentor. The assassination attempts against Nkrumah had clearly been another important factor. From that point on during his presidency, he lived the haunted life of a marked man. People near him said that Nkrumah constantly looked over his shoulder at the slightest sound of footsteps and flinched at the sound of flocking birds.

Against the advice of his leading foreign policy advisors, Kennedy decided to reapprove the American assistance to Ghana for the Volta River dam project that had been withheld by the Eisenhower administration. But Kennedy understood the stakes differently from aides who agreed with Eisenhower that Nkrumah was a lost cause. Engaging with Ghana was not a straightforward move on a black and white checkerboard. Kennedy had no illusions that Nkrumah would line up with the West in its contest with the Soviet Union. More modestly, he hoped to ensure that Nkrumah, who was still the most influential Black African leader, would remain devoted to nonalignment. In exchange for the nearly symbolic American contribution of a $30 million investment in the project, which was needed to secure World Bank financing, Kennedy's biggest ask was that Nkrumah tone down his criticism of the United States, as well as his praise for Moscow.

Hoping to seal this arrangement, Kennedy invited Nkrumah to visit Washington, making him the first foreign leader to be received by his administration at the White House, on March 8, 1961. He even greeted the charismatic Ghanaian upon arrival at the airport in a driving rain. Judging from the statements that were issued, and more still from the photographs taken, the two men hit it off rather well. At fifty-one, Nkrumah was eight years older than Kennedy, but if anything, he looked more youthful than America's young president. He was dressed in a dark suit matching that of his host, and the expressions he wore exuded a natural optimism and self-confidence.

Kennedy heard Nkrumah out at length on the Congo, after which the two leaders agreed that the Belgians should withdraw their troops from the Congo and allow that country's people to determine their future free from foreign intervention or meddling. Nkrumah, for his part, flatly repeated something he had insisted from the outset of his political career in Ghana. He was no communist. If his country and others on the continent sought investment from Moscow and its allies, he said, that was because investment was usually not forthcoming from the West, and even when it was, it often came with excessive foot-dragging.

Laughing and smiling broadly together, the two men radiated optimism. Kennedy took Nkrumah outside for a stroll in the Rose Garden, with its blooming flowers and new central fountain. Then he did something more remarkable. He invited Nkrumah upstairs, into the private quarters of the White House, where he introduced his guest to the First Lady, Jacqueline, who exuded charm in her signature, parted, shoulder-length bob. By her side played the presidential couple's sandy-haired, three-year-old daughter, Caroline. Throughout his visit to the United States, the press constantly emphasized the hospitality lavished on Nkrumah, unprecedented for an African leader. On his return home, Nkrumah addressed a warm personal letter to Kennedy that seemed to augur a strong rebound in relations.[9]

Soon after Nkrumah's return to Ghana, though, other dynamics quickly set in. With George Padmore's death nearly a year in the past, others jockeyed to fill the gulf created by his absence. Many of them, like the rising CPP ideologue Kofi Baako, held much more favorable views toward the USSR than Padmore or even Nkrumah ever had. Some of them advocated abandoning the idea of working with Washington on the Volta Dam project altogether and partnering with Moscow instead.

Some biographers have depicted Nkrumah as a hostage to the ascendant radical wing of the CPP, which controlled the country's radio and leading newspapers in this period. Soon, Washington, too, would take this view. But this represents a serious oversimplification of his decision-making as president. With Ghana's economy in increasing trouble and Arthur Lewis no longer on board as a deeply credentialed advisor, Nkrumah searched for new, more hope-inspiring economic policy guidance, much as a patient facing a grave diagnosis might resort to doctor shopping. This led him to Nicholas Kaldor, another of the most highly reputed international economists of the era.

Kaldor, was a Hungarian-born Briton who trained at the London School of Economics and became internationally influential both as an intellectual disciple of Keynes and as a socialist. The author of a posthumous sketch of him noted:

> It was not only his intellect and passion that made Kaldor dominant and controversial; it was also his style, charm, and sense of fun which made it impossible not to listen to what he had to say. He possessed that rare charisma and magnetic quality which made it difficult not to fall under his spell. When he was an adviser in Ghana in 1961, his hold over the President, Dr. Nkrumah, was likened unto the captivating powers of the ju-ju magicians![10]

The real reason for Kaldor's spell over Nkrumah, though, seems to have been his theories. He held that industry was the best engine of growth for developing countries, and that as it expanded, it would stimulate productivity gains even in other sectors of the economy. This was roughly the opposite of Arthur Lewis's view.

On the strength of advice from Kaldor and from other economists, Nkrumah rejected conditions imposed by the World Bank for its financing for the Volta Dam. This was done largely on the principled basis that a sovereign state should not be held to ransom by an international financial institution. This, however, sparked another showdown that imperiled the project. Kennedy advisors who already loathed Nkrumah invoked this latest twist as another opportunity to pull the plug on the deal. By June 1961, though, Nkrumah was a few weeks away from embarking on a major tour of the Soviet Union, of East Bloc countries, and of China. Here again, Nkrumah was emulating Sukarno, who followed up his triumphal entrance onto the world stage at Bandung by touring both West and East in explicit demonstration of his nonalignment. And this posed a dilemma for the White House. Once again, Barbara Ward helped sway the outcome. She argued that refusing to finance Ghana would risk another Aswan Dam–style setback for the West. That earlier debacle had arisen out of American pique over Egypt supposedly playing

East off West. The Eisenhower administration had withdrawn funding for Nasser's economic centerpiece in July 1956 after Cairo accepted a $1.2 billion Soviet offer to finance the dam's construction. One week later, Nasser nationalized the Suez Canal. Kennedy wrote a letter to Nkrumah at the end of June 1961, informing him that Washington would support the Volta River project, and he put the screws on the World Bank to ensure its participation. With this seeming breakthrough in hand, Nkrumah set off on his eastern tour.

———

ON JULY 9, 1961, KWAME NKRUMAH FLOATED DOWN THE ROLLAWAY STAIRCASE of a Ghana Airways flight at Moscow's Vnukovo Airport as if walking on clouds. He beamed from ear to ear. With a traditional chief's walking stick dangling from his wrist, he took a few steps onto Russian soil and gave a two-kiss embrace to the bald and broadly smiling Nikita Khrushchev. Just a few months earlier, Kennedy had gone out of his way to issue a warm statement of greeting to Nkrumah on an airport apron. Now, the Soviets were pulling out all of the hospitality stops. Standing behind Khrushchev was Brezhnev, his eventual successor, looking equally jubilant. And then came kisses and bouquets from smiling Russian girls, an impressive honor guard, cheers from a troupe of Ghanaian residents, and a long procession into the city led by motorcycle outriders. Natty in a dark suit and tie, Nkrumah waved and smiled from the back seat of an open limousine to crowds who had been assembled in Potemkin-like fashion along the entire route to greet him.

Nkrumah's ten-day state visit to the Soviet Union in July 1961 was part of an extraordinary five-week jaunt through the East that would also take him to Poland, Hungary, Czechoslovakia, Yugoslavia, Albania, Romania, Bulgaria, and even Mao's China. At the time, Beijing was already in the early stages of its clamorous falling out with Moscow. In both a show of self-confidence and a statement of triumph, Nkrumah had traveled with a delegation of sixty or so countrymen. In this voyage there was proof, or at least it so seemed, that an African socialist who was committed to nonalignment could extract benefits from both West and East. For all the niceties and honors they could bestow, though, the world's great powers had other things in mind. Africa would become a collateral victim of the superpower competition in which generosity counted for little. Grave political difficulties lay ahead for Nkrumah, too. Indeed, in retrospect, this half year, bookended by visits to the US and USSR clearly stands out as the diplomatic high-water mark of his presidency. And although it stretched out over five years, the remainder of his rule would be constantly troubled.

Nkrumah's Soviet trip resulted from a year and a half of careful diplomacy. Ghanaian delegations to Moscow had preceded him, and Nkrumah had expended no small amount of energy in trying to reassure the West that a decision to expand relations with the USSR, after years of deliberate distance, would not mean that he was turning his back on Britain and the US. At the same time, however, as Nkrumah wrote to Khrushchev in June as he set off for Moscow, he had firm hopes of Soviet help to assist in Ghana's economic takeoff. His wish list included help in building Tema, in organizing big, state-run farms, and in the construction of other infrastructure projects.

No sooner had Nkrumah returned home from his trip, though, than strong new doubts were raised about American support for the Volta River project. His journey through the communist countries validated the views of many in Washington about what they said was a "lurch to the left" in Ghana. His American skeptics also cited the recent creation of the Kwame Nkrumah Ideological Institute in the somnolent seaside town of Winneba, where Brezhnev had attended the opening ceremony during his Ghanaian stopover.

The faded remains of the Institute—inching gently toward ruin—are now part of the regional University of Education. There, under a canopy of broad-leafed shade trees, I found a handful of squat and neatly designed concrete buildings along with long-abandoned tennis and basketball courts. A handful of men sat just out of reach of the harsh sun on the stairs of the Osagyefo Library. And above the entrance to another building, whose stenciled name had been worn away by the years, I could just make out the slogan, "We Stand For Liberation." The sum effect was hardly spectral.

In the Institute's heyday, students were assigned Nkrumah's plentiful writings on pan-Africanism and liberation along with readings in Marxism. Nkrumah had never concealed his attraction to socialism, so seeing this ideology's forms penetrate strongly into the society here and in other ways, too, should have caused little surprise overseas. The endless toasts during Nkrumah's Eastern tour and the protocols of cooperation he signed were something else, though. Powerful voices arose in the US to oppose help with the big dam project, an unwarranted gift for a leader they viewed as a barely closeted communist. The Nkrumah skeptics so aroused included Tennessee Senator Albert Gore Sr. and Kennedy's most influential adviser, his brother and attorney general, Robert Kennedy.

Other influential officials, such as George Ball, then Undersecretary of State for Economic Affairs, told the president that Nkrumah faced high odds of being overthrown soon and therefore recommended postponing American participation in the VRP. Kennedy inherited a hyperactive CIA that was eager to intervene in many places, including during the failed Bay of Pigs invasion of Cuba, which took place a mere month after Nkrumah visited the White House. In this spirit, it offered to help arrange a coup to overthrow Nkrumah, which Kennedy declined.[11]

Amid this new delay, as more and more voices pressed Kennedy to withdraw from the VRP, Nkrumah spoke with both American and British diplomats to reiterate his previous vows that Ghana was not going communist. But Nkrumah didn't stop there. Showing his elbows, he subtly hinted that if Kennedy backed out of his pledge of support, he would publish the American president's correspondence, exposing the United States as being hostile to nonaligned countries like his and a fickle friend of Africa. It was a risky move, but it seems to have unlocked the logjam and induced Kennedy's final decision to proceed.

At all times, one of the highest purposes of history is to help reveal the gulf between how contemporary events are understood as they unfold and the obscure and hidden more complex realities that underly them. In this final period of his rule, Nkrumah's engagement with the two superpowers serves as a fine illustration of this. Contrary to Washington's fears, the Soviet Union was hardly trying to round up African countries and pull them tight into its ideological embrace. This was mostly a matter of Western projection, for that is precisely what France and some other imperial powers, including Britain to a lesser extent, had been attempting to do. In the early 1960s, Moscow thought precious little of the potential of countries like Ghana, or its West African partners in socialist pan-Africanism like Guinea and Mali, to one day "go communist."

In fact, they saw little potential in Nkrumah, nor any potential in Nkrumahism as a foundation for anything approaching Marxism-Leninism. After his February 1961 stopover in Accra, Brezhnev had written with gentle disparagement about the cult of personality surrounding Nkrumah, and about the rudimentary collectivism at the heart of his ideology. He concluded that Ghana had almost no prospect of advancing toward "scientific socialism."[12]

What the Soviets wanted most from Africa in this era was something very different. The United States and its capitalist allies dominated world trade, placing the USSR at a big economic disadvantage. With Africa, the USSR's goals were twofold. One was increasing trade with new parts of the world and doing so through barter and quasi-capitalist arrangements that would gradually increase Soviet exports and generate revenue. The other aim was to lift the prestige of the Soviet Union by showing that it could strongly boost the economic development of poor countries just emerging from colonial rule. The idea was to have showcase results in low stakes environments as Moscow demonstrated the benefits of planning, of state farms, and of turnkey industrial projects. This is what Khrushchev had meant in 1961, when he mentioned Africa as one of "the most important centers of the revolutionary struggle against imperialism."[13] To counter this, the Kennedy State Department the following year called Africa "the greatest open field of maneuver in the world-wide competition between the Communist Bloc and the non-communist world."[14]

Problems quickly arose. Few yet understood that after a decade of impressive economic growth, the Soviet economy had begun to sharply taper off, and that it would soon encounter increasing difficulty in competing with the West in much of anything beyond nuclear weapons. Soviet agriculture was stalling, and efforts to create big state farms in West Africa met with little success. The reasons for this were varied, ranging from the gulf in management styles and operating culture between Soviet planners and African officials to bureaucratic incompetence on both sides. The poor financial results of these enterprises contributed to economic disarray on the ground in the African client states. And with no good answers available, the Soviet Union became fatigued with frequent demands for additional help.

Another problem was the neocolonialism that Nkrumah had long inveighed against but couldn't escape from. British companies were still so dominant in the trade of Ghana's most valuable commodities, especially cacao, that this left little product to use for barter in financing trade with Moscow.

Ghana, and together with it, Nkrumah, were caught in a fiendish trap, an international economy dominated by big Western companies whose structure offered poor nations almost no chance at real prosperity from the export of harvested crops or raw materials, and by the same token, little help in transforming them locally. Indeed, as any survey of the continent would reveal today, this is a puzzle that has still never been solved.

CHAPTER THIRTY-EIGHT

Twenty-One Guns

During his tour of the Eastern powers, Nkrumah had lain a wreath at Lenin's Tomb. He had sailed on the presidential yacht with Josip Broz Tito, conducting a naval review together. And after signing a mutual friendship treaty in Beijing, he had visited with Mao at a traditional Chinese-style guesthouse on West Lake in the old Southern Song Dynasty Chinese capital, Hangzhou. Four decades later, after China's capitalist opening and transformation, I stayed in one of this same building's rooms as a paying guest and admired the peaked-tile roofs and plum blossom wallpaper.

Back on Ghanaian soil, Nkrumah had no time to savor the grand reception he had received from the Who's Who of the communist world. As it had been before, by 1961, it was suddenly impossible to deny that his country's economy was in perilous trouble. With the price of cacao remaining stubbornly low, growth had stalled. There was runaway inflation, substantially driven by spending on Nkrumah's ambitious nation building agenda. And now many basic goods had become hard to find.

Early in 1961, Ghana began nationalizing industries, something that Cuba had sweepingly undertaken the year before. Nkrumah had not only largely avoided nationalizations in the previous decade, he had foresworn them. This change in direction started with some struggling gold producers but was soon extended to include new industries as they were created as part of the state's manufacturing agenda. This was the beginning of a kind of *fuite en avant*, a long and destructive doubling down by Nkrumah on his vision of a new Ghana made strong through industrialization.

Nkrumah had become aware of a clamor over the spreading economic pain, and of the high living among many of his associates in the political class. Internecine struggles within the CPP had broken out into the open as the left wing, in the ascendancy after Padmore's death in 1959, used the conspicuous consumption of the party's conservatives to discredit them. Invoking the call for one-man one-vote that had powered the CPP's rise toward independence, they mocked their rivals with slogans like "one man, one house," or "one-man, one car."[1] Others denounced what they portrayed as rampant wife stealing, or the luring away of married women with money, as practiced by the nouveau rich. Their biggest target was the finance minister, Komla Gbedemah, who was most outspoken in his pushback against what he called Marxist ideas. The left pushed back by promoting rumors that Gbedemah was involved in an illicit trade in diamonds with a wealthy American businessman named Maurice Tempelsman, who was also deeply involved in the Congo and is said to have played a behind-the-scenes role in the overthrow of Lumumba. (In 1994, when I became the West Africa bureau chief for the *New York Times*, I inherited Tempelsman's name from my predecessors, among many others; he was described as a deeply connected and potentially helpful contact.) By 1961, Nkrumah rightly suspected Gbedemah for maintaining a disloyal, private backchannel to Washington. But although it had been in use for months, Nkrumah had yet to discover its true nature or even its extent.

In a famous speech that April that would become known as the "Dawn Broadcast," Nkrumah denounced the "self-seekers and careerists" among his followers and decreed that "no Minister, Ministerial Secretary or party Member of Parliament should own a business or be involved in anyone else's business, Ghanaian or foreign." He also announced a crackdown on political patronage and apparently rampant overseas travel by civil servants without cabinet or presidential approval.[2] Shortly thereafter, Nkrumah also created a new body called the Budget Bureau to assume some of the functions of the Ministry of Finance and to investigate corruption. When Gbedemah protested, he was reassigned as Minister of Health.

Rather than trimming the sails of his state more systematically, Nkrumah raised taxes on property and required businesspeople and wage earners to invest 5 percent of their income in government bonds under a new emergency national savings scheme. The government required cocoa farmers to invest 10 percent of their earnings under this plan. This was effectively a repeat of an earlier political mistake that had inflamed the Asante heartland, causing great political difficulty for Nkrumah in the previous decade. Then, the price paid to farmers for their cocoa crop was suppressed even as international prices soared. Nkrumah's new tax scheme was coupled with major austerity cuts to the budget that hit social services.

With the outbreak of a railway workers' strike in the twin western cities Takoradi and Sekondi, trouble preceded Nkrumah's return home. This action quickly paralyzed the ports, and other basic services, from sanitation to water supply, and spread from western Ghana to Asante and then nationwide. Amid this unrest, Gbedemah undertook a series of meetings with the American ambassador to Ghana, Francis Russell, in which Gbedemah broached the idea of concocting a legalistic scheme to remove Nkrumah from power. "I would be sorry to have to do it but [the country] has had enough of Nkrumah's arrogance, whims and madness," Gbedemah told Russell. The ambassador was subsequently told by Washington that "the department appreciated the position that [Gbedemah] was taking, and they could count on the support of the American government if he should decide to take certain steps."[3]

On September 14, with Nkrumah still overseas, his government played a card learned from colonial governments, not just in Ghana but all over Africa. It declared a state of emergency. Looking haggard, Nkrumah arrived home two days later and shortly afterward delivered a stern, even menacing national address. He gave striking workers two days to return to their jobs, saying, "Those who do not do so will have given clear indication that they and the instigators behind them are determined to bring about the overthrow of the Constitution by illegal means."[4]

Nkrumah's gambit succeeded, insofar as most workers promptly returned to their jobs. Ghana's troubles, and his own, though, were accelerating. After staring down the strike, the government stepped up surveillance of all kinds and began arresting people on a previously unknown scale. Foreigners came under particular suspicion, with many who had felt a common cause with Nkrumah's pan-Africanism, such as the American expatriate Bill Sutherland, leaving the country.

On September 22, 1961, the day after Nkrumah read the riot act to striking Ghanaian workers, while monitoring an unsecure international phone call between Tempelsman and a man named Grosse, Ghanaian state intelligence listened in on a conversation about Gbedemah's plans to unseat Nkrumah and American support for the idea.[5] Although often denounced as a tyrant by now, Nkrumah made no immediate move against Gbedemah; he only dismissed him from the government a week later, and never ordered his arrest. The following month, Gbedemah departed quietly into exile.

Two days after his ultimatum to workers, Nkrumah announced the firing of the British head of the Ghanaian armed forces, Major General H. T. Alexander, and the complete "Africanization" of the army's officer corps. In his statement on the dismissal, Nkrumah said, "I have also been disturbed by the attitude which the British Government have taken over the question of Katanga in the Congo, and the assistance which the British Government have given to the secessionist elements in Katanga."[6] This was no mere paranoia. The American position on Katanga had long been ambivalent, too. A year earlier, Allen Dulles had argued to Eisenhower that it was "important to preserve Katanga as a separate viable asset," to which the then-President agreed.[7]

Alexander had been pushing back against Nkrumah's efforts to diversify Ghana's relationship with other armed forces. This had notably included Nkrumah's pursuit of having soldiers trained by the Soviets, whose purpose was threefold. The first was to accelerate the growth of Ghana's armed forces to give them more of the heft they would need to meaningfully support liberation efforts in other African colonies. A second aim was to train a presidential guard unit to ensure his own security. And third, by doing so, Nkrumah sought to weaken the enduring grip of Britain, and by extension, the West, on Ghana's military. Nkrumah had also recently purchased a naval patrol ship and was exploring the acquisition of military aircraft. As a stout defender of British interests and as something of a Cold Warrior, Alexander opposed all of these objectives.

The British officer's firing had a more immediate cause, though. For months, Alexander had been stationed in Congo where he commanded Ghana's detachment of peacekeepers amid that country's crisis. While there, he had constantly liaised with the American embassy in Leopoldville and stubbornly pursued what can only be described as his own foreign policy. As the Irish diplomat Conor Cruise O'Brien, a special representative to Hammarskjold in the Congo, wrote, Alexander not only participated in the disarming of troops loyal to Lumumba, many of whom had mutinied early in the crisis, he also proposed to retrain rebels and mercenaries who had fought to help Katanga Province break away from the Congo. These were utterly inimical to Nkrumah's goals, and O'Brien called the idea "scarcely a project that any Secretary-General would relish having to explain to the General Assembly."[8]

Nkrumah interpreted Alexander's behavior in the Congo as evidence that, at least since Lumumba's assassination, the West had abandoned support for anything resembling genuine decolonization in Africa. What it offered instead was a feigned assistance while in fact it was actively scheming to undermine progressive governments on the continent and perpetuate its dominance. After returning to Britain, Alexander didn't exactly disabuse people of this view, either. Speaking about his tour in Ghana in one televised interview, he boldly declared, "I have always wanted to serve with the British Army. But I'll always do what I'm told in the interests of the British Army and Britain."[9]

Nkrumah's defiance of Britain and the West in his firing of Alexander and over the Congo, like his outreach to Moscow for military training, re-aggravated relations with Washington and generated new doubts about its support for the VRP. Citing these issues, Kennedy told Ball that he had "given up" on Nkrumah and was now considering making some token gesture of aid to Ghana instead of the long-promised backing for the VRP.[10] Ball had recently advocated simply postponing the assistance on the theory that Nkrumah would soon be overthrown.

With longstanding plans for Queen Elizabeth to make her rescheduled visit to Ghana in November, the political turbulence and the background radiation emanating from Cold War competition there confronted London with a difficult decision, to cancel her trip or not. Ghana had also recently suffered a spate of bombings, including one that badly damaged the statue of Nkrumah that stood outside of the National Assembly, heightening security concerns. Prime Minister Harold Macmillan wrote to Kennedy to urge him to formalize America's support for the dam. The decision, he said:

> will really depend on whether one thinks that economic aid should really only be given to allies or whether it should be used to "make friends and influence people." In the present state of the world, however much we may dislike it, I think we ought to take the latter view.[11]

Kennedy did not act as quickly as Macmillan had wished, but the Queen's visit went off not only without incident, but with much jubilation. Nkrumah met Elizabeth on the airport tarmac in Accra wearing a white suit coordinated to match her cream-colored lace one. Both African and Western gestures of hospitality were brought to bear: a traditional Ghanaian libation of gin or schnaps was spilled onto the ground to wish for the Queen's continued health and well-being, and a twenty-one-gun salute was sounded. During another event, Nkrumah publicly praised the Commonwealth, easing British anxieties about Ghana's possible exit. The most resonant symbol of the success, though, was the foxtrot Nkrumah danced at a welcome ball with the plainly delighted royal.

Just after Elizabeth's eleven-day stay in Ghana ended, the British prime minister called Kennedy and told him bluntly, "I have risked my Queen. You must risk your money," to which Kennedy agreed verbally, even if he did not act immediately. The American president was still facing pressure from Congress, as well as from within his own government and even his inner circle, to deny help to Nkrumah. For example, when Tennessee's influential Democratic Senator Gore traveled to Ghana, he was told by Nkrumah that the notion that he wished to ally himself with the Soviet Union or even adopt its ideology was completely misplaced. Gore concluded that Nkrumah "was so obsessed with colonialism that he was blind to Soviet colonialism," a remarkable statement about a country that had only just emerged from colonial rule. He advised the president to terminate American support for Ghana on essentially Cold War grounds. In the end, this did not persuade Kennedy, but a secondary argument from the senator was well-founded and underscored the tragedy of the entire dam project endeavor. He said that the VRP's terms were wonderful for Valco, the Kaiser consortium behind the dam, but made little economic sense for Ghana.[12]

DESPITE AT LEAST ONE NEW ROUND OF AMERICAN SIGNALING THAT IT HAD given final approval for the VRP, more back and forth followed in the months after Elizabeth's visit, rubbing leaders raw in both Accra and Washington.

All manner of arguments were still being raised to advocate for abandoning American support. There was Nkrumah's continuing criticism of the West's role in the Congo, his friendly statements toward communist leaders and their nations during his tour of the East, his plans to have four hundred Ghanaian troops sent to the Soviet Union for training, and the Ghanaian's ongoing rhetorical attacks on neocolonialism. Another line of attack on Nkrumah, though, was essentially psychological. He was increasingly held to be mentally not quite right. Earlier in the year, one CIA assessment of Nkrumah, as patronizing as it was damning, had concluded:

> When you cut away all the trappings and the fanfare you are left with a 49-year-old showboy, and a vain opportunist . . . a brilliant politician but not a great statesman, a man with a few set ideas and no great flexibility or depth of vision, a man beginning to slip just a bit and too conceited to see it, a politician to whom the roars of the crowd and the praise of the sycophant are as necessary as the air he breathes.[13]

Some, like the liberal Democrat Adlai Stevenson, the US ambassador to the United Nations who had visited Ghana several times, portrayed Nkrumah as a Soviet puppet and advocated for suspension of all American assistance to the country, not just funds for the VRP. In personal as much as political terms, Kennedy had become deeply invested. The State Department had placed Ghana on a monthly checklist of key countries that was poured over in the Oval Office.[14] Kennedy sent new envoys to Ghana to probe Nkrumah's intentions, demanding to be convinced of his neutrality, of his commitment to safeguarding private investment, and of his tolerance for democracy. In almost every conversation, Nkrumah, increasingly desperate to seal construction of the VRP, offered reassurances, but never to Washington's complete satisfaction.

Kennedy also reached out to other African leaders, awkwardly focusing on two francophone presidents, Léopold Senghor of Senegal, who managed to be both conservative and socialist, and Félix Houphouët-Boigny of the Ivory Coast, an autocrat, and one of the most conservative and pro-Western rulers in all of West Africa. Although very different, both of these men constantly hewed closely to France and opposed Nkrumah's pan-Africanist project. During a helicopter flight over Washington with Kennedy in which they viewed the Lincoln Memorial, Senghor, nonetheless, urged the United States to maintain its support for Ghana's dam. This, he said, would demonstrate that "U.S. aid is not given to purchase friendship." Houphouët-Boigny, who had frequently locked horns with Nkrumah, including over the Ghanaian's support for a small secessionist movement in the Ivory Coast's border region with Ghana, took the opposite position. In a conversation in Abidjan during a visit by Robert Kennedy, the Ivorian spoke of Nkrumah as a dangerous demagogue who sought to dominate the entire region.[15]

On December 6, 1961, with Kennedy presiding, the National Security Council (NSC) met to reach a final decision on the dam, but no consensus about Nkrumah emerged. Some officials likened Nkrumah to an African Castro who they said would propagate communism on the continent. Others emphasized that Kennedy had already committed himself in writing and that to pull back would dishonor the United States. Remarkably, given the long history of loose talk about Nkrumah's supposed communism, John McCone of the CIA flatly denied that Nkrumah was a cat's paw for Moscow.[16]

A recollection from the United States ambassador to Ghana at the time, given years later, provides perhaps the most nuanced and perceptive American assessment of Ghana's president. William P. Mahoney said of Nkrumah:

> He had a scintillating personality. He was a tremendously impressive man to meet. I think he was a man with all kinds of problems, we all have them of course. I think he was kind of mixed up. He was part juju, part Catholic, part Marxist, you name it.[17]

If one takes "juju" to mean Nkrumah's unabashed defense of indigenous systems of belief and tradition—elements of what he called the African personality—this was a concise description of the versatility that Nkrumah had begun to display already in his youth. Mahoney, a fellow Catholic who met with Nkrumah frequently through some of the worst ups and downs of relations between Washington and Accra, likened Nkrumah to Saint John, saying that in his ceaseless advocacy for pan-Africanism, "he was making straight the way." Mahoney also likened Nkrumah's efforts to bring Africa together under his leadership to the Democratic Party politician of the 1960s, Minnesota Senator Eugene McCarthy, who ran and lost a nearly quixotic antiwar presidential primary campaign in 1968. In his 1975 interview, Mahoney also notably went on to remark about Nkrumah's brief against neocolonialism, "I hate to say it, but you know he had a case." At the end of 1961, in fact, events playing out between the United States and Ghana would bear this out.

After the December NSC meeting, Kennedy decided to seek yet more assurances from Nkrumah, dispatching an envoy carrying a letter from him that read, "I have, with some reluctance and misgivings, decided to authorize U.S. financial assistance to the project." Before the envoy had even landed in Accra, the US announced its decision to provide $37 million dollars to Ghana for the VRP. Washington also agreed to lend $96 million and provide investment guarantees worth another $54 million to Valco, the Kaiser-led consortium. The announcement came with warnings by George Ball that the US could still withdraw from the project if unspecified conditions were not met.

Even this seeming end to the saga did not prove conclusive, though. Through Kennedy's envoy, a steel executive named Clarence Randall, Washington demanded that Nkrumah make a public statement addressing its concerns around capitalism and democracy. "While the United States does not wish to interfere internally in Ghana or any other country, it is reasonable to expect that recipient countries share the same basic ideals of freedom and justice as we," Randall explained.[18]

Nkrumah told the Americans he would go on the radio to address their concerns on December 22 and then provided a draft of his address for their review beforehand. The text drew instant complaints from Washington. Respect for private enterprise was covered, but Ambassador Russell found other things to object to, including what he perceived to be digs at the West. Obligingly, Nkrumah agreed to rewrite the speech and once again submitted it to the Americans for review. This draft passed the ambassador's inspection and was given final approval by Dean Rusk, who issued yet another final American assurance that its support for the project would now proceed. It came with a cherry on top. Washington agreed to Nkrumah's request that the signing ceremony be held in Accra.[19]

Nearly two-thirds of a century later, what should one make of all of this back and forth? The first thing is that the Americans come off every bit as unsteady as they considered Nkrumah to be. One benefit enjoyed by the very powerful has always been exemption from the critical standards that they use to assess others. Kennedy had begun his almost romantic obsession with Africa with a vow to break with the Cold War habits of his predecessors. In its generosity, Washington would respect African nonalignment and not lean on newly independent states to accept its ideological priors. This approach was never officially revoked, of course, but it came to an end here with this diplomacy in Ghana. Sorting the continent out along Cold War lines would henceforth become the norm, not just under Kennedy, but under the presidents who followed him.

Senator Albert Gore Sr. of Tennessee had rightly understood that Nkrumah's white whale, the VRP, was no economic homerun for Ghana. It was so costly that it would cripple the country's efforts to pursue more immediate and practical measures to improve the economy, from investing in agriculture to spending more on basic things like roads, education, and public health. Meanwhile, it would not lead to the kind of industrialization that Nkrumah had dreamed of. But it posed even more problems than these. Ghana was effectively subsidizing the production of rich American mining and metals companies by charging Kaiser so little for its electricity from the dam. And that is what the United States would be doing, too, with the financial backing that Nkrumah had so long pleaded and lobbied for. American support for private overseas investment like this was still unusual at the time, and Kaiser had managed to win this through relentless personal and political lobbying of its own.

What had Kennedy won for the United States, though? This, too, must be understood, finally, in Cold War terms. The $37 million to Ghana was a pittance for America, but its most powerful effects were exerted outside of the poor African country it was earmarked for. American support for the VRP can be understood best as a ruse, or what's called a head fake in sports, to fool the Soviets, whose economy was less than half as large, into believing Washington was assigning serious economic importance to the continent, and thereby to greatly raise the economic stakes for Moscow. In the era before a superpower competition of military alliances and strong client relationships had taken off in Africa in the late 1970s, the Volta River project was foremost an American propaganda victory. It was an exhibit in what was shaping up, for now, to be a beauty contest involving trade, investment, and aid—things that the Soviets could not as easily muster. To remain relevant, the USSR, henceforth, would have to pony up funds for big projects here and there, and this would not come easily for Moscow.

Finally, it would be naïve to simply take Washington's concerns about democracy in Ghana at face value. There is no doubt that Nkrumah was moving his country ever deeper into authoritarianism at this time, and that his own political instincts were feeding into a tragedy in the making. The thickening atmosphere of authoritarianism in Ghana was not only true according to American standards or notions of democracy and human rights. The rule of law was in such steep decline and the focus of political life was becoming so concentrated in the person of Nkrumah himself that progressives and socialists who had strongly backed Ghana's push for independence and pan-Africanism began to express their disapproval. These included people with backgrounds as different as C. L. R. James, who maintained an active correspondence with Nkrumah throughout this period, and Bill Sutherland, the African American civil rights pioneer and pacifist. Short, wispy-haired, and mild in manner and tone, Sutherland was a man of tremendous moral fiber. It had carried him through the harsh mistreatment he endured during thirty-eight months of prison for conscientious objection to World War II and through principled struggles against nuclear arms and apartheid in South Africa and its cousin in America. As devoted as he was to African liberation, he was unwilling to compromise on individual rights and protested Nkrumah's tightening grip over his society with his feet, as just mentioned, leaving Ghana for Julius Nyerere's Tanganyika.

The thing is that Washington had never really been put off by dictatorship in Africa before and was steadily growing less inhibited about supporting and even promoting despots there all the time. Examples of this are plentiful. Perhaps the best is one already familiar to readers of this narrative and involves the Congo. There, the United States helped overthrow and plot to assassinate the elected leader of a newly independent country and then engineered his replacement with one of the most notorious and enduring dictators of Africa's twentieth century, Mobutu Sese Seko. Candor compels the conclusion that Washington became Mobutu's strongest backer because having dependable allies on the continent during the Cold War was deemed far more important than democracy, African or otherwise. And Washington's biggest problems with Nkrumah went to this same question: reliability. Nkrumah was far too versatile in the sense we have used here, too independent-minded, and for the leader of a country of Ghana's size, insufficiently servile. His growing antidemocratic tendencies paled before concerns like these. Nkrumah was exasperating to the West. He rubbed the wise men and poohbahs of Washington and London raw, and one can almost hear them wondering, as Napoleon did toward another outsized Black figure on the world stage during the previous century, just who does this N-word think he is?

CHAPTER THIRTY-NINE

Hail Mary

IN 1962, A FEW WEEKS SHY OF THE FIRST ANNIVERSARY OF HIS RETURN FROM his Eastern tour, Nkrumah set off on yet another voyage. This time, he was at work on regional diplomacy, visiting Upper Volta, the land-locked and much poorer former French colony to the north. It was Nkrumah's first big bid to parlay the Volta River project into greater sway in West Africa and, in the bargain, to extract Maurice Yaméogo, the head of state, from the controlling embrace of France and its functional capo in the region, Houphouët-Boigny.

By offering to provide Upper Volta with electricity from his dam, Nkrumah also hoped he might eventually be able to add it to the growing portfolio of states—all French-speaking—in the loose, proto federation that had begun with union agreements signed with Guinea and Mali. Ominous storm clouds, however, were already accumulating all around Nkrumah's rule in Ghana. Critics and foes called his pursuit of pan-Africanism an exorbitant distraction. But it was this, above all, that kept Nkrumah feeling energized and positive.

After heavy rains on the morning of August 1 on his overland return journey from this summit, Nkrumah's motorcade made an unscheduled stop in the remote, northern Ghanaian town of Kulungugu. There, his party was told, villagers wished to organize a welcome ceremony by local schoolchildren for the Osagyefo. An excited crowd formed around Nkrumah's party, and as a girl approached carrying a bouquet of flowers, someone tossed a grenade in the direction of the president. The flower girl was torn apart, as was at least one other person. Many others were hurt. Nkrumah was knocked to the ground and suffered a variety of flesh wounds. He was rushed to the nearest hospital, about eight miles away, where other injured people were also treated.

The headline for the coverage of the incident from Accra in the London *Guardian* read, "Attack on Nkrumah: Escapes Bomb Explosion," and the article went on to say that Queen Elizabeth had been among the first people to reach out to Nkrumah with a message of sympathy. "I have learnt with great concern of the attempt on your life and should like to convey to you the relief of my colleagues in the British Government and myself at your fortunate escape," it said.[1] Close, even obsessive, reporting about Ghana was routine by this time in the African American press, and it struck an entirely different note, one of conspiratorially minded suspicion. Not long after the attack, a front-page headline in the Baltimore *Afro-American*, for example, placed Nkrumah on the List of African Leaders **To Be Murdered** (original emphasis in bold). In a box just below, it went further still, linking the attempt on Nkrumah's life to the elimination of Lumumba and the deaths of other leaders in the Third World:

> List of slain political heads of the Freedom Movement in Asia and Africa already includes:
> Burma's Cabinet, Congo's Lumumba, UN's Hammarskjold, Ceylon's Premier, Prime Minister of Urundi (Africa), Mahatma Ghandi (sic)
> Suspected are 13 gigantic mining companies in control of Africa's resources from Congo to South Africa.[2]

The shock to Nkrumah's mental state was far worse than his bodily wounds, and for similar reasons: like the Afro-American headline writers, he could not help but see the attempt to kill him as part of something much bigger and even more sinister. The series of actions and reactions between Ghana's president and his enemies that the attack set in motion pitched the country rockily forward toward the tumultuous final phase of his rule.

After the railway worker's strike, spurred by the regime's influential, effective second-in-command, Tawia Adamafio, a dynamic and ambitious young leader of the CPP's left-wing faction, there emerged a concerted push to make Ghana a one-party state. The main justification invoked for this was the drag on progress created by the endless parliamentary debates, the stealthy forms of sabotage carried out by the opposition, and above all, the corruption of so-called counterrevolutionary elements within the country. The recently exiled Gbedemah was usually held up as a prime culprit for this last element of dysfunction. With the brazen grenade attack on Nkrumah, though, the push toward one-party rule vaulted into a higher gear, claiming an ever-greater basis for urgency: both from generalized insecurity and direct threats to the regime's survival. A referendum was organized to change the constitution to make the CPP the country's sole political party, although before that could happen the men behind the presidential assassination attempt had to be punished.

Nkrumah had long contemplated the idea of abandoning the Westminster style of government that Ghana had inherited. Historically speaking, authoritarianism had the seductive theoretical advantage of expediency, a common temptation faced by rulers of developing countries. In the preface to his autobiography, published at the very outset of his rule, Nkrumah had even written: "But even a system based on social justice and a democratic constitution may need backing up, during the period following independence, by emergency measures of a totalitarian kind."[3] This, we recall, was a book whose main purpose was to introduce Nkrumah in ways palatable to the Western-dominated world.

By now edging toward paranoia, Nkrumah cast aside all previous caution about concentrating power and eliminating pluralism. His suspicions over the origin of the attack quickly centered on a handful of people who were involved in his regional summit. Three of them—Adamafio; H. H. Cofie-Crabbe, the executive secretary of CPP; and the foreign minister, his friend since Lincoln College days, Ako Adjei—were political insiders and were arrested and tried for attempting to kill the president. In its panic, the regime had begun to commit autophagy, cannibalizing itself. Nkrumah then became infuriated when the three were found not guilty, and he took the fateful step of replacing the country's chief justice and ordering the men to be tried again. Upon their conviction, the three were condemned to life sentences. Nkrumah later commuted these to twenty-year terms.

In September 1962, barely a month after Kulungugu, two new bomb attacks were directed at Nkrumah in Accra. The first of these went off near the presidential offices at Flagstaff House, a long, rectangular, three-story building with a modernist facade fronted by a formal plaza with large shade trees and neat bushes. The complex housed Nkrumah's offices and residence. This blast was set off during a gathering of two thousand people for a celebration that involved song and dance just outside of the gates of the presidential headquarters. As many as five people were killed and sixty-three wounded, but Nkrumah, who was in front of his residence during the explosion, was at a safe distance from the detonation and stunned, but not hurt.

By now, it was almost impossible to blame the state of official alarm on paranoia. This was no manufactured crisis. And yet it was the government's own actions in the wake of these terror attacks that inflicted the most damage on Nkrumah's hold on power. The sub-headline in the front-page *New York Times* coverage of this second bomb attack said, "Dictatorial Pattern

Emerges," detailing the spate of jailings Nkrumah had ordered after the bombing at Kulungugu. "Despite Dr. Nkrumah's professions of nonalignment, his strongly anti-colonialist policies won him a Lenin Peace Prize, presented last July," the newspaper added.[4] In another dispatch a few days later, the *Times* headline stated, "Public Sees Less of Nkrumah Since Aug. 1 Blast: Some Believe He Fears New Attempt on His Life."[5]

Emergency decrees and arrests under the preventive detention law now began following one after another, and officials went into overdrive promoting suspicion of foreigners and spinning stories about Western efforts to destabilize Ghana. While Nkrumah retreated evermore from public view, the circle of those he confided in narrowed sharply.

Erica Powell, Nkrumah's stately and dependable personal secretary and confidante, described the president as demoralized by the attempts on his life. "Time and again when I entered his office and caught him unawares, I saw what seemed a shrunken, smaller version of himself seated at that enormous desk, his eyes gazing sadly into the distance."[6] On one such occasion, she said Nkrumah told her, "You are the only person I feel I can really trust, Erica."[7] Some of the high officials and aides who worked for Nkrumah also sought to freeze Powell out, urging him not to trust her on the premise that she might have been working undercover for the British. Nothing suggests that he ever believed this, but accusations of this nature hurt and rattled Powell and increased the pressure on Nkrumah, along with his sense of isolation.

Perhaps the worst decision he made under these circumstances was derailing judicial independence by placing his three associates in double jeopardy after the grenade attack at Kulungugu. As a result of this action, a wave of disillusionment about Nkrumah's Ghana began to spread among his longest-standing defenders.

In a Dear Francis letter to Nkrumah, C. L. R. James, who, after the deceased Padmore, was perhaps the person Nkrumah held in highest esteem, wrote, "This is a terrible business, bound to have effects far outside Ghana and in Ghana itself." James was tiptoeing, but the subject was clearly Nkrumah's dismissal of the chief justice after he acquitted the three CPP insiders. "I shall have to speak and write about it. . . . What I am concerned about is the impact that Ghana and you are making on the world and on Africa. . . . I hope, my dear Francis, you have people around you able to tell you plainly what is now required from you."[8]

When no reply came, James, then 61, published his letter. He wrote, "I suppose it brings to an end an association of twenty years that I have valued more than most," adding that "When people pointed out what they considered negative aspects of his régime I held my peace because I knew the positive aspects, the immense positive aspects." Foremost among these had been Nkrumah's work with Padmore toward "the expulsion of imperialism from Africa and the development of underdeveloped countries." But if Nkrumah had invited further correspondence, James said that he would have replied, "Mr. President, you cannot dismiss your Chief Justice after he has made a judgment from the Bench. Publicly declare that you made a mistake.... You continue with this dismissal and you dismiss all of us."[9]

By the first half of 1963, a look of worry had taken up permanent residence on Nkrumah's face. Dark bags formed under his eyes. His erstwhile unlined skin now showed furrows between his eyebrows and deep creases in his cheeks instead of smile lines. Standing more alone than ever before, Ghana's leader now presided over an economy in steep decline, leaving him embattled at home while he attempted to launch the second greatest gambit of his life. The first, his spearheading of Ghana's peaceful drive to independence, had seen him rise, bolting out of nowhere to overcome a series of seemingly impossible challenges, not least of which was obliging one of history's mightiest empires to loosen its grip on a prized colony. Remarkably, his new trial, although it involved fellow Africans, stood to be even more difficult.

During the extraordinary wave of independence in 1960, a new country was born almost every month, and sometimes two or three. This peaked with an August bonanza of four independence ceremonies spread widely around the continent. This outburst of freedom was nominal in many cases, given the continuing sway that colonial powers enjoyed. Perversely, though, it meant that realizing Nkrumah's vision of pan-Africanism, never easy to begin with, was becoming vastly more complicated. Instead of the piecemeal efforts of the past that had joined Ghana together, however loosely or ephemerally, with Guinea, Mali, and Congo, what was now required was convincing tens of freshly installed heads of state to cede much of their newly won power to a federation of states that could give Africa more say in the world.

Beyond this practical challenge, Nkrumah's pan-Africanist vision faced many other hindrances. First among them was Nkrumah himself. Many of his fellow African heads of state now saw his bid for continental government as bound up in personal aggrandizement. Not only was he promoting continental leadership, but in their eyes, he was fixated on, even obsessed with, becoming that leader himself. It particularly tried the patience of leaders of much larger countries, like Ghana's near-neighbor, Nigeria. It didn't help that his relations with countries to the immediate east and west, Côte d'Ivoire and

Togo, were contentious; both of them claimed that Ghana was fueling subversion and separatism.

A second objection to pan-Africanism flowed from one of imperialism's most insidious legacies. Africa was divided into language blocs that reflected their colonization by one European nation or another. No divide was deeper than the one between former English- and French-speaking colonies. Although Guinea was a notable exception, many of the French speakers, with persistent encouragement from Paris, were deeply averse to going along with Nkrumah in much of anything. Here, as so often, Félix Houphouët-Boigny, leader of Ghana's next-door neighbor, stood as Nkrumah's direct rival and fierce antagonist.

By 1963, Nkrumah had given decades of thought to African federalism. Many of his ideas were sparked by his experience as a student in the United States, and particularly his reading of *The Federalist Papers*, a collection of essays published in 1788, written by Alexander Hamilton, James Madison, and John Jay. For Nkrumah *The Federalist*'s relevance for Africa lay in its arguments against the decentralization of political power that had weakened American prospects under the Articles of Confederation. That decentralization, *The Federalist* argued, doomed the states to rivalry and conflict with each other. Moreover, and more important for Nkrumah, *The Federalist* argued that a weak association would sharply limit the states' diplomatic power in the world and cripple their attempts to build prosperous economies. The realization of Africa's full potential, he believed, could best be understood by analogy with the political processes that brought the thirteen American colonies together to form the United States.

Nkrumah brought these arguments to the founding conference of the Organization of African Unity (OAU), whose first Summit Conference was held in May 1963, in Addis Ababa. The last consequential international gathering over the future of Africa had been the Berlin Conference in 1884–85, shockingly near the end of the nineteenth century. At that time, the continent counted roughly one hundred million souls, a number that reflected both the African population's low density and its persistent stagnation, a result of the immense human drain and the death toll brought about by the centuries'-long international slave trade and the violence and chaos it generated. Since then the change in Africa's circumstances had been enormous. The population had exploded to two hundred and fifty million people. Like a forest of early spring croci, independence was breaking out everywhere. And for the first time in a major international council over the continent's fate, Africans themselves were in charge.

Bringing the thirty-two African leaders who traveled to Addis Ababa together in and of itself was a major feat. It required overcoming, at least temporarily, the gulf between progressives and conservatives that had deepened since 1957, when Ghana led the way as the first sub-Saharan country to obtain independence. From the outset, Nkrumah's push for pan-Africanism under some kind of federal structure had spurred critical reaction and resistance both from direct rivals of Nkrumah, such as Houphouët-Boigny, and from others, who took a more principled and impersonal stance. Some of them argued that running a newborn state was challenge enough without attempting to construct a continental government on the fly. For them, a relatively loose and toothless association of African states was plenty. To invest more authority in an Africa-wide body, they argued, would invite disaster.

These groups had previously coalesced into rival blocs. Nkrumah and his progressive allies—Algeria, Egypt, Ghana, Guinea, Libya, Mali, and Morocco—came to be known as the Casablanca Group. Pitted against them was the more numerous so-called Monrovia Group, which contained Nigeria, Africa's most populous nation, and most of France's former colonies. Beyond the task of assembling people across the Casablanca-Monrovia divide, the four-day conference brought together a wide array of personalities, from the reserved to the flamboyant, and varied degrees of intellectual and political sophistication. Julius Nyerere, for instance, was known to have translated Shakespeare's *Julius Caesar* into Swahili in his spare time in 1961. The French federalist experimenter Léopold Senghor was a renowned poet who, at one point, devoted a quarter of Senegal's budget to culture. Senghor championed "Negritude," a philosophy that celebrated the African past, along with an esthetics of Blackness. Besides men like these, who could hold their own in any international gathering on the basis of cultivation and intellect, there were many perfectly average or unremarkable figures, as well as some certifiable rogues. These included Jean-Bédel Bokassa, a former army sergeant who fought for the Free French forces in Europe; future self-proclaimed emperor of Central Africa, Mobutu Sese Seko of Zaïre; and Milton Obote, who would rule Uganda corruptly and tyrannically both before and after the dictatorship of Idi Amin.

Addressing his fellow African leaders, Nkrumah gamely likened the convening of heads of state or government of thirty-two countries to the 1787 Philadelphia Congress of twelve restive American colonies.[10] Those delegates had not yet forged anything like a common identity as Americans, let alone the solid institutional bonds and laws that durable nations are built on. They had come together in Philadelphia with little more than plans to strengthen the Articles of Confederation and had ended up with a constitution. Their gathering had at first been "a new and strange experience," Nkrumah said deftly inviting the assembled heads of state to see themselves on the cusp of history in this powerful light of the American analogy.[11] Through dialogue, debate, and compromise, including over the acceptance of slavery, he said, these proto-Americans had found ways to work together toward the building of a workable nation that, in time, became a vast and prosperous continental power. It went unmentioned, but another country had also assumed continental dimensions and tremendous power through amalgamation of a different kind, the Soviet Union.

From there, Nkrumah offered a cautionary counterexample. Africa could fail to meet this appointment with history and end up like Latin America, a continent whose inability to forge continental union had made it "the unwilling and distressed prey of imperialism after one-and-a-half centuries of political independence."[12]

Unfortunately for Nkrumah, and as many believe for Africa, too, Nkrumah's ideas went nowhere at the OAU's founding conference. The host, Haile Selassie, the bearded and diminutive Emperor, wore sober double-breasted suits instead of the military uniforms or imperial regalia he often favored. The seventy-year-old sovereign shared some of Nkrumah's diagnosis about the continent's fragmentation and its consequences and tried to soften the blow by saying that "unity is the accepted goal." He spoke about the importance for continental governance of projecting an African personality, and then he echoed another favorite idea of Nkrumah's, saying, "Our liberty is meaningless unless all Africans are free."[13]

Ethiopia hosted this august convocation of new African leaders in the grand-scale Africa Hall, which had been completed in 1961, to house the UN Economic Commission for Africa. In fact, inside, it looked like a United Nations in miniature, housing a central table with space for five speakers, before which a vast, horseshoe-shaped table was arrayed with seating for each African state.

What the wizened Selassie's response to Nkrumah meant in practice was that for now, the conference should focus on the ways that Africans could cooperate, short of any form of federation, through the OAU. For the foreseeable future, there would be no dismantling of old borders. There would be no continental military or high command to combat apartheid, liberate the remaining Portuguese colonies, or defend African sovereignty in festering crises like those in the Congo. There would be no common market or currency, nor even a continental bank. Nkrumah, gravely disappointed, but powerless to move his fellows further, concluded that without unity, the various forms of cooperation that the conference had agreed upon were "no more than words on paper."[14]

Decades later, in retirement, Julius Nyerere—his nation's Mwalimu, or teacher, and by then the former president and still revered founding father of Tanzania—spoke about Nkrumah's impatience and frustration over the OAU falling short of his goal of continental unity in Addis Ababa in 1963. As an interim measure, the personally modest and sagacious Nyerere said that at the time, he had offered to delay his country's independence if that would provide enough time for Kenya and Uganda to join with his country in an East African federation. By then, in retirement, humbled by his own long years in power, which were spent struggling against seemingly intractable problems of African underdevelopment and division on a mostly national or at best regional scale, he related:

> My differences with Kwame were that Kwame thought there was somehow a shortcut, and I was saying that there was no shortcut. This is what we have inherited, and we'll have to proceed within the limitations that that inheritance has imposed on us. Kwame thought that somehow you could say, "Let there be a United States of Africa" and it would happen. I kept saying, "Kwame, it's a slow process." He had tremendous contempt for a large number of leaders of Africa and I said, "Fine, but they are there. What are you going to do with them? They don't believe as you do—as you and I do—in the need for the unity of Africa.... This is what we have been able to achieve. No builder, after putting the foundation down, complains that the building is not yet finished. You have to go on building and building until you finish; but he was impatient because he saw the stupidity of the others.[15]

So much of Nkrumah's nature is crystalized here: his love of ideas, his profound belief in the power of argument, and in his own force of will, his fundamental urge to race forward toward his goals for the continent and to never be deterred. In Africa, though, he had finally met something immovable, for all his efforts, and although he had no such intimations, by this time, his own political end in Ghana was near.

ON THE EVENING OF NOVEMBER 22, 1963, THE AMERICAN AMBASSADOR TO Ghana received an unexpected telephone call. The voice at the other end of the line that Friday night was that of Kwame Nkrumah. It was only the second time they had spoken by phone. "Is it true?" Nkrumah asked simply, in his large, deep voice. "Yes, I'm afraid it is, Mr. President," came the ambassador's reply. "What can I do?" Nkrumah said. The ambassador, a fellow Catholic, mumbled something about sending a cable to Mrs. Kennedy before urging Nkrumah to say a Hail Mary. "I'm on my knees now," Nkrumah replied, and hung up.[16]

By this time, because of the frequent attempts on his own life, Nkrumah had become a near recluse. The Monday following Kennedy's murder an evening mass was held in Accra's imposing cathedral before a packed gathering. Surely, few who were present had known or even seen Kennedy in person, but tears flowed and muffled sobs could be heard in the crowded pews. Later that night, Nkrumah went on the radio to pay tribute to the fallen American president.[17]

All his life, personal relationships mattered inordinately to Kwame Nkrumah, and in the few years that he had interacted with John F. Kennedy, he had come to admire and possibly even idolize him. Nkrumah was, of course, far from alone. With his optimistic rhetoric and greater willingness to hear out the concerns of leaders in the Third World, Kennedy had been widely embraced. Nkrumah's powerful feelings for Kennedy often overrode his many objections to American leadership in the world, toward the voracious capitalism epitomized by the United States in this era. They also survived the sharp vicissitudes Nkrumah had experienced in dealing with the Kennedy government over the VRP. This included Nkrumah's agreement on the spot when a request was made on Kennedy's behalf to deny the Soviets overflight rights in Ghana's airspace during the Cuban Missile Crisis, as Guinea had also done. "No problem. No questions," Nkrumah told the US ambassador, William P. Mahoney flatly. "Under no circumstances will they be able to do anything vaguely resembling that."[18]

Mahoney, who visited Nkrumah in his book-lined office many times, said it contained three photographs of figures of global political renown, Khrushchev, Mao, and Kennedy, but it was the latter that was given the most prominent display. It was not a widely known image then; it showed the President and his wife, Jacqueline, walking arm in arm out of a chapel together in Palm Beach, Florida. She wore a powder blue outfit and a pillbox hat, her eyes focused on the stairs as they descended. Squinting in the sun, he looked straight ahead, smiling, a crimson prayer book in his right hand.

Even with the personal bond that seemed to exist between Kennedy and Nkrumah, relations between Ghana and the United States had become ever more parlous over the last year of the Kennedy presidency. His administration had come very close to throwing in the towel on Nkrumah, and its support for the dam had barely survived. The ascent of Lyndon Baines Johnson boded ill for Nkrumah, and the bilateral relationship.

IF KENNEDY'S INTEREST IN AFRICA AND HIS COMMITMENT TO PERSONAL diplomacy had favored Nkrumah, Lyndon Baines Johnson's markedly different priorities helped foreclose the Nkrumah experiment. Even though ideology pushed them apart, Kennedy could still not help but identify with the idealist dreamer whom he recognized in Nkrumah. Moreover, he was hardly unmindful of Nkrumah's popular aura and influence as a leader on the continent he somewhat regarded as the world's new frontier. As the first OAU summit revealed, Nkrumah was but one African head of state among many by the time the Johnson presidency began on November 22, 1963. His sway on the continent was greatly diluted even as he was increasingly embattled at home.

Taking office under tragic circumstances, Johnson swore to pursue to completion the civil rights agenda of his predecessor. Because of this, Johnson shared almost none of Kennedy's need to appeal to Black Americans through heavy engagement with Africa. Kennedy had only adopted civil rights as a priority late in his abbreviated presidency and had never articulated a full vision of how to assure legal equality for the country's Black minority. It is not going too far to say that Johnson now made this his political calling, if not his obsession. In this sense, he was the reverse of the Massachusetts brahmin. Johnson, once a keen Texan segregationist, was willing to risk hostility in his native South to win broader national favor, especially in the American North. "We've lost the South for a generation," Johnson is said to have exclaimed about his Democratic Party after the signing of the historic Civil Rights Act of 1964, the most sweeping civil rights legislation in nearly a century.[19]

With the advent of this new administration, Nkrumah had lost Washington right away, and it was as if Africa had been abandoned once again in light of more pressing global obligations. Indeed, Vietnam almost immediately became all-consuming for the US. There was more to it than this, though. As someone whose reputation in politics had been built on vote counting as a former master of the Senate, in his biographer Robert A. Caro's famous words, Johnson was instinctively a "you're either with us or against us" sort of leader: less tolerant of what he saw as standoffishness or defiance in the rulers of small countries.[20] "A curtain dropped," recalled Ambassador Mahoney, in terms of White House interest in Africa, and with presidential interest no longer a priority in Ghana, patience in Washington with Nkrumah evaporated.

Following the assassination attempt at Kulungugu and the explosion outside the presidential residence at Flagstaff House, Nkrumah became haunted and withdrawn. In this bygone era, general circulation newspapers in major cities across the United States covered the world, and the world still very much included Africa. "Ghana's Chief Stays Out of Public View," read one headline in the *Chicago Daily Tribune*.[21] The *Boston Globe* went even further, running a scurrilous article filled with dog whistles that called Nkrumah a frightened fetishist who had secluded himself in his official residence, turning it into a "temple of sorcery." This came under a headline that read, "Ghana President Hated by Nearly Everyone: Chief Fears Death." Even progressive sycophants were plotting a coup against him, the article claimed, adding that Nkrumah "acts frightened, sleeps little, trusts almost no one. His aunt cooks—and tastes—his food."[22]

Ghana soon saw yet more acts of political terror. Bombings in Accra killed dozens of people and injured perhaps three hundred more.[23] On the second day of 1964 came another attempt on Nkrumah's life. Early that afternoon, as he was leaving the presidential office at Flagstaff House, a police constable who was newly assigned to the guard there fired on him with a rifle from about fifty yards. People all around dove for cover.

When Nkrumah's bodyguard rose to survey the scene, he was struck in the head and killed. When the shooter ran out of bullets, Nkrumah jumped up and ran, shouting for help, but drew no assistance, an almost unimaginable tableau, as if JFK, shot, would have had no police or bodyguards coming to his side. In this instance, the shooter pursued the president into the kitchen of his office building, where the two men began to grapple. After being bit on the cheek, the president, who was a fitness buff, got the better of his attacker, knocking him down and out, fueling yet another legend of immortality around Osagyefo. To many, the man now appeared physically invincible, but he was fast approaching the nadir of his power.[24]

With a welter of fear and paranoia now gripping the government, Nkrumah sacked a number of senior police officials and placed his personal security in the hands of the army, instead. Distrusting everyone required constant hedging. Some of his presidential guard was newly trained by the Soviet Union, and others via the traditional method, with its British roots and traditions. Even with this new setup, Nkrumah isolated himself from others more than ever.

Near the end of 1964, after yet another serious assassination attempt on Nkrumah, Ghana moved toward becoming a one-party state by holding a constitutional referendum. Implausibly, 92 percent of Ghanaians voted in favor of eliminating pluralism, a sure indication of fraud. In some regions, such as the Asante, which had long been associated with opposition to Nkrumah, the approval was total. This was one of the oldest delusions of centralizers and authoritarians, that unity could be achieved by writing it into the law. Making the referendum outcome even less believable was the fact that Ghana, by this time, was in deep economic disarray, and discontent about government mismanagement and corruption was widespread. Now, a widely used epithet for Nkrumah's ruling CPP was "Corrupt People's Party."[25] A deep cynicism had also taken hold about the costs of pan-Africanism, which were increasingly blamed as the source of Ghana's economic woes.

Even as he faced an oncoming storm, Nkrumah never trimmed his sails. In 1964, the government officially launched an ambitious agenda called the Programme for Work and Happiness that called for the launching of ever more state-run enterprises and the absorption of 1.1 million citizens into the wage economy by 1970. All the while, Ghana was spending a greater proportion of its GDP on education than many rich nations. These goals were aimed not only at increasing the prosperity and well-being of Ghanaians but also at ensuring that Ghana would be a pacesetter in economic development for the entire continent.

The sad reality was that the means for carrying out these policies no longer existed. Ghana lacked not only capital but human capacity as well. As the United States shifted its economic engagement away from Africa, incoming aid from the Soviet Union and its allies still paled in comparison to Ghana's needs. Even political exhortation, the final tool at Nkrumah's disposal, was failing. Material progress had stalled or even reversed in the lives of most Ghanaians. The more the state and the CPP insisted on loyalty and devotion to the leader and his agenda for the nation and for Africa, the less people believed.

CHAPTER FORTY

The Way Home

For one notable group, Nkrumah's revolution remained vibrant: the generation of international-minded African Americans who struggled in the coterminous civil rights movements of the United States and Africa, but who saw little hope for themselves in their native land. In fact, their enthusiasm for pan-Africanism and Ghana was undiminished and perhaps even rising.

Nkrumah's earliest connections with Black America had been forged three decades prior and had been stoked immeasurably more during Ghana's inspirational rise to independence. In that era Nkrumah had been a cultural and political icon both to leaders and to rank-and-file supporters of the Black rights movement. In the early 1950s, when Bill Sutherland had set off for Ghana, he had been one of a tiny cohort of pioneers. But now, even as Ghana seemed to plunge into a downward spiral, a new generation of African Americans, far younger than Sutherland, was showing up in Ghana in greater numbers.

Less than a century removed from the official end of slavery in the United States, they made their pilgrimage to Ghana in the belief that their best chance at redemption and self-affirmation lay in what they saw as a return to the African motherland and in the embrace of pan-Black unity. They saw Ghana—with a name that harkened back to the era of the continent's great empires, with connections to the birth of the modern world through the production of great quantities of gold, with a dark history of enslavement that helped populate the Americas—as the fountainhead. Many of them despaired that the American civil rights movement, which was contested on every front, could ever deliver unto them full citizenship rights, personal security, and equality in both opportunity and before the law.

One need think only of the headline events of 1963 to grasp their pessimism. Water hoses and fierce police dogs were turned on Black protestors who demanded school integration; people who organized sit-ins at lunch counters throughout the South were beaten. Fannie Lou Hamer was savaged. Medgar Evers was murdered, and Birmingham's 16th Street Baptist Church was bombed, killing four girls. Members of the Student Nonviolent Coordinating Committee (SNCC) who mounted a voter registration drive in benighted Mississippi were attacked viciously. And even as these events were playing out across the South, the Black protest movement and violent reactions against it were newly unfurling in the North, more complicit in the perpetuation of racial segregation than was recognized at the time.

Not everyone knew it, but their "return" to Ghana was the fulfillment of ideals that were much older even than Nkrumah's mid-century pan-Africanism. Nkrumah was now the living incarnation of this ideal, but the unbroken line stretched all the way back to Edward Blyden, Martin Delany, Africanus Horton, Archibald Casely Hayford, and Marcus Garvey.

The written recollections of the early 1960s pilgrims vividly convey the extraordinary sense of the enthusiasm and innocence that they brought to Ghana, whose deep troubles somewhat eluded many of them.

In 1962 Maya Angelou moved from Cairo to Accra with her son, Guy. In her indelible memoir of her three years there, *All God's Children Need Traveling Shoes*, she spoke of "fall[ing] in love, heedless, with the country." She worked at the University of Ghana and frequented the community of Black American pilgrims, in spirit both exiles and returnees. In endless nighttime palavers, these compatriots raised their voices together in "lambasting America and extolling Africa." Angelou and others from this circle, such as Alice Windom and Julian Mayfield, even marched on the American embassy in Accra to denounce American racism and warn of a civil war in the United States.[1]

> We drank gin and ginger ale when we could afford it, and Club beer when our money was short. We did not discuss the open gutters along the streets of Accra, the shacks of corrugated iron in certain neighborhoods, dirty beaches and voracious mosquitoes. And under no circumstances did we mention our disillusionment at being overlooked by the Ghanaians.[2]

"We wanted someone to embrace us and maybe congratulate us because we had survived," Angelou added. "If they felt the urge, they could thank us for having returned." It was only by and by that the newcomers discovered that "our arrival had little impact on anyone but us. We ogled the Ghanaians and few of them even noticed."[3]

One of the most perspicacious memoirs of this time came from the distinguished, two-time Pulitzer Prize–winning African American historian David Levering Lewis, who arrived in Accra in September 1963, armed with a recently minted doctorate in European history from the London School of History and an early release from the US Army because he had received a college teaching offer. It was in Ghana.

The square-jawed Lewis, who favored metal-framed eyeglasses and sported a neatly cropped, sandy-hewed afro, considered himself and others to be answering a call to hegira that Nkrumah had issued to the grandsons and granddaughters of Du Bois's so-called talented tenth. These members of an accomplished and self-confident African American professional class of educators, lawyers, physicians, journalists, and others arrived by the scores as "serenely ill-informed enthusiasts to Accra, the Pan-African Mecca, from Harlem, Atlanta, Chicago, Berkeley, and other American elsewheres."[4]

Like so many others, Lewis had been struck by the resonant symbolism at work in Nkrumah's Ghana—the national flag with its earthy stripes and a bold Garveyite black star at its center, the massive and formal Black Star Square at the heart of Accra with its triumphal arch, and the brick and glass Bauhaus-style African Research Centre named for George Padmore, among others. In Accra, he marveled, in characteristically grand language, that one found "the consummate synthesis of all that African destiny and unity portended." Many of the newcomers found it intoxicating.[5]

In 1961, at Nkrumah's invitation, Du Bois had come to Ghana with his wife Shirley at the age of ninety-one to finish out his life in a new homeland as he tackled his grand final project, the *Encyclopedia Africana*. The United States had revoked his passport in 1950 to sanction his radicalism, and by now, he was so thoroughly disgusted with the land of his birth that, in the twilight of his life, he renounced his American citizenship and legally became Ghanaian.

While researching this book, I wandered the town of Great Barrington, Massachusetts, where Du Bois was born, searching for material signs of his days there, but nowadays, nothing survives of the man's childhood home except a clearing in a sun-dappled patch of pine forest off the highway where songbirds call. In Accra, Nkrumah had provided him with a simple but expansive one-story bungalow in the center of town; today a bust of the old man sits atop a plinth at the head of the walkway. On the day of my most recent visit, I trailed along behind a guide named Ama as she led a group of Black South Carolinian visitors through the villa's musty, book-filled rooms. Framed high on the walls of one room were black and white portraits of Du Bois, Marcus Garvey, Booker T. Washington, Martin Luther King Jr., and Malcolm X. Never mind that Garvey and Du Bois frequently feuded. Here, now together, they were forever intertwined as heroes and patriarchs.

Du Bois finally died at the age of ninety-five, three months before Lewis had arrived in Accra. He had published his doctoral thesis at Harvard, "The Suppression of the African Slave Trade to the United States, 1638–1870," as a monograph in 1896, and his intellectual outpourings and political activism had singularly defined his era. As if slyly arranged by a god of history, his passing came on the very eve of an event that seemed to proclaim a new age: the great civil rights March on Washington for Jobs and Freedom in 1963.

That August 28, I stood in the ferociously bright sun for long hours on the National Mall as an impressionable but only loosely comprehending six-year-old. Together with my siblings and two hundred and fifty thousand others, in what was probably the biggest crowd ever assembled there up to that time, I listened to Martin Luther King's defining "I Have a Dream" oration as Mahalia Jackson whispered into his ear. Whatever history was, I might have thought, it was enormous, full of spectacle and drama, and coming mighty fast. Years later, Lewis would become a Du Bois biographer.

LEWIS FOUND HISTORY COMING ON FAST THEN IN GHANA, TOO. BY THAT point in his brief life, Malcom X was looking for a new home, less a place of physical residence than a global purview for his expansive soul. He had once derided the grand 1963 March on Washington as the "Farce on Washington," holding to the base notion preached by the heterodox Nation of Islam that all white people were fundamentally evil. Confronted about this by Mike Wallace, a CBS journalist in 1959, Malcolm responded:

> You can go to any little Muslim child and ask him where is hell and who is the devil, and he wouldn't tell you that hell was down in the ground and that the devil is something invisible and you can't see. He'll tell you that hell is right where he has been catching it and he'll tell you the one who is responsible for having received this hell is the devil.[6]

During his two visits to Ghana in 1964, Malcolm, who grew up in a Garveyite household, was rapidly molting. He chafed at the lingering prominence of whites in jobs around Nkrumah.[7] But in Egypt, where he had spent time just before Accra, and in a pilgrimage to Mecca, Malcolm had also been struck by the broad palette of racial phenotypes he had seen in public spaces and crowds of Muslim faithful. He understood that it was not only their faith that they held in common, but their humanity.

In a speech at the University of Ghana, Malcolm famously said, "I don't feel that I'm a visitor in Ghana or in any part of Africa. I feel that I am home. I've been away for four-hundred years, but not of my own volition, not of my own will."[8] Lewis witnessed the incendiary visit's speech, writing that Malcolm "strode nervously back and forth on the stage like a lean, young lion." Lewis also heard Malcolm conclude that "racial justice could be achieved only in coalition with people of all colors who believe in equality."[9]

Malcolm's visit to Ghana came at an awkward time for Nkrumah, as he had a simultaneous visit from the aluminum company executive Henry Kaiser and was contending with growing hostility from the Johnson administration. This was not a moment for Nkrumah to embellish his radical reputation, not that American cold warriors needed any encouragement in their skepticism toward him.

The meeting between Nkrumah and Malcolm X was arranged in impromptu fashion by Shirley Graham Du Bois, after she had chatted at length with Malcolm during a reception. "This man is brilliant.... He must meet Kwame," Du Bois concluded. "They have too much in common not to meet."[10] In some respects, Malcolm and Nkrumah were an ill-matched pair: two enormous personalities, both with a love of learning and rapier wit, but both also deeply accustomed to being in the center ring. Secondhand accounts of their private conversation make it sound formal and awkward. In any event, it was too brief to get very deeply into the big topics they mentioned, which ranged from pan-Africanism and civil rights to ancestral connections between Africans and American Blacks.[11]

In between his two African trips Malcolm X publicly embraced the mainstream Sunni form of Islam. He had divorced from the Nation of Islam, disenchanted by the lavish lifestyle and adultery of its leader, Elijah Muhammad. And Muhammad had sanctioned Malcolm over his comment that the Kennedy assassination, an act of political violence, was "merely a case of chickens coming home to roost."[12]

Malcolm's travels on the continent left him a changed man. Nkrumah's pan-Africanism—and especially the living embodiment of Nkrumah's ideas that he had plunged into while in Ghana—stoked his growing ambition of reconnecting African Americans with the broader Black world. On June 28, 1964, Malcolm X launched the Organization of Afro-American Unity (OAAU) at the Audubon Ballroom in New York, the very site where he would be gunned down eight months later. Its first article, under the heading "Restoration," proclaimed that "it is absolutely necessary for the Afro-American to restore communication with Africa." It's second, titled "Reorientation," added, "We can learn much about Africa by reading informative books and by listening to the experiences of those who have traveled there, but many of us can travel to the land of our choice and experience for ourselves."

Nkrumah had a deeper effect still on yet another African American who had risen fast on the national scene, one Stokely Carmichael. He was born in the Trinidad of Padmore and James and lived there to the age of eleven, then moved to New York City in the early 1950s. Under the tutelage of Ella Baker, Carmichael had been among the first freedom riders of the Student Nonviolent Coordinating Committee (SNCC) in 1961, where he had also received copious advice from Bayard Rustin, a gay Black man and committed pacifist who would prove his organizational genius on both sides of the Atlantic.

Carmichael's father, Adolphus, had mostly worked as a carpenter and taxi driver, but he had also been employed in shipping, which had taken him to Ghana, where by an extraordinary coincidence of braided personal histories, he had witnessed Nkrumah's inauguration. When he spoke to his children about this experience later, his "eyes glowed with pride and wonder and a tremor came into his voice."[13] Stokely, in other words, had already been steeped in pan-Africanism as a teenager.

NKRUMAH'S DIRECT INFLUENCE OVER CARMICHAEL, THOUGH, CAME ONLY following Nkrumah's overthrow in 1966. In an exhausted Ghana, after so many attempts to kill or remove him, Nkrumah's overthrow was practically an anticlimax. On February 24, 1966, he was toppled on his way to North Vietnam to propose a peace plan to North Vietnam's leader, Ho Chi Minh, to end the American war in that country. Washington promised to halt the bombing of North Vietnam for the length of Nkrumah's visit, but he never made it to Hanoi.[14]

At the time, and for years afterward, some of Nkrumah's critics savagely mocked this personal diplomacy. It was not enough, they said, that he claimed to speak on behalf of all of Africa, ludicrously now he saw a role for himself in the affairs of the entire world. In casting his attentions abroad, they said, he had ruinously neglected his own country. The most uncharitable of these critics derided the temerity of a Black man for even pretending to have the standing to involve himself in the problems of superpowers.

But such remarks, beyond their implicit racism, misunderstood Nkrumah the man as well as the long and complex tradition that he had emerged from. His entire political career to that point had been attached to peace inflected with Gandhism and was fully consonant with the American civil rights movement, and with even older traditions of Black internationalism. In other words, Nkrumah's timing may have been imprudent, but in proposing peace to Hó Chí Minh, he was being consistent and true to himself, not merely showboating.

During a stopover in Beijing, China's foreign minister informed Nkrumah that he had been overthrown in a violent coup d'état. Nonetheless China's urbane premier, Zhou Enlai, accompanied him to the State Guesthouse in Beijing and hosted him at a banquet that night despite his removal from power. Operation Cold Chop, its code name, had been jointly mounted by elements of the army and the police. Nkrumah's successor, as head of the self-proclaimed National Liberation Council (NLC), was Joseph Ankrah, who had become a brigadier commander during the UN operation in the Congo under the British commander, H. T. Alexander. Another coup leader, Emmanuel Kotoka had also commanded Ghanaian troops in the Congo under Alexander. (Nowadays most people who arrive by air in Accra ignore the fact that the city's international airport was named for Kotoka.)

A definitive account of Nkrumah's overthrow has yet to be published. It is clear, though, that Washington had long known of various plots to depose him and had, at a minimum, provided quiet encouragement.[15]

Little ink has been spilled on just how commonplace such things were in this era, as if the United States had the right to eradicate the leadership of any disobedient banana republic. In 1964, across the ocean in Guyana, the CIA and Britain had fomented opposition to Cheddi Jagan, and the CIA even discussed mounting a coup against him, but later abandoned the idea.[16] Jagan's replacement, Forbes Burnham, won power in coalition with another party that year and would rule as an authoritarian (and later, socialist) for the next twenty-one years.

In her book *White Malice: The CIA and the Covert Recolonization of Africa*, the British author, Susan Williams, chronicles similar American discussions about isolating Nkrumah or removing him from power. By March 11, 1965, Washington was confident enough to assess that Nkrumah would be deposed within a year, and that a military junta would take over.[17] That May, a National Security Council staffer told McGeorge Bundy, Johnson's National Security advisor, that "the plotters are keeping us briefed, and State thinks we're more on the inside than the British. While we're not directly involved (I'm told), we and other Western countries (including France) have been helping to set up the situation by ignoring Nkrumah's pleas for economic aid."[18]

Nkrumah's overthrow sparked a wave of popular jubilation in Ghana, one that toppled or defaced virtually anything that bore the founder's name or image. The new military leaders, in the guise of investigation, ransacked the Bureau of African Affairs and other institutions closely associated with Nkrumah's rule. Ever since, the pervasive rampant destruction or ill storage of archival records has hampered both Ghanaians and historians in their understanding of the Nkrumah years.

In the years that followed, Ghanaians would experience even greater hardships, including disarray under the NLC, restrictions on expression and other civil liberties, ever more brazen corruption, resurgent tribalism, and political executions under a variety of regimes, both military and civilian, several of which were strongly pro-Western. Since 1992, the country has been ruled as a democracy, with regular elections and alternance between parties, but the economic takeoff that Nkrumah dreamed of has never been attained, remaining a mirage ever so elusive on the horizon.

KWAME NKRUMAH, STRICKEN, DEPARTED AND ARRIVED IN CONAKRY, GUINEA, his new home in exile, on March 2, 1966. Many of his close associates over the years had wasted no time politically distancing themselves from him. Even some in his traveling party peeled away, eager to arrive back on African soil on their own, and thus sever their fates from his as quickly as possible. At an enormous rally the next day, though, his host, the ever-forceful Sékou Touré sought to revive Nkrumah's spirits, proclaiming, "The Ghanaian traitors have been mistaken in thinking that Nkrumah is simply a Ghanaian.... He is a universal man."[19]

Touré provided him with a seaside residence in Conakry, Villa Syli, which bore Touré's longtime nickname in politics, big elephant. In fact, it had once been the French colonial governor's residence. In a dramatic act of gratitude, Touré then returned Nkrumah's gesture of 1958, when they had announced the fusion of their two nations, by naming his new guest in exile his copresident and putting Nkrumah's likeness on Guinea's currency. Nkrumah spent five years at Touré's side on important political occasions in Guinea. He would plot and dream about returning to lead his downward spiraling Ghana, and indeed Africa, until the end of his life. From time to time, he broadcast messages back home denouncing the people who had overthrown him, portraying them as stooges of neocolonialism. But Villa Syli would be the last home he knew.

Ten months before the 1966 coup, Erica Powell had left Ghana for Britain, She had been so close to Nkrumah for so long that rumors linking the two as lovers never altogether abated. The two continued to correspond after Nkrumah went into exile, but they never met again. In 1970, she accepted an invitation to work as personal assistant to Siaka Stevens, the president of Sierra Leone.

In a sense, Touré's Guinea was the final redoubt of Nkrumahist pan-Africa. In 1960, Patrice Lumumba had flared as bright as a New Year's fireworks display, but had lasted just as briefly. The erstwhile union between Ghana, Guinea, and Mali had quickly frittered, losing Mali in 1963, after only two years. The mid-1960s saw tumult and violence spread more widely in Africa, with one coup or coup attempt following another. On the heels of Nkrumah's overthrow, a murderous, brutally internecine civil war broke out in Nigeria, caused by the same demons of ethnic division and separatism that Nkrumah had faced. Famine struck down children in breakaway Biafra. In 1971 Idi Amin would seize power in Uganda, creating a garish spectacle of primitive, clownish ignorance that the international media often seemed eager to project onto the entire continent.

Touré did what he could to preserve the pan-Africanist flame, sponsoring Amílcar Cabral, the leader of a war for emancipation next door in Portuguese Guinea (later Guinea-Bissau) against Lisbon's colonial rule. Nkrumah had trained some of Cabral's fighters in Ghana before his overthrow. In November 1970, Portugal, still clinging desperately to colonial power, invaded Guinea in a failed bid to snuff out Cabral and his Partido Africano para a Independência da Guiné e Cabo Verde (PAIGC) in 1970. Less than three years later, in September 1973, a rival from Cabral's own movement murdered him, renewing Portuguese hopes that independence could be forestalled. What happened instead was nearly the opposite: seven years after the murder, Portuguese army captains, inspired by the righteousness of the African liberation struggle, overthrew the country's longtime dictatorship and brought democracy to their country. Impacted by these events, Spain also soon democratized. Here were the latest examples of the European fortune rooted in the tragedies that that continent had inflicted on Africa since the late-Middle Ages.

Cabral, who had drawn amply on the Ghanaian's advice, managed to visit Nkrumah often during his exile years. Their lengthy bull sessions about revolutionary politics and military tactics eased the Ghanaian's sense of isolation and relieved his inevitable feelings of creeping irrelevance. At his memorial Cabral glowingly eulogized him.

Nkrumah's most important understudy in the final phase of his life was not an African but the American Stokely Carmichael. The former SNCC chairman had visited Guinea for the first time in 1967, after a whirlwind tour of revolutionary countries that Washington tagged as hostile, including Cuba, China, North Vietnam, and Algeria. In Beijing he met Shirley Graham Du Bois, and while he was in Hanoi, Ho Chi Minh regaled him with tales of hearing stirring Garvey oratory in Harlem decades earlier.[20]

The United States sought to punish Carmichael, like W. E. B. Du Bois before him, for his political views. His passport, too, was confiscated at one point. Carmichael was targeted by COINTELPRO, the FBI's illegal covert counterintelligence program that spied on civil rights groups, the Black Panthers, the antiwar movement, feminist organizations, environmentalists, and anyone else whom J. Edgar Hoover deemed subversive. With Carmichael in mind, Nicholas Katzenbach, Johnson's Undersecretary of State, also petitioned Congress to pass a law making travel to antagonistic countries punishable by a year in prison.[21]

Beginning in 1961, the Freedom Rides had protested segregation on interstate buses and highway bus stations, prompting widespread violence from marauding Southern whites. Around that time Carmichael famously became associated with the term Black Power, a slogan that quickly grew into a movement. It had originated with the idea of uniting disparate Black communities in the United States—from hamlets in the rural South to urban ghettos—into a stronger, more militant whole. As the contemporary historian Peniel Joseph wrote, Black Power was originally, "an anti-colonial struggle within American borders."[22] Malcolm X too was enriched intellectually by the new anticolonial struggles sweeping Africa. As Robin D. G. Kelley has written, he "viewed the emerging freedom movement in the United States as part of a global assault on empire."[23] Similarly, Carmichael's thinking evolved rapidly as his vision expanded. And in this respect, no one had a greater effect on him than Nkrumah.

In 1968 Carmichael married the South African singer, Miriam Makeba, one of the first African musicians to attain global popularity, beginning with an appearance on *The Steve Allen Show* in 1959 before a national audience of sixty million viewers. Some of Makeba's relatives had been killed in South Africa's 1960 Sharpeville Massacre, after which her South African passport was revoked. Living in New York City, her life soon combined anti-apartheid activism with support for both the American civil rights movement and

African independence. Like Marilyn Monroe, she also performed the song Happy Birthday for President Kennedy in 1962, and the very next year, she was the only singer invited to perform at the founding summit of the Organization of African Unity. Inevitably, Makeba came under the surveillance of both the CIA and FBI because of her relationship with Carmichael who was involved in the Black Panther Party.

Sékou Touré warmly welcomed the couple to Guinea. In his early years there, Carmichael worked as Nkrumah's assistant, meeting with him almost daily and absorbing from him histories of pan-Africanism and advice on world politics and Black liberation.[24] There Carmichael died of prostate cancer at the age of fifty-seven, in 1988, after receiving treatment in both Cuba and the United States.

As a member of Nkrumah's inner circle, one of Carmichael's tasks in Guinea was to engineer his return to power. The group created secret cells in Ghana that mounted scattered acts of sabotage. Talent was recruited from the Black nationalist world in the United States. Plans for a restoration were elaborated and poured over. Even Sékou Touré was said to be on board, making discreet offers of military and diplomatic help. In the final analysis, Kwame Nkrumah insisted that there be no loss of life, and he did not relent from this bottom line. In other ways, though, he seemed to be dragging his feet. It was as if his heart weren't in it, wrote Carmichael:

> [We] kept looking forward to the time of his return to Accra. But he definitely seemed to be putting a brake on those activities. At the time that puzzled me a little bit, but I think I understand better now.... I really think that Nkrumah knew—long before we did—that the cancer he had would not allow him to return to Ghana.[25]

In August 1971, Apollo 15 successfully completed the fourth American mission to land astronauts on the moon. The British government issued a state of exception to habeas corpus laws, suspending the right to a fair trial to facilitate its crackdown on suspected supporters of the Irish Republican Army. And a border clash broke out between Tanzania and Uganda that would end with the overthrow of the Idi Amin dictatorship by the Tanzanian army. That month, Nkrumah left Conakry for Bucharest, Romania, never to return. He had spent the last five years seated at Touré's side on important political occasions in Guinea and had received innumerable visitors. Many of them were unscrupulous characters hoping vainly for money from Nkrumah when they offered him concocted information from Ghana aimed at spurring his belief that a counter-coup was imminent and would pave the way for his return. More inspiring to Nkrumah were the letters on onionskin airmail stationery that flowed in from the moment of his overthrow until the end of his life.

One of the first of these arrived from London in March of 1966:

Dear President Kwame Nkrumah . . .

For five years I have been 47 pound a week Portman in London. I am married with One Child. I do not need any money from you, I do not need any work from you or the Government. But Because I have no mean good FAITH in your Presidentship and your World of Politics, I do here this day of 28/2/66 offer myself to be call for training anywhere, anytime to FIGHT BACK FOR YOUR SAVE [sic] RETURN TO GHANA.

I remain yours,
J.C.N. Akosa[26]

Others wrote in praise of his brainchildren: largescale public works like the Volta River Dam and Tema harbor, and the motorway linking that newly built city to the capital, Accra. Over and over, they expressed the ardent desire to see him return home triumphantly in one way or another. In doing so, they addressed him as Osagyefo and deplored what many of them called the precious time wasted as Ghana drifted in Nkrumah's absence.

Critics wrote, too, in measured words. A woman named Barbara Acquah denounced Nkrumah's use of the preventive detention law and what she called his prestige project, but then added:

People in Ghana now talk as if you had never done anything good in your life, and many of your former friends are now telling the commissions of enquiry that all the bad things they did were planned by you. I should love to see you return to Accra. And stand your trial and show them all up for their false accusations! If you did that, you might stand a chance of becoming President again some day. And it would be more dignified than waiting to be kidnapped and brought back unwillingly.[27]

In the meantime, Nkrumah tended to his book writing, fussing over the editing, and demanding favors with a light but insistent touch from a tiny cenacle of friends overseas. One of them was June Milne, a British historian and publisher who was as devoted to Nkrumah as Erica Powell had been and who became Nkrumah's literary executor. Most of his requests to her consisted of books, of kitchen and household gadgets, and of all manner of potions and supplements intended to keep up his health, all of which had long been among this fastidious man's preoccupations. To stay in shape, he developed a good tennis game and meditated regularly.

But none of this could stop the demons and the physical ills that stalked Nkrumah, privately at first. One of them turned out to be a deadly cancer. In August 1971, he left Conakry for Bucharest, Romania, where he entered a hospital. Shrunken by illness but believing he would be cured almost to the end, he was cared for in a three-bed ward where he was looked after twenty-four hours a day by two Ghanaians, including Nyamekeh, the fellow Nzima whom he had hired as a young man to be his cook and majordomo. He was receiving heavier and heavier doses of narcotics for his excruciating pain.

"He doesn't seem to realise that he is dying," wrote Milne in her notebook in January 1972 on her way from Bucharest back to London after spending long hours with Nkrumah at his bedside. In this period, she served as a kind of personal assistant to him, dutifully hunting down his desiderata. More than that, though, she was his anchor, his strongest remaining link to reality, to the wider world. "He talks of returning to Ghana and leading the party," she wrote. 'I will not be president and go to the airport to meet all those foolish ambassadors, but will be the chairman of the Central Committee.' . . . The only clue that he is wondering about his future was when he turned his eyes toward me and asked: 'June, do you think I will walk again?' I told him: 'Of course, you will.' "[28]

THREE MONTHS LATER, IN APRIL 1972, KWAME NKRUMAH DIED A PAINFUL AND lonely death of metastatic prostate cancer in the Romanian hospital. He was but sixty-two years old.

The announcements, tributes, and eulogies took many forms. The Western press tended toward predictable criticism. The *Los Angeles Times* noted that Ghana and Nkrumah had been the "spearhead of the black advance throughout the world," but called the freshly deceased leader "Africa's greatest disappointment of the 1960s." It quoted the Irish intellectual, Conor Cruise O'Brien, who had served as chancellor of the University of Ghana under Nkrumah, calling him the "equivocal chairman of a corrupt and cynical oligarchy." *The New York Times*, along with many other Western newspapers, called Nkrumah a megalomaniac.[29]

The African American press that had followed Nkrumah closely for years could not have remembered him more differently. Black newspapers were filled with celebrations and remembrances and eloquent encomiums from correspondents who had experienced the excitement of independence. Under the title "A Betrayed Redeemer," the *New Pittsburgh Courier* published one of the most incisive and remarkable assessments of Nkrumah. "In the whole punctuated course of the African Liberation history no one was more worthy of the title redeemer—with all its majestic and dolorous implications than Kwame Nkrumah." The *Courier* spoke of his "ingenious political strategy" and "personal sacrifice" in enduring prison to free his land from British rule.[30]

Nkrumah brought "the black continent into the forefront of world affairs," the *Courier* said, "together with a degree of recognition and respectability never before enjoyed by Africans," which made him "the greatest figure in modern African history." The paper wondered if the price he paid for this was the involvement of the CIA, which it and others speculated might have had a hand in his overthrow. Most astute of all was the *Courier*'s political judgment, a corrective to the standard Cold War analyses of the day:

> [Nkrumah] was often accused of Marxist leaning. The truth is that he sought to evolve an economic theory that would be more in step with African resources and traditions by extracting what was good in both the socialist and capitalistic culture. His insistence on the principle of non-alignment was based on cooperation with all states whether they be capitalist, socialist or have a mixed economy.[31]

A more down-to-earth measure of Nkrumah's resonance was the state funeral that Sékou Touré put on for his old comrade. The more than forty delegations it drew came from all over Africa and around the world. Erica Powell attended. Fifty thousand mourners, nearly all dressed in white, filled Conakry's main stadium, where Nkrumah's coffin was placed on a caisson and driven about slowly for all to see, including his widow, Fathia, who sat at Touré's side. Afterward, soldiers marched and saluted crisply to the sounds of military bands, and dances were performed in Nkrumah's honor. Respect for the Ghanaian in death was such that one of the African leaders who presided over the funeral was Liberia's conservative president, William Tolbert, a stalwart of the Monrovia Group that had firmly stood in opposition to Nkrumah's federal plans for Africa in 1963.

In 1978, Stokely Carmichael paid what was perhaps the deepest homage of all, legally changing his name to Kwame Ture, to honor the president of Guinea who had hosted him, and to honor Nkrumah, his greatest mentor. As Peniel Joseph writes, the Ghanaian had persuaded Carmichael that pan-Africanism, and only pan-Africanism, could one day free Black Americans. This reconnection with ancient roots on the continent from which they had been torn away was, he wrote, "the highest political expression of Black power."[32]

CODA

Strange Fruit

DURING THE TURBULENT FINAL YEARS OF HIS RULE, KWAME NKRUMAH concentrated ever more decision-making power in his own hands. As he became increasingly distrustful of others, he was widely criticized in the West as a tyrant. With his overthrow in 1966, many of his longtime domestic opponents claimed vindication; after all, they had always said he was a dictator in the making.

By the mid-1960s, there was certainly enough grist in the historical record to build a damning picture of the man. The passage of time and the emergence of much more scholarly information, though, reveal that views like this of Nkrumah and of his record are incomplete, if not skewed and inaccurate.

It is undisputed that Nkrumah's concentration of power accelerated in 1960, with a constitutional switch to a republican form of government. This was followed by the proclamation of a one-party system after a national referendum in 1964. As he accumulated increasing nominal authority, culminating with the title President for Life, Nkrumah became more embattled, and his opposition ever more ruthless and determined.

This produced deplorable overreactions by Nkrumah, such as the repeated jailing of his greatest rival, J. B. Danquah, who had recruited Nkrumah from London. With a career steeped in British law, the urbane Danquah righteously denounced Nkrumah's interference in decisions by Ghana's judiciary. Nkrumah's government arrested the aged Danquah for a second time in January 1964, alleging that he was involved in plotting against the president and ignored his requests for urgent medical attention. Danquah would die tragically behind bars a year later, earning Nkrumah strong new waves of denunciation for his government's increasingly dictatorial tendencies.

Nothing good can be said about Nkrumah's treatment of Danquah, even with the passage of time. However, it is worthwhile to try to understand some of Nkrumah's behavior from his own perspective, and to place his political decisions, including some of those that were most widely deplored at the time, in a deeper historical context.

The period from 1957 to 1960 had given Nkrumah the sense that Ghana did not have, and was perhaps incapable of developing anytime soon, a loyal opposition. His political rivals' repeated bids to assassinate him were the worst of it. His opponents attempted to build political parties largely based on ethnic or regional identity. What followed were two outright secession drives among the Asante and Ewe, a sustained push for a fragmentary federal political system, and a parliamentary opposition that devolved into reflexive obstruction and crude gamesmanship.

Nkrumah's 1957 autobiography displayed such intuitive understanding. "Unless [Ghana] is, as it were, 'jet propelled' it will lag behind and thus risk everything for which it had fought."[1] Language like this has been used to charge Nkrumah with rash impatience, and worse, the kind of exaggerated ambition often associated with dictators, but this ignores a tremendous amount of historical context. Nowadays, it is all too easy to forget the paroxysms of anxiety felt in Western circles about the rapid economic growth of the Soviet Union in the 1950s. In 1956 Khrushchev vowed in the presence of Western diplomats in Poland in 1956, "We will bury you," which the capitalist world took to mean that Moscow would outstrip Western democracies economically and would build a nuclear weapons arsenal. Until the late 1960s, the nearly universally used college economics textbook written by Paul Samuelson predicted that the economy of the USSR would surpass that of the US in production per head before 2000.[2] Soviet advances stoked the ambitions of a great many new nations, including Ghana.

The new leaders of many young states reserved a strong role for the state in planning, economic ownership, and management, and hoped that they could thereby achieve and sustain high rates of growth. But few of these countries—again, Ghana included—adopted Soviet style rule or ideology. Even in the West, the consensus among well-established development economists, including Arthur Lewis, held that only a major state-led investment drive, or "big push," could enable newly enfranchised nations to escape from the poverty trap.

In biology, scientists speak of evolutionary convergence, a phenomenon in which unrelated species scattered over far-flung geographies or epochs develop uncannily similar morphologies and strategies. The Tasmanian tiger, for example, was an extinct marsupial, but it had a form and hunting style that mirrored those of large and familiar predatory cat species. Nkrumah's evolutionary convergence, as it were, was with Julius Nyerere, who was born a decade and a half after him and became leader of Tanganyika (later Tanzania) at independence from Britain in 1961.

The political choices that Nyerere made during his early years in power closely track with some of the decisions of Nkrumah that drew the strongest opprobrium, both from his domestic political rivals and Western critics. Perhaps because these decisions were taken in Nkrumah's wake, and indeed were echoed in many parts of the continent, including by regimes with sharply divergent ideologies, Nyerere drew much less of the denunciation that was directed at the Ghanaian leader.

Nyerere came to these views on his own, but like Nkrumah, he believed deeply that the most important prerequisite for his country's success and that of the continent was unity at the national level. This meant curbing regionalism and tribalism, while emphasizing pan-African concertation and consolidation. Nyerere warned that the continent, newly freed from European domination, would soon be confronted with a Second Scramble for Africa, in which one nation was "going to be divided against another nation to make it easier to control Africa by making her weak and divided against herself."[3] As a brief description of the Cold War in Africa, one could do much worse. Unity was the only arm that Africans possessed to defend their independence.

Like Nkrumah, Nyerere inherited a bare-bones and ill-adapted colonial administration, and he concluded even more quickly than the Ghanaian that it would be foolhardy to expect holdovers from the imperial past to help local Africans build a new and thriving state of their own. Nyerere expressed this most famously in a 1970 speech, in which he said, "the development of people means rebellion."[4] It meant never forgetting that the old order that Tanzania was struggling to emerge from was innately hostile to its national interests.

Already by 1962, which is to say two years after Nkrumah had led Ghana across this threshold, Tanzania under Nyerere also jettisoned the Westminster model of government for Tanzania and adopted a presidential-style constitution. "There must be no confusing outward forms which are meaningless in the light of our experience and history," he wrote in a letter to the *London Observer* defending the change:

> Our constitution differs from the American system in that it . . . enables the executive to function without being checked at every turn. . . . Our need is not for brakes to social change . . . our lack of trained manpower and capital resources, and even our climate, act too effectively already.

We need accelerators powerful enough to overcome the inertia bred by poverty, and the resistances which are inherent in all societies.[5]

It was but a short step from there to concluding that, amid the new nation's dire development struggle, multiparty politics was also a costly distraction amid the new nation's dire development struggle. A mere two months after the prime minister's office was eliminated and Nyerere, like Nkrumah, became president, the executive council of the ruling Tanganyika African National Union (TANU) party considered the idea of adopting a one-party political model. Strong opposition to some of the political changes afoot came from trade unions and armed forces, and parts of the latter mutinied. Nyerere's government responded by employing a preventive detention act that was similar in scope to the one employed by Nkrumah, which itself copied practices common under colonial rule. In the end, the police swept up five hundred people, including roughly two hundred trade unionists. This led to the creation of a single national trade union, as in Ghana, and consolidation of political control over the army. In 1965, a new, interim constitution formalized these changes, formally rendering Tanzania into a one-party state.

The justification used for these changes was that if Tanzania was going to meet the rude challenges of freedom (*uhuru* in Swahili) including economic development and the construction of a fairer and more inclusive new society, it required social and political unity (*umoja* in Swahili)—behind a strong national leadership.

This all echoed the political logic of Nkrumah's Ghana. If Tanzania and Ghana were the only two new countries in Africa that put such precepts in place, that would be one thing. But the move to single-party constitutions became the rule, not the exception, throughout Africa in the 1960s, and if the justifications employed often resembled each other from country to country, the range of ideologies, behaviors, and outcomes varied enormously from place to place. The counterpart of progressives like Nkrumah and Nyerere were conservatives like Houphouët-Boigny of the Ivory Coast, who also placed their concentration of power in the service of highly articulated national programs. Many other new single-party leaders presided over the worst kinds of human rights abuses and the most flagrant forms of kleptocracy seen on the continent. In those countries, the violent suppression of critics and rivals was widespread, as were blatant ethnic favoritism, the muzzling of journalists, and extreme forms of personalized rule. During my first visit to Zaïre in the late-1970s, I was stupefied by a televised montage that opened the nightly news: it showed that country's dictator, Mobutu, descending on a throne from the clouds amid rays of heavenly light like some demigod.

For anyone who attempts to understand Africa today, it is vital to try to make sense of its convergent evolution in this era. So is tracing that evolution backward in time. Because Ghana's independence came first, it is too often considered as a singular, iconoclastic political entity, but this impedes our understanding of Nkrumah's pioneering role.

Tanzania provides illuminating parallels with that of Ghana. TANU, the political party that Nyerere would lead, held its first mass meeting in 1955, eight years after Nkrumah had done so with the CPP. As in Ghana, the British were stunned by Nyerere's party's rapid growth. Incredulous that their former African subjects could sustain any kind of coherent political activity on their own, the colonial government attributed TANU's rise to outside support, darkly hinting at communism—once again, as in Ghana. The British authorities, just as they had pilloried Nkrumah and the CPP leadership, painted the TANU leadership, with Nyerere at its center, as "hooliganish, unreasonable and extreme."[6] British charges like these quickly became associated with race-based claims.

Tanganyika's colonial governor, Edward Twining, like Arden-Clarke in Ghana, saw it as his mission to rein Nyerere in, as if he were some malevolent teenage delinquent, and keep him under the governor's control. The truth is that early in the independence era Europe's colonizers treated all Africans but the most eager collaborationists as dangerous provocateurs and demagogues. In the Gold Coast, that even included J. B. Danquah and other members of the smallish British-educated elite. The Colonial Office spoken of them simultaneously as the "ruling class of the future" and as only semi-adults.[7]

One of the standard defenses of colonial rule in Africa was a somewhat wayward form of white saviorism: that the imperial nations had the best interests of their subjects at heart, and that only slowly, through their careful and patient ministrations, could Africans slowly be rendered competent for assuming control over their own affairs. This was from a colonial power that by independence had only trained two indigenous engineers and three doctors.[8]

In Tanzania, the colonial government accused TANU of "racialism, of wanting for Tanganyika a Government of Africans only, of wanting independence in five years," and, of course, of being anti-British.[9] This British response to the African will to become independent was strikingly akin, by the way, to America's nineteenth century racial gradualism. The charge once commonly levied by American slaveowners against their chattels, whenever someone among their movable property managed to escape to a free state was: how could they be so ungrateful and disloyal?

In fact, almost all arguments for the enfranchisement of Africans in Tanganyika were met with British alarm, even when Nyerere vowed to pursue a nonracial approach to citizenship. In response, he said, the British often lectured him that democracy is "alright in civilised countries, but it is a dangerous thing in the hands of uncivilized colonial people." Others justified European rule as a matter not of race, but merely of "government by the best" over the colony's Black majority.[10]

When none of London's efforts to blunt TANU's political momentum seemed to be working, Governor Twining, a member the Twining tea family who had been appointed as governor of a tea-producing colony, wrote in 1957:

> I feel that there can be no getting away from the fact that unless Nyerere entirely changes his attitude and policy, he and his movement will have to be suppressed, and it is a question of whether we should wait until he does something stupid—which will almost certainly lead to bloodshed—or whether we should anticipate this by closing him down now. If it was not for the difficult external influences which are at work, I am quite sure the right thing to do would be to close him down now.[11]

As a result of such views, Nyerere and other leaders of his party were banned from holding rallies. Nor did London's efforts, even in the late 1950s, to suppress a nationalist independence movement stop at its colony's borders, either. As Nyerere's biographer Ng'wanza Kamata has written, it also intervened with the British press to prevent any coverage that could paint Nyerere in a favorable light or elevate his profile internationally, much as Stokely Carmichael was smeared as a dangerous radical in my own country.

Seen even in this limited light, colonial rule's view of itself as a school for liberal (in the classic sense), democratic self-rule is hard to sustain. And that is without even taking into account its stolen labor; its arbitrary and nearly unlimited powers of arrest and detention; its use of banishment, its land appropriation, its explicit racial favoritism for whites in employment and in business; its frequent attacks on the press and infringement on rights of association; and its taxation without representation. One could go on and on.

Here, we have spoken of just two countries, Ghana and Tanganyika, but these two share a lot and are reasonably good surrogates for all of British-ruled sub-Saharan Africa. A broader study would show that the pre-independence paternalism and post-independence meddling by France were far stronger still.

THE SECOND EMANCIPATION

IN THE DECADE AFTER THE YEAR OF AFRICA IN 1960, WEST AND EAST JOUSTED fiercely over ideology. They debated capitalism and socialism, the proponents of each denouncing the other across a deepening divide. By the late 1960s and especially in the 1970s, East and West heavily promoted avatars and proxies of their rival ideologies on the continent, each warning that the other was leading only toward exploitation and political perdition. Samir Amin, an economist who worked for the Malian government between 1960 and 1963, captured some of this intensity when he wrote of his encounters with experts from East and West. "The Soviets kept churning out the same 'principles': it's good when the state intervenes, bad when this is not planned.... But the World Bank people were, and are, of exactly the same type, and also speak a totally ideological language, even if their basic principle ('it's good whenever the private sector takes charge') is the diametrical opposite."[12] Six and a half decades later what is most remarkable to me is the immense waste brought on by this blind contest of ideology; the ideologies proved, over time, to matter little in terms of delivering African people into solid economic development.

To illustrate the point, few better examples exist than a couple that we have talked about often here: Nkrumah of Ghana and Houphouët-Boigny of the Ivory Coast. The one an ardent African socialist and the other a fervent proponent of Western-style capitalism, the two men literally placed a bet between them as to whose "way" would triumph. Sadly, for Africa, the outcome was that neither exemplar delivered strong and durable economic growth and socioeconomic equality.

For decades, following the crumbling of Nkrumah's system, Ghana appeared to have lost this bet. The capitalist Ivory Coast became a commodity-exporting powerhouse and grew smartly. I visited Accra for the first time in 1976, when Ghana was led by Ignatius Acheampong, the army officer who had seized power in 1972. The country was experiencing runaway inflation, and the value of the national currency, the cedi, seemed to shrink by the hour, requiring massive wads of it to be surreptitiously sold on the black market to obtain just a few dollars. Even the better hotels lacked most menu items. For years after Nkrumah's ouster, power changed hands, usually by coup, but none of the would-be saviors, stern critics of Nkrumah among them, seemed to have any clue as to how to cure the country's woes. Acheampong's most memorable reform was to switch the country from the imperial to the metric system and to have cars drive on the right side of the road rather than the left. People had complained about Nkrumah's ambitions. What stood out about his successors, though, was not their ideas, but how readily they served themselves through corruption.

Well before 2000, though, France's supposed showcase on the continent hit a ceiling and stalled. Houphouët-Boigny had fulfilled his vow to rule for life, incurring little Western criticism; following his death in 1993, succession crises ensued, as did a violent and ruinous civil war, something Ghana has never suffered. In terms of economic statistics today, there is little to pick from between the two countries. Neither showed the way to broad prosperity.

This encapsulation is the tragedy of Africa. A great many strategies have been tried to lift countries up onto a higher plane of economic life to rejoin the rest of the world, but no formula has proved successful. In 1960, when the continental GDP per capita was $1,320, a third of the global average, Africa had nothing but bad choices. Nor are there any obviously good choices now, when Africa's average GDP per capita is a mere $1,980, while the global average has risen to $10,636.

Most of this cannot be explained in the usual way, by placing the blame on Africans' ineptitude and corruption. The rich world has been strikingly miserly toward Africa, given what it removed, while many of Africa's own leaders have been almost equally unaccountable to their peoples. This story, therefore, is rich in failure, both structural and human.

During the Nkrumah era, idealism was occasionally wedded to power and Africans labored boldly and purposefully to change the world and the global distribution of power. For me that era ended, not with Nkrumah's death, but with the murder in 1987 of the young and stirringly progressive army captain Thomas Sankara, a man who had ruled in the inland, semi-arid, former French colony to Ghana's north, a place that had been known by its bland colonial name as Upper Volta. Sankara's assassination was arranged by his close associate, Blaise Compaoré, who went on to govern for decades in close concert with Côte d'Ivoire. Enabled and protected by Paris, Compaoré built an immense fortune, while Sankara was buried in an out-of-the-way, trash-strewn cemetery in an unmarked pauper's grave.

Three years earlier I took a trundling overnight train trip from Abidjan, where I then lived, to Ouagadougou, a capital composed of tin shack dwellings. The route itself served up unmistakable lessons in geography and political economy. Downtown Abidjan sparkled with evidence of recent wealth—glimmering new buildings, shiny new cars, and smart new boulevards then gave way to the fetid slums inhabited by immigrants drawn from poorer countries who did most of the hard and unpleasant work. Rich commodity plantations slid past as we progressed northward—cocoa, coffee, pineapple, rubber—before finally yielding to savannah. At Ouagadougou, the terminus, it was the crushing traffic and pallid smog of cheap Japanese motorbikes, not cars, which few there could afford, that ruled the road. I had come to get a close-up sense for myself of a new kind of leader who had just taken power. How had Sankara managed to stir hope deeply in a country of hardscrabble subsistence farmers, as so many people said he had?[13] In the beginning, the answer lay with easy, even gimmicky-sounding things, like changing the name of his country to Burkina Faso, or Land of Upright People.

Burkina Faso had a brutal past as a land that had long served as a reservoir of the slave trade and then of colonial labor mercilessly forced to grow cotton commercially. By no means did Sankara, at thirty-three, have all the answers. What he did have, though, was sincerity and personal integrity, as well as the ability to articulate a vision, a good part of which was fired by memories of Nkrumah's pan-Africanism. It was a vision based on looking inwardly for whatever resources Africans could muster at home, not by becoming dogmatic about this, but by emphasizing self-reliance, rather than slavishly following the ever-changing recipes and dictates that have always been foisted upon Africa by those richer and more powerful.

I got to know Sankara a bit on that visit, and I returned often. How much he unnerved France in the mid-1980s was plain to see. Paris had long seduced the leaders of its African client-states to do its bidding by protecting them against coups and allowing them to park their ill-gotten wealth in French banks and luxury real estate. Sankara freely denounced the corruption this fostered, and even as Paris labored to undermine him, he remained outspoken about the hypocrisy of the world's rich countries and their exploitation of the weak. He embraced a kind of participatory politics that placed the needs of the rural population and the poor at the forefront of his agenda. He prioritized simple-seeming but long-neglected basics such as introducing rudimentary primary healthcare clinics in villages, leveling ill-kept direct roads, and digging hundreds of new wells for safe drinking water. He got rid of fancy cars and first-class travel for members of government and did not tolerate illicit enrichment. He promoted women to positions of influence in government and preached gender equality to the entire population. Like Nkrumah, he invested heavily in education. He mobilized campaigns to plant trees to protect his drought-vulnerable country's fragile environment.

West Africa proved to be too mean a place for this program to last, though, and it was his childhood friend and right-hand man who had him killed and restored all of the country's old crooked ways.

IN A WORLD THAT HAS IN SIGHT NO OBVIOUS QUICK SOLUTIONS FOR AFRICA, maybe it all comes down to this: starting with can-do vision, and figuring out how to connect people, across a multitude of frontiers of ethnicity, religion, colonial languages, and borders, while never losing sight of the needs of the ordinary people.

Let us hope for more of this in an altogether different future.

ACKNOWLEDGMENTS

THIS BOOK HAS HAD AN UNUSUAL, IF FELICITOUS, ORIGIN STORY. AS I write in the Introduction, its birth grows in substantial part out of my formative experiences in Ghana and of West Africa, first as a wide-eyed college student and then, after graduation, as an eager apprentice of journalism. It was this field that set me in motion as a curious young man, sending me to almost every region of the continent, where I labored to understand a host of complex societies—all undergoing dramatic mutations—while learning the ways of a new craft.

I owe my introduction to the continent, and thus my first thanks, to my parents. They both participated deeply in the American civil rights struggle and supported African independence—the two great movements whose stories come braided together in this narrative. But it was their decision to move to West Africa just as I was entering university in America that physically brought me to the continent during breaks in the school calendar, and therefore gave me my first enthralling tastes of life in a new part of the world. Without that start, it is unlikely that I would have ever written a book like this.

It was in Abidjan, where my family lived, that I met Avouka, the woman I married and built a life with, and mother to my children. I am thankful to her in so many ways, including for her informal guidance to Nzema culture and to all things Akan, Ghana's largest ethnic cluster. This additional family background was just as indispensable in putting my life on a path that led, however circuitously, to this book. I am also grateful to my brother-in-law, Ngamah Kofi, who generously accompanied me on the road in Ghana for some of the research that went into this account.

After several fond years of working as a novice "freelance" reporter in Africa, I was hired by *The New York Times*, where I was soon assigned to cover other parts of the world. For a time, I resisted the entreaties of my editors that I return to Africa because it seemed clear to me that the interest of the American press in the continent was shallow and episodic. In the wake of the Rwandan genocide, I allowed myself to be persuaded to return to the region of the continent that I have always known best: West Africa. From my base there I covered a broad swath of the continent in unusually turbulent times.

The experiences I had during those years—of seemingly interminable war and dictatorship in places like Zaïre, Nigeria, Sierra Leone, and in Ivory Coast, where I had started as a reporter—got me thinking about many of the themes that fill these pages, especially how and under what circumstances African countries had achieved their independence, and why in so many places had this turned into a false start?

After that second stint on the continent, the *Times* sent me much farther afield, first to cover Japan and the Koreas and then to cover China. Physically, it is hard to get much farther away from Africa, but these distant outposts turned into very good vantage points from which to think about that continent. While in Japan I wrote my first book, a memoir of my time as a reporter in Africa, and in China I caught early wind of the rebirth of interest in that then-fast-rising country in a continent that Beijing had first seriously courted during the Mao years. This eventually led to another book, this one about China's search for deepened human and economic relations with Africa.

I have produced other books that are solely about China, a country that continues to fascinate me, but I am grateful that Africa has never released its hold on me. As I was working on *Born in Blackness*, the book that preceded this one, my editor at Liveright, Bob Weil, repeatedly appealed to me to consider writing a book about Kwame Nkrumah. In my experience, it was most unusual to have an editor propose and almost insist, I should say, on a topic for a new book project. I hope that readers will agree that it was also fortuitous.

Rebecca Homiski and Luke Swann of Norton both lent me their unfailing support. This book benefitted from the careful work of two copyeditors, Janet Biehl and Rebecca Rider, each of whom helped me untangle sentences, chase down details, and improve things in a multitude of ways. Thank you.

Thanks go also, as always, to my longtime agent, the wonderful Gloria Loomis.

Like many of my books, this work has been immeasurably facilitated by the libraries and staff of Columbia University. My research has also drawn heavily on the archival resources and staff assistance of several other libraries. Key among them have been the Langston Hughes Memorial Library at Lincoln University; the Moorland-Spingarn Research Center at Howard University; the Schomburg Center for Research in Black Culture at the New York Public

Library; the George Padmore Research Library on African Affairs, in Accra, Ghana; and the Special Collections and University Archives of the W.E.B. Du Bois Library at the University of Massachusetts–Amherst.

I have been blessed with the assistance, friendly or collegial encouragement, and intellectual companionship of a great many people—too many, indeed, to name. Their generosity has left a deep mark on this work, and on me personally.

Frederick Cooper, an outstanding historian of Africa and of empire, who has been so kind to me in the past, read this book in manuscript while he was traveling to Japan and offered many astute observations. David Levering Lewis, the author of two remarkable biographies of W.E.B. Du Bois, among other notable books, was similarly generous, and the commentary he shared led to numerous enhancements. Jeffrey Ahlman, a brilliant scholar of Nkrumah, was also extremely helpful, offering archival and logistical suggestions early in my research and reading the manuscript in full. I have also learned a great deal from Jeffrey's work and am grateful to him and to the many other scholars of Nkrumah and of pan-Africanism whose writings I have drawn from and often quoted here.

Anakwa Dwamena, a young Ghanaian scholar and writer also read the book in manuscript and sustained an illuminating discussion with me about how Nkrumah is seen and remembered by the present generation. Many other friends in Ghana contributed in innumerable informal ways. A very short list would include Audrey Gadzekpo, Chrys Placca, Bright Simons, Selase Kove-Seyram, Kwame Karikari, and Promise. You all and numerous other unnamed friends in Ghana and throughout West Africa have my full gratitude.

I would be remiss if I did not say that if all the forms of help and acts of kindness that I've mentioned above contributed to making this a better book, the assessments and conclusions herein are mine alone, as is the responsibility for any of its shortcomings.

My deepest thanks go, finally, to my readers. The past remembered here belongs to all of you.

NOTES

INTRODUCTION

1. Issa G. Shivji, *Rebellion without Rebels*, Book Three of *Development as Rebellion: A Biography of Julius Nyerere*, by Issa G. Shivji, Saida Yahya-Othman, and Ng'wanza Kamata (Dar es Salaam, Tanzania: Mkuki na Nyota Publishers, 2020), xxv.
2. Kwame Nkrumah, *Ghana: The Autobiography of Kwame Nkrumah* (New York: International Publishers, 1971), 5.
3. See, for example, W. E. B. Du Bois, *The World and Africa: An Inquiry into the Part which Africa Has Played in World History* (New York: International Publishers, 1946).
4. Harold Cruse, *The Crisis of the Negro Intellectual: A Historical Analysis of the Failure of Black Leadership* (New York: New York Review of Books, 2005), 5.
5. Marcus Garvey, "The True Solution to the Negro Problem—1922," in *Philosophy and Opinions of Marcus Garvey*, Part 1, ed. Amy Jacques Garvey (London: Frank Cass and Co. Publishers 1923), 17.
6. Thomas Borstelmann, *The Cold War and the Color Line: American Race Relations in the Global Arena* (Cambridge, MA: Harvard University Press, 2001), 22–23.
7. Woodrow Wilson, "The Reconstruction of the Southern States," in *Woodrow Wilson: Essential Writings and Speeches of the Scholar-President*, ed. Mario R. Dinunzio (New York: New York University Press, 2006), 206.
8. Gerald Horne, "Race from Power: U.S. Foreign Policy and the General Crisis of 'White Supremacy'," *Diplomatic History* 23, no. 3 (July 1999): 450.
9. See, for example, Linda Gordon, *The Second Coming of the KKK: The Ku Klux Klan of the 1920s and the American Political Tradition* (New York: Liveright, 2018).
10. Zachary D. Carter, *The Price of Peace: Money, Democracy, and the Life of John Maynard Keynes* (New York: Random House, 2020), 59.
11. James Baldwin, "Letter from a Region in My Mind," *New Yorker*, November 9, 1962.
12. Aimé Césaire, *Discourse Sur le colonialisme*, trans. Howard W. French (Paris: Editions Présence Africaine, 1955), 77.
13. Langston Hughes, "Beaumont to Detroit, 1943," in *The Collected Poems of Langston Hughes*, ed. David Roessel (New York: Vintage, 1995), 281.
14. Joint Statement by President Roosevelt and Prime Minister Churchill, August 14, 1941, Foreign Relations of the United State Diplomatic Papers, 1941, General, The Soviet Union, Vol. 1, 740.00116 European War 1939/14593, Office of the Historian, Foreign Service Institute, US Department of State.
15. Jason C. Parker, "Made-in-America Revolutions? The 'Black University' and the Decolonization of the Black Atlantic," *Journal of American History* 96, no. 3 (December 2009): 742.
16. Kwame Nkrumah, "At Long Last, the Battle Has Ended!," speech at independence, March 6, 1957, posted by the BBC World Service Programmes, last updated March 2, 2007.
17. James Baldwin, "They Can't Turn Back" (1960), in *James Baldwin: Collected Essays*, ed. Toni Morrison (New York: Library of America, 1998), 629; Nicholas Buccola, *The Fire Is upon Us: James Baldwin, William F. Buckley Jr., and the Debate Over Race in America* (Princeton: Princeton University Press, 2019), 109.
18. John Henrik Clarke, "Kwame Nkrumah: His Years in America," *Black Politics*, October 1974, 15.
19. C. L. R. James, "Kwame Nkrumah: Founder of African Emancipation," *Black World/Negro Digest*, July 1972, 4.

20. James, "Kwame Nkrumah," 4.
21. Louis Menand, *The Free World: Art and Thought in the Cold War* (New York: Farrar, Straus and Giroux, 2021), 198.
22. George Lamming, *The Pleasures of Exile* (London: M. Joseph, 1960).
23. Odd Arne Westad, *The Cold War: A World History* (Basic Books: New York, 2017), 279.
24. Adom Getachew, *Worldmaking after Empire: The Rise and Fall of Self-Determination* (Princeton, NJ: Princeton University Press, 2019), 59.
25. Westad, *Cold War*, 262.

CHAPTER ONE: SATURDAY'S CHILD

1. Kwame Nkrumah, *Ghana: The Autobiography of Kwame Nkrumah* (New York: International Publishers, 1957), [Au: pg #?].
2. David Birmingham, *Kwame Nkrumah: The Father of African Nationalism* (Athens: Ohio University Press, 1990), 10.
3. Nkrumah, *Ghana: Autobiography*, 27.
4. Basil Davidson, *The Black Man's Burden: Africa and the Curse of the Nation-State* (New York: Times Books, 1992), 76.
5. Robert Addo-Fening, "Ghana Under Colonial Rule: An Outline of the Early Period and the Interwar Years," *Transactions of the Historical Society of Ghana* 15 (2013): 60.
6. Addo-Fening, "Ghana Under Colonial Rule,"60.
7. J. E. Casely Hayford, *Gold Coast Native Institutions, with Thoughts upon a Healthy Imperial Policy for the Gold Coast and Ashanti* (London: Sweet and Maxwell, 1903), ix; Esperanza Brizuela-Garcia, "Cosmopolitanism: Why Nineteenth Century Gold Coast Thinkers Matter in the Twenty-First Century," *Ghana Studies* 17 (2014): 203–21.
8. Jules François Camille Ferry, "Speech before the French Chamber of Deputies, March 28, 1884," in *Discours et Opinions de Jules Ferry*, ed. Paul Robiquet (Paris: Armand Collin, 1897), 1.
9. Frederick D. Lugard, *The Amalgamation and Administration of Southern and Northern Nigeria, 1912–1919* (London: HMSO, 1920), 19.
10. Nkrumah, *Ghana: Autobiography*, 4.
11. Nkrumah, *Ghana: Autobiography*, 5.
12. Nkrumah, *Ghana: Autobiography*, 9.
13. Minutes from July 24, 1886, by Hemming in David Kimble, *A Political History of Ghana* (London: Oxford University Press, 1963), 91.
14. General Act of the Berlin Conference on West Africa, February 26, 1885, Jus Mundi.
15. Great Britain, Foreign Office, Historical Section, *Gold Coast* (London: H.M. Stationery Office, 1920), PDF from the Library of Congress online collection.
16. Prince Young Aboagye, "Inequality of Education in Colonial Ghana: European Influences and African Responses," *Economic History of Developing Regions* 36, no. 3 (2021): 367–91. Also see Addo-Fening, "Ghana Under Colonial Rule," 66.
17. F. G. Guggisberg and A. G. Fraser, *The Future of the Negro* (London: Student Christian Movement, 1929), 152.
18. Pamela Newkirk, *Tuskegee, Achimota and Construction of Black Transcultural Identity* (PhD thesis, Columbia University, 2012), 173.
19. Newkirk, *Tuskegee, Achimota and Black Transcultural Identity*, 142, citing *The New York Age*, January 7, 1928.
20. In my discussion of Aggrey and Washington I have drawn broadly on an illuminating 2012 doctoral thesis in Philosophy—Newkirk, *Tuskegee, Achimota and Black Transcultural Identity*.
21. Edwin William Smith, *Aggrey of Africa: A Study in Black and White* (Freeport, NY: Books for Libraries Press, 1971), 123.
22. Newkirk, *Tuskegee, Achimota and Black Transcultural Identity*, 9.
23. J. E. Kwegyir Aggrey to Thomas Jesse Jones (of the Phelps Stokes Fund), April 8, 1926, quoted in Smith, *Aggrey of Africa*, 256.
24. Newkirk, *Tuskegee, Achimota and Black Transcultural Identity*, 69.
25. Nnamdi, Azikiwe, *My Odyssey: An Autobiography* (New York: Praeger, 1970), 37–38.
26. Newkirk, *Tuskegee, Achimota and Black Transcultural Identity*, 117.
27. A plaque bearing this quote can be found on the Achimota campus today.
28. Nkrumah, *Ghana: Autobiography*, 14.
29. Nkrumah, *Ghana: Autobiography*, 14.
30. For more on this subject, see Frederick Cooper, *Africa in the World: Capitalism, Empire, Nation-State* (Cambridge, MA: Harvard University Press, 2014), 22–24.
31. On colonial correspondence, see Stanley Shaloff, "Press Controls and Sedition Proceedings in the Gold Coast, 1933–39," *African Affairs* 71, no. 284 (July 1972): 241.

32. Marika Sherwood, *Kwame Nkrumah: The Years Abroad, 1935–1947* (Legon, Ghana: Freedom Publications, 1996), 15.
33. Basil Davidson, *Black Star: A View of the Life and Times of Kwame Nkrumah* (New York: Praeger, 1973), 29.
34. Shaloff, "Press Controls and Sedition Proceedings," 225.
35. Leo Spitzer and LaRay Denzer, "I. T. A. Wallace-Johnson and the West African Youth League," *International Journal of African Historical Studies* 6, no. 3 (1973): 441–42.
36. Nkrumah, *Ghana: Autobiography*, 22–23.
37. Shaloff, "Press Controls and Sedition Proceedings," 255.
38. Nkrumah, *Ghana: Autobiography*, 22.
39. Sherwood, *Nkrumah: The Years Abroad*, 24.
40. Nnamdi Azikiwe, *Renascent Africa* (Accra, Gold Coast: self-published, 1937), 43.
41. Nkrumah, *Ghana: Autobiography*, 23.
42. Sherwood, *Nkrumah: The Years Abroad*, 25.

CHAPTER TWO: BLACK IS A COUNTRY

1. John Locke, "Second Treatise," chap. 16, in *Two Treatises of Government*.
2. Wallerstein's review of Christopher Fyfe, *Africanus Horton, 1835–1883: West African Scientist and Patriot* (New York: Oxford University Press, 1972).
3. Fyfe, *Africanus Horton*, 110.
4. Hakim Adi and Marika Sherwood, *Pan-African History: Political Figures from Africa and the Diaspora since 1787* (Abingdon, Oxfordshire, UK: Routledge, 2003), 88.
5. Fyfe, *Africanus Horton*, 158.
6. David Walker, *Walker's Appeal, in Four Articles* (Boston: David Walker, 1830), 34.
7. W. E. B. Du Bois, *The Souls of Black Folk* (Chicago: A.C. McClurg and Co., 1904), 4.
8. Michael O. West, "Garveyism Root and Branch: From the Age of Revolution to the Onset of Black Power," in *Global Garveyism*, eds. Ronald J Stephens and Adam Ewing (Gainesville: University Press of Florida, 2019), 15–58.
9. Martin R. Delany, *Blake; or The Huts of America*, ed. Jerome McGann (Cambridge, MA: Harvard University Press, 2017), xviii.
10. Gloria Chuku, "African Intellectuals as Cultural Nationalists: A Comparative Analysis of Edward Wilmot Blyden and Mbonu Ojike," *Journal of African American History* 99, no. 4 (2014): 350–78.
11. Edward W. Blyden, *Our Origin, Dangers, and Duties. The Annual Address before the Mayor and Common Council of the City of Monrovia, 26 July 1865* (New York: 1865), 36.
12. Adi and Sherwood, *Pan-African History*, 12.
13. Kwame Nkrumah, "At Long Last, the Battle Has Ended!," speech at independence, March 6, 1957, posted by the BBC World Service Programmes, last updated March 2, 2007.
14. Louis Menand, *The Free World: Art and Thought in the Cold War* (New York: Farrar, Straus and Giroux, 2021), 199.
15. J. E. Casely Hayford, *Gold Coast Native Institutions: With Thoughts upon a Healthy Imperial Policy for the Gold Coast and Ashanti* (London: Sweet and Maxwell, 1903), 22.
16. As used by Casely Hayford, "Ethiopian" meant person of African descent in the broadest possible sense. This encompassed the furthest reaches of the Atlantic world, and indeed wherever else an African diaspora might be found.
17. Yogita Goyal, *Romance, Diaspora, and Black Atlantic Literature* (Cambridge, UK: Cambridge University Press, 2010), 104.
18. Kelefa Sanneh, "The Wizard: Before There Was a Black American President, Black America Had a President," *New Yorker*, January 25, 2009.
19. Benjamin Quarles, *The Negro in the Making of America* (New York: Collier Books, 1987), 167.
20. Adam Ewing, *The Age of Garvey: How a Jamaican Activist Created a Mass Movement and Changed Global Black Politics* (Princeton: Princeton University Press, 2014), 37.
21. Magnus J. Sampson, ed., *West African Leadership: Public Speeches Delivered by J. E. Casely Hayford* (London: Frank Cass and Company, 1969), 75.
22. Gerald Horne, "Looking Forward/Looking Backward: The Black Constituency for Africa Past & Present," *Black Scholar* 29, no. 1 (Spring 1999): 30–33.
23. Goyal, *Romance, Diaspora, and Black Atlantic Literature*, 122; J. Casely Hayford, *Ethiopia Unbound: Studies in Race Emancipation* (London: C. M. Phillips, 1911), 183.
24. Casely Hayford, *Ethiopia Unbound*, 170.
25. Brandon Kendhammer, "DuBois the Pan-Africanist and the Development of African Nationalism," *Ethnic and Racial Studies* 30, no. 1 (January 2007): 61.
26. Casely Hayford to W. E. B. Du Bois, June 8, 1904, in W. E. B. Du Bois Papers (MS 312), Special Collections and University Archives, University of Massachusetts at Amherst.
27. Casely Hayford, *Ethiopia Unbound*, 181.

28. "Nationalism as a West African Ideal: Casely Hayford's Address to the Union on November 5, 1926," *Wāsù: Journal of the West African Students' Union of Great Britain* 2 (December 1926): 23–34.
29. Robert Addo-Fening, "Ghana Under Colonial Rule: An Outline of the Early Period and the Interwar Years," *Transactions of the Historical Society of Ghana* 15 (January 2013): 62.
30. Quoted in Sampson, *West African Leadership*, 156–157, as seen in Marika Sherwood, *Kwame Nkrumah: The Years Abroad, 1935–1947* (Legon, Ghana: Freedom Publications, 1996), 14.
31. "Casely Hayford, Joseph Ephraim," in *The Oxford Encyclopedia of African Thought*, ed. F. Abiola Irele and Biodun Jeyifo (Oxford: Oxford University Press, 2010), 59.
32. Goyal, *Romance, Diaspora, and Black Atlantic Literature*, p. 122.
33. Wayne J. Urban, *Black Scholar: Horace Mann Bond, 1904–1972* (Athens: University of Georgia Press, 1992), 124.
34. Ralph Ellison, *Invisible Man* (New York: Vintage, 1947), 367.
35. Muhammad Ali, "How Come Is Everything White?," interview with Sir Michael Parkinson, BBC, October 17, 1971.
36. George Padmore and Tiemoko Garan Kouyat, "Inventing the Black International," in *The Practice of diaspora: Literature, Translation, and the Rise of Black Internationalism*, by Brent Hayes Edwards (Cambridge, MA: Harvard University Press, 2003), 241–305.
37. Harold Cruse, *The Crisis of the Negro Intellectual* (1967; repr., New York: New York Review of Books, 2005), 133.
38. Ewing, *The Age of Garvey*, 42.
39. Marcus Garvey, "The Negro's Greatest Enemy," *Current History* 18, no. 6 (1923): 953.
40. Jeffrey C. Stewart, *The New Negro: The Life of Alain Locke* (New York: Oxford University Press, 2018), 231.
41. Booker T. Washington, Atlanta Exposition speech, Atlanta, GA, September 18, 1895, State Historical Society of Iowa.
42. Robert J. Norrell, *Up from History: The Life of Booker T. Washington* (Cambridge, MA: Harvard University Press, 2011), 124.
43. Colin Grant, *Negro with a Hat: The Rise and Fall of Marcus Garvey and His Dream of Mother Africa* (London: Jonathan Cape, 2008), 298.
44. Nell Irvin Painter, *Creating Black Americans: African-American History and Its Meaning, 1619 to the Present* (New York: Oxford University Press, 2006), 189.
45. Kwame Nkrumah, *Ghana: The Autobiography of Kwame Nkrumah* (New York: International Publishers, 1957), 45.
46. Marcus Garvey, "The British West Indies in the Mirror of Civilization: History Making by Colonial Negros," *African Times and Orient Review* (London), October 1913, reproduced in Robert A. Hall ed., *The Marcus Garvey and Universal Negro Improvement Association Papers*, vol. 1 (Berkeley: UC Press, 1983), 27.
47. David Killingray, "British Racial Attitudes towards Black People during the Two World Wars, 1914–1945," in *Colonial Soldiers in Europe 1914–1945: Aliens in Uniform in Wartime Societies*, ed. Eric Storm and Ali Al Tuma (New York: Routledge, 2016), 100.
48. Grant, *Negro with a Hat*, 139.
49. Quarles, *Negro in the Making of America*, 186.
50. W. E. B. Du Bois, "Returning Soldiers," *The Crisis*, May 1919.
51. Marcus Garvey at UNIA Madison Square Garden Conference, New York City, August 3, 1920, in Amy Jacques Garvey, ed., *Philosophy and Opinions of Marcus Garvey* (The Journal of Pan-African Studies, 2009), 23, ebook.
52. Frederick Cooper, *Africa Since 1940: The Past of the Present* (Cambridge, UK: Cambridge University Press, 2002), 25.
53. Marcus Garvey, "The Negro's Place in World Organization," *Negro World*, March 24, 1923.
54. Ewing, *The Age of Garvey*, 92.
55. Kwegyir Aggrey in *Evening Telegram*, Toronto, December 5, 1923, James Aggrey Papers, Moorland-Spingarn Research Center, Howard University.

CHAPTER THREE: SO MUCH TO DO, SO LITTLE DONE

1. Marika Sherwood, *Kwame Nkrumah: The Years Abroad, 1935–1947* (Legon, Ghana: Freedom Publications, 1996), 21.
2. Kwame Nkrumah, *Ghana: The Autobiography of Kwame Nkrumah* (New York: International Publishers, 1957), 24.
3. Nkrumah, *Ghana: Autobiography*, 24.
4. Nkrumah, *Ghana: Autobiography*, 26.
5. Nkrumah, *Ghana: Autobiography*, 26.
6. Nkrumah, *Ghana: Autobiography*, 12.
7. Nkrumah, *Ghana: Autobiography*, 38.
8. Nkrumah, *Ghana: Autobiography*, 36.

9. Nkrumah, *Ghana: Autobiography*, 41.
10. Nkrumah, *Ghana: Autobiography*, 56.
11. Nkrumah, *Ghana: Autobiography*, 21.
12. George Orwell, *The Road to Wigan Pier* (San Diego: Mariner Books Classics, 1958), 79.
13. George Orwell, *Road to Wigan Pier*, 136.
14. Nkrumah, *Ghana: Autobiography*, 27.
15. Psalms 63:31, King James Bible.
16. Gersham A. Nelson, "Rastafarians and Ethiopianism," in *Imagining Home: Class, Culture and Nationalism in the African Diaspora*, eds. Sydney J. Lemelle and Robin D. G. Kelley (London: Verso, 1994), 73.
17. "J. A. Rogers Tells Why We Should Help Ethiopia," *Pittsburgh Courier*, July 20, 1935.
18. "Italy May Take Decades and Then Not Subdue the Ethiopians," *The Pittsburgh Courier*, October 10, 1935.
19. On African American activism on behalf of Ethiopia, see: Nell Irvin Painter, *Creating Black Americans* (New York: Oxford University Press, 2006), 212.
20. Sherwood, *Nkrumah: The Years Abroad*, 63.
21. Nkrumah, *Ghana: Autobiography*, 28.
22. Kwame Nkrumah, application for admittance, March 1, 1935, Nkrumah archives, Lincoln University.
23. Kwame Nkrumah, application.
24. W. E. B. Du Bois, *The Souls of Black Folk* (1903; reprint Greenwich, CT: Crest Reprints, 1961), 31.
25. Leonard Leslie Bethel, "1939—The Role of Lincoln University (Pennsylvania) in the Education of African Leadership: 1854–1970" (PhD diss., Rutgers University, 1975), 7.
26. Bethel, "Role of Lincoln University," 4.
27. Evelyn Rowand, *The Effect of Lincoln University Upon the Leaders of British West Africa* (MA thesis, University of Alberta, 1964), 3.
28. Rowand, *Effect of Lincoln University*, 3.
29. Ama Biney, *Kwame Nkrumah: An Intellectual Biography* (PhD thesis, University of London, 2007), 37.
30. Kwame Nkrumah, application.
31. Adam Ewing, *The Age of Garvey: How a Jamaican Activist Created a Mass Movement and Changed Global Black Politics* (Princeton: Princeton University Press, 2014), 43.
32. Sherwood, *Nkrumah: The Years Abroad*, 22.
33. Nkrumah, *Ghana: Autobiography*, 29.
34. Claude Brown, *Manchild in the Promised Land* (1965; repr., New York: Scribner, 2011), ix.
35. Ralph Ellison, *Shadow and Act* (New York: Knopf Doubleday Publishing Group, 2011), 15.
36. Lawrence Jackson, *Ralph Ellison: Emergence of Genius* (New York: John Wiley and Sons, 2002), 163.
37. Ralph Ellison to Ida Bell, August 30, 1937, in *The Selected Letters of Ralph Ellison*, ed. John F. Callahan. (New York: Penguin, 2019), 88.
38. David Levering Lewis, *When Harlem Was in Vogue* (Oxford, UK: Oxford University Press, 1979), 156.
39. Nkrumah, *Ghana: Autobiography*, 22.

CHAPTER FOUR: ACE BOY

1. Wil Haygood, *Showdown: Thurgood Marshall and the Supreme Court Nomination That Changed America* (New York: Vintage, 2016), 43.
2. Leonard Leslie Bethel, *The Role of Lincoln University (Pennsylvania) in the Education of African Leadership: 1854–1970* (PhD diss., Rutgers University, 1975), 53.
3. Marika Sherwood, *Kwame Nkrumah: The Years Abroad, 1935–1947* (Legon, Ghana: Freedom Publications, 1996), 31.
4. Kwame Nkrumah, *Ghana: The Autobiography of Kwame Nkrumah* (New York: International Publishers, 1957), 30.
5. Nkrumah, *Ghana: Autobiography*, 31.
6. Sherwood, *Nkrumah: The Years Abroad*, 34.
7. Nkrumah, *Ghana: Autobiography*, 29.
8. The Abyssinian Baptist Church was founded in 1809 after seamen from the Kingdom of Ethiopia joined arms with African American worshippers to protest against segregation in the church pews of New York City.
9. Nkrumah, *Ghana: Autobiography*, 28.
10. Wil Haygood, *King of the Cats: The Life and Times of Adam Clayton Powell, Jr.* (New York: Houghton Mifflin, 1993), 74.
11. Cheryl Greenberg, "The Politics of Disorder: 'Reexamining Harlem's Riots of 1935 and 1943,'" *Journal of Urban History* 18, no. 4 (1992): 395.
12. Sherwood, *Nkrumah: The Years Abroad*, 35.
13. Nkrumah, *Ghana: Autobiography*, 32.
14. Sherwood, *Nkrumah: The Years Abroad*, 53.
15. W. E. B. Du Bois, "The Future and Function of the Private Negro College," *Crisis* 53 (August 1946): 254.
16. E. Franklin Frazier, "A Note on Negro Education," *Opportunity* 2 (March 1924): 75.

17. David Levering Lewis, *When Harlem Was in Vogue* (Oxford, UK: Oxford University Press, 1979), 161.
18. Raymond Wolters, *The New Negro on Campus: Black College Rebellions of the 1920s* (Princeton: Princeton University Press, 1975), 279.
19. Brenda Gayle Plummer, *Rising Wind: Black Americans and U.S. Foreign Affairs, 1933–1960* (Chapel Hill: University of North Carolina Press, 1996), 34.
20. Bethel, *Role of Lincoln University in African Leadership*, 48–49.
21. Nkrumah, *Ghana: Autobiography*, 35.
22. Nkrumah, *Ghana: Autobiography*, 37.
23. Nkrumah, *Ghana: Autobiography*, 36.
24. Nkrumah, *Ghana: Autobiography*, 37.
25. "Aggrey Memorial Services," *The African Interpreter* 1, no. 1 (February 1, 1943): 9, Lincoln University Archives.
26. Kwame Nkrumah to Dean Johnson, April 24, 1943, Nkrumah archives, Lincoln University.
27. Ama Biney, *Kwame Nkrumah: An Intellectual Biography* (PhD thesis, University of London, 2007) 149.
28. Kwame Nkrumah, *Africa Must Unite* (New York: Praeger, 1963), 43.
29. Nkrumah, *Ghana: Autobiography*, 18.
30. Nkrumah, *Ghana: Autobiography*, 42.
31. Nkrumah, *Ghana: Autobiography*, 33.
32. Sherwood, *Nkrumah: The Years Abroad*, xx.
33. George Johnson to Harvard, recommendation letter, Lincoln University archives.
34. Nkrumah, *Ghana: Autobiography*, 33.
35. Sherwood, *Nkrumah: The Years Abroad*, 50.

CHAPTER FIVE: YOURS AFRICANLY

1. This second thesis was titled *Mind and Thought in Primitive Society: A Study in Ethno-Philosophy with Special Reference to the Akan Peoples of the Gold Coast*.
2. Daniel Immerwahr, "A New History of World War II," *The Atlantic*, April 4, 2022.
3. Kwame Nkrumah, *Ghana: The Autobiography of Kwame Nkrumah* (New York: International Publishers, 1957), 46.
4. Nkrumah thesis, National Archives of Ghana, as quoted in Ama Biney, *Kwame Nkrumah: An Intellectual Biography* (PhD thesis, University of London, 2007), 48.
5. Marika Sherwood, *Kwame Nkrumah: The Years Abroad, 1935–1947* (Legon, Ghana: Freedom Publications, 1996), 64.
6. Sherwood, *Nkrumah: The Years Abroad*, 32.
7. Nkrumah, *Ghana: Autobiography*, 32.
8. Nkrumah, *Ghana: Autobiography*, 44.
9. Nkrumah, *Ghana: Autobiography*, 44.
10. Kal Raustiala, *The Absolutely Indispensable Man: Ralph Bunche, the United Nations, and the Fight to End Empire* (New York: Oxford University Press, 2023), 62.
11. Ralph Bunche, "Africa and the Current World Conflict," in *Ralph J. Bunche: Selected Speeches and Writings*, ed. Charles P. Henry (Ann Arbor: University of Michigan Press, 1995), 146.
12. Sherwood, *Nkrumah: The Years Abroad*, 74.
13. Sherwood, *Nkrumah: The Years Abroad*, 78.
14. Wil Haygood, *King of the Cats: The Life and Times of Adam Clayton Powell, Jr.* (New York: Houghton Mifflin, 1993), 78.
15. C. L. R. James, "Nkrumah: Founder of African Emancipation," *Black World* 29, no. 9 (July 1972): 4–5.
16. Sherwood, *Nkrumah: The Years Abroad*, xx.

CHAPTER SIX: EUSTON STATION

1. Kwame Nkrumah, *Ghana: The Autobiography of Kwame Nkrumah* (New York: International Publishers, 1957), 49.
2. Cynthia Davis and Verner D. Mitchell, *Images in the River: The Life and Work of Waring Cuney* (Lubbock: Texas Tech University Press, 2024), 5.
3. Alain Locke, "Enter the New Negro," *Survey Graphic: Harlem, Mecca of the New Negro* 53, no. 11 (March 1925): 631–34.
4. "Alain Locke: The Legacy of the Ancestral Arts, 1925" in *Primitivism and Twentieth Century Art: A Documentary History*, eds. Jack Flam and Miriam Deutch (Berkeley: University of California Press, 2003), 197.
5. Jeffrey C. Stewart, *The New Negro: The Life of Alain Locke* (New York: Oxford University Press, 2018), 149.
6. Marc Greif, "Black and White Life," *London Review of Books* 29, no. 21 (November 1, 2007): 4.
7. Leslie James, *George Padmore and Decolonization from Below: Pan-Africanism, the Cold War, and the End of Empire* (London: Palgrave Macmillan, 2015), 28.
8. Tridup Suhrud, "'You Are Today the One Person in the World Who Can Prevent a War.' Read Gandhi's Letters to Hitler," *Time*, September 25, 2019.

9. Joe Appiah, *Joe Appiah: The Autobiography of an African Patriot* (New York: Praeger, 1990), 171.
10. Tufuku Zuberi, *African Independence: How Africa Shapes the World* (London: Rowman and Littlefield, 2015), 39.
11. Mark Mazower, *No Enchanted Palace: The End of Empire and the Ideological Origins of the United Nations* (Princeton: Princeton University Press, 2013), 151.
12. Tony Judt, *Postwar: A History of Europe Since 1945* (New York: Penguin Books, 2005), 278.
13. Richard Toye, *Churchill's Empire: The World That Made Him and the World He Made* (New York: Henry Holt and Co., 2010), 261.
14. Appiah, *Autobiography of an African Patriot*, 163.
15. Toye, *Churchill's Empire*, 230.
16. Orwell, *The Road to Wigan Pier* (San Diego: Mariner Books Classics, 1958), 210–11.
17. Orwell, *Road to Wigan Pier*, 211.
18. Frederick Cooper, "Reconstructing Empire in British and French Africa," *Past and Present* 210, no. 6 (2011): 204.
19. See Frederick Cooper, *Decolonization and African Society: The Labor Question in French and British Africa* (Cambridge: Cambridge University Press, 1996), 204.
20. Caroline Elkins, *Legacy of Violence: A History of the British Empire* (New York: Knopf, 2022), 468. Other estimates range even higher.
21. James, *Padmore and Decolonization from Below*, 54.
22. James, *Padmore and Decolonization from Below*, 81.
23. James, *Padmore and Decolonization from Below*, 56.
24. James, *Padmore and Decolonization from Below*, 42.

CHAPTER SEVEN: THE DAWN OF ACTION

1. Joe Appiah, *Joe Appiah: The Autobiography of an African Patriot* (New York: Praeger, 1990), 163.
2. Appiah, *Autobiography of an African Patriot*, 163.
3. Ashley Robertson Preston, *Mary McLeod Bethune the Pan-Africanist* (Gainesville: University Press of Florida, 2023), 12.
4. Martha S. Jones, "Mary McLeod Bethune Was at the Vanguard of More Than 50 Years of Black Progress," *Smithsonian Magazine*, July 2020.
5. Kal Raustiala, *The Absolutely Indispensable Man: Ralph Bunche, the United Nations, and the Fight to End Empire* (Oxford: Oxford University Press, 2022), 110.
6. Appiah, *Autobiography of an African Patriot*, 164.
7. Peter Abrahams, "Nkrumah, Kenyatta, and the Old Order," *The Star* (Nairobi), April 13, 2013.
8. For an account of this see, for example, Bankole Timothy, *Kwame Nkrumah: His Rise to Power* (London: George Allen and Unwin, 1963), 36.
9. Kwame Nkrumah, *Ghana: The Autobiography of Kwame Nkrumah* (New York: International Publishers, 1957), 60.
10. Nkrumah, *Ghana: Autobiography*, 57.
11. Nkrumah, *Ghana: Autobiography*, 56.
12. "The Untold Story of Dr. Ako Adjei," *Christian Messenger* (Accra), July 1–14, 1992, as quoted in Marika Sherwood, *Kwame Nkrumah: The Years Abroad, 1935–1947* (Legon, Ghana: Freedom Publications, 1996), 55.
13. Nkrumah, *Ghana: Autobiography*, 61.
14. Nkrumah, *Ghana: Autobiography*, 61.
15. Nkrumah, *Ghana: Autobiography*, 62.
16. Nkrumah, *Ghana: Autobiography*, 62.
17. Nkrumah, *Ghana: Autobiography*, 62.
18. Marika Sherwood, "Kwame Nkrumah: The London Years," in *Africans in Britain*, ed. David Killingray (London: Routledge, 1994), 168.
19. Sherwood, *Nkrumah: The Years Abroad*, 161.
20. Appiah, *Autobiography of an African Patriot*, 170.
21. Kojo Botsio, who had been the treasurer of WANS, would become Nkrumah's right-hand man during his years in power and was at his side even at the moment of his overthrow. Appiah, *Autobiography of an African Patriot*, 171.
22. Sherwood, *Nkrumah: The Years Abroad*, 129.
23. Charles de Gaulle, *Mémoires de Guerre*, trans. Howard French (Paris: Librairie Plon, 1954), 1.
24. Nkrumah, *Ghana: Autobiography*, 61.
25. Kwame Nkrumah, *Africa Must Unite* (London: Heinemann, 1963), 135.
26. Abrahams, "Nkrumah, Kenyatta, and the Old Order."
27. Kwame Arhin, *A View of Kwame Nkrumah, 1909–1972: An Interpretation* (Accra: Sedco Publishing, 1990), 6.
28. Murithi Mutiga, "Jomo Kenyatta's Troubled Years in London That Drove Him to Greatness," *Nation*, July 2, 2020.

CHAPTER EIGHT: THE DARKER NATIONS

1. Vijay Prashad, *The Darker Nations: A People's History of the Third World* (New York: The New Press, 2007), 28.
2. Louis Menand, *The Free World: Art and Thought in the Cold War* (New York: Farrar, Straus and Giroux, 2021), 9.
3. Telegram from Kennan (Charge in the Soviet Union) to the Secretary of State, February 22, 1946, 861.00/2-2246, National Security Archive of George Washington University.
4. Winston Churchill, "Sinews of Peace" address (also known as the "Iron Curtain" speech), given at Westminster College, Fulton Missouri, March 5, 1946, from press release by British Information Services, transcript at UK National Archives website.
5. Jeffrey Frank, *The Trials of Harry S. Truman: The Extraordinary Presidency of an Ordinary Man, 1945–1953* (New York: Simon and Schuster, 2022), 115.
6. Telegram from Kennan to the Secretary of State.
7. Kennan, as Menand has written, was "firmly anti-majoritarian, not only in foreign affairs, where he considered public opinion a menace, but also in governmental decision-making generally" and loathed declarations about the rights of peoples of self-determination (Menand, *Free World*, 9, 21).
8. Hans J. Morgenthau, *Politics Among Nations: The Struggle for Power and Peace* (New York: Knopf, 1948), 196.
9. Menand, *Free World*, xii.
10. Tony Chafer, *The End of Empire in French West Africa: France's Successful Decolonization?* (Oxford: Oxford University Press, 2002), 85.
11. Frantz Fanon, *The Wretched of the Earth* (New York: Grove Press, 2021), 2.
12. Frank Dikötter, *China After Mao: The Rise of a Superpower* (New York: Bloomsbury, 2022), 23.
13. Caroline Elkins, *Legacy of Violence: A History of the British Empire* (New York: Vintage, 2023), 462.
14. Elkins, *Legacy of Violence*, 480, 511, 517.
15. Robert Templer, "General Vo Nguyen Giap Obituary," *Guardian*, October 4, 2013.
16. David Halberstam, *The Fifties* (New York: Villard Books, 1993), 403.
17. Bernard B. Fall, "Bernard Fall on the Battle of Dien Bien Phu," *Parallel Natives* (blog), n.d.
18. Bernard B. Fall, "Dienbienphu: Battle to Remember," *New York Times*, May 3, 1964.
19. Elizabeth A. Cobbs, "Decolonization, the Cold War, and the Foreign Policy of the Peace Corps," *Diplomatic History* 20, no. 1 (January 1996): 79–105.

CHAPTER NINE: LAND AND FREEDOM

1. From Ashley Jackson, *The British Empire and the Second World War* (London: Hambledon, 2006), 171.
2. Jackson, *British Empire and Second World War*, 213.
3. France preserved this practice of requiring its former colonies to bank their hard currency reserves with the French treasury according to the terms of membership in a common, nominally African currency, the African Financial Community franc, or CFA, that it has helped maintain for decades after formal independence.
4. Harold Evans, "Studies in War-Time Organisation: (2) The Resident Ministry in West Africa," *African Affairs* 43, no. 173 (October 1944): 152–58.

CHAPTER TEN: NOTHING TO LOSE BUT CHAINS

1. See for example Emmanuel Asiedu-Acquah, *"And Still the Youth Are Coming": Youth and Popular Politics in Ghana, c. 1900–1979* (PhD diss., Harvard University, 2015).
2. Franklin D. Roosevelt and Winston S. Churchill, "Joint Statement by President Roosevelt and Prime Minister Churchill, August 14, 1941," in *Foreign Relations of the United States Diplomatic Papers, 1941, General, The Soviet Union, Volume I*, Document 372, eds. Matilda F Axton, N. O. Sappington, Shirley L. Phillips, Rogers P. Churchill, and Irving L. Thomson (Washington DC: US Government Printing Office, 1959).
3. William B. Cohen, *Rulers of Empire: The French Colonial Service in Africa* (Stanford: Hoover Institution Press, 1971), 167.
4. Tony Chafer, *The End of Empire in French West Africa: France's Successful Decolonization?* (Oxford: Berg Publishers, 2002), 57.
5. Robert Cornevin, "Le corps des administrateurs de la France d'Outremer durant la 2e guerre mondiale," in *Institut d'Histoire du Temps Present, Les Chemins de la decolonisation de l'empire francais 1936–56* (CNRS Éditions, 1986), 456, as seen in Chafer, *End of Empire in French West Africa*, 60.
6. African soldiers were deliberately removed from French resistance units to whiten them prior to the final liberation of Paris in order to promote de Gaulle's claim that France had essentially freed itself.
7. Chafer, *End of Empire in French West Africa*, 46–47.
8. Chafer, *End of Empire in French West Africa*, 95.
9. Jane Burbank and Frederick Cooper, *Post-Imperial Possibilities: Eurasia, Eurafrica, Afroasia* (Princeton: Princeton University Press, 2023), 8.

CHAPTER ELEVEN: SALTPOND

1. Kwame Nkrumah, *Ghana: The Autobiography of Kwame Nkrumah* (New York: International Publishers, 1957), 64.
2. Nkrumah, *Ghana: Autobiography*, 65.
3. Nkrumah, *Ghana: Autobiography*, 60.
4. Nkrumah, *Ghana: Autobiography*, 60.
5. Nkrumah, *Ghana: Autobiography*, 70.
6. Nkrumah, *Ghana: Autobiography*, 70.
7. Nkrumah, *Ghana: Autobiography*, 70.
8. Dennis Austin, *Politics in Ghana: 1946–1960* (Oxford: Oxford University Press, 1964), 54.
9. Austin, *Politics in Ghana*, 54, 55.

CHAPTER TWELVE: THE MONGOOSE

1. Basil Davidson, *Black Star: A View of the Life and Times of Kwame Nkrumah* (New York: Praeger, 1973), 60.
2. Bankole Timothy, *Kwame Nkrumah: His Rise to Power* (Chicago: Northwestern University Press, 1963), 168.
3. Dennis Austin, *Politics in Ghana: 1946–1960* (Oxford: Oxford University Press, 1964), 53.
4. Kwame Nkrumah, *Ghana: The Autobiography of Kwame Nkrumah* (New York: International Publishers, 1957), 71.
5. Nkrumah, *Ghana: Autobiography*, 72.
6. Nkrumah, *Ghana: Autobiography*, 72.
7. Nkrumah, *Ghana: Autobiography*, 74.
8. John H. Dalton, "Colony and Metropolis: Some Aspects of British Rule in Gold Coast and the Implications for and Understanding of Ghana Today," *Journal of Economic History* 21, no. 4 (December 1961): 556.
9. Dalton, "Colony and Metropolis," 556.
10. Austin, *Politics in Ghana*, 68.
11. David Rooney, *Kwame Nkrumah: The Political Kingdom in the Third World* (London: I. B. Taurus and Co., 1988), 35.
12. Nkrumah, *Ghana: Autobiography*, 75.
13. Nkrumah, *Ghana: Autobiography*, 76.
14. Austin, *Politics in Ghana*, 74. Other accounts say that three ex-servicemen were killed in the shooting.
15. Austin, *Politics in Ghana*, 75.
16. Rooney, *Political Kingdom in the Third World*, 79.
17. Nkrumah, *Ghana: Autobiography*, 80.
18. Nkrumah, *Ghana: Autobiography*, 82.
19. Nkrumah, *Ghana: Autobiography*, 86.
20. Rooney, *Political Kingdom in the Third World*, 40.
21. Nkrumah, *Ghana: Autobiography*, 87.
22. Davidson, *Black Star*, 64.
23. Davidson, *Black Star*, 65.

CHAPTER THIRTEEN: POSITIVE ACTION

1. "Interview with Komla Gbedema," *People's Century: Freedom Now, 1947–1997*, PBS.org, n.d.
2. Profile-Kwame Nkrumah, *The Observer*, February 11, 1951.
3. Dennis Austin, *Politics in Ghana: 1946–1960* (Oxford: Oxford University Press, 1964), 85.
4. Basil Davidson, *Black Star: A View of the Life and Times of Kwame Nkrumah* (New York: Praeger, 1973), 68.
5. Kwame Nkrumah, *Ghana: The Autobiography of Kwame Nkrumah* (New York: International Publishers, 1957), 103; Davidson, *Black Star*, 69.
6. Nkrumah, *Ghana: Autobiography*, 104.
7. Austin, *Politics in Ghana*, 85.
8. Davidson, *Black Star*, 73.
9. Ooi Keat Gin, *Post-War Borneo, 1945–1950: Nationalism, Empire and State Building* (Abingdon, Oxfordshire, UK: Routledge, 2013), 78.
10. Nkrumah, *Ghana: Autobiography*, 103.
11. Austin, *Politics in Ghana*, 90.
12. David Rooney, *Kwame Nkrumah: The Political Kingdom in the Third World* (London: I. B. Taurus and Co., 1988), 50.
13. Rooney, *Political Kingdom in the Third World*, 51.
14. Nkrumah, *Ghana: Autobiography*, 116.
15. Nkrumah, *Ghana: Autobiography*, 116.
16. Nkrumah, *Ghana: Autobiography*, 118.

17. Austin, *Politics in Ghana*, 90.
18. Rooney, *Political Kingdom in the Third World*, 55.
19. Austin, *Politics in Ghana*, 90.

CHAPTER FOURTEEN: SEEK THE POLITICAL KINGDOM

1. William Fulton, "British Rulers Whitewashed in African Riots: Firing by Police Head Called Justified," *Chicago Daily Tribune*, September 6, 1948.
2. "Interview with Komla Gbedema," *People's Century: Freedom Now, 1947–1997*, PBS.org, n.d.
3. Kwame Nkrumah, *Ghana: The Autobiography of Kwame Nkrumah* (New York: International Publishers, 1957), 128.
4. Gbedemah, "Interview with Komla Gbedemah."
5. Dennis Austin, *Politics in Ghana: 1946–1960* (Oxford: Oxford University Press, 1964), 90.
6. Jonathan Derrick, *Africa, Empire and Fleet Street: Albert Cartwright and West Africa Magazine* (New York: Oxford University Press, 2018), 138.
7. *West Africa*, December 1950.
8. Austin, *Politics in Ghana*, 150.
9. Austin, *Politics in Ghana*, 118.
10. Gbedema, "Interview with Komla Gbedema."
11. Nkrumah, *Ghana: Autobiography*, 141.
12. Austin, *Politics in Ghana*, 112.
13. Gbedema, "Interview with Komla Gbedema."
14. Gbedema, "Interview with Komla Gbedema."
15. Gbedema, "Interview with Komla Gbedema."
16. Gbedema, "Interview with Komla Gbedema."
17. Gbedema, "Interview with Komla Gbedema."
18. Gbedema, "Interview with Komla Gbedema."
19. Nkrumah, *Ghana: Autobiography*, 135.
20. Nkrumah, *Ghana: Autobiography*, 136.
21. "Profile-Kwame Nkrumah," *The Observer*, February 11, 1951, 2.
22. "Gold Coast: Tomcat Triumphant," *Newsweek* 37 (February 19, 1951): 41–42.
23. "Lincoln Graduate Released As Party Wins Africa Polling," *The Philadelphia Tribune*, February 20, 1951.
24. Nkrumah, *Ghana: Autobiography*, 169.
25. Austin, *Politics in Ghana*,150–51.
26. Frederick Cooper, "Decolonization and African Society: The Labor Question in French and British Africa," *African Studies*, Series no. 89 (Cambridge: Cambridge University Press, 1996), 214.
27. David Rooney, *Kwame Nkrumah: The Political Kingdom in the Third World* (London: I. B. Taurus and Co., 1988), 61.
28. Rooney, *Political Kingdom in the Third World*, 64.
29. Davidson, Black Star, 80.
30. Rooney, *Political Kingdom in the Third World*, 63.
31. Rooney, *Political Kingdom in the Third World*, 63.

CHAPTER FIFTEEN: AFTER THE BALL (THE DRUMS ARE HEAVY)

1. Dennis Austin, *Politics in Ghana: 1946–1960* (Oxford: Oxford University Press, 1964), 156.
2. Kwame Nkrumah, *Ghana: The Autobiography of Kwame Nkrumah* (New York: International Publishers, 1957), 151.
3. Erica Powell, *Private Secretary (Female)/Gold Coast* (London: C. Hurst and Co., 1984), 10.
4. Powell, *Private Secretary*, 11.
5. Nkrumah, *Ghana: Autobiography*, 150.
6. Basil Davidson, *Black Star: A View of the Life and Times of Kwame Nkrumah* (New York: Praeger, 1973), 97.
7. Nkrumah, *Ghana: Autobiography*, 144.
8. Powell, *Private Secretary*, 76.
9. Bankole Timothy, *Kwame Nkrumah: His Rise to Power* (London: George Allen and Unwin, 1955), 157.

CHAPTER SIXTEEN: THE RACE MEN

1. Kwame Nkrumah, *Ghana: The Autobiography of Kwame Nkrumah* (New York: International Publishers, 1957), 157.
2. Wayne J. Urban, *Black Scholar: Horace Mann Bond, 1904–1972* (Atlanta: University of Georgia Press, 1992), 146.
3. James T. Campbell, *Middle Passages: African American Journeys to Africa, 1787–2005* (New York: Penguin Press, 2006), 240.
4. W. E. B. Du Bois, "Little Portraits of Africa," *The Crisis*, April 1924, 273.

NOTES

5. Richard I. McKinney, *Mordecai, the Man and His Message: The Story of Mordecai Wyatt Johnson* (Washington, DC: Howard University Press, 1997), 99.
6. Jason C. Parker, "'Made in America Revolutions'? The 'Black University' and the American Role in the Decolonization of the Black Atlantic," *The Journal of American History* 96, no. 3 (December 2009): 732.
7. Nnamdi Azikiwe, *My Odyssey: An Autobiography* (Ann Arbor, MI: C. Hurst, 1970), 144. Also see Parker, "'Made in America Revolutions'?," 732.
8. Marika Sherwood, *Origins of Pan-Africanism: Henry Sylvester Williams, Africa, and the African Diaspora* (London: Routledge, 2011), 40.
9. J.R. Hooker, "The Pan-African Conference 1900," *Transition* 46 (1974): 20–24.
10. Du Bois, W. E. B. (William Edward Burghardt), 1868–1963. Memoranda on the future of Africa, ca. January 1919. W. E. B. Du Bois Papers (MS 312). Special Collections and University Archives, University of Massachusetts Amherst Libraries.
11. Chad L. Williams, *The Wounded World: W. E. B. Du Bois and the First World War* (New York: Farrar, Straus and Giraud, 2023), 125.
12. Williams, *The Wounded World*, 140.
13. "W. E. B. Du Bois to Charles Evans Hughes, U.S. Secretary of State," New York, June 23, 1921, *African Series Sample Documents* IX (June 1921–December 1922), UCLA African Studies Center.
14. Matthew F. Delmont, *Half American: The Epic Story of African Americans Fighting World War II at Home and Abroad* (New York: Viking, 2022), 296.
15. Richard M. Dalfiume, "The 'Forgotten Years' of the Negro Revolution," *Journal of American History* 55, no. 1 (June 1968): 93.
16. Les Payne and Tamara Payne, *The Dead Are Arising: The Life of Malcolm X* (New York: Liveright, 2020), 187.
17. Mark Dunton, "Black GIs Arrive in Britain (Part Two)," *The National Archives* (blog), October 20, 2022.
18. James G. Thompson, "Should I Sacrifice to Live 'Half-American'?," *Pittsburgh Courier*, January 31, 1942.
19. Philip S. Foner and Yuval Taylor, eds., *Frederick Douglass: Selected Speeches and Writings* (Chicago: Chicago Review Press, 2000), 533.
20. W. E. B. Du Bois, "Returning Soldiers," *The Crisis*, May 1919, 13.
21. Jervis Anderson, "Early Voice I—A. Philip Randolph's Radical Harlem: How a Labor Organizer's Disputes with Marcus Garvey Helped Set the Stage for the Civil-Rights Triumphs of the Nineteen-Sixties," *New Yorker*, November 24, 1972.
22. Anderson, "Randolph's Radical Harlem."
23. W. E. B. Du Bois, "Close Ranks," July 1918, in *Let Nobody Turn Us Around: Voices of Resistance, Reform, and Renewal; An African American Anthology*, eds. Manning Marable and Leith Mullings (New York: Bowman and Littlefield, 2000), 242–243.
24. Melvin L. Rogers and Jack Turner, *African American Political Thought: A Collective History* (Chicago: University of Chicago Press, 2021), 300.
25. Michael McCann, "A. Philip Randolph: Radicalizing Rights at the Intersection of Class and Race," in *African American Political Thought: A Collected History*, eds. Melvin L. Rogers and Jack Turner (Chicago: University of Chicago Press, 2021), 290–313.
26. Eric Arnesen, "A. Philipp Randolph, Black Anticommunism, and the Race Question," in *Rethinking U.S. Labor History: Essays on the Working-Class Experience, 1756–2009*, eds. Donna T. Haverty-Stacke, Daniel J. Walkowitz (New York: Continuum, 2010), 146.
27. Delmont, *Half American*, 50.
28. Cynthia Taylor, *A. Philip Randolph: The Religious Journey of an African American Labor Leader* (New York: New York University Press, 2006), 130.
29. Delmont, *Half American*, 50.
30. Jonathan Eig, *King: A Life* (New York: Farrar, Straus and Giroux, 2023), 47.
31. Delmont, *Half American*, 56.
32. Delmont, *Half American*, 57.
33. John Hope Franklin and August Meier, *Black Leaders of the Twentieth Century* (Champaign: University of Illinois Press, 1982), 155.
34. Eig, *King: A Life*, 48.
35. Thomas Borstelmann, *The Cold War and the Color Line* (Cambridge, MA: Harvard University Press, 2003), 107.
36. Manning Marable, *Malcolm X: A Life of Reinvention* (New York: Penguin, 2011), 163.
37. Eig, *King: A Life*, 184.

CHAPTER SEVENTEEN: THE RAPE OF DECENCY

1. Matthew F. Delmont, *Half American: The Epic Story of African Americans Fighting World War II at Home and Abroad* (New York: Viking, 2022), 243.
2. Delmont, *Half American*, 263–64

3. Delmont, *Half American*, 275, 276. I have drawn extensively on Delmont's valuable account for some of the historical background in this chapter.
4. David Halberstam, *The Fifties* (New York: Villard Books, 1993), 142.
5. Halberstam, *The Fifties*, 141.
6. Delmont, *Half American*, 267.
7. Ira Katznelson, *When Affirmative Action Was White: An Untold History of Racial Inequality in Twentieth-Century America* (New York: W. W. Norton, 2005), 116.
8. Katznelson, *When Affirmative Action Was White*, 128.
9. Katznelson, *When Affirmative Action Was White*, 116.
10. Wayne J. Urban, *Black Scholar: Horace Mann Bond, 1904–1972* (Atlanta: University of Georgia Press, 1992), 135.
11. Urban, *Black Scholar*, 135.
12. Kevin E. Grimm, "Symbol of Modernity: Ghana, African Americans, and the Eisenhower Administration" (PhD diss., Ohio University, 2012), 54. Original emphasis.
13. Grimm, "Symbol of Modernity," 55. Here and throughout this section, I have benefitted from the extensive archival research of Kevin E. Grimm.
14. Grimm, "Symbol of Modernity," 60.
15. Grimm, "Symbol of Modernity," 54.
16. *The Pittsburgh Courier*, "Because! Ten Cardinal Points in Courier's Campaign for Army and Navy Equality," March 26, 1938.
17. Bond to W. Montague Cobb, December 1, 1949, Bond Papers, 3.18.2B, cited in Urban, *Black Scholar*, 148.

CHAPTER EIGHTEEN: THE NEGRO CIRCUIT

1. Kwame Nkrumah, *Ghana: The Autobiography of Kwame Nkrumah* (New York: International Publishers, 1957).
2. Ian Fleming, *You Only Live Twice* (New York: New American Library of World Literature, 1964), chapter 4.
3. Nkrumah, *Ghana: Autobiography*, 158.
4. Nkrumah, *Ghana: Autobiography*, 158.
5. "Gold Coast Wields Big Power: Nkrumah Called West Africa's 'Gandhi'—Attitude Toward West Closely Watched Could Lead All Africans Favors Congress of Peoples," *New York Times*, June 3, 1951.
6. Susan Williams, *White Malice: The CIA and the Covert Recolonization of Africa* (New York: Hachette Books Group, 2021), 491.
7. Nkrumah, *Ghana: Autobiography*, 163.
8. Nkrumah, *Ghana: Autobiography*, 166.
9. Kwame Nkrumah's Commencement Address, Lincoln University, June 5, 1951. Horace Mann Bond Papers (MS 411), Special Collections and University Archives, University of Massachusetts Amherst Libraries.
10. Kwame Nkrumah's Commencement Address.
11. "'Cultural Bridge' to Africa Sought: Gold Coast Official Here Asks for Aid to 'See Imperialism Wiped Off Continent' Standards of Living," *New York Times*, June 10, 1951.
12. *New York Times*, June 18, 1951.
13. Kevin E. Grimm, "Symbol of Modernity: Ghana, African Americans, and the Eisenhower Administration" (PhD diss., Ohio University, 2012), 75.
14. Horace Mann Bond to James L. Brown, Secretary of African Opinion, May 28, 1951. Horace Mann Bond Papers (MS 411), Special Collections and University Archives, University of Massachusetts Amherst Libraries.
15. Horace Mann Bond to Colonel A. T. Walden, May 25, 1951. Horace Mann Bond Papers (MS 411), Special Collections and University Archives, University of Massachusetts Amherst Libraries.
16. Bond to Walden, Bond Papers (MS 411).
17. Grimm, "Symbol of Modernity," 75.
18. Richard Wright, *Black Power: A Record of Reactions in a Land of Pathos* (New York: Harper: 1954), 222.
19. Michael Krenn, *Black Diplomacy: African Americans and the State Department, 1945–69* (London: Routledge, 1999), 29–30.
20. Vijay Prashad, *The Darker Nations: A People's History of the Third World* (New York: New Press, 2007), 68.
21. Brenda Gayle Plummer, *Rising Wind: Black Americans and U.S. Foreign Affairs, 1935–1960* (Chapel Hill: University of North Carolina Press, 1996), note 13, chapter 4.
22. James H. Meriwether, *Proudly We Can Be Africans: Black Americans and Africa, 1935–1961* (Chapel Hill: University of North Carolina Press, 2002), 65.
23. George McGhee, "Africa's Role in the Free World Today," *Department of State Bulletin* 25, no. 629 (July 16, 1951): 97–99.
24. Michael L. Krenn, *The History of United States Cultural Diplomacy: 1770 to the Present Day* (New York: Bloomsbury Academic, 2017), 85.
25. Krenn, *Black Diplomacy*, 32.
26. Earl Warren. *The Memoirs of Earl Warren* (Garden City, NY: Doubleday, 1977), 191.

NOTES

27. Krenn, *Black Diplomacy*, 89.
28. David Halberstam, *The Fifties* (New York: Villard Books, 1993), 426.
29. Halberstam, *The Fifties*, 425.
30. Krenn, *Black Diplomacy*, 90.
31. "Memorandum for the Files: Meeting of Negro Leaders with the President," The White House, Washington, DC, June 23, 1958.

CHAPTER NINETEEN: LAND OF MY FATHERS

1. Zachary Karabell, *Architects of Intervention: The United States, the Third World, and the Cold War 1946–1962* (Baton Rouge: Louisiana State Press, 1999), 111.
2. Stephen Kinzer, *The Brothers: John Foster Dulles, Allen Dulles, and Their Secret World War* (New York: Times Books, 2013), 149.
3. Kinzer, *The Brothers*, 156.
4. "Nkrumah Says All Must Help Africa Gain Freedom," *Philadelphia Tribune*, June 9, 1951.
5. Kwame Nkrumah's Commencement Address, Lincoln University, June 5, 1951. Horace Mann Bond Papers (MS 411), Special Collections and University Archives, University of Massachusetts Amherst Libraries.
6. Arnold J. Toynbee, "A War of the Races? No." *New York Times*, August 7, 1960.
7. "34. Memorandum of a Conference with the President, White House, July 31, 1956," in *Foreign Relations of the United States 1955–1957, Vol. XVI, Suez Crisis, July 26–December 31, 1956*, ed. Nina J. Noring (Washington, DC: US Government Printing Office, 1990).
8. Natalia Telepneva, *Cold War Liberation: The Soviet Union and the Collapse of the Portuguese Empire in Africa, 1961–1975* (Chapel Hill: University of North Carolina Press, 2022), 15–16.
9. James T. Campbell, *Middle Passages: African American Journeys to Africa 1787–2005* (New York: Penguin, 2006), 286.
10. Campbell, *Middle Passages*, 286.
11. Richard Wright, *Black Power: A Record of Reactions in a Land of Pathos* (New York: Harper: 1954), 102.
12. Langston Hughes, *The Big Sea: An Autobiography* (New York: Thunder's Mouth Press, 1940), 102.
13. Wright, *Black Power*, 299.
14. Tommie Shelby, "Richard Wright: Realizing the Promise of the West," in *African American Political Thought: A Collected History*, eds. Melvin L. Rogers and Jack Turner (Chicago: University of Chicago Press, 2021), 416.
15. Era Bell Thompson, *Africa, Land of My Fathers* (New York: Doubleday, 1954), 76.
16. Thompson, *Africa, Land of My Fathers*, 75.

CHAPTER TWENTY: THE MOTION OF DESTINY

1. Kwame Nkrumah, "Motion of Destiny. Today We Are Here to Claim This Right to Our Independence," speech given before the Gold Coast National Assembly, July 10, 1953.
2. Nkrumah, "Motion of Destiny."
3. Kwame Nkrumah, *Ghana: The Autobiography of Kwame Nkrumah* (New York: International Publishers, 1957), 200.
4. Nkrumah, "Motion of Destiny."
5. Basil Davidson, *Black Star: A View of the Life and Times of Kwame Nkrumah* (New York: Praeger, 1973), 130.
6. Davidson, *Black Star*, 98.
7. Richard Wright, *Black Power: A Record of Reactions in a Land of Pathos* (New York: Harper, 1954), 221.
8. Dennis Austin, *Politics in Ghana: 1946–1960* (Oxford: Oxford University Press, 1964), 214.
9. Davidson, *Black Star*, 148.
10. Jean Marie Allman, *The Quills of the Porcupine: Asante Nationalism in an Emergent Ghana* (Madison: University of Wisconsin Press, 1993), 22.
11. Allman, *Quills of the Porcupine*, 72.

CHAPTER TEWNTY-ONE: IMAGINED COMMUNITIES

1. Erica Powell, *Private Secretary (Female)/Gold Coast* (London: C. Hurst and Co., 1984), 20.
2. Powell, *Private Secretary*, 50.
3. Powell, *Private Secretary*, 19, 28.
4. Powell, *Private Secretary*, 97.
5. Jean Marie Allman, *The Quills of the Porcupine: Asante Nationalism in an Emergent Ghana* (Madison: University of Wisconsin Press, 1993), 87.
6. Powell, *Private Secretary*, 96.
7. "Opening Speech Given by Sukarno (Bandung, 18 April 1955)," in *Asia-Africa Speak from Bandung* (Jakarta, Indonesia: Ministry of Foreign Affairs, 1955), 19–29.
8. Dennis Austin, *Politics in Ghana: 1946–1960* (Oxford: Oxford University Press, 1964), 334.

9. David Rooney, *Kwame Nkrumah: The Political Kingdom in the Third World* (London: I. B. Taurus and Co., 1988), 114–115.
10. Powell, *Private Secretary*, 40.

CHAPTER TWENTY-TWO: BIRTHDAY PARTY

1. Dennis Austin, *Politics in Ghana: 1946–1960* (Oxford: Oxford University Press, 1964), 123.
2. Austin, *Politics in Ghana*, 124.
3. Basil Davidson, *Black Star: A View of the Life and Times of Kwame Nkrumah* (New York: Praeger, 1973), 153.
4. David Rooney, *Kwame Nkrumah: The Political Kingdom in the Third World* (London: I. B. Taurus and Co., 1988), 124.
5. Kwame Nkrumah, *Ghana: The Autobiography of Kwame Nkrumah* (New York: International Publishers, 1957), 282.
6. Nkrumah, *Ghana: Autobiography*, 285.
7. Nkrumah, *Ghana: Autobiography*, 290.

CHAPTER TWENTY-THREE: NEW AFRICANS

1. AfricaSon, "Kwame Nkrumah's Speech on Independence Day: 6th March, 1957," *AfricaSon* (blog), September 27, 2014.
2. AfricaSon, "Kwame Nkrumah's Speech."
3. Kwame Nkrumah, *Ghana: The Autobiography of Kwame Nkrumah* (New York: International Publishers, 1957), 290.
4. Laurence Bergreen, *Louis Armstrong: An Extravagant Life* (New York: Broadway Books, 1997), 460.
5. Erica Powell, *Private Secretary (Female)/Gold Coast* (London: C. Hurst and Co., 1984), 108–9.
6. James Warren, "He's Back: Nixon Tapes Offer Insights on Shah, World," *Chicago Tribune*, August 21, 2021.
7. Kevin E. Grimm, "Symbol of Modernity: Ghana, African Americans, and the Eisenhower Administration" (PhD diss., Ohio University, 2012), 224.
8. Martin Meredith, *The Fate of Africa: A History of the Continent Since Independence* (New York: Public Affairs, 2011), 26.
9. Kevin K. Gaines, *American Africans in Ghana: Black Expatriates and the Civil Rights Era* (Chapel Hill: University of North Carolina Press, 2008), 80; Lawrence D. Reddick, *Crusader without Violence: A Biography of Martin Luther King, Jr.* (New York: Harper, 1958), 179–81.
10. James H. Meriwether, *Proudly We Can Be Africans: Black Americans and Africa, 1935–1961* (Chapel Hill: University of North Carolina Press, 2002), 160.
11. Juliana Spahr, *Du Bois's Telegram: Literary Resistance and State Containment* (Cambridge, MA: Harvard University Press, 2018), 1.
12. Spahr, *Du Bois's Telegram*, 2.
13. "The South: Attack on the Conscience," *Time*, February 18, 1957.
14. Grimm, "Symbol of Modernity," 224.
15. Jonathan Eig, *King: A Life* (New York: Farrar, Straus and Giroux, 2023), 183.
16. David J. Garrow, *Bearing the Cross: Martin Luther King, Jr., and the Southern Christian Leadership Conference* (New York: William Morrow, 2004), 91.
17. Garrow, *Bearing the Cross*, 75.
18. Eig, *King, A Life*, 24.
19. "Martin Luther King Jr. interview with Etta Moten Barnett, March 6, 1957, Accra, Ghana," in *The Papers of Martin Luther King, Jr., Volume IV Symbol of the Movement, January 1957–December 1958*, ed. Clayborn Carson (Berkeley: University of California Press, 2000), 145.
20. Ebere Nwaubani, *The United States and Decolonization in West Africa, 1950–1960* (Rochester, NY: University of Rochester Press, 2001), 165.
21. Gaines, *American Africans in Ghana*, 82.

CHAPTER TWENTY-FOUR: KEEP ON KEEPING ON

1. James Baldwin, *Notes of a Native Son* (New York: The Library of America, 1998), 45.
2. Horace Cayton, "A New Black Nation on the World Scene," *Pittsburgh Courier*, February 9, 1957.
3. Ethel Payne, "Ghana's Independence, Africa' Biggest Event," *Chicago Defender*, February 16, 1957.
4. "The Courier Salutes Ghana: An Editorial," *Pittsburgh Courier*, March 9, 1957.
5. Kevin E. Grimm, "Symbol of Modernity: Ghana, African Americans, and the Eisenhower Administration" (PhD diss., Ohio University, 2012), 220. In writing about this period, I have valued Kevin F. Grimm's doctoral archival research into newspaper coverage of the era.
6. James H. Meriwether, *Proudly We Can Be Africans: Black Americans and Africa, 1935–1961* (Chapel Hill: University of North Carolina Press, 2002), 163.
7. Alyson Hobbs, "A Hundred Years Later, 'The Birth of a Nation' Hasn't Gone Away," *New Yorker*, December 13, 2015.

8. Martin Luther King, Jr., "'The Birth of a New Nation,' sermon delivered at Dexter Avenue Baptist Church," Montgomery, Alabama, April 7, 1957, The Martin Luther King Jr. Research and Education Institute, Stanford University. This source is used throughout this chapter wherever this sermon is referenced.
9. A full treatment of this history lies at the center of my book, *Born in Blackness* (New York: Liveright, 2021).
10. On November 13, 1956, after the Supreme Court's final decision affirming a lower court decision outlawing bus segregation in Montgomery, King had declared, "The universe is on the side of justice." David J. Garrow, *Bearing the Cross: Martin Luther King and the Southern Christian Leadership Conference* (New York: William Morrow, 1986), 80.

CHAPTER TWENTY-FIVE: FRENEMIES

1. Jon Woronoff, *West African Wager: Houphouët versus Nkrumah* (Metuchen, NJ: Scarecrow Press, 1972), 11.
2. Walter Rodney, *How Europe Underdeveloped Africa* (London: Verso Books, 2018), 344.
3. Woronoff, *West African Wager*, 36.
4. Tony Chafer, *The End of Empire in French West Africa: France's Successful Decolonization?* (Oxford: Oxford University Press, 2002), 164.
5. Chafer, *End of Empire*, 77.
6. Emmanuel Akyeampong, *Independent Africa: The First Generation of Nation Builders* (Bloomington: Indiana University Press, 2023), 115
7. Woronoff, *West African Wager*, 12.
8. Woronoff, *West African Wager*, 13.

CHAPTER TWENTY-SIX: *QUAND ON REFUSE ON DIT NON*

1. For an extended description of the Mali Empire, see my *Born in Blackness* (New York: Liveright, 2021).
2. Carol A. Johnson, "Conference of Independent African States," *International Organization* 16, no. 2 (Spring 1962): 426–29.
3. In Frank Gerits, *The Ideological Scramble for Africa: How the Pursuit of Anticolonial Modernity Shaped a Postcolonial Order, 1945–1966* (Ithaca, NY: Cornell University Press, 2023), 65.
4. David Van Reybrouk, *Revolusi: Indonesia and the Birth of the Modern World* (New York: W. W. Norton, 2024), 493.
5. Gerits, *Ideological Scramble for Africa*, 70.
6. Tony Chafer, *The End of Empire in French West Africa: France's Successful Decolonization?* (Oxford: Oxford University Press, 2002), 166.
7. A brilliant discussion of these debates, which go beyond the scope of this book, can be found in Jane Burbank and Frederick Cooper's *Post-Imperial Possibilities: Eurasia, Eurafrica, Afroasia* (Princeton, NJ: Princeton University Press, 2023).
8. Chafer, *End of Empire*, 174n27.
9. Jaap van Ginneken, *The Profile of Political Leaders: Archetypes of Ascendancy* (London: Palgrave, 2016), 46.
10. David Halberstam, "Touré's Country—'Africa Incarnate'," *New York Times Magazine*, July 8, 1962.
11. See Elizabeth Schmidt, "Cold War in Guinea: The Rassemblement Démocratique Africain and the Struggle over Communism, 1950–1958," *Journal of African History* 48, no. 1 (2007): 95–121.
12. Frederick Cooper, *Citizenship between Empire and Nation: Remaking France and French Africa, 1945–1960* (Princeton, NJ: Princeton University Press, 2014), 300.
13. Cooper, *Citizenship between Empire and Nation*, 306.
14. Kris Manjapra, *Black Ghost of Empire: The Long Death of Slavery and the Failure of Emancipation* (New York: Scribner, 2022), 62. Manjapra has written one of the best recent accounts of the financial jeopardy imposed by France and other Western powers on Haiti.

CHAPTER TWENTY-SEVEN: KEEP YOUR JUICE

1. Kevin E. Grimm, "Symbol of Modernity: Ghana, African Americans, and the Eisenhower Administration" (PhD diss., Ohio University, 2012), 261.
2. Kevin K. Gaines, *American Africans in Ghana: Black Expatriates and the Civil Rights Era* (Chapel Hill: University of North Carolina Press, 2008), 105; "Bill Sutherland, Pan African Pacifist, 1918–2010," *War Resisters' International*, January 6, 2010.
3. "Interview with Bill Sutherland," Michigan State University, September 2004, https://projects.kora.matrix.msu.edu/files/210-808-946/BillSutherland11-4-11.pdf.
4. James Baldwin, *Notes of a Native Son* (New York: The Library of America, 1998), 70.
5. E. Fredric Morrow, *Black Man in the White House: A Revealing Diary of the Eisenhower Administration by the First Negro Presidential Aide in History* (New York: Coward-McCann, 1963), 175.
6. Grimm, "Symbol of Modernity," 254.
7. "Gbedemah Meets Colour Bar in the United States," *Ghana Evening News*, October 10, 1957; "Restaurant Bars African Leader," *New York Times*, October 9, 1957.

8. Derek A. Bell Jr. "*Brown v. Board of Education* and the Interest-Convergence Dilemma," *Harvard Law Review* 93, no. 3 (January 1980): 518.
9. "The Life of a Negro Isn't Worth a Whistle," *Freies Volk*, September 28, 1955.
10. David Margolick, "The Day Louis Armstrong Made Noise," *New York Times*, September 23, 2007.
11. James H. Meriwether, *Proudly We Can Be Africans: Black Americans and Africa, 1935–1961* (Chapel Hill: University of North Carolina Press, 2002), 167.
12. Andrew Glass, "Eisenhower Apologizes for Racial Insult, Oct. 10, 1957," *Politico*, October 10, 2018.
13. Morrow, *Black Man in the White House*, 175.
14. Grimm, "Symbol of Modernity," 254.
15. David Rooney, *Kwame Nkrumah: The Political Kingdom in the Third World* (London: I. B. Taurus and Co., 1988), 147.

CHAPTER TWENTY-EIGHT: HIGH WATER

1. Kevin E. Grimm, "Symbol of Modernity: Ghana, African Americans, and the Eisenhower Administration" (PhD diss., Ohio University, 2012), 259.
2. James H. Meriwether, *Proudly We Can Be Africans: Black Americans and Africa, 1935–1961* (Chapel Hill: University of North Carolina Press, 2002), 168.
3. Stephen G. Rabe, *John F. Kennedy: World Leader* (Washington, DC: Potomac Books, 2000), 164.
4. Meriwether, *Proudly We Can Be Africans*, 173.
5. Kwame Nkrumah, May Craig, Clifton Daniel, Richard Cluman, and Patrick O'Donovan, "Sunday, July 27, 1958 with guest Dr. Kwame Nkrumah, Prime Minister of Ghana," *Meet the Press* (television program transcript) (3 MIM Press Co: 1972), microfiche. This interview is referenced repeatedly in this passage.
6. Meriwether, *Proudly We Can Be Africans*, 177.
7. Meriwether, *Proudly We Can Be Africans*, 173–74.
8. Meriwether, *Proudly We Can Be Africans*, 175.
9. Meriwether, *Proudly We Can Be Africans*, 175.
10. I am indebted to the historian, Kevin E. Grimm, for his collection of these revealing popular responses. "Symbol of Modernity," 272.
11. Letter to the Editor, Peter Mosley, "The People Speak: Inspired by Dr. Nkrumah," *Chicago Defender*, August 6, 1958, A1.

CHAPTER TWENTY-NINE: THE BUREAU OF AFRICAN AFFAIRS

1. Late in life, Padmore would distance himself from Trotskyites.
2. George Shepperson and St. Clair Drake, "The Fifth Pan-African Conference, 1945 and the All African People's Congress, 1958," *Contributions in Black Studies* 8, no. 1 (1986–1987): 63.
3. Charles Arden-Clarke, untitled note, October 4, 1956, 'Odd Oddments'—file containing miscellaneous materials, Papers of Sir Charles Noble Arden-Clarke, MS 380596/03. Special Collections, SOAS Library.
4. Cyril Lionel Robert James, *At the Rendezvous of Victory: Selected Writings* (London: Allison and Busby, 1984), 54.
5. Kwame Nkrumah, *Padmore, the Missionary: An Address on the Opening of the George Padmore Memorial Library in Accra on 30th June, 1961* (Accra, Ghana: Ministry of Information, 1961), Lincoln University Archives, Box 14a.
6. Nkrumah, *Padmore, the Missionary*.

CHAPTER THIRTY: SLOGANS AND MANIFESTOS

1. Leslie James, *George Padmore and Decolonization from Below: Pan-Africanism, the Cold War, and the End of Empire* (London: Palgrave Macmillan, 2014), 136.
2. W. Scott Thompson, *Ghana's Foreign Policy, 1957–1966: Diplomacy, Ideology, and the New State* (Princeton, NJ: Princeton University Press, 1969), 68.
3. Alan Gray, "Quarterly Chronicle," *African Affairs* 58, no. 230 (1959): 2.
4. J. N. Webster, A. A. Boahen, and H. O. Idowu, *The Growth of African Civilisation: The Revolutionary Years—West Africa Since 1800* (London: Longman Group, 1967), 383.
5. David Rooney, *Kwame Nkrumah: The Political Kingdom in the Third World* (London: I. B. Taurus and Co., 1988),149n13.
6. Eric Opoku Mensah, "Establishing Ethos and Envisioning a New Africa: Kwame Nkrumah's Invention at the 1958 All-African People's Conference," *Journal for Studies in Humanities and Social Sciences* 4, no. 1–2 (2015): 103–15.
7. Moumié was assassinated with radioactive thallium by the French secret service on November 3, 1960, in Geneva, Switzerland, less than a year after his country had been granted independence.
8. Chambi Seithy Chachage, "Nyerere: Nationalism and Post-Colonial Developmentalism," *African Sociological Review* 8, no. 2 (2004): 158.
9. Chachage, "Nationalism and Post-Colonial Developmentalism," 161.

10. Manning Marable, *African and Caribbean Politics: From Kwame Nkrumah to the Grenada Revolution* (New York: Verso Books, 1987), 123.
11. Marable, *African and Caribbean Politics*, 121.
12. Stuart A. Reid, *The Lumumba Plot: The Secret History of the CIA and a Cold War Assassination* (New York: Alfred A. Knopf, 2023), 56.
13. Patrice Lumumba, *Congo, My Country* (New York: Fredrick A. Praeger, 1962), 146.
14. Reid, *The Lumumba Plot*, 43.
15. See Leslie James, *George Padmore and Decolonization from Below: Pan-Africanism, the Cold War, and the End of Empire* (London: Palgrave Macmillan, 2015), 182n79.
16. Reid, *Lumumba Plot*, 58.
17. Jeffrey S. Ahlman, "The Algerian Question in Nkrumah's Ghana, 1958–1960: Debating 'Violence' and 'Nonviolence' in African Decolonization," *Africa Today* 57, no. 2 (2010), 74.
18. Joby Fanon, *Frantz Fanon, My Brother: Doctor, Playwright, Revolutionary* (Lanham, MD: Lexington Books, 2014), 38.
19. "Contributions de l'Algerie a la Construction de. L'Afrique," *El Moudjahid*, Dec. 24, 1958.
20. "Africa Tired of Foreign Domination," *Accra Evening News*, December 10, 1958.
21. David Macey, *Frantz Fanon: A Biography* (New York: Picador, 2000), 368.
22. George M. Houser, "Assessing Africa's Liberation Struggle," *Africa Today* 34, no. 4 (1987): 21.
23. Frantz Fanon, *The Wretched of the Earth* (New York: Grove Press, 2021), 1.
24. Fanon, *Wretched of the Earth*, 96.
25. Kevin E. Grimm, "Symbol of Modernity: Ghana, African Americans, and the Eisenhower Administration" (PhD diss., Ohio University, 2012), 282.

CHAPTER THIRTY-ONE: IMITATION IS THE SINCEREST FORM

1. Anakwa Dwamena, "The Insufficiency of Pan-Africanism as We Know It," *The Nation*, July 7, 2016.
2. David Rooney, *Kwame Nkrumah: The Political Kingdom in the Third World* (London: I. B. Taurus and Co., 1988), 144.
3. Dwamena, "Insufficiency of Pan-Africanism."
4. Erica Powell, *Private Secretary (Female)/Gold Coast* (London: C. Hurst and Co., 1984), 126.
5. Powell, *Private Secretary*, 125–26.
6. Kwame Botwe-Asamoah, *Kwame Nkrumah's Politico-Cultural Thought and Politics: An African-Centered Paradigm for the Second Phase of the African Revolution* (London: Routledge, 2013), 93.
7. Komla Alfred, "Hitler's Victory," *Ashanti Pioneer* (Kumasi), July 2, 1956.
8. Basil Davidson, *Black Star: A View of the Life and Times of Kwame Nkrumah* (New York: Praeger, 1973), 170.
9. "Nkrumah Escapes Assassin 5th Time; Security Guard Fatally Shot—Assailant Is Arrested," *New York Times*, January 3, 1964.
10. "Lim's Cleanup Gets Mixed Press Reception," *The Times*, London, August 24, 1957.
11. James H. Meriwether, *Proudly We Can Be Africans: Black Americans and Africa, 1935–1961* (Chapel Hill: University of North Carolina Press, 2002), 180.
12. Ayi Kwei Armah, *The Beautyful Ones Are Not Yet Born* (Oxford: Pearson Education, 1988), 62.
13. Manning Marable, *African and Caribbean Politics: From Kwame Nkrumah to the Grenada Revolution* (New York: Verso Books, 1987), 124.
14. Ebenezer Obiri Addo, *Kwame Nkrumah: A Case Study of Religion and Politics in Ghana* (New York: University Press of America, 1999), 107.
15. For a full treatment of this sort of political use of iconography, see Harcourt Fuller, *Building the Ghanaian Nation-State: Kwame Nkrumah's Symbolic Nationalism* (London: Palgrave Macmillan, 2014).

CHAPTER THIRTY-TWO: FORWARD TO INDEPENDENCE

1. For an account of the exploitation of Congo under Leopold, see Adam Hochschild's *King Leopold's Ghost: A Story of Greed, Terror, and Heroism in Colonial Africa* (Boston: Houghton Mifflin, 1998).
2. Johan Op de Beeck, *Leopold II: het hele verhall* (The Whole Story) (Horizon, 2020).
3. Stuart A. Reid, *The Lumumba Plot: The Secret History of the CIA and a Cold War Assassination* (New York: Alfred A. Knopf, 2023), 35.
4. Reid, *The Lumumba Plot*, 23.
5. Reid, *The Lumumba Plot*, 26.
6. "Conflict in the Congo," *Africa Today* 7, no. 5 (September 1960): 5.
7. Reid, *The Lumumba Plot*, 45.
8. Reid, *The Lumumba Plot*, 45.
9. "Discours pronouncé par le général de Gaulle, président du Conseil, à Brazzaville (Congo), 24 août 1958" (Speech of General de Gaulle, president of the Council, in Brazzaville [Congo], August 24, 1958), *Élysée*. Excerpt translated by the author.
10. Reid, *The Lumumba Plot*, 53.

11. "Speech by the Prime Minister of Ghana at the Opening Session of the All-African People's Conference," Accra, Ghana, December 8, 1958, from course materials provided for "Main Currents in African History," Columbia University.
12. "Speech by the Prime Minister of Ghana."
13. Speech by the Prime Minister of Ghana."
14. Susan Williams, *White Malice: The CIA and the Covert Recolonization of Africa* (New York: Public Affairs, 2021), 96.
15. Koning Boudewijn, "35 jaar dialoog met de natie. Een keuze uit de koninklijke toespraken van 1951 tot 1986" [35 Years of Dialogue with the Nation: A Selection of Royal Speeches from 1951–1986] (Tielt, Belgium: Lannoo-Brussels, 1986), 124.
16. Reid, *The Lumumba Plot*, 102.
17. Williams, *White Malice*, 103.
18. Reid, *The Lumumba Plot*, 111, 112.
19. "Colonization and Independence in Africa: How Did Africans Resist European Colonialism?," Choices Program (Providence, RI: Watson Institute, Brown University, 2013), 36–37.
20. "Letter from King Leopold II of Belgium to Colonial Missionaries, 1883," *Africa: The Trouble with Africa's Political Development* (blog), AllAfrica, October 8, 2005.
21. Harry Gilroy, "Lumumba Assails Colonialism as Congo Is Freed," *New York Times*, July 1, 1960.
22. Ludo de Witte, "Patrice Lumumba's Speech: Ludo de Witte Revisits the Birth of the Republic of Congo, 30th June 1960," Verso Books, January 19, 2016.
23. "Congolese Independence Speech by King Baudouin on June 30, 1960," Wikisource.org, July 16, 2021.
24. Gilroy, "Lumumba Assails Colonialism."
25. Gilroy, "Lumumba Assails Colonialism."

CHAPTER THIRTY-THREE: NEI LUAN WAI HUAN

1. Kwame Nkrumah, *I Speak of Freedom* (Bedford, UK: Panaf, 2009), 179.
2. Richard Wright, *The Color Curtain: A Report on the Bandung Conference* (Jackson: University Press of Mississippi, 1995), 140.
3. "Kwame Nkrumah 1900–72: Ghanaian Statesman, Prime Minister 1957–60, President 1960–6," *Oxford Essential Quotations*, 4th ed., ed. Susan Ratcliffe (Oxford Reference, 2016).
4. Isabelle Lasserre, "Le jour où la France a conquis la bombe," *Le Figaro*, February 13, 2010.
5. *Ghana Evening News*, February 17, 1960.
6. Jean Allman, "Nuclear Imperialism and the Pan-African Struggle for Peace and Freedom: Ghana, 1959–1962," *Souls: A Critical Journal of Black Politics, Culture, and Society* 10, no. 2 (2008): 97.
7. Howard W. French, *Everything Under the Heavens: How the Past Helps Shape China's Push for Global Power* (New York: Knopf, 2017), 7–8.
8. Kwame Nkrumah, *Ghana: The Autobiography of Kwame Nkrumah* (New York: International Publishers, 1957), x.
9. David Birmingham, *Kwame Nkrumah: The Father of African Nationalism* (Athens: Ohio University Press, 1998), p. 44
10. Jeffrey S. Ahlman, *Living with Nkrumahism: Nation, State, and Pan-Africanism in Ghana* (Athens: Ohio University Press, 2017).
11. Ahlman, *Living with Nkrumahism*, 55.
12. Suzy Hansen, *Notes on a Foreign Country: An American Abroad in a Post-American World* (New York: Farrar Straus and Giroux, 2018), 111.
13. Abena Dove Osseo-Asare and John Krzyzaniak, "Interview: Nuclear Research and the Quest for Scientific Equity in Ghana, *Bulletin of the Atomic Scientists*, October 15, 2019.
14. Ahlman, *Living with Nkrumahism*, 58.
15. Birmingham, *Father of African Nationalism*, 60.
16. Birmingham, *Father of African Nationalism*, 60.
17. Ahlman, *Living with Nkrumahism*, 62.
18. Robert L. Tignor, *W. Arthur Lewis and the Birth of Development Economics* (Princeton, NJ: Princeton University Press, 2020), 119.
19. "Sir Arthur Lewis, Biographical," in *Nobel Lectures, Economics 1969–1980*, ed. Assar Lindbeck (Singapore: World Scientific Publishing Co., 1992).
20. Tignor *Lewis and Birth of Development Economics*, 17.
21. Tignor, *Lewis and Birth of Development Economics*, 110.
22. Tignor, *Lewis and Birth of Development Economics*, 125.

CHAPTER THIRTY-FOUR: DAM(N) VOLTA

1. Robert L. Tignor, *W. Arthur Lewis and the Birth of Development Economics* (Princeton, NJ: Princeton University Press, 2020), 195.
2. White Paper on the Volta River Aluminum Scheme (Cmd. 8702 of 1952), *Nature*, February 21, 1953.

NOTES

3. Tignor, *Lewis and the Birth of Development Economics*, 195.
4. Gold Coast Legislative Assembly Debates, April 18, 1952, cited in Tignor, *Lewis and Birth of Development Economics*, 197.
5. Gold Coast Legislative Assembly Debates, in Tignor, *Lewis and Birth of Development Economics*, 197.
6. Stephan F. Miescher, "'Nkrumah's Baby': The Akosombo Dam and the Dream of Development in Ghana, 1952–1966," *Water History* 6 (December 24, 2014): 348.
7. Tignor, *Lewis and the Birth of Development Economics*, 196.
8. Miescher, "'Nkrumah's Baby,'" 353.
9. Tignor, *Lewis and the Birth of Development Economics*, 199.
10. Miescher, "'Nkrumah's Baby,'" 354.
11. Miescher, "'Nkrumah's Baby,'" 354.
12. Tignor, *Lewis and the Birth of Development Economics*, 200.
13. Tignor, *Lewis and the Birth of Development Economics*, 200.
14. Tignor, *Lewis and the Birth of Development Economics*, 200, 173.
15. Ama Biney, *The Political and Social Thought of Kwame Nkrumah* (New York: Palgrave Macmillan, 2011), 53.
16. Philip E. Muehlenbeck, *Betting on the Africans: John F. Kennedy's Courting of African Nationalist Leaders* (Oxford: Oxford University Press, 2014), 20.
17. David Birmingham, *Kwame Nkrumah: The Father of African Nationalism* (Athens: Ohio University Press, 1998), 67.

CHAPTER THIRTY-FIVE: HARD PLACES

1. William L. Ryan, "Independent Congo Suffering National Nervous Breakdown," *Los Angeles Times*, July 17, 1960.
2. "Telegram from the Mission at the United Nations to the Department of State," September 7, 1960, Document 202 in *Foreign Relations of the United States, 1958–1960, Africa, Volume XIV*, ed. Harriet Dashiell Schwar and Stanley Shaloff (Washington, DC: US Government Printing Office, 1992).
3. Sergey Mazov, "A Fragile Alliance: The Congo Crisis and Soviet-Ghanaian Relations 1960–61," *Twentieth Century Communism: A Journal of International History* 2018, no. 15 (2018): 3.
4. Susan Williams, *White Malice: The CIA and the Covert Recolonization of Africa* (New York: Public Affairs, 2021), 213.
5. Jeffrey S. Ahlman, "The Algerian Question in Nkrumah's Ghana, 1958–1960: Debating "Violence" and "Nonviolence" in African Decolonization," *Africa Today*, 57, no. 2 (Winter 2010): 73.
6. Adam Shatz, *The Rebel's Clinic: The Revolutionary Lives of Frantz Fanon* (New York: Farrar, Straus and Giroux, 2024), 248.
7. Philip C. Naylor, *France and Algeria: A History of Decolonization and Transformation* (Gainesville: University Press of Florida, 2000), 52–53.
8. Stuart A. Reid, *The Lumumba Plot: The Secret History of the CIA and a Cold War Assassination* (New York: Alfred A. Knopf, 2023), 178–79.
9. Reid, *The Lumumba Plot*, 195, 202.
10. Reid, *The Lumumba Plot*, 257.
11. Ebere Nwaubani, "Eisenhower, Nkrumah and the Congo Crisis," *Journal of Contemporary History* 36, no. 4 (October 2001): 610.
12. Mazov, "A Fragile Alliance," 4.
13. Sergei Mazov, "Soviet Aid to the Gizenga Government in the Former Belgian Congo (1960–61) as Reflected in Russian Archives," *Cold War History* 7, no. 3 (August 2007): 7.
14. Williams, *White Malice*, 247.
15. Mazov, "A Fragile Alliance," 6.
16. Edward McWhinney, Introductory Note for "Declaration on the Granting of Independence to Colonial Countries and Peoples, New York, 14 December 1960," Audiovisual Library of International Law, August 2008.
17. Manning Marable, *Malcolm X: A Life of Reinvention* (New York: Penguin Books, 2011), 172.
18. Nwaubani, "Eisenhower, Nkrumah and the Congo Crisis," 618.
19. "Memorandum of Conversation, September 22, 1960. Subject: President Nkrumah's Call on the President," in *Foreign Relations of the United States, 1958–1960, Africa, Volume XIV*, Document 301, eds. Harriet Dashiell Schwar and Stanley Shaloff (Washington, DC: US Government Printing Office, 1992).
20. Mazov, "A Fragile Alliance," 7.
21. Mazov, "A Fragile Alliance," 13.
22. Nwaubani, "Eisenhower, Nkrumah and the Congo Crisis," 616.
23. Kwame Nkrumah, "Osagyefo at the United Nations," September 23, 1960, (box 154-15, folder 49), Nkrumah Papers, Manuscript Division, Moorland-Spingarn Research Center, Howard University, Washington, DC.
24. Nwaubani, "Eisenhower, Nkrumah and the Congo Crisis," 614.

25. Jim Newton, *Eisenhower, The White House Years* (New York: Knopf Doubleday Publishing Group, 2012), 583.
26. Dwight D. Eisenhower, *Waging Peace: The White House Years, A Personal Account, 1956–1961* (New York: Doubleday and Company, 1965), 586.
27. Nwaubani, "Eisenhower, Nkrumah and the Congo Crisis," 619.

CHAPTER THIRTY-SIX: A WAY IN THE WORLD

1. Michael Merschel, "The Presidential Heart Attack That Changed America, " Heart.org, February 15, 2024.
2. Philip E. Muehlenbeck, *Betting on the Africans: John F. Kennedy's Courting of African Nationalist Leaders* (Oxford: Oxford University Press, 2014), 76.
3. LTC Roger T. Housen, Army, "Why Did the US Want to Kill Prime Minister Lumumba of the Congo?" (Report, National Defense University, National War College, 2002), 8.
4. "The United Nations: The Bear's Teeth," *Time*, February 24, 1961.
5. "The United Nations: The Bear's Teeth."
6. Dana Adams Schmidt, "Nkrumah Divides Diplomatic Visits: Ghanaian Sees Eisenhower and Then Makes Call on Soviet Premier," *New York Times*, September 23, 1960.
7. Richard Mahoney, *JFK: Ordeal in Africa* (Oxford: Oxford University Press, 1983), 50.
8. Via M.E. Landricina, "From 'Our Experiment' to the 'Prisoner of the West': Ghana's Relations with Great Britain, the United States of America and West Germany during Kwame Nkrumah's Government (1957–1966) (PhD. Thesis, Univerità Degli Studi Di Roma Tre Dipartimento Di Scienze Politiche, 2016), 133. United Nations General Assembly, Official Records, 867th Plenary Meeting, 22.09.1960m document GA_1960_NL600697 [15.06.215].
9. "Telegram from the Embassy in Belgium to the Department of State, July 19, 1960,"in *Foreign Relations of the United States, 1958–1960, Africa, Volume XIV*, Document 136, eds. Harriet Dashiell Schwar and Stanley Shaloff (Washington, DC: US Government Printing Office, 1992).
10. Landricina, "From 'Our Experiment,'" 170.
11. "National Affairs: Battleground," *Time*, October 3, 1960.
12. Ebere Nwaubani, "Eisenhower, Nkrumah and the Congo Crisis," *Journal of Contemporary History* 36, no. 4 (October 2001): 601.
13. Nana Osei-Opare, "Uneasy Comrades: Postcolonial Statecraft, Race, and Citizenship, Ghana-Soviet Relations, 1957–1966," *Journal of West African History* 5, no. 2 (Fall 2019): 96.
14. Osei-Opare, "Uneasy Comrades," 86.
15. Osei-Opare, "Uneasy Comrades," 95.
16. Alessandro Iandolo, *Arrested Development: The Soviet Union in Ghana, Guinea, and Mali, 1955–1968* (Ithica, NY: Cornell University Press, 2022), 78.
17. Osei-Opare, "Uneasy Comrades," 95.
18. John Pratos and Arturo Jimenez-Bacardi, "CIA Covert Operations: The 1964 Overthrow of Cheddi Jagan in British Guiana," National Security Archive, April 6, 2020.
19. "Guinea Life Expectancy 1950–2023," Macrotrends.net, accessed November 11, 2023.
20. Iandolo, *Arrested Development*, 156.
21. Osei-Opare, "Uneasy Comrades," 103.
22. Osei-Opare, "Uneasy Comrades," 99.
23. "Soviet Bloc Aid to Underdeveloped Countries in the Field of Electric Power," Central Intelligence Agency, Economic Intelligence Report, Office of Research and Reports, March 1963.
24. Osei-Opare, "Uneasy Comrades," 99.
25. David Rooney, *Kwame Nkrumah: The Political Kingdom in the Third World* (London: I.B. Taurus and Co., 1988), 158–59.
26. Adom Getachew, *Worldmaking After Empire: The Rise and Fall of Self-Determination* (Princeton: Princeton University Press, 2019).
27. Howard W. French, *China's Second Continent: How a Million Migrants Are Building a New Empire in Africa* (New York: Alfred A. Knopf, 2014), 199.

CHAPTER THIRTY-SEVEN: SOUTHERN STRATEGIES

1. Mark Stern, "John F. Kennedy and Civil Rights: From Congress to the Presidency," *Presidential Studies Quarterly: Foreign Policy, Human Rights, and Political Alignment* 19, no. 4 (Fall 1989): 799.
2. Louis Menand, *The Free World: Art and Thought in the Cold War* (New York: Farrar, Straus and Giroux, 2021), 382.
3. Philip E. Muehlenbeck, *Betting on the Africans: John F. Kennedy's Courting of African Nationalist Leaders* (Oxford: Oxford University Press, 2014), 35.
4. "Remarks of Senator John F. Kennedy in the Senate, Washington, D.C., July 2, 1957," Papers of John F. Kennedy, Pre-Presidential Papers, Senate Files, Box 784, "Algeria Speech," John F. Kennedy Presidential Library (JFK Library), Boston, MA.

NOTES

5. Gregory L. Garland, "Kennedy, Nixon and the Competition for Mr. Africa, 1952–1960," *The Foreign Service Journal*, September 2022.
6. Muehlenbeck, *Betting on the Africans*, 17–18.
7. Muehlenbeck, *Betting on the Africans*, 70.
8. Muehlenbeck, *Betting on the Africans*, 75.
9. I have drawn here on the work by Muehlenbeck, *Betting on the Africans*.
10. "Nicholas Kaldor: 1908–1986," *Proceedings of the British Academy* 73 (1987): 519.
11. Muehlenbeck, *Betting on the Africans*, 83.
12. Alessandro Iandolo, *Arrested Development: The Soviet Union in Ghana, Guinea, and Mali, 1955–1968* (Ithaca, NY: Cornell University Press, 2022), 161.
13. Iandolo, *Arrested Development*, 57.
14. State Department Paper, "Africa: Guidelines for Policy and Operations," March 1962, National Security Files, (Box 2: "Africa". Folder "General, 3/62–4/62"), JFK Library, Boston, MA.

CHAPTER THIRTY-EIGHT: TWENTY-ONE GUNS

1. Susan Williams, *White Malice: The CIA and the Covert Recolonization of Africa* (New York: Public Affairs, 2021), 445.
2. *Dawn Broadcast* (Accra, Ghana: Government Printing Department, April 8, 1961) from the archives of Lincoln University.
3. Williams, *White Malice*, 445.
4. Jeffrey S. Ahlman, *Living with Nkrumahism: Nation, State, and Pan-Africanism in Ghana* (Athens: Ohio University Press, 2017), 139.
5. Richard D. Mahoney, *JFK: Ordeal in Africa* (New York: Oxford University Press, 1983), 174.
6. Conor Cruise O'Brien, "Changing the Guard," *New York Review of Books*, June 23, 1966.
7. Williams, *White Malice*, 236.
8. Williams, *White Malice*, 236.
9. Adeyinka Makinde, "Aftermath of Major General H.T. Alexander's Sacking by President Kwame Nkrumah, September 1961," YouTube, April 21, 2022.
10. "Memorandum of Telephone Conversation between President Kennedy and the Acting Under Secretary of State (Ball)," in *Foreign Relations of the United States, 1961–1963, Volume XXI, Africa*, Document 232, ed. Nina Davis Howland (Washington, DC: US Government Printing Office, 1995).
11. Philip E. Muehlenbeck, *Betting on the Africans: John F. Kennedy's Courting of African Nationalist Leaders* (Oxford: Oxford University Press, 2014), 88.
12. David Rooney, *Kwame Nkrumah: The Political Kingdom in the Third World* (London: I. B. Taurus and Co., 1988), 164; Gore to Kennedy, November 13, 1961, Ghana, National Security Files (Box 99), JFK Library, Boston, MA.
13. US Central Intelligence Agency, "Kwame Nkrumah," March 1961, President's Office Files, Box 117a, cited in Thomas J. Noer, "The New Frontier and African Neutralism: Kennedy, Nkrumah, and the Volta River Project," *Diplomatic History* 8, no. 1 (Winter 1984): 61–79.
14. William P. Mahoney Oral History interview by William W. Moss, transcript, May 14, 1975 (JFK#1, 5/14/1975), 100, JFK Library, Boston, MA.
15. Mahoney by Moss interview, 74.
16. Mahoney by Moss interview, 76.
17. Mahoney by Moss interview, 40.
18. Thomas. J. Noer, "The New Frontier and African Neutralism: Kennedy, Nkrumah, and the Volta River Project," *Diplomatic History* 8, no. 1 (Winter 1984):76.
19. Noer, "New Frontier and African Neutralism," 77.

CHAPTER THIRTY-NINE: HAIL MARY

1. "Attack on Nkrumah: Escapes Bomb Explosion," *Guardian*, August 3, 1963.
2. Charles Howard, "Nkrumah on the List of African Leaders To Be Murdered," *Afro-American*, September 29, 1962, A1.
3. Kwame Nkrumah, *Ghana: The Autobiography of Kwame Nkrumah* (New York: International Publishers, 1957), x.
4. "Two Killed by Bomb at Nkrumah Palace," *New York Times*, September 9, 1962.
5. "Public Sees Less of Nkrumah Since Aug. 1 Blast: Some Believe He Fears New Attempt on His Life. His Failure to Read Speech to Congress Is Noted," *New York Times*, September 17, 1962.
6. Erica Powell, *Private Secretary (Female)/Gold Coast* (London: C. Hurst and Co., 1984), 194.
7. Cyril Lionel Robert (C. L. R.) James, *Nkrumah and the Ghana Revolution* (London: L. Hill, 1977), 153.
8. C. L. R. James, *Nkrumah and the Ghana Revolution*, 181.
9. C. L. R. James, *Nkrumah and the Ghana Revolution*, 183.
10. Rhode Island, the thirteenth colony, did not send a delegate to the Congress.
11. Kwame Nkrumah, "Address to the Summit Conference of the O.A.U.," May 24, 1963, *Voice of Africa* 5

(September–October 1965). Here, I have also drawn from arguments made by Adom Getachew in *World-making after Empire: The Rise and Fall of Self-Determination* (Princeton: Princeton University Press, 2019), 116. Nkrumah, in fact, had been calling for a United States of Africa at least since the All-African People's Conference he hosted in 1958.

12. African Union Founders, *Speeches and Statements Made at the First Organization of African Unity (O.A.U.) Summit* (Addis Ababa, Ethiopia: African Union, May 1963), 44.
13. "Speeches and Statements Made at the First Organisation of African Unity (OAU) Summit" African Union, May 1963, 8.
14. Getachew, *Worldmaking after Empire*, 136.
15. Chambi Chachage, "Excerpt from Interview with Bill Sutherland: Nyerere vs Nkrumah on Pan-Africanism," Centre for Consciencist Studies and Analyses (CENSCA), WordPress, September 5, 2008.
16. William P. Mahoney Oral History interview by William W. Moss, transcript, May 14, 1975 (JFK#1, 5/14/1975), 70, JFK Library, Boston, MA.
17. Mahoney by Moss interview, 70.
18. Mahoney by Moss interview, 76.
19. DeNeen L. Brown, "60 Years Ago, the Civil Rights Act of 1964 Changed American Justice," *Washington Post*, July 1, 2024.
20. See also Robert B. Rakove, *Kennedy, Johnson, and the Nonaligned World* (Cambridge, UK: Cambridge University Press, 2013), xxvi.
21. Robert Lindsay, "Ghana's Chief Stays Out of Public View," *Chicago Daily Tribune*, September 17, 1962.
22. Russell Howe, "Ghana President Hated by Nearly Everyone: Chief Fears Death," *Boston Globe*, October 21, 1962.
23. David J. Finlay, Ole R. Holsti, and Richard R. Fagan, *Enemies in Politics* (Chicago: Rand McNally, 1967), 163.
24. British High Commissioner in Accra to Foreign Secretary Rt. Hon Duncan Sandys, "January 2nd, 1964: Police Constable Ametewee Fails in Assassination Attempt on Nkrumah," Edward A. Ulzen Memorial Foundation, January 2, 2018.
25. Ahlman, *Living with Nkrumahism*, 201.

CHAPTER FORTY: THE WAY HOME

1. Alex White, "Maya Angelou's Newly Uncovered Writing from Egypt and Ghana Reveals a More Radical Side to Her Career," *The Conversation*, April 3, 2024.
2. Maya Angelou, *All God's Children Need Traveling Shoes* (New York: Vintage Books: 1991), 19.
3. Angelou, *All God's Children*, 21.
4. David Levering Lewis, "Ghana, 1963: A Memoir," *American Scholar* 68, no. 1 (Winter 1999): 41.
5. Lewis, "Ghana, 1963," 41.
6. Manning Marable and Garrett Felber, eds., *The Portable Malcolm X Reader: A Man Who Stands for Nothing Will Fall for Anything* (New York: Penguin Books, 2013), 154–55.
7. Peter Goldman, *The Death and Life of Malcolm X* (Champaign: University of Illinois Press, 2013), 179.
8. ICIT Digital Library, Malcolm X at University of Ghana (May 13, 1964).
9. Lewis, "Ghana 1963," 59.
10. Angelou, *All God's Children*, 141.
11. Malcolm X and Alex Haley, *The Autobiography of Malcolm X: As Told by Alex Haley* (New York: Ballantine Books, 1992), 389.
12. "God's Judgment of White America," Dec. 1, 1963, The Malcolm X Papers, folder 6, Schomburg Center for Research in Black Culture, New York Public Library, folder 6.
13. Stokely Carmichael with Michael Ekwueme Thelwell, *Ready for the Revolution: The Life and Struggles of Stokely Carmichael (Kwame Ture)* (New York: Scribner, 2003), 81.
14. Osei Boateng, "How Nkrumah Was Lured to His End," *New African*, December 1999.
15. "Action Memorandum from the Assistant Secretary of State for African Affairs (Williams) to the Under Secretary of State for Political Affairs (Harriman), April 9, 1964," in *Foreign Relations of the United States 1964–1968, Volume XXIV, Africa*, Document 250, ed. Nina Davis Howland (Washington, DC: US Government Printing Office, 1999).
16. John Pratos and Arturo Jimenez-Bacardi, "CIA Covert Operations: The 1964 Overthrow of Cheddi Jagan in British Guiana," National Security Archive, April 6, 2020.
17. Susan Williams, *White Malice: The CIA and the Covert Recolonization of Africa* (New York: Public Affairs, 2021), 491.
18. Williams, *White Malice*, 491.
19. Williams, *White Malice*, 497–98.
20. Peniel E. Joseph, *Waiting 'Til the Midnight Hour: A Narrative History of Black Power in America* (New York: Henry Holt and Co., 2006), 194.
21. Joseph, *Waiting 'Til the Midnight Hour*, 204.
22. Joseph, *Waiting 'Til the Midnight Hour*, 193.

23. Robin D. G. Kelley, *Freedom Dreams: The Black Radical Imagination* (Boston: Beacon Press, 2022), 63.
24. Carmichael with Thelwell, *Ready for Revolution*, 622.
25. Carmichael with Thelwell, *Ready for Revolution*, 694.
26. MSRC Staff, "NKRUMAH, Kwame," *Manuscript Division Finding Aids*, 149, (Box 154-1) Moorland Spingarn Research Center, Howard University.
27. MSRC Staff, "NKRUMAH, Kwame."
28. June Milne, *Kwame Nkrumah: The Conakry Years, His Life and Letters* (Bedford, UK: Panaf, 2009), 410.
29. Stanley Meisler, "Kwame Nkrumah: The Disappointment Matched Promise," *Los Angeles Times*, April 30, 1972.
30. "A Betrayed Redeemer," *New Pittsburgh Courier*, May 27, 1972.
31. "A Betrayed Redeemer."
32. Joseph, *Waiting 'Til the Midnight Hour*, 257.

CODA: STRANGE FRUIT

1. Kwame Nkrumah, *Ghana: The Autobiography of Kwame Nkrumah* (New York: International Publishers, 1957), xv–xvi.
2. J. Bradford DeLong, *Slouching Towards Utopia: An Economic History of the Twentieth Century* (New York: Basic Books, 2022), 455.
3. Issa G. Shivji, *Rebellion without Rebels*, Book Three of *Development as Rebellion: A Biography of Julius Nyerere*, by Issa G. Shivji, Saida Yahya-Othman, and Ng'wanza Kamata (Dar es Salaam, Tanzania: Mkuki na Nyota Publishers, 2020), 26.
4. Shivji, *Rebellion without Rebels*, 11.
5. Shivji *Rebellion without Rebels*, 27
6. Ng'wanza Kamata, *Becoming Nationalist*, Book Two of *Development as Rebellion*, 33.
7. Frederick Cooper, *Decolonization and African Society: The Labor Question in French and British Africa* (Cambridge, UK: Cambridge University Press, 1996), 214.
8. Emmanuel Kwaku Akyeampong, *Independent Africa: The First Generation of Nation Builders* (Bloomington: Indiana University Press, 2023), 55.
9. Akyeampong, *Independent Africa*, 33–34.
10. Akyeampong, *Independent Africa*, 35.
11. Akyeampong, *Independent Africa*, 38–39.
12. Samir Amin, *A Life Looking Forward: Memoirs of an Independent Marxist*, trans. Patrick Camiller (London: Zed Books, 2006), 118.
13. Howard W. French, "Enemies of Progress," *New York Review*, October 7, 2021.

CREDITS

PHOTOGRAPHS USED IN TEXT

iv: Adobe Stock • 19: Lincoln University • 123: Shutterstock • 251: Album / World History Archive

PHOTOGRAPHS USED IN GALLERY

Aside from the images listed below, photographs were taken by Howard W. French.

Yearbook photo, Who's Who at Lincoln, Nkrumah's letter: Lincoln University, Langston Hughes Memorial Library, Special Collections, Kwame Nkrumah

Nkrumah with his wife, Fathia Rizk, presenting a gift to W.E.B. Du Bois: Photographs and Prints Division, Schomburg Center for Research in Black Culture, The New York Public Library

Nkrumah at Ghana's independence ceremonies: Bettmann

Nkrumah at the All-African People's Conference: Phillippe Le Tellier / Paris Match Archive

Nkrumah and Ralph Bunche: Library of Congress, Prints & Photographs Division.

Nkrumah dances with Queen Elizabeth: Universal History Archive / Bridgeman Images

Nkrumah greets Patrice Lumumba: Bridgeman Images

Nkrumah with John F. Kennedy: Abbie Rowe. White House Photographs. John F. Kennedy Presidential Library and Museum, Boston

Nkrumah visits Harlem: Photographs and Prints Division, Schomburg Center for Research in Black Culture, The New York Public Library

INDEX

Page numbers in *italic* indicate a figure on the corresponding page.

Abako party (Congo), 328, 330–31
Abernathy, Ralph, 258, 342
Abidjan, Ivory Coast, 1–3, 133, 267, 399, 439, 443
abolitionism, 23, 37, 40, 269
Abrahams, Peter, 102, 104, 110
Abyssinia. *See* Ethiopia
Abyssinian Baptist Church, Harlem, 70, 74, 263, 451
Accra, 12, 22
   Accra Central constituency, 171, 175
   Achimota College, 27–32, 55, 82, 141, 143, 138, 168, 257, 448
   African Research Centre, 419
   Black Star Square, 313, 419
   Christianborg Castle, 149, 158, 168, 176, 178, 238, 248, 296, 310
   the European Club in, 184
   Flagstaff House, 406, 415
   James Fort Prison, 166, 175–76
   "Lagos Town," 186, 239
   National Museum, 321, 346
   Palladium Cinema, 148
   polo grounds, 149, 244, 253–54
   states of emergency in, 166, 316, 395
   University of Ghana, 418, 421, 429
   Ussher Fort, 150
   West Accra Arena, 157–59, 163–65, 176
Accra Community Centre, 302, 313–14, 346
Accra Evening News (newspaper), 156, 160, 163, 166, 169, 174, 234, 345, 374

Acheampong, Ignatius, 438
Acheson, Dean, 114
Achimota College, Accra, 27–32, 55, 82, 141, 143, 138, 168, 257, 448
Acquah, Barbara, 428
activism
   abolitionism, 23, 37, 40, 269
   Du Bois's "talented tenth," 47, 192, 226, 419
   global networks of, 101–3, 218
   labor union activism, 33, 100, 273
   moments galvanizing, 55, 63–64, 253
   pan-African activism, 42, 46, 51
   student activism, 88, 92
   See also civil disobedience; civil rights movement; decolonization
Adamafio, Tawia, 405, 406
Addis Ababa, Ethiopia, 36, 384, 409–10, 412
Adegbite, Victor, 346
Adjei, Ebenezer Ako, 61, 105, 107, 138, 153, 175, 406
Adjety, Sargeant, 158
Adwa, Battle of (1896), 68
Africa, xiii–xiv, 20, *124*
   in African American media, 224–27
   Akan peoples of, 22, 26, 44, 234, 271
   Baoulé people of the Ivory Coast, 269, 271
   division above and below the Sahara, 38, 161, 222, 248, 270, 273, 275–76, 312–13, 437–38
   division into language blocs, 2, 5–6, 39, 242, 341, 409, 441

Ewe people of West Africa, 145, 233, 242, 244–45, 314, 315, 433
Ga ethnic group, 314, 347
kente cloth, 180, 285, 289, 321
"Negritude," 410
after Nkrumah, 438–41
postwar awakening of, 125–28, 129–35
white settler colonies in, 127, 159, 222, 307
women of the markets, 134, 154, 173, 226
in World War II, 9–10
See also African economies; African politics; West Africa; *specific countries and peoples, present and former*
Africa: Britain's Third Empire (Padmore), 268
"Africa for Africans," 7, 32, 41, 51
Africa Hall, Addis Ababa, 411
Africa: Land of My Fathers (Wright), 226
African American people and communities, 54, 68
   African Redemption movement, 48–56, 417
   African Studies, as an academic discipline, 89, 190
   athletes, 117
   "Black Is Beautiful," 49
   Black Panther Party, 426–27
   Black Power, 32, 51, 292, 426, 431
   in Chicago, 68, 237, 287, 288, 326, 419
   as conscientious objectors, 194, 281, 402
   as depicted in racist minstrel shows, 194, 213–41

African American people and
    communities (continued)
  Double V (Victory) campaign, 195–96
  in the Eisenhower administration, 215–20
  exchanges with Africans in the 1950s, 188–201
  and federal civil rights, 381–82
  Friends of Ghana associations, 224
  Great Migration from the Deep South, 69, 82
  impact of the Depression on, 79
  Nation of Islam (NOI), 200, 420–21
  New Negro movement, 54, 76, 93
  in the Republican Party, 219
  toward the term *African American*, 208
  in the Union Army, 41
  watershed events of 1963, 417–20
  women serving as nurses during war, 202
  in World War I, 8–9
  in World War II and after, 194–95, 202–8
  See also Black diaspora; Black intellectuals; civil rights movement
African American press, 11–12, 98, 101, 168, 200, 214, 224–27, 259, 262, 287, 382, 405, 429–30
  Chicago Daily Tribune, 168–69, 415
  Chicago Defender, 11, 98, 262, 286, 292, 358
  Ebony, 225, 226
  Negro World, 52
  New Pittsburgh Courier, 430
  The New York Age, 30
  New York Amsterdam News, 98, 203, 213
  Philadelphia Tribune, 67, 176, 213–14
  Pittsburgh Courier, 11, 63, 98, 194–96, 199, 208, 262–63, 282, 358, 430
African and Orient Review, 52
African Association (London), 191
African Communities (Imperial) League, 8
African diaspora. *See* Black diaspora; Black intellectuals
African economies
  classic commodity booms, 349, 356

compared to Asian economies, 260–61
continental GDP per capita, 439
industrialization, 137, 261, 344, 350, 351, 355, 388, 393, 401
inflation after World War I, 130, 147–48, 154, 393, 438
Keynesianism, 354
neocolonialism, 32, 98, 254, 301, 333, 348, 360, 368, 392, 400, 425
plantation slavery/plantation economies, 15, 37, 41, 55, 72, 88, 92, 117, 125, 127, 146, 260, 269–70, 291, 326, 439–40
the private sector among African people, 184, 318, 438
seemingly intractable problems of African underdevelopment, 408, 213, 412
Syrian and Lebanese merchants in Africa, 147, 149, 165
trade with the Soviet Union, 391–92
urbanization, 129, 268, 345
See also colonialism; slavery and the slave trade
African Financial Community franc (CFA), 454
African Friends of Abyssinia, 35, 63
African Interpreter (newspaper), 81, 105
African Morning Post (newspaper), 33, 95, 98, 268
African politics
  administrative/political vacuum(s) left by decolonization, 185, 187, 326
  African leaders and the habits of their erstwhile masters, 322
  "Africanization" of government, 184–85, 395
  Casablanca-Monrovia divide, 410, 430
  cults of personality, 4–5, 108, 111, 173, 240, 309, 315, 320–21
  fragmentation, 38–39, 86–87, 233, 299, 330, 368, 411, 433
  Katangan separatism in the Congo, 361, 363, 372, 385–86, 395–96
  local ethnic/linguistic group hegemony in, 4, 39–40, 48, 126, 144, 274, 317–18, 330, 348, 424, 434

Nzima ethnic group, 5–6, 21–22, 58, 61, 187, 271
  origins of African nationalism, 37–39
  postwar awakening of, 125–28, 129–35
  projecting an "African personality," 42, 81, 286, 306, 330–31, 399–400, 411
African Redemption movement, 48–56, 417
African Research Centre, Accra, 419
"African Roots of War, The" (Du Bois), 14
African Studies, as a discipline, 89, 190
"Africanization," 184–85, 395
Aggrey, J. E. Kwegyir, 22, 30–32, 34–35, 55–56, 81, 248, 255
Ahlman, Jeffrey, 348
Ajena Dam, Ghana, 356, 359
Akan peoples, 22, 26, 44, 234, 271
Akosombo Dam, Ghana, 344, 352, 356, 359, 361, 366, 377–79, 384–85
Akufo-Addo, Edward, 153
Alabama
  in the African mind, 257
  Birmingham, 175, 203, 258, 418
  Dexter Avenue Baptist Church, Montgomery, 252, 262–66
  Montgomery Bus Boycott of 1956–57, 12, 217, 258–60, 266
  Tuskegee Institute, 30, 44–45, 50, 69
  white supremacist terrorism in, 217–18, 258, 316, 384, 418
Albania, 389
Alcan, 355–57
Alexander, Henry Templer (H. T.), 365, 395–97, 423
Algeria, 410, 426
  Front de Libération National (FLN), 307
  independence of, 119, 121, 246, 270, 275, 297, 307–8, 342, 363, 382, 385
  nuclear test zone in, 341–43
Ali, Dusé Mohamed, 52
Ali, Muhammad, 49
All God's Children Need Traveling Shoes (Angelou), 418
All-African People's Conference (AAPC), 302–7, 309, 314, 468
aluminum/bauxite, 126, 213, 281, 285, 344, 347, 352–59, 421

INDEX

American Colonization Society, 66
American Friends Service Committee, 281
American Jewish community, 75, 292
American Negro Labor Congress, 94
Amin, Idi, 322, 410, 425, 427
Amin, Samir, 438
Amsterdam News (newspaper), 98, 301, 214
Anderson, Benedict, 242
Anderson, Jervis, 197
Anderson, Marian, 78
Angelou, Maya, 418
Anglo American Oil Company, 118
Angola, 304, 305
Ankrah, Joseph, 423
Antor, S. G., 315
Apollo 15 space mission, 427
Apollo Theater, Harlem, 70
Appiah, Joe, 92, 100, 102, 106–8, 240
Arab-Israeli conflict over Palestine, 140, 153, 290
Árbenz, Jacobo, 221–22
Arden-Clarke, Charles
　during the colonial legislative elections of 1951, 170–72, 175–81, 182–83, 232, 234, 237
　at the end of colonial government, 246–48, 295–96, 357–58
　as governor of the Gold Coast, 159–67
　after Nkrumah becomes prime minister, 238–39
Armah, Ayi Kwei, 319
Armstrong, Louis, 256, 284
Armstrong, Lucille, 256, 257
Aron, Raymond, 270
Articles of Confederation, 409–11
Arusha Declaration, 319
Asante people, 23–24, 43, 92–93, 229, 233–37, 238–46, 271, 316–18, 332, 348–49, 415–16, 433
Ashanti Confederacy, 235
Ashanti Pioneer (newspaper), 98, 107
Ashanti Royal Council, 236
Ashmun, Jehudi, 66
assimilation, 38, 96, 135, 326
Association of West African Merchants (AWAM), 148
Atlantic Charter, the, 10, 129, 130
Atlantic world among Black intellectuals, xiii, 11, 22, 37–38, 41, 46, 55, 95, 193, 210, 291, 329–30

Atlantic, The (magazine), 14
Atta, William Ofori, 153, 354
authoritarianism
　consider the "Era of Good Feelings" of early America, 303
　in Ghana, 16, 234, 316–17, 320, 402, 406, 416
　in Guyana, 423
　one-party rule, 4, 375, 405, 415, 432, 435–36
Avoidance of Discrimination Act, 314
Avriel, Ehud, 305
Axim, Ghana, 57
Ayeke, Kodzo, 315
Azikiwe, Nnamdi, 22, 33–36, 55, 57, 58, 67–69, 71, 77, 191, 206, 316
　newspapers of, 98, 105, 107, 156, 268
　Renascent Africa, 35

Baako, Kofi, *123*, 387
"Back to Africa," 54, 214. *See also* Garvey, Marcus
Baker, Ella, 422
Baldwin, James, 9, 12–13, 262, 283, 289
Balfour Declaration of 1926, 159
Balkanization, 6, 109
Ball, George, 390–91, 397, 400
Baltimore Afro-American (newspaper), 98, 206, 405
Banda, Hastings, 102, 107, 321–22
Bandung Conference of 1955, 222–23, 243, 258, 264, 266, 275–76, 388
Baoulé people of the Ivory Coast, 269, 271
Baudouin of Belgium, 330–39
bauxite/aluminum, 126, 213, 281, 285, 344, 347, 352–59, 421
Bay of Pigs invasion, 391
Bechuanaland (later Botswana), 159
Belgian Empire
　army of, 333
　"civic merit cards," 327
　the Congo as royal property and not as a possession of Belgium, 325
　the Congo Crisis, 4, 89, 305–7, 323–39, 360–69, 373, 385–87
　the Order of the Crown, 338
　the Table Ronde in Brussels, 331–32, 335
Belgium, 305, 307, 323, 324, 342, 385
Bell, Derek, 283

Benin, *124*
Bergen-Belsen concentration camp, 100–101
Beria, Lavrentiy, 228
Berlin Airlift, 115, 153
Berlin Conference of 1884–885, 14, 28, 38, 43, 45–46, 51, 68, 268, 336, 409
Bethune, Mary McLeod, 11, 101, 216
Bevan, Aneurin, 97
Biafra, 425
"Big Four" of the American civil rights movement, 219
Big Sea, The (Hughes), 226
"Big Six, the" of Ghanaian independence, 151–56
Biney, Ama, 358
Birmingham, Alabama, 175, 203, 258, 418
Birmingham, David, 348
Birth of a Nation, The (film), shown in the White House, 198
"Birth of a New Nation, The" sermon (King), 264
Black diaspora, 7, 11, 15, 42, 53
　African students and other expats/exiles, 105–6
　bitterness, 146, 180, 219–20, 266
　convergent evolution in, 433, 436
　"creole" cultures, 39
　global phase shifts in the, 101, 112, 132
　towards a "kingdom of culture," 40
　pride in Blackness, 31, 52, 67, 101, 189, 207–8, 213, 225–26, 289
　in the West Indies, 41, 49–52, 54–55, 68, 91–98, 104, 192, 207, 296, 314
　See also African American people and communities; education; slavery and the slave trade
Black intellectuals
　African Studies, as a discipline, 89, 190
　the Atlantic world among Black intellectuals, xiii, 11, 22, 37–38, 41, 46, 55, 95, 193, 210, 291, 329–30
Black internationalism, 15, 49, 104, 201, 423
Black nationalism, 41, 50–54, 67, 94, 206–7, 427
　"double consciousness" of, 45
　global color line, 7, 11–13, 98–99, 103, 194, 368

Black intellectuals (*continued*)
gradualism among, 104, 156–57, 160, 179, 192, 327, 357, 436–37
impact of Garveyism in Africa, 55–56
towards a global Blackness, 14, 30–31, 38–39, 41, 46, 49, 52, 56, 88, 93–94, 291, 349, 410
postwar awakening of, 125–28, 129–35
See also African American press; African politics; decolonization
"Black Is Beautiful," 49
Black Jacobins, The (C. L. R. James), 13
Black newspapers. *See* African American press
Black Panther Party, 426–27
Black Power (cultural movement), 32, 51, 292, 426, 431
Black Power (Wright), 225–26
Black Skin, White Masks (Fanon), 307
Black Star Line shipping company, 51
Blackness, 14, 30–31, 38–39, 41, 46, 49, 52, 56, 88, 93–94, 291, 349, 410
Blake (Delany), 41
Blyden, Edward W., 30, 41–43, 48–51, 88, 94, 418
Bokassa, Jean-Bédel, 322, 410
Bond of 1844, 254–65
Bond, Horace Mann, 11, 72, 77, 188–90, 205–8, 210, 212–15, 224, 257
Bond, Julian, 72
Bonne, Nii Kwabena, 147–48
Born in Blackness (French), 14
Borneo, 126, 159
Boston Globe (newspaper), 415
Botsio, Kojo, 108, *123*, 136, 180, 209–11, 275, 305, 453
Botswana, 159
Bourgerie, E. M., 215, 216–17
Brandenburg-Prussia, 264
Brazil, 15
Brazzaville Conference (1944), 130–32
Brazzaville, French Central Africa, 130–32, 277, 329
Bretton Woods monetary system, 216
Brezhnev, Leonid, 384–85, 389–91
Britain
Black people and communities in, 37, 68, 96
Conservative Party, 377
Edwardian British attitudes, 23

Labour Party (UK), 96–98, 156, 161, 243
Magna Carta, 152
Manchester Pan-African Congress of 1945, 92, 102–5, 109, 151, 160, 192, 293, 299, 303–4
Privy Council, 340
"Wind of Change" speech (Macmillan), 377. *See also* London
British Army, 23, 39–40, 118, 396
British Empire, 71, 96–97, 316
Cape Colony, 162
civil service in the, 159, 172, 177, 183–86, 188, 231
Colonial Office, 27, 126, 155, 170, 246, 353, 436
Committee on Constitutional Reform, 155
Commonwealth of Nations, 159, 161, 248, 321, 344, 374, 397
Coussey Committee report, 156–63, 170, 173, 177
"direct" vs. "indirect" rule, 23, 25
the Gold Coast as a model colony, 3, 23–24, 138, 143–44, 146–47, 150, 237
in Iran, 118, 221, 342
Malaya, 98, 117, 126, 153, 159
Royal African Company of England, 166
Special Powers Act (Northern Ireland), 317
sterling zone, 98, 127, 231, 353
United Africa Company, 141, 147, 149, 151
United Fruit Company, 49, 222
Westminster model of government, 177, 179, 230, 247, 318, 406, 434
British Guiana (later Guyana), 102, 118, 375, 423
British Library, London, 49
Brooke, James, 159
Brotherhood of Sleeping Car Porters (BSCP), 197–98, 200–201
Brown v. Board of Education, 15, 217–18, 283
Brown, Claude, 69
Brown, Irving, 309
Brown, John, 41
Bucharest, Romania, 7, 427–29
Budget Bureau (Ghana), 394
Buffalo Soldiers of the 92nd Infantry Division, 8, 52
Bui dam, Ghana, 356, 377–79, 385
Bulgaria, 389

Bunche, Ralph, 11, 88–89, 101, 190–91, 213, 257, 290–91
Bundy, McGeorge, 423
Bureau of African Affairs (BAA), 294–98, 341, 424
Burkina Faso (Upper Volta), *124*, 153, 162, 341–42, 303, 439–40
Burma, during World War II, 10, 147, 193
Burma, independence of, 140
Burnham, Forbes, 102, 423
Burns constitution, 143–44, 154
Burns, Alan, 143
Burroughs, Edgar Rice, 150
Busia, Kofi, 314

Cabral, Amílcar, 297, 425–26
cacao. *See* cocoa
Cameroon, 304, 377, 462
Camp Thiaroye, Senegal, 132
Candace of Ethiopia, 45
Cape Coast, Ghana, 24, 140, 151, 156, 161, 167, 229, *252*
Carmichael, Adolphus, 422
Carmichael, Stokely, 51, 422, 426–27, 430–31, 437
Caro, Robert A., 414
Carr, Robert K., 217
Carter, W. Beverly, 76
Cartwright, Marguerite, 282, 286
Casablanca-Monrovia divide, 410, 430
Casely Hayford, Archibald, 167, 180, 418
Casely Hayford, Joseph Ephraim (J. E.), 7, 24–25, 35, 42–48, 51, 67, 131, 138, 229, 255, 268
Ethiopia Unbound, 7, 44–45, 47, 449
Gold Coast Native Institutions, 24, 43, 46
cash crops, 32, 127, 325
classic commodity booms, 349, 356
coffee, 126–27, 134, 269, 329–40
cotton, 69, 126, 127, 195, 325–26, 440
rubber, 23, 116–17, 126, 137, 159, 325–26, 440
See also cocoa
Castro, Fidel, 228, 366–67, 399
Castro, Raúl, 228
Catholicism
in America, 204, 214, 399–400, 413
Catholic Africans, 268, 304, 334–35
Catholic institutions in Africa, 325, 328, 334–35

INDEX

Nkrumah's Catholic devotion, 16, 21, 27, 34, 73, 80, 82, 140, 204, 214, 399–400, 413
CBS, 219, 420
Central African Republic, 192, 322
Cephron, the Master of Egypt, 45
Ceres, Albert, 280, 287
Césaire, Aimé, 9
Chafer, Tony, 133
Chicago Daily Tribune (newspaper), 168–69, 415
Chicago Defender (newspaper), 11, 98, 262, 286, 292, 358
Chicago, 68, 237, 287, 288, 326, 419
China, People's Republic of
 Communist China's admission into the UN, 368
 Hangzhou, 393
 "losing" China to the communists, 358–59
 Nkrumah in Beijing, 393, 423, 426
 Tazara Railway project (Tanzania/Zambia), 17
China, Republic of (Taiwan), 162, 261, 368
Chinese Communist Party, 116
Christianborg Castle, Accra, 149, 158, 168, 176, 178, 238, 248, 296, 310
Christianity, Islam, and the Negro Race (Blyden), 49–50
Christianity
 Egyptian Coptic Christians, 310, 312
 missionaries in the Congo, 325
 missionaries in the Gold Coast, 27, 39, 73
 Montgomery, Alabama's Dexter Avenue Baptist Church, 252, 262–66
Churchill, Winston, 10, 97, 114, 118, 129, 161
CIA
 in Angola, 304
 assessments of Nkrumah, 211, 309, 377, 398–99, 430
 assessments of Stokely Carmichael, 426
 in the Congo, 307, 365–66, 372, 385–86, in Cuba, 390–91
 in Guyana, 423
"Circle, The," 110–11, 138, 151, 154, 222
citizenship, 109, 190–94, 131, 219, 262–63, 277, 319, 417, 437

"civic merit cards," 327
civil disobedience, 160, 162–65
 Gandhiism, 96, 160–61, 175, 201, 224, 210, 259, 265, 303, 329, 423
 "useful trouble," 341
 See also activism; civil rights movement
Civil Rights Act of 1957 (US), 382
Civil Rights Act of 1964 (US), 414
civil rights movement
 the "Big Four" of the, 219
 Brown v. Board of Education, 15, 217–18, 283
 "Don't Buy Where You Can't Work" campaign in Harlem, 75, 89
 federal civil rights laws, 381–82
 Freedom Rides, 422, 426
 March on Washington for Jobs and Freedom, August 28, 1963, 199–201, 420
 sit-ins, 12, 200, 342, 418
civil service in Ghana, 188, 231, 289, 318, 349, 351, 358, 394
civil service in the British Empire, 159, 172, 177, 183–86, 188, 231
civil service in the French Empire, 277
civil wars, 66, 77–78, 116, 234, 304, 425, 439
Clark, Joseph S., Jr., 211
Clarke, John Henrik, 13, 16
Clemenceau, Georges, 192
Coast Native Institutions (Casely Hayford), 24, 43, 46
cobalt mining, 126, 326, 361
Cocoa Marketing Board (Ghana), 348
Cocoa Purchasing Company (Ghana), 235
cocoa/cacao, 3, 32–33, 98, 116–17, 127, 134, 146–47, 266, 233, 235–36, 240, 243–44, 261, 280, 392–93
 British control over, 145–47
 classic commodity booms, 349, 356
 swollen shoot disease, 146–47, 154
coffee, 126–27, 134, 269, 329–40
Cofie-Crabbe, H. H., 406
COINTELPRO, 426
Cold War, 9, 14, 112–15, 430, 434
 breakdown of empire after World War II, 115–20
 Bretton Woods monetary system, 216

 in the Congo, 4, 89, 305–7, 323–39, 360–69, 373, 385–87
 Eisenhower's New Look, 120–21
 Kennan's Long Telegram, 113–14
 the Korean War, 228, 281–82
 "losing China," 358–59
 proxy wars, 438
 realism in international relations, 114–15
 in Vietnam, 115, 119–20, 126, 130, 140, 174, 264, 270, 275, 288, 382, 414, 422
 See also nuclear weapons
Colonial Aid to Britain in the Great War (Padmore), 98
colonialism
 assimilation and, 38, 96, 135, 326
 Berlin Conference of 1884–1885, 14, 28, 38, 43, 45–46, 51, 68, 268, 336, 409
 Britain's sterling zone, 98, 127, 231, 353
 colonial dependence on imperial powers, 86–87, 99, 183, 343, 345, 359
 colonies as "the slums of the world," 101
 Europe's dependence on its colonies, 10, 54, 96–98, 215
 ferocious tenacity of Western imperialism, 116
 Global South, 115, 209, 221, 222, 294
 palm oil extraction, 23, 127, 226, 322
 Scramble for Africa, 28, 308, 325, 434
 second wave of, 117
 shared experience of imperial rule, 191
 the threat of Balkanization in Africa, 6, 109
 timber, 116–17, 140, 173, 233
 West African settler colonies, 37, 41–42
 white settler colonies in Africa, 127, 159, 222, 307
 See also cash crops; mining; slavery and the slave trade
Color and Democracy (Du Bois), 101
color line, global, 7, 11–13, 98–99, 103, 194, 368
"color-blindness," 204
Colored Women's League of Washington, DC, 192
Coltrane, John, 255
Comintern, 32

Commissioner for Africanization (Gold Coast), 172
Committee on Constitutional Reform (UK), 155
Committee on Youth Organization (CYO), 157–58
Commonwealth of Nations, 159, 161, 248, 321, 344, 374, 397
communism
　Comintern, 32
　First Red Scare, 94
　Leninist, 94, 376–77, 383–84, 391
　nationalization of industry, 359, 393–94
　Trotskyism, 13, 90, 293
　See also Cold War; Marxism
Communist Party of France, 132, 268, 274
Communist Party of the United States, 75, 94, 207
Compaoré, Blaise, 439
Conakry, 278, 424–25, 427, 430
concentration camps, 100, 224
Concorde supersonic jets, 5
Confederation Générale du Travail (Guinea), 273
Conference of Independent African States (CIAS), 275–76, 303
Congo (Belgian), 4, 89, 305–7, 323–39, 360–69, 373, 385–87
　Abako party, 328, 330–31
　Brazzaville Conference (1944), 130–32
　Catholic University of Lovanium, 328
　educated class of the, 328
　Elisabethville (Lubumbashi), 362
　évolués of the, 326–29
　independence of, 323, 327, 334–39
　Katangan separatism, 361, 363, 372, 385–86, 395–96
　Kinshasa (Leopoldville), 306, 323, 327, 329–30, 362–65, 372, 386, 396
　Lingala, the lingua franca of western Congo, 332, 335
　Onalua village, 324–25
　Stanleyville, 325–29, 331, 365, 385
Congo (French Central Africa), 130–32, 277, 329
Congo, Land of the Future. Is It Threatened? (Lumumba), 328–29
Congolese Army, 333, 337, 365, 378
Congress of Black Writers and Artists, Paris, 258

Conservative Party (UK), 377
Convention People's Party (CPP), 157–66, 169–76
　after the election of 1950, 182–83, 212–13, 222, 225, 230
　after the election of 1954, 232–36, 240–44, 246, 254, 281
　toward a one-party state, 313–15, 319, 341, 348, 349, 354, 358, 387, 393–94, 405–7, 416, 436
　today, 313
Cooper, Anna Julia, 191–92
Cooper, Frederick, 133
copper, 326, 361, 372
Copts, 310, 312
Cordier, Andrew, 365
corruption
　"featherbedding," 319
　in Ghanaian politics, 240–41, 313–19
　Mobutu's "Versailles in the Jungle," 4–5
　Nigeria's "national cake," 241
　patronage jobs for party loyalists, 185, 231, 235, 240–41, 319, 394
Costa Rica, 49
Côte d'Ivoire. See Ivory Coast
cotton, 69, 126, 127, 195, 325–26, 440
Council on African Affairs (CAA), 207
coups d'état and covert actions, 115, 221, 319, 377, 391, 415, 423, 424
Coussey Committee report, 156–63, 170, 173, 177
Coussey, James Henley, 154
Creasy, Gerald, 151, 152, 154
"creole" cultures, 39
Cripps, Stafford, 98
Crisis, The (magazine), 53, 189, 196, 198
Cuba, 343, 426
　Bay of Pigs invasion, 391
　Cuban Missile Crisis, 384, 413
　Guantanamo Bay, 317
　the Cuban Revolution, 228, 366
cults of personality, 4–5, 108, 111, 173, 240, 309, 315, 320–21
Czechoslovakia, 389

Dachau concentration camp, 100–101
Daily Worker (UK), 151
Dakar, 132–33, 269, 276–77, 278

Daley, Richard J., 288
Danish Empire, 149, 284
Danquah, J. B., 35, 48, 61, 106–8, 138, 141–45, 148–53
　break with Nkrumah, 158, 169–70, 179, 232–34, 314–15, 321, 348–49
　death of, 432–33, 436
Davidson, Basil, 33
Davis, Miles, 255, 289
de Gaulle, Charles
　at the Brazzaville Conference (1944), 130–32
　during the French Fifth Republic, 270, 271, 275–79, 299, 329, 334, 342, 383, 454
　government in exile, 131–32
　Guinean independence and, 277–79, 299, 383
　Ivory Coast and, 271, 278
　nuclear testing in Algeria, 342
　after World War II, 95–96, 109
De Schryver, August, 334
Debs, Eugene V., 198
Declaration on the Granting of Independence of Colonial Countries and Peoples (1960), 366
decolonization
　administrative/political vacuum(s) left by, 185, 187, 326
　colonial dependence on imperial powers, 86–87, 99, 183, 343, 345, 359
　Europe's dependence on its colonies, 10, 54, 96–98, 215
　notions of citizenship, 109, 190–94, 131, 219, 262–63, 277, 319, 417, 437
Defiance Campaign (South Africa), 282
Dei-Anang, Michael, 143
Delany, Martin, 7, 41, 418
Delmont, Matthew, 193
Democratic Party (US), 199, 204, 286–87, 373, 382, 397, 400, 414
democratization
　America's deep-seated hypocrisy about, 217, 225, 160
　Cold War racism and the prospects of democracy in Africa, 113–15, 241–42
　"economic democracy," 103–4
　failure in Africa, 17
　making the world "safe for democracy," 8–9, 53, 195–98

INDEX

self-defined, 173
Westminster model of government, 177, 179, 230, 247, 318, 406, 434
Denmark, 149, 264
Deportation Act of 1957 (Ghana), 315
de-Stalinization, 228
Dexter Avenue Baptist Church, Montgomery, 252, 262–66
Diagne, Blaise, 54, 192
diamonds, 322, 326, 352, 394
Điện Biên Phủ, Battle of, 119, 121, 130
Diggs, Charles C., Jr., 257, 291
Diop, Alioune, 258
Discourse on Colonialism (Césaire), 9
Disneyland, Kennedy and Touré in, 384
Divine, Major Jealous, 80–81
Djin, Andrew, 365
Dosumu-Johnson, Thomas, 67–69, 74, 79
Double V (Victory) campaign, 195–96
Douglass, Frederick, 30, 51, 196
Drew, Jane, 346
drinking water, 440
Du Bois, Shirley Graham, 312, 419, 421, 426
Du Bois, W. E. B., 6–7, 14, 40, 45–47, 50–51, 56, 104–5, 190–98
"The African Roots of War," 14
Color and Democracy, 101
The Crisis, 53, 189, 196, 198
on education, 65, 76–77
Encyclopedia Africana, 419
first visit to Africa, 189
the global color line, 7, 11–13, 98–99, 103, 194, 368
later life and death in Ghana, 419–20
"Memorandum on the Future of Africa," 192
The Philadelphia Negro, 7, 82
relationship with the U.S. State Department, 216, 258
The Souls of Black Folk, 7, 45, 46, 197
the "talented tenth," 47, 192, 226, 419
Dulles, Allen, 221, 372, 396
Dulles, John Foster, 221, 257, 288
Dutch Empire, 41, 140, 142, 150, 162. *See also* Indonesia

Eastland, James O., 202–3
Ebony (magazine), 225, 226
"economic democracy," 103–4

economic development. *See* African economies; colonialism
Economist, The (magazine), 357, 475
Education of the Negro in the American Social Order (H. M. Bond), 188–89
education, 10–11, 27, 45, 66, 133, 205, 327, 345, 416, 440
under Belgian rule, 331
under British rule, 27–31
Brown v. Board of Education, 15, 217–18, 283
GI Bill (US), 203–4
Kumasi College of Science and Technology, 233, 345–46
Nkrumah's time at Achimota College, 27–32, 55, 82, 141, 143, 168
Nkrumah's time at Lincoln University, 19, 11, 35–36, 64–70, 71–84, 85–90, 105, 188, 205, 211, 280
public education in the US, 27
in the struggle for African liberation, 40
Tuskegee Institute, 30, 44–45, 50, 69
University of Ghana, 418, 421, 429
University of Pennsylvania, 82–85, 87, 205, 280
See also Historically Black Colleges and Universities (HCBUs)
Edusei, Krobo, 153, 319
Edwards, Brent H., 49
Egypt
Coptic Christians, 310, 312
searching for a wife for Nkrumah, 310–12, 430
Suez Crisis, 223, 242–43, 246, 389
Suez Dam, 289
Eisenhower, Dwight D., 120–21, 129, 217–20
African American in government, 215–20, 284
desegregating schools, 283–84
heart attack, 371
lack of interest in Africa, 221
New Look, 120–21
Elisabethville (Lubumbashi), Congo, 362
Elizabeth II of England, 340, 397–98, 405
Elkins, Caroline, 117
Ellison, Ralph, 49, 69–70, 75, 79, 80, 93–94

emancipations
"mental emancipation" of Africans, 35
"race emancipation," 44
understanding Nkrumah's "second emancipation," 15–28, 200
Encyclopedia Africana (Du Bois), 419
England. *See* Britain; British Empire; London
"Era of Good Feelings" of 1820s America, 303
Ethiopia
Addis Ababa, 36, 384, 409–10, 412
Battle of Adwa (1896), 68
Candace, queen of, 45
Haile Selassie I, 63, 411
Italy's invasion of, 22–23, 35, 62–64, 68, 77, 95, 126, 253, 342, 346
Ethiopia Unbound (Casely Hayford), 7, 44–45, 47, 449
European Club of Accra, 184
European Convention on Human Rights, 270
European imperialism. *See* colonialism; *specific imperial powers*
Evers, Medgar, 418
évolués of the Congo, 326–29
Ewe people of West Africa, 145, 233, 242, 244–45, 314, 315, 433
Ewe Togoland region of Ghana, 145, 244–45
Ex-Servicemen's Union (Ghana), 148
Eyskens, Gaston, 333

Face the Nation (news show), 288
Fair Employment Practices Committee (US), 200
Fall, Bernard, 119–20
famine in Biafra, 425
Fanon, Frantz, 116, 118, 307–8, 363
Fante Confederacy, 24
Fante ethnic group, 2, 5, 7, 24, 43–44, 81, 236, 264
Faubus, Orval, 283
FBI (Federal Bureau of Investigation), 211, 426, 427
"featherbedding," 319
federalism/confederation, 6–7, 15, 102, 106, 110, 138, 141, 233, 242, 245, 270–73, 404, 408–12
Federalist Papers, The, 409
Ferry, Jules, 25
"feudalism," 182, 221, 235, 243

INDEX

Fifth Pan-African Congress of 1945 (Manchester), 92, 102–5, 109, 151, 160, 192, 293, 299, 303–4
First Red Scare, 94
First World War. *See* World War I
Fischer, George, 27
Fisk University, Nashville, 65, 93
Flagstaff House, Accra, 406, 415
Fleming, Ian, 209–10
Flower, Elizabeth, 64
Fort Amsterdam, 142
Fourah Bay College, Sierra Leone, 39, 43
"Fourteen Points" speech (Wilson), 8–9
France
 Communist Party of France, 132, 268, 274
 Congress of Black Writers and Artists, 258
 during the French Fifth Republic, 270, 271, 275–79, 299, 329, 334, 342, 383, 454
 National Assembly of, 109, 132–33, 269–70, 276–77
 organized labor in, 273
 pan-African congress of 1919, 192
 See also French Empire
Franco, Francisco, 78
Fraser, Alec Garden, 28–29
Fraternité Matin (newspaper), 321
Frazier, E. Franklin, 11, 77, 88
Free French forces, 130, 307, 410
"Freedom Now!" slogan, 7, 192, 353
Freedom Rides, 422, 426
Freetown, Sierra Leone, 39, 136–39
French Communist Party, 132, 268, 274
French Empire
 and the African Financial Community franc (CFA), 454
 Battle of Điện Biên Phủ, 119, 121, 130
 cadre unique (equal pay and benefits system), 134
 calls for unlimited migration, 135
 civil service in the, 277
 dreams of a French Union, 131, 133, 270, 276–77
 Free French forces, 130, 307, 410
 French Central Africa, 130–32, 277, 329

French West Africa, 130–35, 276
 in Indochina, 115, 119–20, 126, 130, 140, 174, 270, 275
 Konkouré River dam, 279
 Loi Cadre (enabling act), 276–77
 in Mali, 341
 in Martinique, 9, 133, 307
 after World War II, 95–96
Friends of Ghana associations, 224
Front de Libération National (FLN), 307
Fry, Maxwell, 346
fugu traditional cotton smocks of Ghana, 165, 253

Ga ethnic group, 314, 347
Gabon, 273
Gambia, 29, *124*
Garvey, Amy Ashwood, 92
Garvey, Marcus, 7–8, 41, 48–56, 62–63, 67–68, 197, 214
 Ethiopianist movement, 75
 Garveyism in Africa, 53, 55–56, 87, 368
 Philosophy and Opinions of Marcus Garvey, 51, 87
 shipping company, the Black Star Line, 51
 Universal Negro Improvement Association (UNIA), 7–8, 51–52, 54, 55, 67–68, 257
Gbedemah, Komla, *123*, 168–76, 180, 182, 280–85, 302, 357, 358, 394–95, 405
George V of England, Orwell, 62
George VI of England, 180
Germany
 Berlin Conference of 1884–1885, 14, 28, 38, 43, 45–46, 51, 68, 268, 336, 409
 rearmament of, 62, 78
 in Tanganyika, 126
Getachew, Adom, 378
Ghana, xiii–xiv
 authoritarianism in, 16, 234, 316–17, 320, 402, 406, 416
 Axim, 57
 the "Big Six," the founding fathers of, 151–56
 Budget Bureau (Ghana), 394
 Cape Coast, 24, 140, 151, 156, 161, 167, 229, *252*
 civil service in, 188, 231, 289, 318, 349, 351, 358, 394
 during the Congo Crisis, 362, 365–68, 372, 411
 in the context of West African geography, *124*

Deportation Act of 1957, 315
 elections of 1956, 243–45
 Elizabeth II's visit to, 397–98
 Half Assini, 4–6, 26–27
 Kulungugu, 404, 406–7, 415
 Kumasi, 153, 147, 233, 236, 244, 247, 316, 379
 Lawra, 153
 Malcolm X's visits to, 420–22
 map of, *252*
 Martin Luther King Jr. at Ghana's independence ceremonies, 258–61, 263–66
 Nkroful village, 3, 4, 6, 21, 26, 76, *252*, 325
 Northern Territories, 145, 234, 246
 as a republic, 340–44
 Saltpond, 140, 141–42, 144, 150, 151, *252*
 Sekondi, 40, 165, 394
 Sunyani, *252*, 377, 379
 Takoradi, 3, 58, 137–38, 394
 Tamale, 153
 Tarkwa, 139–40, 148, 165
 Tema, 316, 347, 359, 390, 428
 Togoland, 145, 244–45
 Winneba, *252*, 390
 See also Accra
Ghana Chamber of Commerce, 148
Ghana Congress Party, 234
Ghana Evening News (newspaper), 283, 342
Ghana National College, Cape Coast, Ghana, 156
Ghana: The Autobiography of Kwame Nkrumah, 3
Ghanaian culture
 Asante people of, 23–24, 43, 92–93, 229, 233–37, 238–46, 271, 316–18, 332, 348–49, 415–16, 433
 Fante ethnic group, 2, 5, 7, 24, 43–44, 81, 236, 264
 fugu traditional cotton smocks, 165, 253
 Ga ethnic group of, 314, 347
 Highlife music of, 2, 254
 invented traditions of, 322
 new national iconography of public spaces, 346–47
 ntoma, traditional togas, 289
 Nzima ethnic group, 5–6, 21–22, 58, 61, 187, 271
 Voice of Africa broadcast service, 341
Ghanaian economics
 bauxite and aluminum production in, 126, 213, 281, 285, 344, 347, 352–59, 421

INDEX

economic development and modernization, 344–51
foreign aid, 366–67
nationalization of industries, 359, 393–94
Programme for Work and Happiness, 416
transitioning to cash economy, 21
See also cocoa; Volta River Project (VRP)
Ghanaian politics
accession to the UN, 262
in the African American press, 262–63
"Africanization" of the army's officer corps, 395–96
the army as locus of power in, 415, 423, 425, 438–39
Avoidance of Discrimination Act, 314
Budget Bureau, 394
Bureau of African Affairs, 294–98
civil service in, 188, 231, 289, 318, 349, 351, 358, 394
corruption in, 240–41, 313–19
Deportation Act of 1957 (Ghana), 315
dignitaries at the independence ceremonies, 255–61
diplomatic relations with China, 369
drifting in Nkrumah's absence, 428
earliest sovereign relations with the US, 280–85
Ewe Togoland region of Ghana, 145, 244–45
Ex-Servicemen's Union, 148
first anniversary of independence, 286
flag of, 51, 253, 419
general election of 1956, 232, 235, 241, 243–36
growing authoritarianism in, 319–22
Guinea and, 299–302
independence of, 246–49
from model colony to model for other colonies, 138, 143–44, 146–47, 150, 224, 237, 343
petty corruption in, 240–41
"power sweet," 318
Preventive Detention Act of July 1958, 288–89, 315–17, 320, 407, 428, 435
the rule of law in, 13, 402

struggles with political cohesion and corruption, 313–19
Supreme Court of, 154
Tanzania and, 434–37
Trade Union Council (TUC), 164–66, 274, 319
United Gold Coast Convention (UGCC), 61, 105–9, 138–57, 159, 162, 169, 171–75, 179, 212, 232, 240
United Party (UP) of Ghana, 314–15
See also Convention People's Party (CPP)
GI Bill (US), 203–4
Giáp, Võ Nguyên, 119
Gilroy, Harry, 337
Gizenga, Antoine, 365
Global South, 115, 209, 221, 222, 294
globalization. See Black diaspora; Cold War; colonialism
Gold Coast Aborigines' Rights Protection Society (GCARPS), 34–35, 43, 45, 229
Gold Coast Echo (newspaper), 43
Gold Coast, xiii–xiv, 23–24, 159–67
Bond of 1844, 254–65
British control over cocoa, 145–47
Burns constitution, 143–44, 154
Christian missionaries in the, 27, 39, 73
civil service in the Gold Coast, 159, 172, 177, 183–86, 188, 231
Commissioner for Africanization, 172
constitutional "reform" in the, 155
Friends of Ghana associations, 224
lack of indigenous education in, 27–28
Nkrumah's final address before the colonial assembly, 253–55
Nkrumah's speaking tour throughout the Gold Coast, 145–48
opposition to the Land Bill, 43
the "prison graduates" of, 123, 171, 175–76, 180, 253, 260
the "verandah boys" of the, 150, 156, 173, 180, 236
violence against veterans, 149–51

Watson Commission, 153–54, 168
See also Ghana
gold mining, 275
Gore, Albert, Sr., 390, 397–98, 401
governance. See African politics; Ghanaian politics; various forms of governance
Granger, Lester, 219–20, 257, 291
Grant, George "Paa," 61, 64, 105, 140, 142, 144, 173, 179
Great Depression, 61, 79
Greatest Generation, 14, 193, 204
Guadeloupe, 133
Guantanamo Bay, Cuba, 317
Guardian, The (newspaper), 404–15
Guatemala, 221–22
Guggisberg, Gordon, 28–29
Guinea, 124, 207, 273–79, 342, 369, 409, 410, 413
Conakry, 278, 424, 427, 430
Confédération Générale du Travail, 273
de Gaulle and Guinean independence, 277–79, 299, 383
Ghana and, 299–302, 425
Soviet overflights and airspace, 384
Guinea-Bissau, 124, 425
Guyana, 102, 118, 375, 423

Haile Selassie I of Ethiopia, 63, 411
Haiti, 13–14, 41, 92, 189, 279
Half Assini, Ghana, 4–6, 26–27, 252
Halm, W. M. Q., 373
Hamer, Fannie Lou, 418
Hammarskjöld, Dag, 364–69, 396, 405
Hangzhou, China, 393
Hansberry, Lorraine, 190
Hansberry, William Leo, 11, 77, 89, 190, 191
Harlem, 49, 52–54, 69–70, 71, 74–77, 197–98, 287, 366–67
Abyssinian Baptist Church, 70, 74, 263, 451
Apollo Theater, 70
Audubon Ballroom, 421
"Don't Buy Where You Can't Work" campaign, 75, 89
first modern race riot, 74–75
Hotel Theresa on 125th, 366
Jewish store owners in, 75
Savoy Ballroom, 70
Speakers' Corner on 135th Street, 52

INDEX

Harlem Hellfighters, 290
Harlem Hospital, 75
Harlem Renaissance, 54, 70, 92–93, 226
Harriman, Averill, 288
"Has the African a God?" (Wallace-Johnson), 33–34
Haygood, Wil, 75
Hemming, A. W. L., 27
Hershey Chocolate Company, 280
Herskovits, Melville J., 88
Herter, Christian, 218, 285, 368–69, 373, 374
Himes, Chester, 70
Historically Black Colleges and Universities (HBCUs), 11, 36, 65, 72, 77, 93, 191
  Fisk University, 65, 93
  Howard University, 11, 65, 72, 77, 88–89, 93–94, 190–91, 195–96, 257, 291
"History and Philosophy of Imperialism, With Special Reference to Africa, The" (Nkrumah), 85
History of the British Empire, A (Elkins), 117
Hitler, Adolf, 10, 62, 78, 94, 113, 165, 194, 198, 299
Ho Chi Minh, 119, 422, 423, 426
Hodson, Arnold, 34
Holocaust, 100–101
Hood, Timothy, 203
Hoover, J. Edgar, 211, 426
Horton, Africanus (James Beale), 39–40, 136
Houphouët-Boigny, Félix, 4–5, 109, 132–34, 267–78, 300, 321, 399, 404, 409–10, 435, 438–39
House Un-American Activities Committee, 207
How Britain Rules Africa (Padmore), 97–98
Howard Johnson's of Dover Delaware, 282–85, 357–58
Howard University, 11, 65, 72, 77, 88–89, 93–94, 190–91, 195–96, 257, 291
Howard, William James, 52
Hughes, Langston, 9–10, 69–70, 71, 93, 225–26
Hungary, 389
Hunton, William Alphaeus, 11, 190, 207, 216
Hurston, Zora Neale, 70
hydroelectric power. *See* Volta River Project (VRP)

"I Saw a New Heaven and a New Earth" sermon (Nkrumah), 212
"imagined communities," 242

Impellitteri, Vincent R., 214
imperialism. *See* colonialism; decolonization; *specific imperial powers and their possessions*
indentured labor, 192, 326
"Indépendence Cha Cha," 335
independence movements. *See* decolonization; Black diaspora
India
  authoritarianism in, 317
  comparing Africans to Indians, 164–65
  Gandhiism 96, 160–61, 175, 201, 224, 210, 259, 265, 303, 329, 423
  independence of, 10, 97, 116–17, 126, 140, 160–61, 185, 294
  under Nehru, 276, 366, 369
  in the United Nations, 342
Indian Ocean slave trade, 325
Indochina, 115, 119–20, 126, 130, 140, 174, 270, 275
Indonesia, 116, 140, 162, 221, 276. *See also* Bandung Conference of 1955
industrialization, 137, 261, 344, 350, 351, 355, 388, 393, 401
inflation after World War I, 130, 147–48, 154, 393, 438
intelligentsia. *See* Black diaspora; Black intellectuals
International African Friends of Abyssinia, 63
International African Opinion (newspaper), 92
International African Service Bureau (IASB), 92
International Monetary Fund, 281
International Trade Union Committee of Negro Workers (ITUCNW), 32, 94
Invisible Man (Ellison), 49, 75, 79, 80
Iran, 118, 221, 342
Irish Americans, 381
Irish Republican Army, 427
"Iron Curtain" speech (Churchill), 114
Islam, Nation of, 200, 420–21
Israel, 292, 305, 342
  Arab-Israeli conflict over Palestine, 140, 153, 290
  during the Suez Crisis, 223
Italian Americans, 208, 292
Italian nationalism of the nineteenth century, 87
Italy's invasion of Ethiopia, 22–23, 35, 62–64, 68, 77, 95, 126, 253, 342, 346

Ivory Coast, *124*, 267–72, 300, 438–39
  Abidjan, 1–3, 133, 267, 399, 439, 443
  Baoulé people of the, 269, 271
  Port-Bouët and the Vridi Canal, 271
  Robert Kennedy's visit to the, 399
  travail forcé, 269

Jackson, Mahalia, 420
Jackson, Robert, 384
Jadotville prison, Congo, 332
Jagan, Cheddi, 118, 375–76, 423
Jamaica, 52, 359
James Fort Prison, Accra, 166, 175–76
James, Cyril Lionel Robert (C. L. R.), 11, 13, 89–90, 91–93, 102–3, 281, 296, 374, 402, 407–8
James, Leslie, 94, 98
Janssens, Émile, 333
Japan
  modernization during the Meiji Restoration, 44
  Russo-Japanese War of 1904–5, 44
  during World War II, 101, 159, 198, 218
Jawara, Dawda, 29
Jefferson Memorial, Washington, DC, 213
Jefferson, Thomas, 37, 66, 346
Jet (magazine), 225
Jewish community in the US, 75, 292
Jim Crow United States, 11, 193, 198, 201, 202–4, 281, 341
Johnson Publishing Company, 225
Johnson, George (Lincoln University), 81–83
Johnson, Lyndon B., 414, 421, 423, 426
Johnson, Mordecai Wyatt, 190, 257, 291
Johnson, Walter I., 73–74
Johnson, William Hallock, 66, 70
Jones, Norton, 353
Joseph, Peniel, 426, 431
Judt, Tony, 96
"just wars," 38

Kabasele, Joseph, 335
Kadzamira, Cecilia, 321
Kaiser Aluminum Corporation, 285, 367, 377
Kaiser, Edgar, 357–59, 401
Kaiser, Henry J., 285, 421
Kaldor, Nicholas, 388
Kamata, Ng'wanza, 437

INDEX

Kanza, Thomas, 336
Kasa-Vubu, Joseph, 306, 325, 328, 330, 333, 337, 362–63, 365, 370, 385
Katangan separatism, 361, 363, 372, 385–86, 395–96
Katzenbach, Nicholas, 426
Kaunda, Kenneth, 4, 297, 304
Keïta, Modibo, 376
Kelley, Robin D. G., 426
Kennan's Long Telegram, 113–14, 454
Kennedy, Caroline, 387
Kennedy, Jacqueline, 387, 413
Kennedy, John F.
  and African liberation, 382–84
  assassination of, 412–14
  civil rights under, 381–82
  Nkrumah and, 251, 287, 371–73, 384–89, 397–403, 413
Kennedy, Robert, 390, 399
kente cloth, 180, 285, 289, 321
Kenya, 55, 118, 127–28, 130, 224, 297, 304, 321
  Kenya Land and Freedom Army (the "Mau Mau"), 118, 127–28, 224, 237, 317
  Kikuyu ethnic group of, 118, 128
Kenyatta, Jomo, 102, 111, 321
Keynes, John Maynard, 216, 350
Keynesianism, 354
Khrushchev, Nikita, 222–23, 364, 367–69, 384, 389–92, 413, 433
Kikuyu ethnic group of Kenya, 118, 128
King, Coretta Scott, 257, 259
King, Martin Luther, Jr.
  "The Birth of a New Nation" sermon, 264
  at the Dexter Avenue Baptist Church, Montgomery, 252, 262–66
  at Ghana's independence ceremonies and upon return, 258–61, 263–66
  "I Have a Dream" speech, 420
  from jail in Birmingham, Alabama, 175
  March on Washington for Jobs and Freedom, August 28, 1963, 199–201, 420
  "passive resistance," 259
King, Michael, 260
"kingdom of culture," 40
Kinloch, Alice Victoria, 191
Kinshasa (Leopoldville), Belgian Congo, 306, 323, 327, 329–30, 362–65, 372, 386, 396

Kitson, Albert, 352–53, 356, 359, 377, 379
kleptocracy, 435. *See also* corruption
Korea, Democratic Republic of (North Korea), 322, 378, 444
Korea, Republic of (South Korea), 261
Korean War, 228, 281–82
Kotoka, Emmanuel, 423
Ku Klux Klan, 8, 10, 77, 258
Kufuor, John, 379
Kulungugu, Ghana, 404, 406–7, 415
Kumasi College of Science and Technology, 233, 345–46
Kumasi, Ghana, 153, 147, 233, 236, 244, 247, 316, 379
Kusi, B. F., 236
Kwame Nkrumah Ideological Institute, Winneba, Ghana, 390

La Communauté (newspaper), 132
labor
  Brotherhood of Sleeping Car Porters (BSCP), 197–98, 200–201
  Hidastrut Zionist labor organization, 305
  indentured labor, 192, 326
  Negro Bureau of the Red International of Labor Unions, 94
  strikes, 10, 96, 130, 134, 164, 273–75, 395
  travail forcé, 269
  union activism, 33, 100, 273
  See also slavery and the slave trade
Labour Party (UK), 96–98, 156, 161, 243
"Lagos Town," 186, 239
Lagos, Nigeria, 48, 57, 129, 372
Lamine-Guèye, Amadou, 109
Laos, 119
Las Palmas, Canary Islands, 58
Latin America, 112, 217, 223, 411
Lawra, Ghana, 153, *252*
"Le Grand Kallé," 335
League of Nations, 51, 342
Lenin Peace Prize, 376, 407
Lenin, Vladimir, 94. *See also* communism; Marxism
Leopold II of Belgium, 325–26, 330, 336–37
Leopoldville (Kinshasa), Belgian Congo, 306, 323, 327, 329–30, 362–65, 372, 386, 396

Levittown, New York, 204
Lewis, David Levering, 70, 419–21, 433
Lewis, John, 341
Lewis, W. Arthur, 349–51, 354–49, 388, 433
Liberia, 7, 21, 37–38, 41–42, 94, 101, 189, 257, 275, 342, 430. *See also* Garvey, Marcus
Libya, 275, 342, 410
Licorish, David, 263
Lie, Trygve, 213
Life (magazine), 193, 224
Lincoln Memorial, Washington, DC, 213
Lincoln University, Oxford Pennsylvania, *19*, 11, 35–36, 64–70, 71–84, 85–90, 105, 188, 205, 211, 280
Lincoln, Abraham, 176
Lingala, the lingua franca of western Congo, 332, 335
Little Rock High School, desegregation of, 217, 219, 283–84
Little, Malcolm. *See* Malcolm X
Liverpool, 61, 136
Livingstone College, Salisbury, North Carolina, 30
Locke, Alain, 11, 50, 69, 93–94, 191
Locke, John, 38
Logan, Rayford, 11, 190, 196, 216
Loi Cadre (enabling act), 276–77
London
  African students in, 64
  British Library, 49
  the Great Smog, 209
  Speakers' Corner in Hyde Park, 49
Long Telegram (Kennan), 113–14, 454
Los Angeles Times, 361, 429
"Lost Cause" and "Redemption" of the South, 189
Louverture, Toussaint, 13–14, 30, 51, 92, 279
Lugard, Frederick John, 25
Lumumba, Patrice, 305–7, 309, 323–39, 360–78
  arrests and incarceration of, 332–34, 366
  assassination of, 322, 372, 384–87, 396, 405, 425
  Congo, Land of the Future. Is It Threatened?, 328–29

Macmillan, Harold, 377, 397
Madagascar, 115, 126
Magna Carta, 152

INDEX

Mahoney, William P., 399–400, 413–14
Makeba, Miriam, 426–27
Makonnen, T. Ras, 102–3, 104, 110
Malawi, 102, 107, 320–21
Malaya (now Malaysia), 98, 117, 126, 153, 159–60, 163, 167
Malcolm X, 8, 54, 194, 200, 282, 366, 420–22, 426
Mali Empire, 273
Mali, 124, 341, 376, 391, 404, 408, 410, 425
Malik, Yakov Alexandrovich, 375
Manchester Pan-African Congress of 1945, 92, 102–5, 109, 151, 160, 192, 293, 299, 303–4
Mandela, Nelson, xiii, 13, 181, 282
manganese, 126, 352
Manley, Norman, 257–48
Mao Zedong, 116, 162, 222–23, 393, 413, 444
Marable, Manning, 366–67
March on Washington for Jobs and Freedom, August 28, 1963, 199–201, 420
Marina, the Duchess of Kent, 256
Marquis, Fredrik (Lord Woolton), 127
Marshall Plan, 14, 115, 204, 271
Marshall, George C., 120, 217
Marshall, Thurgood, 11, 71, 206, 291
Martinique, 9, 133, 307
Marxism
anti-Marxism in the context of conservative nationalism, 87
among Black intellectuals and leaders, 49, 89–90, 94, 110, 222, 260, 318, 394
gauging Nkrumah's revolutionary bona fides, 13, 16, 110, 118, 137, 176, 390–91, 399, 430
Marxist-Leninist dream of the state that withers away, 242
See also communism; Cold War
massive retaliation, 120
"Mau Mau" rebellion, 118, 127–28, 224, 237, 317
Mayfield, Julian, 418
Mays, Willie, 188
Mazzini, Giuseppe, 87
Mboya, Tom, 304, 308
McCarthy, Eugene, 400
McCarthy, Joseph, 174, 207, 282

McCone, John, 399
McGhee, George, 216
McLean, Tony, 106
"Memorandum on the Future of Africa" (Du Bois), 192
Menand, Louis, 382, 454
Menelik II of Ethiopia, 68
Menen Asfaw of Ethiopia, 63
Mensah, E. T., 255
Messenger Magazine, 200
Messenger, The (magazine), 198
Meuse-Argonne campaign of World War II, 52
Mexico City Olympics (1968), 117
Miller, Doris "Dorie," 195–96
Milne, June, 428–29
mining
cobalt, 126, 326, 361
copper, 326, 361, 372
gold, 274
diamonds, 322, 326, 352, 394
manganese, 126, 352
uranium, 326, 331
minstrel shows, 194, 213–41
Mississippi, 27, 127, 202–3, 204, 284, 326, 418
Mobutu Sese Seko, 4–5, 322, 332, 365–66, 378, 402, 410, 435–36
modernism, 69, 112, 346–47, 406
modernity, 255, 360, 384
modernization, 24, 44, 133, 144, 355, 345–47, 379. See also African economies; Ghanaian economics
Mogambo (film), 126
"Monroe Doctrine for Africa," 276
Monroe, James, 37, 66
Monrovia Group of African nations, 410, 430
Monrovia, Liberia, 66, 137
Montgomery Bus Boycott of 1956–57, 12, 217, 258–60, 266
Montgomery, Alabama's Dexter Avenue Baptist Church, 252, 262–66
Morgenthau, Hans, 115
Morgue, Efua, 282
Morocco, 275, 342, 410
Morrison, Herbert, 97
Morrow, E. Frederic, 218–19, 284
Moscow Daily News, 358
Moscow New Times, 151
Mosely, Peter, 292
Moses, Robert, 214
Mossadegh, Mohammad, 118, 221
"Motion of Destiny" speech (Nkrumah), 228–31, 233–34

Motley, Archibald Jr., 70
Moumié, Félix-Roland, 304, 462
Mountbatten, Louis, 117
Mouvement National Congolais (MNC), 305, 330–31, 333
Mouvement Nationaliste Africain, 132
Mozambique, 359
Mugabe, Robert, 29
Muhammad, Elijah, 421
Mussolini, Benito, 22–23, 62–63, 68, 126, 342, 346
Mwalimu ("teacher"), 321, 412
Myth of the Negro Past, The (Herskovits), 88
Mzee ("revered elder"), 321

Namibia (South West Africa), 97
Napoleon I of France, 279
Nasser, Gamal Abdel, 223, 276, 289, 305, 311, 366, 389
Nasserism, 309
Nation of Islam (NOI), 200, 420–21
National Association for the Advancement of Colored People (NAACP), 54, 68, 189, 199–200, 206, 219, 281, 291
National Congress of British West Africa (NCBWA), 7, 47, 48, 67, 229
National Guard of the United States, 283–84, 290
National Liberation Council (NLC), 423–24
National Liberation Movement (NLM), 236, 240, 243–44, 246, 248, 296
National Maritime Union, Philadelphia, 80
National Museum, Accra, 321, 346
National Press Club, Washington, DC, 288
National Security Council (NSC), 399, 423
National Urban League, 219, 257, 291
nationalism
"Africanization" of government, 184–85, 395
Black nationalism, 41, 50–54, 67, 94, 206–7, 427
"imagined communities," 242
origins of African nationalism, 37–39
race-based nationalism, 94
Zionism, 305
See also decolonization
nationalization of industry, 359, 393–94

INDEX

Native Son (Wright), 69x
NBC's *Face the Nation*, 288
"Negritude," 410
Negro Bureau of the Red International of Labor Unions, 94
"Negro circuit," 218
Negro Family in the United States, The (Frazier), 88
Negro World (newspaper), 52
Nehru, Jawaharlal, 276, 366, 369
nei luan, wai huan, 343
neocolonialism, 32, 98, 254, 301, 333, 348, 360, 368, 392, 400, 425
Netherlands/Dutch Empire, 41, 140, 142, 150, 162. *See also* Indonesia
New African, The (magazine), 104
New Deal, 76, 204
New Look, 120–21
New Negro movement, 54, 76, 93
New Pittsburgh Courier (newspaper), 430
New York Age, The (newspaper), 30
New York Amsterdam News (newspaper), 98, 203, 213
New York City, 54, 288, 290. *See also* Harlem
New York Times Magazine, 223
New York Times, The, 151, 210, 214, 278, 283, 316, 337, 339, 406–7, 429
Newkirk, Pamela, 31
newspapers. *See* African American press
Newsweek, 176
Nigeria, *124*, 130, 295, 408, 410
breakaway Biafra, 425
civil war in, 425
Ibadan, 331
Ife, 226
Lagos, 48, 57, 129, 372
the "national cake" in, 241
north-south cleavage in, 234
Nimitz, Chester W., 195
Nixon, Richard, 12, 224, 256–59, 262, 284, 286, 288, 317, 383
Nkomo, Joshua, 304
Nkrumah, Francis Nwia Kofi, xiii–xiv, 2–4
at Achimota College, 27–32, 55, 82, 141, 143, 168
African students and other expats/exiles, 105–6
Catholic devotion of, 16, 21, 27, 34, 73, 80, 82, 140, 204, 214, 399–400, 413
children of, 59, 312

death and legacy of, 427–31, 438–41
early life of, 4–6, 21–23, 25–27
George Padmore and, 91–95, 98–99, 100–103
in Harlem for the first time, 74–76
his father, 21, 28
his lifelong assistant Nyamekeh, 166, 187, 429
his mother, Elizabeth Nyaniba, 26, 140, 310, 311
his personality, 15–17, 108, 185, 413
his wife Fathia Halim Rizk, 310–12, 430
honorary doctorate from Lincoln University, 188, 209–15
the international education of, 35–36, 57–61
likeness on Guinea's currency, 424
at Lincoln University, *19*, 11, 35–36, 64–70, 71–84, 85–90, 105, 188, 205, 211, 280
in Liverpool, 61
in London, 62–64, 91–99, 100–11
Nkroful village, 3, 4, 6, 21, 26, 76, *252*, 325
like Obama, but blacker and cooler, 289–90
in Paris, 110–11
religion in the life of, 16
return home 1947, 137–42
women in his life, 60, 211–12
Nkrumah, Kwame
absence from the Bandung Conference, 243
Africa after Nkrumah, 438–41
appearance on *Face the Nation*, 288
arrest by British authorities, 151–54
"The Circle," 110–11, 138, 151, 154, 222
and the Committee on Youth Organization (CYO), 157–58
in the context of decolonization and desegregation, 13–17
in the context of nonalignment, 221–24
"Dawn Broadcast," 394
early influences, 32–36, 85–90
the early organizing of, 109–11

economic development and modernization, 344–51
during the elections of 1956, 243–45
at the 15th UN General Assembly, 366–70, 373–74
files on, 211
final address before the colonial assembly, 253–55
Flagstaff House, 406, 415
foreign policy balancing acts (late 1950s–1960s), 374–77
"Freedom Now!" slogan, 7, 192, 353
Gbedemah and, 168–70
Ghanaian independence as the first step of African liberation, 246–49
growing authoritarianism of, 404–8, 414–16, 432–33
his cult of personality, 4, 108, 111, 173, 240, 309, 315, 320–21
his mother Elizabeth Nyaniba, 21, 26–27, 58, 139–40, 148, 186–87, 310–11
"I Saw a New Heaven and a New Earth" sermon, 212
Joe Appiah and, 100–102
Kennedy and, *251*, 371–73, 384–89, 397–403
Kulungugu assassination attempt, 404, 406–7, 415
as "leader of government business," 177, 182–87
Motion of Destiny speech, 228–31, 233–34
on neocolonialism, 32, 98, 254, 301, 333, 348, 360, 368, 392, 400, 425
nonalignment and, 369
opposition to the Coussey Committee Report, 161–67
Osagyefo ("victor in war"), 234, 271, 319–21, 390, 404, 415, 428
as "our little Hitler," 165
overthrow and exile of, 423–29
pan-Africanism's ironic end, 408–9
personal diplomacy of, 206, 214–15, 384, 414, 422
the political opposition to, 240–43
political victory from prison, 168–81
politics of "positive action," 160–61, 163–66, 175, 224, 231–32, 265
as "President for Life," 432

INDEX

Nkrumah, Kwame (*continued*)
  as president of the republic, 340–44
  as a "prison graduate," *123*, 171, 175–76, 180, 253, 260
  as prime minister, 231–37
  as a secular Christian socialist, 16
  "Self-Government Now," 157–58
  speaking tour throughout the Gold Coast, 145–48
  supposed megalomania of, 343, 429
  "tactful action," 232, 295
  "tactical action," 177, 232
  Towards Colonial Freedom, 86–87
  and the United Gold Coast Convention (UGCC), 61, 105–9, 138–57, 159, 162, 169, 171–75, 179, 212, 232, 240
  unsigned Communist Party card from Britain, 137, 151
  the violent opposition to, 238–40, 316, 386, 433
  visit to Russia and other eastern powers, 389–90, 393
  visit to the US as head of state, 286–92
  visits to Beijing, 393, 423, 426
  the West's view of, 13–14
  winner of the Lenin Peace Prize, 407
Nkrumah, Samia, 313
Nobel Prizes and Nobel Peace laureates, 13, 89, 282, 290, 349
Non-Aligned Movement, 130, 221, 223, 274–75, 288, 343, 383, 386. *See also* Bandung Conference of 1955
North Korea, 322, 378, 444
North Star, The (newspaper), 41
North Vietnam, 422, 426
Northern People's Party (NPP), 233–34, 244
Northern Rhodesia (later Zambia), 297, 304, 359
Northern Territories, Ghana, 145, 234, 246
NSC-68, 14
ntoma, traditional togas of Ghana, 289
nuclear power, 346, 378–79
nuclear weapons, 120–21, 282, 392, 433
  Algerian nuclear testing zone, 341–43
  massive retaliation, 120
  mutually assured destruction, 121
Nurse, Malcolm. *See* Padmore, George
Nyame, Kankan, 311
Nyamekeh, 166, 187, 429
Nyaniba, Elizabeth, 21, 26–27, 58, 139–40, 148, 186–87, 310–11
Nyasaland (now Malawi), 102, 107, 320–21
Nyerere, Julius, 4, 282, 304–5, 318–19, 321, 410, 412, 434–37
  Arusha Declaration, 319
  the honorific Mwalimu ("teacher"), 321, 412
  nonracial approach to citizenship, 437
Nzima ethnic group, 5–6, 21–22, 58, 61, 187, 271

Obama, Barack, 289–90
Obetsebi-Lamptey, Emmanuel, 153
Obote, Milton, 410
O'Brien, Conor Cruise, 396, 429
Observer, The (UK), 434
Ocansey, Alfred, 33
Onalua, Congo, 324–25
"one-man, one-house," 394
one-party rule, 4, 375, 405, 415, 432, 435–36
Operation Barbarossa, 94
Operation Cold Chop, 423
Operation Crossroads Africa (organization), 257
Order of the Crown (Belgium), 338
Organization of African Unity (OAU), 384, 409–12, 414, 427
Organization of Afro-American Unity (OAAU), 421–22
Orwell, George, 62, 97, 195
Osagyefo ("victor in war"), 234, 271, 319–21, 390, 404, 415, 428
Ouagadougou, 439–40
Out of Africa (film), 126
Owusu Addo, John, 346
Oxford Union debate society, 77
Oxford, Pennsylvania. *See* Lincoln University

Padmore, George, 32–33, 91–99, 100–103
  Africa: Britain's Third Empire, 268
  as an agent of the Comintern, 32–33
  Colonial Aid to Britain in the Great War, 98
  criticism of Nkrumah, 107
  death of, 374, 386
  falling out with the Soviet Union, 94–95
  How Britain Rules Africa, 97–98
  in London, 95, 101
  mentorship of Nkrumah, 90, 91–92, 95–96, 100–103, 107–8, 173, 180, 210, 212, 222, 282, 293–94
  move to Ghana, 293–96
  Richard Wright and, 225
  and the union between Guinea and Ghana, 299–300, 302
Pakistan, 116, 317
Palestine, 140, 153, 290
palm oil, 23, 127, 226, 322
PANAFEST festival of theater arts, 282
Pan-Africa (magazine), 151
Pan-African Federation, 102, 104
pan-Africanism
  All-African People's Conference (AAPC) of 1958, 302–7, 309, 314, 468
  complications, 300
  early forms of, 39–48
  Pan-African Conference of 1900 (London), 191–92
  Pan-African Conference of 1919 (Paris), 192, 305
  Pan-African Congress of 1945 (Manchester), 92, 102–5, 109, 151, 160, 192, 293, 299, 303–4
  Paris 1919 congress, 192
  after Nkrumah, 438–41
  under Nkrumah's presidency, 340–44
  a "United States of Africa," 54, 134, 304, 412, 468
Panama, 49
Paris, 192, 258
Parks, Rosa, 258, 341
Parti Démocratique de Guinée (PDG), 273
Partido Africano para a Independência da Guiné e Cabo Verde (PAIGC), 425
pass laws/pass books, 218, 224
"passing" as white, 89
passport control, 258, 377, 419, 426
Pasteur, Louis, 146
Payne, Ethel, 262
Pearl Harbor, Japanese attack on, 195, 198, 218
Pedler, Frederick, 98

INDEX

People's Progressive Party (Guiana), 375
personality cults. *See* cults of personality
Phelps Stokes Fund, 30
Phi Beta Sigma Fraternity, 73
Philadelphia
   Blyden Society, 88
   National Maritime Union, 80
   University of Pennsylvania, 82–85, 87, 205, 280
Philadelphia Negro, The (Du Bois), 7, 82
Philadelphia Tribune (newspaper), 67, 176, 213–14
Philippines, 10, 116, 120, 126, 140
Philosophy and Opinions of Marcus Garvey, 51, 87
Pittsburgh Courier (newspaper), 11, 63, 98, 194–96, 199, 208, 262–63, 282, 358, 430
Pizer, Dorothy, 294
plantation slavery/plantation economies, 15, 37, 41, 55, 72, 88, 92, 117, 125, 127, 146, 260, 269–70, 291, 326, 439–40
Pleven, René, 130
Poland, 389, 433
politics. *See* African politics; Ghanaian politics
Port-Bouët and the Vridi Canal, Ivory Coast, 271
Portugal, 342, 411
Portuguese Empire, 264, 308, 411, 425
Portuguese Guinea (later Guinea-Bissau), *124*, 425
Positive Action Conference for Peace and Security in Africa, 342
positive action, 160–61, 163–66, 175, 224, 231–32, 265
Powell, Adam Clayton, Jr., 12, 89, 257–58, 263, 291
Powell, Erica, 90, 184–87, 238, 239–40, 242, 244, 256, 312, 407, 425, 428–30
"power sweet," 318
Présence Africaine (journal), 258
"President for Life," 321, 432
President's Committee on Civil Rights (PCCR), 217
Preventive Detention Act of July 1958 (Ghana), 288–89, 315–17, 320, 407, 428, 435
Primus beer, 332
"prison graduates," *123*, 171, 175–76, 180, 253, 260

Profiles in Courage (J. F. Kennedy), 382
Programme for Work and Happiness (Ghana), 416
protests. *See* civil disobedience; civil rights movement
Pullman Company, 198
Pye, Lucian, 345–46
pyrethrum, 126

Quaison-Sackey, Alex, 366
Quist, Emmanuel, 179

"race consciousness," 93, 208, 226
"race emancipation," 44
"race men," 189, 205, 293–93
racism
   apartheid in South Africa, 13, 48, 153, 162, 202, 218, 224, 282, 297, 368, 374, 402, 411, 426–27
   global color line, 7, 11–13, 98–99, 103, 194, 368
   implicit racism in the mainstream press, 424–23
   Jim Crow United States, 11, 193, 198, 201, 202–4, 281, 341
   Ku Klux Klan, 8, 10, 77, 258
   "Lost Cause" and "Redemption" of the South, 189
   minstrel show "Amos 'n Andy," 213
   Truman's screening of *The Birth of a Nation* in the White House, 198
   white supremacist terrorism in Alabama, 217–18, 258, 316, 384, 418
   white supremacy, 8, 95–97, 189, 195–96, 207, 296, 343
Railway Workers' Federation of French West Africa, 133–34
Randall, Clarence, 400
Randolph, A. Philip, 190, 197–201, 219, 257, 291
Rankin, John E., 204
Rassemblement Démocratique Africain (RDA), 270, 273
realism in international relations, 114–15
"receptives," 38–39
Reconstruction, 53, 189, 198
Red Summer of 1919, 53
"Redemption" of the American South, 189
Reid, Stuart A., 323, 334
religion. *See specific belief systems and denominations*
Renascent Africa (Azikiwe), 35
Republican Party (US), 219, 382–83

Rhodes, Cecil, 36, 65, 67–68
Rizk, Fathia Halim, 310–12, 430
Roberto, Holden, 304, 305
Robeson, Paul, 258, 349
Robinson, Jackie, 291
Robinson, James, 257
Rockefeller, Nelson, 223
Rogers, J. A., 63
Romania, 7, 389, 427–29
Roosevelt, Eleanor, 382
Roosevelt, Franklin D.
   Atlantic Charter, 10, 129, 130
   death of, 129
   Executive Order 8802, 200
   making the US the "arsenal of democracy," 198
   New Deal, 76, 204
Roosevelt, Theodore, 45
Rostow, Walt, 345
Royal African Company of England, 166
rubber, 23, 116–17, 126, 137, 159, 325–26, 440
Rusk, Dean, 217, 400
Russell, Francis, 395, 400
Russo-Japanese War of 1904–5, 44
Rustin, Bayard, 200–201, 282, 341, 422

Sahara Desert, and the politics of Africa, 38, 161, 222, 248, 270, 273, 275–76, 312–13, 437–38
Sahara Protest, 341–42
Saint Thomas, 41
Saloway, Reginald, 163–65, 174, 183
Saltpond, Ghana, 140, 141–42, 144, 150, 151, *252*
Samuelson, Paul, 433
San Francisco Conference, 51, 96–97, 101, 216
Sankara, Thomas, 162, 439–40
Sarawak, 159–60, 163, 167
Satterthwaite, Joseph C., 369
Savoy Ballroom, Harlem, 70
Schlesinger, Arthur M., Jr., 375
school. *See* education
Schuyler, George, 194
Scott, Julius, 55
Scottsboro Boys, 281
Scramble for Africa, 28, 308, 325, 434
Second World War. *See* World War II
segregation. *See* education
Sekondi, Ghana, 40, 165, *252*, 394
"Self-Government Now," 157–58

self-government/self-rule, 10, 33, 40, 131, 144–45, 157–61, 165, 172, 174, 177, 181, 185, 191, 229, 233, 236
Senegal, 10, 54–55, 74, 109, *124*, 132
   Camp Thiaroye, 132
   Dakar, 132–33, 269, 276–77, 278
   de Gaulle's visit to, 278
   Kennedy's policy towards, 399
   labor unrest in, 130
   lack of education in, 133
   Nixon's visit to, 257
   prisoners of war returning to, 132
Senghor, Lamine, 15
Senghor, Léopold, 109–10, 133–34, 277, 399, 410
settler colonialism. *See* colonialism
Sharpeville massacre, South Africa (1960), 218, 426
Sherwood, Marika, 83, 107
Shuttlesworth, Fred, 258
Sierra Leone, 37–38, 39, 41, *124*
   Fourah Bay College, 39,.43
   Freetown, 39, 136–39
Sinare, Alhaji Saleh Said, 312
Singapore, 261, 317, 350
single-party rule, 4, 375, 405, 415, 432, 435–36
Sisulu, Walter, 282
sit-ins, 12, 200, 342, 418
16th Street Baptist Church, Birmingham, Alabama, 418
slavery and the slave trade, 15, 15, 41, 409, 41, 409
   abolitionism, 23, 37, 40, 269
   Indian Ocean slave trade, 325
   Middle Passage, 88, 149–50
   plantation slavery/plantation economies, 15, 37, 41, 55, 72, 88, 92, 117, 125, 127, 146, 260, 269–70, 291, 326, 439–40
   "recaptives," 38–39
   Slavery Convention of 1926, 15
Smuts, Jan, 224
socialism. *See* African economies; Cold War; communism; Marxism
Socialist Party (US), 197
Solod, Daniel, 376–77
Somalia, 335
Souls of Black Folk (Du Bois), 7, 45, 46, 197
South Africa, 13, 36, 55, 97, 101–2, 113, 160, 162, 192, 218, 224, 342, 343

apartheid, 13, 48, 153, 162, 202, 218, 224, 282, 297, 368, 374, 402, 411, 426–27
Sharpeville Massacre of 1960, 218, 426
South Korea, 261
South West Africa (Namibia), 97
"South, the." *See* race/racism
Southern Christian Leadership Council, 342
Southern Rhodesia (later Zimbabwe), 29, 304
Soviet Red Army, 113
Soviet Union, 391
   agriculture, 392
   aid, 416
   de-Stalinization, 228
   economy, 392
   Ghana and the, 377–78
   lack of an Africa policy, 324
   Lenin Peace Prize, 376, 407
   requests for overflight rights, 384, 413
   at the sidelines at Ghana's independence ceremonies, 375
   struggle to remain relevant, 401
Spain, 342, 425
Spanish Civil War, 77, 78
Special Powers Act (Northern Ireland), 317
Sri Lanka, 185, 372
Stalin, Joseph, 222–23, 228
Stanley, Henry Morton, 325–26
Stanleyville (later Kisangani), 325–29, 331, 365, 385
Steve Allen Show, The (TV show), 426
Stevens, Siaka, 425
Stevenson, Adlai, 371, 398
Stewart, Duncan, 160
Street Life, Harlem (painting), 70
Stuart, Jeffrey C., 93
student activism. *See* education
Student Nonviolent Coordinating Committee (SNCC), 418, 422
Sudan, 130, 275, 310, 360
Suez Crisis, 223, 242–43, 246, 389
Suez Dam, 289
Sukarno, 162, 221, 243, 264, 276, 369, 388
Sunni Islam, 421
Sunyani, Ghana, 377, 379
Supreme Court of Ghana, 154
Supreme Court of the United States, 15, 71, 218–19, 283, 461
Sutherland, Bill, 281–82, 341, 395, 402, 417

swollen shoot disease, 146–47, 154
Syrian and Lebanese merchants in Africa, 147, 149, 165

Table Ronde, Brussels, 331–32, 335
Taiwan, 162, 261, 368
Takoradi, Ghana, 3, 58, 137–38, 394, *252*
"talented tenth," 47, 192, 226, 419
Tamale, Ghana, 153, *252*
Tambo, Oliver, 282
Tanganyika (later Tanzania), 126, 130, 304, 434, 436–57
Tanganyika African National Union (TANU), 318–19, 435–37
Tanzania, 4, 76, 282, 318, 321, 412
   Ghana and, 434–37
   into a one-party state., 434–36
   in the overthrow of Idi Amin, 427
   Tazara Railway project, 17
Tarkwa, Ghana, 139–40, 148, 165, *252*
Taylor, Maxwell, 288
Tazara Railway project (Tanzania/Zambia), 17
Teitgen, Pierre-Henri, 270
Tema, Ghana, *252*, 316, 347, 359, 390, 428
Tempelsman, Maurice, 394, 395
Tettegah, John, 319
"thin veneer of civilization," 150
"Third World, the," 2, 14, 113, 216, 222, 294, 413
Thompson, Era Bell, 225–27
Thompson, James, 196
Thompson, Kojo, 33
Till, Emmett, 284
timber, 116–17, 140, 173, 233
Time (magazine), 214, 258
Timothy, Bankole, 315
Tito, Josip Broz, 366, 369, 393
Togo, *124*, 314, 418, 409
Togoland, Ghana, 145, 244–45
Tolbert, William, 430
Touré, Ahmed Sékou, , 273–79, 375–76, 383–84, 424, 427
Tours, Kenneth, 349, 351
Towards Colonial Freedom (Nkrumah), 86–87
Toynbee, Arnold J., 223
Trade Union Council (TUC), 164–66, 274, 319
travail forcé, 269
Treichville neighborhood of Abidjan, 1–2

INDEX

tribal identities. *See* African politics
Trinidad and Tobago, 13, 32–33, 89–90, 422
Trotskyism, 13, 90, 293
Truman, Harry S., 10, 14, 114, 120, 129–30, 198, 200, 215, 217
Tubman, William V. S., 137
Tunisia, 130, 275, 342
Ture, Kwame. *See* Carmichael, Stokely
Ture, Samori, 273
Tuskegee Institute, 30, 44–45, 50, 69
Tutu, Desmond, 282
Twi language, 100, 347
Twining, Edward, 436–37

Uganda, 322, 410, 412, 425, 427
Unilever, 149
"Union of African Socialist Republics," 110
Union of Meteorological Workers (Ghana), 164
unions. *See* labor
United Africa Company, 141, 147, 149, 151
United Arab Republic, 275, 303, 309
United Fruit Company, 49, 222
United Gold Coast Convention (UGCC), 61, 105–9, 138–57, 159, 162, 169, 171–75, 179, 212, 232, 240
United Kingdom. *See* Britain; British Empire
United Nations, 112–13
  admission of the People's Republic of China to the, 368
  in the Congo Crisis, 362, 365–68, 372, 411
  Declaration on the Granting of Independence of Colonial Countries and Peoples (1960), 366
  emerging Afro-Asiatic block at the United Nations, 342
  General Assembly, 112–13, 130, 366–69, 373–74, 396
  Ghana's admission to the, 262
  Nkrumah before the 15th UNGA, 366–70, 373–74
  peace-keeping forces, 372
  San Francisco Conference, 51, 96–97, 101, 216
  Security Council, 112, 367–68, 399, 421
  Trustee Division, 213

UN Economic Commission for Africa, 411
"Year of Africa," 335, 438
United Party (UP) of Ghana, 314–15
"United States of Africa," 54, 134, 304, 412, 468
United States of America
  American Jewish community, 75, 292
  Communist Party of the United States, 75, 94, 207
  "Era of Good Feelings" of the early 1820s, 303
  The Federalist Papers, 409
  Italian Americans, 208, 292
  Jewish community in the US, 75, 292
  Reconstruction, 53, 189, 198
  Voting Rights Act of 1965 (US), 15
  See also Alabama; Cold War; Harlem; *specific departments and agencies*
Universal Negro Improvement Association (UNIA), 7–8, 51–52, 54, 55, 67–68, 257
University of Ghana, 418, 421, 429
University of Pennsylvania, 82–85, 87, 205, 280
Up from Slavery (Booker T. Washington), 49–50
Upper Volta (later Burkina Faso), *124*, 153, 162, 341–42, 303, 439–40
uranium, 326, 331
urban planning, 346
urbanization, 129, 268, 345
US Army, 188–89
US Congress, 204, 207, 426
US State Department, 215, 218, 281, 401
US Supreme Court, 15, 71, 218–19, 283, 461
"useful trouble," 341
Ussher Fort, Accra, 150
USSR (Union of Socialist Soviet Republics). *See* Soviet Union

Valco, 398, 400
Van Bilsen, A. A. J., 327–28
Van Rensselaer, Cortlandt, 66
Van Vechten, Carl, 92
Vardaman, James K., 27
"verandah boys," 150, 156, 173, 180, 236
"Versailles in the Jungle," 4–5
Veterans Administration, 204
Veterans of Foreign Wars (VFW), 280, 287
Vietnam War, 264, 288, 382, 414, 422

Vietnam, 119–20, 130, 174, 264, 382, 414
Villa Syli, Conakry, 424–25
Vindication of the African Race, A (Blyden), 42
Voice of Africa broadcast service, 341
Volta River Project (VRP), 352–60
  Ajena Dam, 356, 359
  Akosombo Dam, 344, 352, 356, 359, 361, 366, 377–79, 384–85
  Bui dam, 356, 377–79, 385
  tragedy of, 398
  World Bank financing of, 357, 359, 366, 386, 389, 438
Voting Rights Act of 1965 (US), 15

Walker, David, 40
Wallace, Mike, 420
Wallace-Johnson, Isaac Theophilus Akunna (I. T. A.), 33–34, 137, 316
Wallerstein, Immanuel, 38
War Resisters League, 282
Ward, Barbara, 384, 388
warfare
  civil wars, 66, 77–78, 116, 234, 304, 425, 439
  conscientious objectors in the US, 194, 281, 402
  devastating and protracted wars, 308
  IQ tests in army recruiting, 188
  "just wars," 38
  violence against Gold Coast veterans, 149–51
  See also specific conflicts and campaigns
Warren, Earl, 218
Washington, Booker T.
  Tuskegee Institute, 30, 44–45, 50, 69
  Up from Slavery, 49–50
Washington, DC, 80, 213, 287, 331
  Howard University, 11, 65, 72, 77, 88–89, 93–94, 190–91, 195–96, 257, 291
  March on Washington for Jobs and Freedom, August 28, 1963, 199–201, 420
  National Press Club, 288
  Youth Marches for Integrated Schools, 218
Watson Commission (Gold Coast), 153–54, 168

INDEX

West Africa, *124*
    Black settler colonies in, 37, 41–42
    the end of French West Africa, 130–35
    Ewe people of, 145, 233, 242, 244–45, 314, 315, 433
    settler colonies of, 37, 41–42
West African Countries and Peoples, British and Native, with the Requirements Necessary (Horton), 40
West African National Secretariat (WANS), 104, 106, 109–10, 137, 141, 154, 453
West African Pilot (Nigeria), 98
West African Students' Union (WASU), 68, 100, 104–5, 107, 109
West African Youth League, 33
West Indies, 41, 49–52, 54–55, 68, 91–98, 104, 192, 207, 296, 314. *See also specific countries in the region*
"West, the." *See* Cold War; colonialism
Western Echo (newspaper), 43
Westminster model of government, 177, 179, 230, 247, 318, 406, 434
White Malice: The CIA and the Covert Recolonization of Africa (S. Williams), 423
White Man's Burden, 337
White Rajahs of Sarawak, 159
white settler colonies in Africa, 127, 159, 222, 307
white supremacy, 8, 95–97, 189, 195–96, 207, 296, 343
White, Walter, 199
"wife stealing," 394

Wilkins, Roy, 216, 219, 257, 291, 292
Williams, Eric, 11, 89, 349
Williams, Henry Sylvester, 191
Williams, Susan, 423
Wilson, Frank, 72, 78
Wilson, Woodrow, 8–9, 10, 198
"Wind of Change" speech (Macmillan), 377
Windom, Alice, 418
Winneba, Ghana, *252*, 390
women
    education for women and girls, 40
    in government, 440
    of the markets in Africa, 134, 154, 173, 226
    in Nkrumah's life, 60, 211–12
    "wife stealing," 394
Wood, Samuel R., 34–35, 63
World Affairs Council, 211
World Bank, 281, 357, 359, 366, 386, 389, 438
World War I, 8–9, 1–15, 52–55
    Africa's material contributions to the war effort, 352–53, 378
    African American veterans and activism, 8–9, 14, 52–55, 93, 196–98
    African imperial veterans of, 15, 52
    the global order after, 36, 52–53
    inflation after, 130, 147–48, 154, 393, 438
    League of Nations, 51, 342
    as rooted in European imperialism, 14, 126
World War II, 9–13
    Atlantic Charter, 10, 129, 130

    global phase shift after the, 112
    Japanese attack on Pearl Harbor, 195, 198, 218
    liberation of the concentration camps, 100–101
    Marshall Plan, 14, 115, 204, 271
    Meuse-Argonne campaign of, 52
    myths for the Greatest Generation, 14, 193, 204
    Operation Barbarossa, 94
    pan-Africanism after, 190–92
    as rooted in European imperialism, 85–86, 125–26
    roots of independence in Africa and beyond, 55
Wretched of the Earth, The (Fanon), 118, 307–8
Wright, Richard, 69–70, 102, 190, 215, 224–26, 234, 281, 340–41
Wuo, Nana Kojo, 379–80

Yaméogo, Maurice, 404
Yamoussoukro, Ivory Coast, 5, 269
Yankey, Ambrose, 311
"Year of Africa," 335, 438
Youth Marches for Integrated Schools, Washington, DC, 218
Yugoslavia, 366, 389

Zaïre, 4, 322, 410, 435, 444
Zambia, 4, 207, 297, 304, 335, 359
Zanzibar, 130
Zimbabwe, 29, 304
Zionism, 305

ABOUT THE AUTHOR

Howard W. French has been a professor at the Columbia University Graduate School of Journalism since 2008. After teaching at the University of Abidjan in Côte d'Ivoire in the early 1980s, he began a career in journalism writing about Africa for *The Washington Post*, *Africa News*, *The Economist*, and other publications. Later, after joining *The New York Times*, where he became a foreign correspondent and senior writer, he reported from Central America, the Caribbean, West and Central Africa, Japan, and China; wrote a global-affairs column for the *International Herald Tribune*; and was twice nominated for the Pulitzer Prize. French is the author of several books on both Africa and East Asia, including, most recently, *Born in Blackness: Africa, Africans, and the Making of the Modern World, 1471 to the Second World War*. In addition to his native English, he speaks Chinese, French, Japanese, and Spanish. French was born in Washington, DC, and now lives in New York with his wife, Avouka.